IMAGES OF ORGANIZATION

Updated Edition of the International Bestseller

*In memory of my parents
Idris and Rachel Morgan*

Contents

Preface

It is with real pleasure that I write this Preface to the latest edition of *Images of Organization*.

Since the first edition was published in 1986, there have been huge changes in the corporate world. Large centralized bureaucracies have given way to more decentralized and fluid forms of organization, and globalization has proceeded at a tremendous pace—changing the face of the world economy. Yet the basic ideas underlying the book remain as relevant as ever, because it seeks, above all else, to empower its reader with a way of thinking that can help us navigate some of the ambiguity and flux.

The central message is presented in two short chapters: the Introduction (Chapter 1) and the Postscript (Chapter 12). They show, very simply, (a) how different metaphors give rise to different theories of organization and management, (b) how an understanding of the process can help us master the strengths and limitations of different viewpoints, and (c) how we can use this knowledge to become more effective leaders and managers.

By reading these two chapters, one can understand the basic theory. But it is by reading and absorbing the ideas presented in Chapters 2 to 9 and *experiencing* how they can help us understand what is going on in the world around us, that the book's central messages really hit home. These chapters present eight very different metaphorical perspectives on organization—drawing out their strengths, limitations, and implications for practice. My aim is to give a practical demonstration of the power of metaphor and how it can be used to generate deep understandings of the nature of organizations and organizational life.

In the twenty years since *Images* was first published, interest in the role of metaphor has grown enormously. Organization and management practitioners, theorists, and researchers have developed many new metaphors for thinking about organization. For example, metaphors derived from chaos and complexity science, from the field of jazz, "improv" theater and movie making, from law and accounting, from the field of ecology and sustainability, from cyberspace, and from the mosaic-like diversity of the global economy have all been used to create frameworks for thinking about modern organization. And the list will no doubt continue to grow as management practitioners and researchers seek yet other metaphors to deal with the new realities being faced.

Hence, in producing the current edition, I have run up against the obvious questions: "Should I go back to the beginning and start writing the book all over again?" "Should I try to take account of all the new metaphors that have appeared?"

I confronted the same questions in writing the 1997 edition of *Images* and have reached the same conclusion. The structure and approach adopted in the original version still serve the book's main purpose very well. Now, as then, my aim is not to present an exhaustive account of every conceivable metaphor that can be used to understand and shape organizational life. Rather, it is to reveal, through illustration, the power of metaphor in shaping organization and management and how the ultimate challenge is not to be seduced by the power or attractiveness of a single metaphor—old or new—so much as to develop an ability to integrate the contributions of different points of view.

Hence, in the current edition, I have limited the revisions to an updating of the references and bibliographic notes to ground the book's thesis in some of the most recent literature. I have also updated some factual data on the role of multinationals in the global economy but left the basic structure, arguments, and illustrations unchanged. As you read each chapter, I'm sure that you'll find yourself making connections with many contemporary issues and developments, such as the following:

- The crises associated with high-profile scandals at Enron and elsewhere in relation to corporate governance and the role, management, and motivations of large corporations in the global economy ("The Ugly Face," discussed in Chapter 9)
- The increasing relevance of chaos and complexity science in explaining the unpredictable nature of organizational change (Chapter 8)
- The importance of understanding organizational power and politics (Chapter 6)
- How the classic machine model of organization (Chapter 2) continues to underwrite many franchising systems worldwide and the methods of low-cost manufacturing and outsourcing systems in developing countries, re-creating the old industrial revolution in a new twenty-first-century form

- How the increasing use of teams and "24/7" modes of global operation are giving rise to new "species" of organization (Chapter 3), requiring new cultural norms and practices and an in-depth understanding of the links between organization, management and culture (Chapter 5)
- How the internet and other forms of information technology supporting instant networking and continuous learning are making the image of "organizations as brains," discussed in Chapter 4, more and more of a reality
- How conscious and unconscious motivations continue to shape organizations and the political and social landscape in deep and hidden ways (Chapter 7)

These links with contemporary developments are spelled out in the Bibliographic Notes and provide a useful trail for further in-depth reading.

As always, my work has benefited from the contributions of many people. They are recognized in the Acknowledgments section on page xv. I offer them all my sincere thanks.

—Gareth Morgan
Toronto, Canada 2006

Acknowledgments

M y thanks on this project go to many people over many years. Friends, colleagues, and students at Lancaster, Penn State, and York universities, together with participants at executive and research workshops throughout Europe and North America, have contributed to many of the insights developed in this book. I am especially grateful to Asaf Zohar at York University for his valuable contributions and to Dean Desző Horvath at York's Schulich School of Business for his long-standing support. The Social Sciences and Humanities Research Council of Canada played an important role in launching my early research on the role of metaphor in the study of organization and has been helpful in supporting doctoral students working on the theory and practice of self-organization.

Rhea Copeland provided outstanding secretarial support in the production of the original manuscript, and as always, my friends at Sage Publications have made numerous contributions to its final form. I also want to thank Jean Adams, Vicki Casey, and Brenda Turgeon for their contributions to the updated edition.

My family provides an indispensable foundation for all that I do. Karen, Evan, and Heather have played a crucial role in helping me find the creative space needed to develop and work on my ideas. They provide a loving atmosphere full of positive energy and fun.

To all, my sincere thanks.

—Gareth Morgan

PART I

AN OVERVIEW

On the nature of metaphor and its role in understanding organization and management

1

Introduction

Effective managers and professionals in all walks of life have to become skilled in the art of "reading" the situations they are attempting to organize or manage.

This skill usually develops as an intuitive process, learned through experience and natural ability. Although at times a person may actually declare that he or she needs to "read what's happening in a particular situation" or to "get a handle on a particular problem," the process of reading and rereading often occurs at an almost subconscious level. For this reason it is often believed that effective managers and problem solvers are born rather than made and have a kind of magical power to understand and transform the situations they encounter.

If we take a closer look at the processes used, however, we find that this kind of mystique and power is often based on an ability to develop deep appreciation of the situations being addressed. Skilled leaders and managers develop the knack of reading situations with various scenarios in mind and of forging actions that seem appropriate to the understandings thus obtained.

They have a capacity to remain open and flexible, suspending immediate judgments whenever possible, until a more comprehensive view of the situation emerges. They are aware that new insights often arise as one approaches situations from "new angles" and that a wide and varied reading can create a wide and varied range of action possibilities. Less effective managers and problem solvers, however, seem to interpret everything from a fixed standpoint. As a result, they frequently hit blocks they cannot get around; their actions and behaviors are often rigid and inflexible.

This book explores and develops the art of reading and understanding organizational life. It is based on a very simple premise: that all theories of organization and management are based on implicit images or metaphors that lead us to see, understand, and manage organizations in distinctive yet partial ways.

Metaphor is often regarded just as a device for embellishing discourse, but its significance is much greater than this. The use of metaphor implies *a way of thinking* and *a way of seeing* that pervade how we understand our world generally. For example, research in a wide variety of fields has demonstrated that metaphor exerts a formative influence on science, on our language, and on how we think, as well as on how we express ourselves on a day-to-day basis.

We use metaphor whenever we attempt to understand one element of experience in terms of another. Thus, metaphor proceeds through implicit or explicit assertions that A *is* (or is like) B. When we say "the man is a lion," we use the image of a lion to draw attention to the lionlike aspects of the man. The metaphor frames our understanding of the man in a distinctive yet partial way.

One of the interesting aspects of metaphor is that it always produces this kind of one-sided insight. In highlighting certain interpretations it tends to force others into a background role. Thus, in drawing attention to the lionlike bravery, strength, or ferocity of the man, the metaphor glosses over the fact that the same person may well also be a pig, a devil, a saint, a bore, or a recluse.

Another interesting feature rests in the fact that metaphor *always* creates distortions (Exhibit 1.1). Metaphor uses evocative images to create what may be described as "constructive falsehoods," which, if taken literally, or to an extreme, become absurd.

"The man is a lion."

He is brave, strong, and ferocious.

But he is *not* covered in fur and does not have four legs, sharp teeth, and a tail!

Metaphor invites us to see the similarities

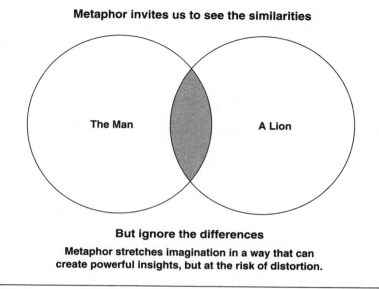

But ignore the differences

Metaphor stretches imagination in a way that can create powerful insights, but at the risk of distortion.

Exhibit 1.1   The Nature of Metaphor

When we approach metaphor in this way we see that our simple premise that *all theory is metaphor* has far-reaching consequences. We have to accept that any theory or perspective that we bring to the study of organization and management, while capable of creating valuable insights, is also incomplete, biased, and potentially misleading.

To illustrate, consider the popular idea that "the organization is a machine." The metaphor may create valuable insights about how an organization is structured to achieve predetermined results. But the metaphor is incomplete. For example, it ignores the human aspects. The metaphor is biased. For example, it elevates the importance of the rational and structural dimensions. The metaphor is misleading. For example, the organization is *not* a machine and can never really be designed, structured, and controlled as a set of inanimate parts.

Metaphor is inherently paradoxical. It can create powerful insights that also become distortions, as the way of seeing created through a metaphor becomes a way of *not* seeing.

Yet when we recognize this we can begin to mobilize the true power of metaphor and its role in management. In recognizing theory as metaphor, we quickly appreciate that no single theory will ever give us a perfect or all-purpose point of view. We realize that the challenge is to become skilled in the art of using metaphor: to find fresh ways of seeing, understanding, and shaping the situations that we want to organize and manage.

The following chapters illustrate how this can be done by exploring the implications of different metaphors for thinking about the nature of organization. Some of the metaphors tap familiar ways of thinking; others develop insights and perspectives that will be rather new. Collectively, they demonstrate how we can use metaphor to generate a range of complementary and competing insights and learn to build on the strengths of different points of view.

Thus, Chapter 2 examines the image of organizations as machines and illustrates how this style of thought underpins the development of bureaucratic organization. When managers think of organizations as machines they tend to manage and design them as machines made up of interlocking parts that each play a clearly defined role in the functioning of the whole. At times, this can prove highly effective; at others, it can have many unfortunate results. One of the most basic problems of modern management is that the mechanical way of thinking is so ingrained in our everyday conceptions of organization that it is often very difficult to organize in any other way. In demonstrating this, the chapter helps us become more open to other ways of thinking.

Chapter 3 examines the idea that organizations are like organisms. This popular metaphor focuses attention on understanding and managing organizational "needs" and environmental relations. We come to see different types of organization as belonging to different species, of which the bureaucratic type is just one. We see that different species are suited to different environments. We are encouraged to understand how organizations are born, grow, develop, decline, and die and how they can adapt to changing circumstances. We are also encouraged to consider relations between species and the evolutionary patterns found in the broader ecology. As in the case of the mechanical metaphor, this kind of imagery leads us to see and understand organizations from a unique perspective that has already contributed a great deal to the theory of modern management.

In Chapter 4, we pursue the implications of yet another metaphor. What if we view organizations as brains? What if we attempt to design them as brains? The metaphor draws attention to the importance of information processing, learning, and intelligence and provides a frame of reference for understanding and assessing modern organizations in these terms. It also provides a set of principles for creating "learning organizations."

Chapter 5 explores the idea that organizations are cultures. This focus, which has received increasing attention over the past few years from writers on corporate culture, gives us yet another way of managing and designing organizations: by focusing on the values, ideas, beliefs, norms, rituals, and other patterns of shared meaning that guide organizational life.

In Chapter 6 we use a political metaphor to focus on the different sets of interests, conflicts, and power plays that shape organizational activities. The chapter explores organizations as systems of government and the detailed factors shaping the politics of organizational life.

In Chapter 7 the focus shifts to a more abstract metaphor: the idea that organizations are "psychic prisons" where people become trapped by their own thoughts, ideas, and beliefs or by the unconscious mind. Could it be that our favored modes of organizing manifest an unconscious preoccupation with control? A form of repressed sexuality? A fear of death? The image of a psychic prison invites us to examine organizational life to see if, and in what ways, we have become trapped by conscious and unconscious processes of our own creation. It offers many important insights about the psychodynamic aspects of organization and favored styles of management.

Chapter 8 investigates another image. This time we are invited to understand organization as flux and transformation by focusing on the logics of change shaping social life. The chapter examines four such "logics." In effect, they offer four different metaphors for studying change. One emphasizes how organizations are self-producing systems that create themselves in their own image. The second draws on insights from the study of chaos and complexity, viewing organizational life through images of competing "attractor patterns." The third views organization as the product of circular flows of positive and negative feedback. The fourth explores how the features of modern organization are the product of a dialectical logic whereby every phenomenon generates its opposite. The insights help us to understand and manage organizational change and to appreciate some of the forces shaping the nature of organization at a societal level.

Chapter 9 explores the idea that organizations are instruments of domination. Here the focus is on the potentially exploitative aspects of corporate life. The chapter shows how organizations often use their employees, their host communities, and the world economy to achieve their own ends. An extension of the political metaphor examined in Chapter 6, the chapter helps us understand aspects of modern organization that have radicalized labor-management relations and the negative impacts of global corporations. This metaphor is particularly useful for understanding organizations from the perspective of exploited groups and for understanding how actions that are rational from one viewpoint can prove exploitative from another.

As you read these different chapters you are going to *experience* the core message of this book. Each chapter invites you to engage in a mode of thinking that generates important insights while having major limitations. You are likely to be attracted to certain metaphors and be impatient with others. Or you may find competing metaphors equally compelling or attractive. As you pursue a favored perspective you are going to find the insights of others eliminated from view.

In this way the book invites you to explore and deal with the paradox of metaphor. So, absorb and enjoy the process. Gain comfort in dealing with competing viewpoints, for this is one of the key competencies that needs to be developed as a basis for effective management.

Chapters 10, 11, and 12 develop this theme, showing how we can use and integrate the insights of different metaphors from a managerial perspective. Chapters 10 and 11 focus on the use of metaphor as a tool for improving our ability to see, understand, and interpret key aspects of organizational life. Chapter 12 sketches the broader implications for managing in a turbulent world.

Each chapter is accompanied by a set of bibliographic notes. They appear toward the end of the book and have been designed to provide comprehensive references and discuss specific points and arguments in greater depth, without disrupting the flow of the text.

The book thus stands as a treatise on metaphorical thinking that contributes to both the theory and the practice of management. The metaphors discussed have been selected to illustrate a broad range of ideas and perspectives. But they by no means exhaust the possibilities. As you read, you may find yourself disagreeing with the importance of the metaphors that have been chosen and wish to add ones of your own. That is the way it should be, for the aim is to open dialogue and extend horizons rather than to achieve closure around an all-embracing perspective.

In this respect, *Images of Organization* is very different from most management books. It has a clear point of view: that metaphor is central to the way we "read," understand, and shape organizational life. But at no point will you find that view being brought down to advocacy of a single perspective. There are no right or wrong theories in management in an absolute sense, for every theory illuminates and hides.

The book offers a means of coping with this paradox. It offers a *way of thinking* that is crucial for understanding, managing, and designing organizations in a changing world.

PART II

SOME IMAGES OF ORGANIZATION

The following chapters demonstrate how metaphor can be used to develop theories of organization and management. Some focus on metaphors that have already been well explored. Others open newer territory. Collectively, they show how we can use metaphor to generate a range of complementary and competing insights about the nature of organizations and how they can be designed and managed.

2

Mechanization
Takes Command
Organizations as Machines

The Chinese sage Chuang-tzu, who lived in the fourth century B.C., relates the following story:

As Tzu-gung was traveling through the regions north of river Han, he saw an old man working in his vegetable garden. He had dug an irrigation ditch. The man would descend into the well, fetch up a vessel of water in his arms, and pour it out into the ditch. While his efforts were tremendous, the results appeared to be very meager.

Tzu-gung said, "There is a way whereby you can irrigate a hundred ditches in one day, and whereby you can do much with little effort. Would you not like to hear of it?" Then the gardener stood up, looked at him, and said, "And what would that be?"

Tzu-gung replied, "You take a wooden lever, weighted at the back and light in front. In this way you can bring up water so quickly that it just gushes out. This is called a draw-well."

Then anger rose up in the old man's face, and he said, "I have heard my teacher say that whoever uses machines does all his work like a machine. He who does his work like a machine grows a heart like a machine, and he who carries the heart of a machine in his breast loses his simplicity. He who has lost his simplicity becomes unsure in the strivings of his soul.

"Uncertainty in the strivings of the soul is something which does not agree with honest sense. It is not that I do not know of such things; I am ashamed to use them."

If the old man were to visit the modern world he would no doubt be very dismayed. Machines now influence virtually every aspect of our existence. They have increased our productive abilities a thousandfold, but they have also done much more, shaping almost every aspect of our lives. The debate initiated by Tzu-gung and the old man continues. In the view of many, mechanization has brought mainly gain, raising mankind from competitors with nature to virtual masters of nature. For others, the old man's vision of human alienation recurs in various forms, as they contemplate the high price of mechanical progress in terms of the transition from craft to factory production, the exchange of rural community for urban sprawl, the general degradation of the environment, and the assault of rationalism upon the human spirit.

Regardless of the stand one takes, the wisdom of the old man's vision regarding the pervasive influence of machines remains beyond dispute. The use of machines has radically transformed the nature of productive activity and has left its mark on the imagination, thoughts, and feelings of humans throughout the ages. Scientists have produced mechanistic interpretations of the natural world, and philosophers and psychologists have articulated mechanistic theories of human mind and behavior. Increasingly, we have learned to use the machines as a metaphor for ourselves and our society and to mold our world in accordance with mechanical principles.

This is nowhere more evident than in the modern organization. Consider, for example, the mechanical precision with which many of our institutions are expected to operate. Organizational life is often routinized with the precision demanded of clockwork. People are frequently expected to arrive at work at a given time, perform a predetermined set of activities, rest at appointed hours, and then resume their tasks until work is over. In many organizations, one shift of workers replaces another in methodical fashion so that work can continue uninterrupted twenty-four hours a day every day of the year. Often, the work is very mechanical and repetitive. Anyone who has observed work in the mass-production factory or in any of the large "office factories" processing paper forms such as insurance claims, tax returns, or bank checks will have noticed the machinelike way in which such organizations operate. They are designed like machines, and their employees are in essence expected to behave as if they were parts of machines.

Fast-food restaurants and service organizations of many kinds operate in accordance with similar principles, with every action preplanned in a minute way, even in areas where personal interactions with others are concerned. Employees are frequently trained to interact with customers according to a detailed code of instructions and are monitored in their performance. Even the most casual smile, greeting, comment, or suggestion by a sales assistant is often programmed by company policy and rehearsed to produce authentic results. The management observation checklist used by a famous fast-food restaurant to monitor employee performance (Exhibit 2.1) indicates the degree to which a simple task like serving a customer can be mechanized, observed, and evaluated in a mechanical way.

Machines, Mechanical Thinking, and the Rise of Bureaucratic Organization

Organizations that are designed and operated as if they were machines are now usually called bureaucracies. But most organizations are bureaucratized in some degree, for the mechanistic mode of thought has shaped our most basic conceptions of what organization is all about. For example, when we talk about organization we usually have in mind a state of orderly relations between clearly defined parts that have some determinate order. Although the image may not be explicit, we are talking about a set of mechanical relations. We talk about organizations as if they were machines, and as a consequence we tend to expect them to operate as machines: in a routinized, efficient, reliable, and predictable way.

In certain circumstances, which are discussed in the concluding section of this chapter, a mechanical mode of organization can provide the basis for effective operation. But in others it can have many unfortunate consequences. It is thus important to understand how and when we are engaging in mechanistic thinking and how so many popular theories and taken-for-granted ideas about organization support this thinking. One of the major challenges facing many modern organizations is to replace this kind of thinking with fresh ideas and approaches, such as those discussed in subsequent chapters. Let us turn, therefore, to the story behind the development of our mechanistic concepts of organization.

Greeting the customer	Yes	No
1. There is a smile.		
2. It is a sincere greeting.		
3. There is eye contact.		
Other:		
Taking the order	Yes	No
1. The counter person is thoroughly familiar with the menu ticket. (No hunting for items)		
2. The customer has to give the order only once.		
3. Small orders (four items or less) are memorized rather than written down.		
4. There is suggestive selling.		
Other:		
Assembling the order	Yes	No
1. The order is assembled in the proper sequence.		
2. Grill slips are handed in first.		
3. Drinks are poured in the proper sequence.		
4. Proper amount of ice.		
5. Cups slanted and finger used to activate.		
6. Drinks are filled to the proper level.		
7. Drinks are capped.		
8. Clean cups.		
9. Holding times are observed on coffee.		
10. Cups are filled to the proper level on coffee.		
Other:		
Presenting the order	Yes	No
1. It is properly packaged.		
2. The bag is double folded.		
3. Plastic trays are used if eating inside.		
4. A tray liner is used.		

5. The food is handled in a proper manner.		
Other:		
Asking for and receiving payment	**Yes**	**No**
1. The amount of the order is stated clearly and loud enough to hear.		
2. The denomination received is clearly stated.		
3. The change is counted out loud.		
4. Change is counted efficiently.		
5. Large bills are laid on the till until the change is given.		
Other:		
Thanking the customer and asking for repeat business	**Yes**	**No**
1. There is always a thank-you.		
2. The thank-you is sincere.		
3. There is eye contact.		
4. Return business was asked for.		
Other:		

Exhibit 2.1   A Management Observation Checklist Used to Evaluate the Performance of Counter Staff in a Fast-Food Restaurant

THE ORIGINS OF MECHANISTIC ORGANIZATION

Organizations are rarely established as ends in themselves. They are instruments created to achieve other ends. This is reflected in the origins of the word *organization*, which derives from the Greek *organon*, meaning a tool or instrument. No wonder, therefore, that ideas about tasks, goals, aims, and objectives have become such fundamental organizational concepts, for tools and instruments are mechanical devices invented and developed to aid in performing some kind of goal-oriented activity.

This instrumentality is evident in the practices of the earliest formal organizations of which we know, such as those that built the great pyramids, empires, churches, and armies. However, it is with the invention and proliferation of machines, particularly along with the industrial revolution in Europe and North America, that those concepts of organization really became mechanized. The use of machines, especially in industry, required that organizations be adapted to the needs of machines.

If we examine the changes in organization accompanying the industrial revolution, we find an increasing trend toward the bureaucratization and routinization of life generally. Many self-employed family groups and skilled artisans gave up the autonomy of working in their homes and workshops to work on relatively unskilled jobs in factory settings. At the same time, factory owners and their engineers realized that the efficient operation of their new machines ultimately required major changes in the design and control of work. Division of labor at work, which was praised by the Scottish economist Adam Smith in his book *The Wealth of Nations* (1776), became intensified and increasingly specialized as manufacturers sought to increase efficiency by reducing the discretion of workers in favor of control by their machines and their supervisors. New procedures and techniques were also introduced to discipline workers to accept the new and rigorous routine of factory production.

Much was learned from the military, which since at least the time of Frederick the Great of Prussia has emerged as a prototype of mechanistic organization. Frederick, who ruled from 1740 to 1786, inherited an army composed for the most part of criminals, paupers, foreign mercenaries, and unwilling conscripts—an unruly mob. He was determined to change this and quickly set about making reforms. He borrowed much from the practice of Roman legions and the reformed European armies of the sixteenth century but also introduced numerous innovations of his own. Many of these were inspired by the mechanical inventions of his day.

In particular, Frederick was fascinated by the workings of automated toys such as mechanical men, and in his quest to shape the army into a reliable and efficient instrument he introduced many reforms that actually served to reduce his soldiers to automatons. Among these reforms were the introduction of ranks and uniforms, the extension and standardization of regulations, increased specialization of tasks, the use of standardized equipment, the creation of a command language, and systematic training that involved army drills. Frederick's aim was to shape the army into an efficient mechanism operating through means of standardized parts. Training procedures allowed these parts to be forged from almost any raw material, thus allowing the parts to be easily replaced when necessary, an essential characteristic for wartime operation. To ensure that his military machine operated on command, Frederick fostered the principle that the men must be taught to fear their officers more than the enemy. And to ensure that the military machine was used as wisely as possible, he developed the distinction between advisory and command functions, freeing specialist advisers (staff) from the line of command to plan activities. In time, further refinements were introduced, including the idea of decentralizing controls to create greater autonomy of parts in different combat situations.

Many of these ideas and practices had great relevance for solving problems created by the development of factory systems of production and were adopted in a piecemeal fashion throughout the nineteenth century as entrepreneurs struggled to find organizational forms suited to machine technology. The new technology was thus accompanied and reinforced by mechanization of human thought and action. Organizations that used machines became more and more like machines. Frederick the Great's vision of a "mechanized" army gradually became a reality in factory and office settings as well.

During the nineteenth century, a number of attempts were made to codify and promote the ideas that could lead to the efficient organization and management of work. Thus, Adam Smith's praise of the division of labor was followed in 1801 by Eli Whitney's public demonstration of mass production, showing how guns could be assembled from piles of interchangeable parts. In 1832, Charles Babbage, inventor of one of the earliest forms of the mathematical computer, published a treatise advocating a scientific approach to organization and management and emphasizing the importance of planning and an appropriate division of labor. However, it was not until the early twentieth century that these ideas and developments were synthesized in a comprehensive theory of organization and management.

One major contribution to this theory was made by the German sociologist Max Weber, who observed the parallels between the mechanization of industry and the proliferation of bureaucratic forms of organization. He noted that the bureaucratic form routinizes the process of administration exactly as the machine routinizes production. In his work we find the first comprehensive definition of bureaucracy as a form of organization that emphasizes precision, speed, clarity, regularity, reliability, and efficiency achieved through the creation of a fixed division of tasks, hierarchical supervision, and detailed rules and regulations.

As a sociologist Weber was interested in the social consequences of the proliferation of bureaucracy and, rather like the old man in Chuang-tzu's story, was concerned about the effect it would have on the human side of society. He saw that the bureaucratic approach had the potential to routinize and mechanize almost every aspect of human life, eroding the human spirit and capacity for spontaneous action. He also recognized that it could have grave political consequences in undermining the potential for more democratic forms of organization. His writings on bureaucracy are thus pervaded by a great skepticism, of which we will have more to say in Chapter 9.

The other major contribution was made by a group of management theorists and practitioners in North America and Europe who set the basis for what is now known as "classical management theory" and "scientific management." In contrast with Weber, they were firm advocates of bureaucratization and devoted their energies to identifying detailed principles and methods through which this kind of organization could be achieved. Whereas the classical management theorists focused on the design of the total organization, the scientific managers focused on the design and management of individual jobs. It is through the ideas of these theorists that so many mechanistic principles of organization have become entrenched in our everyday thinking. It is thus worth examining their work in some detail.

CLASSICAL MANAGEMENT THEORY: DESIGNING BUREAUCRATIC ORGANIZATIONS

Typical of the classical theorists were the Frenchman Henri Fayol, the American F. W. Mooney, and the Englishman Col. Lyndall Urwick. They were all interested in problems of practical management and sought to codify their experience of successful organization for others to follow. The basic thrust of their thinking is captured in the idea that management is a process of planning, organization, command, coordination, and control. Collectively, they set the basis for many modern management techniques, such as management by objectives (MBO); planning, programming, budgeting systems (PPBS); and other methods stressing rational planning and control. Each theorist codified his insights, drawing on a combination of military and engineering principles. Exhibit 2.2 summarizes some of the general principles of classical management theory.

If we implement these principles, we arrive at the kind of organization represented in the familiar organization chart (Exhibit 2.3): a pattern of precisely defined jobs organized in a hierarchical manner through precisely defined lines of command or communication. If we examine these principles closely, we find that the classical theorists were in effect designing the organization exactly as if they were designing a machine.

When an engineer designs a machine the task is to define a network of interdependent parts arranged in a specific sequence and anchored by precisely defined points of resistance or rigidity. The classical theorists

Unity of command: an employee should receive orders from only one superior.

Scalar chain: the line of authority from superior to subordinate, which runs from top to bottom of the organization; this chain, which results from the unity-of-command principle, should be used as a channel for communication and decision making.

Span of control: the number of people reporting to one superior must not be so large that it creates problems of communication and coordination.

Staff and line: staff personnel can provide valuable advisory services, but must be careful not to violate line authority.

Initiative: to be encouraged at all levels of the organization.

Division of work: management should aim to achieve a degree of specialization designed to achieve the goal of the organization in an efficient manner.

Authority and responsibility: attention should be paid to the right to give orders and to exact obedience; and appropriate balance between authority and responsibility should be achieved. It is meaningless to make someone responsible for work if they are not given appropriate authority to execute that responsibility.

Centralization (of authority): always present in some degree, this must vary to optimize the use of faculties of personnel.

Discipline: obedience, application, energy, behavior, and outward marks of respect in accordance with agreed rules and customs.

Subordination of individual interest to general interest: through firmness, example, fair agreements, and constant supervision.

Equity: based on kindness and justice, to encourage personnel in their duties; and fair remuneration, which encourages morale yet does not lead to overpayment.

Stability of tenure of personnel: to facilitate the development of abilities.

Esprit de corps: to facilitate harmony as a basis of strength.

These principles, many of which were first used by Frederick the Great and other military experts to develop armies into "military machines," provided the foundation of management theory in the first half of the twentieth century. Their use is very widespread today.

Exhibit 2.2   Principles of Classical Management Theory

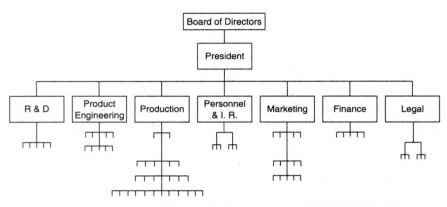

Chart A **ORGANIZATIONAL STRUCTURE OF A MANUFACTURING FIRM**

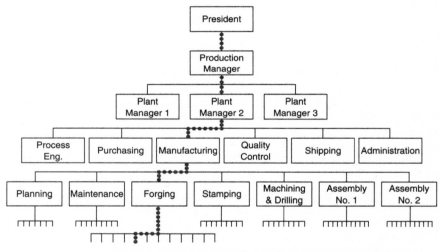

Chart B **DETAILED STRUCTURE OF THE PRODUCTION DEPARTMENT**

Chart A illustrates an organization divided on the principle of functional special-ization. Each functional department has its own hierarchical mode of organiza-tion. Chart B illustrates details relating to the production department. Note the chain of command that runs from top to bottom of the organization. From any place at the bottom of the hierarchy there is only one route to the top, a reflection of the principle that each subordinate should have no more than one superior. An example is indicated by the highlighted line. Note the different "spans of control." The chief executive in Chart A has a span of control equal to seven. The foreman of the forging section in the production department (Charts A and B) has a span of control of twelve. The production manager has a span of three. Note how the advisory or "staff" departments (e.g., finance, personnel, legal, R&D) have no direct authority over "line" departments such as the production department.

Exhibit 2.3   Organization Chart Illustrating the Principles of Classical Management Theory and Bureaucratic Organization

were attempting to achieve a similar design in their approach to organization. We see this in the way the organization is conceived as a network of parts: functional departments such as production, marketing, finance, personnel, and research and development, which are further specified as networks of precisely defined jobs. Job responsibilities interlock so that they complement each other as perfectly as possible and are linked together through the scalar chain of command expressed in the classical dictum "one man, one boss."

The motions of the organizational structure thus produced are made to operate as precisely as possible through patterns of authority—for example, in terms of job responsibilities and the right to give orders and to exact obedience. Patterns of authority serve as points of resistance and coordinate activities by restricting activity in certain directions while encouraging it in others. By giving detailed attention to patterns of authority and to the general process of direction, discipline, and subordination of individual to general interest, the classical theorists sought to ensure that when commands were issued from the top of the organization they would travel throughout the organization in a precisely determined way to create a precisely determined effect.

These principles are basic to both centralized bureaucracy (illustrated in Exhibit 2.3) and the modified form found in the divisionalized organization, where various units are allowed to operate in a semiautonomous manner under general rather than detailed supervision and the control of those with ultimate authority. Just as the military introduced decentralization to cope with difficult combat situations, the classical management theorists recognized the necessity of reconciling the contrary requirements of centralization and decentralization to preserve an appropriate flexibility in different parts of large organizations.

The ability to achieve this kind of decentralization has been greatly advanced during the course of the twentieth century through the development of management techniques like MBO and PPBS and the design of sophisticated management information systems (MIS), which are often used to establish the kinds of "top-down" control advocated by the classical theorists. For example, forms of MBO are often used to impose a mechanistic system of goals and objectives on an organization. These are then used to control the direction in which managers and employees can take the organization—for example, through the development of performance targets consistent with these goals and various budgetary systems. Computerized information systems now allow performance to be subjected to almost complete surveillance and control.

In this way, the ideas of the classical management theorists are reinforced under the guise of modern management. This often occurs because the people designing these management systems have come to think about organization mechanistically and are unaware of other ways in which these techniques could be used—for example, to promote the kind of organizational learning and inquiry discussed in Chapter 4, or the participative corporate cultures or systems of organizational democracy discussed in Chapters 5 and 6.

The whole thrust of classical management theory and its modern application is to suggest that organizations can or should be rational systems that operate in as efficient a manner as possible. While many will endorse this as an ideal, it is easier said than done, because we are dealing with people, not inanimate cogs and wheels.

In this regard it is significant that the classical theorists gave relatively little attention to the human aspects of organization. Although they frequently recognized the need for leadership, initiative, benevolence, equity, esprit de corps, and other factors that might influence human motivation, organization as such was mainly understood as a technical problem. The classical theorists recognized that it was important to achieve a balance or harmony between the human and technical aspects, especially through appropriate selection and training procedures, but their main orientation was to make humans fit the requirements of mechanical organization.

For this they have been much criticized. Yet modern managers and management consultants often continue to introduce the same bias into their way of thinking. The most recent example is found in the "reengineering movement" that swept across North America and much of Europe in the 1990s. Recognizing that the bureaucratic form of organization with its emphasis on rigid departmentalization had outlived its usefulness, the reengineering movement urged a new mechanistic design, building around key business processes instead of bureaucratic functions. As in the old classical theory, the basic assumption is that if you get the engineering right the human factor will fall into place. Needless to say, this is not always the case. As a result, the reengineering movement has encountered exactly the same problems and failures experienced by older-style classical management principles. The human factor often subverts the reengineering process, leading to massive failure rates.

SCIENTIFIC MANAGEMENT

In Frederick the Great's approach to military organization we thus find many of the basic principles later elaborated by the classical management theorists. We also find many of the principles elaborated by the other great Frederick of organization theory, Frederick Taylor, who pioneered what is now known as scientific management.

Taylor was an American engineer and a flamboyant if somewhat disturbed personality. By his death in 1915 he had gained a reputation as a major "enemy of the working man," having been summoned in 1911 to defend his system of management before a committee of the U.S. House of Representatives. Although one of the most maligned and criticized of all organization theorists, he has also proved to be one of the most influential. His principles of scientific management provided the cornerstone for work design throughout the first half of the twentieth century, and in many situations prevail right up to the present day.

Taylor advocated five simple principles, which can be summarized as follows:

1. *Shift all responsibility for the organization of work from the worker to the manager.* Managers should do all the thinking relating to the planning and design of work, leaving the workers with the task of implementation.

2. *Use scientific methods* to determine the most efficient way of doing work. Design the worker's task accordingly, specifying the *precise* way in which the work is to be done.

3. *Select* the best person to perform the job thus designed.

4. *Train* the worker to do the work efficiently.

5. *Monitor* worker performance to ensure that appropriate work procedures are followed and that appropriate results are achieved.

In applying these principles Taylor advocated the use of time-and-motion study as a means of analyzing and standardizing work activities. His scientific approach called for detailed observation and measurement of even the most routine work to find the optimum mode of performance. Under Taylor's system, menial tasks such as pig-iron handling and earth shoveling became the subjects of science. He fused the perspective of an engineer with an obsession for control.

Prominent models of his approach to scientific management are found in numerous manufacturing firms, retail organizations, and offices. Consider, for example, the fast-food chains serving hamburgers, pizzas, and other highly standardized products. Here work is often organized in the minutest detail on the basis of designs that analyze the total process of production, find the most efficient procedures, and then allocate these as specialized duties to people trained to perform them in a very precise way. All the "thinking" is done by the managers and designers, leaving all the "doing" to the employees. The management observation checklist presented in Exhibit 2.1 provides the perfect illustration of Taylor's approach to management, showing how a simple job such as taking and serving a customer's order can be split into many separate elements that can each be observed and evaluated. Taylor would have been well pleased with such a system of work evaluation.

The same approach to work design is also found in traditional forms of assembly-line manufacturing and in production processes that are tightly controlled and monitored by computer technology. Here Taylor's ideas are built into the technology itself, making the workers servants or adjuncts to machines that are in complete control of the organization and pace of work.

Taylor's principles also had a major influence on the organization of office work through "organization and methods" and "work study" projects that broke integrated tasks into specialized components that could then be allocated to different employees. For example, in mechanized systems for processing insurance claim forms, one employee would often be responsible for checking a claim against a policy, another would initiate an evaluation process, another would conduct the evaluation, yet another would evaluate the evaluation, and so on. Systematically applied, Taylor's five principles led to the development of "office factories" where people performed fragmented and highly specialized duties in accordance with an elaborate system of work design and performance evaluation.

The effect of Taylor's scientific management on the workplace has been enormous, increasing productivity manyfold while accelerating the replacement of skilled craftspeople by unskilled workers. It is for these reasons that it has been so influential yet so maligned, for the increases in productivity have often been achieved at great human cost, reducing many workers to automatons, just as the army reforms of Frederick the Great did to his soldiers over 150 years earlier. The trend is so pervasive that it is now often described as one of "McDonaldization": to capture how the organizational principles underlying the design of the McDonald's chain of fast-food restaurants, with its emphasis on ruthless efficiency, quantification, predictability, control, and deskilled jobs (often described as "McJobs"), is providing an icon for organization throughout society. The principles advocated by Taylor and perfected by McDonald's and other fast-food restaurants have found their way into the organization of hospitals, factories, retail outlets, schools, universities, and other institutions seeking to rationalize their operations.

The human problems resulting from such methods of organization have been glaringly obvious ever since they were first introduced. For example, when Henry Ford established his first assembly line to produce the Model T, employee turnover rose to approximately 380 percent per annum. Only by doubling wages to his famous "$5 a day" was he able to stabilize the work situation and persuade workers to accept the new technology. For most people, assembly-line work is simply boring or alienating. Job cycles are often very short, with workers sometimes being asked to complete work involving seven or eight separate operations every forty or fifty seconds, seven or eight hours a day, fifty weeks a year. When General Motors decided to tighten up on efficiency in its Lordstown plant in the late 1960s, at the height of its commitment to this technology, the speed of the assembly line was raised to increase output from 60 to 100 cars per hour. At this new pace some workers had only thirty-six seconds to perform at least eight different operations, such as walking, lifting, handling, raising a carpet, bending to fasten bolts, fastening them by air gun, replacing the carpet, and putting a sticker on the hood.

The principle of separating the planning and design of work from its execution is often seen as the most pernicious and far-reaching element of Taylor's approach to management, for it effectively "splits" the worker, advocating the separation of hand and brain. As Taylor was fond of telling his workers, "You are not supposed to think. There are other people paid for thinking around here." Men and women were no more than "hands" or "manpower": the energy or force required to propel the organizational machine. The jobs they were required to perform were simplified to the ultimate degree so that workers would be cheap, easy to train, easy to supervise, and easy to replace. Just as the system of mass production required that products be assembled from interchangeable parts, Taylor's system rationalized the workplace so that it could be "manned" by interchangeable workers.

Over the years, Taylor's approach to management has been extended and refined in many ways, most notably through the development of franchising systems that are faced with the challenge of offering consistent products and services through decentralized operations and through the science of ergonomics, which studies the use of energy in the workplace. Interestingly, Taylor's principles have crossed many ideological barriers, being extensively used in the former USSR and Eastern Europe as well as in capitalist countries. This fact signifies that Taylorism is as much a tool for securing general control over the workplace as it is a means of generating profit. Although noncapitalist countries and institutions are rarely averse to profitable use of productive resources, one of the great attractions of Taylorism rests in the power it confers to those in control.

Although Taylor is often seen as the villain who created scientific management, it is important to realize that he was really part of a much broader social trend involving the mechanization of life generally. For example, the principles underlying Taylorism are now found on the football field and athletics track, in the gymnasium, and in the way we rationalize and routinize our personal lives. Taylor gave voice to a particular aspect of the trend toward mechanization, specialization, and bureaucratization that Max Weber saw as such a powerful social force. Taylorism was typically imposed on the workforce. But many of us impose forms of Taylorism on ourselves as we train and develop specialized capacities for thought and action and shape our bodies to conform with preconceived ideals. Under the influence of the same kind of mechanism that has helped make Taylorism so powerful, we often think about and treat ourselves as if we were machines.

The really distinctive feature of Taylorism thus is not the fact that Taylor tried to mechanize the organization of people and work, but the *degree* to which he was able to do this. Taylor's workers were expected to be as reliable, predictable, and efficient as the robots that are now replacing them. History may well judge that Taylor came before his time. His principles of scientific management make superb sense for organizing production when robots rather than human beings are the main productive force, and organizations can truly become machines.

Strengths and Limitations of the Machine Metaphor

- "Set goals and objectives and go for them."
- "Organize rationally, efficiently, and clearly."
- "Specify every detail so that everyone will be sure of the jobs that they have to perform."
- "Plan, organize, and control, control, control."

These and other similar ideas are often ingrained in our way of thinking about organization and in the way we evaluate organization practice. For many people, it is almost second nature to organize by setting up a structure of clearly defined activities linked by clear lines of communication, coordination, and control. Thus, when a manager designs an organization he or she frequently designs a formal structure of jobs into which people can then be fitted. When a vacancy arises in an organization, managers frequently talk about having "a slot" to fill. Much of our training and education is often geared to making us "fit in" and feel comfortable in our appointed place, so that the organization can proceed in a rational and efficient way.

Classical management theory and scientific management were each pioneered and sold to managers as the "one best way to organize." The early theorists believed that they had discovered *the* principles of organization, which, if followed, would more or less solve managerial problems forever. Now, we only have to look at the contemporary organizational scene to find that they were completely wrong on this score. Indeed, if we look closely, we find that their management principles often lie at the basis of many modern organizational problems.

Images or metaphors only create partial ways of seeing, for in encouraging us to see and understand the world from one perspective they discourage us from seeing it from others. This is exactly what has happened in the course of developing mechanistic approaches to organization. In understanding organization as a rational, technical process, mechanical imagery tends to underplay the human aspects of organization and to overlook the fact that the tasks facing organizations are often much more complex, uncertain, and difficult than those that can be performed by most machines.

The strengths and limitations of the machine as a metaphor for organization are reflected in the strengths and limitations of mechanistic organization in practice.

The strengths can be stated very simply. Mechanistic approaches to organization work well only under conditions where machines work well: (a) when there is a straightforward task to perform; (b) when the environment is stable enough to ensure that the products produced will be appropriate ones; (c) when one wishes to produce exactly the same product time and again; (d) when precision is at a premium; and (e) when the human "machine" parts are compliant and behave as they have been designed to do.

Some organizations have had spectacular success using the mechanistic model because these conditions are all fulfilled. As noted earlier, McDonald's and many firms in the fast-food industry provide the best examples. Look closely, and we find that the McDonald's situation meets all the conditions described above. The firm has built a solid reputation for excellent performance in the fast-food industry by mechanizing the organization of all its franchise outlets all over the world so that each can produce a uniform product. It serves a carefully targeted mass market in a perfectly regular and consistent way, with all the precision that "hamburger science" can provide. (The firm actually has its own "Hamburger U" for teaching this science to its managers, and has a detailed operating manual to guide franchisees in the daily operations of the McDonald's system.) The firm is exemplary in its adoption of Tayloristic principles and recruits a nonunionized labor force, often made up of high school and college students and part-time workers, that will be happy to fit the organization as designed. And the "machine" works perfectly most of the time. Of course, the company also has a dynamic and innovative character, but this is for the most part confined to its central staff who do the thinking (i.e., the policy development and design work) for the corporation as a whole.

Many franchising systems have used the same Tayloristic approach with great effect, centralizing the design and development of products or services and decentralizing implementation in a highly controlled way. The use of scientific methods to determine the work to be performed, manuals that set standards and codify performance in minute detail, well-developed recruitment and training plans, and comprehensive systems of job evaluation often provide the recipe for success, provided that the service or product is amenable to definition and control in this way.

Surgical wards, aircraft maintenance departments, finance offices, courier firms, and other organizations where precision, safety, and clear accountability are at a premium are also often able to implement mechanistic approaches successfully, at least in certain aspects of their operations.

However, despite these successes, mechanistic approaches to organization often have severe limitations. In particular they (a) can create organizational forms that have great difficulty in adapting to changing circumstances; (b) can result in mindless and unquestioning bureaucracy; (c) can have unanticipated and undesirable consequences as the interests of those working in the organization take precedence over the goals the organization was designed to achieve; and (d) can have dehumanizing effects upon employees, especially those at the lower levels of the organizational hierarchy.

Mechanistically structured organizations have great difficulty adapting to changing circumstances because they are designed to achieve predetermined goals; they are not designed for innovation. This should come as no surprise, for machines are usually single-purpose mechanisms designed to transform specific inputs into specific outputs and can engage in different activities only if they are explicitly modified or redesigned to do so.

Changing circumstances call for different kinds of action and response. Flexibility and capacities for creative action become more important than narrow efficiency. It becomes more important to do the right thing in a way that is timely and "good enough" than to do the wrong thing well or the right thing too late. In these respects, mechanistic organization falls victim to the kind of "segmentalism" that Rosabeth Moss Kanter and others have shown plagues so many modern corporations. The compartmentalization created by mechanistic divisions between different hierarchical levels, functions, roles, and people tends to create barriers and stumbling blocks.

For example, when new problems arise they are often ignored because there are no ready-made responses. Or they are approached in a fragmented rather than a holistic way so that they can be tackled through existing organizational policies, procedures, and patterns of expertise. But standardized procedures and channels of communication are often unable to deal effectively with new circumstances, necessitating numerous ad hoc meetings and committees, which, because they have to be planned to fit rather than disrupt the normal mode of operation, are often too slow or too late for dealing with issues. Problems of inaction and lack of coordination thus become rife. In such circumstances the organization frequently becomes clogged with backlogs of work because normal routine has been disrupted, and complex issues float up the organizational hierarchy as members at each level find in turn that they are unable to solve them. On the way, information often gets distorted, as people hide errors and the true nature and magnitude of problems for fear of being held responsible for them. Those in command of the organization thus frequently find themselves facing issues that are inappropriately defined, and which they have no real idea of how to approach. They are often forced to delegate them to special task forces or teams of staff experts or consultants—who, since they are often remote from the concrete problems being experienced, further increase the delay and inadequacy of response.

The difficulty of achieving effective responses to changing circumstances is often further aggravated by the high degree of specialization in different functional areas within the organization (e.g., production, marketing, finance, product engineering). Interdepartmental communications and coordination are often poor, and people often have a myopic view of what is occurring, there being no overall grasp of the situation facing the enterprise as a whole. As a result the actions encouraged by one element of the organization often entail negative consequences for others, so that one element ends up working against the interests of another.

These problems are often compounded by the fact that mechanistic definitions of job responsibilities encourage many organizational members to adopt mindless, unquestioning attitudes such as "it's not my job to worry about that," "that's his responsibility, not mine," or "I'm here to do what I'm told." Although often seen as attitudes that employees "bring to work," they are actually inherent in the mechanistic approach to organization. Defining work responsibilities in a clear-cut manner has the advantage of letting everyone know what is expected of them. But it also lets them know what is *not* expected of them. Detailed job descriptions have this two-edged character, creating many problems when the organization faces changing circumstances that call for initiative and flexibility in response.

This institutionalized passivity and dependency can even lead people to make and justify deliberate mistakes on the premise that they're obeying orders. The hierarchical organization of jobs builds on the idea that control must be exercised *over* the different parts of the organization (to ensure that they are doing what they are designed to do), rather than being built *into* the parts themselves. Supervisors and other hierarchical forms of control do not just monitor the performance of workers—they also remove responsibility from workers, because their function really becomes operational only when problems arise. In a similar way, a system of quality control on a production line often institutionalizes the production of defective goods. People realize that they are allowed a quota of errors.

Much of the apathy, carelessness, and lack of pride so often encountered in the modern workplace is thus not coincidental: it is fostered by the mechanistic approach. Mechanistic organization discourages initiative, encouraging people to obey orders and keep their place rather than to take an interest in, and question, what they are doing. People in a bureaucracy who question the wisdom of conventional practice are viewed more often than not as troublemakers. Therefore, apathy often reigns as people learn to feel powerless about problems that collectively they understand and ultimately have the power to solve.

These difficulties are often linked to another set of problems: the development of subgoals and sets of interests that undermine the organization's ability to meet its primary objectives. Functional specialization is supposed to create a system of cooperation. Yet it often ends up creating a system of competition as individuals and departments compete for scarce resources or job positions higher up the hierarchy. Empire building, careerism, the defense of departmental interests, pet projects, and the padding of budgets to create slack resources may subvert the working of the whole. If the organization is staffed by rational men and women who behave in accordance with the formal interests and aims of the total organization, "fitting in" rather than using the organization for other purposes, then this may not occur. But humans are human, and the best-laid plans have a habit of turning in ways never intended by their creators. Formal organizations thus often become guided toward the achievement of informal ends, some of which may be quite contrary to the aims underlying the original design.

A final set of problems relate to human consequences. The mechanistic approach to organization tends to limit rather than mobilize the development of human capacities, molding human beings to fit the requirements of mechanical organization rather than building the organization around their strengths and potentials. Both employees and organizations lose from this arrangement. Employees lose opportunities for personal growth, often spending many hours a day on work they neither value nor enjoy, and organizations lose the creative and intelligent contributions that most employees are capable of making, given the right opportunities.

Mechanistic approaches to organization have proved incredibly popular, partly because of their efficiency in the performance of tasks that can be successfully routinized and partly because they offer managers the promise of tight control over people and their activities. In stable times, the approach worked from a managerial point of view. But with the increasing pace of social and economic change, the limitations have become more and more obvious.

As we enter the twenty-first century we find bureaucracies and other modes of mechanistic organization coming under increasing attack because of their rigidities and other dysfunctional consequences. The total quality movement (TQM) and emphasis on flexible, team-based organization that came into prominence in the 1980s and 1990s signaled an early response to these problems and the need to find other nonmechanical ways of organizing. From a historical perspective, the mechanistic approach to organization belongs to the mechanical age. Now that we are entering an age with a completely new technological base drawing on microelectronics, new organizational principles are likely to become increasingly important. Some of the images of organization considered in the following chapters give a glimpse of what may be both possible and appropriate for managing in these new times.

3

Nature Intervenes

Organizations as Organisms

Let's think about organizations as if they were organisms. We find ourselves thinking about them as living systems, existing in a wider environment on which they depend for the satisfaction of various needs. And as we look around the organizational world we begin to see that it is possible to identify different species of organization in different kinds of environments. Just as we find polar bears in arctic regions, camels in deserts, and alligators in swamps, we notice that certain species of organization are better "adapted" to specific environmental conditions than others. We find that bureaucratic organizations tend to work most effectively in environments that are stable or protected in some way and that very different species are found in more competitive and turbulent regions, such as the environments of high-tech firms in the aerospace and microelectronics industries.

In this simple line of inquiry we find the crux of many of the most important developments in organization theory over the past sixty years, for the problems of mechanistic visions of organization have led many organization theorists away from mechanical science and toward biology as a source of ideas for thinking about organization. In the process, organization theory has become a kind of biology in which the distinctions and relations among *molecules, cells, complex organisms, species,* and *ecology* are paralleled in those between *individuals, groups, organizations, populations (species) of organizations,* and their *social ecology.* In pursuing this line of inquiry, organization theorists have generated many new ideas for understanding how organizations function and the factors that influence their well-being.

In this chapter we will explore these ideas, showing how the organismic metaphor has helped organization theorists identify and study different organizational needs and focus on the following:

- Organizations as "open systems"
- The process of adapting organizations to environments
- Organizational life cycles
- Factors influencing organizational health and development
- Different species of organization
- The relations between species and their ecology

Collectively, these ideas have had an enormous impact on the way we now think about organization. Under the influence of the machine metaphor, organization theory was locked into a form of engineering preoccupied with relations between goals, structures, and efficiency. The idea that organizations are most like organisms has changed all this, guiding our attention toward the more general issues of survival, organization-environment relations, and organizational effectiveness. Goals, structures, and efficiency now become subsidiary to problems of survival and other more "biological" concerns.

Discovering Organizational Needs

Not surprisingly, organization theory began its excursion into biology by developing the idea that employees are people with complex needs that must be satisfied if they are to lead full and healthy lives and to perform effectively in the workplace. In retrospect, this hardly appears a profound insight because from a modern perspective this seems an obvious fact of life. We all know that employees work best when motivated by the tasks they have to perform and that the process of motivation hinges on allowing people to achieve rewards that satisfy their personal needs. However, in the nineteenth and early twentieth centuries this idea was by no means obvious. For many people, work was a basic necessity, and those who designed and managed early organizations treated it as such. Hence, as we saw in the previous chapter, people like Frederick Taylor and the other classical management theorists were able to view the design of organizations as a *technical* problem, and the task of encouraging people to comply with the requirements of the organizational machine was reduced to a problem of "paying the right rate for the job." Although esprit de corps was viewed as a valuable aid to management, management was viewed primarily as a process of controlling and directing employees in their work.

Much of organization theory since the late 1920s has rested in overcoming the limitations of this perspective. We can start the story with the Hawthorne Studies. These were conducted in the 1920s and 1930s under the leadership of Elton Mayo, at the Hawthorne Plant of the Western Electric Company in Chicago. At the outset the studies were primarily concerned with investigating the relation between conditions of work and the incidence of fatigue and boredom among employees. As the research progressed, however, it left this narrow Taylorist perspective to focus on many other aspects of the work situation as well, including the attitudes and preoccupations of employees and factors in the social environment outside work. The studies are now famous for identifying the importance of social needs in the workplace and the way that work groups can satisfy these needs by restricting output and engaging in all manner of unplanned activities. In identifying that an "informal organization" based on friendship groups and unplanned interactions can exist alongside the formal organization documented in the "blueprints" designed by management, the studies dealt an important blow to classical management theory. They showed quite clearly that work activities are influenced as much by the nature of human beings as by formal design and that organization theorists must pay close attention to this human side of organization.

With the Hawthorne Studies, the whole question of work motivation thus became a burning issue, as did the relations between individuals and groups. A new theory of organization began to emerge, built on the idea that individuals and groups, like biological organisms, operate most effectively only when their needs are satisfied.

Theories of motivation such as that pioneered by Abraham Maslow presented the human being as a kind of psychological organism struggling to satisfy its needs in a quest for full growth and development. This theory, which suggested that humans are motivated by a hierarchy of needs progressing through the physiological, the social, and the psychological, had very powerful implications, for it suggested that bureaucratic organizations that sought to motivate employees through money or by merely providing a secure job confined human development to the lower levels of the need hierarchy. Many management theorists were quick to see that jobs and interpersonal relations could be redesigned to create conditions for personal growth that would simultaneously help organizations achieve their aims and objectives.

Thus, the idea of integrating the needs of individuals and organizations became a powerful force. Organizational psychologists like Chris Argyris, Frederick Herzberg, and Douglas McGregor began to show how bureaucratic structures, leadership styles, and work organization generally could be modified to create "enriched," motivating jobs that would encourage people to exercise their capacities for self-control and creativity. Under their influence, alternatives to bureaucratic organization began to emerge.

Particular attention was focused on the idea of making employees feel more useful and important by giving them meaningful jobs and by giving as much autonomy, responsibility, and recognition as possible as a means of getting them involved in their work. Job enrichment, combined with a more participative, democratic, and employee-centered style of leadership, arose as an alternative to the excessively narrow, authoritarian, and dehumanizing work orientation generated by scientific management and classical management theory.

Developed in countless ways, these ideas provided a powerful framework for the development of what is now known as human resource management. Employees were to be seen as valuable resources that could contribute in rich and varied ways to an organization's activities if given an appropriate chance. Maslow's theory suggested a whole repertoire of means (summarized in Exhibit 3.1) through which employees could be motivated at all levels of the need hierarchy. Much of this theorizing has proved extremely attractive in management circles, for it offered the possibility of motivating employees through "higher level" needs in a way that could increase involvement and commitment without paying them any more money.

Since the 1960s, management and organizational researchers have given much attention to shaping the design of work to increase productivity and job satisfaction while improving work quality and reducing employee absenteeism and turnover. Human resource management has become a major focus of attention and the need to integrate the human and technical aspects of work an important principle.

This dual focus is now reflected in the view that organizations are best understood as "sociotechnical systems." The term was coined in the 1950s

TYPE OF NEED

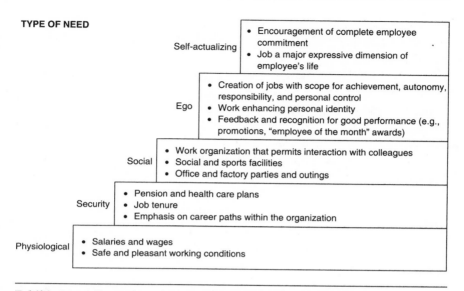

Self-actualizing	• Encouragement of complete employee commitment • Job a major expressive dimension of employee's life	
Ego	• Creation of jobs with scope for achievement, autonomy, responsibility, and personal control • Work enhancing personal identity • Feedback and recognition for good performance (e.g., promotions, "employee of the month" awards)	
Social	• Work organization that permits interaction with colleagues • Social and sports facilities • Office and factory parties and outings	
Security	• Pension and health care plans • Job tenure • Emphasis on career paths within the organization	
Physiological	• Salaries and wages • Safe and pleasant working conditions	

Exhibit 3.1   Examples of How Organizations Can Satisfy Needs at Different Levels of Maslow's Hierarchy

by members of the Tavistock Institute of Human Relations in England to capture the interdependent qualities of work. In their view, these aspects of work are inseparable because the nature of one element in this configuration *always* has important consequences for the other. When we choose a technical system (whether in the form of an organizational structure, job design, or particular technology) it always has human consequences, and vice versa.

This has been particularly well illustrated in many Tavistock studies, such as that conducted by Eric Trist and Ken Bamforth on technological change in coal mining in England in the late 1940s. The attempt to mechanize the mining process through the introduction of the "long-wall method," which in effect brought assembly-line coal cutting to the coal face, created severe problems by destroying the informal fabric of social relations present in the mine. The new technology promised increases in efficiency yet brought all the social problems now associated with the modern factory, compounded many times by much worse physical conditions. The resolution of the problems rested in finding a means of reconciling human needs and technical efficiency.

Work in most parts of the world has now shown that in designing or managing any kind of social system, whether it be a small group, an organization, or a society, the interdependence of technical and human needs must be kept firmly in mind.

The principle now seems very obvious and is clearly recognized in most popular theories of organization, leadership, and group functioning. But there is still a tendency in management to fall back into a strictly technical view of organization. As noted in Chapter 2, this has been the primary problem facing the "reengineering movement," which more or less dominated Western management practice in the early 1990s. Aspiring "reengineers" paid a heavy price for ignoring the social dimension. By placing primary emphasis on the design of technical "business systems" as the key to change, the majority of reengineering programs mobilized all kinds of social, cultural, and political resistance that undermined their effectiveness.

Recognizing the Importance of Environment: Organizations as Open Systems

When we recognize that individuals, groups, and organizations have needs that must be satisfied, attention is invariably drawn to the fact that they depend on a wider environment for various kinds of sustenance. It is this kind of thinking that now underpins the "open systems approach" to organization, which takes its main inspiration from the work of Ludwig von Bertalanffy, a theoretical biologist. Developed simultaneously on both sides of the Atlantic in the 1950s and 1960s, the systems approach builds on the principle that organizations, like organisms, are "open" to their environment and must achieve an appropriate relation with that environment if they are to survive.

Developed at a theoretical level, the open-systems approach has generated many new concepts for thinking about organizations (Exhibit 3.2, page 40). These are often presented as general principles for thinking about *all* kinds of systems owing to von Bertalanffy's having developed the principles of General Systems Theory as a means of linking different scientific disciplines. However, he achieved this integration by taking the living organism as a model for understanding complex open systems, thus reproducing ideas primarily developed for understanding biological systems in order to understand the world at large. Early systems theory thus developed as a biological metaphor in disguise.

At a pragmatic level, the open-systems approach usually focuses on a number of key issues. First, there is the emphasis on the environment in which organizations exist. Surprising as it may now seem, the classical management theorists devoted relatively little attention to the environment. They treated the organization as a "closed" mechanical system and became preoccupied with principles of internal design. The open-systems view has changed all this, suggesting that we should always organize with the environment in mind. Thus, much attention has been devoted to understanding the immediate "task" or "business environment," defined by the organization's direct interactions with customers, competitors, suppliers, labor unions, and government agencies, as well as the broader "contextual" or "general environment." All this has important implications for organizational practice, stressing the importance of being able to scan and sense changes in task and contextual environments, of being able to bridge and manage critical boundaries and areas of interdependence, and of being able to develop appropriate operational and strategic responses. Much of the widespread interest in corporate strategy is a product of this realization that organizations must be sensitive to what is occurring in the world beyond.

A second focus of the open-systems approach defines an organization in terms of interrelated subsystems. Systems are like Chinese boxes in that they always contain wholes within wholes. Thus, organizations contain individuals (who are systems on their own account) who belong to groups or departments that belong to larger organizational divisions. And so on. If we define the whole organization as a system, then the other levels can be understood as subsystems, just as molecules, cells, and organs can be seen as subsystems of a living organism, even though they are complex open systems on their own account.

Systems theorists are fond of thinking about intra- and interorganizational relations in these terms, using configurations of subsystems to depict key patterns and interconnections. One popular way of doing this is to focus on the key "business processes" or sets of needs the organization must satisfy to survive and emphasize the importance of managing relations between them. Thus, the sociotechnical view of organization discussed earlier is often expanded to take account of relations between technical, social, managerial, strategic, and environmental requirements (Exhibit 3.3). As we will see, this way of thinking has helped us recognize how everything depends on everything else and find ways of managing the relations between critical subsystems and the environment.

A third focus in the pragmatic use of the systems approach rests in the attempt to establish congruencies or "alignments" between different systems and to identify and eliminate potential dysfunctions. Just as a sociotechnical approach to work design emphasizes the importance of matching human and technical requirements, open-systems theory more generally encourages a matching of the kind of subsystems illustrated in Exhibit 3.3 on page 43. Here the principles of requisite variety, differentiation and integration, and other systems ideas (discussed in Exhibit 3.2)

These principles, derived primarily from the study of biological systems, are now often used in the analysis of organizations as systems:

The concept of an "open system." Organic systems at the level of the cell, complex organism, and population of organisms exist in a continuous exchange with their environment. This exchange is crucial for sustaining the life and form of the system, as environmental interaction is the basis of self-maintenance. It is thus often said that living systems are "open systems," characterized by a continuous cycle of input, internal transformation (throughout), output, and feedback (whereby one element of experience influences the next). The idea of openness emphasizes the key relationships between the environment and the internal functioning of the system. Environment and system are to be understood as being in a state of interaction and mutual dependence. The open nature of biological and social systems contrasts with the "closed" nature of many physical and mechanical systems, although the degree of openness can vary, as some open systems may be responsive only to a relatively narrow range of inputs from the environment. Towers, bridges, and even clockwork toys with predetermined motions are closed systems. A machine that is able to regulate its internal operation in accordance with variations in the environment may be considered a partially open system. A living organism, organization, or social group is a fully open system. (But note the critique of the concept of openness presented in Chapter 8.)

Homeostasis. The concept of homeostasis refers to self-regulation and the ability to maintain a steady state. Biological organisms seek a regularity of form and distinctness from the environment while maintaining a continuous exchange with that environment. This form and distinctness is achieved through homeostatic processes that relate and control system operation on the basis of what is now called "negative feedback," where deviations from some standard or norm initiate actions to correct the deviation. Thus, when our body temperature rises above normal limits, certain bodily functions operate to try to counteract the rise (e.g., we begin to perspire and breathe heavily). Social systems also require such homeostatic control processes if they are to acquire enduring form.

Entropy/negative entropy. Closed systems are entropic in that they have a tendency to deteriorate and run down. Open systems, on the other hand, attempt to sustain themselves by importing energy to try to offset entropic tendencies. It is thus said that they are characterized by negative entropy.

Structure, function, differentiation, and integration. The relationship between these concepts is of crucial importance for understanding living systems. It is easy to see organization as a structure of parts and to explain

Exhibit 3.2   A Glossary of Some Open-Systems Concepts

system behavior in terms of relations between the parts, causes and effects, stimulus and response. Our understanding of living systems warns against such reduction, emphasizing that structure, function, behavior, and all other features of system operation are closely intertwined. Although it is possible to pursue the study of organisms through the study of anatomy, a full understanding of such systems calls for much more. Even the life of the simple cell is dependent on a complex web of relations between cellular structure, metabolism, gas exchange, the acquisition of nutrients, and numerous other functions. The cell as a system is a system of functional interdependence that is not reducible to a simple structure. Indeed, the structure at any one time depends on the existence of these functions and in many respects is only a manifestation of them. The same is true of more complex organisms, which reflect increased differentiation and specialization of function (e.g., with specialized organs performing specific functions)—and which thus require more complex systems of integration to maintain the system as a whole (e.g., through the operation of a brain). Similar relationships between structure, function, differentiation, and integration can also be seen in social systems such as organizations.

Requisite variety. Related to the idea of differentiation and integration is the principle of requisite variety, which states that the internal regulatory mechanisms of a system must be as diverse as the environment with which it is trying to deal. For only by incorporating required variety into internal controls can a system deal with the variety and challenge posed by its environment. Any system that insulates itself from diversity in the environment tends to atrophy and lose its complexity and distinctive nature. Thus, requisite variety is an important feature of living systems of all kinds.

Equifinality. This principle captures the idea that in an open system there may be many different ways of arriving at a given end state. This is in contrast to more closed systems where system relations are fixed in terms of structure to produce specific patterns of cause and effect. Living systems have flexible patterns of organization that allow the achievement of specific results from different starting points with different resources in different ways. The structure of the system at a given time is no more than an aspect or manifestation of a more complex functional process; it does not determine that process.

System evolution. The capacity of a system to evolve depends on an ability to move to more complex forms of differentiation and integration, and greater variety in the system facilitating its ability to deal with challenges and opportunities posed by the environment. This involves a cyclical process of variation, selection, and retention of the selected characteristics.

can be brought into play. For example, the principle of requisite variety is particularly important in designing control systems or for the management of internal and external boundaries—for these must embrace the complexity of the phenomena being controlled or managed to be effective. As we shall see later, the principle of differentiation and integration is useful for organizing different kinds of tasks within the same organization.

Collectively, these ideas have pointed the way to theories of organization and management that allow us to break free of bureaucratic thinking and to organize in a way that meets the requirements of the environment. These insights are now usually marshaled under the perspective known as "contingency theory" and in the practice of organizational development.

Contingency Theory: Adapting Organization to Environment

- "Organizations are open systems that need careful management to satisfy and balance internal needs and to adapt to environmental circumstances."
- "There is no one best way of organizing. The appropriate form depends on the kind of task or environment with which one is dealing."
- "Management must be concerned, above all else, with achieving alignments and 'good fits.'"
- "Different approaches to management may be necessary to perform different tasks within the same organization."
- "Different types or 'species' of organizations are needed in different types of environments."

In a nutshell, these are the main ideas underlying the contingency approach to organization, which has established itself as a dominant perspective in modern organizational analysis.

One of the most influential studies establishing the credentials of this approach was conducted in the 1950s by two British researchers, Tom Burns and G. M. Stalker. Their work is famous for establishing the distinction between "mechanistic" and "organic" approaches to organization and management.

Organization, like organisms, can be conceived of as sets of interacting subsystems. These subsystems can be defined in many ways. Here is one example stressing relations between the different variables that influence the functioning of an organization, thereby providing a useful diagnostic tool.

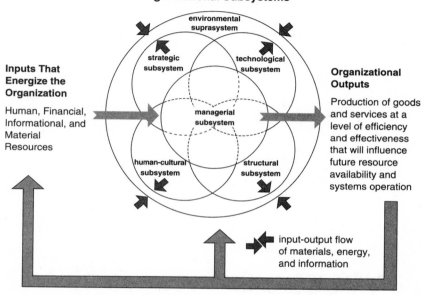

Organizational Subsystems

Inputs That Energize the Organization

Human, Financial, Informational, and Material Resources

Organizational Outputs

Production of goods and services at a level of efficiency and effectiveness that will influence future resource availability and systems operation

Exhibit 3.3   How an Organization Can Be Seen as a Set of Subsystems

SOURCE: Adapted from CONTINGENCY VIEW OF ORGANIZATION AND MANAGE-MENT by Fremont E. Kast and James E. Rosenzweig. © 1973, Science Research Associates.

Focusing on firms in a variety of industries (e.g., man-made fibers, engineering, and electronics), Burns and Stalker illustrated that when change in the environment becomes the order of the day, as when changing technological and market conditions pose new problems and challenges, open and flexible styles of organization and management are required. Exhibit 3.4 captures salient aspects of their study, illustrating patterns of organization and management in four successful firms experiencing different rates of environmental change.

The rayon mill faced a relatively stable environment, employed a technology that was routine and well understood, and was organized in a highly mechanistic way. The firm had a "factory bible," which was held by every head of a department and defined required action in almost every situation. People in the organization thus knew precisely what was

	Rayon Mill	Switch-gear Firm	Radio and Television Firm	Electronics Firm
Nature of environment	Relatively stable: technological and market conditions well understood	Moderate rate of change: expanding market coupled with opportunities for improved products	High degree of change: dynamic technological and market conditions with predictable rate of novelty	Highly unpredictable: rapid technological advance and boundless market opportunities
Nature of task facing the firm	Efficient production of standard product	Efficient production and sale of basic product, subject to modification according to customer requirements	Efficient design, production, and marketing of new products highly competitive in environment	Exploitation of rapid technical change through innovation and exploration of new market situations
Organization of work	Clearly defined jobs arranged in hierarchical pattern	Rough division of job responsibilities according to functional and hierarchical pattern, modified to meet contingencies; no stable division of functions	Consistent blurring of organizational positions; every section of management concerned with the focal task of competitive selling	Deliberate attempt to avoid specifying individual tasks; jobs defined by the individuals concerned through interaction with others
Nature of authority	Clearly defined and vested in formal position in hierarchy; seniority important	Not clearly defined but following the hierarchy except in specially convened committees and meetings	Limits of authority and responsibility not defined; authority vested in people with ability to solve problems at hand	Pattern of authority informal and constantly changing as roles become redefined with changing circumstances;

Exhibit 3.4   Patterns of Organization and Management in Four Successful Organizations Facing Different Rates of Environmental Change

(Continued)

Exhibit 3.4 (Continued)

	Rayon Mill	Switch-gear Firm	Radio and Television Firm	Electronics Firm
				vested in individuals with appropriate skills and abilities
Communications system	According to pattern specified in various rules and regulations; mainly vertical	According to rules and conventions but supplemented by regular system of committees and meetings; junior staff free to consult with top management group	Frequent meetings in a context of constant consultation across all levels and parts of the firm	Completely free and informal; the process of communication was unending and central to the concept of organization
Nature of employee commitment	Commitment to responsibilities associated with their own particular jobs; loyalty and obedience important	Commitment to own job but recognizing the need for flexibility in dealing with contingencies arising from the total situation	Commitment to demands of one's own functional positions reconciled with wider demands for cooperation and flexible interpretation of function	Full commitment to the central tasks facing the concern as a whole and an ability to deal with considerable stress and uncertainty
	MECHANISTIC	←——————————————→		ORGANIC

SOURCE: Based on Burns and Stalker (1961).

expected of them and attended to their job responsibilities in a narrow yet efficient way to create a competitively priced product. The firm was relatively successful in meeting the demands placed upon it, treating problematic situations as temporary deviations from the norm and doing whatever it could to stabilize its operating environment. For example, the sales office was sometimes asked to restrain sales in the interests of sustaining an even and trouble-free production schedule.

In other successful organizations facing more uncertain and turbulent environmental conditions, the mechanistic approach to organization tended to be abandoned; more organic and flexible approaches to organization were required for successful operation. Thus, in a switch-gear firm operating in an area of the engineering industry, where product developments hinged on improvements in design and cutting costs and where products were frequently made to customer specifications, systems of authority, communication, and work organization were geared to the contingencies of changing situations. Great use was made of meetings as a means of exchanging information and identifying problems, particularly those relating to the coordination of work, so that an alternative system of organization existed alongside the formal hierarchy defining relationships between specialist tasks.

In successful firms in the electronics industry, the departure from the mechanistic mode was even more pronounced. For example, in a firm involved in radio and television manufacture, at the more stable end of the electronics spectrum, the need to keep abreast of market and technological change through frequent product modification and the need to link developments in research and production called for free and open collaboration and communication across departments and levels of seniority. Meetings were again a central feature, driving and dominating day-to-day work activities. This approach to organization has grown in prominence since the publication of Burns and Stalker's work. It is most evident in the "project" or "matrix" form of organization, which makes use of project teams to deal with the continuous flow of problems and projects associated with changes in corporate policy and the external environment.

In successful organizations in even more unpredictable areas of the electronics field, where the need to innovate was an essential condition for survival, the mode of organization was even more open. Here, jobs were allowed to shape themselves, people being appointed to the organization for their general ability and expertise and allowed and encouraged to find their own place and define the contribution that they could make.

This style of open, "organic" management is fully consistent with the way the electronics industry has evolved. When the first commercial electronics firms began operating at the end of World War II, there was no commercial market for electronics products to speak of, for peacetime applications of this newly emerging technology had yet to be found. The electronics industry literally had to invent both products and markets and at the same time cope with the rapid technological change that has converted computers from room-size giants into devices that fit our pockets. As we are all so well aware, countless new applications have been found for the basic technology.

From the start, firms in this industry operated in an organic and flexible manner, creating or searching for opportunities in the environment and adapting themselves to take advantage of these opportunities. In the firms observed by Burns and Stalker, the process of finding out what one should be doing proved unending, defining a mode of organization linking inquiry and action, and the process has continued. Successful electronics firms avoided organizational hierarchies and avoided narrow departmentalization, with individuals and groups defining and redefining roles in a collaborative manner in connection with the tasks facing the organization as a whole. They created innovative, team-based organizations having more in common with an amoeba than a machine.

Burns and Stalker's idea that it is possible to identify various organizational forms ranging from mechanistic to organic and that more flexible forms are required to deal with changing environments quickly received support from other studies conducted in the late 1950s and early 1960s. For example, Joan Woodward, in a study of firms in England, discerned a relationship between technology and the structure of successful organizations. She showed that the principles of classical management theory were not always the right ones to follow, for different technologies impose different demands on individuals and organization that have to be met through *appropriate* structure. Her evidence suggested that bureaucratic-mechanistic organization might be appropriate for firms employing mass-production technologies but that firms with unit, small-batch, or process systems of production needed a different approach.

Woodward's findings also suggested that given any technology a range of possible organizational forms may be employed. Although suggesting that successful organizations matched structure and technology, she demonstrated that this relationship was ultimately one of strategic choice. Burns and Stalker also made a similar point in stressing that there was absolutely no guarantee that firms would find the appropriate mode of organization for dealing with their environment. Their study emphasized that successful adaptation of organization to environment depended on the ability of top management to interpret the conditions facing the firm in an appropriate manner and to adopt relevant courses of action. Both these studies thus demonstrated that, in the process of organizing, a lot of choices have to be made and that effective organization depends on achieving a balance or compatibility between strategy, structure, technology, the commitments and needs of people, and the external environment.

We find here the essence of modern contingency theory. But it took an important study by several Harvard researchers, led by Paul Lawrence and Jay Lorsch, to hammer the point home. Their research was built around two principal ideas: (a) that different kinds of organizations are needed to deal with different market and technological conditions and (b) that organizations operating in uncertain and turbulent environments need to achieve a higher degree of internal differentiation (e.g., between departments) than those in environments that are less complex and more stable. To test their ideas, they studied high- and low-performance organizations in three industries experiencing high, moderate, and low rates of growth and technological and market change. The plastics industry was selected as an example of a turbulent environment and the standardized container industry as an example of a stable environment, with the food industry in between. Lawrence and Lorsch's results supported their hypotheses, showing that successful firms in each environment achieved an appropriate degree of differentiation and integration and that the degree of differentiation between departments tended to be greater in the plastics industry than in the food industry, which was in turn greater than that in the standardized container industry.

The Lawrence and Lorsch study thus refined the contingency approach by showing that styles of organization may need to vary between organizational subunits because of the detailed characteristics of their subenvironments. At the time of their study, production departments typically faced task environments characterized by more clear-cut goals and shorter time horizons. They adopted more formal or bureaucratic modes of interaction. Research and development departments, especially those engaged in fundamental as opposed to applied research, faced even more ambiguous goals, had longer time horizons, and usually adopted even more informal modes of interaction. The study showed that the degree of required differentiation in managerial and organizational styles between departments varied according to the nature of the industry and its environment and that an appropriate degree of integration was also needed to tie the differentiated parts together again.

The study also yielded important insights on modes of integration. For example, in relatively stable environments, conventional bureaucratic modes of integration such as hierarchy and rules appeared to work quite well. But in more turbulent environments they needed to be replaced by other modes, such as the use of multidisciplinary project teams and the appointment of personnel skilled in the art of coordination and conflict resolution. The successful use of these integrative devices was also shown to be dependent on achieving an intermediate stance between the units being coordinated; on the power, status, and competence of those involved; and on the presence of a structure of rewards favoring integration.

Lawrence and Lorsch gave precision and refinement to the general idea that certain organizations need to be more organic than others, suggesting that the degree of organicism required varies from one organizational subunit to another. Using their ideas, we can appreciate that even in the dynamic context of an electronics firm, where the dominant ethic may be to remain open, flexible, and innovative, there may be exceptions to the rule. For example, certain aspects of production or financial administration may require clearer definition and control than work in other areas.

The Lawrence and Lorsch study thus reinforced and developed the ideas emerging from the other studies discussed above, marking an important turning point in favor of contingency theory. This work served to popularize the idea that in different environmental circumstances some species of organization are better able to survive than others and that since the relations between organization and environment are the product of human choices, they may become maladapted. In such cases, organizations are likely to experience many problems both in dealing with the environment and in their internal functioning. Such ideas naturally give rise to a desire to know more about the nature of organizational species and the requirements for designing and maintaining healthy organizations. Not surprisingly, these concerns have been an important feature of recent research.

The Variety of the Species

The ideas discussed in the previous sections go a long way toward showing us what species of organization are successful and under what conditions. But since the 1960s, hundreds of research studies have further addressed the job of specifying organizational characteristics and their success in dealing with different tasks and environmental conditions. These studies have added rich insight to the mechanistic-organic continuum developed by Burns and Stalker.

Consider, for example, the work of Henry Mintzberg of McGill University, which identifies five configurations or species of organization: the *machine bureaucracy*, the *divisionalized form*, the *professional bureaucracy*, the *simple structure*, and the species that we refer to as the *adhocracy*. The thrust of this work, which has been extended and refined in many ways by Mintzberg's colleagues Danny Miller and Peter Friesen, is to show that effective organization depends on developing a cohesive set of relations between structural design; the age, size, and technology of the firm; and the conditions of the industry in which it is operating.

The work of the McGill researchers confirms that the machine bureaucracy and the divisionalized form (both of which were discussed in Chapter 2) tend to be ineffective except under conditions where tasks and environment are simple and stable. Their highly centralized systems of control tend to make them slow and ineffective in dealing with changing circumstances. While appropriate for firms that are "production driven" or "efficiency driven," they are often inappropriate for firms that are "market" or "environment driven."

The professional bureaucracy modifies the principles of centralized control to allow greater autonomy to staff and is appropriate for dealing with relatively stable conditions where tasks are relatively complicated. This has proved an appropriate structure for universities, hospitals, and other professional organizations where people with key skills and abilities need a large measure of autonomy and discretion to be effective in their work. But, since the 1980s, its effectiveness has been severely challenged by the changing environments with which these kinds of organizations have had to deal. The structure of the professional bureaucracy tends to be fairly flat, tall hierarchies being replaced by a decentralized system of authority. Standardization and integration are achieved through professional training and the acceptance of key operating norms rather than through more direct forms of control.

The simple structure and "adhocracy" tend to work best in unstable environmental conditions. The former usually comprises a chief executive, often the founder or an entrepreneur, who may have a group of support staff along with a group of operators who do the basic work. Organization is very informal and flexible and, although run in a highly centralized way by the chief executive, is ideal for achieving quick changes and maneuvers. This form of organization works very well in entrepreneurial organizations where speedy decision making is at a premium, provided that tasks are not too complex. It is typical of successful young and innovative companies.

The "adhocracy," a term coined by Warren Bennis to characterize organizations that are temporary by design, approximates Burns and Stalker's organic form of organization. It is a form highly suited for the performance of complex and uncertain tasks in turbulent environments.

The adhocracy usually involves project teams that come together to perform a task and disappear when the task is over, with members regrouping in other teams devoted to other projects. Sometimes, this kind of enterprise is called a "virtual" or "network" organization, especially when teams and team members are spread geographically, using electronic technology and occasional face-to-face meetings to integrate their activities.

Adhocracies, "virtual teams," and "virtual organizations" now abound in innovative firms in the electronic and other high-tech and rapidly changing industries. They are the norm in all kinds of project-oriented companies, such as consulting firms and advertising agencies, and in the movie industry. This form of organization also sometimes emerges as a differentiated unit of a larger organization: for example, an ad hoc task group or project team performing a limited assignment or contributing to the strategic planning and development of the organization as a whole. It is also frequently used in R&D work.

As organizational environments have become more complex, differentiated, and turbulent, more and more "species" of organizations seem to have emerged. Charles Handy identifies "federal" and "shamrock" organizations, James Brian Quinn talks about "cluster" organizations, and, of course, there's the well-known "matrix" form. Each species seems to have distinct characteristics and distinctive niches in which it excels.

More often than not, the label or name applied to these different types of organizations seeks to capture the visual configuration that appears when the basic structure or "skeleton" is drawn on paper. Consider, for example, the concept of "matrix organization," a species with many variations, some of which look like modified bureaucracies while others have more free-flowing forms.

The term *matrix organization* was coined to capture a visual impression or organizations that systematically attempt to combine the kind of functional or departmental structure of organization found in a bureaucracy with a project-team structure (Exhibit 3.5). The functional units are equivalent to the columns of a matrix, while the teams form the rows.

The fully developed matrix is team driven, in that priority is given to business, program, product, or project areas, with functional specialisms providing support. In this form, it is like the adhocracy: The focus on an end product rather than on functional contributions encourages flexible, innovative, and adaptive behavior. In some matrix organizations, however, the functional divisions retain most of the control, so the teams are set within a bureaucratic structure from which it is often difficult to break free. As a result, they often fail to innovate and perform their project tasks in an effective way.

Matrix and other team-based organizations provide a means of breaking down the barriers between specialisms and allowing members from different functional backgrounds to fuse their skills and abilities in an

Matrix organizations, sometimes described as "project organizations," adapt the functional-bureaucratic form to meet the demands of special situations through the establishment of subunits or teams with membership drawn from different functional areas or departments:

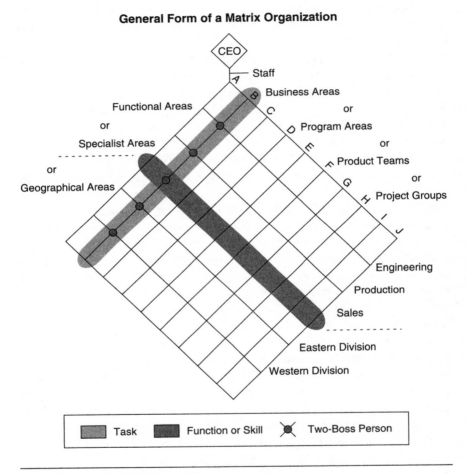

General Form of a Matrix Organization

Exhibit 3.5   Matrix Organization

SOURCE: Diagram from Kolodny (1981: 20). Copyright, 1981, by the Foundation for the School of Business at Indiana University. Reprinted by permission.

attack on common problems. Such organizations may establish project teams to cope with the design and production of specific products, to tackle a corporate planning problem, or to deal with ad hoc issues such as the relocation of a plant or offices. Some organizations may establish few teams; others may be dominated by team activity. Teams may be temporary and be treated as a departure from normal operations, or they may be seen as a feature of the way business ought to be done.

Team-based organization typically increases the adaptability of organizations in dealing with their environments, improves coordination between functional specialisms, and makes good use of human resources. The approach also diffuses influence and control, allowing people at the middle and lower levels of an organization to make contributions that might otherwise be denied. The fusion of functional expertise with a product, client, project, or other business orientation also helps create a healthy competition for internal resources while preserving a focus in relation to key business challenges and the external environment.

Problems do arise, however, especially when conflicts develop between departmental and team loyalties and responsibilities. This is particularly true in formal matrix organizations where project teams are superimposed on a strong bureaucratic structure. In such situations, team members are often seen as *representatives* of functional departments and held accountable for their actions by departmental heads upon whose favor their career may ultimately depend. They are often confined to "sitting in" on team meetings with the responsibility of "reporting back" to their boss. They thus find it difficult to become fully committed members of their team, and the dual loyalties and responsibilities usually erode team effectiveness. In fully developed matrix organizations, this tension between team and departmental loyalties and responsibilities is usually resolved in favor of an emphasis on team commitments. Appropriate authority and rewards are stacked in ways that encourage dynamic teams. Otherwise, the organization gets the worst of both worlds, producing an inefficient form of bureaucracy. Matrix and other team-based organizations tend to be driven by meetings that, at times, can be very time-consuming but when working effectively can be incredibly productive. In terms of effective management, close attention has to be paid to the conflicts that inevitably develop, and team members need to possess a high degree of collegiality and interpersonal skill.

Our discussion of the varieties of matrix organization illustrates some of the difficulties encountered in attempting to identify discrete types of organization, for unlike in nature, where species are distinguished by discrete clusters of attributes, organizational characteristics are often distributed in a more continuous way. One form often tends to blend with another, producing organizations that have hybrid characteristics.

However, if we focus on *successful* organizations, their specieslike character becomes much clearer. Successful organizations seem to share "configurations" or "patterns" of distinctive characteristics that are appropriate for dealing with their particular environments.

For example, as organizational researchers such as Raymond Miles, Charles Snow, and Danny Miller have shown, highly successful companies that strive to keep on the edge of change invariably pursue strategies of constant innovation and product breakthrough backed by flexible, organic structures. Successful companies that seek to build competitive advantage around high-quality, cost-effective "second-generation" products that are highly innovative but not always at the leading edge combine flexibility and control in a more structured way. Organizations that have a well-established niche that they can defend through low-cost, high-quality strategies that keep potential competitors away have bureaucratized tightly controlled structures.

Like organizations in the natural world, it seems that successful organizations evolve appropriate structures and processes for dealing with the challenges of their external environments. The basic pattern revealed by Burns and Stalker in the 1960s seems to be confirmed time and again, although the proliferation of species equipped to deal with high degrees of change seems to be a major trend. As technological and market changes challenge traditional niches, many old-style bureaucracies are becoming extinct and being replaced by more nimble competitors. However, despite a high degree of consensus about the nature of this basic trend, organization and management researchers are deeply split in terms of their explanations of *how* organizations can strike an appropriate relationship with the environment. One school of thought argues that managers can use the insights of contingency theory to develop a "good fit" between organization and environment; the other argues that, although short-term innovation and adjustments are always possible, the forces of natural selection and the environment are ultimately in control. These contrasting views are explored in the following sections of this chapter.

Contingency Theory: Promoting Organizational Health and Development

- How can an organization systematically achieve a good "fit" with its environment?
- How can it adapt to changing environmental circumstances?
- How can it ensure that internal relations are balanced and appropriate?
- What does this mean in operational terms?

These and related questions have become the focus of attention for numerous consultancy-oriented researchers working in the field of organizational development, popularly known as "OD." They have helped bring the insights generated by the contingency theorists and by the systems approach right down to earth by developing diagnostic and prescriptive models to identify organizational ailments and to prescribe some kind of cure. In effect, they have adopted the role of "organizational doctors."

Given an understanding of the ideas discussed in previous sections, it is easy to see how such diagnosis and prescription can proceed. All we really need to do is take the insights generated about organizational subsystems and pose a series of questions about the existing relations internally and between organization and environment:

1. *What is the nature of the organization's environment?* Is it simple and stable or complex and turbulent? Is it easy to see interconnections between various elements of the environment? What changes are occurring in the economic, technological, market, labor relations, and sociopolitical dimensions? What is the chance of some development transforming the whole environment—some development that will create a new opportunity or challenge the viability of existing operations?

2. *What kind of strategy is being employed?* Is the organization adopting a nonstrategy, simply reacting to whatever change comes along? Is the organization attempting to defend a particular niche that it has created in the environment? Is the organization systematically analyzing the environment to identify new threats and opportunities? Is the organization adopting an innovative, proactive stance, constantly searching for new opportunities and evaluating existing activities? Is the stance toward the environment competitive or collaborative?

3. *What kind of technology (mechanical and nonmechanical) is being used?* Are the processes used to transform inputs into outputs standardized and routinized? Does the technology create jobs with high or low scope for responsibility and autonomy? Does the technology rigidify operations, or is it flexible and open-ended? What technological choices face the organization? Can it replace rigid systems with more flexible forms?

4. *What kinds of people are employed, and what is the dominant "culture" or ethos within the organization?* What orientations do people bring to their work? Is a narrow "I'm here for the money" commitment the norm, or are people searching for challenge and involvement? What are the core values and beliefs shaping patterns of corporate culture and subculture?

5. *How is the organization structured, and what are the dominant manager-ial philosophies?* Is the organization bureaucratic, or are matrix/organic forms of organization the norm? Is the dominant managerial philosophy authoritarian, stressing accountability and close control? Or is it more democratic, encouraging initiative and enterprise throughout the organi-zation? Does the philosophy stress safe but sure approaches, or is it inno-vative and risk taking?

This scheme of questioning can be used to identify organizational characteristics and to determine the compatibility between the different elements. In asking these questions we are building on the idea that the organization consists of interrelated subsystems of a strategic, human, technological, structural, and managerial nature (see Exhibit 3.3 discussed earlier), which need to be internally consistent and adapted to environ-mental conditions. Our answers can be plotted as shown in Exhibit 3.6, to reveal congruencies and incongruencies.

Three examples of congruent relations between organizational and environmental characteristics are represented by the positions (A), (B), and (C) in Exhibit 3.6. In accordance with the conclusions of contingency theory, each is likely to be highly effective. Position (A) represents an organization in a stable environment adopting a defensive strategy to pro-tect its niche. Perhaps it is an organization commanding a secure market on the basis of a good-quality product produced in a cost-efficient way. The organization employs a mass-production technology and is struc-tured and managed mechanistically. The people employed are content with their narrowly defined roles, and the organization operates in an efficient and trouble-free manner.

Position (C) represents an organization encountering a moderate degree of change in its environment. Technological developments are occurring at a regular pace, and markets are in a constant state of transi-tion. The organization has to keep abreast of these developments, analyz-ing emergent trends, updating production methods, and creating a flow of product modifications rather like the radio and television firm in Burns and Stalker's study. It is not on the cutting edge of innovation. Its com-petitive advantage rests in being able to produce a better product in a cost-effective way. The organization adopts an effective project-driven matrix organization and commands the required flexibility and commit-ment from its staff.

Position (B) represents the case of a firm in a highly turbulent environ-ment where products and technologies are constantly changing and often have a very short life span. This means that it has to search for new ideas and opportunities on a continuous basis. The firm is a kind of "prospector,"

Profile of Organizational Characteristics

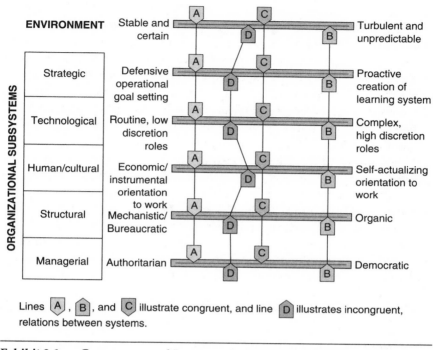

Lines A , B , and C illustrate congruent, and line D illustrates incongruent, relations between systems.

Exhibit 3.6   Congruence and Incongruence Between Organizational Subsystems

SOURCE: Adapted from Burrell and Morgan (1979: 177).

always looking for new places where it can strike gold. It relies on getting there first, recognizing that type (C) organizations will soon move in with a competitive product. Innovation is the lifeblood of this organization. It employs people who are prepared to make massive commitments to their work and who are motivated and managed in an organic way. Again, this organization is balanced internally and in relation to its environment.

Position (D) presents a set of relations where the strategic stance, technology, and approach to organization and management are incongruent with the nature of the environment and the general orientations of the people within the organization. The situation is characteristic of an organization that is overbureaucratized, being more inclined to defend the position it has achieved than to search out new opportunities. It is a frustrating place in which to work because the employees are looking for more open and demanding jobs than the strategy, technology, organization, and managerial style allow. Contingency theorists suggest that the organization should be designed and managed like organization (C). If a way could be found to allow the people who are highly involved with the organization to initiate changes in the required direction, it could achieve a much more effective configuration of relations. At present, the incongruencies get in the way of effective operations, and the organization is likely to find difficulty in sustaining its position within the industry.

The kind of analytical diagnosis presented above can first be conducted at the level of a total organization or major division, but it will also need to be conducted at the level of subunits within the organization to take account of Lawrence and Lorsch's point about the need for appropriate differentiation and integration. The analysis at this level will identify the pattern of relations necessary for dealing with various subenvironments and show the required differentiation and integration. However, in an analysis at this subunit level, care must be taken to ensure that the requirements of the parts do not take priority over those of the whole and that critical competencies are kept firmly in mind. For example, in organizations where frontline innovation is the basis of survival, the design and management of subunits must accommodate the primary task of innovation rather than the reverse.

Our discussion thus demonstrates how contingency theory and an understanding of organization needs can provide the basis for a detailed organizational analysis. The analysis helps us describe detailed patterns of organizational relations, and it shows us possible solutions to the problems revealed. For example, organizational development practitioners confronted with the situation in organization (D) could attempt to improve the alignment of relations by persuading management to move closer to a (C) configuration. This organizational change strategy could involve action on a number of fronts—in relation to strategy, technology, organization structure, and management style. It would also involve an attempt to change the culture of the organization, namely, the systems of belief and practice that hold the organization in its ineffective configuration.

The task of successful organizational change and development thus often hinges on bringing variables into closer alignment so that the organization can meet the challenges and opportunities posed by the environment. In nature we find that organisms are endowed with a harmonious pattern of internal and external relations as a result of evolution. In organizations, however, the degree of internal harmony and fit with the environment is a product of human decision, action, and inaction so that incongruence and conflict are often the rule. As a result, there are usually many problems to keep managers and organizational consultants favoring a contingency approach very busy.

Natural Selection: The Population-Ecology View of Organizations

Up to now our use of the organismic metaphor has focused on organizations as the key units of analysis. We have discussed how organizations and their members can be seen as having different sets of "needs" and examined how organizations can develop patterns of relations that allow them to adapt to their environment. Survival has been presented as a problem of adaptation, with contingency theory offered as a means of identifying patterns of "good fit" and showing how these can be achieved.

Popular as this approach has been, in recent years it has attracted growing criticism from theorists and researchers subscribing to a "natural selection" view of organizations. In their opinion, the idea that organizations can adapt to their environments attributes too much flexibility and power to the organization and too little to the environment as a force in organizational survival. They advocate that we must counteract this imbalance by focusing on the way environments "select" organizations and that this can best be done by analysis at the level of *populations* of organizations and their wider ecology.

This "population ecology" view of organization brings Darwin's theory of evolution right into the center of organizational analysis. In essence, the argument is as follows. Organizations, like organisms in nature, depend for survival on their ability to acquire an adequate supply of the resources necessary to sustain existence. In this effort, they have to face competition from other organizations, and since there is usually a resource scarcity, only the fittest survive. The nature, numbers, and distribution of organizations at any given time are dependent on resource availability and on competition within and between different species of organizations. The environment is thus the critical factor in determining which organizations succeed and which fail, "selecting" the most robust competitors through elimination of the weaker ones.

As Darwin frequently emphasizes in his writings, although selection may be the mechanism through which evolution occurs, it depends on there being variation in individual characteristics. Without variation there is nothing to select. Most applications of Darwin's theory thus build on a cyclical model that allows for the *variation, selection, retention,* and *modification* of species characteristics. Variations in a species typically arise as a result of cross-reproduction and random variation of characteristics. Some of these variations may confer a competitive advantage in the survival process, leading to a better chance of selection, or of evolving along with changes in the environment. Because the surviving members of a species, or emerging new species, provide a foundation for the next stage of reproduction, there is a strong chance that the new characteristics will be retained. In turn, these characteristics will be subject to random modification, creating the variety that allows the process to continue. In this way, new species and ecological patterns evolve from variations in the old.

Although evolution occurs through modification of individual members of a species, the population ecologists argue that it is more important to understand evolutionary dynamics at the level of the population. When the environment changes or when a new species makes an inroad on the resource niche traditionally held by another, ultimately the change is reflected in population structure. Because members of a species tend to share similar strengths and weaknesses, it is the whole species that tends to survive or fail. Although some individual members may be fitter than others, they are often not as fit as the incoming species and thus tend to share the fate of their population in the long run.

This population perspective opens many new avenues of inquiry, for it encourages us to understand the dynamics influencing whole populations of organizations. Thus, as Howard Aldrich, John Freeman, Michael Hannan, and others who have popularized the approach suggest, organizational analysis shifts from explaining how individual organizations adapt to their environments to understanding how different species rise and decline in importance. Why are there so many different kinds of organizations? What factors influence their numbers and distribution? What factors influence a population's ability to acquire or retain a resource niche?

Under the influence of these and related questions the population ecologists have begun to develop a form of organizational demography. Numerous research studies are attempting to identify species or populations (typically defined as sets of organizations sharing certain characteristics or a common fate with regard to environmental circumstances) and the birth rates, death rates, and general factors influencing organizational life cycles, growth, and decline. Considerable attention has also been devoted to understanding organizations and their environments in terms of "resource dependencies" and the patterning and availability of resource niches.

The perspective has created many interesting insights. For example, in critiquing the "adaptation" view of organization, the population ecologists have highlighted the importance of inertial pressures that often prevent organizations from changing in response to their environments. Specialization of production plants and personnel, established ideas and "mind-sets" of top managers, inadequate information, the difficulty of restructuring technology and personnel in unionized plants, the force of tradition, barriers to entry created by legal, fiscal, and other circumstances, and many other factors may make it impossible for organizations to engage in timely and efficient changes. Faced with new kinds of competition or environmental circumstances, whole industries or types of organization may come and go. Large traditional steel mills may give way to small, technologically advanced competitors. Department stores may give way to specialty stores in shopping malls or to "factory outlets." Coal mines and oil companies may give way to entrepreneurial solar energy firms. Bureaucracies may give way to more flexible project-oriented firms, or "market driven" competitors. Firms offering traditional products and services throughout the economy may find themselves eliminated by information technology companies serving customers in a completely different way. Public sector organizations in government, education, or health care may find once secure niches completely eroded by more nimble service-oriented firms in the private sector.

In the population ecologists' view, it is the ability to obtain a resource niche and outperform one's competitors that is all-important, and in the long run, relative superiority in being able to command resources applies to whole populations of organizations. Perhaps one particularly skillful or efficient steel mill or department store may be able to hold off new forms of competition a little longer than other members of their species, but in the long run they too may become extinct as a result of environmental changes they are ill equipped to deal with compared with species of better fit.

Two other important insights generated by the population-ecology approach are the importance of resource limitations in shaping the growth, development, and decline of organizations and the role of successful innovations in shaping new species of organization. An awareness of the changing structure of critical resource niches and patterns of resource dependencies can make important contributions to our understanding of the success and power of different organizations. The way that new populations of organizations can emerge through the dissemination of innovations or new practices, as has happened in the computer and electronics sector, does much to explain the changing structure of industry.

However, while there is much to commend the population-ecology view, many organization theorists believe that it is far too deterministic a theory to provide a satisfactory explanation of how organizations actually evolve. For example, if we accept at face value the theory that environments select organizations for survival, then in the long run it really doesn't matter what managers and decision makers do. Even an efficient and successful firm that adapts to its environment is liable to fail as the result of environmental changes that influence the structure of its resource niche. Not surprisingly, therefore, the population-ecology view has been much criticized for downplaying the importance of the choice of strategic direction for an organization. Despite inertial pressures, an organization may be able to transform itself from one kind of organization into another or shift from a declining niche to a more profitable one. Take, for example, how companies like General Electric have shifted out of their core business, in this case the electrical business, to become diversified conglomerates spanning many different sectors.

The population-ecology approach has also been criticized for offering a rather one-sided view of the evolutionary process. In particular, the emphasis on resource scarcity and competition, which lie at the basis of selection, underplays the fact that resources can be abundant and self-renewing and that organisms can collaborate as well as compete. Organizations that focus on value *creation* may be able to create resource niches that never existed before. For example, many aspects of development in the information technology industry, bioengineering, and the electronic media business are fueled by this kind of process. Social and economic resources, especially in a knowledge economy, are inherently self-generating. When these neglected aspects of population ecology are brought into consideration, a more optimistic view of the ecology of organizations begins to emerge.

Organizational Ecology:
The Creation of Shared Futures

The population-ecology and contingency views of organization both view organizations as existing in a state of tension or struggle with their environments. Both presume that organizations and environments are separate phenomena. Under the influence of developments in modern systems theory, however, this kind of assumption has attracted increasing criticism. Organizations, like organisms, are not really discrete entities, even though it may be convenient to think of them as such. They do not live in isolation and are not self-sufficient. Rather, they exist as elements in a complex ecosystem.

Many biologists now believe that it is the whole ecosystem that evolves and that the process of evolution can really be understood only at the level of the total ecology. This has important implications because it suggests that organisms do not evolve by adapting to environmental changes or as a result of these changes selecting the organisms that are to survive. Rather, it suggests that evolution is always evolution of a pattern of relations embracing organisms *and* their environments. It is the *pattern*, not just the separate units composing this pattern, that evolves. Or as Kenneth Boulding has put it, evolution involves the "survival of the fitting," not just the survival of the fittest.

When we attempt to understand the ecology of organizations with this perspective in mind, it becomes necessary to understand that organizations and their environments are engaged in a pattern of co-creation, where each produces the other. Just as in nature, where the environment of an organism is composed of other organisms, organizational environments are in large measure composed of other organizations. Once we recognize this, it becomes clear that organizations are, in principle, able to influence the nature of their environment. They can play an active role in shaping their future, especially when acting in concert with other organizations. Environments then become in some measure always negotiated environments rather than independent external forces.

If we look at the organizational world, we find that, as in nature, collaboration is often as common as competition. Organizations in the same industry frequently get together under the umbrella of trade and professional associations to collaborate in relation to shared interests. Formal and informal cartels for price fixing, agreements regarding areas of competition and market sharing, and the joint sponsorship of lobbies designed to influence government legislation are obvious examples. The Tobacco Trust, which was established by leading U.S. tobacco companies to help shape research on the link between cancer and smoking, presents a particularly striking example of cooperation between firms that are normally engaged in fierce competition.

Examples of day-to-day collaborative relations between organizations in different industries or in different parts of the same industry are also very common. For example, firms often cultivate interlocking directorships to create a measure of shared decision making and control, engage in joint ventures to pool expertise or share risk in research and development, strike agreements with suppliers or manufacturers to achieve a measure of "vertical integration" of production, and engage in numerous kinds of informal networking. They also sometimes establish informal joint organizations to link firms that have an interest in special problems or lines of development. For example, in the financial services industry it is not uncommon for banks, trust companies, insurance firms, and other interested agencies to offer joint services, in effect creating a new form of organization at the level of the industry. Similar developments can be seen in many other areas as well.

An ecological perspective that emphasizes the importance of collaboration can make an important contribution to how we understand and manage the world of organizations. Under the influence of interpretations of evolution that emphasize the survival of the fittest, competition is often encouraged as the basic rule of organizational life. Under the influence of more ecological interpretations stressing the "survival of the fitting," the ethic of collaboration receives much more attention.

A number of social scientists inspired by the work of the late Eric Trist have now begun to develop this view of organizational ecology, investigating the possibility of developing new patterns of interorganizational relations that can help shape the future in a proactive way. Building on the observation that these relations emerge as a natural response to complexity and turbulence in the environment, Trist argued that they should be encouraged to help make the turbulence more manageable. In several "action projects," he and his colleagues sought to develop "referent organizations" to regulate relations between stakeholders in broad-based "domains." The idea of such domain-based organizations is to embrace the organization-environment relations of a whole set of constituent organizations so that what were once external relations—for example, between competing or interdependent firms or between labor and management—now in some measure become internal relations that are open to collaborative action. The approach has been applied in a wide variety of settings to tackle problems of environmental pollution, regional and community economic development, and the development of industrial associations. Trist and his colleagues also encourage the development of informal learning networks that can generate domain-based exchange and discussion, promote shared appreciations of concerns and problems, facilitate the emergence of common values and norms, and thus possibly find new solutions to shared problems.

The concern in both cases is to allow the ecology of organizational relations to evolve and survive. Just as natural ecologists are concerned about the disastrous effects of industrial pollution on the natural world, Trist and his successors believe that our organizational ecology is menaced by highly individualistic lines of action that threaten to make the social world completely unmanageable. The concept of organizational ecology is thus marshaled as a new and creative way of thinking and acting in relation to these problems.

Strengths and Limitations of the Organismic Metaphor

We began this chapter with the invitation to view organizations as organisms and have ended up with a review of some of the central ideas of modern organization theory. This is because most modern organization theorists have looked to nature to understand organizations and organizational life. The ideas identified provide an excellent illustration of how a metaphor can open our minds to a systematic and novel way of thinking. By exploring the parallels between organisms and organizations in terms of organic functioning, relations with the environment, relations between species, and the wider ecology, it has been possible to produce different theories and explanations that have very practical implications for organization and management.

Given the rich and varied insights thus generated, it is difficult to identify strengths and limitations that apply equally to all variations of the metaphor. However, there are a number of important commonalities.

One of the main strengths of the metaphor stems from the emphasis placed on understanding relations between organizations and their environments. The mechanical theories explored in Chapter 2 more or less ignored the role of the environment, treating organizations as relatively closed systems that could be designed as clearly defined structures of parts. In contrast, the ideas considered in this chapter stress that organizations are open systems and are best understood as ongoing *processes* rather than as collections of parts. Using the image of an organism in constant exchange with the environment, we are encouraged to take an open and flexible view of organization. We can recognize that so long as key processes are functioning in an effective manner, everything may be going well.

This leads us to the second strength of the metaphor: The management of organizations can often be improved through systematic attention to the "needs" that must be satisfied if the organization is to survive. The metaphor emphasizes survival as the key aim or primary task facing any organization. This contrasts with the classical focus on specific operational goals. Survival is a process, whereas goals are often targets or end points to be achieved. This reorientation gives management an increased flexibility, for if survival is seen as the primary orientation, specific goals are framed by a more basic and enduring process that helps prevent them from becoming ends in themselves, a common fate in many organizations. The focus on the use and acquisition of resources also helps emphasize that the process of organizing is much broader and more basic than the task of achieving specific goals.

The focus on "needs" also encourages us to see organizations as interacting processes that have to be balanced internally as well as in relation to the environment. Thus, we see strategy, structure, technology, and the human and managerial dimensions of organization as subsystems with living needs that must be satisfied in a mutually acceptable way.

Otherwise, the openness and health of the overall system suffer. Imagine a socio-technical system where human needs characteristic of the higher reaches of Maslow's need hierarchy meet a technology characterized by routine, boring, low-discretion jobs. The result is one of human boredom and alienation where game playing and sabotage often emerge as means of gaining self-respect. The abrasive interaction between subsystems in this case is likely to produce an ongoing battle between workers and management, high absenteeism, job turnover when new jobs are freely available, poor-quality products, and low organizational self-image. The socio-technical approach suggests that, by accommodating and balancing basic needs, strategic management can create a much more harmonious and productive work environment.

The third principal advantage of the metaphor is that in identifying different "species" of organization we are alerted to the fact that in organizing we always have a range of options. The ideas relating to matrix and other team-based and organic forms of organization and the research showing how effective organization is contingent on environmental circumstances emphasize that managers and those involved in organization design always have choice and that effective organization depends on the quality of choice. Although those favoring a population-ecology perspective may adopt the rather pessimistic stance that this choice will never count for much because environmental forces ultimately have the upper hand in determining the fate of an organization, the contingency view offers a new flexibility of approach.

The fourth major strength of the metaphor is that it stresses the virtue of organic forms of organization in the process of innovation. It would be an exaggeration to suggest that mechanistic organizations do not innovate, but the point contains an important kernel of truth. The ideas explored in this chapter are at one in suggesting that if innovation is a priority, then flexible, dynamic, project-oriented matrix or organic forms of organization will be superior to the mechanistic-bureaucratic ones.

Another obvious strength of the organismic metaphor rests in its contributions to the theory and practice of organizational development, especially through the contingency approach. The metaphor has also had a major impact upon the theory and practice of corporate strategy, which for the most part now focuses on achieving an appropriate fit between organization and environment.

Finally, the metaphor is making important contributions through a focus on "ecology" and interorganizational relations. Researchers adopting ecological views have reinforced the idea that a theory of interorganizational relations is necessary if we are to understand how the world of organization actually evolves. If the organizational ecologists are correct, it may also be necessary to create new forms of interorganizational relations to deal with the complex environments that modern organizations now face.

As noted in Chapter 1, a way of seeing is a way of not seeing. Now that the organismic image of organization has established its powerful credentials, it is difficult to see how the classical theorists could have given so little attention to the influence of the environment. It is also difficult to see how they could have believed that there are uniform principles of management worthy of universal application. Yet we have to remember that the organizational world was much simpler then. The rise in importance of the organismic metaphor is in many respects a product of changing times that have undermined the efficiency of bureaucratic organizations. Organization theorists did not simply discover the organismic metaphor; they needed it to keep abreast of developments, and as we have seen, they have exploited its insights in many different ways.

This said and done, the metaphor does have major limitations, most of which are associated with the basic way of seeing that the metaphor encourages. The first of these is the fact that we are led to view organizations and their environments in a way that is far too concrete. We know that organisms live in a natural world with material properties that determine the life and welfare of its inhabitants. We can see this world. We can touch and feel it. Nature presents itself as being objective and real in every aspect. However, this image breaks down when applied to society and organization because organizations and their environments can, at least to some extent, be understood as socially constructed phenomena. As we will discuss in some detail in Chapter 5, organizations are very much products of visions, ideas, norms, and beliefs, so their shape and structure is much more fragile and tentative than the material structure of an organism. True, there are many material aspects of organizations, such as land, buildings, machines, and money, but organizations fundamentally depend for life— in the form of ongoing organizational activity—upon the creative actions of human beings. Organizational environments can also be seen as being products of human creativity because they are made through the actions of the individuals, groups, and organizations who populate them.

In view of this, it is misleading to suggest that organizations need to "adapt" to their environments, as do the contingency theorists, or that environments "select" the organizations that are to survive, as do the population ecologists. Both views tend to make organizations and their members dependent upon forces operating in an external world rather than recognizing that they are active agents operating with others in the construction of that world. The natural selection view of organizational evolution in particular gives the individual organization little influence in the struggle for survival. This view undermines the power of organizations and their members to help make their own futures. Organizations, unlike organisms, have a choice as to whether they are to compete or to collaborate. We may agree that an organization acting in isolation can have little impact on the environment, and hence that the environment presents itself as external and real in its effects, but it is quite a different matter when we consider the possibility of organizations collaborating in pursuit of plural interests to shape the environment they desire.

A second limitation of the organismic metaphor rests in its assumption of "functional unity." If we look at organisms in the natural world we find them characterized by a functional interdependence where every element of the system under normal circumstances works for all the other elements. Thus, in the human body the blood, heart, lungs, arms, and legs normally work together to preserve the homeostatic functioning of the whole. The system is unified and shares a common life and a common future. Circumstances in which one element works in a way that sabotages the whole, as when appendicitis or a heart attack threatens one's life, are exceptional and potentially pathological.

If we look at most organizations, however, we find that the times at which their different elements operate with the degree of harmony discussed above are often more exceptional than normal. Most organizations are not as functionally unified as organisms. The different elements of an organization are usually capable of living separate lives and often do so. Although organizations *may* at times be highly unified, with people in different departments working in a selfless way for the organization as a whole, they may at other times be characterized by schism and major conflict.

The organismic metaphor has had a subtle yet important impact on our general thinking by encouraging us to believe in a state of unity where everyone is "pulling together." This style of thought usually leads us to see "political" and other self-interested activity as abnormal or dysfunctional features that should be absent in the healthy organization. As will become apparent from discussion in Chapter 6, where we will be examining organizations as political systems, the emphasis upon unity rather than conflict as the normal state of organization may be an inherent weakness of the organismic metaphor. In recent years, those favoring the metaphor have begun to recognize this weakness by giving more attention to the role of power in organizations, but they rarely have gone so far as to abandon the ideal of functional unity. There are good reasons for this. The idea that organizations can work in a functionally unified way is popular, particularly among managers charged with the task of holding organizations together.

The above point brings us to the final limitation of the organismic metaphor to be considered here: the danger of the metaphor becoming an ideology. This is always a problem in applied social science where images or theories come to serve as normative guidelines for shaping practice. We have already seen the impact of the machine metaphor on classical management theory: The idea that the organization is a machine sets the basis for the idea that it ought to be run like a machine. With the organismic metaphor, this "ought" takes a number of forms. For example, the fact that organisms are functionally integrated can easily set the basis for the idea that organizations *should* be the same way. Much of organizational development attempts to achieve this ideal by finding ways of integrating individual and organization—for example, by designing work that allows people to satisfy their personal needs *through* the organization. Whereas Frederick Taylor's scientific management provided an ideology based on the idea that "efficiency and productivity is in the interests of all," ideologies associated with "OD" tend to emphasize that we can live full and satisfying lives if we fulfill our personal needs through the organizations that dominate the contemporary scene. Many argue that this style of thinking runs the danger of producing an organizational society populated by the "organization man" and the "organization woman." People become resources to be developed rather than human beings who are valued in themselves and who are encouraged to choose and shape their own future. This issue directs attention to the values that underlie much organizational development and, by implication, to the values associated with the use of the organismic metaphor as a basis for theorizing.

Another important ideological dimension of some of the theories discussed in this chapter is found in their links with the social philosophy of the nineteenth century. For example, the population-ecology view of organizations revives the ideology of social Darwinism, which stressed that social life is based on the laws of nature and that only the fittest will survive. Social Darwinism arose as an ideology supporting the early development of capitalism in which small firms competed for survival on a free and open basis. The population-ecology view of organization in effect develops an equivalent ideology for modern times, holding up a mirror to the organizational world and suggesting that the view we see reflects a law of nature. In effect, natural law is invoked to legitimize the organization of society. Obviously, there are real dangers in doing this because when we take the parallels between nature and society too seriously we fail to see that human beings, in principle, have a large measure of influence and choice over what their world can be.

4

Learning and Self-Organization

Organizations as Brains

In his book *The Natural History of the Mind*, science writer G. R. Taylor offers the following observations on some of the differences between brains and machines:

In a famous experiment, the American psychologist Karl Lashley removed increasing quantities of the brains of rats which had been taught to run in a maze. He found that, provided he did not remove the visual cortex and thus blind them, he could remove up to ninety percent of their cortex without significant deterioration in their power to thread their way through the maze. There is no man-made machine of which this is true. Try removing nine-tenths of your radio and see if it still brings in a signal! It would seem that each specific memory is distributed in some way over the brain as a whole.

Similarly, you can remove considerable amounts of the motor cortex without paralyzing any one group of muscles. All that happens is a general deterioration of motor performance. The evolutionary advantages of such an arrangement are manifest: when pursued, it is better to run clumsily than not at all. But how this remarkable distribution of function is achieved we do not really understand. We see, at all events, that the brain relies on patterns of increasing refinement and not (as man-made machines do) on chains of cause and effect. The fact is, the brain is not comparable with anything else.

Taylor's comments raise intriguing questions. Is it possible to design "learning organizations" that have the capacity to be as flexible, resilient, and inventive as the functioning of the brain? Is it possible to distribute capacities for intelligence and control *throughout* an enterprise so that the system as a whole can self-organize and evolve along with emerging challenges?

These issues are the focus of this chapter, which pursues the basic question "What if we think about organizations as living brains?"

Images of the Brain

As *Newsweek* reporters Sharon Begley and R. Sawhill have noted, in the 2,400 years since Hippocrates located the seat of intellect in the skull, humans have been presented with the paradox that their greatest thoughts and achievements, and even their deepest emotions, may stem from a three-pound glob of matter with the consistency of Jell-O. Through persistent research, especially over the past 100 years, scientists and philosophers of all kinds have gradually begun to probe and reveal the mysteries of this prized area of anatomy. As might be expected, numerous metaphors have been summoned to shape understanding.

Many of these images focus on the idea that the brain is an information processing system. For example, the brain has been conceived as

- A control system similar to a complex computer or telephone switchboard, transmitting information through electronic impulses
- A kind of television system with a capacity to reassemble coherent patterns and images from millions of separate pieces of data
- A sophisticated library or memory bank for data storage and retrieval
- A complex system of chemical reactions that transmit messages and initiate actions
- A mysterious "black box" linking stimuli and behavior
- A linguistic system operating through a neural code that translates information into thoughts, ideas, and actions, rather like the code

represented in an alphabet can be converted into prose through words and sentences

More recently, the brain has been compared to a holographic system, one of the marvels of laser science. Holography, invented in 1948 by Dennis Gabor, uses lenseless cameras to record information in a way that stores the whole in all the parts. Interacting beams of light create an "interference pattern" that scatters the information being recorded on a photographic plate, known as a hologram, which can then be illuminated to recreate the original information. One of the interesting features of the hologram is that, if broken, any single piece can be used to reconstruct the entire image. Everything is enfolded in everything else, just as if we were able to throw a pebble into a pond and see the whole pond and all the waves, ripples, and drops of water generated by the splash *in each and every one of the drops of water thus produced.*

Holography demonstrates that it is possible to create processes where the whole can be encoded in all the parts, so that each and every part represents the whole. Neuroscientist Karl Pribram of Stanford University has suggested that the brain functions in accordance with holographic principles: that memory is distributed throughout the brain and can thus be reconstituted from any of the parts. If he is correct, this may explain why the rats in Karl Lashley's experiments were able to function reasonably well even when major portions of their brain had been removed.

Debate about the true nature and functioning of the brain continues at an intense level, and the evidence remains inconclusive. Each metaphor used to shape understanding seems to catch key insights but falls short on other accounts. For example, the information processing images capture how the human brain manages to process billions of bits of data every second, transforming them into patterns and routines that help us deal with the world around us. But the explanations tend to overcentralize the process. The holographic evidence favors a more decentralized, distributed form of intelligence. When it comes to brain functioning it seems that there is no center or point of control. The brain seems to store and process data in many parts simultaneously. Pattern and order *emerge from the process;* it is not imposed.

Holographic explanations stress the "all over the place" character of brain functioning. Different elements are involved in systems of "parallel processing," generating signals, impulses, and tendencies that make contributions to the functioning and character of the whole. But the holographic explanation can go too far in that it underplays the fact that despite this distributed character there is also a strong measure of system specialization. The brain, it seems, is *both* holographic *and* specialized!

This paradox is clearly illustrated, for example, in the results of "split brain" research. This shows how the brain's right hemisphere plays a dominant role in creative, intuitive, emotional, acoustic, and pattern recognition functions and controls the left side of the body. The left hemisphere is more involved with rational, analytic, reductive, linguistic, visual, and verbal functions while controlling the right side of the body. There is undoubtedly a high degree of specialization on the part of each hemisphere, but both are always involved in any given activity. It is just that one hemisphere seems to be more active or dominant than the other as different functions are brought into play. The complementarity is also illustrated in the evidence that although different people may bring a right- or left-brain dominance to a specific task, both hemispheres are necessary for effective action or problem solving to occur.

When it comes to understanding the brain, we have to be able to embrace this kind of paradox and develop explanations that acknowledge how logical reduction and creative expansiveness may be elements of the same process; how high degrees of specialization and distributed function can coexist; how high degrees of randomness and variety can produce a coherent pattern; how enormous redundancy and overlap can provide the basis for efficient operation; and how the most highly coordinated and intelligent system of which we are aware has no predetermined or explicit design.

Interestingly, some of the most powerful insights on these issues are emerging from the field of artificial intelligence, where experiments in the construction of brainlike machines are actually showing how we can create the capacities that G. R. Taylor refers to in the quotation presented at the beginning of this chapter.

For example, in the construction of mobile robots, called "mobots," ways are being found of reconciling principles of centralized and decentralized intelligence. Mobots with large centralized "brains" require so much supporting hardware that they get overwhelmed and immobilized by the high ratio of body to brain. And when the "body problem" is solved by putting "the brain" in a central but remote location, communication processes tend to get distorted by all kinds of random "noise" that creates a constant tendency toward system failure. The most successful innovations seem to involve systems of distributed intelligence where integration and coherence are built from the "bottom up" in a way that allows "higher" or more evolved forms of intelligence to emerge.

Consider, for example, the mobot called "Genghis," created by Rodney Brooks at MIT and described by Kevin Kelly in his book *Out of Control*. Genghis has been designated as a kind of "mechanical cockroach" that has six legs but no brain. Each leg has its own microprocessor that can act as a sensing device that allows it to "think for itself" and determine its actions. Within the body of the machine other semi-independent "thinking" devices coordinate communications between the legs. The walking process emerges as a result of the piecemeal intelligence. The independence of the legs gives great flexibility and avoids the mammoth task of processing all the information that would be necessary to coordinate the operation of the six legs as an integrated process.

Genghis offers a metaphor for understanding how intelligent action can emerge from quasi-independent processes linked by a minimal set of key rules, making the whole system appear to have an integrated, purposeful, well-coordinated intelligence. By building around a pattern of simple "If . . . then . . ." routines, the "cockroach" walks without knowing how it does so. Rodney Brooks describes some of the key design principles as follows:

> There is no central controller which directs the body where to put each foot or how high to lift a leg should there be an obstacle ahead. Instead, each leg is granted a few simple behaviors and each independently knows what to do under various circumstances. For instance, two basic behaviors can be thought of as "If I'm a leg and I'm up, put myself down," or "If I'm a leg and I'm forward, put the other five legs back a little." These processes exist independently, run at all times, and fire whenever the sensory preconditions are true. To create walking then, there just needs to be a sequencing of lifting legs (this is the only instance where any central control is evident). As soon as a leg is raised it automatically swings itself forward, and also down. But the act of swinging forward triggers all the other legs to move back a little. Since those legs happen to be touching the ground, the body moves forward.

Now return to the brain. Could it be that sophisticated forms of intelligence emerge from the "bottom up," as the result of the integration of more modest capacities and intelligences? This, indeed, is close to the view offered by cognitive philosopher Daniel Dennett of Tufts University, who suggests that what we see and experience in the brain as a highly ordered stream of consciousness is really the result of a more chaotic process where multiple possibilities—what he calls "multiple drafts"—are generated as a result of activity distributed throughout the brain. There is no master, centralized intelligence! The brain as a system engages in an incredibly diverse set of parallel activities that make complementary and competing contributions to what eventually emerges as a coherent pattern.

So, the question *What if we view organizations as brains?* raises many interesting possibilities.

Clearly, there are many possibilities!

In the following sections we will explore and develop the insights discussed above by viewing organizations in three interconnected ways: as information processing brains; as complex learning systems; and as holographic systems combining centralized and decentralized characteristics.

Organizations as Information Processing Brains

If one thinks about it, every aspect of organizational functioning depends on information processing of one form or another. Bureaucrats make decisions by processing information with reference to appropriate rules. Strategic managers make decisions by developing policies and plans that then provide a point of reference for the information processing and decision making of others. Computers automate complex information flows, and with the development of the Internet, corporate "intranets," and other webs of electronic communication, we are finding that organizations are becoming synonymous with the decisions, policies, and data flows that shape day-to-day practice.

Organizations are information systems. They are communication systems. And they are decision-making systems. We can thus go a long way toward understanding them as information processing brains!

This approach to understanding organization, originally known as "the decision-making approach," was pioneered in the 1940s and 1950s by Nobel Prize winner Herbert Simon and colleagues like James March while at the Carnegie Institute of Technology (now Carnegie-Mellon University). Exploring the parallels between human decision making and organizational decision making, Simon is famous for arguing that organizations can never be perfectly rational because their members have limited information processing abilities. Arguing that people (a) usually have to act on the basis of incomplete information about possible courses of action and their consequences, (b) are able to explore only a limited number of alternatives relating to any given decision, and (c) are unable to attach accurate values to outcomes, Simon challenged the assumptions made in economics about the optimizing behavior of individuals. He concluded that individuals and organizations settle for a "bounded rationality" of "good enough" decisions based on simple rules of thumb and limited search and information.

In Simon's view, these limits on human rationality are institutionalized in the structure and modes of functioning of our organizations. Hence, his theory of decision making leads us to understand organizations as kinds of institutionalized brains that fragment, routinize, and bound the decision-making process to make it manageable. As we look at organizations from this vantage point, we come to see that the various job, departmental, and other divisions within an organization do not just define a structure of work activity. They also create a structure of attention, information, interpretation, and decision making that exerts a crucial influence on an organization's daily operation.

Since Simon and his colleagues first introduced this way of thinking about organizations, numerous researchers and consultants have devoted considerable attention to understanding organization from an information processing standpoint with a view to enhance organizational rationality in practice. Paradoxically, although Simon's main contribution has been to show that organizations can never be fully rational and thus have to be content with "satisficing," the main impact of his work has been to reinforce the rational model.

For example, scientists working in the fields of operations research (OR), management decision systems (MDS), and management information systems (MIS) have been inspired to find ways of developing information processing and decision-making tools that can lead to more rational decisions. This has resulted in complex theories and systems for data management in relation to logistics, production, distribution, finance, sales, marketing, and other areas of activity and to the creation of planning, design, and implementation teams and departments that can "think" for the rest of the organization and control overall activities. In effect, this development has given many complex organizations the equivalent of a centralized brain that regulates overall activity. Large, complex organizations that rely on vast amounts of data processing to manage their customers, production, or distribution activities would now find it impossible to function without this kind of support.

Other important work in line with the rational model has been conducted by organization theorists wishing to understand organizational structure in terms of information processing models. For example, Jay Galbraith has given attention to the relationship between uncertainty, information processing, and organization design to explain the reasons for different styles of organization such as the mechanistic and organic approaches discussed in Chapter 3. Uncertain tasks require that large amounts of information be processed between decision makers during task performance. The greater the uncertainty, the more difficult it is to program and routinize activity by preplanning a response. Thus, as uncertainty increases, organizations typically find ways of controlling outputs (e.g., by setting goals and targets) rather than controlling behaviors (e.g., through rules and programs) and by relying on continuous feedback as a means of control. Hierarchy provides an effective means for controlling situations that are fairly certain but in uncertain situations can encounter information and decision overload.

The information processing perspective has created a fresh way of thinking about organization. But there are two major criticisms, each of which opens a new line of development.

The first is that most decision-making and information processing views have had a "left-brain bias" and an overcentralized view of the nature of organizational intelligence. As Simon himself acknowledges, in his early writings he specifically sought to use logic, with its emphasis on drawing conclusions from premises, as a central metaphor for describing the decision-making process. This is why his findings reinforced the bureaucratic model. The emphasis was placed on rational, analytical, reductive approaches to information processing and problem solving. More intuitive nonlinear approaches, characteristic of a more "right-brain" orientation, were underemphasized.

A more fully developed decision-making perspective would balance and integrate left and right brain capacities. Simon himself has taken important steps in this direction, recognizing how left and right brain capacities are intertwined, rather than being polar opposites, and how much of what passes as nonlogical, intuitive judgment can be understood as the result of complex information processing skills based on pattern recognition rather than formal logic and analysis. The theory is that intuitive managers learn to recognize clusters or chunks of information and act accordingly. While their behavior often seems nonrational, in that the managers concerned are unable to give formal accounts or justifications of why a particular decision has been made, implicit analytical processes are involved.

This more intuitive, nonlogical approach to organizational decision making has also been developed by James March, Simon's former colleague, and other associates who have interested themselves in understanding the fluid and informal aspects of organizations. They have used many unconventional metaphors, such as the idea that organizations are like "garbage cans," "organized anarchies," "seesaws," and "camping grounds," to capture the unpredictable ways in which solutions go looking for problems (rather than the reverse), how rational explanations are often imposed on decisions *after* they have been made, and how one organizational pattern or design may give way to another without any explicit rational analysis. Instead of just focusing on how managers and their organizations can find ways of trying to reduce or eliminate uncertainty, as has been the case with most rational approaches to decision making and organizational design, attention has been focused on confronting and flowing with that uncertainty. The challenge has been to find ways of opening thinking styles and decision making that take us beyond the rationality model.

The second major criticism is that too much emphasis has been placed on using the image of the limited information processing capacities of a *single individual*, as a model for understanding decision making in organizations generally. This is the implicit premise of Simon's view of "bounded rationality." The limited intelligence of individuals is used to justify the limited intelligence of organizations.

All this is now changing, as developments in information technology and forms of "networked intelligence" are giving a completely different twist to the information processing view of organization and its implications for organizational design.

Consider, for example, how computerized stock control and checkout facilities in supermarkets and other large retail stores have transformed the organizations using them. In applying a laser beam to precoded labels on the items being sold, the sales assistant records price and product and inputs data into various kinds of financial analyses, sales reports, inventory controls, reordering procedures, and numerous other automated information and decision-making activities. The system of organization embedded in the design of such information systems replaces more traditional modes of human interaction, eliminating armies of clerks, stockroom attendants, and middle managers. It also links organizations that used to have distinct identities—manufacturers, suppliers, banking and finance companies—into an integrated information web.

Organization in such circumstances increasingly rests *in* the information system. Indeed, microprocessing technology has created the possibility of organizing without having an organization in strictly physical terms. For example, a manufacturing organization "based" in the outskirts of New York City may coordinate the assembly of parts delivered from several Asian manufacturing plants at a location in Taiwan. The resulting product will be delivered to retailers throughout Europe and North America by independent distributors. Customer inquiries or problems with the product may be routed via a "Help Line" to customer service representatives employed in Ireland, Denmark, or New Brunswick. The accounting to support such transactions is performed in the Far East, and "Accounts Receivable" is delegated to a firm in Atlanta. The company based in New York City has a small staff of central coordinators and provides a marketing and R&D function. It is a "virtual organization." Information technology is used to dissolve the constraints of space and time, linking "knowledge workers" and factory operators in remote locations across the globe into an integrated set of activities.

We find the same pattern in "just-in-time" (JIT) systems of manufacturing, where the components to be used in producing a product are delivered by independent suppliers just minutes or hours before they are needed. This innovation has transformed the very concept of what it means to be "an organization." Under older systems of production where suppliers provided the parts or raw materials to be used in manufacturing a product, such as an automobile, the automobile manufacturer (e.g., Ford, GM, or Volkswagen) was a clearly defined organization. It had a physical boundary and a distinct workforce. But with JIT such boundaries and patterns of membership dissolve. Suppliers may locate their production activities on the premises of Ford or GM to streamline the delivery process and make the "just-in-time" period shorter and more reliable. To an outsider, it may be impossible to distinguish who is working for whom. The fundamental organization really rests in the complex information system that coordinates the activities of all the people and firms involved rather than in the discrete organizations contributing different elements to the process. JIT has transformed organizational relationships throughout the world, linking what used to be discrete organizations into integrated systems of intelligence and activity. We also see the same process occurring in financial services and throughout the service sector.

Consider, for example, how the Internet and other webs of electronic information exchange are transforming retailing and electronic commerce. Large computer software companies are collaborating with manufacturers, distributors, and credit card and finance companies to produce a pattern of direct interaction between customers and manufacturers. Besides eliminating intermediary firms, such as retailers, the development is enhancing possibilities for mass customization. For example, a person wishing to order a shirt or suit of clothes from a manufacturer can select the desired product from an electronic catalogue, submit height, weight, and other personal measurements for complete customization, pay electronically, and expect to receive delivery without further action.

We have here a system of organization. Or is it better described and understood as a system of intelligence? It reflects the shift that is occurring toward a fully fledged information economy. Organizations are rapidly evolving into global information systems that are becoming more and more like electronic brains. What once seemed to rest within the domain of science fiction—peopleless factories coordinated by peopleless offices, producing services on demand—is rapidly becoming reality.

All these developments break the old assumptions about how the structure and capacities of our organizations are limited by the "bounded rationality" described by Herbert Simon. While human intelligence is still the driving force, networked computing is able to realize organizational possibilities that, just a few decades ago, were no more than a dream.

In this world, where rapid change and transformation are becoming the norm, organizations face new challenges. In addition to planning and executing tasks in an efficient rational way, they face the challenge of constant learning and, perhaps even more important, of learning to learn. It is to this aspect of the brain that we now turn.

Creating Learning Organizations

How can one design complex systems that are capable of learning in a brainlike way? This question has been of special concern to a group of information theorists who have interested themselves in problems of artificial intelligence under the umbrella of what is now known as cybernetics.

CYBERNETICS, LEARNING, AND LEARNING TO LEARN

Cybernetics is a relatively new interdisciplinary science focusing on the study of information, communication, and control. The term was coined in the 1940s by MIT mathematician Norbert Wiener as a metaphorical application of the Greek *kubernetes*, meaning "steersman." The Greeks developed the concept of steersmanship, probably from their understanding of the processes involved in the control and navigation of watercraft, and extended its use to the process of government and statecraft. Wiener used this imagery to characterize processes of information exchange through which machines and organisms engage in self-regulating behaviors that maintain steady states.

The origins of modern cybernetics are diverse, but they are found most concretely in the research activities of Wiener and his colleagues during World War II, particularly in the attempt to develop and refine devices for the control of gunfire. The problem of firing a gun at a moving target, such as an airplane, presents a difficult problem of steersmanship involving complex statistical forecasting and computation. Along with considering the speed and position of the plane at a given time and the direction and speed of the missile to be fired, allowance must also be made for variable wind effects and the likelihood that the plane will engage in diversionary flight patterns. Cybernetics emerged from this design challenge, as scientists expert in mathematics, communications theory, engineering, and social and medical science combined their skills and insights to create machines with the computational and adaptive capacities of a living brain.

The core insight emerging from this early work was that the ability of a system to engage in self-regulating behavior depends on processes of information exchange involving *negative feedback*. This concept is central to the process of steersmanship. If we shift a boat off course by taking the rudder too far in one direction, we can get back on course again only by moving it in the opposite direction. Systems of negative feedback engage in this kind of error detection and correction automatically so that movements beyond specified limits in one direction initiate movements in the opposite direction to maintain a desired course of action.

The concept of negative feedback explains many kinds of routine behavior in a very unconventional way. For example, when we pick up an object from a table we typically assume that our hand, guided by our eye, moves directly toward the object. Cybernetics suggests not. This action occurs through a process of error elimination, whereby deviations between hand and object are reduced *at each and every stage of the process*, so that in the end no error remains. We pick up the object by avoiding not picking it up (Exhibit 4.1).

These cybernetic principles are evident in many kinds of systems. The "governor" regulating the speed of the steam engine invented by James Watt in the nineteenth century provides an early example. Two steel balls were suspended from a central shaft attached to the engine. The shaft rotated with the speed of the engine, swinging the balls in an outward direction as speed increased, thus closing the throttle. The reverse actions occurred when speed was reduced. The machine thus acted as a form of a communication system in which an increase in speed initiated actions leading to a decrease in speed and vice versa. This is negative feedback: More leads to less, and less to more. Similar principles are incorporated in a house thermostat. Living organisms operate in a parallel manner. When our body heat rises, the brain and central nervous system initiate action that leads us to slow down, sweat, and breathe heavily in order to initiate changes in the opposite direction. Similarly, when we get cold, we are led to shiver, stamp our feet, and attempt to increase body temperature, keeping body functioning within the critical limits necessary for survival.

Cybernetics thus leads to a theory of communication and learning stressing four key principles:

1. Systems must have the capacity to sense, monitor, and scan significant aspects of their environment.

2. They must be able to relate this information to the operating norms that guide system behavior.

We pick up an object by avoiding not picking it up!

In a similar way, we manage to ride a bicycle by means of a system of information flows and regulatory actions that help us to avoid falling off.

Negative feedback eliminates error: It creates desired system states by avoiding noxiant states.

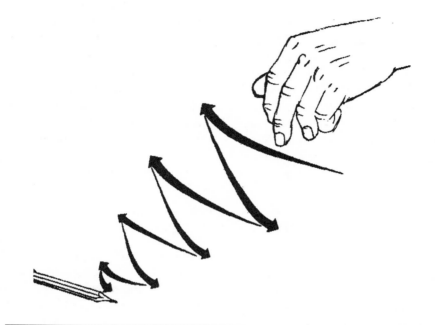

Exhibit 4.1   Negative Feedback in Practice

3. They must be able to detect significant deviations from these norms.

4. They must be able to initiate corrective action when discrepancies are detected.

If these four conditions are satisfied, a continuous process of information exchange is created between a system and its environment, allowing the system to monitor changes and initiate appropriate responses. In this way the system can operate in an intelligent, self-regulating manner. However, the learning abilities thus defined are limited in that the system can maintain only the course of action determined by the operating norms or standards guiding it. This is fine so long as the action defined by those standards is appropriate for dealing with the changes encountered. But when this is not the case, the intelligence of the system breaks down, for the process of negative feedback ends up trying to maintain an inappropriate pattern of behavior.

This has led modern cyberneticians to draw a distinction between the process of learning and the process of learning to learn. Simple cybernetic systems, like house thermostats, are able to learn in the sense of being able to detect and correct deviations from predetermined norms, but they are unable to question the appropriateness of what they are doing. For example, a simple thermostat is unable to determine what level of temperature is appropriate to meet the preferences of the inhabitants of a room and to make adjustments to take account of this. More complex cybernetic systems such as the human brain or advanced computers have this capacity. They are often able to detect and correct errors in operating norms and thus influence the standards that guide their detailed operations. It is this kind of self-questioning ability that underpins the activities of systems that are able to learn to learn and self-organize. The essential difference between these two types of learning is sometimes identified in terms of a distinction between "single-loop" and "double-loop" learning (Exhibit 4.2).

CAN ORGANIZATIONS
LEARN TO LEARN?

All the above ideas raise very important questions for modern organizations. Are they able to learn in an ongoing way? Is this learning single-loop or double-loop? What are the main barriers to learning? Are these barriers intrinsic to the nature of human organization? Can they be overcome?

As a result of the pioneering work conducted by Chris Argyris at Harvard University and by Donald Schön at MIT, these issues have now been brought to the forefront of management attention. Conceived as a challenge of creating "learning organizations," and popularized by the work of Peter Senge in the United States and independently through Reg Revans's concept of "action learning" in Europe, the idea of developing capacities for individual and organizational learning has established itself as a key priority in designing and managing organizations that can deal with the challenges of a turbulent world.

The principles of modern cybernetics provide a framework for thinking about how this can be achieved.

For example, many organizations have become proficient at single-loop learning, developing an ability to scan the environment, set objectives, and monitor the general performance of the system in relation to these objectives. This basic skill is often institutionalized in the form of information systems designed to keep the organization "on course."

Single-loop learning rests in an ability to detect and correct error in relation to a given set of operating norms:

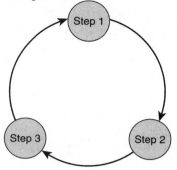

Double-loop learning depends on being able to take a "double look" at the situation by questioning the relevance of operating norms:

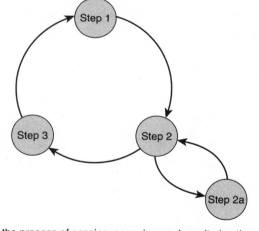

Step 1 = the process of sensing, scanning, and monitoring the environment.
Step 2 = the comparison of this information against operating norms.
Step 2a = the process of questioning whether operating norms are appropriate.
Step 3 = the process of initiating appropriate action.

Exhibit 4.2   Single- and Double-Loop Learning

For example, budgets and other management controls often maintain single-loop learning by monitoring expenditures, sales, profits, and other indications of performance to ensure that organizational activities remain within established limits. Advances in computing have done much to foster the use of this kind of single-loop control.

However, the ability to achieve proficiency at double-loop learning often proves more elusive. Although some organizations have been successful in institutionalizing systems that review and challenge basic paradigms and operating norms, many fail to do so. This failure is especially true of bureaucratized organizations, whose fundamental organizing principles often operate in a way that actually *obstructs* the learning process.

For example, bureaucratization tends to create fragmented patterns of thought and action. Where hierarchical and horizontal divisions are particularly strong, information and knowledge rarely flow in a free manner. Different sectors of the organization thus often operate on the basis of different pictures of the total situation, pursuing subunit goals almost as ends in themselves.

The existence of such divisions tends to emphasize the distinctions between different elements of the organization and fosters the development of political systems that place yet further barriers in the way of learning. The bounded rationality inherent in organizational design thus actually *creates* boundaries! Employees are usually encouraged to occupy and keep a predefined place within the whole, and are rewarded for doing so. Situations in which policies and operating standards are challenged tend to be exceptional rather than the rule. Under these circumstances, single-loop learning systems are reinforced and may actually serve to keep an organization on the wrong course.

Barriers to double-loop learning can also be created by processes of bureaucratic accountability and other systems for rewarding or punishing employees. As Chris Argyris and Donald Schön have shown, when people feel threatened or vulnerable they often engage in "defensive routines" designed to protect themselves and their colleagues. They find ways of obscuring or burying issues and problems that will put them in a bad light and of deflecting attention elsewhere. They become skilled in all kinds of impression management that can make situations for which they are responsible look better than they actually are. They often ignore or fail to report deep-seated problems and often "hold back" or dilute other bad news, giving senior managers rosy pictures of a situation or telling them what they think they would like to hear. The sequence of events and burying of problems leading to the U.S. space shuttle *Challenger* disaster provides an excellent example. The desire to launch "on time" overrode knowledge of serious problems with the O-ring seals that triggered the shuttle explosion.

Argyris and Schön suggest that such problems are systemic and universal. They are found in many different kinds of organizations and transcend cultural boundaries. The "defensive routines" they express seem to be learned early in life and hinge on various kinds of face-saving processes through which people seek to protect themselves and others from embarrassment or threat. In organizational contexts, formal structures, rules, job descriptions, and various conventions and beliefs offer themselves as convenient allies in the process of self-protection and are used both consciously and unconsciously for this purpose. Defensive routines can also become a central part of the culture of an organization, generating shared norms and patterns of "groupthink" that prevent people from addressing key aspects of the reality with which they are dealing.

GUIDELINES FOR "LEARNING ORGANIZATIONS"

Given all these potential pathologies, it is not surprising that so many organizations find difficulty in learning and evolving in a fluid way. Indeed, as Peter Senge of MIT has pointed out, most organizations seem to have severe learning disabilities; most "die" before the age of forty.

But the good news here is that awareness of a problem is often the first important step toward a solution. We can thus take the insights about cybernetics and learning and begin to define the requirements of learning organizations in practice.

In a nutshell, cybernetics suggests that learning organizations must develop capacities that allow them to do the following:

- Scan and anticipate change in the wider environment to detect significant variations.
- Develop an ability to question, challenge, and change operating norms and assumptions.
- Allow an appropriate strategic direction and pattern of organization to emerge.

Also, in achieving these aims, they must

- Evolve designs that allow them to become skilled in the art of double-loop learning, to avoid getting trapped in single-loop processes, especially those created by traditional management control systems and the defensive routines of organizational members.

The task of realizing these characteristics in practice, of course, is a difficult one and very much a "work in progress." Many organizations are struggling to find ways of breaking free of traditional modes of operation to enhance continuous learning. However, the above guidelines provide clear indications of the direction in which to move.

Scanning and Anticipating Environmental Change

Learning organizations have to develop skills and mind-sets that embrace environmental change as a norm. They have to be able to detect "early warning" signals that give clues to shifting trends and patterns. And they often have to find ways of inventing completely new ways of seeing their environment. For it is by seeing and thinking about the context of their industry and activities in new ways that they are able to envisage and create new possibilities.

As Ikujiro Nonaka and Hiro Takuchi have shown in their study of innovation in successful Japanese companies, genuine learning and the ability to develop breakthrough products and services have to go beyond the collection and processing of information. They must embrace the *creation* of insight and knowledge. Like the human brain, successful learning organizations need to be skilled in the art of representation. They need to be able to create appropriate maps of the reality with which they have to deal. But the process has to be active rather than passive. It has to embrace views of potential futures as well as of the present and the past.

The process is well illustrated in the work of Gary Hamel and C. K. Prahalad, who have shown how many of the most innovative companies worldwide possess an ability to envisage and create completely new industries or business niches. This allows them to invent and reinvent themselves, and their relationships with competitors, customers, and the broader environment, on a continuous basis. For example, Apple Computer's vision of a world where everyone has a PC helped reinvent the computer industry. CNN's vision of an international "around-the-clock" system of news reporting helped create a major transformation in broadcasting. Canon's vision of small user-friendly photocopiers using disposable parts created a major new niche in the maturing photocopier business. British Airways' drive to globalization initiated major transformations in the airline industry. The vision of a world where everyone will possess their own mobile telephone number and where telecommunications and other media services will be completely user driven is setting a new stage for the development of media, computer, and other electronic services. Similarly, the vision of electronic merchandising is changing the shape of retailing and creating personal relationships between mass, yet fully customized, manufacturers and the people who buy their products and services.

Intelligent learning systems use information about the present to ground their activities in a business reality. But they are also skilled in spotting the "fracture lines," signals, and trends that point to future possibilities. They are skilled at imagining and anticipating possible futures and acting in the present in ways that help make those futures realities. Often, the skill is not just cognitive but intuitive, emotional, and tactile as well.

As many successful companies have shown, it is impossible to truly know one's customers, potential customers, or products and services at a distance. One has to join them. One has to share their experiences. One has to understand products and services from *their* point of view. A learning organization thus has to become skilled in breaking the boundaries separating it from its environment, to engage and experience the environment as fully as possible.

The view of learning involved here goes well beyond the passive information processing characteristics of simple cybernetic machines. It embraces the kind of active intelligence characteristic of the human brain and its extension through the nervous system. And, like the products of the human brain, the actions of a learning organization actually change the environment in which it exists. We are a long way, here, from the bounded rationality of a mechanistic organization monitoring its environment, shielding itself from uncertainty and seeking to maintain a stable internal system and a fixed niche. We are involved with a much more fluid sense of intelligence that uses, embraces, and at times creates uncertainty as a resource for new patterns of development.

Challenging Operating
Norms and Assumptions

The kind of learning orientation described above must be rooted in key competencies within the organization concerned. As has been shown, the principles of double-loop learning give clear guidance on what's needed. To learn and change, organizational members must be skilled in understanding the assumptions, frameworks, and norms guiding current activity and be able to challenge and change them when necessary. In this way the organization can adjust internal operations to meet changing strategic and environmental requirements and avoid being locked into the past. "Double-loop" learning depends on what is sometimes described as the art of framing and reframing, which, as Donald Schön has shown, is crucial for the kind of self-reflective practice that underpins intelligent action. In concrete terms, it means that organizational members must be skilled in understanding the paradigms, metaphors, mind-sets, or mental models that underpin how the organization operates. They must be able to develop new ones when appropriate. Most of what Peter Senge tells us about learning organizations fits here. In essence, he invites organizational members to challenge how they see and think about organizational reality, using different templates and mental models, especially those generated by "systems thinking," to create new capacities through which organizations can extend their ability to create the future.

- What business are we in, and is it the right business?
- Can we create fundamentally new products and services?
- Can we redefine the boundaries between different industries and services so that new niches emerge?
- Can we structure our organization around business processes that reflect a customer viewpoint rather than the influence of traditional departmental structures?
- Can we redesign business processes in a way that will increase the quality of production *and reduce* costs?
- Can we replace our organizational hierarchy with a network of self-managing teams?

All these questions contain a double-loop learning potential because they invite the questioner to examine the status quo and consider alternative modes of operation. They encourage us to understand key organizational attributes from the standpoint of a new frame.

This is what it takes to reinvent existing modes of operation. Many organizations get trapped by the status quo. They become myopic, accepting their current reality as *the* reality. To learn and change they must be prepared to challenge and change the basic rules of the game at both strategic and operational levels.

The practice of double-loop learning has become well established at a strategic level. Most organizations have recognized the importance of challenging key business paradigms, using brainstorming sessions and other forms of creative thinking to create new directions. As a result of the pathbreaking work by Edwards Deming, Joseph Juran, and other leaders of the "quality movement," the philosophy of promoting continuous improvement (the Japanese concept of *Kaizen*) and total quality management (TQM) has done much to institutionalize the practice of challenging taken-for-granted norms and practices at an operational level (Exhibit 4.3).

The challenge, of course, is to ensure that the strategic and operational dimensions are in sync, and this is where problems often arise. Strategic development may run ahead of organizational reality because of the tendency for current operations to get caught in patterns of single-loop

> The power of TQM, *Kaizen,* and other methods of generating continuous improvement rests in the fact they encourage double-loop learning:
>
> - Employees are asked to dig beneath the surface of recurring problems and uncover the forces that are producing them.
> - They are encouraged to examine existing modes of practice and find better ones.
> - They are encouraged to create "languages," mind-sets, and values that make learning and change a major priority.
>
> In challenging operating norms and assumptions in this way, the approaches create information, insights, and capacities through which a system can evolve to new levels of development.

Exhibit 4.3   TMQ and Double-Loop Learning

learning. Indeed, the TQM movement has suffered badly from this problem. Despite an outright commitment to constant improvement, many TQM programs have got caught in old bureaucratic patterns and cultural norms, leading to failure rates in the region of 70 percent. Such is the strength of pressures toward single-loop learning. When change threatens the status quo, defensive routines "kick in," diluting or diverting the attack on established practice.

For successful double-loop learning to occur, organizations must develop cultures that support change and risk taking. They have to embrace the idea that in rapidly changing circumstances with high degrees of uncertainty, problems and errors are inevitable. They have to promote an openness that encourages dialogue and the expression of conflicting points of view. They have to recognize that legitimate error, which arises from the uncertainty and lack of control in a situation, can be used as a resource for new learning. They have to recognize that genuine learning is usually action based and thus must find ways of helping to create experiments and probes so that they learn through doing in a productive way.

All this, of course, can raise high levels of anxiety in an organization. In particular, it is difficult for managers who want to be "on top of the facts" and "in control" to ride the kind of creative chaos on which innovation thrives. Yet this is precisely the competence that double-loop learning requires. Under its reign, managers and employees at all levels have to find ways of embracing uncertainty in a manner that allows new patterns of action to emerge.

Encouraging "Emergent" Organization

The intelligence of the human brain is not predetermined, predesigned, or preplanned. Indeed, it is not centrally driven in any way. It is a decentralized *emergent* phenomenon. Intelligence *evolves*.

This aspect of the brain metaphor has enormous implications because it counters the traditional view of management as requiring strong direction, leadership, and control that, in effect, imposes goals and objectives from "above" for execution "below."

As has been shown, a "top down" approach to management, especially one focusing on control through clearly defined targets, encourages single-loop learning but discourages the double-loop thinking that is so important for an organization to evolve.

This creates interesting paradoxes for management, for how can one manage in a coherent way without setting clear goals and objectives?

The answer derived from cybernetics is that the behavior of intelligent systems requires a sense of the vision, norms, values, limits, or "reference points" that are to guide behavior. Otherwise, complete randomness will prevail. But these "reference points" must be defined in a way that creates a space in which many possible actions and behaviors can emerge *including those that can question the limits being imposed!* Targets tend to create straitjackets. Cybernetic points of reference create space in which learning and innovation can occur.

The contrast between these two approaches is beautifully illustrated in a story told by management writer William Ouchi on how American and Japanese managers view objectives (Exhibit 4.4).

In the American view, objectives should be hard-and-fast and clearly stated for all to see. In the Japanese view, objectives *emerge* from a more fundamental process of exploring and understanding the values through which a firm is or should be operating. As the Japanese bank president in Ouchi's example suggests, if his managers could absorb the basic philosophy of the bank and how it wants its staff to deal with customers and competitors, appropriate objectives and behaviors in any situation would become very apparent. They wouldn't have to be set or be imposed by a third party.

The core values of the bank are cybernetic reference points that allow self-regulating behavior to occur. They create coherence. But they also give a lot of space. In any situation a manager is free to choose whatever action or behavior seems appropriate to the situation at hand. This opens the way to sustained innovation at a local level. This, in turn, creates a potential for double-loop learning, as significant innovations can be used to modify operating norms.

William Ouchi reports on differences in the style of American and Japanese managers working in the U.S. headquarters of a Japanese bank:

The basic mechanisms of management control in a Japanese company are so subtle, implicit, and internal that they often appear to an outsider not to exist. That conclusion is a mistake. The mechanisms are thorough, highly disciplined, and demanding, yet very flexible. Their essence could not be more different from methods of managerial control in Western organizations.

In an interview with the American vice presidents, I asked how they felt about working for this Japanese bank. "They treat us well, let us in on the decision making and pay us well. We're satisfied." "You're very fortunate," I continued, "but tell me, if there were something that you could change about this Japanese bank, what would it be?" The response was quick and clearly one that was very much on their minds: "These Japanese just don't understand objectives, and it drives us nuts!"

Next I interviewed the president of this bank, an expatriate Japanese who was on temporary assignment from Tokyo headquarters to run the United States operation, and asked about the two American vice presidents. "They're hard-working, loyal, and professional. We think they're terrific," came the reply. When asked if he would like to change them in any way, the president replied, "These Americans just don't seem to be able to understand objectives."

With each side accusing the other of an inability to understand objectives, there was a clear need for further interviewing and for clarification. A second round of interviews probed further into the issue. First, the American vice presidents: "We have all the necessary reports and numbers, but we can't get specific targets from him. He won't tell us how large a dollar increase in loan volume or what percent decrease in operating costs he expects us to achieve over the next month, quarter, or even year. How can we know whether we're performing well without specific targets to shoot for?" A point well taken, for every major American company and government bureau devotes a large fraction of its time to the setting of specific, measurable performance targets. Every American business school teaches its students to take global, fuzzy corporate goals and boil them down to measurable performance targets. Management by objective (MBO), program planning and evaluation, and cost-benefit analysis are among the basic tools of control in modern American management.

When I returned to reinterview the Japanese president, he explained, "If only I could get these Americans to understand our philosophy of banking. To understand what the business means to us—how we feel we should deal with customers and our employees. What our relationship should be to the

Exhibit 4.4   American and Japanese Styles of Management: The Contrast Between Mechanistic and Cybernetic Styles of Decision Making

(Continued)

Exhibit 4.4 (Continued)

---

local communities we serve. How we should deal with our competitors, and what our role should be in the world at large. If they could get that under their skin, then they could figure out for themselves what an appropriate objective would be for any situation, no matter how unusual or new, and I would never have to tell them, never have to give them a target."

SOURCE: Pages 33–34 in William Ouchi, *Theory Z* (adapted material). © 1981 by Addison-Wesley, Reading, Massachusetts.

Suppose, for example, that managers working within the framework of the bank's philosophy and values find means of meeting customer needs in a new way or of providing a new service. A system that is open to this kind of innovation from below can acknowledge, disseminate, and use the information and ideas in a way that actually influences the operating rules of the system. For example, the principles or values through which the bank seeks to serve its customers or deal with a competitor or potential competitor can evolve in a way that incorporates and builds on the successful innovation.

Many aspects of Japanese management have a cybernetic quality that promotes learning through innovation and the questioning of operating norms. It is no accident, for example, that the "quality movement" first took off in Japan. Quality circles, where people come together to share issues and problems and find ways of making improvements to the overall system in which they are working, offer a perfect illustration of double-loop learning in practice. The principles are also evident in the ritual of *ringi*, a collective decision-making process through which companies seek to test the robustness of policy initiatives and other developments. Under this process, a policy document is circulated among a group of managers or other personnel for approval. If a person disagrees with what is being proposed, he or she is free to amend the document, and it is circulated again. The process in effect explores the values, premises, and details relating to a project from multiple points of view until an agreed-on position that satisfies all critical concerns and parameters emerges. The process can be extremely time-consuming because in important decisions a very large number of people may be involved. But when the decision is made, one can be fairly certain that key assumptions will have been challenged and that most errors will have been detected and corrected.

This is what double-loop learning is all about. The *ringi* serves the dual function of allowing people to challenge core operating principles and, in both the process and the outcome, to affirm and reaffirm the values that are to guide action. Paradoxically, it is a process that mobilizes disagreement to create consensus. It is also a process that allows innovation to be driven from all directions and for "intelligence" to evolve to higher and higher levels.

We can see here how cybernetic functioning based on double-loop learning can allow a system to get smarter and smarter. Interestingly, the process is completely paradoxical because learning has to be guided by key operating norms that, in turn, have to be constantly challenged.

Learning always seems to involve this kind of paradox because whenever we try to do something new, established modes of behavior are threatened. For example, when a corporation seeks to reinvent itself and create a new business orientation, if often encounters resistance from the "old business." The fear is that *everything* will be lost in the transition. Or when a traditional bureaucracy tries to create "empowered teams," they are often undermined as the old hierarchy tries to retain control. The existing norms of a system "rise up" and in effect say "don't change." To facilitate the double-loop process of learning to learn, people have to be skilled in managing this kind of paradox, a point to which we will return in Chapter 8. They have to be able to find ways of managing the tensions generated through the learning process in a way that allows new operating norms to emerge. Otherwise, the system will almost certainly remain trapped in the old pattern.

Cybernetics also shows us that in facilitating double-loop learning, managers have to be aware of the importance of understanding the *limits* to be placed on action. Here again we find ourselves challenging central principles of Western management theory.

Return, for example, to the whole issue of setting objectives and targets. When we try to achieve goals or targets as end states, for example, a cost reduction of 20 percent or sales growth of $200 million, the target can dominate attention and obliterate other key aspects of the overall situation. Attention and action tend to be oriented to a fixed point in the future, and the environment tends to be manipulated in a way that will allow the organization to get there. In the process, all kinds of dysfunctions and unintended consequences arise. Managers may gain their 20 percent cut in costs but in the process do irreversible damage to the corporate culture as a result of employee layoffs. The sales department may achieve its new target of $200 million but alienate a part of the company's future customer base because substandard product has been shipped to get the sales on time.

Corporate life is full of these kinds of horror stories. In retrospect, they always seem blatantly stupid and short-sighted. More fundamentally, they are systemic. They are inevitable in any situation where people are encouraged to edit their understanding of reality to suit narrow purposes.

A cybernetic view of the problem shows us that while goals and targets often reflect noble *intentions*, the achievement of any goal must always be moderated by an understanding of the *limits* that need to be placed on behavior. Put more forcefully, successful system evolution has to be guided as much by the "avoidance of noxiants" as the pursuit of desired ends.

To illustrate, return to the operation of a simple cybernetic system. Look at how system behavior is guided by the *avoidance of undesirable system states*. A thermostat achieves its "goal" of a warm, comfortable room by ensuring that the room does *not* get too warm or too cold. The system avoids noxious outcomes.

We see the same cybernetic principle operating in more complex areas of social life. It is no coincidence, for example, that most of the great codes of behavior are framed in terms of "Thou shalt *not*." Whether we examine the Ten Commandments or contemporary legal systems, we find the principle of avoiding noxiants defining a space of acceptable behavior within which individuals can act, innovate, or self-organize as they please.

Interestingly, the same process is evident in the evolution of the Internet, which offers a perfect example of the problems of design in complex, open-ended systems. No one can say what form the Internet should take. No one knows its true potential or what its future should look like. It cannot be predesigned in any authoritative way.

Hence, this de facto design principle: Give would-be users advice on what they should *not* do. For example: "Don't offend other users." "Don't overload them with information." "Don't send junk mail." "Don't reveal confidential information." "Never respond to provocation."

As a result, the Internet is evolving within the space defined by key parameters. Experience and practice test the limits thus defined, giving rise to a redefinition of limits when appropriate. In this way, the Internet is self-organizing in a way that is producing an emergent design. As in the developing intelligence of the brain, resonant innovations become embedded in the evolving "architecture." Inappropriate lines of development stall or die.

Western management, with its enormous emphasis on the achievement of predetermined goals, objectives, and operational targets, overasserts desired *intentions* and underplays the importance of recognizing the *limits* that need to guide behavior. Much of the turbulence of the modern environment is created as a by-product. Independent lines of action collide as organizations jostle to achieve their targets, with a solution "here" creating a problem elsewhere. The message of cybernetics: learn from *ringi*. Be sure to surface the noxiants associated with favored lines of action, because in surfacing the negatives, we can produce a creative redefinition of the space in which positive patterns of behavior can unfold.

Cybernetics shows us that effective management depends as much on the selection of the limits that are to be placed on behavior as on the active pursuit of desired goals. If management encourages an appropriate dialogue about the limits or constraints to be placed on action, it creates a space in which desirable futures and appropriate strategies and modes of organization can develop. The system becomes "learning driven." Detailed goals become an emergent phenomenon. They look after themselves! These ideas challenge many established management assumptions.

"Designs" That Facilitate Learning

In all that has been said above, considerable emphasis has been placed on how the creation of double-loop learning and emergent forms of organization depend on an ability to transcend the constraints of the single-loop processes and defensive routines that tend to tie an organization to the past. Part of the challenge hinges on adopting an appropriate management philosophy that views and encourages the capacity of learning to learn as a key priority. It also rests in encouraging organizational principles and designs that can support this process.

This brings us to the topic of our next section: the holographic approach to organization. As we will see, the ideas generated through this image provide many interesting and practical insights into the qualities that organizations must possess if they are to have the flexible self-organizing capacities of a brain.

Organizations as Holographic Brains

The metaphor of a hologram invites us to think of systems where qualities of the whole are enfolded in all the parts so that the system has an ability to self-organize and regenerate itself on a continuous basis.

Recall the image of a broken holographic plate, where any part can be used to regenerate the information contained in the whole.

Think of a holographic sculpture of a dancer in an art gallery. As you walk around the laser beam the dancer changes position as the information encoded in the beam is engaged in different ways.

Or think of how the brain is able to reorganize itself when specific parts are injured or removed. As we have seen, rats are able to thread their way through a maze with up to 90 percent of their cortex missing. Young children who lose a complete hemisphere of their brain are often able to recover lost functions as the remaining hemisphere takes over. In a similar way, adults experiencing severe brain injury involving amnesia sometimes develop completely new personalities as the brain self-organizes and relearns all the skills, emotions, and capacities needed to create a new life.

Now think of designing organizations that possess these abilities.

They would be organizations that have wonderful memories that are organized and accessed in a highly decentralized way. They would be capable of processing massive amounts of information and of shaping it for different purposes. They would be comfortable with managing many different points of view. They would be organizations where individuals, teams, and other units are able to take on almost any challenge and find ways of organizing for the needs at hand. They would be capable of functioning when major sections become obliterated or immobilized. They would be organizations where capacities, intelligence, and control are distributed in a way that allows any single element to become a vital part of the whole. They would be organizations that are able to grow, develop, and change their personalities along with changing experiences. They would, in short, be intelligent, self-organizing brains that reflect all the qualities of what we have described as a "learning organization."

Presented in this way the holographic image seems to offer an almost impossible ideal. But if one examines *existing* organizational reality it is surprising to find that many of these qualities already exist. For example, every individual working in an organization has a wonderful brain. Even though it may not be used effectively, the potential is there. Similarly, decentralized local computer networks as well as the Internet, the World Wide Web, and other electronic databases extend and distribute memory and intelligence in a way that can be accessed at many points and in many forms. The potential for new forms of intelligence to emerge from this vast network of connections is enormous.

The regenerative capacities that allow an organization to form and reform itself to deal with destructive circumstances are also present. For example, when organizations encounter disaster that immobilizes major functions, the healthy parts often rise to the new challenge. Note, for example, how government, health, telecommunications, transportation, and other service companies in San Francisco were able to reorganize in response to the great earthquake of 1989. Within hours or days, revised services were in operation. Staid organizations transformed themselves. Dynamic organizations became even more dynamic.

The process is also observed, from a completely different perspective, in the experience of a small Norwegian shipping company, which, as a result of a charter plane crash, lost half its employees, including many managers. As Espen Anderson, who reports the story, observes, the company was initially shocked and immobilized by the event. But it was soon able to function very much as before. The remaining staff shared much of the original intelligence of the company and by pooling their knowledge were able to reconstruct the functions performed by the people who perished.

Holographic aspects of organization are always asserting their presence. But in many situations they are suppressed or negated by conventional assumptions about organization design. So let's explore some ways that holographic qualities can be encouraged.

PRINCIPLES OF HOLOGRAPHIC DESIGN

In certain respects it is a paradox to talk of "holographic design" because the holographic style of organization is very much a self-organizing, emergent phenomenon. However, there are several key principles that can help create contexts in which holographic self-organization can flourish. They are discussed here under the five headings summarized in Exhibit 4.5.

Principle 1: Build the "Whole" Into All the "Parts"

At first sight, this principle seems to express an impossible ideal. But there are at least four ways in which the "whole in parts" philosophy can be realized in practice: by focusing on corporate culture, information systems, structure, and roles.

Corporate "DNA." The visions, values, and sense of purpose that bind an organization together can be used as a way of helping every individual understand and absorb the mission and challenge of the whole enterprise. Just as DNA in nature carries a holographic code that contains the information required to unfold the complete development of the human body, it is possible to encode key elements of a "complete organization" in the cultural and other codes that unite its members.

An appreciation of an organization's vision, aspirations, core values, operating norms, and other dimensions of corporate culture, discussed in detail in the next chapter, creates a capacity for each person to embody and act in a way that represents the whole. This is one of the reasons why companies like the Norwegian shipping firm, discussed earlier, are able to recreate themselves in new situations. Culture has a holographic

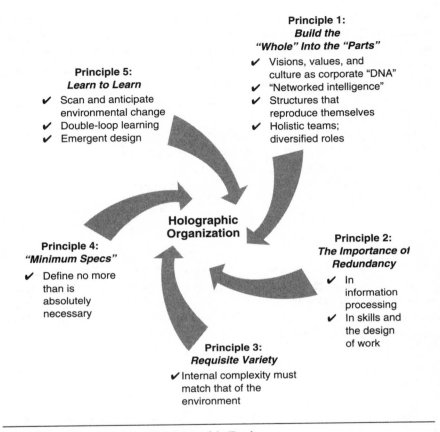

Principle 1:
Build the
"Whole" Into the "Parts"

✔ Visions, values, and culture as corporate "DNA"
✔ "Networked intelligence"
✔ Structures that reproduce themselves
✔ Holistic teams; diversified roles

Principle 5:
Learn to Learn

✔ Scan and anticipate environmental change
✔ Double-loop learning
✔ Emergent design

Principle 4:
"Minimum Specs"

✔ Define no more than is absolutely necessary

Holographic Organization

Principle 2:
The Importance of Redundancy

✔ In information processing
✔ In skills and the design of work

Principle 3:
Requisite Variety

✔ Internal complexity must match that of the environment

Exhibit 4.5   Principles of Holographic Design

quality—a quality that is arguably its major source of power as a factor influencing effective management.

To create brainlike capacities for self-organization, however, it is vital that the cultural codes uniting an organization foster an open and evolving approach to the future. Cultures that embody closed visions and self-sealing values tend to die. In line with the principles of cybernetic learning discussed earlier, visions, values, and other dimensions of culture must create space in which productive innovation can occur. In this way, the culture that unites an organization can have an enduring yet changing form, as the visions, values, and operating codes get expressed in different ways at different times and evolve with changing circumstances.

"Networked intelligence." The second way of building "the whole" into "the parts" of an organization is through the

design of appropriate information systems. This is the true significance and power of what's being called "networked intelligence." Information systems that can be accessed from multiple points of view create a potential for individuals throughout an enterprise, even those in remote locations, to become full participants in an evolving system of organizational memory and intelligence. They can learn from and contribute to the organization's information base and the ideas expressed. Just as the Internet and the World Wide Web create an opportunity for the evolution of a kind of "global mind," organizational information systems create a capacity for the evolution of a shared "organizational mind."

Developments in information technology and associated global networks are creating quantum breakthroughs insofar as the holographic metaphor is concerned. They create a practical context in which information that used to be shaped, manipulated, and controlled through organizational hierarchies in an exclusive manner can become widely assembled and disseminated and used as a new source of intelligence and growth throughout an enterprise.

Holographic structure. A third way of building "the whole" into "the parts" rests in the design of organizational structures that can grow large while staying small. Consider, for example, the case of Magna International, an auto parts manufacturer that has grown at a rapid rate from a single factory employing twenty people in the mid-1950s to a corporation with sales in excess of $4 billion in the mid-1990s. The Magna philosophy is encoded in a simple set of business principles and the rule that operating factories must remain on a small scale to avoid becoming impersonal. Thus, once an enterprise reaches a size in the region of 200 people, the only way it can grow is by spinning off another unit. In this way, Magna spawns clusters of organizations that, in turn, spawn further clusters (Exhibit 4.6), creating a highly diversified enterprise where each part in effect develops as an integrated whole. The process has a "fractal" quality in that the same basic pattern reproduces itself over and over again.

As a second example, consider the information processing company that has achieved a spectacular rate of growth over the past ten years through a process of holographic reproduction. Within the context of a broadly defined vision of superior customer service it has formulated the broad operational rule that growth can occur only through the development of new service units. When a unit reaches an optimal size, yet wishes to serve a larger customer base, three people from the unit, typically a manager and two service specialists, break away to launch a new enterprise. In this way the culture, character, and skill base of the whole organization are encoded into the new part. The "part" quickly

It is possible to grow large while staying small.

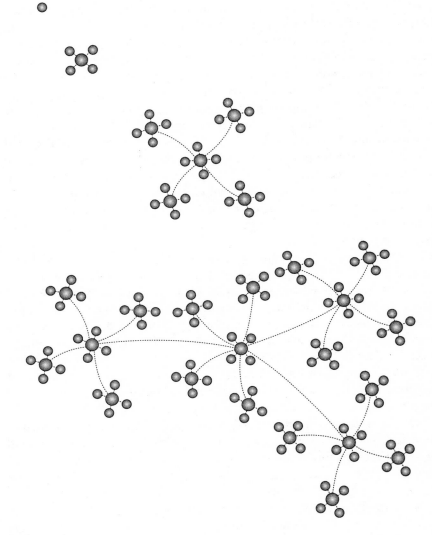

And so on!

Exhibit 4.6   Holographic Reproduction

becomes synonymous with the whole as new staff joining the unit absorb and "live" the qualities that lend the organization its distinctive character. Using information technology and a strong sense of values and corporate culture as unifying forces, it is able to operate in a completely decentralized fashion, adjusting to the special circumstances met in local environments. Yet it remains a tightly integrated enterprise.

Holistic teams and diversified roles. A fourth way of building "the whole" into "the parts" rests in how work tasks are designed. Under old mechanistic principles work processes were usually fragmented into narrow and highly specialized jobs, linked through some means of coordination. The whole was the sum of the parts thus designed. Think, for example, of Adam Smith's famous description of how the making of a simple pin can be split into many discrete tasks, or of the definition of jobs under Frederick Taylor's scientific management, discussed in Chapter 2. Fragmentation rules.

The holographic approach to job design moves in exactly the opposite direction by defining work holistically. The basic unit of design is a work team that is made responsible for a complete business process, such as assembling the seat of a car, meeting the needs of a group of customers, or steering the development of a new product from inspiration to prototype production. Within the team, roles or jobs are then broadly defined with individuals being trained in multiple skills so that they are interchangeable and can function in a flexible, organic way.

The prototype of this mode of operation is found in offices and factories built around self-managing work groups. Consider, for example, the electronics firm that assembles modular units for use in computers through the work of autonomous work teams of 14 to 18 people. These operating teams have complete responsibility for production, from the arrival of supplies in the plant to the shipment of finished products. Every employee is multiskilled and able to perform the operating tasks needed to produce the whole product. The teams meet daily to make decisions about production, to divide work, and to attend to special issues such as improvements in work design, problems in supplies or shipping, or the hiring of new members. Members of the team are responsible for setting their own hours of work and production schedules and conduct their own quality control. They even administer skills-certification tests to their colleagues. Each operating team has a leader or manager who acts as a resource, coach, and facilitator and who has special concern for the team's identity.

In effect, the teams have absorbed many of the functions that, in a bureaucratic organization, would be performed by staff in many separate departments, such as planning, personnel, training, quality control, and engineering. This pattern is evident in autonomous work groups of all kinds. There seems to be a natural tendency to "embrace the whole" in the sense that teams that are responsible and rewarded for effective performance of a set of tasks soon realize that work becomes a lot easier and more effective if they are able to influence and shape the context and conditions influencing their performance. Thus, rather than just trying to achieve their production bonus through methods and guidelines suggested by production engineering staff, they frequently develop innovations of their own. They see how a simplification of product design could lead to many production efficiencies. Rather than accept new team members chosen by the personnel department, they realize the benefits of handling the recruitment process themselves. Rather than relying on training programs mandated by the training department, they prefer to shape and select their own. Although the teams may require professional support from outside their ranks from technical, administrative, and other specialist staff, especially in terms of ongoing development and integration with the wider enterprise, the team approximates the whole organization just as each multiskilled team member embodies the vision, outlook, and skills of the whole team.

The four broad practices discussed above offer concrete strategies through which holographic organization can become a reality. Although, at first sight, the notion of "building the whole into all the parts" seems a paradoxical and unattainable ideal, there are clear ways in which it can be made to happen.

There is, however, an important qualification that needs to be made with regard to the balance that often has to be struck between demands for specialization and demands for generalization. Recall earlier discussion of the brain. The brain is both specialized *and* generalized. While memory and the capacities to perform different functions have a strong holographic quality, it is also possible to see strong specialist tendencies, for example, in the orientations of the left and right hemispheres; in how the cortex has distinct functional areas; in how the hypothalamus is concerned with survival activity; and so on.

A similar synthesis may be required in organizational contexts. Thus, in a company like Magna International, the "whole in parts" philosophy does not lead to the development of identical units. There may be considerable differences between parts of the company specializing in the assembly of electrical components compared with those producing car seating modules. The company's central office will be different from the manufacturing cells.

Similarly, in the information processing company discussed above, the process of holographic diffusion may produce a variety of "spin-off" units that are differentiated in terms of the relations struck with different clients. Different environmental niches may require that the company avoid producing "clones" and find ways of delivering core services in a manner tailored to meet specific needs. Different spin-offs may thus develop distinct competencies.

Self-organizing work groups in office or factory settings are also likely to reflect similar variations, as they develop their own modes of operation and distinctive character.

The pattern reflected in each of these examples is illustrated in Exhibit 4.7.

The point being made here is that, in practice, the "whole in parts" principle does not always result in "clones" and has to be interpreted and implemented in a creative manner.

As another source of inspiration, recall our earlier discussion about mobots. They provide an excellent image for thinking about the whole/part problem. Consider Genghis the "mechanical cockroach." It is a system composed of six "thinking legs" linked by a few simple rules that allow walking, as a kind of higher-order "intelligence," to emerge.

It operates through loosely coupled subsystems that are skilled in dealing with the challenges of their immediate environment. When bound together Genghis becomes more than the sum of its parts.

There is an important lesson for organizational design here. When organizational units are allowed to develop in a manner that enhances local intelligence, whether in the form of a self-organizing work group committed to continuous process and product innovation, or a decentralized company with semiautonomous units each meeting the needs of different environmental niches, capacities for intelligent self-organization of the whole system are much enhanced.

The "whole in parts" principle is perhaps the key idea underlying holographic design. But it needs to be supported by an understanding of the four other principles illustrated earlier in Exhibit 4.5.

Principle 2: The Importance of "Redundancy"

Any system with an ability to self-organize must have a degree of redundancy: a kind of excess capacity that can create room for innovation and development to occur. Without redundancy, systems are fixed and completely static.

In the human brain we find this redundancy in the vast networks of connectivity through which each neuron, or nerve cell, is connected with thousands upon thousands of others. It is estimated that with 10 billion neurons, each having 1,000 connections, the brain has the equivalent of 60,000 miles of "circuitry" that can be traveled in countless different ways. This enormous capacity generates considerable evolutionary potential. It

This "whole in parts" principle does not always result in "clones."

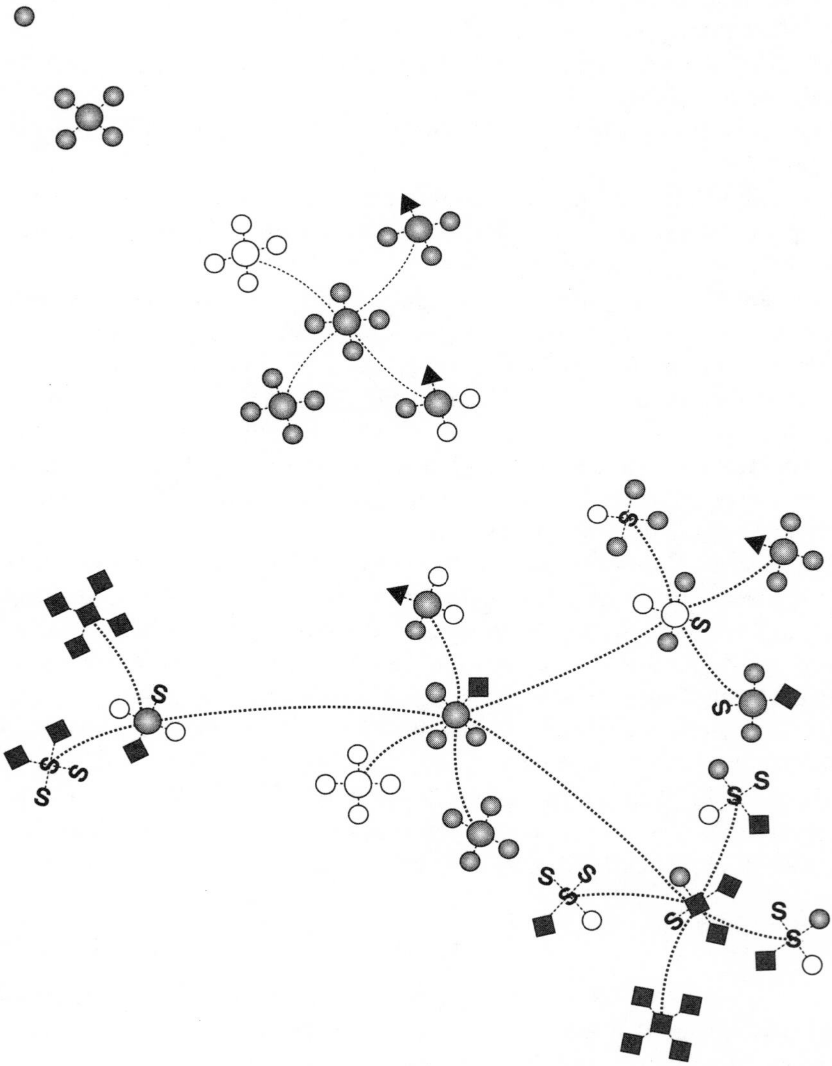

Exhibit 4.7   Holographic Yet Differentiated

allows vast amounts of information processing from which thousands of potential patterns of development can emerge, contributing to the brain's constantly evolving structure, refinement, and intelligence.

A lot of the brain's activity seems to be completely random and characterized by a massive amount of distributed and parallel information processing. At any one time many parts of the brain may be involved with the same activity or information. This redundancy allows initiatives to be generated from many locations at once, thus reducing dependence on the activities of any single location. The process generates the multiple, competing "drafts" of intelligence from which an evolving pattern eventually emerges. The redundancy reflected in this system of parallel processing is vital in generating a range of potential outcomes, in coping with error, and in contributing to the brain's flexibility, creativity, and adaptiveness.

In an organizational context, redundancy can play a similar role. "Parallel processing" and sharing of information can be a source of creativity, shared understanding, trust, and commitment. We see this in the *ringi* process discussed earlier. This shared decision-making system contains massive redundancy. It is, however, very effective in exploring issues from multiple perspectives and in testing the robustness of emerging decisions and actions. The process offers a wonderful example of how intelligent action can emerge from "multiple drafts."

We see the same process in the way Japanese and many Western companies approach problem solving or product innovation from multiple perspectives: by giving the same project to different teams, who work independently and then come together to share progress, information, ideas, and insights. The process, like the *ringi*, creates an enormous degree of shared understanding of issues and problems. It broadens the range of investigation. It opens the process to random variation. It counteracts premature "groupthink." It creates a fertile ground in which promising ideas or innovations can strike resonant chords of acceptance and appreciation.

As Nonaka and Takuchi show in their study of knowledge creation and innovation in successful Japanese companies, this kind of redundancy can do much to create deep levels of tacit understanding that go well beyond the cognitive and intellectual realm. Their vision of what they call the "hypertext organization," based on the image of modern user-friendly computer programs that allow one to search large quantities of information from multiple points of view, and to formulate an investigation at many different levels and in many different forms, has a great deal in common with the holographic model described here.

Redundancy can also be built into the skills and mind-sets within an organization. Australian systems theorist Fred Emery has made an important contribution here, suggesting that there are two methods for designing redundancy into a system. The first involves *redundancy of parts*, where each part is precisely designed to perform a specific function, special parts being added to the system for the purpose of control and to back up or replace operating parts whenever they fail. This is the old mechanistic design principle, creating a hierarchy of roles where managers and supervisors become responsible for the work of others. In effect, managers are "spare parts" that come into operation when things go wrong.

The second design method incorporates a *redundancy of functions*. Instead of spare parts being added to a system, extra functions are added to each of the operating parts, so that each part is able to engage in a range of functions. This is the principle guiding the self-organizing work groups discussed earlier. Members acquire multiple skills so that they are able to perform each other's jobs and substitute as the need arises. And the team as a whole absorbs an increasing range of functions as it develops more effective ways of approaching its work. At any one time, each team member possesses skills that are redundant in the sense that they are not being used for the job at hand. However, this organizational design possesses great flexibility and creates a capacity for self-organization within each and every part of the system.

The two design principles show us different ways of creating flexibility. Holographic, self-organizing processes require a *redundancy* of *functions* approach. The shift to self-organizing work groups, the use of quality circles and TQM, and the flattening of organizational structures all reflect a major shift to this in practice. Holographic design encourages people to get involved in the challenges at hand, whatever they may be and wherever they come from, rather than focusing on narrow job descriptions and adopting the "that's not my responsibility" attitude typical of more mechanistic approaches to management.

From a mechanistic standpoint, redundancy seems unnecessary and inefficient. It is something that needs to be eliminated. That is why it is so important to understand its role in fostering self-organization and innovative practice.

However, as discussed in relation to the "whole in parts" principle, another paradox arises: How much redundancy should be built into a system?

This is where the principle of requisite variety comes into play.

Principle 3: Requisite Variety

Clearly, it is impossible to give everybody all possible information about everything. It is impossible for people to become skilled in all possible tasks and activities. So where does one draw the line?

The principle of *requisite variety*, originally formulated by the English cybernetician W. Ross Ashby, suggests that the internal diversity of any self-regulating system must match the variety and complexity of its environment if it is to deal with the challenges posed by that environment. Or, to put the matter slightly differently, any control system must be as varied and complex as the environment being controlled.

In the context of holographic design, this means that all elements of an organization should embody critical dimensions of the environment with which they have to deal so that they can self-organize to cope with the demands they are likely to face.

The principle of requisite variety thus gives clear guidelines as to how the ideas about getting the "whole into the parts" and redundant functions should be applied. It suggests that redundancy (variety) should always be built into a system where it is *directly* needed rather than at a distance. This means that close attention must be paid to the boundary relations between organizational units and their environments to ensure that requisite variety always falls within the unit in question. What is the nature of the environment being faced? Can all the skills for dealing with this environment be possessed by every individual? If so, then build around multifunctioned people, as in the model of the self-organizing work groups discussed earlier. If not, then build around multifunctioned teams that collectively possess the requisite skills and abilities and where each individual member is as generalized as possible, creating a pattern of overlapping skills and knowledge bases in the team overall. It is here that we find a means of coping with the problem that everyone cannot be skilled in everything. Organization can be developed in a cellular manner around self-organizing, multidisciplined groups that have the requisite skills and abilities to deal with the environment in a holistic and integrated way.

The principle of requisite variety has important implications for the design of almost every aspect of organization. Whether we are talking about the creation of a strategic business unit, a corporate planning group, a product development or research team, or a work group in a factory, it argues in favor of a proactive embracing of the environment in all its diversity. Very often, managers do the reverse, reducing variety to achieve greater internal consensus. For example, corporate planning teams are often built around people who think along the same lines rather than around a diverse set of stakeholders who can actually represent the complexity of the problems with which the team ultimately has to deal. Or, in launching a strategic business unit, corporate headquarters may be persuaded to retain vital functions for themselves so that they can continue to exert a measure of direction and control.

The principle of requisite variety points to the fallacy of this. If a business unit or team is to be successful in dealing with the challenges of a complex task, or of a difficult environment, it is vital that it be allowed to possess sufficient internal complexity. As was indicated in earlier discussion of the development of self-organizing work teams, the practical value and wisdom of this principle is well recognized. Teams absorb more and more functions—recruitment, training, quality control, process, and product design—so that they can become more effective in dealing with their environment.

The principle of requisite variety is not just an abstract concept. It is a vital management principle. If a team or unit is unable to recognize, absorb, and deal with the variations in its environment, it is unlikely to evolve and survive. The principle suggests that when variety and redundancy are built at a local level—at the point of interaction with the environment rather than at several stages removed, as happens under hierarchical design—evolutionary capacities are enhanced. Individuals, teams, and other units are empowered to find innovations around local issues and problems that resonate with their needs. This also provides a resource for innovation within the broader organization, as the variety and innovation thus experienced is shared and used as a resource for further learning. The principle of requisite variety can play a vital role in developing evolutionary capacities throughout an enterprise.

Principle 4: Minimum Specs

The three principles discussed above create a capacity to evolve. But systems also need the freedom to evolve. This is where the principle of "minimum critical specification," summarized as *minimum specs*, comes into play.

The central idea here is that if a system is to have the freedom to self-organize it must possess a certain degree of "space" or autonomy that allows appropriate innovation to occur. This seems to be stating the obvious. But the reality is that in many organizations the reverse occurs because management has a tendency to overdefine and overcontrol instead of just focusing on the *critical* variables that need to be specified, leaving others to find their own form.

Thus, to take an example, a senior manager responsible for a strategic business unit may fall under the influence of the old bureaucratic mind-set, trying to define relations as clearly and as precisely as possible. Instead of focusing on critical elements, such as the vision or strategy that will guide the unit, expected resource flows, time lines, and anticipated results, and using these to create a broad structure of accountability, he or she ends up specifying detailed rules, protocol, and targets that in effect bind the organization into a specific mode of operation. The overcontrol negates any redundancy, variety, and innovative potential that the unit may possess because attention gets focused on the internal rules and controls instead of absorbing and dealing with the external challenges being faced.

The principle of minimum specs suggests that managers should define no more than is absolutely necessary to launch a particular initiative or activity on its way. They have to avoid the role of "grand designer" in favor of one that focuses on facilitation, orchestration, and boundary management, creating "enabling conditions" that allow a system to find its own form. The challenge is to help operating units, whether they be spin-off businesses, work teams, research groups, or individuals, find and operate within a sphere of "bounded" or "responsible autonomy." The challenge is to avoid the anarchy and the completely free flow that arises when there are no parameters or guidelines, on the one hand, and overcentralization, on the other.

If a manager does a good job in creating a holographic sense of the vision that is to guide a subunit's operation, discussed earlier as a strategy for getting the "whole into the parts," the additional specifications can often be quite minimal because an element of guidance is already built into the system. The experience and needs of the unit or work group concerned can then become the driving force in the emerging design. The manager plays an integrating role, with a focus on the issues linking the team to the wider organization.

The principle of minimum specs helps preserve the capacities for self-organization that bureaucratic principles and mind-sets usually erode. It helps create a situation where systems can be self-designing as opposed to being "designed" in a traditional sense.

Principle 5: Learning to Learn

This final principle of holographic design brings us back to our earlier discussion of organizational learning. As has been emphasized, there is a strong tendency in most organizations to get trapped in single-loop systems that reinforce the status quo. Continuous self-organization requires a capacity for double-loop learning that allows the operating norms and rules of a system to change along with transformations in the wider environment.

The holographic design principles presented above create a potential for this to occur. But they must be supported by managerial philosophies that help to create a context that encourages the process of "learning to learn." All the ideas discussed on pages 81–97 thus have relevance here.

As indicated in Exhibit 4.5, our design principles have a circular quality. They are interconnected and blend with each other. Although presented as *design* principles, they don't offer a blueprint or recipe.

Rather, they define a mind-set and approach through which we can mobilize key insights about the holographic qualities of the brain in organizational contexts.

Strengths and Limitations
of the Brain Metaphor

Discussion in much of this chapter has looked to the future. While our chapters on the machine and organismic metaphors were able to focus on how these metaphors have already been used to shape organization theory and practice, our discussion of the brain metaphor has had to chart newer ground and adopt a more normative and prescriptive tone.

The main strengths of the metaphor hinge on the contributions made to our ability to create "learning organizations." In discussing the organismic metaphor in Chapter 3 much was made of the importance of creating organizations that are able to innovate and evolve to meet the challenges of changing environments. The ideas presented in this chapter offer concrete guidelines on how this can be achieved.

As we shift into what Peter Drucker has described as the new "knowledge economy," where human intelligence, creativity, and insight is the key resource, we can expect the ideas and principles involved in creating brainlike organizations to become more and more a reality. As has been discussed, the potential is already there. Every person has a brain, and developments in electronic technology are demonstrating how we can mobilize intelligence on a broad front.

One of the major advantages of the brain metaphor is that it identifies the requirements of "learning organizations" in a comprehensive way and how different elements need to support each other. As has been discussed, many management writers have done an outstanding job in identifying the requirements and pathologies of the learning process and in specifying elements of organizational designs that are needed to make learning a reality. The strength of the brain metaphor is that it brings all these together and shows how to move forward on a broad front.

In this regard, the metaphor offers a powerful way of thinking about the implications of new information technology and how it can be used to support the development of learning organizations. Historically, there has been a tendency to use the new technology to reinforce bureaucratic principles and centralized modes of control. As we have seen, this misses the true potential, which rests in creating networks of interaction that can self-organize and be shaped and driven by the intelligence of everyone involved. The holographic design principles presented in this chapter show how this can be achieved.

The metaphor also invites us to rethink key management principles in a way that lays the foundation for a completely new theory of management. Consider, for example, how an understanding of the functioning of the brain challenges traditional assumptions about the importance of strong central leadership and control; about the wisdom of setting clear goals and objectives; about the role of hierarchy; about the concept of organizational design; and about the wisdom of trying to develop and impose systems from the top down.

All these ideas are central to the managerial mind-sets that have dominated the industrial age. But, as has been shown, they are all open to major challenge as organizing principles for the new information age.

It is impossible to reproduce all the detailed arguments presented in this chapter. But the essence of the critique is this: Leadership needs to be diffused rather than centralized; even though goals, objectives, and targets may be helpful managerial tools, they must be used in a way that avoids the pathologies of single-loop learning; goal seeking must be accompanied by an awareness of the "limits" needed to avoid noxious outcomes; and hierarchy, design, and strategic development must be approached and understood as self-organizing, emergent phenomena.

The brain is a paradoxical phenomenon, and the management principles it inspires are equally paradoxical. We see this running throughout the chapter and the issues presented above. Managers have to grapple with this sense of paradox. That is the main reason why the design principles offered here have been presented as aspirations rather than blueprints. Traditional management practice based on a mechanical frame of reference thrives on blueprints and "how-to" manuals. Yet the message of the brain is that we need to remain more open than this.

The brain metaphor thus has many strengths insofar as the development of intelligent organization is concerned. But there are also several limitations.

First, in using the brain as a metaphor of organization we are posed with an interesting problem of self-reference—of brains looking at brains! As has been shown, no sooner do we evoke the brain as a metaphor of organization than we find ourselves looking for other metaphors to make sense of what we see. Thus, during the course of the chapter we have evoked images of holograms, mobots, DNA, and other self-organizing phenomena. As it turns out, there is no coherent image of the brain to which everyone subscribes. We are thus left with the problem of evoking metaphors to elaborate the implications of a metaphor, a point to which we will return in Chapter 11.

Second, in developing the implications of the brain as a way of creating capacities for learning and self-organization there is a danger of overlooking important conflicts that can arise between learning and self-organization, on the one hand, and the realities of power and control, on the other. Any move away from hierarchically controlled structures toward more flexible, emergent patterns has major implications for the distribution of power and control within an organization, as the increase in autonomy granted to self-organizing units undermines the ability of those with ultimate power to keep a firm hand on day-to-day activities and developments. Moreover, the process of learning requires a degree of openness and self-criticism that is foreign to traditional modes of management.

Both these factors tend to generate resistance from the status quo. Managers are often reluctant to trust self-organizing processes among their staff and truly "let go." Many early experiments in self-organizing work designs encountered this problem, and they still do. There is such a strong belief that order means clear structure and hierarchical control that any alternative seems to be a jump in the direction of anarchy and chaos. As has been suggested, successful self-organizing systems always require a degree of hierarchical ordering. But this hierarchy must be allowed to emerge and change as different elements of the system take a lead in making their various contributions. In such systems, hierarchy and control have an emergent quality; they cannot be predesigned and imposed.

Application of ideas associated with the brain metaphor thus requires both a "power shift" and a "mind shift." Few will probably quarrel with the ideal of creating "learning organizations" that are able to evolve and adapt along with the challenges they encounter. But when ideal comes to reality, many forces of resistance can be unleashed.

Finally, we have to be aware of the strong normative bias of the brain metaphor. As suggested above, few will quarrel with the aim of increased learning. But what are the purposes to be served? As will be clear from discussion in Chapter 8, a future where learning organizations devote all their energies to outwitting other learning organizations is a recipe for enormous turbulence. Imagine the uncertainty and upheaval that this would create. Continuous learning may seem fine as an end in itself. But in practice it needs to be accompanied by an awareness of the cybernetic limits that will help make it a positive process from a societal perspective.

5

Creating Social Reality

Organizations as Cultures

Ever since the rise of Japan as a leading industrial power, organization theorists and managers alike have become increasingly aware of the relationship between culture and management. During the 1960s, the confidence and impact of American management and industry seemed supreme. Gradually, but with increasing force, throughout the 1970s the performance of Japanese automobile, electronics, and other manufacturing industries began to change all this. Japan began to take command of international markets, establishing a solid reputation for quality, reliability, value, and service. With virtually no natural resources, no energy, and over 110 million people crowded in four small mountainous islands, Japan succeeded in achieving the highest growth rate, the lowest level of unemployment, and, at least in some of the larger and more successful organizations, one of the best-paid and healthiest working populations in the world. Out of the ashes of World War II the country built an industrial empire second to none.

Although different theorists argued about the reasons for this transformation, most agreed that the culture and general way of life of this mysterious Eastern country played a major role. "Culture" thus became a hot topic in management in the 1980s and early 1990s, with the special character of Japan prompting Western management theorists to take special interest in the culture and character of their *own* countries and the links with organizational life.

Culture and Organization

But what is this phenomenon we call culture? The word has been derived metaphorically from the idea of cultivation: the process of tilling and developing land. When we talk about culture we are usually referring to the pattern of development reflected in a society's system of knowledge, ideology, values, laws, and day-to-day ritual. The word is also frequently used to refer to the degree of refinement evident in such systems of belief and practice, as in the notion of "being cultured." Both these usages derive from nineteenth-century observations of "primitive" societies conveying the idea that different societies manifest different levels of social development. Nowadays, however, the concept of culture does not necessarily carry this old evaluative stance, being used more generally to signify that different groups of people have different ways of life.

When talking about society as a culture we are thus using an agricultural metaphor to guide our attention to very specific aspects of social development. It is a metaphor that has considerable relevance for our understanding of organizations.

In this chapter, we first explore the idea that organization is itself a cultural phenomenon that varies according to a society's stage of development. We then focus on the idea that culture varies from one society to another and examine how this helps us understand cross-national variations in organizations. Next, we explore patterns of corporate culture and subculture between and within organizations. Finally, we take a detailed look at how patterns of culture are created and sustained and how organizations are socially constructed realities.

ORGANIZATION AS A
CULTURAL PHENOMENON

Political scientist Robert Presthus has suggested that we now live in an "organizational society." Whether in Japan, Germany, Hong Kong, Great Britain, Russia, the United States, or Canada, large organizations are likely to influence most of our waking hours in a way that is completely alien to life in a remote tribe in the jungles of South America. This may seem to be stating the obvious, but many characteristics of culture rest in the obvious. For example, why do so many people build their lives around distinct concepts of work and leisure, follow rigid routines five or six days a week, live in one place and work in another, wear uniforms, defer to authority, and spend so much time in a single spot performing a single set of activities? To an outsider, daily life in an organizational society is full of peculiar beliefs, routines, and rituals that identify it as a distinctive cultural life when compared with that in more traditional societies.

Anthropologists and sociologists have long observed these differences. For example, in societies where households rather than formal organizations are the basic economic and productive units, work has a completely different meaning and often occupies far less of a person's time. The distinctions drawn between means and ends and between occupational activities and other aspects of social life tend to be far more blurred.

The French sociologist Emile Durkheim has shown that the development of organizational societies is accompanied by a disintegration of traditional patterns of social order, as common ideals, beliefs, and values give way to more fragmented ones based on the occupational structure of the new society. The division of labor characteristic of industrial societies creates a problem of integration, or what may be more accurately described as a problem of "cultural management." Ways have to be found of binding the society together again. Government, religion, the media, and other institutions and individuals concerned with shaping opinion and belief play important roles in this process.

In a sense, we can thus say that people working in factories and offices in Detroit, Moscow, Liverpool, Paris, Tokyo, and Toronto all belong to the same industrial culture. They are all members of organizational societies. Their work and life experience seem qualitatively different from those of individuals living in more traditional societies dominated by domestic systems of production. If nothing else, modern office and factory workers share basic expectations and skills that allow organizations to operate on a day-to-day basis. Although we often regard the routine of organizational life as just that, routine, it does in point of fact rest on numerous skillful accomplishments. Being a factory or office worker calls on a depth of knowledge and cultural practice that, as members of an organizational society, we tend to take for granted.

For these reasons, some social scientists believe that it is often more useful to talk about the culture of industrial *society* rather than of industrial societies because the detailed differences between countries often mask more important commonalities. Many of the major cultural similarities and differences in the world today are occupational rather than national, the similarities and differences associated with being a factory worker, a janitor, a government official, a banker, a store assistant, or an agricultural worker being as significant as those associated with national identity. Important dimensions of modern culture are rooted in the structure of industrial society, the organization of which is itself a cultural phenomenon.

ORGANIZATION AND
CULTURAL CONTEXT

However, although all modern societies share much in common, it would be a mistake to dismiss cross-national differences in culture as being of little significance. The course of history has fashioned many variations in national social characteristics and views of the meaning of life and in national style and philosophies of organization and management. The recent success of Japan, the decline of industrial Great Britain, the fame of American enterprise, and the distinctive characteristics of many other organizational societies are all crucially linked with the cultural contexts in which they have evolved.

For example, if we examine the Japanese concept of work and the relations between employees and their organizations we find that they are very different from those prevailing in the West. The organization is viewed as a collectivity to which employees belong rather than just a workplace comprising separate individuals. The collaborative spirit of a village or commune often pervades work experience, and there is considerable emphasis on interdependence, shared concerns, and mutual help. Employees frequently make lifelong commitments to their organization, which they see as an extension of their family. Authority relations are often paternalistic and highly traditional and deferential. Strong links exist between the welfare of the individual, the corporation, and the nation. For example, at Matsushita, one of Japan's largest and most successful corporations, these principles permeate company philosophy (Exhibit 5.1).

Murray Sayle, an Australian expert on Japan, has offered an intriguing theory of the historical factors accounting for this solidarity. He believes that Japanese organizations combine the cultural values of the rice field with the spirit of service of the samurai. Whereas the former is crucial for understanding solidarity in the factory, the latter accounts for many characteristics of management and for the pattern of interorganizational relations that has played such a crucial role in Japan's economic success.

Basic Business Principles

To recognize our responsibilities as industrialists, to foster progress, to promote the general welfare of society, and to devote ourselves to the further development of world culture

Employees' Creed

Progress and development can be realized only through the combined efforts and cooperation of each member of our Company. Each of us, therefore, shall keep this idea constantly in mind as we devote ourselves to the continuous improvement of our Company.

The Seven "Spiritual" Values

1. National Service Through Industry
2. Fairness
3. Harmony and Cooperation
4. Struggle for Betterment
5. Courtesy and Humility
6. Adjustment and Assimilation
7. Gratitude

These values, taken to heart, provide a spiritual fabric of great resilience. They foster consistent expectations among employees in a workforce that reaches from continent to continent. They permit a highly complex and decentralized firm to evoke an enormous continuity that sustains it even when more operational guidance breaks down.

"It seems silly to Westerners," says one executive, "but every morning at 8:00 a.m., all across Japan, there are 87,000 people reciting the code of values and singing together. It's like we are all a community."

Exhibit 5.1   Company Philosophy at Matsushita Electric Company

SOURCE: Pascale and Athos (1981: 75–76, 73).

Rice growing in Japan has always been a precarious activity because of the scarcity of land and the short growing season. In retrospect, the process of building a civilization on this crop appears to be a prototype of the Japanese ability to take on projects that seem impossible. Above all else, traditional rice cultivation is a cooperative affair. As Sayle has observed, there is no such thing as a solitary, independent, pioneering rice farmer. The growing process calls for intensive teamwork in short backbreaking bursts of planting, transplanting, and harvest. Everyone is expected to perform to the best of his or her ability to ensure that the collective outcome is as good as it can be. If one family fails to maintain their irrigation ditches in good repair, the whole system suffers. When the crop fails because of disastrous weather conditions, the whole group is punished. There are no individual winners or losers. Under such circumstances, conformity and tradition are favored over opportunism and individuality. Respect for and dependence on one another are central to the way of life. It is this rice culture that was originally transferred to the Japanese factory.

Rice farmers in Japan were always willing to share their crop with those who were able to look after them. Such was the case in relation to the samurai, the "men of service" who depended on the farmers for their rice and physical existence. They played an important role in Japanese military and bureaucratic history and are now paralleled in the managerial "clans" or elites that run Japanese society. Protection of one's employees, service to each other, and acceptance of one's place in and dependence on the overall system are dominant characteristics. This service orientation extends to relations between organizations and the wider society, as reflected in the Matsushita philosophy. It is also crucial in explaining the close and collaborative relations between the banking system and Japanese industry. In contrast with the West, where the banks tend to act as independent judges and controllers of corporate investment, in Japan they assume a responsibility to provide help when and where it is needed.

Coupled with an amazing capacity to borrow and adapt ideas from elsewhere, first from China and later from the West, the cultures of rice field and samurai blended to create a hierarchical yet harmonious form of social organization within a modern industrial context. The managerial echelons were elitist and highly meritocratic, as they had been for centuries. Workers readily contributed to the material goals of their industrial masters and deferred to their authority because that had always been the traditional relationship between worker and samurai. No surprise, therefore, that so many people have been prepared to sing the company song and commit a lifetime to the corporate family.

The basic system of organization is feudal rather than modern, and from outside the culture seems distinctly oppressive, particularly as mobility between ranks is highly restricted, being determined for each individual from a very early age. However, it is important to realize that the kind of submissiveness and deference to authority found in Japan is not necessarily experienced as demeaning. Hierarchy in a Japanese corporation is as much a system of mutual service as one of top-down control. As Robert Dore, a well-known commentator on Japanese society, has noted, there seem to be different relations between subordination and self-respect in Japan. In many Western countries, individualistic culture leads us to seek and gain self-respect by competing with others, or against the wider "system," thus emphasizing our uniqueness and separateness. In Japan, cultural conditions allow workers to achieve self-respect through service *within* the system, even though there may be many aspects of the system that they find distasteful. In this regard, the spirit of the samurai pervades the whole culture.

It is difficult to judge a culture from the outside. What seems unacceptable from a Western viewpoint may be completely acceptable from within. That said, however, there is often a tendency in management reports of Japanese organizations to celebrate overall accomplishments while ignoring some of the more distasteful aspects of the work experience. Dazzling success stories tell of the way the Japanese arrive at work early or stay late to find ways of improving efficiency through the activities of voluntary "quality circles," or of how the dedicated Honda workman straightens the windshield-wiper blades on all the Hondas he passes on his way home each evening. Far less attention is devoted to the disgruntlement with which many workers accept the burdens of factory life. In this regard, the firsthand account of work in a Toyota factory by Japanese journalist Satoshi Kamata helps provide a refreshing balance. Although perhaps untypical of Japanese industry as a whole, it shows how Toyota's relentless drive for success in the early 1970s was accompanied by much personal deprivation on the part of many workers, particularly those living hundreds of miles away from their families in camps rigidly policed by company guards. Although the workplace was characterized by the genuine spirit of cooperation found in the rice field, it was also characterized by constant pressures to achieve demanding work targets and fulfill the requirements of company values and norms. The exercise of company authority—whether in the form of an arbitrary transfer from one workplace to another, of a call for extra work effort, or of canceled leave—was often resented, even though accepted with a grumble and a joke as an inevitable feature of life. Kamata's account suggests that day-to-day life in a Japanese factory can be at least as grueling as that in any Western manufacturing plant. The important difference is that the Japanese seem to have a greater capacity to grin and bear it!

Many discussions of Japanese management tend to ignore the cultural-historical circumstances that allow Japanese management to flourish as it does. They tend to overestimate the ease with which techniques and policies can be transplanted from one context to another, for it is the context that often makes the difference between success and failure. Debates regarding the merits of the Japanese system continue. For some writers, it offers a model for practice throughout the world. For others, it represents the remnants of a feudal system that may be well on the verge of major transformation as a restless youth culture, exposed to Western rather than samurai and rice field values, exerts its influence on work and society. When people grow up in a city environment in a "TV" and "multimedia" age, the rice field is an alien environment. The new experience is a transforming force.

Our focus on Japan is intended to be no more than illustrative. The point is that culture, whether Japanese, Arabian, British, Canadian, Chinese, French, or American, shapes the character of organization. Thus, in Great Britain, generations of social change and class conflict often perpetuate antagonistic divisions in the workplace that no amount of conciliation and management technique seems able to overcome. In contrast with the Japanese, British factory workers have traditionally defined themselves in opposition to a system they perceive as having exploited their ancestors as it now exploits them. Managerial elites assumed a basic right to rule "workers," whom they saw as having a "duty to obey" (Exhibit 5.2). Antagonism and strife rather than "factory solidarity" became the order of the day.

If we turn to the United States for illustrations of how culture shapes management, the ethic of competitive individualism is probably the one that stands out most clearly. Many American corporations and their employees are preoccupied with the desire to be "winners" and with the need to reward and punish successful and unsuccessful behavior. In this regard, it is significant that the American expert on Japan Ezra Vogel, writing in the 1970s, posed the Japanese challenge in an American way, titling his book *Japan as Number One*. From an American perspective, industrial and economic performance is often understood as a kind of game, and the general orientation in many organizations is to play the game for all it's worth: set objectives, clarify accountability, and "kick ass" or reward success lavishly and conspicuously.

In an essay written in the early 1940s on the relation between morale and national character, anthropologist Gregory Bateson drew attention to differences among parent-child relations in North America, England, and elsewhere. He noted the American practice of encouraging certain forms of boastful and exhibitionistic behavior on the part of children still in a dependent and subordinate position, whereas in England, children were encouraged to be submissive spectators in adult company and rewarded for being "seen but not heard." Bateson suggests that these child-rearing

The antagonism that often runs throughout the British workplace is gently yet clearly illustrated in the following account offered by management writer Charles Handy:

When Auntie Came to Dinner

My aunt by marriage is a splendid character, but from a bygone age. Her father never worked, nor his father before him, nor, of course, had she ever earned a penny in her life. Their capital worked for them, and they managed their capital. Work was done by workers. She sees all governments today as insanely prejudiced against capital, all workers as inherently greedy and lazy, and most managements as incompetent. No wonder the world is in a mess and she getting poorer every day.

Tony is a friend from work. His father was a postman. He started life as a draftsman in a large engineering firm. He grew up believing that inherited capital was socially wrong. He had never met any man who did not or had not worked for his living.

They met, by chance, at my house over a meal. It started quietly, politely. The she inquired what he did. It transpired that he had recently joined his staff union. Auntie had never met a union member.

"Good Heavens, how could you?" she said.

"It makes very good sense," said Tony, "to protect your rights."

"What rights? What poppycock is this? If people like you spent more time at their work and less looking after their own interests, this country wouldn't be in its present mess."

"Don't you," said Tony, "spend your time looking after your rights?"

"Of course," she said, "but then, I've rights. I provide the money that makes it possible for people like you to live."

"I provide the labor that keeps your money alive, although why I should work to preserve the capital of rich people whom I've never met is something that puzzles me."

"You talk like a Communist, young man, although you dress quite respectably. Do you know what you're saying?"

"You don't have to be a Communist to question the legitimacy of inherited wealth."

My aunt turned to me.

"You see why I'm worried about this country?" she said.

Each regarded the other as an example of an unnatural species. Given their opposed "core beliefs," no proper argument or dialogue was possible, only an exchange of slogans or abuse. It is a score that is replicated at negotiating tables as well as dinner tables.

Exhibit 5.2   Antagonistic Attitudes and the Workplace

SOURCE: From C. Handy, *Gods of Management*, Souvenir Books of London, 1978, pp. 161–162.

practices have considerable implications for later life—in the American case, creating a great deal of room for self-appreciation and self-congratulation as a basis for independence and strength. We see this in the "We're No. 1" syndrome. We also find it in an organizational context in the opportunities created for conspicuous achievement on the part of those in subordinate roles combined with expressive congratulation from those in superior roles.

Consider, for example, some of the illustrations presented in Tom Peters and Robert Waterman's *In Search of Excellence*, a book that can be understood as an early American management response to the rise of Japan. The idea of rewarding and motivating employees so that they come to see themselves as winners is a dominant theme. For example, Thomas Watson, Sr., of IBM is reported to have made a practice of writing out a check on the spot for achievements he observed in wandering about the organization. At Tupperware, the process of positive reinforcement is described as being ritualized every Monday night when all the saleswomen attend a "Rally" for their distributorship. At the rally, everyone marches up on stage in the reverse order of the previous week's sales, a process known as "Count Up," while their peers celebrate them by joining in "All Rise." Almost anyone who has done anything at all receives a pin or badge or several pins and badges. The ceremony combines head-on competition with a positive tone that suggests that everyone wins. Applause and hoopla are reported as surrounding the entire event.

The above examples provide splendid illustrations of Gregory Bateson's point about how the culture of the United States re-creates patterns found in American parent-child relations. However, the most colorful example emerging from the Peters and Waterman research is found in the early years of a company named Foxboro, where a technical advance was desperately needed for survival. Late one evening, a scientist rushed into the president's office with a working prototype. Dumbfounded at the elegance of the solution and bemused about how to reward it, the president rummaged through the drawers in his desk, found something, and leaning toward the scientist said, "Here!" In his hand was a banana, the only reward he could immediately put his hands on. As Peters and Waterman report, from that day on a small "gold banana" pin has been the highest accolade for scientific achievement at Foxboro.

Positive reinforcement is practiced in many Japanese, British, French, and other non-American corporations, often with considerable influence on employee motivation and performance. However, the United States stands supreme in the extent to which a concern for winning and direct reward for appropriate behavior have established themselves as important features of the culture and corporate life.

While it is a mistake to talk about any country as if there is an integrated, homogeneous culture, especially when societies are becoming so culturally diverse, important cross-national differences definitely exist. By understanding these differences we are able to get a much better appreciation of "foreign" practice. At the same time, we are able to gain a much better appreciation of our own. One of the interesting aspects of culture is that it creates a form of "blindness" and ethnocentricism. In providing taken-for-granted codes of action that we recognize as "normal," it leads us to see activities that do not conform with these codes as abnormal. A full awareness of the nature of culture, however, shows us that we are all equally abnormal in this regard. There is considerable value in adopting the standpoint of the cultural stranger because, in becoming aware of the stranger's point of view, we can see our own in a refreshingly new perspective.

CORPORATE CULTURES
AND SUBCULTURES

The influence of a host culture is rarely uniform. Just as individuals in a culture can have different personalities while sharing much in common, so too with groups and organizations.

It is this phenomenon that is now recognized as "corporate culture." Organizations are mini-societies that have their own distinctive patterns of culture and subculture. One organization may see itself as a tight-knit team or family that believes in working together. Another may be permeated by the idea that "we're the best in the industry and intend to stay that way." Yet another may be highly fragmented, divided into groups that think about the world in very different ways or that have different aspirations as to what their organization should be. Such patterns of belief or shared meaning, fragmented or integrated, and supported by various operating norms and rituals can exert a decisive influence on the overall ability of the organization to deal with the challenges that it faces.

One of the easiest ways of appreciating the nature of corporate culture and subculture is simply to observe the day-to-day functioning of a group or organization to which one belongs, *as if one were an outsider*. Adopt the role of anthropologist. The characteristics of the culture being observed will gradually become evident as one becomes aware of the patterns of interaction between individuals, the language that is used, the images and themes explored in conversation, and the various rituals of daily routine. As one explores the rationale for these aspects of culture, one usually finds that there are sound historical explanations for the way things are done.

An excellent illustration of this kind of analysis has been provided by my colleague Linda Smircich, who studied the top executive group of an American insurance company. The company was a division of a much larger organization offering a broad range of insurance services to agricultural organizations and to the general public. Sustained observation of day-to-day management generated two key impressions.

First, the company seemed to emphasize cooperative values and an identity rooted in the world of agriculture rather than in that of competitive business. The staff were polite and gracious and always seemed prepared to give help and assistance wherever it was needed. This ethos was reflected in one of the company mottoes: "We grow friends."

However, coexisting with this surface of friendly cooperation was a second dimension of organizational culture that suggested that the cooperative ethos was at best superficial. Meetings and other public forums always seemed dominated by polite yet disinterested exchange. Staff rarely got involved in any real debate and seemed to take very little in-depth interest in what was being said. For example, hardly anyone took any notes, and the meetings were in effect treated as ritual occasions. This superficiality was confirmed by observed differences between the public and private faces of the organization. Whereas in public, the ethos of harmony and cooperation ruled, in private, people often expressed considerable anger and dissatisfaction with various staff members and with the organization in general.

Many organizations have fragmented cultures of this kind, where people say one thing and do another. One of the interesting features of Linda Smircich's study was that she was able to identify the precise circumstances that had produced the fragmentation within the company and was able to show why it continued to operate in its somewhat schizophrenic fashion. Ten years earlier, when the organization was just four years old, it had passed through a particularly "traumatic" period that witnessed the demotion of its president, the hiring and firing of his successor, and the appointment of a group of professionals from the insurance industry at large. These events led to the development of separate subcultures. The first of these was represented by the original staff, or the "inside group" as they came to be known, and the second by the new professionals—"the outside group." Most of the outside group had been recruited from the same rival insurance company and brought with them very strong beliefs as to what was needed in their new organization. "This was how we did it at . . ." became a frequent stance taken in discussion. They wanted to model the new organization on the old.

The new president, appointed after the firing of the second, was a kind and peace-loving man. He set out to create a team atmosphere that would bind the organization together. However, rather than encourage a situation where organizational members could explore and resolve their differences in an open manner, he adopted a style of management that really required organizational members to put aside or repress their differences. The desire for harmony was communicated in a variety of ways, particularly through the use of specific rituals. For example, at special management meetings, the staff became an Indian tribe. Each member was given an Indian name and a headband with a feather. The aim was to forge unity between inside and outside groups. During this ritual, the practice of levying a 50-cent fine on anyone who mentioned the name of the rival insurance firm was introduced.

In both subtle and more obvious ways, the president continued to send messages about the need for harmony. He introduced regular staff meetings to review operations at which calm, polite cooperation quickly established itself as a norm. As some staff members reported,

We sit in the same seats, like cows always go to the same stall.

It's a real waste of time. It's a situation where you can say just about anything and no one will refute it.

People are very hesitant to speak up, afraid to say too much. They say what everyone else wants to hear.

Harmony and teamwork were also sought through the use of imagery to define the desired company spirit—for example, the slogan "wheeling together." The logo of a wagon wheel was spread through the company. The idea of "putting one's shoulder to the wheel" or "wheeling together" featured in many discussions and documents. An actual wagon wheel, mounted on a flat base, was moved from department to department.

The effect of this leadership style was to create a superficial appearance of harmony while driving conflict underground. This created the divergence between the public and private faces of the organization observed by Smircich and led to a situation where the organization became increasingly unable to deal with real problems. Because the identification of problems or concerns about company operation frequently created controversy the organization didn't really want to handle, the staff tended to confine their discussion of these issues to private places. In public, the impression that all was well gained the upper hand. When problematic issues were identified, they were always presented in the form of "challenges" to minimize the possibility of upsetting anyone. Driven underground by a style of management that effectively prevented the discussion of differences, genuine concerns were not given the attention they deserved. Not surprisingly, the organization no longer exists as a separate entity; the parent group eventually decided to reabsorb the insurance division into the main company.

In this case study, we see how corporate culture develops as an ethos (e.g., "let's bury our differences and keep the peace") created and sustained by social processes, images, symbols, and ritual. Rituals are often embedded in the formal structure of the organization, as in the case of the president's weekly staff meeting, the real function of which was to affirm that senior members of the organization were at some form of peace with each other. The case also illustrates the crucial role played by those in power in shaping the values that guide an organization. In this example, even though the president was perceived by the staff as being relatively weak, he managed to exert a decisive influence on the nature of the organization. The case also shows how historical circumstances, in this case the conflict between inside and outside groups, can shape the present. We also see how the fundamental nature of an organization rests as much in its corporate culture as in the more formal organization chart and codes of procedure. Indeed, it is probably no exaggeration to suggest that, in this case, corporate culture may have been the single most important factor standing between success and failure.

The idea of building a team of integrated players is a powerful one, and the president of the insurance company was probably not at fault in choosing this metaphor. Rather, the problems lay in the way it was coupled with norms favoring passivity. Had the metaphor been linked with an ethos favoring openness and innovation, and had team players been encouraged to make active contributions, the company's fortunes could have turned out very differently indeed.

Such is the case with Hewlett-Packard (H-P), a recognized leader in the microelectronics business. H-P was started in the 1940s by Bill Hewlett and Dave Packard and has established a corporate culture famed for strong team commitment coupled with a philosophy of innovation through people. The company decided to put the team ethos on the line early in its history, adopting a policy that it would not be "a hire and fire company." This principle was severely tested on a couple of occasions in the 1970s, as it has been many times since then, when declines in business forced the company to adopt the policy of a "nine-day fortnight," whereby staff took a 10 percent pay cut and worked 10 percent fewer hours. Whereas other companies resorted to layoffs, H-P kept its full complement of staff, thus emphasizing that all members of the H-P team shared the same fortune and that a measure of job security was possible even in unfavorable times.

Being a member of this team, of course, carried a set of obligations. Enthusiasm for work and an ethos of sharing problems and ideas in an atmosphere of free and open exchange were values the organization actively encouraged. Much of this ethos stemmed from the day-to-day example set by Hewlett and Packard, the founding heroes who established a reputation for hands-on management throughout the company. The ethos was also fostered by ritual "beer busts" and "coffee klatches" and by numerous ad hoc meetings that created regular opportunities for informal interaction.

Stories, legends, and myths about corporate heroes circulated through the organization and did much to communicate and sustain the cultural values underlying H-P's success. New recruits were treated to slide presentations that showed how "Bill and Dave" started the company in Bill's garage and used the Hewlett oven for making some of the first products. On another occasion they learned that when Bill Hewlett visited a plant one Saturday and found the lab stock area locked he immediately cut the padlock, leaving a note saying, "Don't ever lock this door again. Thanks, Bill." Along with more formal statements of company philosophy, the message soon hits home: At H-P we trust and value you. You're free to be enthusiastic about your job even if it's Saturday and to innovate and contribute in whatever way you can. Even though Hewlett-Packard is now spread across many continents, the founding spirit of "Bill and Dave" still pervades the company.

For a very different example of the development of corporate culture, let us now turn to the development of ITT under the tough and uncompromising leadership of Harold Geneen. The story here is one of success built on a ruthless style of management that converted a medium-sized communications business with sales of $765 million in 1959 into one of the world's largest and most powerful and diversified conglomerates, operating in over ninety countries, with revenues of almost $12 billion in 1978. Under Geneen's twenty-year reign, the company established a reputation as one of the fastest-growing and most profitable American companies— and, following its role in overseas bribery and the downfall of the Allende government in Chile, as one of the most corrupt and controversial.

Geneen's managerial style was simple and straightforward. He sought to keep his staff on top of their work by creating an intensely competitive atmosphere based on confrontation and intimidation. The foundation of his approach rested in his quest for what were known as "unshakable facts." He insisted that all managerial reports, decisions, and business plans be based on irrefutable premises, and he developed a complete information system, a network of special task forces, and a method of cross-examination that allowed him to check virtually every statement put forward.

Geneen possessed an extraordinary memory and an ability to absorb vast amounts of information in a relatively short time. This made it possible for him to keep his executives on their toes by demonstrating that he knew their situations as well as, if not better than, they did. His interrogation sessions at policy review meetings have become legendary. These meetings, which have been described as "show trials," were held around an enormous table capable of seating over fifty people, each executive being provided with a microphone into which to speak. It is reported that Geneen's approach was to pose a question to a specific executive or to sit back listening to the reports being offered while specially appointed staff people cross-examined what was being said. As soon as the executive being questioned showed evasiveness or lack of certainty, Geneen would move in to probe the weakness. In complete command of the facts, and equipped with a razor-sharp ability to cut to the center of an issue, he would invariably also cut the floundering executive and his argument to shreds. It is said that these experiences were so grueling that many executives were known to break down and cry under the pressure.

Geneen's approach motivated people through fear. If an executive was making a presentation, there was every incentive to stay up preparing throughout the night to ensure that all possible questions and angles were covered. This intimidating style was set by Geneen from the very beginning of his tenure. For example, it is reported that early in his career with ITT he would call executives at all hours, perhaps in the middle of the night, to inquire about the validity of some fact or obscure point in a written report. The message was clear: ITT executives were expected to be company men and women on top of their jobs at all times. The idea that loyalty to the goals of the organization should take precedence over loyalty to colleagues or other points of reference was established as a key principle.

ITT under Geneen was a successful corporate jungle. High executive performance was undoubtedly achieved but at considerable cost in terms of staff stress and in terms of the kind of actions that this sometimes produced, such as the company's notorious activities in Chile. The pressure on ITT executives was above all to perform and deliver the goods they had promised. Their corporate necks were always on the line. Geneen's approach typifies the managerial style that psychoanalyst Michael Maccoby has characterized as that of the "jungle fighter": the power-hungry manager who experiences life and work as a jungle where it is eat or be eaten and where winners destroy losers.

The "cut and thrust" corporate culture of ITT under Geneen stands poles apart from the "let's bury our differences" culture of the humble insurance company considered earlier. It also stands poles apart from the successful team atmosphere created at Hewlett-Packard. As in the case of our cross-cultural comparisons between Japan, Great Britain, and the

United States, the examples are just illustrative. They show how different organizations can have different cultures. Extending the principle, we see that IBM is very different from Microsoft. Both are unlike Compaq, Apple, Coca-Cola, or Boeing.

A focus on the links between leadership style and corporate culture often provides key insights into why organizations work the way they do. However, there are other factors that need to be considered.

For example, gender may also be a powerful cultural force.

"Macho" case studies such as those of Harold Geneen do an excellent job in bringing this to light in an extreme way. But the influence of gender is far more pervasive than this. For example, as researchers such as Carol Gilligan and Sally Helgesen have suggested, traditional forms of organization are often dominated and shaped by male value systems. For example, the emphasis on logical, linear modes of thought and action, and the drive for results at the expense of network and community building, from a gender standpoint, express values and approaches to life that are much more "male" than "female."

We will have a lot more to say on this in Chapters 6 and 7 because a strong case can be made for the idea that many aspects of the corporate world have been trapped within a male archetype creating what Betty Harragan has vividly described as "no-woman's land." Until recently, it has been a man's world where women and associated gender styles were physically and psychologically marginalized or excluded from the male-dominated reality.

This has led to the creation of organizations that often have strong female subcultures standing in tension and, at times, opposition with male power structures. Often, this unleashes powerful forces that can politicize a corporate culture along gender lines, a point further discussed in the next chapter.

From a cultural standpoint, organizations shaped around "female" values are more likely to balance and integrate the rational-analytic mode with values that emphasize more empathic, intuitive, organic forms of behavior. Interestingly, the new flat, network forms of organization that are emerging to cope with the uncertainty and turbulence of modern environments require managerial competencies that have more in common with the female archetype than the male. As this develops, we can expect to see the transformation of many corporate cultures and subcultures away from the dominant influence of male values and associated modes of behavior.

The trend is already evident in the way that new-style corporate leaders such as Anita Roddick of the Body Shop are forging different styles of management and creating very different niches for their organization. For example, as Roddick puts it, "I run my company according to feminine principles—principles of caring, making intuitive decisions, not getting hung up on hierarchy or all those dreadfully boring business-school management ideas; having a sense of work as being part of your life, not separate from it; putting your labor where your love is; being responsible to the world in how you use your profits; recognizing the bottom line should stay at the bottom."

This quotation is taken from the work of Sally Helgesen, who, in her book *The Female Advantage*, shows how women like Frances Hesselbein of the Girl Scouts of the USA, Barbara Grogan of Western Industrial Contractors, Nancy Badore of Ford Motor Company's Executive Development Center, and Dorothy Brunson of Brunson Communications, like Anita Roddick, bring distinctively female styles of management to the workplace. They help create cultures where hierarchy gives way to "webs of inclusion." They manage by placing themselves "in the middle of things," building communities based on inclusive relationships characterized by trust, support, encouragement, and mutual respect. They help to produce organizations that are truly "networked," where the *process* of doing things is as important as the end result or product. Through their actions and successes they are modeling ways of producing corporate cultures that seem to have a lot in common with the brainlike forms of organization explored in Chapter 4.

In developing these points about the importance of gender values, it is interesting to note that we have again ended up focusing on the links between leadership and corporate culture. Powerful leaders seem to symbolize so many aspects of their organizations. But it is really important to recognize that formal leaders do not have any monopoly on the ability to create shared meaning. The leader's position of power may lend him or her a special advantage in developing corporate value systems and codes of behavior because formal leaders often have important sources of power through which they can encourage, reward, or punish those who follow their lead. However, others are also able to influence the process by acting as informal opinion leaders or simply by acting as the people they are. Culture is not something that can be imposed on a social setting. Rather, it develops during the course of social interaction.

In any organization there may be different and competing value systems that create a mosaic of organizational realities rather than a uniform corporate culture. Besides gender, race, language, and ethnicity, religious, socioeconomic, friendship, and professional groups can have a decisive impact on the cultural mosaic.

For example, different professional groups may each have a different view of the world and of the nature of their organization's business.

Accountants may subscribe to one kind of philosophy and marketing people to another. The frame of reference guiding development engineers may be different from the perspective of members of the production department, marketing, and sales. Each group may have developed its own specialized language and set of favored concepts for formulating business priorities.

Social or ethnic groupings may also give rise to different norms and patterns of behavior with a crucial impact on day-to-day functioning, especially when the ethnic groupings coincide with different organizational activities. An excellent example of this has been provided by sociologist W. F. Whyte in his studies of restaurants, where status and other social differences between kitchen staff and those waiting on tables often create many operational problems. When a high-status group interacts with a low-status group, or when groups with very different occupational attitudes are placed in a relation of dependence, organizations can become plagued by a kind of subcultural warfare. Different norms, beliefs, and attitudes to time, efficiency, or service can combine to create all kinds of contradictions and dysfunctions. These can be extremely difficult to tackle in a rational manner because they are intertwined with all kinds of deep-seated personal issues that in effect *define* the human beings involved.

Subcultural divisions may also arise because organization members have divided loyalties. Not everyone is fully committed to the organization in which he or she works. People may develop specific subcultural practices as a way of adding meaning to their lives (e.g., by getting involved with friendship and other social groupings at work) or by developing norms and values that advance personal rather than organizational ends. For example, the politicking through which organizational members sometimes advance careers or specific interests can result in the development of coalitions sustained by specific sets of values. These coalitions sometimes develop into forms of counterculture, in opposition to the organizational values espoused by those formally in control.

Many organizations are characterized by such informal divisions of opinion within the top management group and sometimes in the organization at large. Typically, these divisions usually result in a struggle for control, which in certain important respects can be understood as a struggle for the right to shape corporate culture. As in politics, such struggles are often closely linked to questions of ideology.

Foremost among all organizational countercultures, of course, are those fostered by trade unions. It is here that the battle for ideological control is often most clearly defined, for trade unions are in effect counterorganizations in the sense that their existence stems from the fact that the interests of employee and employer may not be synonymous. Trade unions have their own specific cultural histories, which vary from industry to industry and from organization to organization within an industry. The philosophy, values, and norms of union culture usually exert an important impact on the mosaic of culture, subculture, and counterculture that characterizes life in any organization.

Creating Organizational Reality

Shared values, shared beliefs, shared meaning, shared understanding, and shared sense making are all different ways of describing culture. In talking about culture we are really talking about a process of reality construction that allows people to see and understand particular events, actions, objects, utterances, or situations in distinctive ways. These patterns of understanding help us to cope with the situations being encountered and also provide a basis for making our own behavior sensible and meaningful.

But how does this occur? How is culture created and sustained? How do we construct our realities? We have already begun to answer these questions in general terms, but it is useful to take a closer and more systematic look at the process involved.

CULTURE: RULE FOLLOWING
OR ENACTMENT?

Sociologist Harold Garfinkel has demonstrated that the most routine and taken-for-granted aspects of social reality are in fact skillful *accomplishments*. When we travel on a subway car, visit a neighbor, or act as a normal person walking down the street, we employ numerous social skills of which we are only dimly aware. Just as a tightrope walker might think nothing of running across a high wire to collect his or her possessions at the end of rehearsal, oblivious to the skill that this involves, so too in the most mundane accomplishments of daily life.

Garfinkel elucidates our taken-for-granted skills by showing us what happens if we deliberately attempt to disrupt normal patterns of life. Look a fellow subway passenger in the eye for a prolonged period of time. He or she will no doubt look away at first but get increasingly uncomfortable as your gaze continues. Perhaps he will eventually inquire what's wrong, change seats, or get off at the next stop. Behave in your neighbor's house as if you live there. Disrupt the smooth and continuous line of your walk down a crowded street with a series of random stops and turns or with the shifty manner of a suspicious character. In each case, you will gradually discover how life within a given culture flows smoothly only insofar as one's behavior conforms with unwritten codes. Disrupt these norms and the ordered reality of life inevitably breaks down.

In one sense, then, we can say that the nature of a culture is found in its social norms and customs and that if one adheres to these rules of behavior one will be successful in constructing an appropriate social reality. Thus, a businessperson visiting overseas, or even visiting a client or another organization at home, may be well advised to learn the norms that will allow him or her to "go native." For example, in visiting an Arab state it is important to understand the different roles played by men and women in Arab society and the local rules regarding the flexible nature of time. In general, Arabs in their home country have reservations about conducting business with women. Also, they like to take their time in building business trust and sound relationships before they make decisions, refuse to be hurried, and do not necessarily see a 2:00 p.m. appointment as meaning 2:00 p.m. People who unwittingly break these rules and attempt to keep a fixed schedule or to rush their business will frequently get nowhere. Their actions are likely to be as disruptive as those of the norm-breaking passenger on the subway car.

However, there seems to be more to culture than rule following. This has been illustrated in several important studies conducted by Garfinkel and his colleagues, which show that the ability to apply a rule calls for much more than a knowledge of the rule itself, as rules are invariably incomplete. For example, sociologist David Sudnow has illustrated that even in the administration of justice, an area of human activity where action is supposed to be determined by clearly defined rules, the application of a specific law calls upon background knowledge on the part of the legal officer or judge that goes well beyond what is stated in the law itself. His studies show that cases of child molesting or burglary, for example, are typically assigned to legal categories on the basis of images and judgments as to what constitutes a "normal crime" in these areas. A series of subjective decisions are thus made on the nature of the case before any rule is applied. Lawyers and judges do not follow the rules. Rather, they invoke rules as a means of making a particular activity or particular judgment sensible and meaningful to themselves and to others. In effect, the parties involved in this process are involved in a definition of the rules that are to be applied. This process often involves negotiation—for example, among the defendant and his or her lawyer, the public prosecutor, and the judge, all of whom may subscribe to competing definitions of the situation being considered.

If we return to consider how we accomplish the everyday realities of riding a subway car, visiting a neighbor, or walking down the street, we will find the same process at work. As in judgments within the legal system, our constructions of the situation influence what rules and codes of behavior are to be summoned as appropriate to the situation. Suppose that we are visiting a neighbor to party and drink beer. Our understanding of the nature of the situation will lead us to invoke certain rules (e.g., that it is OK to go to the refrigerator to fetch another beer or to search for a bottle opener in the kitchen drawers), even though these rules might be considered quite inappropriate on another occasion. The point is that the norms operating in different situations have to be invoked and defined in the light of our understanding of the context. We implicitly make many decisions and assumptions about a situation before any norm or rule is applied. Many of these decisions and assumptions are made quite unconsciously, as a result of our previous socialization and taken-for-granted knowledge, so that action appears quite spontaneous. And in most circumstances, the sense-making process or justification for action will occur only if the behavior is challenged.

Organizational psychologist Karl Weick has described the process through which we shape and structure our realities as a process of *enactment*. Like Garfinkel's concept of accomplishment, Weick's concept stresses the proactive role that we unconsciously play in creating our world. Although we often see ourselves as living in a reality with objective characteristics, life demands much more of us than this. It requires that we take an active role in bringing our realities into being through various interpretive schemes, even though these realities may then have a habit of imposing themselves on us as "the way things are."

The point is well illustrated in a wonderful tale related by Charles Hampden-Turner about a man whose wife's portrait was being painted by Picasso. One day the man called at the artist's studio. "What do you think?" asked Picasso, indicating the nearly finished picture. "Well . . . ," said the husband, trying to be polite, "it isn't how she really looks." "Oh," said the artist, "and how does she really look?" The husband decided not to be intimidated. "Like this!" said, he producing a photograph from his wallet. Picasso studied the photograph. "Mmm . . . ," he said, "small, isn't she?"

In recognizing that we accomplish or enact the reality of our everyday world, we have a powerful way of thinking about culture. It means that we must attempt to understand culture as an ongoing, proactive process of reality construction. This brings the whole phenomenon of culture alive. When understood in this way, culture can no longer just be viewed as a simple variable that societies or organizations possess or something that a leader brings to his or her organization. Rather, it must be understood as an active, living phenomenon through which people jointly create and re-create the worlds in which they live.

Organization: The Enactment of a Shared Reality

This enactment view of culture has enormous implications for how we understand organizations as cultural phenomena, for it emphasizes that we must root our understanding of organization in the processes that produce systems of shared meaning.

What are shared frames of reference that make organization possible?

Where do they come from?

How are they created, communicated, and sustained?

These questions now become central to the task of organizational analysis and effective management. They help us see that organizations are in essence socially constructed realities that are as much in the minds of their members as they are in concrete structures, rules, and relations.

The power of this insight has been mobilized with great effect by management writers like Tom Peters and Robert Waterman, who emphasize that successful organizations build cohesive cultures around common sets of norms, values, and ideas that create an appropriate focus for doing business. For example, in their famous book *In Search of Excellence*, they showed how America's leading companies built around core values and ideas such as:

"IBM means service."

"Never kill a new product idea." (3M)

"Sell it to the sales staff." (Hewlett-Packard)

The focus at IBM was to create a service-driven organization where staff at every level made the needs of the customer a core priority. The focus at 3M was on the need for constant innovation as a means of creating a flow of new products. At Hewlett-Packard, a company operating in a sector where technical innovation can easily run away with itself, the focus was on marketability. In each case, the core ideas helped create a corporate culture that diffused fundamental values and operating principles throughout the organization to create a basis for success.

In a similar way, the "total quality" and "customer service" movements that dominated managerial thinking and practice in the 1980s and 1990s have sought to create a cultural change in management at large. The various theories and techniques advocated by these movements offered new mind-sets and new values for doing business, backed by a detailed "language" and protocol through which organizational members could begin to think, talk, and act in new ways. Their implicit aims were to create a kind of "cultural revolution" that would replace the old bureaucratic way of life with a focus on a new "customer and quality driven" business logic. To the extent that the new cultural values were able to replace the bureaucratic ones, initiatives spawned by these movements were extremely successful. For example, many organizations succeeded in revolutionizing and reinventing themselves through the values of "quality" and "customer service." But, as noted in Chapter 4, it is estimated that as many as 70 percent of the firms that set off on this new path were unsuccessful, largely because they failed to replace the bureaucratic logic governing the old mode of operation. Their quality and service programs became no more than programs. Despite all the money and effort that was spent, they failed to dent the dominant culture and the political dynamic that often supports it. The "reengineering" and "empowerment" movements have encountered a similar experience. To be effective they needed to transform prevailing organizational mind-sets and political patterns. But in the majority of cases, they failed to do so.

There can be little doubt that the culture metaphor offers a fresh way of thinking about organization. It shows that the challenge of creating new forms of organization and management is very much a challenge of cultural change. It is a challenge of transforming the mind-sets, visions, paradigms, images, metaphors, beliefs, and shared meanings that sustain existing business realities and of creating a detailed language and code of behavior through which the desired new reality can be lived on a daily basis. Viewed in this way, the creation of a particular corporate culture is not just about inventing new slogans or acquiring a new leader. It is about inventing what amounts to a new way of life.

Those who understand the challenge of cultural change recognize the enormity of this task because it involves the creation of shared systems of meaning that are accepted, internalized, and acted on at every level of the organization. In the most fundamental sense, culture has a holographic quality. Characteristics of the whole must be encoded in all the parts. Otherwise, the parts fail to express and act on the character of the whole. The best teams, and the free-flowing organizations that have discarded bureaucratic forms of management, constantly reflect this quality. They are organized through core meanings that people own and share. It is this quality that allows them to be flexible, adaptive, and nonbureaucratic. Organizationally, shared meanings provide alternatives to control through external procedures and rules.

There is thus much more to culture and corporate culture than meets the eye. Many management theorists and practitioners influenced by the metaphor fail to recognize this. As a result, they think and talk about culture at what may be described as "the level of slogans." As a result, their methods and techniques of cultural change usually do little more than dent surface reality.

To come to grips with an organization's culture, it is necessary to uncover the mundane as well as the more vivid aspects of the reality-construction process. Sometimes, these are so subtle and all-pervasive that they are very difficult to identify. Recall our discussion of how Japanese organizations are shaped by the values of the rice field or of how some British organizations reproduce attitudes rooted in a long history of class conflict. These values may have very little to do with the actual organizations in which they are found, being imported in an invisible way. Yet they can play a crucial role in upsetting all attempts at cultural change.

Or take the way in which financial considerations may be allowed to shape the reality of an organization through the routine operation of financial information systems. Under the influence of these kinds of controls, people or organizational units, whether they be pupils in schools, patients in hospitals, or work teams in manufacturing plants, may be translated into profit centers generating costs and revenues. These systems may not be seen as cultural in nature. But they definitely are. Their influence may be far more pervasive than other policies and programs that are explicitly designed to create cultural change, for example, in relation to the enhancement of "quality production" or the "empowerment of staff."

Although it is not usual to regard accountants as "reality constructors" exerting a decisive influence on an organization's culture, this is exactly the role that they play. They can shape the reality of an organization by persuading people that the interpretive lens of "financial performance" should be given priority in determining the way that the organization is to be run. This, of course, is not to say that financial considerations are unimportant. The point is that thinking about organization in financial terms is but one way of thinking about that organization. There are always others, and these are usually forced into the background as financial considerations gain a major hold on the definition of organizational reality.

Organizational structure, rules, policies, goals, missions, job descriptions, and standardized operating procedures perform a similar interpretive function, for they act as primary points of reference for the way people think about and make sense of the contexts in which they work.

Although typically viewed as among the more objective characteristics of an organization, an enactment view emphasizes that they are cultural artifacts shaping the ongoing reality.

Just as a tribal society's values, beliefs, and traditions may be embedded in kinship and other social structures, many aspects of an organization's culture are thus embedded in routine aspects of everyday practice. These define the socially constructed stage on which organizational members lend their culture living form. More mundane than the vivid ritual and ceremony that decorated meetings at the insurance company discussed earlier, the weekly "Rally" at Tupperware, the gold banana awards at Foxboro, or the new corporate philosophies and programs through which an organization is trying to improve "quality" or "customer service," they are incredibly important in understanding how organizations work when no one is really looking and why established practice may be so resistant to change.

As we explore corporate culture with this frame of reference in mind, it is amazing to see the extent to which *every* aspect of organization is rich in symbolic meaning and how the familiar often appears in a new light. That weekly meeting or annual planning cycle that everyone knows is a waste of time assumes a new significance: as a ritual serving various kinds of hidden functions. We begin to realize that the everyday language of bureaucracy is one of the means through which the organization actually creates its bureaucratic characteristics. We see that the aggressive character of an organization is sustained by an implicit military mentality that leads it to shape aggressive relations with its environment and the local labor union. We find that organizations end up being what they think and say, as their ideas and visions realize themselves.

As we look at the everyday relations between people in an organization with an eye on the reality-construction process, new insights on group functioning and leadership also emerge. We find that the formation of a group and the process of becoming a leader ultimately hinges on an ability to create a shared sense of reality. We find that cohesive groups are those that arise around shared understandings, while fragmented groups tend to be those characterized by multiple realities. In seeing organizations as cultures, we can see almost every aspect in a new way.

Strengths and Limitations of the Culture Metaphor

In an essay on the use of statistics as a basis for public policy published in 1954, British economist Ely Devons drew parallels between decision-making processes in formal organizations and magic and divination in tribal societies. He noted that, although organizational decision makers would not normally think of examining the entrails of a chicken or of consulting an oracle about the fortunes of their organization or the state of the economy, many of the uses of statistics have much in common with the use of primitive magic. In primitive society, magic decides whether hunting should proceed in one direction or another, whether the tribe should go to war, or who should marry whom, giving clear-cut decisions in situations that might otherwise be open to endless wrangling.

In formal organizations, techniques of quantitative analysis seem to perform a similar role. They are used to forecast the future and analyze the consequences of different courses of action in a way that lends decision making a semblance of rationality and substance. The use of such techniques does not, of course, reduce risks. The uncertainties surrounding a situation still exist, hidden in the assumptions underlying the technical analysis. Hence Devon's point. The function of such analysis is to increase the credibility of action in situations that would otherwise have to be managed through guesswork and hunch. Like the magician who consults entrails, many organizational decision makers insist that the facts and figures be examined before a policy decision is made, even though the statistics provide unreliable guides as to what is likely to happen in the future. And, as with the magician, they or their magic are not discredited when events prove them wrong. Just as the magician may attribute failure to imperfect execution or the unanticipated intervention of some hostile force, the technical expert is allowed to blame the model used, or the turn of events, as a means of explaining why forecasts are inaccurate. The analysis is never discredited. The appearance of rationality is preserved.

Modern organizations are sustained by belief systems that emphasize the importance of rationality, and their legitimacy in the public eye usually depends on their ability to demonstrate rationality and objectivity in action. It is for this reason that anthropologists often refer to rationality as the myth of modern society, for, like primitive myth, it provides us with a comprehensive frame of reference, or structure of belief, through which we can negotiate day-to-day experience and help to make it intelligible. The myth of rationality helps us see certain patterns of action as legitimate, credible, and normal. It helps us avoid the wrangling and debate that would arise if we were to recognize the basic uncertainty and ambiguity underlying many of our values and the situations with which we have to deal.

One of the major strengths of the culture metaphor is that it directs attention to the symbolic significance of almost every aspect of organizational life. As we have seen, even the most concrete and rational aspects of organization—whether structures, hierarchies, rules, or organizational routines—embody social contructions and meanings that are crucial for understanding how organization functions day by day. For example, meetings are more than just meetings. They carry important aspects of organizational culture: norms of passivity in the insurance company; fear and respect for unshakable facts in Geneen's intimidation rituals. Even the nature of an empty meeting room conveys something about the general organizational culture, for these rooms generally reflect and reproduce the structures of interaction expected in the organization. Straight lines of chairs and note pads, each guarded by a water glass, communicate a sense of conformity and order. The friendly chaos and casualness of more informal meeting rooms extend a more open invitation to self-organization. In highlighting the symbolic significance of these and other aspects of organization, the culture metaphor thus focuses attention on a human side that other metaphors ignore or gloss over.

A second major strength of the metaphor is that it shows how organization ultimately rests in shared systems of meaning, hence in the actions and interpretive schemes that create and re-create that meaning. Under mechanical and organismic metaphors, primary emphasis tends to be placed on the importance of organizational *design*: the design of organizational structures or the design of adaptive processes. The culture metaphor points toward another means of creating and shaping organized activity: by influencing the ideologies, values, beliefs, language, norms, ceremonies, and other social practices that ultimately shape and guide organized action.

This is the aspect of the culture metaphor that has had the greatest impact on organizational practice to date. Since the 1980s there has been growing realization that the fundamental task facing leaders and managers rests in creating appropriate systems of shared meaning that can mobilize the efforts of people in pursuit of desired aims and objectives.

The two key words here are "appropriate" and "shared."

For example, the shared vision that "IBM means service" served the company extremely well in an era dominated by mainframe computers. The company had an industry dominance that allowed it to lavish high-priced attention on key customers through its service philosophy. However, under different circumstances, the very same vision became a liability. As the result of the meteoric rise of the personal computer, networked computing, a rapidly developing software industry, an era of global communication systems, plus dozens of competitors with high-quality, state-of-the-art, low-priced products, the core values that helped IBM achieve dominance were no longer enough. Like other once successful corporations, the organization has been faced with the challenge of reinventing and repositioning itself through new visions and shared values that can help mobilize a new-style corporate culture capable of dealing with the new reality.

The challenge, of course, is enormous because corporate culture is not a simple phenomenon. It is not something that can be mandated, designed, or made. It is a living, evolving, self-organizing reality that can be shaped and reshaped but not in an absolute way. The challenge of changing corporate culture is always difficult. But as shown in this chapter, a broad understanding of the nature of the metaphor can offer important insights in approaching this task.

Under the influence of the culture metaphor, leaders and managers come to see themselves as people who ultimately help to create and shape the meanings that are to guide organized action. This involves a major reframing of their roles.

When leaders and managers ask themselves, "What impact am I having on the social construction of reality in my organization?" and "What can I do to have a different and more positive impact?" they penetrate to a new level of understanding about the significance of what they are truly doing.

Under more traditional views of management they could use their formal authority, function, and role as a kind of protective device to insulate themselves from many of the realities of organizational life. They could persuade themselves that, so long as they were doing what was mandated, they were doing the right thing: "To hell with what others think. I'm doing my job."

To this kind of attitude the culture metaphor responds "No you're not!" You are what you are *seen and experienced as being*, not what you think you are or what your job title or job description says you are. This obliges the leader and manager to understand their roles and significance in terms of actual impacts on the reality construction process.

This is a major strength of the metaphor because it makes people own their impact on the way things are and shows that it is their responsibility to change when appropriate. They can no longer hide behind formal structures and roles or excuse themselves for having unfortunate personality traits. From a cultural standpoint, the impact on shared meaning is all-important.

A third major strength of the metaphor is that it encourages us to recognize that the relations between an organization and its environment are also socially contructed. As Karl Weick puts it, they are a social enactment. Organizations choose and structure their environment through a host of interpretive decisions that are extensions of corporate culture. This point has also been made in a different context by anthropologist Gregory

Bateson in saying that mind and nature are intertwined; our understandings of nature are always cultural.

This has profound implications for how we understand organization-environment relations and strategic management, for in stressing the fundamental interconnection between these phenomena we recognize that our environments are extensions of ourselves. (This idea is explored in some detail in Chapter 8.) We choose and operate in environmental domains according to how we construct conceptions of what we are and what we are trying to do (e.g., "be an organization in the computer industry," "produce and sell automobiles," "be a leader in our field," "whip the competition"). And we act in relation to these domains through the definitions that we impose on them. For example, firms in an industry typically develop a language for making sense of their market, technology, and relations with other segments of the economy, aligning their actions in relation to the pattern of threats and opportunities that this set of interpretations makes visible. Firms organize their environments exactly as they organize their internal operations, enacting the realities with which they have to deal.

Of course, the environment may not be so easily controlled as internal operations. Other organizations also inhabit this domain, shaping action in accordance with *their* favorite interpretive schemes and thus influencing the environment to which others are trying to adapt and react. Environmental turbulence and change is a product of this ongoing process of enactment. Environments are enacted by hosts of individuals and organizations each acting on the basis of his or her interpretation of a world that is in effect mutually defined. A competitive ethos produces competitive environments. Visions of recession produce recession. The beliefs and ideas that organizations hold about who they are, what they are trying to do, and what their environment is like have a much greater tendency to realize themselves than is usually believed.

This has considerable relevance for the way organizations should approach strategy formulation. By appreciating that strategy making is a process of enactment that *produces* a large element of the future with which the organization will have to deal, it is possible to overcome the false impression that organizations are adapting or reacting to a world that is independent of their own making. This can help empower organizations to take responsibility for the future in an active way and help them appreciate that they themselves often create the constraints, barriers, and situations that cause them problems. For example, in the 1970s, the American automobile industry saw the Japanese challenge as lying at the heart of their problems and tried to deflect the challenge through import restrictions and regulation. A closer look at the situation would have led them to see that members of their industry had enacted the conditions that helped to make the Japanese challenge successful (e.g., by ignoring the possibility that the American market might be amenable to the idea of buying smaller cars).

A final strength of the culture metaphor is the contribution that it makes to our understanding of organizational change. Traditionally, the change process has been conceptualized as a problem of changing technologies, structures, and the abilities and motivations of employees. Although this is in part correct, effective change also depends on changes in the images and values that are to guide action.

Without this support it is unlikely that these other changes will have the desired effect. The message of the culture metaphor is that change programs must give attention to the kind of corporate ethos required in the new situation and find how this can be developed. Since organization ultimately resides in the heads of the people involved, effective organizational change always implies cultural change. Changes in technology, rules, systems, procedures, and policies are just not enough.

As has already been noted, the insights generated by the culture metaphor have encouraged many managers and management theorists to find ways of managing corporate culture. Most are now aware of the symbolic consequences of organizational values, and many organizations have started to explore the pattern of culture and subculture that shapes day-to-day action. On the one hand, this can be seen as a positive development, since it recognizes the truly human nature of organizations and the need to build organization around people rather than techniques. However, there are a number of potentially negative consequences.

Persuaded by the ideas that there are good and bad cultures, that a strong organizational culture is essential for success, or that modifications to an existing culture will lead employees to work harder and feel more content, many managers and management consultants have begun to adopt new roles as change agents attempting to create new forms of corporate consciousness. Although many managers approach this task on the assumption that what's good for the organization will inevitably be in the best interests of its employees, critics feel that this trend is a potentially dangerous one, developing the art of management into a process of ideological control or what is sometimes described as "values engineering."

Of course, management has always been to some extent an ideological practice, promoting appropriate attitudes, values, and norms as means of motivating and controlling employees. What is new in many recent developments is the not-so-subtle way in which ideological manipulation and control is being advocated as an essential managerial strategy. There is a certain ideological blindness in much of the writing about corporate culture, especially by those who advocate that managers attempt to become folk heroes shaping and reshaping the culture of their organizations. The fact that such manipulation may well be accompanied by resistance, resentment, and mistrust and that employees may react against being manipulated in this way receives scant attention. There is an important distinction to be drawn between attempts to create networks of shared meaning that link key members of an organization around visions, values, and codes of practice so essential to the holographic self-organization described in Chapter 4 and the use of culture as a manipulative tool. To the extent that the insights of the culture metaphor are used to create an Orwellian world of "corporate newspeak," where the culture controls rather than expresses human character, the metaphor may prove quite manipulative and totalitarian in its influence.

When we observe a culture, whether in an organization or in society at large, we are observing an evolved form of social practice that has been influenced by many complex interactions between people, events, situations, actions, and general circumstance. Culture is self-organizing and is always evolving. Although at any given time it can be seen as having a discernible pattern (e.g., reflecting an ethos of competition or cooperation), this pattern tends to be a snapshot abstraction imposed on the culture from the outside. It is a pattern that helps the observer to make sense of what is happening in the culture. But it is not synonymous with experience in the culture itself. Recall, for example, Western interpretations versus Japanese experience of hierarchical relationships. From the Western standpoint, Japanese hierarchy may be seen as a pattern of domination. Internally, it may be experienced as a process of mutual service.

The message: observer beware. There is often more to culture than meets the eye, and our understandings are usually much more fragmented and superficial than the reality itself.

This is an important point because many management theorists view culture as a phenomenon with clearly defined attributes. Like organizational structure, culture is often reduced to a set of discrete variables such as values, beliefs, stories, norms, and rituals that can be documented and manipulated in an instrumental way.

It is this kind of mechanistic attitude that underlies many perspectives advocating the management of culture. But, as has been discussed, culture seems more holographic than mechanistic. Where corporate culture is strong and robust, a distinctive ethos pervades the whole organization: employees exude the characteristics that define the mission or ethos of the whole—for example, outstanding commitment to service, perseverance against the odds, a commitment to innovation, or in less fortunate circumstances, lethargy or a sense of helplessness or futility.

Corporate culture rests in distinctive capacities and incapacities that are built into the attitudes and approaches of organizational members. Culture is not something that can be measured on a scale because it is a form of lived experience. Managers can influence that experience by being aware of the symbolic consequences of their actions and by attempting to foster desired values. But they can never control culture in the sense that many management writers advocate. The holographic diffusion of culture means that it pervades activity in a way that is not amenable to direct control by any single group of individuals. An understanding of organizations as cultures opens our eyes to many crucial insights that elude other metaphors, but they do not always provide the easy recipe for solving managerial problems that many managers and management writers hope for.

When anthropologist Franz Boas entertained a Kwakiutl from the Pacific Northwest in New York City in the early twentieth century, his visitor reserved most of his intellectual curiosity for the brass balls on hotel banisters and the bearded ladies then exhibited in Times Square. His attention was caught by the bizarre rather than the fundamental aspects of the culture. This experience contains a valuable caution for those interested in understanding organizational culture, for in this sphere too, attention may be captured by the hoopla and ritual that decorate the surface of organizational life rather than by the deeper and more fundamental structures that sustain these visible aspects. In studies of organizational culture, enactment is usually seen as a voluntary process under the direct influence of the actors involved. This view can be important in empowering people to take greater responsibility for their world by recognizing that they play an important part in the construction of their realities. But it can be misleading to the extent that it ignores the stage on which the enactment occurs. We all construct or enact our realities but not necessarily under circumstances of our own choosing. There is an important power dimension underlying the enactment process that the culture metaphor does not always highlight to the degree possible. When this is taken into account, the culture metaphor becomes infused with a political flavor that has close links with the perspectives to be explored in subsequent chapters.

6

Interests, Conflict, and Power

Organizations as Political Systems

I live in a democratic society. Why should I have to obey the orders of my boss eight hours a day? He acts like a bloody dictator, ordering us around and telling us what we should be thinking and doing. What right does he have to act in this way? The company pays our wages, but does this mean it has the right to command all our beliefs and feelings? It certainly has no right to reduce us to robots who must obey every command.

This rather angry comment of a factory worker exasperated by the grinding and oppressive experience of daily work life captures an aspect of organization that has escaped us up to now. He recognizes that his rights as a citizen and as a paid employee are in conflict with each other. As a citizen in a democratic society he is theoretically free to hold his own opinions, make his own decisions, and be treated as an equal. As an employee he is denied all these rights. He is expected to keep his mouth shut, do what he is told, and submit to the will of his superior. For eight hours a day, five days a week, he is expected to forget about democracy and get on with his work. His only democratic right rests in the freedom to find another job and move on. Or as his manager put it, "You can vote with your feet. If you don't like it here, you don't have to stay."

The situation described is an extreme one. Not all organizations are characterized by such entrenched relations between managers and workers or by such dictatorial modes of rule. But the situation is more common than we often like to think, especially in industrial organizations where battle lines have developed between labor and management. Typical or not, the point of our illustration is that it invites us to understand organizations as political systems.

Managers frequently talk about authority, power, and superior-subordinate relations. It takes but a small step to recognize these as political issues involving the activities of rulers and ruled. If we develop this idea, it is clear that we can understand organizations as systems of government that vary according to the political principles employed.

Some, like the one considered above, may be highly authoritarian while others may be model democracies. By recognizing that organization is intrinsically political, in the sense that ways must be found to create order and direction among people with potentially diverse and conflicting interests, much can be learned about the problems and legitimacy of management as a process of government and about the relation between organization and society.

The political metaphor can also be used to unravel the politics of day-to-day organizational life. Most people working in an organization readily admit in private that they are surrounded by forms of "wheeling and dealing" through which different people attempt to advance specific interests. However, this kind of activity is rarely discussed in public. The idea that organizations are supposed to be rational enterprises in which their members seek common goals tends to discourage discussion of political motive. Politics, in short, is seen as a dirty word.

This is unfortunate because it often prevents us from recognizing that politics and politicking may be an essential aspect of organizational life and not necessarily an optional and dysfunctional extra. In this regard, it is useful to remember that in its original meaning the idea of politics stems from the view that, where interests are divergent, society should provide a means of allowing individuals to reconcile their differences through consultation and negotiation. For example, in ancient Greece, Aristotle advocated politics as a means of reconciling the need for unity in the Greek *polis* (city-state) with the fact that the *polis* was an "aggregate of many members." Politics, for him, provided a means of creating order out of diversity while avoiding forms of totalitarian rule. Political science and many systems of government have built on this basic idea, advocating politics and the recognition of the interplay of competing interests as a means of creating a noncoercive form of social order.

By attempting to understand organizations as systems of government and by attempting to unravel the detailed politics of organizational life, we are able to grasp important qualities of organization that are often glossed over or ignored.

Organizations as Systems of Government

In April 1979, *BusinessWeek* ran a cover story on the Ford Motor Company. The cover featured a cartoon of Henry Ford II sitting in a thronelike driving seat with a driving wheel between his hands. Behind the throne stands a shadowy figure—we are left to guess who. The prominent Ford-like nose suggests that it may be Henry Ford I, founder of the Ford dynasty, scrutinizing the way his grandson was driving the company. The focus of the story was on the problem of succession. After thirty-four years as chief executive officer, Henry II was contemplating retirement, but there was no obvious successor capable of taking the wheel. Up until his demotion and dismissal in summer 1978, the popular candidate had been Lee Iacocca, the highly successful Ford executive who later became head of Chrysler. The firing of Iacocca added depth to the imagery conveyed in the cartoon, for it symbolized the authoritarian nature of Ford under the two Henrys. Iacocca's dismissal was merely the most recent and controversial in a list of firings that had included the names of seven company presidents since 1960. Iacocca was a popular and powerful figure at the Ford company but obviously not popular where it mattered most: His dismissal was solely linked to the fact that he did not have Henry II's approval. Henry II is reported as having presented an "it's him or me" ultimatum to his board's organization review committee and won. The formal reason given by Henry II to *Business-Week* was that Iacocca did not fit into his way of looking at things. Informally, it is speculated that Iacocca's fate was sealed by the fact that he had become too powerful within the company. Although the guiding philosophy of Ford was reported to be toward a General Motors style of "group management," *Business Week* stated that it believed Henry had found it difficult to reconcile himself with the loss of personal power that this kind of decentralization involved.

The story at Ford is by no means unique. Many organizations are ruled by authoritarian managers who wield considerable power as a result of their personal characteristics, family ties, or skill in building influence and prestige within the organization. Obvious examples are the owner-operated firm where the principle that "It's my business and I'll do as I like" holds sway; the family business ruled through "iron hands" that respect family interest and tradition above all else; large corporations such as ITT under Harold Geneen; and business firms, labor unions, and even voluntary organizations or clubs dominated by self-perpetuating oligarchies. The basis of day-to-day order in these organizations tends to be autocratic rather than democratic in that the ultimate power to shape action rests in the hands of a single individual or group, who typically makes all the important decisions. Although it is rare in practice to find an organization that is completely autocratic, many organizations have strong autocratic tendencies and characteristics.

When we summon terms like autocracy and democracy to describe the nature of an organization we are implicitly drawing parallels between organizations and political systems. As indicated in Exhibit 6.1, we do the same when we talk about organizations as bureaucracies or technocracies because in each case we are characterizing the organization in terms of a particular style of political rule. In each of these words the suffix *cracy*, which derives from the Greek *kratia*, meaning power or rule, is coupled with a prefix that indicates the precise nature of the power or rule employed. Thus, the word autocracy signifies the kind of absolute and often dictatorial power associated with ruling by oneself. In a bureaucracy, rule is associated with use of the written word and is exercised by bureaucrats who sit behind their *bureaux*, or desks, making and administering the rules that are to guide organizational activity. Power and accountability in such organizations are intimately connected with one's knowledge and use of the rules and with the lawlike form of administration that this implies.

In technocratic organizations, such as the flexible and ever-changing firms that thrive in the electronics industry and other turbulent environments, power and accountability are directly linked to one's technical knowledge and expertise. Whereas in autocracies and bureaucracies the pattern of power and authority is fairly stable and clearly defined, in technocracies it is often in flux as different individuals and groups rise and decline in power along with the value of their technical contributions. Power and influence often tend to follow the "whiz kids" and other knowledgeable people who seem capable of addressing dominant concerns or of opening new paths to corporate fame and fortune.

Organizations, like governments, employ some system of "rule" as a means of creating and maintaining order among their members. Political analysis can thus make a valuable contribution to organizational analysis. The following are among the most common varieties of political rule found in organizations:

Autocracy: absolute government where power is held by an individual or small group and supported by control of critical resources, property or ownership rights, tradition, charisma, and other claims to personal privilege

Bureaucracy: rule exercised through use of the written word, which provides the basis for a rational-legal type of authority, or "rule of law"

Technocracy: rule exercised through use of knowledge, expert power, and the ability to solve relevant problems

Codetermination: the form of rule where opposing parties combine in the joint management of mutual interests, as in coalition government or corporatism, each party drawing on a specific power base

Representative democracy: rule exercised through the election of officers mandated to act on behalf of the electorate and who hold office for a specified time period or so long as they command the support of the electorate, as in parliamentary government and forms of worker control and shareholder control in industry

Direct democracy: the system where everyone has an equal right to rule and is involved in all decision making, as in many communal organizations such as cooperatives and kibbutzim. It encourages self-organization as a key mode of organizing

It is rare to find organizations that use just one of these different kinds of rule. More often, mixed types are found in practice. For example, although some organizations are more autocratic, more bureaucratic, or more democratic than others, they often contain elements of other systems as well. One of the tasks of political analysis is to discover which principles are in evidence, where, when, why, and how.

Exhibit 6.1   Organizations and Modes of Political Rule

Finally, in democratic organizations, the power to rule rests with the *demos*, or populace. This power may be exercised through representative forms of management, where different stakeholders are formally represented in decision-making processes, as in systems of codetermination or coalition government and in forms of worker or shareholder control. Democratic power may also be exercised directly through participative forms of rule where everyone shares in the management process.

Many people hold the belief that there is a separation between business and politics and that they should be kept apart. Hence, when someone proposes the idea that workers should sit on boards of directors or that there is a case for employee control of industry, that person is often viewed as taking an unwarranted political stand. However, the foregoing discussion shows that this interpretation is not quite correct. The person advocating the case of employee rights or industrial democracy is not introducing a political issue so much as arguing for a different approach to a situation that is already political. Organizations that are autocratic, bureaucratic, or technocratic have as much political significance as those dominated by systems of worker control. Their political nature is simply of a different kind, drawing on different principles of legitimacy.

The system of industrial codetermination that developed in West Germany and other European countries after World War II explicitly recognizes the rival claims to legitimate rule that can be advanced by owners of capital, on the one hand, and by employees, on the other. Under this system, owners and employees codetermine the future of their organizations by sharing power and decision making. The system varies widely in application. For example, in Germany, codetermination varies from industry to industry. In the coal and steel industries, legislation dating from the 1950s provides for the appointment of supervisory boards comprising eleven members, five to be elected by shareholders and five by employees, the remaining member being appointed by the other ten. The supervisory board is then responsible for appointing a managing board of three members to run the day-to-day affairs of the organization. One member of this board must be a business specialist, another a production specialist, and the other a trade unionist. Elections to these boards are held every three years. The boards are designed to give capital and labor equal rights, although many would argue that this does not always work out in practice. A modification of the codetermination principle in other European and North American countries is found in the appointment of worker directors, as in Denmark, Norway, and Sweden, where a certain number of seats on corporate boards are usually allocated to union representatives. Another application of the principle is found in the forms of corporatism where management, unions, and government join together to consult and collaborate with each other on issues of mutual interest.

Although such developments recognize the rights of labor to participate in the management of an enterprise, they have not always been readily embraced by those in the labor movement. The reason for this is found in another political principle: that in healthy systems of government those in power should be held in check by some form of opposition. Many people concerned with the rights of labor fear that direct involvement in the management process creates a situation that co-opts or incorporates, and hence reduces, the power of dissent. By being a part of a decision-making process one loses one's right to oppose the decisions that are made. Many advocates of labor rights have thus suggested that employee interests can best be protected through associations such as labor unions or professional bodies that adopt an oppositional role in order to shape policy without owning it.

This problem of "incorporation" often accompanies changes in organization favoring increased employee participation in decision making. The fear of many opponents of such changes is that employees will be allowed to exercise their democratic rights in decisions of minor importance while being excluded from major ones. "We're allowed to choose the color of the wallpaper but little else" is a familiar complaint. As these critics see it, partial movements toward industrial democracy are often motivated by a managerial intent to divert or diffuse potential opposition by sharing the less important aspects of control. For these reasons, advocates of industrial democracy suggest that participation is not enough and that organizations should move toward styles of management based on fully developed forms of workers' control.

These have been widely employed in Eastern European countries such as the former Yugoslavia, where workers elected their managers and where the principle of self-management provided a key organizational value. This kind of system differs from schemes of codetermination that recognize that owners of capital and labor have equal rights by dissolving the distinction between capital and labor. In countries where industry is state owned, this form of self-management is fairly easily achieved, but elsewhere it has run into difficulties from those who wish to protect the rights of owners.

The most obvious large-scale experiments in workers' control in capitalist countries have occurred in ailing firms and industries where changes in fortune have increased the probability of unemployment and plant closures and prompted the desire of owners to sell their interest in the organization. The employee response has occasionally been to buy and run the company, often with mixed success, partly because the organizations are in declining industries and partly because of the problems of co-option that arise when workers become or appoint managers of an organization operating in a capitalist system. Like other managers in nondemocratic organizations, they find that survival in the system calls for certain kinds of action that are not always popular with their fellow owner-employees. The system has a logic of its own, and being an owner does not necessarily imply freedom of action.

Whether we are discussing the management of the Ford Motor Company under a member of the Ford dynasty or the management of a worker-controlled cooperative, it is clear that organizational choice always implies political choice. Although the language of organization theory often presents ideas relating to the management and motivation of people at work in relatively neutral terms—for example, as issues of leadership style, autonomy, participation, and employer-employee relations—they are by no means as neutral as they seem. In understanding organizations as political systems we have a means of exploring the political significance of these issues and the general relation between politics and organization.

Organizations as Systems of Political Activity

An analysis of organization from the perspective of comparative government can place our understanding of organizations in a refreshing perspective. However, in order to understand the day-to-day political dynamics of organization, it is also necessary to explore the detailed processes through which people engage in politics. For this purpose, it is useful to return to Aristotle's idea that politics stems from a diversity of interests, and trace how this diversity gives rise to the "wheeling and dealing," negotiation, and other processes of coalition building and mutual influence that shape so much of organizational life.

An organization's politics is most clearly manifest in the conflicts and power plays that sometimes occupy center stage, and in the countless interpersonal intrigues that provide diversions in the flow of organizational activity. More fundamentally, however, politics occurs on an ongoing basis, often in a way that is invisible to all but those directly involved.

We can analyze organizational politics in a systematic way by focusing on relations between *interests, conflict,* and *power.* Organizational politics arise when people think differently and want to act differently. This diversity creates a tension that must be resolved through political means. As we have already seen, there are many ways in which this can be done: autocratically ("We'll do it this way"); bureaucratically ("We're supposed to do it this way"); technocratically ("It's best to do it this way"); or democratically ("How shall we do it?"). In each case the choice between alternative paths of action usually hinges on the power relations between the actors involved. By focusing on how divergent interests give rise to conflicts, visible and invisible, that are resolved or perpetuated by various kinds of power play, we can make the analysis of organizational politics as rigorous as the analysis of any other aspect of organizational life.

ANALYZING INTERESTS

In talking about "interests" we are talking about predispositions embracing goals, values, desires, expectations, and other orientations and inclinations that lead a person to act in one way rather than another. In everyday life we tend to think of interests in a spatial way: as areas of concern that we wish to preserve or enlarge or as positions that we wish to protect or achieve. We live "in" our interests, often see others as "encroaching" on them, and readily engage in defenses or attacks designed to sustain or improve our position. The flow of politics is intimately connected with this way of positioning ourselves.

There are many ways in which we can define and analyze this pursuit and defense of interests. One way that has particular relevance for understanding organizational politics is to conceive interests in terms of three interconnected domains relating to one's organizational task, career, and personal life (Exhibit 6.2). *Task interests* are connected with the work one has to perform. The manager of a production plant has to ensure that products are produced in a timely and efficient manner. A salesperson must sell his or her quota of goods and sustain customer relations. An accountant must maintain appropriate records and produce regular accounts. However, work life always involves more than just doing one's job. Employees bring to the workplace aspirations and visions as to what their future may hold, providing the basis for *career interests* that may be independent of the job being performed. They also bring their personalities, private attitudes, values, preferences, and beliefs and sets of commitments from outside work, allowing these *extramural interests* to shape the way they act in relation to both job and career.

The relations among the three sets of interests are best understood if we examine a specific situation. Consider, for example, the position of a corporate executive working in a large organization. He may be highly committed to his job, ambitious, and also highly involved with family life. In his work experience, he may desire to manage all three: to do a good job, move ahead in the organization, and strike a reasonable balance between work and leisure so that he can spend weekends and most evenings with his family. In some situations, all three may coincide; in others, two spheres of interest may be compatible; whereas in others, the different interests may have no relation with each other. Life runs very smoothly for the executive in the first case (e.g., he gets a great idea that

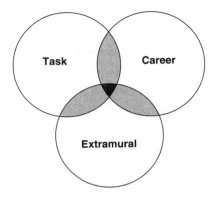

The above diagram illustrates the relationships and tensions that often exist between one's job (task), career aspirations, and personal values and lifestyle (extramural interests). The three domains can interact (the shaded areas) and also remain separate. In working in an organization we try to strike a balance between the three sets of interests. Most often, the balance is an uneasy and ever-changing one, creating tensions that lie at the center of political activity. The fact that the area of complete convergence of interests is often small (the darkest area) is one reason why organizational (or task) rationality is such a rare phenomenon. The degree of overlap varies from situation to situation.

Exhibit 6.2   Organizational Interests: Task, Career, and Extramural

contributes to his job performance and promotion prospects and gives him more leisure time as well) but gets difficult in the latter cases. His great idea may improve performance and career prospects but mean more work and less leisure. Or it may enable him to reduce his workload but in a way that makes him less visible and hence a less obvious candidate for promotion. Sometimes, the idea will be great for getting on with his job but have no other significance at all. The executive's attitude and relation to tasks, ideas, and the suggestions of others are all likely to be crucially affected by where the tasks, ideas, or suggestions fall on the map of interests depicted in Exhibit 6.2. The tensions existing between the different interests that he wishes to pursue make his relation to work inherently "political," even before we take into account the existence and actions of other organizational members. These tensions are inherent in work life in Western society because of the latent contradictions between the demands of work and leisure, on the one hand, and the demands of present and future, on the other.

The orientation of different people toward these tensions varies from situation to situation, producing a great variety of styles of behavior.

Some people are committed to doing their job as an end in itself; others are more careerist. Yet others spend most of their energy attempting to make work life less onerous or as comfortable and consistent with their personal preferences as possible. Many people manage to achieve considerable degrees of overlap between competing aims and aspirations, shaping their general task or mission in a way that allows them to achieve all their aims at once. Others have to content themselves with compromise positions.

This way of understanding different kinds of interests provides us with a means of decoding the personal agendas underlying specific actions and activities. We can begin to understand how people relate to their work through their own personal concerns and detect the motivating factors that underpin the varied styles of careerism, gamesmanship, task commitment, rigidity, "turf protection," zealousness, detachment, and freewheeling that lend the politics of organizational life its detailed character.

By simply following one's personal inclinations, the drama of organizational life is shaped by a political script. However, the political content increases manyfold when we begin to recognize the existence of other players, each with interest-based agendas to pursue. The politicking to which this gives rise becomes particularly visible in situations that present choices between different avenues for future development and in other transitional contexts such as the influx of new people or the succession of one person by another.

For the purpose of illustration, consider the following case example.

Mr. X was the flamboyant marketing vice president in a medium-size cosmetics firm. After five years, he had a solid reputation within his firm, having steered many successful campaigns designed to establish the firm's products as premier brands available in up-market retail outlets. Although he had encountered difficult times in persuading his colleagues that it was preferable to concentrate on relatively low-volume, high-quality products rather than to go for the mass market, over the years they had come to accept his viewpoint. His marketing philosophy and vision were in keeping with his personality, reflecting an interest and involvement with the social elites with whom he felt at home. The settings and themes of the firm's ads were selected by Mr. X and, as noted by many of his colleagues, were very much a reflection of his personal lifestyle. Crucial to the adoption of this marketing strategy and the line of corporate development it involved was the support of key members of the board who shared family connections and a taste for the style of life symbolized by Mr. X and his marketing philosophy. Other, less well-connected members who were appointed for their professional knowledge and links with the industry at large, along with the chief executive officer and a number of vice presidents, felt that many opportunities were being lost by the need to preserve an elite image. Whenever possible, they thus tried to mobilize an awareness of the need to consider other policy options, but the success of the company muted their inclination to press their concerns too far. So long as Mr. X's charismatic influence remained an important driving force, the firm was thus committed to preserving and developing its elite status.

An opportunity for change dropped by chance in the mailbox of Mr. Y, vice president for corporate planning and one of those most concerned about the lost opportunities. A friend and former colleague, now chief of a prestigious "head-hunting" firm, had written asking if he could recommend possible candidates for the position of marketing VP in the new North American branch of a European firm dealing in high-society fashion. A vision of Mr. X smiling in the midst of furs, diamonds, and Paris fashions immediately floated into Y's mind. Within the hour he had made an off-the-record call to his friend suggesting that Mr. X might well be approached. Within two months, Mr. X had been offered and had accepted the job.

Mr. X's successor at the cosmetics firm, Ms. Z, was a relatively young and ambitious woman with a liking for the glossy life. She had been a compromise selection, the board having been split on two other candidates. Ms. Z seemed to strike the balance between the dashing style to which X's allies had become accustomed and the promise of new initiative favored by those who had felt constrained by the direction set by X's philosophy. Even though neither group was delighted with the appointment, they both felt that Ms. Z was eminently capable of handling the job, especially since she would inherit a successful operation.

For Ms. Z, the job was a great opportunity. She felt that the time was right to make her mark in the industry and saw in the steady direction steered by X a base on which to launch new initiatives. In her interview discussions with X's former supporters she had made much of the need to conserve what had been achieved. In her discussions with those less committed to this philosophy she had stressed the promise of new markets. Her first year in the new job was spent developing an initiative that would bring these goals together: By retaining the up-market image but broadening marketing outlets to include selected chains of retail drug and department stores. She knew that she had to come up with a philosophy that set her apart from X, but that she must retain the support of the board and the senior executives who were essential for ensuring success. Her colleagues ready for a change were willing partners, and excellent working relations soon developed through a give-and-take approach that helped define ideas and opportunities where all seemed to gain. Her task in relation to those who still equated the style and personality of Mr. X with what the company stood for was much more difficult. Resistance and heated exchange became a feature of boardroom discussion. Over a period of three years, however, most came to accept the idea that the broadening of the market was still consistent with the image of a high-status product, particularly since the changing strategy was sweetened by its obvious financial success. As one board member put it while looking at the latest returns, "I think I'll be able to live with even more ads in those dreadful magazines if I think about these figures."

Our case only sketches the dynamics of the situation in broadest out-line. However, it serves to illustrate the politics intrinsic to any situation where people wish to pursue divergent interests. Mr. X had a vision that others were persuaded to share. His charismatic personality allowed him to use the organization to express himself through a strategy that com-bined task, career, and extramural interests in a coherent way. The col-leagues who bought into his strategy did so to the extent that their aims were achieved as well. Those opposed to the strategy had other aspira-tions. They wanted to see the organization go elsewhere. For this reason Mr. Y took advantage of a chance opportunity to change the situation. The state of transition opened up new opportunities. Rival coalitions formed around the candidates who people thought would be able to advance their interests. Ms. Z, the very able compromise candidate, read and played the situation well. She saw a convergence between personal and corporate opportunity and used her new job to further both. Given her ambitions there was no way that she could accept the status quo. Her personal style and career aspirations required her to "be a mover" and "make her mark." X's philosophy, although solidly successful, thus had to change. Others were prepared to join Z in shaping a new corporate direc-tion in return for prizes of their own. The confidence of the rival coali-tions, although doubtful at times, was retained because the new situation resulted in a transformation that most could identify with. Even though our discussion glosses over the power relations and other aspects of this case, the interactions between these few key actors and their supporters illustrate the thick and rich political dynamic of organizational life. The diversity of interests that Aristotle observed in the Greek city-state is evi-dent in every organization and can be analyzed by tracing how the ideas and actions of people collide or coincide.

In contrast with the view that organizations are integrated rational enterprises pursuing a common goal, the political metaphor encourages us to see organizations as loose networks of people with divergent interests who gather together for the sake of expediency (e.g., making a living, developing a career, or pursuing a desired goal or objective).

Organizations are coalitions and are made up of coalitions, and coalition building is an important dimension of almost all organizational life.

Coalitions arise when groups of individuals get together to cooperate in relation to specific issues, events, or decisions or to advance specific values and ideologies. Organizations fit this definition of coalitions in the sense that they comprise groups of managers, workers, shareholders, customers, suppliers, lawyers, governmental agents, and other formal and informal groups with an interest or stake in the organization but whose goals and preferences differ. The organization as a coalition of diverse stakeholders is a coalition with multiple goals.

Some organization theorists draw a distinction between cliques that become aware of common goals and coalitions of two or more such groups who unite to pursue a joint interest, often working against a rival network. Clearly, people in organizations can pursue their interests as individuals, specific interest groups, or more generalized coalitions, so this distinction is often a useful one. In many organizations, there is often a dominant coalition that controls important areas of policy. Such coalitions usually build around the chief executive or other key actors in the organization, each participant making demands on and contributions to the coalition as a price of participation. All coalitions have to strike some kind of balance between the rewards and contributions necessary to sustain membership, a balance usually influenced by factors such as age, organizational position, education, time spent in the organization, and values and attitudes.

Most approaches to organization actually foster the development of cliques and coalitions, as functional and other divisions fragment interests—for example, allocating different goals and activities to subunits such as departments or project teams. The "bounded rationality" discussed in Chapter 4 thus assumes a political dimension as salespeople become preoccupied with sales objectives, production people with production, and project teams with their group projects. Given such fragmentation, there is often considerable disagreement about specific objectives, requiring the organization to function with a minimal degree of consensus. This allows the organization to survive while recognizing the diversity of the aims and aspirations of its members. The organization often has to be content with satisfactory rather than optimal solutions to problems, with negotiation and compromise becoming more important than technical rationality.

Coalition development offers a strategy for advancing one's interests in an organization, and organization members often give considerable attention to increasing their power and influence through this means. Sometimes, coalitions are initiated by less powerful actors who seek the support of others. At other times, they may be developed by the powerful to consolidate their power; for example, an executive may promote people to key positions where they can serve as loyal lieutenants. Whether formal or informal, confined to the organization or extended to include key interests outside, coalitions and interest groups often provide important means of securing desired ends.

UNDERSTANDING CONFLICT

Conflict arises whenever interests collide. The natural reaction to conflict in organizational contexts is usually to view it as a dysfunctional force that can be attributed to some regrettable set of circumstances or causes. "It's a personality problem." "They're rivals who always meet head-on." "Production people and marketing people never get along." "Everyone hates auditors and accountants." Conflict is regarded as an unfortunate state that in more favorable circumstances would disappear.

Our analysis in the previous section suggests otherwise. Conflict will always be present in organizations. Conflict may be personal, interpersonal, or between rival groups or coalitions. It may be built into organizational structures, roles, attitudes, and stereotypes or arise over a scarcity of resources. It may be explicit or covert. Whatever the reason, and whatever the form it takes, its source rests in some perceived or real divergence of interests.

As Scottish sociologist Tom Burns has pointed out, most modern organizations actually encourage organizational politics because they are designed as systems of simultaneous competition and collaboration. People must collaborate in pursuit of a common task, yet are often pitted against each other in competition for limited resources, status, and career advancement. These conflicting dimensions of organization are most clearly symbolized in the hierarchical organization chart, which is both a system of cooperation, in that it reflects a rational subdivision of tasks, *and* a career ladder that people are motivated to climb. The fact that there are more jobs at the bottom than at the top means that competition for the top places is likely to be keen and that in any career race there are likely to be far fewer winners than losers. The system more or less ensures the kinds of competitive struggle on which organizational politics thrives. One does not have to be consciously cunning or deviously political to end up playing organizational politics. The corporate Machiavellis who systematically wheel and deal their way through organizational affairs merely illustrate the most extreme and fully developed form of a latent tendency present in most aspects of organizational life.

The literature on organization theory is full of examples of how everyday organizational life produces "political" forms of behavior. Some of the most vivid of these are found in reports by sociologists who have infiltrated the workplace in the role of participant observers. The setting of budgets and work standards, the day-to-day supervision and control of work, and the pursuit of opportunity and career are often characterized by sophisticated forms of gamesmanship. Take, for example, the situations reported by W. F. Whyte in his classic study *Money and Motivation*. These reveal the guile with which factory workers are able to control their pace of work and level of earnings, even when under the close eye of their supervisors or of efficiency experts trying to find ways of increasing productivity. The workers know that to maintain their positions they have to find ways of beating the system and do so with great skill and ingenuity.

For example, Starkey, an experienced factory worker, finds ways of building extra movements into his job when work standards are being set so that the job can be made easier under normal circumstances. He also finds completely new ways of working at high speeds when his supervisor is not around, thus allowing him to create slack time elsewhere in his day. Ray, famed among his fellow workers for his skill in outthinking and outperforming his controllers, finds ways of getting his machine to destroy the product on which he is working when he is asked to work at too fast a pace. He also has a great ability to look as if he is working harder than he is, generating a profuse sweat to impress and deceive his observers. Workers share ideas on how to get better work standards, to restrict output, to cash in on "gravy" jobs, or to land their competitors with the "stinkers." Such collaboration is often used against management and at other times against other workers or work teams. Management, of course, often knows that this is happening but is frequently powerless to do anything about it, particularly where plants are unionized. Sometimes, management gains control of the problem at hand, only to find another one arising elsewhere. The relationship is essentially combative. The status and self-respect of each group rest on their ability to outwit or control the other.

Similar relations are found in office settings, where staff manage impressions and schedules in a way that makes them seem busier and more productive than they actually are. Also, in budget-setting and other decision-making sessions, managers often attempt to outwit their own managers by padding their estimates to create slack resources or by negotiating easy work targets to allow room for error or to allow them to look good when the next salary review comes around.

Politicking is also latent in the horizontal relations between specialist units and within multidisciplinary teams. As noted earlier, people begin to identify with the responsibilities and objectives associated with their specific role, work group, department, or project team, in a way that often leads them to value achievement of these responsibilities and objectives over and above the achievement of wider organizational goals. This is especially true when reward systems and one's general status and sense of success are linked with good performance at the level of one's specialized responsibilities.

Even when people recognize the importance of working together, the nature of any given job often combines contradictory elements that create various kinds of role conflict. For example, the politicized interactions so often observed between production and marketing staff or between accountants and the users of financial services often rest in part on the fact that they are being asked to engage in activities that impinge on each other in a negative way. The product modification requested by marketing creates problems in the design and sequencing of production. The accountant's concern for firm control over expenditures proves an unwelcome constraint for executives in the spending department. As the actors in their various roles attempt to do the job for which they have been appointed, interpreting their task interests in a way that seems ideally suited for the achievement of organizational goals, they are set on a collision course. Similar conflicts are often observed between "line" managers responsible for day-to-day results and "staff" people such as planners, lawyers, accountants, and other experts who perform an advisory role; between professionals seeking to extend their sphere of autonomy and bureaucrats seeking to reduce it in the interests of improving control; and so on.

The potential complexity of organizational politics is mind-boggling, even before we take account of the personalities and personality clashes that usually bring roles and their conflicts to life. Sometimes, the conflicts generated are quite explicit and open for all to see. At other times, they lie beneath the surface of day-to-day events. For example, relations in meetings may be governed by various hidden agendas of which even the participants are unaware. In some organizations, disputes may have a long history, decisions and actions in the present being shaped by conflicts, grudges, or differences that others believe long forgotten or settled. The manager of a production department may align with the marketing manager to block a proposal from the production engineer not because he disagrees with the basic ideas but because of resentments associated with the fact that he and the production engineer have never gotten along. Although such resentments may seem petty, they are often powerful forces in organizational life.

Many organizational conflicts often become institutionalized in the attitudes, stereotypes, values, beliefs, rituals, and other aspects of organizational culture. In this socialized form, the underlying conflicts can be extremely difficult to identify and to break down. Here again, history can shape the present in subtle ways. However, by remembering Aristotle's injunction to understand the source of politics in the diversity of interests to which conflicts merely lend visible form, organizational analysts have a means of penetrating the surface of any conflict situation to understand its genesis. We will examine some of the ways in which conflicts can be managed when we discuss the politics of pluralist organizations later in this chapter.

EXPLORING POWER

Power is the medium through which conflicts of interest are ultimately resolved. Power influences who gets what, when, and how.

In recent years, organization and management theorists have become increasingly aware of the need to recognize the importance of power in explaining organizational affairs. However, no really clear and consistent definition of power has emerged. While some view power as a resource (i.e., as something one possesses), others view it as a social relation characterized by some kind of dependency (i.e., as an influence *over* something or someone).

Most organization theorists tend to take their point of departure from the definition of power offered by American political scientist Robert Dahl, who suggests that power involves an ability to get another person to do something that he or she would not otherwise have done. For some theorists, this definition leads to a study of the "here-and-now" conditions under which one person, group, or organization becomes dependent on another, whereas for others it leads to an examination of the historical forces that shape the stage of action on which contemporary power relations are set. As listed in Exhibit 6.3, the sources of power are rich and varied, providing those who wish to wheel and deal in the pursuit of their interests with many ways of doing so. In the following discussion we will examine how these sources of power are used to shape the dynamics of organizational life. In so doing we will be creating an analytical framework that can help us understand the power dynamics within an organization and identify the ways in which organizational members can attempt to exert their influence.

Formal Authority

The first and most obvious source of power in an organization is formal authority, a form of legitimized power that is respected and acknowledged by those with whom one interacts. As

---

The following are among the most important sources of power:

1. Formal authority

2. Control of scarce resources

3. Use of organizational structure, rules, and regulations

4. Control of decision processes

5. Control of knowledge and information

6. Control of boundaries

7. Ability to cope with uncertainty

8. Control of technology

9. Interpersonal alliances, networks, and control of "informal organization"

10. Control of counterorganizations

11. Symbolism and the management of meaning

12. Gender and the management of gender relations

13. Structural factors that define the stage of action

14. The power one already has

   The sources of power provide organizational members with a variety of means for enhancing their interests and resolving or perpetuating organizational conflict.

Exhibit 6.3   Sources of Power in Organizations

sociologist Max Weber has noted, legitimacy is a form of social approval that is essential for stabilizing power relations. It arises when people recognize that a person has a right to rule some area of human life and that it is their duty to obey. Historically, legitimate authority has been underpinned by one or more of three characteristics: charisma, tradition, or the rule of law (see Exhibit 9.1 in Chapter 9 for further details).

   Charismatic authority arises when people respect the special qualities of an individual (*charisma* means "gift of grace") and see those qualities as defining the right of the individual to act on their behalf. Traditional authority arises when people respect the custom and practices of the past and vest authority in those who symbolize and embody these traditional values. Monarchs and others who rule because of some kind of inherited status acquire their right to rule through this kind of principle. Bureaucratic or rational-legal authority arises when people insist that the exercise of power depends on the correct application of formal rules and procedures. Those who exercise bureaucratic authority must win their rights to power through procedural means—for example, by demonstrating ownership or property rights in a corporation, through election in a democratic system, or by demonstrating appropriate professional or technical qualifications in a meritocracy.

Each of these three kinds of formal authority may be found in modern organizations. A hero figure may acquire immense charismatic power that allows that person to control and direct others as he or she wishes. The owner of a family firm may exercise authority as a result of membership in the founding family. A bureaucrat may exercise power as a result of the formal office held. So long as those who are subject to the kind of authority in use respect and accept the nature of that authority, the authority serves as a form of power. If it is not respected, the authority becomes vacuous, and power depends on the other sources named in Exhibit 6.3.

The most obvious type of *formal* authority in most organizations is bureaucratic and is typically associated with the position one holds, whether as sales manager, accountant, project coordinator, secretary, factory supervisor, or machine operator. These different organizational positions are usually defined in terms of rights and obligations, which create a field of influence within which one can legitimately operate with the formal support of those with whom one works. A factory manager may be given a "right" to direct those under his or her control. A sales manager may be given the "right" to influence policy on sales campaigns—but not on financial accounting. The formal positions on an organization chart thus define spheres of delegated authority. To the extent that authority is translated into power through the assent of those falling under the pattern of command, the authority structure is also a power structure. Although the authority is often seen as flowing down from the top of the organization chart, being delegated by one's superior, our discussion of the nature of legitimacy suggests that this is only partly true. The authority becomes effective only to the extent that it is legitimized from below. The pyramid of power represented in an organization chart thus builds on a base where considerable power belongs to those at the bottom of the pyramid as well as to those at the top. Trade unionization has of course recognized this, channeling the power existing at the lower levels of the pyramid to challenge the power at the top. To the extent that trade union power is legitimized by the rule of law and the right to unionize, it too represents a type of formal authority. We will have more to say on this later in our discussion of "counterorganizations."

Control of Scarce Resources

All organizations depend for their continued existence on an adequate flow of resources, such as money, materials, technology, personnel, and support from customers, suppliers, and the community at large. An ability to exercise control over any of these resources can thus provide an important source of power within and between organizations. Access to funds, possession of a crucial skill or raw material, control of access to some valued computer program or new technology, or even access to a special customer or supplier can lend individuals considerable organizational power. If the resource is in scarce supply and someone is dependent on its availability, then it can almost certainly be translated into power. Scarcity and dependence are the keys to resource power!

When we begin to talk about the power associated with resources, attention usually focuses on the role of money, for money is among the most liquid of all resources and can usually be converted into the others. A person with a valued skill, a supplier with a precious raw material, or a person holding information on a new project opportunity can often be persuaded to exchange his or her valued resource for an attractive price. Money can also be converted into promotions, patronage, threats, promises, or favors to buy loyalty, service, support, or raw compliance.

No wonder therefore that so much organizational politics surrounds the process of budgeting and the control and allocation of financial resources. As Jeffrey Pfeffer of Stanford University has suggested, the use of such power is critically linked with one's ability to control the discretionary use of funds. It is not necessary to have full control over financial decisions. One needs to have just enough control to pull the crucial strings that can create changes at the margin. The reason for this is that most of the financial resources available to an organization are committed to sustaining current operations. Changes to these operations are usually incremental, decisions being made to increase or reduce current expenditure. It is the ability to increase or decrease this flow of funds that gives power.

Hence, if a manager can acquire access to uncommitted resources that can be used in a discretionary way (e.g., as a slush fund or to support a new initiative), he or she can exert a major influence over future organizational development and at the same time buy commitment from those who benefit from this use of funds. Similarly, someone outside an organization who is responsible for deciding whether his or her financial support to that organization should be continued is in a position to exercise considerable influence on the policies and practices of the organization. Often, this influence is out of all proportion with the amount actually given, as organizations are often critically dependent on marginal funds to create room to maneuver. Organizations often have a tendency to use their slack in one year in ways that create commitments or expectations for the next year—for example, by giving a raise in salary that will be expected to be repeated next year, by appointing staff whose appointments will need to be renewed, or by launching a new program that staff will wish to continue—thus lending considerable power to the marginal funder.

The principles that we have discussed in relation to the use of financial power apply to other kinds of resource power as well. The important point is that power rests in controlling resources on which the organization is dependent for current operations or for creating new initiatives. There must be a dependence before one is able to control, and such control always derives its power from there being a scarcity of, or limited access to, the resource in question. Whether we are talking about the control of finance, skills, materials, or personnel, or even the provision of emotional support to a key decision maker who has come to value one's support and friendship, the principles remain the same. The more Machiavellian among us will quickly see how these principles point the way to a strategy for increasing power by *creating* dependence through the planned control of critical resources.

One's power can also be increased by reducing one's dependence on others. This is why many managers and organizational units like to have their own pockets of resources. The seemingly needless duplication of resources where each unit has the same underemployed machine, technical experts, or reserve of staff that can be used in rush periods is often a result of attempts to reduce dependence on the resources of others. The idea of "stockpiling" staff and expertise used to be a very familiar sign of organizational power. With the streamlining that comes with "cost cutting" and efficiency drives, and the possibility of gaining the required flexibility through "outsourcing" or subcontracting, it has now become less common.

Use of Organizational Structure, Rules, Regulations, and Procedures

Most often, organizational structure, rules, regulations, and procedures are viewed as rational instruments intended to aid task performance. A political view of these arrangements, however, suggests that in many situations they are best understood as products and reflections of a struggle for political control.

Consider the following example drawn from research that I conducted on British "new town" development corporations. The corporation in question was established in the early 1960s to develop a new town in an old industrial area. A functional organization was established with separate departments (finance, law, administration, commercial development, housing, architecture and planning, and engineering services) reporting to a general manager, who reported to the board. A few years later, an energetic businessman became chairman of the board. He made the corporation's chief legal officer the new general manager and split the now vacant legal officer's post into two parts, creating the post of corporation secretary and leaving the new legal officer with a narrower range of functions. The corporate secretary's post was filled by a nominee of the chairman who had worked with him in a similar capacity at another organization. The chairman and secretary began to work closely together, and the board eventually agreed that the secretary should have direct access to the board without having to go through the general manager. The chairman involved himself in the day-to-day running of the organization, often bypassing the general manager, whose role became very difficult to perform.

This situation came to a rather abrupt end with the surprise resignation of the chairman in response to a controversy over policy issues. With the appointment of a new chairman who was interested in delegating the task of running the organization to the general manager, power relations within the corporation changed dramatically. The general manager gradually established his control over his department heads, many of whom had become quite powerful through the interventions of the former chairman. His approach was to bring many of the functions that had been allocated to the secretary under his own control and to reorganize other departmental responsibilities. For example, he split the functions of the architecture and planning department, establishing a new planning department and a new department dealing with surveys. This move left the chief architect, who had become a strong executive during the reign of the previous chairman, with but a fraction of the department he once ran. These structural redesigns were later accompanied by further changes that in effect demoted the heads of the functional departments, and it was not long before a number left the organization, including the secretary and the chief architect.

Although these structural changes were justified in technical terms, they were also motivated by political considerations relating to issues of control. The initial changes created by the corporation's energetic chairman were designed to enhance his own control of the organization by weakening that of the general manager. The changes introduced after the chairman's resignation were primarily designed to help the general manager regain control over powerful department heads. Structural change was part of a power play to limit the role and influence of other key individuals.

The circumstances of this case may be unique, but the pattern is quite general; organizational structure is frequently used as a political instrument. Plans for organizational differentiation and integration, designs for centralization and decentralization, and the tensions that can arise in matrix organizations often entail hidden agendas related to the power, autonomy, or interdependence of departments and individuals.

The tensions surrounding the process of organizational design and redesign provide many insights on organizational power structures. People and departments often cling to outdated job descriptions and resist change because their power and status within the organization are so closely tied with the old order. Or they learn to use key aspects of organizational structure for their own ends. Consider, for example, how job descriptions can be used by employees to define what they are not prepared to do ("that's not part of my job" or "I'm not paid to do that!"). Rules and regulations in general can prove to be two-edged swords.

Take, for example, the case of the old state-owned British Rail, where employees discovered the power of "working to rule." Rather than going on strike to further a claim or address a grievance, a process that proved costly to employees because they forfeited their pay, the union acquired the habit of declaring a "work to rule," whereby employees did exactly what was required by the regulations developed by the railway authorities. The result was that hardly any train left on time. Schedules went haywire, and the whole railway system quickly slowed to a snail's pace, if not a halt, because normal functioning required that employees find shortcuts or at least streamline procedures.

The case is by no means unique. Many organizations have comprehensive systems of rules that, as almost every employee knows, can never be applied if the system is to achieve any degree of operational effectiveness.

What, then, is the real significance of the rules? Although their formal purpose may be to protect employees, customers, or the public at large, they also are there to protect their creators.

For example, if an accident occurs in a railway system, it is possible to launch an investigation comparing practice against the rules to find who or what was in error. Sometimes, gaps in the rules are found. Sometimes, gross negligence is discovered. But often the accident is no more than what Charles Perrow of Yale University calls a "normal accident," in the sense that its probability is built into the nature of the system. The broken rules that accompany the accident have often been broken thousands of times before as part of normal work practice, since normal work is impossible without breaking the rules. The railwaymen in Britain, like others who have adopted the "work to rule" practice, discovered how a weapon designed to control and possibly punish them could be used to control and punish others.

Rules and regulations are often created, invoked, and used in either a proactive or retrospective fashion as part of a power play. All bureaucratic regulations, decision-making criteria, plans and schedules, promotion and job-evaluation requirements, and other rules that guide organizational functioning give potential power to both the controllers and those controlled. Rules designed to guide and streamline activities can almost always be used to block activities. Just as lawyers make a profession out of finding a new angle on what appears to be a clear-cut rule, many organizational members are able to invoke rules in ways that no one ever imagined possible. An ability to use the rules to one's advantage is thus an important source of organizational power and, as in the case of organizational structures, defines a contested terrain that is forever being negotiated, preserved, or changed.

Control of Decision Processes

An ability to influence the outcomes of decision-making processes is a well-recognized source of power that has attracted considerable attention in the organization-theory literature. In discussing the kinds of power used here, it is useful to distinguish between control of three interrelated elements: decision *premises,* decision *processes,* and decision *issues and objectives.*

By influencing decision *premises* one can control the foundations of decision making—preventing crucial decisions from being made and fostering those that one actually desires. Hence, the attention is devoted to the control of decision agendas and to strategies for guiding or deflecting people's attention to the grounds or issues defining a favored point of view. As Charles Perrow has noted, an unobtrusive or unconscious element of control can also be built into vocabularies, structures of communication, attitudes, beliefs, rules, and procedures. Though often unquestioned, they exert a decisive influence on decision outcomes by shaping how we think and act. Our understandings of problems and issues often act as mental straitjackets that prevent us from seeing other ways of formulating basic concerns and finding the alternative courses of action. Many of these unobtrusive controls are "cultural" in the sense that they are built into organizational assumptions, beliefs, and practices about "who we are" and "the way we do things around here."

Control of decision-making *processes* is usually more visible than the control of decision premises. How should a decision be made? Who should be involved? When will the decision be made? By determining whether a decision can be taken and then reported to appropriate quarters, whether it must go before a committee and which committee, whether it must be supported by a full report, whether it will appear on an agenda where it is likely to receive a rough ride (or an easy passage), the order of an agenda, and even whether the decision should be discussed at the beginning or end of a meeting, a manager can have a considerable impact on decision outcomes. The ground rules to guide decision making are thus important variables that organization members can manipulate and use to stack the deck in favor of or against a given action.

A final way of controlling decision making is to influence the *issues and objectives* to be addressed and the evaluative criteria to be employed. An individual can shape issues and objectives most directly through preparing the reports and contributing to the discussion on which the decision will be based. By emphasizing the importance of particular constraints, selecting and evaluating the alternatives on which a decision will be made, and highlighting the importance of certain values or outcomes, decision makers can exert considerable influence on the decision that emerges from discussion. Eloquence, command of the facts, passionate commitment, or sheer tenacity or endurance can in the end win the day, adding to a person's power to influence the decisions with which he or she is involved.

Control of Knowledge and Information

Evident in much of the above discussion, particularly with regard to the control of decision premises, is the idea that power accrues to the person who is able to structure attention to issues in a way that in effect defines the reality of the decision-making process. This draws attention to the key importance of knowledge and information as sources of power. By controlling these key resources a person can systematically influence the definition of organizational situations and can create patterns of dependency. Both these activities deserve attention on their own account.

The American social psychologist W. I. Thomas once observed that if people define situations as real, they are real in their consequences. Many skillful organizational politicians put this dictum into practice on a daily basis by controlling information flows and the knowledge that is made available to different people, thereby influencing their perception of situations and hence the ways they act in relation to those situations. These politicians are often known as "gatekeepers," opening and closing channels of communication and filtering, summarizing, analyzing, and thus shaping knowledge in accordance with a view of the world that favors their interests. Many aspects of organizational structure, especially hierarchy and departmental divisions, influence how information flows and are readily used by unofficial gatekeepers to advance their own ends. Even by the simple process of slowing down or accelerating particular information flows, thus making knowledge available in a timely manner or too late for it to be of use to its recipients, the gatekeeper can wield considerable power.

Often, the quest for control of information in an organization is linked to questions of organizational structure. For example, many battles have been fought over the control and use of centralized computer systems because control of the computer often carries with it control over information flows and the design of information systems. The power of many finance and other specialist information processing departments is often tied up with this fact. Finance staff are important not only because they control resources but because they also define and control information about the use of resources. By influencing the design of budgeting and cost-control information systems they are able to influence what is perceived as being important within the organization both on the part of those who use the information as a basis for control and among those who are subject to these controls. Just as decision-making premises influence the kind of decisions that are made, the hidden and sometimes unquestioned assumptions that are built into the design of information systems can be of crucial importance in structuring day-to-day activity.

Many of the hot issues regarding the merits and problems of microprocessing hinge on the question of power. The new information processing technology creates the possibility of multiple points of access to common databases and the possibility of local rather than centralized information systems. In principle, the technology can be used to increase the power of those at the periphery or local levels of the organization by providing them with more comprehensive, immediate, and relevant data relating to their work, facilitating self-control rather than centralized control. In practice, the technology is often used to sustain or to increase power at the center. The designers and users of such systems have been acutely aware of the power in information, decentralizing certain activities while centralizing ongoing surveillance over their performance. Thus executives in remote parts of the world, airline reservation staff in unsupervised offices, and workers on the factory floor perform under the watchful eye of the computer, which reports almost every move to someone or some point at the heart of the information system.

Besides shaping definitions of organizational realities or exercising control, knowledge and information can be used to weave patterns of dependency. By possessing the right information at the right time, by having exclusive access to key data, or by simply demonstrating the ability to marshal and synthesize facts in an effective manner, organizational members can increase the power they wield within an organization. Many people develop these skills in a systematic way and jealously guard or block access to crucial knowledge to enhance their indispensability and "expert" status. Obviously, other organizational members have an interest in breaking such exclusivity and widening access. There is thus usually a tendency in organizations to routinize valued skills and abilities whenever possible. There is also a tendency to break down dependencies on specific individuals and departments by acquiring one's own experts. Thus, departments often prefer to have their own specialist skills on hand, even if this involves duplication and some redundancy of specialisms within the organization as a whole.

A final aspect of expert power relates to the use of knowledge and expertise as a means of legitimizing what one wishes to do. "The expert" often carries an aura of authority and power that can add considerable weight to a decision that rests in the balance or, though already having been made in the minds of key actors, needs further support or justification.

Control of Boundaries

Any discussion of power in organizations must give attention to what is sometimes known as "boundary management." The notion of boundary is used to refer to the interface between different elements of an organization. Thus we can talk about the boundaries between different work groups or departments or between an organization and its environment. By monitoring and controlling boundary transactions, people are able to build up considerable power. For example, it becomes possible to monitor changes occurring outside one's group, department, or organization and initiate timely responses. One acquires knowledge of critical interdependencies over which one may be able to secure a degree of control. Or one gains access to critical information that places one in a particularly powerful position to interpret what is happening in the outside world and thus help define the organizational reality that will guide action. One can also control transactions across boundaries by performing a buffering function that allows or even encourages certain transactions while blocking others.

Most people in leadership positions at all levels of an organization can engage in this kind of boundary management in a way that contributes to their power. The process is also an important element of many organizational roles, such as those of a secretary, special assistant, or project coordinator, and of liaison people of all kinds. People in such roles are often able to acquire power that goes well beyond their formal status. For example, many secretaries and special assistants are able to exert a major impact on the way their boss views the reality of a given situation by determining who is given access to the manager and when and by managing information in a way that highlights or downplays the importance of events and activities occurring elsewhere in the organization. One of the most famous examples of boundary management is found in the management of the White House under the Nixon administration, where Nixon's top aides Richard Erlichman and Bob Haldeman exercised tight control over access to the president. In doing so, it seems they were able to manage the president's view of what was happening in the White House and elsewhere. One of the main issues in the notorious Watergate affair and the collapse of the presidency was whether Nixon's aides had allowed the president to receive the critical information regarding the Watergate burglary. Erlichman and Haldeman were experts at boundary management, and their basic strategy for acquiring power is found in many different kinds of organizations all over the world.

Boundary management can help integrate a unit with the outside world, or it can be used to isolate that unit so that it can function in an autonomous way. The quest for autonomy—by individuals, groups, and even departments—is a powerful feature of organizational life because many people like to be in full control over their life space. Boundary management aids this quest, for it often shows ways in which a unit can acquire the resources necessary to create autonomy and points to strategies that can be used to fend off threats to autonomy. Groups and departments often attempt to incorporate key skills and resources within their boundaries and to control admissions through selective recruitment. They also often engage in what sociologist Erving Goffman has described as "avoidance rituals," steering clear of issues and potential problems that will threaten their independence.

The quest for autonomy is, however, often countered by opposing strategies initiated by managers elsewhere in the system. They may attempt to break down the cohesiveness of the group by nominating their own representatives or allies to key positions, find ways of minimizing the slack resources available to the group, develop information systems that make activities transparent to outsiders, or encourage organizational redesigns that increase interdependence and minimize the consequences of autonomous actions. Boundary transactions are thus often characterized by competing strategies for control and countercontrol. Many groups and departments are successful in acquiring considerable degrees of autonomy and in defending their position in a way that makes the organization a system of loosely coupled groups and departments rather than a highly integrated unit.

Ability to Cope With Uncertainty

One source of power implicit in much that has been discussed above is the ability to cope with the uncertainties that influence the day-to-day operation of an organization. Organization implies a certain degree of interdependence, so that discontinuous or unpredictable situations in one part of an organization have considerable implications for operations elsewhere. An ability to deal with these uncertainties gives an individual, group, or subunit considerable power in the organization as a whole.

The ability to cope with uncertainty is often intimately connected with one's place in the overall division of labor in an organization. Generally speaking, uncertainty is of two kinds. Environmental uncertainties (e.g., with regard to markets, sources of raw materials, or finance) can provide great opportunities for those with the contacts or skills to tackle the problems and thus minimize their effects on the organization as a whole. Operational uncertainties within the organization (e.g., the breakdown of critical machinery used in factory production or data processing) can help troubleshooters, maintenance staff, or others with the requisite skills and abilities acquire power and status as a result of their ability to restore normal operations. The degree of power that accrues to people who can tackle both kinds of uncertainty depends primarily on two factors: the degree to which their skills are substitutable, and hence the ease with which they can be replaced; and the centrality of their functions to the operations of the organization as a whole.

Organizations generally try to reduce uncertainties whenever possible, usually by "buffering" or through processes of routinization. For example, stocks of critical resources may be built up from different sources, maintenance programs may be developed to minimize technological failures, and people may be trained to deal with environmental contingencies. However, some uncertainty almost always remains, for, by their nature, uncertain situations cannot always be accurately predicted and forestalled. Then, too, those who see the power deriving from their capacity to deal with uncertainty often preserve their power base by ensuring that the uncertainties continue and sometimes by manipulating situations so that they appear more uncertain than they actually are.

In understanding the impact of uncertainty on the way an organization operates, we thus have an important means of understanding the power relations between different groups and departments. We also get a better understanding of the conditions under which the power of the expert or troubleshooter comes into play and of the importance of the various kinds of power deriving from the control of resources discussed earlier. The existence of uncertainty and an ability to cope with uncertainty are often reasons explaining why and when these other kinds of power become so critical in shaping organizational affairs.

Control of Technology

From the beginning of history, technology has served as an instrument of power, enhancing the ability of humans to manipulate, control, and impose themselves on their environment. The technology employed in modern organizations performs a similar function. It provides its users with an ability to achieve amazing results in productive activity, and it also provides them with an ability to manipulate this productive power and make it work effectively for their own ends.

Organizations usually become vitally dependent on some form of core technology as a means of converting organizational inputs into outputs. This may be a factory assembly line, a telephone switchboard, a centralized computer or record-keeping system, or perhaps a capital-intensive plant like those used in oil refining, the production of chemicals, or power generation. The kind of technology employed influences the patterns of interdependence within an organization and hence the power relations between different individuals and departments. For example, in organizations where the technology creates patterns of sequential interdependence, as in a mass-production assembly line where task A must be completed before task B, which must be completed before task C, the people controlling any one part of the technology possess considerable power to disrupt the whole. In organizations where the technology involves more autonomous systems of production, the ability of one individual or group to influence the operation of the whole is much more limited.

The fact that technology has a major impact on power relations is an important reason why attempts to change technology often create major conflicts between managers and employees and between different groups within an organization, for the introduction of a new technology can alter the balance of power. The introduction of assembly-line production into industry, designed to increase managerial control over the work process, also had the unintended effect of increasing the power of factory workers and their unions. In standardizing jobs, the technology standardized employee interests in a way that encouraged collective action, and also gave employees the power over the production process to make that action extremely effective. A strike on any part of an assembly line can bring the work of hundreds or even thousands of people to a complete halt. The technology is designed in a way that makes collective action by a small group of people extremely effective.

The system of production based on the use of autonomous work groups and other forms of "cellular technology," however, fragments the interests of workers. Work and rewards accrue to the work team as a primary organizational unit. The interests of an employee thus often become more closely associated with those of his team than with those of a general type of employee or occupational group, making unionization and collective action much more difficult, especially as competitive relations may develop between different work teams. Under the group system, a withdrawal of work does not affect overall operations unless other work groups do the same. Hence the power of workers and their unions tends to be reduced quite substantially.

The introduction of new production methods, machines, computing facilities, or any kind of technological change that increases the power of one group or department at the expense of another thus tends to develop into a hot political issue. Groups of employees usually have a clear understanding of the power relations inherent in current work arrangements and are usually ready to marshal all their resources and ingenuity to fight changes that threaten their position.

The power associated with the control of technology becomes most visible in confrontations and negotiations surrounding organizational change or when groups are attempting to improve their lot within the organization. However, it also operates in more subtle ways. In working with a particular machine or work system, an employee learns the ins and outs of its operation in a way that often lends that person considerable power. Earlier in this chapter we discussed how machine operators were able to use their knowledge of their machines to outwit the experts attempting to set work standards. They were able to control the use of their technology to improve their wages and control their pace of work. This kind of process is used for many purposes in different kinds of work settings every day. People manipulate and control their technology just as they twist and turn rules, regulations, and job descriptions. Technology designed to direct and control the work of employees frequently becomes a tool of workers' control!

Interpersonal Alliances, Networks, and
Control of "Informal Organization"

Friends in high places, sponsors, mentors, ethnic or cultural affiliations, coalitions of people prepared to trade support and favors to further their individual ends, and informal networks for touching base, sounding out, or merely shooting the breeze—all provide a source of power to those involved. Through various kinds of interlocking networks, individuals can acquire advance notice of developments that are relevant to their interests, exert various forms of interpersonal influence to shape these developments in a manner that they desire, and prepare the way for proposals they are interested in advancing. The skilled organizational politician systematically builds and cultivates such informal alliances and networks, incorporating whenever possible the help and influence of all those with an important stake in the domain in which that person is operating. Alliances and coalitions are not necessarily built around an identity of interests; rather, the requirement for these forms of informal organization is that there be a basis for some form of mutually beneficial exchange. Successful networking or coalition building involves an awareness that besides winning friends it is necessary to incorporate and pacify potential enemies. It also requires an ability to see beyond immediate issues and find ways of trading help in the present for promises in the future. The successful coalition builder recognizes that the currency of coalition building is one of mutual dependency and exchange.

The coalitions, alliances, and networks built through these processes may remain highly informal and to a degree invisible. The coalition building may occur over the telephone, through old-boy networks and other friendship groups, through the golf club, or through chance contacts. For example, people sharing a meeting on one project may find that they share an interest in relation to another area of their work and use informal exchanges at the meeting to lay the groundwork for cooperative action elsewhere. Much of the coalition building found in organizational life occurs through this kind of chance encounter or through planned informal meetings such as lunches and receptions. Sometimes, however, alliances and networks are forged through various kinds of institutionalized exchange, such as meetings of professional groups and associations, and may themselves eventually become institutionalized in enduring forms such as project teams, advisory boards, joint ventures, or cartel-like organizations. As is clear from the above examples, networks may be internal to an organization or extend to include key people outside. Sometimes, they are explicitly interorganizational, such as interlocking directorships where the same people serve on the boards of different organizations. In all networks, some players may take an active central role, and others may operate at the fringes. Some will contribute to and derive power from the network more than others, according to the pattern of mutual dependence on which the alliance builds.

Besides drawing power from networking and coalition building, many members of an organization may draw power from their role in the social networks known as the "informal organization." All organizations have informal networks where people interact in ways that meet various kinds of social needs. Groups of coworkers may make a habit of going to lunch together or drinking on Fridays after work or may evolve means of enhancing the quality of their life at work. They may share similar ethnic or cultural backgrounds and have affiliations that extend beyond the workplace. Informal group leaders may become as powerful an influence on their network or group as any rule, regulation, or manager. In a culturally diverse workforce, such leaders can acquire enormous power as "gatekeepers," "boundary managers," and representatives and inter- preters of reality for the groups they lead.

One other variant of informal organization arises in situations where one member of an organization develops a psychological or emotional depen- dency on another. This becomes particularly significant when the depen- dent party draws considerable power from other sources. The history of corporate and public life is full of examples where a key decision maker has become critically dependent on his or her spouse, lover, secretary, or trusted aide or even on a self-proclaimed prophet or mystic. In the power-behind- the-throne syndrome that results, the informal collaborator exerts a critical influence on how the decision maker's power is used. Such relations often develop by chance, but it is by no means uncommon for people to rise to power by cultivating such dependencies in a Machiavellian way.

Control of Counterorganizations

Another route to power in organizations rests in the establishment and control of what can be called "counterorganiza- tions." Trade unions are the most obvious of these. Whenever a group of people manages to build a concentration of power in relatively few hands it is not uncommon for opposing forces to coordinate their actions to cre- ate a rival power bloc. Economist John Kenneth Galbraith has described the process as one involving the development of "countervailing power." Thus, unions develop as a check on management in industries where there is a high degree of industrial concentration; government and other regulatory agencies develop as a check on the abuse of monopoly power;

and the concentration of production is often balanced by the development of large organizations in the field of distribution—for example, chain stores often develop in ways that balance the power exercised by the large producers and suppliers.

The strategy of exercising countervailing power thus provides a way of influencing organizations where one is not part of the established power structure. By joining and working for a trade union, consumers' association, social movement, cooperative, or lobby group—or by exercising citizens' rights and pressuring the media, one's political representative, or a government agency—one has a way of balancing power relations. Many people make a career out of doing this. Thus, a shopfloor worker may spend a major part of his leisure time working for his union, perhaps rising through the ranks of the union bureaucracy to a level at which he deals with senior management face-to-face. A spokesperson or advocate for a social, ethnic, or cultural minority may build considerable influence in a way that mobilizes power bases both within that person's organization and within the wider community. For many people at the lower levels or marginalized areas of an organization, the only effective way that they can influence their work life is through this form of countervailing power.

Consumer advocates like Ralph Nader also illustrate the potential of countervailing power. Nader and his colleagues have been able to exert a much greater influence on American industry by acting as critics and champions of consumer rights than they would have had as employees of any of the organizations they have criticized. Many socially conscious lawyers, journalists, academics, and members of other professional groups have also found an effective route to influence by criticizing rather than joining the organizations that are the object of their concern.

The principle of countervailing power is also often employed by the leaders of large conglomerates, who in effect play a form of chess with their environment, buying and selling organizations as corporate pawns. More than one multinational has attempted to counter the power of its competitors or bargain with its host government with the principle of countervailing power in mind.

Symbolism and the Management of Meaning

Another important source of power in organizations rests in one's ability to persuade others to enact realities that further the interests one wishes to pursue. Leadership ultimately involves an ability to define the reality of others. While the authoritarian leader attempts to "sell," "tell," or force a reality on his or her subordinates, more democratic leaders allow definitions of a situation to evolve from the views of others. The democratic leader's influence is far more subtle and symbolic. He or she spends time listening, summarizing, integrating, and guiding what is being said, making key interventions and summoning images, ideas, and values that help those involved to make sense of the situation with which they are dealing. In managing the meanings and interpretations assigned to a situation, the leader in effect wields a form of symbolic power that exerts a decisive influence on how people perceive their realities and hence the way they act. Charismatic leaders seem to have a natural ability to shape meaning in this way.

We will focus upon three related aspects of symbolic management: the use of imagery, the use of theater, and the use of gamesmanship.

Images, language, symbols, stories, ceremonies, rituals, and all the other attributes of corporate culture discussed in Chapter 5 are tools that can be used in the management of meaning and hence in shaping power relations in organizational life. Many successful managers and leaders are aware of the power of evocative imagery and instinctively give a great deal of attention to the impact their words and actions have on those around them. For example, they often encourage the idea that the organization is a team and the environment a competitive jungle, talk about problems in terms of opportunities and challenges, symbolize the importance of a key activity or function by giving it high priority and visibility on their own personal agenda, or find other ways of creating and massaging the systems of belief deemed necessary to achieve their aims. In managing the meaning of organizational situations in these ways, they can do much to shape patterns of corporate culture and subculture that will help them achieve desired aims and objectives.

Many organizational members are also keenly aware of the way in which theater—including physical settings, appearances, and styles of behavior—can add to their power, and many deserve organizational Oscars for their performances. We have all walked into senior executives' offices that exude power in terms of decor and layout, shouting out that someone of considerable influence works there. An executive's office is the stage on which that person performs and is often carefully organized in ways that help that performance. In one area we may find a formal desk with a thronelike chair where the executive plays authoritarian roles. In another we may find casual chairs around a coffee table, setting a more convivial scene. When one is summoned to such an office, one often senses the likely tone of the meeting according to where one is seated. If you are guided to a low-level chair facing a desk where the manager can physically look down and thus dominate you, you can almost be sure that you are in for a hard time. Situations often speak louder than words and do much to express and reproduce the power relations existing within an organization.

Appearances can also count for a great deal. For example, most people in an organization soon learn the rules of dress and other unwritten requirements for successful progress to higher ranks. In some organizations, it is possible to distinguish marketing people, accountants, or even those who work on a certain floor according to their choice of fashion and general demeanor. Many aspiring young executives quickly learn the value of carrying the *Wall Street Journal* to work and ensuring that it is always visible, even if they never actually manage to read it. Some people symbolize their activity with paper-strewn desks, and others demonstrate their control and mastery of their work with a desk where no trace of paper is ever seen. In organizational contexts, there is usually more to appearance than meets the eye.

Style also counts. It is amazing how you can symbolize power by being a couple of minutes late for that all-important meeting where everyone depends on your presence or how visibility in certain situations can enhance your status. For example, in many organizations, senior executives dramatize their presence at high-profile events but fade into the woodwork at low-status functions. It is reported that in the White House people often dramatize their access to the president by making sure they arrive at least half an hour early so that others can see that they are seeing the president. Access to the president is itself both a reflection and a source of power, but if others know that you have such access, it can usually be used to acquire even more power. Those who are aware of how symbolism can enhance power often spend a great deal of time dramatizing their work, using "impression management" to influence the systems of meaning surrounding them and their activities.

Finally, we must note the skills of "gamesmanship." The organizational game player comes in many forms. Sometimes, he is reckless and ruthless, "shooting from the hip," engaging in boardroom brawls, and never missing an opportunity to intimidate others. Other kinds of game players may be more crafty and low profile, shaping key impressions at every turn. In seeing organization—with its rewards of success, status, power, and influence—as a game to be played according to their own sets of unwritten rules, organizational game players often have a significant influence on the structure of power relations.

Gender and the Management of Gender Relations

It often makes a great deal of difference if you're a man or a woman! Many organizations are dominated by gender-related values that bias organizational life in favor of one sex over another. Thus, as many feminist writers have emphasized, organizations often segment opportunity structures and job markets in ways that enable men to achieve positions of prestige and power more easily than women. It is sometimes called the "glass ceiling" effect. Women can see opportunities at the top of their organizations, but the path is often blocked by gender biases. These biases also shape how organizational reality is created and sustained on a day-to-day basis. This is most obvious in situations of open discrimination and various forms of sexual harassment but often pervades the culture of an organization in a way that is much less visible.

Consider, for example, some of the links between gender stereotypes and traditional principles of organization. Exhibit 6.4 counterposes a series of characteristics that are often used to differentiate between male and female. The links between the male stereotype and the values that dominate many ideas about the nature of organization are striking. Organizations are often encouraged to be rational, analytical, strategic, decision-oriented, tough, and aggressive, and so are men. This has important implications for women who wish to operate in this kind of world, for insofar as they attempt to foster these values, they are often seen as breaking the traditional female stereotype in a way that opens them to criticism (e.g., for being "overly assertive" and "trying to play a male role"). Of course, in organizations that cultivate values that are closer to those of the female stereotype, women can have an advantage, reversing the traditional imbalance.

These and other gender biases are also found in the language, rituals, myths, stories, and other modes of symbolism that shape an organization's culture. General conversation and day-to-day ritual can serve to include or to exclude and is sometimes constructed to achieve this end. A lone man or woman can quickly feel outnumbered or "out on a limb" when others talk about matters that this individual cannot share or when language and jokes assume a derogatory form. Such people can miss important conversation by not being in the same locker room and can be subjected to all kinds of subtle degradation through the stories and myths that circulate on the organizational grapevine. All the factors shaping corporate culture discussed in Chapter 5 are relevant for understanding the gender realities constructed in an organization. They also identify the means through which a person can begin to counter and reshape the power relations thus produced.

The subtleties associated with gender often create different experiences of the same organizational situation and present many practical problems for the way men and women interact on a daily basis. Sometimes, the difficulties created are so significant that they give rise to conscious and unconscious strategies for "gender management."

Relations between men and women are frequently shaped by predefined stereotypes and images as to how they are expected to behave. Here are some of the common traits traditionally associated with being male and female in Western society:

The Male Stereotype	*The Female Stereotype*
Logical	Intuitive
Rational	Emotional
Aggressive	Submissive
Exploitative	Empathic
Strategic	Spontaneous
Independent	Nurturing
Competitive	Cooperative
"A leader and decision maker"	"A loyal supporter and follower"

Under the influence of the "gender revolution," these stereotypes are now in flux and transition.

Exhibit 6.4   Traditional Male and Female Stereotypes

Consider the following situation, drawn from research conducted by my colleague Deborah Sheppard:

Susan Jones is a marketing research manager in a male-dominated industry. She frequently has to give presentations to her male colleagues and feels a need to ensure that she "blends in" by managing her appearance and behavior so that conventional expectations and norms relating to sex roles are maintained. She strives to be "credible" while not overly challenging the status quo and monitors herself on a continuing basis. She is particularly careful not to act in a masculine way, and much of her "impression management" rests in avoiding giving offense because she is a woman. In her oral presentations she tries to demonstrate competence while avoiding being assertive. She stands in the same place rather than engaging in the more aggressive act of walking around, even if the presentation lasts three hours. She attempts to get her ideas across gently. She does not raise her voice, finding other ways of emphasizing critical points (e.g., using overheads) but being sure never to use a pointer. She avoids wearing pants or three-piece suits with a vest and is always careful to balance her more formal attire with a feminine blouse.

Susan Jones works in a male-dominated reality and spends a lot of her time living on other people's terms. Ms. Jones knows exactly what she is doing: She feels that to succeed in her organization she must try to fit in as best she can.

Many people would challenge her style of gender management and suggest that she should be more assertive and confront and change the status quo. Many women in organizations do this very effectively or, like their male counterparts, adopt a variety of other roles for managing gender relations, such as those illustrated in Exhibit 6.5.

But the point about the case for present purposes rests in the fact that it shows how life in organizations is often guided by subtle and not so subtle power relations that guide attention and behavior in one direction rather than in another. To do a good job in a male-dominated organization, Susan Jones has to put much greater effort into accomplishing everyday reality than her male colleagues do.

The gender balance in many organizations is changing rapidly as gender and equal opportunity issues hit the political "hot list." Also, as discussed in Chapter 5, the shift from hierarchical to flat, networked forms of organization is creating a major political shift that favors what have been traditionally seen as female styles of management. The ability to weave "webs of inclusion," build consensus, mobilize insight and intuition, and pay more attention to "process" than "product" are all part of the shifting balance.

As recently as the 1980s, the best advice to women wishing to succeed in organizational life was to "fit in" and beat men at their own game. For example, Betty Harragan's influential *Games That Mother Never Taught You* in effect offered a guide for playing the male-dominated game. Many of the most prominent female leaders have also reflected skill in succeeding within the male archetype. For example, Margaret Thatcher, one of the strongest political leaders of the twentieth century, has been openly and only half-jokingly described as "the best man the British Conservative Party has ever had"—and that includes the wartime leadership of Sir Winston Churchill, a major hero and role model for Thatcher.

Now, a lot of the advice given women is to change the rules of the game. Switch the archetype. In a networked as opposed to hierarchical world, new skills and competencies are needed. The characteristics of the female archetype have much to offer here.

Gender politics are in a state of flux. Everyone's power is shaped to some degree by his or her position on the gender continuum, whether male, female, or somewhere in between. We shall have much more to say about the nature of gender issues in Chapter 7, where we discuss the role of sexuality and the patriarchal family in corporate life.

As one looks around the organizational world it is possible to identify different ways in which people manage gender relations. Here are a variety of popular strategies. Each can be successful or unsuccessful, according to the persons and situations involved.

Some Female Strategies	
Queen Elizabeth I	Rule with a firm hand, surrounding oneself as far as possible by submissive men. Margaret Thatcher provides a modern example.
The First Lady	Be content to exercise power behind the throne: a tactic adopted by many "corporate wives" such as executive secretaries and special assistants.
The Invisible Woman	Adopt a low profile and try and blend with one's surroundings, exercising influence in whatever ways one can.
The Great Mother	Consolidate power through caring and nurturing.
The Liberationist	Play rough and give as good as you get; be outspoken and always make a stand in favor of the role of women.
The Amazon	Be a leader of women. This style is especially successful when one can build a powerful coalition by placing like-minded women in influential positions.
Delilah	Use the powers of seduction to win over key figures in male-dominated organizations.
Joan of Arc	Use the power of a shared cause and mission to transcend the fact that you are a woman and gain widespread male support.
The Daughter	Find a "father figure" prepared to act as sponsor and mentor.
Some Male Strategies	
The Warrior	Frequently adopted by busy executives caught up in fighting corporate battles. Often used to bind women into roles as committed supporters.
The Father	Often used to win the support of younger women searching for a mentor.
King Henry VIII	Use of absolute power to get what one wants, attracting and discarding female supporters according to their usefulness.
The Playboy	Use of sex appeal (both real and imagined) to win support and favor from female colleagues. A role often adopted by executives lacking a more stable power base.

Exhibit 6.5   Some Strategies for the Management of Gender Relations

(Continued)

Exhibit 6.5 (Continued)

The Jock	Based on various kinds of "display behavior" intended to attract and convince women of one's corporate prowess. Often used to develop administration and support from women in subordinate or lateral positions.
The Little Boy	Often used to try to "get one's way" in difficult situations, especially in relation to female co-workers and subordinates. The role may take many forms—for example, the "angry little boy" who throws a temper tantrum to create a stir and force action; the "frustrated or whining little boy" who tries to cultivate sympathy; and the "cute little boy" who tries to curry favor, especially when he's in a jam.
The Good Friend	Often used to develop partnerships with female colleagues, either as confidants or as key sources of information and advice.
The Chauvinist Pig	Often used by men who feel threatened by the presence of women. Characterized by use of various "degradation" rituals that seek to undermine the status of women and their contributions.

Structural Factors That
Define the Stage of Action

One of the surprising things one discovers in talking with members of an organization is that hardly anyone will admit to having any real power. Even chief executives often say that they feel highly constrained, that they have few significant options in decision making, and that the power they wield is more apparent than real. Everyone usually feels in some degree hemmed in either by forces within the organization or in terms of requirements posed by the environment. Given the numerous and varied sources of power already discussed, these attitudes present us with a paradox. How is it that there can be so many sources of power, yet so many feelings of powerlessness?

One possible answer is that access to power is so open, wide, and varied that to a large extent power relations become more or less balanced. Whereas some people may be able to amass considerable personal power, this is offset by the power of others, and even the powerful thus feel constrained. We will give more attention to this "pluralist" view later in the chapter.

Another possible explanation rests in the idea that it is important to distinguish between the surface manifestations and the deep structure of power. This view is linked with perspectives on organization to be explored in Chapters 8 and 9. It suggests that while organizations and society may at any one time comprise a variety of political actors drawing on a variety of power bases, the stage on which they engage in their various kinds of power play is defined by economics, race, class relationships, and other deep-structural factors shaping the social epoch in which they live.

This view summons the idea that organization and society must be understood from a historical perspective. To illustrate, let us examine an analogy from the natural world. Suppose that we are considering the ecology of a river valley. We can understand that ecology in terms of the "power relations" between the various species of tree, shrub, fern, and undergrowth and the soil from which they draw sustenance. But these power relations are underpinned by the basic structure of the river valley, as determined by the impact of glaciation millennia before. One species of tree may be more powerful and thus dominate another, but the conditions of this domination are structurally determined.

Applying this analogy to organizational life, we see how underlying structures or logics underpin power relations. A manager may control an important budget, have access to key information, and be excellent at impression management and be a powerful person for all these reasons. But his ability to draw on and use these sources of power is underpinned by various structural factors, such as intercorporate power plays or an impending merger that will eliminate his job. Many powerful managers have been the victims of downsizing. Similarly, a factory worker may possess considerable power to disrupt production as a result of his or her role on an assembly line. Knowing the way in which production can be disrupted is the immediate source of power, but the ultimate source is the structure of productive activity that makes such power significant. A black manager may be extremely skilled in mobilizing ideas and valued resources, only to find himself blocked by racial prejudice.

These considerations encourage us to see people as agents or carriers of power relations embedded in the wider structure of society. As such, people may be no more than semiautonomous pawns moving themselves around in a game where they can learn to understand the rules but have no power to change them. This phenomenon may explain why even the powerful often feel that they have little real choice as to how they should behave. For example, a chief executive may face some of these wider rules of the game in terms of the economic conditions that influence the survival of her organization. Insofar as she wishes the organization to survive, she may perceive herself as having no real options about what must be done to ensure its survival.

This view of the deep structure of power leads us to recognize the importance of factors such as economics, race, and class relations in determining the roles we occupy within organizations and hence the kind of opportunity structure and power to which we have access. It draws attention to the way educational systems and other processes of socialization shape basic elements of culture. It draws attention to the logic of capital accumulation that shapes the structure of industry, levels of employment, patterns of economic growth, and the ownership and distribution of wealth. We will consider these underlying factors in more detail in the following chapters. They define the stage on which organizational members act and moderate the influence of the other sources of power to which one has access.

The Power One Already Has

Power is a route to power, and one can often use power to acquire more. The biographies of many consummate politicians illustrate this fact. For example, politicians within organizations and in public life frequently tie the use of power to informal IOU agreements where help or favor begs its return in kind at a later date. Thus a manager may use his or her power to support X in a struggle with Y, knowing that when X is successful it will be possible to call upon similar (if not more) support from X: "Remember last July. Your future was on the line, and I risked everything to help out. Surely you'll now do a small favor for me?" Often, the exchanges are more subtle than this, but the message is essentially the same. Power used in a judicious way takes the form of an investment and, like money, often becomes useful on a rainy day.

It is also possible to take advantage of the honey-pot characteristic of power. The presence of power attracts and sustains people who wish to feed off that power and actually serves to increase the power holder's power. In the hope of gaining favor, people may begin to lend the power holder uninvited support or buy into that person's way of thinking to show that they're on the same side. When the time comes for the power holder to recognize this interest with active support, people then actually become indebted to the power holder, with all kinds of IOUs coming into a play. Power, like honey, is a perpetual source of sustenance and attraction among fellow bees.

Finally, there is the empowering aspect of power. When people experience progress or success, they are often energized to achieve further progress and success. In this way, a sense of power can actually lead to more power. This perspective has received considerable attention in the 1990s as a result of the "New Age" human potential movement, which stresses how individuals have access to all kinds of personal power that can be unleashed by feeling powerful.

The approach emphasizes the importance of developing proactive "Can Do!" mind-sets that lead people to see and act on their world in a way that will produce the results they desire. The process is most evident in situations where people who believe that they have absolutely no power or ability fight and win a small victory or achieve unbelievable things, like running over hot coals or bungee-cord jumping from the top of a cliff. The experience of success becomes a transforming force as they realize that one victory can lead to another. Many organizations and communities have been transformed by this kind of experience in quite unexpected ways.

The Ambiguity of Power

Although we have identified numerous sources of power, which are probably far from being exhaustive, it is difficult to tie down exactly what the phenomenon is. We know that it has a great deal to do with asymmetrical patterns of dependence whereby one person or unit becomes dependent on another in an unbalanced way, and that it also has a great deal to do with an ability to define the reality of others in ways that lead them to perceive and enact relations that one desires. However, it is far from clear whether power should be understood as an interpersonal behavioral phenomenon or as the manifestation of deep-seated structural factors. It is not clear whether people have and exercise power as autonomous human beings or are simply carriers of power relations that are the product of more fundamental forces. These and other issues—such as whether power is a resource or a relationship, whether there is a distinction between power and processes of societal domination and control, whether power is ultimately linked to the control of capital and the structuring of the world economy, or whether it is important to distinguish between actual manifest power and potential power—continue to be the subject of considerable interest and debate among those interested in the sociology of organization.

These problems aside, however, it is clear that our discussion of possible sources and uses of power provides us with an inventory of ideas through which we can begin to decode power plays and political dynamics in organizational contexts. Like our analysis of interests and our discussion of conflict, it provides us with a working tool with which we can analyze organizational politics and, if we so wish, orient our action in a politicized way.

Managing Pluralist Organizations

The image of organizations developed above reflects what is sometimes known as a "pluralist" frame of reference, for it emphasizes the plural nature of the interests, conflicts, and sources of power that shape organizational life. The term *pluralism* is used in political science to characterize idealized kinds of liberal democracies where potentially authoritarian tendencies are held in check by the free interplay of interest groups that have a stake in government. The pluralist vision is of a society where different groups bargain and compete for a share in the balance of power and use their influence to realize Aristotle's ideal of politics: a negotiated order that creates unity out of diversity.

This pluralist philosophy stands in contrast with an older organic or "unitary" frame of reference. The unitary view pictures society as an integrated whole where the interests of individual and society are synonymous. This unitary view emphasizes the sovereignty of the state and the importance of individuals subordinating themselves in the service of society as a means of realizing and satisfying their true interests and the common good. It is an ideology that has grown in importance along with the development of the nation-state and the idea that individuals should place the interests of the state above all else.

The pluralist view also contrasts with the so-called "radical" frame of reference, which views society as comprising antagonistic class interests characterized by deep-rooted social and political cleavages and held together as much by coercion as by consent. This radical view, influenced by a Marxian perspective, suggests that the interests of disadvantaged groups can be furthered in a substantial way only through radical changes in the structure of society that displace those currently in power.

These three frames of reference (Exhibit 6.6) have considerable relevance for understanding organizations and the ideologies that shape management practice. Some organizations tend to function like unitary teams, others as vibrant political systems with the kind of pluralist politics discussed earlier in this chapter, and others as battlefields where rival groups engage in ongoing warfare.

Organization can be understood as mini-states where the relationship between individual and society is paralleled by the relationship between individual and organization. The unitary, pluralist, and radical views of organization can be characterized in the following terms:

	Unitary	Pluralist	Radical
Interests	Places emphasis on the achievement of common objectives. The organization is viewed as being united under the umbrella of common goals and striving toward their achievement in the manner of a well-integrated team.	Places emphasis on the diversity of individual and group interests. The organization is regarded as a loose coalition with just a passing interest in the formal goals of the organization.	Places emphasis on the oppositional nature of contradictory "class" interests. The organization is viewed as a battleground where rival forces (e.g., management and unions) strive for the achievement of largely incompatible ends.
Conflict	Regards conflict as a rare and transient phenomenon that can be removed through appropriate managerial action. Where it does arise it is usually attributed to the activities of deviants and troublemakers.	Regards conflict as an inherent and ineradicable characteristic of organizational affairs and stresses its potentially positive or functional aspects.	Regards organizational conflict as inevitable and as part of a wider class conflict that will eventually change the whole structure of society. It is recognized that conflict may be suppressed and thus often exists as a latent rather than manifest characteristic of both organizations and society.

Exhibit 6.6   Unitary, Pluralist, and Radical Frames of Reference

(Continued)

Exhibit 6.6 (Continued)

	Unitary	Pluralist	Radical
Power	Largely ignores the role of power in organizational life. Concepts such as authority, leadership, and control tend to be preferred means of describing the managerial prerogative of guiding the organization toward the achievement of common interests.	Regards power as a crucial variable. Power is the medium through which conflicts of interests are alleviated and resolved. The organization is viewed as a plurality of power holders drawing their power from a plurality of sources.	Regards power as a key feature of organization, but a phenomenon that is unequally distributed and follows class divisions. Power relations in organizations are viewed as reflections of power relations in society at large and as closely linked to wider processes of social control (e.g., control of economic power, the legal system, and education).

SOURCE: Based on Burrell and Morgan (1979: 204–388).

Unitary characteristics are most often found in organizations that have developed a cohesive culture based on respect for management's right to manage, especially those that have a long and continuous history of paternalistic management. Organizations where there are sharp racial or class distinctions between different categories of employee, where there are strong divisions between blue- and white-collar workers such as those found in many heavy industries, or where there has been a history of conflict between management and labor, tend to reflect the characteristics of the radical model. Organizations primarily made up of white-collar staff, particularly where there is room for employees to acquire considerable autonomy, often tend to fit the pluralist model. Sometimes, the three models apply to different parts of the same organization. It is often a salutary experience for a person to ask, "Which frame of reference applies to my organization?" By using the model presented in Exhibit 6.6 to assess the general pattern of interests, conflicts, and power, one can often gain a useful initial grasp on the character of the political system with which one is dealing.

Besides serving as analytical tools, the three frames of reference often serve as organizational ideologies. Thus, managers or employees may encourage the idea that "we're a team, let's work together" or that "we all want different things, so let's talk about and resolve our differences so we can all gain" or that "we're at war, I don't trust you, so we'll have to fight it out." Clearly, the ideology in use will determine the character of the organization. If a manager believes that he or she is managing a team and can persuade employees to believe that this is the case, harmonious cooperation with a three musketeers' attitude of "all for one and one for all" may gain ground. If the radical frame of reference provides the major context for interpreting organizational events, then a battle-torn organizational life is almost certain. These ideologies may emerge and be used as a management tool as a means of shaping the organization to conform with the image that best suits specific ends. This, after all, is the role of ideology in organizations, as in society.

Each frame of reference leads to a different approach to management. If one believes that one is managing a team, one tends to expect and demand that people rally around common objectives and to respect "the right of the manager to manage and the duty of employees to obey." Employees are expected to perform the roles for which they have been appointed. No less, no more. Conflict is seen as a source of trouble and as an unwanted intrusion. Hence, the orientation of the unitary manager is usually to eliminate or suppress conflict whenever possible. Given this ideology, there is no room to recognize or accept the kind of organizational politics discussed earlier in this chapter. Unitary managers tend to see formal authority as the only legitimate source of power and thus rarely acknowledge the right or ability of others to influence the management process. Unions are seen as a scourge, and the pursuit of individual interest through use of different kinds of power is viewed as a form of malpractice.

Although this unitary view may seem somewhat narrow and old-fashioned, it is often extremely pervasive and influential and is supported by many theories of management. For example, theories based on the mechanical and organismic metaphors discussed in Chapters 2 and 3 often encourage this unitary view, emphasizing the importance of designing or adapting the organization to achieve common goals. Hence, they provide primary resources for the unitary manager who wishes to believe that an enterprise *ought* to possess the unity and shared sense of direction that we find in carefully designed machines or in organisms in the natural world. The team idea is often much more attractive than the idea of a somewhat chaotic political system that wishes to move in many directions at once. Hence, many managers often unconsciously take refuge in this team ideology rather than deal with political realities.

Also, unitary ideology can serve as a resource for a crafty manager who recognizes that espousing the attitude that "we're a team" may help create unity among divergent elements. By identifying conflict as a *source* of trouble, the manager may be able to unite the rest of the organization against those who are key actors in the trouble. This tactic is often used to unite employees against individuals or groups who are seen as disruptive elements in an otherwise harmonious and rational enterprise. The unitary frame of reference is a powerful ideology among the public at large, and managers can often use this public ideology as a strategy for mobilizing support and achieving control in the pluralist or radical power plays that characterize their organization. The fact that managers who at times espouse the unitary ideology may not actually believe in that ideology themselves can make it difficult to determine which ideology has a controlling influence in an organization. However, the person who has an awareness of the role played by rhetoric and espoused ideology has a means of understanding when this form of power play is occurring. The unitary manager is often a pluralist in unitary clothing!

The hallmark of the pluralist manager is that he or she accepts the inevitability of organizational politics, recognizing that because individuals have different interests, aims, and objectives, employees are likely to use their membership in the organization for their own ends. Management is thus focused on balancing and coordinating the interests of organizational members so that they can work together within the constraints set by the organization's formal goals, which really reflect the interests of shareholders and others with ultimate control over the fate of the organization. The pluralist manager recognizes that conflict and power plays can serve both positive and negative functions; hence, the main concern is to manage conflict in ways that will benefit the overall organization or, more selfishly, in ways that will promote his or her own interests within the organization. The pluralist manager is, after all, not politically neutral. He or she is an active player in the politics of organization and uses the roles of organizational power broker and conflict manager to maximum effect.

For example, the pluralist manager may seek ways of using conflict as an energizing force to counteract staleness and keep people "on their toes." Conflict can encourage self-evaluation and challenge conventional wisdom. It may cause a certain degree of pain within an organization but can also do much to stimulate learning and change. It can help an organization keep abreast of a changing environment and be a source of constant innovation.

This is particularly true in group decision-making situations, where the absence of conflict often produces conformity and "groupthink." The existence of rival points of view and of different aims and objectives can do much to improve the quality of decision making. Conflict can also serve as an important release valve that gets rid of pent-up pressures. It facilitates processes of mutual accommodation through the exploration and resolution of differences, often in a way that preempts more subversive or explosive resolutions. Somewhat paradoxically, conflict can at times serve to stimulate change and at other times help maintain the status quo.

One of the main tasks of the pluralist manager is to find ways of maintaining just the right level of conflict. Too much conflict can immobilize an organization by channeling the efforts of its members into unproductive activities, but too little conflict may encourage complacency and lethargy. In the former case, the manager may need to employ conflict resolution techniques or reorient conflict in more productive directions. In the latter he or she may need to find ways of promoting appropriate conflicts, often by making hidden conflicts overt, or perhaps by actually creating conflict. Although this may at times help to enliven the atmosphere and performance of an organization, it can also be perceived as a form of unwarranted manipulation, with disastrous results for relations between managers and their employees.

In approaching the task of conflict management, the pluralist manager is faced with a choice of styles, which hinge on the extent to which he or she wishes to engage in assertive or cooperative behavior (Exhibit 6.7). Although a manager may have a preferred style, all the different styles are likely to be appropriate at one time or another (Exhibit 6.8). Even in the realm of politics, contingency theory thus has an important place. On some occasions, the manager may wish to buy time through various kinds of avoidance behavior. On others, head-on competition, collaboration, accommodation, or compromise may prove more effective. While some managers prefer to battle it out in a way that all can see, others prefer more subtle fly-fishing techniques that depend on an intimate knowledge of the situation and the skillful use of the right bait at the right time for the right people. The choice of the style and tactics to be used in a given situation is crucial, but unfortunately it cannot be explored in detail here.

Regardless of style, successful pluralist management always depends on an ability to read developing situations. The manager must be able to analyze interests, understand conflicts, and explore power relations so that situations can be brought under a measure of control. This requires a keen ability to be aware of conflict-prone areas, to read the latent tendencies and pressures beneath the surface actions of organizational life, and to initiate appropriate responses. In general, the manager can intervene to change perceptions, behaviors, and structures in ways that will help redefine or redirect conflicts to serve constructive ends.

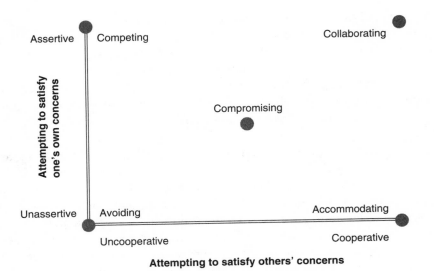

The five styles can be characterized in terms of the following kinds of behavior:

Avoiding:
- Ignoring conflicts and hoping that they'll go away.
- Putting problems under consideration or on hold.
- Invoking slow procedures to stifle the conflict.
- Using secrecy to avoid confrontation.
- Appealing to bureaucratic rules as a source of conflict resolution.

Compromise:
- Negotiating.
- Looking for deals and trade-offs.
- Finding satisfactory or acceptable solutions.

Competition:
- Creating win-lose situations.
- Using rivalry.
- Using power plays to get one's ends.
- Forcing submission.

Accommodation:
- Giving way.
- Submitting and complying.

Collaboration:
- Problem-solving stance.
- Confronting differences and sharing ideas and information.
- Searching for integrative solutions.
- Finding situations where all can win.
- Seeing problems and conflicts as challenging.

Exhibit 6.7   Conflict Management: A Question of Style

SOURCE: Adapted from Thomas (1976: 900). Used by permission of Marvin Dunnette.

Situations in which to use the five conflict-handling modes, as reported by twenty-eight chief executives

Competing

1. When quick, decisive action is vital (e.g., emergencies).
2. On important issues where unpopular actions need implementing—e.g., cost cutting, enforcing unpopular rules, discipline.
3. On issues vital to company welfare when you know you're right.
4. Against people who take advantage of noncompetitive behavior.

Collaborating

1. To find an integrative solution when both sets of concerns are too important to be compromised.
2. When your objective is to learn.
3. To merge insights from people with different perspectives.
4. To gain commitment by incorporating concerns into a consensus.
5. To work through feelings that have interfered with a relationship.

Compromising

1. When goals are important, but not worth the effort or potential disruption of more assertive modes.
2. When opponents with equal power are committed to mutually exclusive goals.
3. To achieve temporary settlements to complex issues.
4. To arrive at expedient solutions under time pressure.

5. As a backup when collaboration or competition is unsuccessful.

Avoiding

1. When an issue is trivial, or more important issues are pressing.
2. When you perceive no chance of satisfying your concerns.
3. When potential disruption outweighs the benefits of resolution.
4. To let people cool down and regain perspective.
5. When gathering information supersedes immediate decision.
6. When others can resolve the conflict more effectively.
7. When issues seem tangential or symptomatic of other issues.

Accommodating

1. When you find you are wrong—to allow a better position to be heard, to learn, and to show your reasonableness.
2. When issues are more important to others than to yourself—to satisfy others and maintain cooperation.
3. To build social credits for later issues.
4. To minimize loss when you are outmatched and losing.
5. When harmony and stability are especially important.
6. To allow subordinates to develop by learning from mistakes.

Exhibit 6.8   When to Use the Five Conflict-Handling Styles

SOURCE: Thomas (1977: 487). © 1977 *Academy of Management Review*. Reprinted with permission of the *Academy of Management Review* and the author.

Many organizational conflicts can be fruitfully resolved through pluralist means, but not all. This is particularly true in radicalized organizations where conflicts between managers and employees run deep, and there are no "win-win" solutions. Here, issues often have to be negotiated in fairly formal terms if progress is to be made, or else grind their way to a bitter end through the raw interplay of structural forces embedded in the economic and industrial structure of society itself. Disputes leading to head-on clashes between management and unions, such as those relating to the replacement of skilled employees by automation or the closing and relocation of plants, are obvious examples. The underlying power relations and bitterness between the parties involved often encourage a winner-take-all or fight-to-the-death attitude that makes compromise extremely difficult, often leading to painful outcomes such as unemployment or bankruptcy of the organizations involved. Even though the intransigence that often accompanies such disputes can seem senseless to outside observers, it is intelligible in terms of the basic premises on which the radical frame of reference builds. We will examine these in Chapter 9.

Strengths and Limitations of the Political Metaphor

One of the curious features of organizational life is that although many people know they are surrounded by organizational politics they rarely come out and say so. One ponders politics in private moments or discusses it off the record with close confidants and friends or in the context of one's own political maneuverings with members of one's coalition. One knows that manager A is pushing for a particular project because it will serve her own aims or that B got a particular job because of his associations with C, but one can rarely say so. It breaks all the rules of organizational etiquette to impute private motive to organizational acts, which are supposed to serve the organization's interests above all else. For these and other reasons, including the fact that privatization and secrecy can serve political ends, organizational politics becomes a taboo subject, which at times makes it extremely difficult for organization members to deal with this crucially important aspect of organizational reality.

The discussion presented in this chapter helps us accept the reality of politics as an inevitable feature of organizational life and, following the Aristotelian view, to recognize its constructive role in the creation of social order. The political metaphor encourages us to see how *all* organizational activity is interest based and to evaluate all aspects of organizational functioning with this in mind. Organizational goals, structure, technology, job design, leadership style, and other seemingly formal aspects of organizational functioning have a political dimension as well as the more obvious political power plays and conflicts. The model of interests, conflict, and power developed in this chapter provides a practical and systematic means of understanding the relationship between politics and organization and emphasizes the key role of power in determining political outcomes. The metaphors considered in earlier chapters tend to underplay the relation between power and organization. The political metaphor overcomes this deficiency, placing a knowledge of the role and use of power at the center of organizational analysis.

The metaphor also helps explode the myth of organizational rationality. Organizations may pursue goals and stress the importance of rational, efficient, and effective management. But rational, efficient, and effective for whom? Whose goals are being pursued? What interests are being served? Who benefits? The political metaphor emphasizes that organizational goals may be rational for some people's interest but not for others. An organization embraces many rationalities because rationality is always interest based and thus changes according to the perspective from which it is viewed. Rationality is always political. No one is neutral in the management of organizations—even managers! They, like others, use the organization as a legitimizing umbrella under which to pursue a variety of task, career, and extramural interests. Like others, they often use the idea of rationality as a resource for pursuing political agendas—justifying actions that suit their personal aspirations in terms that appear rational from an organizational standpoint. The idea of rationality is as much a resource to be used in organizational politics as a descriptive term describing the aims of organization.

These considerations suggest a reevaluation of the ideological significance of the concept of rationality. Above all else, the idea of rationality seems to be invoked as a myth to overcome the contradictions inherent in the fact that an organization is simultaneously a system of competition and a system of cooperation. The emphasis on rationality attempts to bind together a political system that, because of the diversity of interests on which it builds, always has a latent tendency to move in diverse directions and sometimes to fall apart.

This leads us to another strength of the political metaphor: that it helps us find a way of overcoming the limitations of the idea that organizations are functionally integrated systems. As will be recalled from discussion in Chapter 3, much organization theory has built on the assumption that organizations, like machines or organisms, are unified systems that bind part and whole in a quest for survival. The political metaphor suggests otherwise, pointing to the disintegrative strains and tensions that stem from the diverse sets of interests on which organization builds.

The strains have become increasingly apparent with the organizational "downsizing movement" of the 1990s. Organizations that have promoted the unitary ideology that "we're a family" or "we're a team" have found themselves firing team members in order to cut costs. If team members are so dispensable, is the organization really a team? Or is the team idea merely used to promote a sense of unity? Is the more fundamental reality that of diverse and often incompatible interests? Genuinely pluralist organizations recognize that a high degree of integration and commitment is problematic and ultimately depends on the degree to which people *really* need each other. In such circumstances it is much better to think about the organization as a coalition of changing interests and manage it that way than to pretend that it has more integrated properties.

Many organizations are more likely to have the characteristics of loosely coupled systems, where semiautonomous parts strive to maintain a degree of independence while working under the name and framework provided by the organization, than the characteristics of a completely integrated organism. In organizations where a desire for autonomy or subunit goals becomes more important than the aims of the wider organization, schismatic tendencies may be a constant feature and transforming force. Such organizations usually spawn new organizations when key members or subunits spin off into entities of their own. Or different elements may end up fighting and destroying each other. An analysis of organizational politics in terms of the interplay among rival interests, conflicts, and sources of power can help us understand and manage these forces.

Another strength of the metaphor is the fact that it politicizes our understanding of human behavior in organizations. We may not agree with Nietzsche that humans have a will to power, mastery, and control, or with writers who suggest that politics and game playing are fundamental to human nature, but we are obliged to recognize that tensions between private and organizational interests provide an incentive for individuals to act politically. Whereas some people view such action as a manifestation of the selfish or "dark" side of human personality, the analysis presented here suggests that there is usually a structural as well as a motivational basis. Even the most altruistic persons may find their action following a political script in the sense that their orientation to organizational life is influenced by the conflicting sets of interests that they bring to issues of immediate concern. Although some people are no doubt more political in orientation than others, employing gamesmanship and other forms of wheeling and dealing as a basic strategy, the enactments of everyone are, at least in part, of a political nature. The political metaphor encourages us to recognize how and why the organizational actor is a political actor and to understand the political significance of the patterns of meaning enacted in corporate culture and subculture.

Finally, the metaphor also encourages us to recognize the sociopolitical implications of different kinds of organization and the roles that organizations play in society. Recall the quotation that opened this chapter. Should people be prepared to surrender their democratic rights when they begin work each morning? Is it possible to have a democratic society if the majority of the population spend their working lives obeying the commands of others? Should organizations be allowed to play politics by lobbying in an attempt to influence legislation and other government policies? Should there be closer or more distant relations between business and government? The political metaphor brings questions such as these to the center of our attention. Although it is common to draw strict divisions between organization theory and political science, it is clear that business and organization is always to some extent political and that the political implications of organization need to be systematically explored.

Against these strengths of the metaphor, it is necessary to identify a number of important limitations. The first can be framed as a potential danger. When we analyze organizations in terms of the political metaphor it is almost always possible to see signs of political activity. This can lead to an increased politicization of the organization, for when we understand organizations as political systems we are more likely to behave politically in relation to what we see. We begin to see politics everywhere and to look for hidden agendas even where there are none. For this reason, the metaphor must be used with caution. There is a very real danger that its use may generate cynicism and mistrust in situations where there was none before. In a course that I teach on the nature of organizational politics I usually begin by warning my students that by the second or third week there is a danger that they will be looking for hidden motives everywhere, even wondering whether a colleague's innocent offer to buy the coffee is really a political act. Although at first my warning is seen as a joke, by week two or three its gravity and significance usually hit home. Under the influence of a political mode of understanding, everything becomes political. The analysis of interests, conflicts, and power easily gives rise to a Machiavellian interpretation that suggests everyone is trying to outwit and outmaneuver everyone else. Rather than use the political metaphor to generate new insights and understandings that can help us deal with divergent interests, we often reduce the metaphor to a tool to be used to advance our own personal interests.

This kind of manipulative stance is reflected in many contemporary writings on the politics of organization, which have a tendency to emphasize the cynical, selfish, ruthless, get-ahead-at-all-costs mentality that so often turns organizations into corporate jungles. These writings "sell" the insights of the metaphor through statements such as "Find out where the real power is and use it," "Understand and harvest the grapevine," "Win through intimidation," "Protect your job by knowing your enemies," or "Seize power and wield clout." This use of the metaphor breeds mistrust and encourages the idea that organization involves a zero-sum game where there must be winners and losers. There may be a measure of truth in this, in that many organizations are dominated by competitive relations, yet the effect is to reduce the scope for genuine openness and collaboration. This kind of thinking loses sight of the more general implications of the political metaphor, such as the Aristotelian vision of politics as a constructive force in the creation of social order, and the possibility of using political principles to examine and restructure the relationship between organization and society.

A final limitation of the metaphor, and one to which I have briefly alluded, relates to the assumptions of pluralism. Is it realistic to presume a plurality of interests and a plurality of power holders? Are more radical organization theorists correct in seeing class, racial, and other social divisions as primary forces defining unequal and antagonistic structures of interest and power?

A strong case can be made for the idea that the interests of individuals or small coalitions may best be served if they recognize affinities of a "class" kind and act in a unified manner. Such is they logic of trade unionism, although the trade union movement has fragmented along sectionalist rather than class lines. A strong case can also be made for the idea that, although everyone has access to sources of power, ultimate power rests with the people or forces that are able to define the stage of action on which the game of politics is played. From a radical standpoint, pluralist power may be more apparent than real. Ultimately, some people have much more power than others. These considerations, which will be examined in more detail in Chapters 8 and 9, suggest that pluralist politics may be restricted to the resolution of marginal, narrow, and superficial issues and may fail to take account of the structural forces that shape the nature of those issues. As a result, the political metaphor may overstate the power and importance of the individual and underplay the system dynamics that determine what becomes political and how politics occurs.

7

Exploring Plato's Cave

Organizations as Psychic Prisons

Human beings have a knack for getting trapped in webs of their own creation. In this chapter we will examine some of the ways this occurs by exploring the idea of organizations as psychic prisons. This metaphor joins the idea that organizations are ultimately created and sustained by conscious and unconscious processes, with the notion that people can actually become imprisoned in or confined by the images, ideas, thoughts, and actions to which these processes give rise. The metaphor encourages us to understand that while organizations may be socially constructed realities, these constructions are often attributed an existence and power of their own that allow them to exercise a measure of control over their creators.

The idea of a psychic prison was first explored in Plato's *The Republic* in the famous allegory of the cave where Socrates addresses the relations among appearance, reality, and knowledge. The allegory pictures an underground cave with its mouth open toward the light of a blazing fire. Within the cave are people chained so that they cannot move. They can see only the cave wall directly in front of them. This is illuminated by the light of the fire, which throws shadows of people and objects onto the wall. The cave dwellers equate the shadows with reality, naming them, talking about them, and even linking sounds from outside the cave with the movements on the wall. Truth and reality for the prisoners rest in this shadowy world, because they have no knowledge of any other.

However, as Socrates relates, if one of the inhabitants were allowed to leave the cave, he would realize that the shadows are just reflections of a more complex reality and that the knowledge and perceptions of his fellow cave dwellers are distorted and flawed. If he were then to return to the cave, he would never be able to live in the old way, since for him the world would be a very different place. No doubt he would find difficulty in accepting his confinement and would pity the plight of his fellows. However, if he were to try and share his new knowledge with them, he would probably be ridiculed for his views. For the prisoners, the familiar images of the cave would be much more meaningful than a world they had never seen. Moreover, as the person espousing the new knowledge would now no longer be able to function with conviction in relation to the shadows, his fellow inmates would likely view the world outside as a dangerous place, something to be avoided. The experience could actually lead them to tighten their grip on their familiar way of seeing.

In this chapter we will use this image of a psychic prison to explore some of the ways in which organizations and their members become trapped by constructions of reality that, at best, give an imperfect grasp on the world. We will start by examining how people in organizations can become trapped by favored ways of thinking. We will then explore how organizations can become trapped by unconscious processes that lend organization a hidden significance. As we shall see, the perspective puts familiar patterns in a fresh light and contributes much to our understanding of why people and organizations often find it so difficult to change.

The Trap of Favored Ways of Thinking

Consider the following examples:

Following the OPEC oil crisis of 1973 the Japanese automobile industry began to make massive inroads on the North American market. Caught up in the mind-set of the American way of producing cars, the large U.S. manufacturers were completely ill equipped to meet the

Japanese challenge. For years they had taken their superior resources, technical competence, and skills in engineering and marketing as a given. Oriented to the large-car market and kept alive by annual model changes, the large firms ignored the potential of small, fuel-efficient cars. The myopia allowed the Japanese to capture a stronghold on their traditional market base.

A similar pattern can be observed in the computer industry where IBM established a dominant position in the 1970s and early 1980s. The IBM view of the world was dominated by "hardware" and the development of large powerful computer systems. It was a view that blocked out the possibility of a computer industry driven by software and networks of "PCs." The myopia created the opportunity for Bill Gates's Microsoft and other organizations to create a world completely at odds with the one in which IBM wanted to live.

In times of change it is possible to look at almost any industry and find once successful firms struggling to survive. In 1982, Tom Peters and Robert Waterman wrote about excellent companies such as IBM. By the 1990s, many were struggling. Their particular style of excellence had become a trap that prevented them from thinking in new ways and from transforming themselves to meet new challenges.

In his book *The Icarus Paradox*, Danny Miller offers a comprehensive analysis of some of the reasons why this occurs, arguing that organizations can get caught in vicious circles whereby victories and strengths become weaknesses leading to their downfall. Icarus was the figure in Greek mythology who, flying with his artificial wax wings, soared so close to the sun that the wings melted, whereupon he plunged to his death. The power created through the wings ultimately led to his downfall. In a similar way, strong corporate cultures can become pathological. Powerful visions of the future can lead to blind spots. Ways of seeing become ways of not seeing. All the forces that help people and their organizations create the shared systems of meaning that allow them to negotiate their world in an orderly way, can become constraints that prevent them from acting in other ways.

Communications theorist Marshall McLuhan noted that the last thing a fish is likely to discover is the water it is swimming in. The water is so fundamental to the fish's way of life that it is not seen or questioned. The organizational world is full of similar examples.

To illustrate, consider how manufacturing systems perfected throughout the twentieth century locked thousands of North American and European organizations into modes of industrialized inefficiency. Their mechanistic design required the creation of certainty. Thus assembly lines and other modes of mass manufacture were typically designed to prevent errors or unacceptable variances from traveling throughout a system. For example, buffer stocks of inventory or work in progress were typically held at different stages of the production process to "protect" one part from another. The procedure seemed inevitable and quickly became adopted as a foundation for effective production design.

However, these very same buffer stocks that guaranteed the continuous operation of the system perpetuated inefficiency. Buffer stocks create "slack" in a system. They represent unused resources. They allow one part of the manufacturing process to become separate from another. They create the kind of autonomy and space on which politics and empire building thrive. People are able to struggle for control over their particular part of the system. The existence of adequate stocks of high-quality work in process also institutionalizes errors and sloppy work. If a person or machine produces a defective product, production can still continue at its regular pace. Traditional systems of quality control institutionalized the error-producing process further by accepting a certain percentage of damaged products, waste, and inefficiency as the norm.

The challenge to this method of manufacturing, naturally enough, came from outside the system: in the form of "just-in-time" methods of production where parts and raw materials are delivered just before they are needed and in the related concept of "zero inventory." Both were pioneered in Japan. From the Japanese perspective, buffer stocks represented costs that could be eliminated. By building systems of production that *relied* on high-quality work being performed at *every* stage, the Japanese were able to develop production systems that resulted in high-quality, high-volume, low-cost production every time.

When there are no buffer stocks to absorb error, there is no room for error. Systems of production must thus become error free.

When people are no longer buffered from each other they must recognize the nature of their interdependence. Collaboration and mutual problem solving are encouraged. Activities have to be synchronized. Root problems must be confronted and eliminated.

"Just-in-time" manufacturing systems were unthinkable from a Western point of view. They contradicted all that seemed logical in designing manufacturing systems that could cope with the inevitable uncertainties of our uncertain world. The Western response was to try to eliminate and protect against uncertainty. The Japanese response was to learn from uncertainty and flow with it.

Of course, just-in-time systems are now widely used in Western manufacturing. But until they were demonstrated in reality by the Japanese they remained an unthinkable or crazy ideal.

Such is the nature of psychic prisons. Favored ways of thinking and acting become traps that confine individuals within socially constructed worlds and prevent the emergence of other worlds. As in the case of Plato's allegory of the cave, disruption usually comes from the outside. But the hold of favored ways of thinking can be so strong that even the disruption is often transformed into a view consistent with the reality of the cave.

Sometimes, this process is described as one of *groupthink*, a term coined by Irving Janis to characterize situations where people are carried along by group illusions and perceptions that have a self-sealing quality. One of the most famous examples is found in the abortive invasion of Cuba at the Bay of Pigs by 1,200 anti-Castro exiles. Launched on April 17, 1961, by the Kennedy administration, it almost led to nuclear war. "How could we have been so stupid?" President Kennedy later remarked. In retrospect, the plan looked completely misguided. Yet it had never seriously been questioned or challenged.

Kennedy and his advisers had unwittingly developed shared illusions and operating norms that interfered with their ability to think critically and to engage in the required reality testing. The president's charisma and a sense of invulnerability set the momentum for all kinds of self-affirming processes that produced conformity among key decision makers and advisers. Strong rationalizing tendencies mobilized support for favored opinions. A strong sense of "assumed consensus" inhibited people from expressing their doubts. Self-appointed people worked informally to protect the president from information that might damage his confidence. As a result, the CIA-planned invasion went ahead with a minimum of debate about the core assumptions on which its success depended.

This kind of "groupthink" has been reproduced in thousands of decision-making situations in organizations of all kinds. It may seem overly dramatic to describe the phenomenon as reflecting a kind of "psychic prison." Many people would prefer to describe it through the culture metaphor, seeing the pathologies described in all the above examples as the product of particular cultural beliefs and norms. But there is great merit in recognizing the prisonlike qualities of culture.

Culture gives us our world. And it traps us in that world! The psychic prison metaphor alerts us to pathologies that may accompany our ways of thinking and encourages us to question the fundamental premises on which we enact everyday reality. Plato's allegory draws attention to blind spots in *conscious* awareness. But, as we shall see, there are also many *unconscious* dimensions to how we construct the reality of organizational life. When we explore this realm, the image of a psychic prison takes on a new quality.

Organization and the Unconscious

If the psychoanalysts are correct, much of the rational and taken-for-granted reality of everyday life expresses preoccupations and concerns that lie beneath the level of conscious awareness. This places the study of organization and management in an interesting perspective, suggesting that much of what happens at a surface level must take account of the hidden structure and dynamics of the human psyche.

As is well known, the basis for this kind of thinking was laid by Sigmund Freud, who argued that the unconscious is created as humans repress their innermost desires and private thoughts. He believed that in order to live in harmony with one another humans must moderate and control their impulses, and that the unconscious and culture are really two sides of the same coin. He saw culture as the visible surface of the "repression" that accompanied the development of human sociability. It was in this sense that he talked about the essence of society being the repression of the individual, and about the essence of the individual as being the repression of himself or herself.

Since Freud's early work, the whole field of psychoanalysis has become a battleground between rival theories of the origin and nature of the unconscious. While Freud placed importance on its links with various forms of repressed sexuality, others have stressed its links with the structure of the patriarchal family, with fear of death, with anxieties associated with early infancy, with the collective unconscious, and so on.

Common to all these different interpretations is the idea that humans live their lives as prisoners or products of their individual and collective psychic history. The past is seen as living in the present through the unconscious, often in ways that create distorted and uncomfortable relations with the external world. Whereas Plato saw the route to enlightenment in the pursuit of objective knowledge and the activities of philosopher-kings, the psychoanalysts seek it in forms of self-understanding that show how in encounters with the external world, people are really meeting hidden dimensions of themselves.

As we shall see, the detailed images and ideas that have shaped the field of psychoanalysis have great relevance for how we understand organizational life.

ORGANIZATION AND
REPRESSED SEXUALITY

Frederick Taylor, the creator of "scientific management," was a man totally preoccupied with control. He was an obsessive, compulsive character, driven by a relentless need to tie down and master almost every aspect of his life. His activities at home, in the garden, and on the golf course, as well as at work, were dominated by programs and schedules, planned in detail and rigidly followed. Even his afternoon walks were carefully laid out in advance; it was not unknown for him to observe his motions, to measure the time taken over different phases, and even to count his steps.

These traits were evident in Taylor's personality from an early age. Living in a well-to-do household dominated by strong puritan values (emphasizing work, discipline, and the ability to keep one's emotions decently in check), Taylor quickly learned how to regiment himself. Childhood friends described the meticulous "scientific" approach that he brought to their games. Taylor insisted that all be subjected to strict rules and exact formulas. Before playing a game of baseball he would often insist that accurate measurements be made of the field so that everything would be in perfect relation, even though most of a sunny morning was spent ensuring that measurements were correct to the inch. Even a game of croquet was subject to careful analysis, with Fred working on the angles of the various strokes and calculating the force of impact and the advantages and disadvantages of understroke and overstroke. On cross-country walks, the young Fred would constantly experiment with his legs to discover how to cover the greatest distance with a minimum of energy, or the easiest method of vaulting a fence, or the ideal length of a walking stick. As an adolescent, before going to a dance, he would be sure to make lists of the attractive and unattractive girls likely to be present so that he could spend equal time with each.

Even during sleep this same meticulous regulation was brought into operation. From about the age of twelve Taylor suffered from fearful nightmares and insomnia. Noticing that his worst dreams occurred while he was lying on his back, he constructed a harness of straps and wooden points that would wake him whenever he was in danger of getting into this position. He experimented with other means of overcoming his nightmares, constructing a canvas sheet hung between two poles so that he could keep his brain cool. The insomnia and sleeping devices stayed with him in one way or another throughout his life. In later years he preferred to sleep in an upright position, propped by numerous pillows. This made spending nights away from home a rather difficult business, and in hotels where pillows were in short supply he would sometimes spend the night propped up by bureau drawers.

Taylor's life provides a splendid illustration of how unconscious concerns and preoccupations can have an effect on organization, for it is clear that his whole theory of scientific management was the product of the inner struggles of a disturbed and neurotic personality. His attempt to organize and control the world, whether in childhood games or in systems of scientific management, was really an attempt to organize and control himself.

From a Freudian perspective, Taylor's case presents a classic illustration of the anal-compulsive type of personality. As is well known, Freud's theory of human personality emphasizes that character traits in adult life emerge from childhood experience, and in particular from the way the child manages to reconcile the demands of his or her sexuality and the forces of external control and constraint. Freud's view of sexuality was a very broad one, embracing all kinds of libidinal desires and gratifications. He believed that children typically developed through different phases of sexuality, and that difficult experiences could lead to various forms of repression that resurface in later life. As illustrated in Exhibit 7.1, repression may set the basis for all kinds of defense mechanisms that displace and redirect these unconscious strivings so that they appear in other less threatening and more controlled forms.

From a Freudian standpoint, excessive concerns with parsimony, order, regularity, correctness, tidiness, obedience, duty, and punctuality are direct corollaries of what is learned and repressed as the child copes with early anal experiences. Taylor's life is permeated with many of these preoccupations and with "reaction formations" that manifest the opposite.

For example, much of Taylor's life reflects an inner struggle with the puritanical discipline and authority relations of his childhood. There is good reason to believe that the relations that his scientific management struck between managers and working men were rooted in the disciplinary structure under which he grew up. His relish in the dirt and grime of factories and his identification with the workers (he always claimed that he was one of them) can be understood as reactions against the same family situation. Amid all the conflict surrounding the introduction of scientific management, including direct insults, threats on his life, and his appearance before a special U.S. House of Representatives subcommittee on Taylorism, where he was presented as the "enemy of the working man," Taylor clung to the view that he had the friendship of those whom he sought to control. Within Taylor's mind the aggression of scientific management was turned into its opposite: the idea that it promoted harmony. It was this view that allowed him to see himself as an industrial peacemaker at the very same time that scientific management was one of the major forces creating industrial unrest.

Taylor had a productive neurosis! His preoccupations and ideas dovetailed perfectly with the concerns of the organizations of his day. Hence, rather than be dismissed as a crank he became a kind of infamous hero. The resolution of his own internal struggle resulted in productive innovations, ideas, and methods of control that had wide social impact.

Freudian psychology emphasizes how human personality is shaped as the human mind learns to cope with raw impulses and desires. Freud believed that in the process of maturation these are brought under control or banished to the unconscious. The unconscious thus becomes a reservoir of repressed impulses. The adult person deals with this reservoir in a variety of ways, engaging in various defense mechanisms to keep them in check. Here are some of the important defenses that have been identified by Freud and his followers:

Repression: "Pushing down" unwanted impulses and ideas into the unconscious

Denial: Refusal to acknowledge an impulse-evoking fact, feeling, or memory

Displacement: Shifting impulses aroused by one person or situation to a safer target

Fixation: Rigid commitment to a particular attitude or behavior

Projection: Attribution of one's own feelings and impulses to others

Introjection: Internalizing aspects of the external world in one's psyche

Rationalization: Creation of elaborate schemes of justification that disguise underlying motives and intentions

Reaction formation: Converting an attitude or feeling into its opposite

Regression: Adoption of behavior patterns found satisfying in childhood in order to reduce present demands on one's ego

Sublimation: Channeling basic impulses into socially acceptable forms

Idealization: Playing up the good aspects of a situation to protect oneself from the bad

Splitting: Isolating different elements of experience, often to protect the good from the bad

Exhibit 7.1   Glossary of Some Freudian and Neo-Freudian Defense Mechanisms

SOURCE: Hampden-Turner (1981: 40–42) and Klein (1980: 1–24).

The relationship between Taylor's anal-compulsive approach to life and the mode of organization embraced by scientific management raises a number of intriguing questions about styles of organization generally. For example, to what extent is it possible to understand organization as an external reflection of unconscious strivings? What are the detailed links between the rise of formal organization and libidinal repression? To what extent do modes of organization institutionalize defense mechanisms? Is there a pattern? Do tightly controlled bureaucratic forms reflect the influence of compulsive preoccupations? Do they attract and reward people who share these characteristics? Do organic and other forms of organization reflect and institutionalize preoccupations concerned with Freud's other personality types?

These questions may seem rather far fetched. But interesting links can be drawn. For example, it is clear that there has always been a highly visible connection between the rise of formal organization and the control of sexuality. If we return to the Middle Ages we find a libidinal society where few distinctions were drawn between public and private life. Open displays of sexual behavior were common. As my colleague Gibson Burrell of Warwick University has shown, even in medieval monasteries, convents, and churches, outrageous sexual behaviors presented a major problem. Manuscripts from the seventh and eighth centuries reveal that punishments for different classes of sexual misconduct were calculated in elaborate detail. Some of the most extreme offenses called for castration; others required extensive penitentials. Thus, a monk found guilty of simple fornication with unmarried persons could expect to fast for a year on bread and water, whereas a nun could expect three to seven years of fasting and a bishop twelve years. The punishment for masturbation in church was forty days' fasting (sixty days' psalm singing for monks and nuns). A bishop caught fornicating with cattle could expect eight years' fasting for a first offense and ten years' fasting for each subsequent offense.

The very fact that these schedules existed indicates the extent to which these behaviors posed an ever-present problem to the order and routine of monastic life, one of the earliest modes of formal organization. They provide a graphic illustration of Freud's point that to promote social order and "civilized" behavior the libido has to be brought under control.

In the view of the French historian Michel Foucault this conflict between organization and sexuality should come as no surprise, for mastery and control of the body is fundamental for control over social and political life. He thus encourages us to note the parallels between the rise of formal organization and the routinization and regimentation of the human body. This is evident in the examples above, in how Frederick the Great made a disciplined Prussian army out of an unruly mob (discussed in Chapter 2), and in early forms of industrial organization. For example, the British "Factory Acts" of 1833 gave much attention to the problem of controlling sexual behavior at work. Modern legislation on sexual harassment seeks to tackle the residue of this problem in today's workplace. Virtues of abstinence, restraint, and clean living were actively promoted in the Industrial Revolution of the eighteenth and nineteenth centuries. Many of the early industrialists in Europe and North America had Quaker and Puritan affiliations, the background against which Frederick Taylor was later to emerge.

In Freudian terms this process of acquiring control over the body hinges on a social process in which the kind of organization and discipline of the anal personality becomes dominant. This sublimation has provided much of the energy underlying the development of industrial society.

As we examine the bureaucratic form of organization, therefore, we should be alert to the hidden meaning of the close regulation and supervision of human activity, the relentless planning and scheduling of work, and the emphasis on productivity, rule following, discipline, duty, and obedience. The bureaucracy is a mechanistic form of organization but an anal one, too. Not surprisingly, some people are able to work in this kind of organization more effectively than others.

Historically, a strong case can be made for the idea that anality has been the major form of repressed sexuality shaping the nature of organizations. However, as we look around the organizational world, it is easy to see signs of other forms. Take, for example, the more flamboyant, flexible, organic, innovative firms now making such an impact on the corporate world. These organizations often call for a creative looseness of style that is quite alien to the bureaucratic personality. Freudian theory would suggest that the corporate cultures of these organizations often institutionalize various combinations of oral, phallic, and genital sexuality.

Consider, for example, the driving ambition behind boardroom conquests, acquisitions, and mergers or the exhibitionistic "me-oriented" behaviors through which managers and organizations may lavish attention on themselves. In aggressive, individualistic organizations the corporate culture is often characterized by what Wilhelm Reich would describe as a phallic-narcissistic ethos, where satisfaction is derived from being visible, adored, and "a winner." Such organizations regard and encourage this kind of narcissistic behavior exactly as rigid bureaucracies institutionalize anality.

Freudian theory thus provides an interesting twist to the kind of exhibitionistic behavior found in some of the corporate cultures discussed in Chapter 5. It suggests a new kind of contingency theory. Organizations are shaped not just by their environments. They are also shaped by the unconscious concerns of their members and the unconscious forces shaping the societies in which they exist.

ORGANIZATION AND THE
PATRIARCHAL FAMILY

While the Freudian perspective creates many novel interpretations of organizational life, in the view of many critics Freud was too hung up on sexuality and took the argument too far. Notable among these critics are members of the contemporary women's movement who see Freud as a man espousing male values and trapped in his own unconscious sexual preoccupations, especially as they interacted with the Victorian morality of his day. Rather than place emphasis on repressed sexuality as a driving force behind modern organization, these critics suggest that we ought to try and understand organization as an expression of patriarchy. From their standpoint, patriarchy operates as a kind of conceptual prison, producing and reproducing organizational structures that give dominance to males and traditional male values.

The evidence for a patriarchal view of organization is easy to see. Formal organizations typically build upon characteristics associated with Western male values and, historically, have been dominated by males, except in those jobs where the function is to support, serve, flatter, please, and entertain. Thus men have tended to dominate organizational roles and functions where there is a need for aggressive and forthright behavior, whereas women have, until fairly recently, been socialized to accept roles placing them in a subordinate position, as in nursing, clerical, and secretarial work, or roles designed to satisfy various kinds of male narcissism. The bureaucratic approach to organization tends to foster the rational, analytic, and instrumental characteristics associated with the Western stereotype of maleness, while downplaying abilities traditionally viewed as "female," such as intuition, nurturing, and empathic support. In the process it has created organizations that in more ways than one define "a man's world," where men, and the women who have entered the fray, joust and jostle for positions of dominance like stags contesting the leadership of their herd.

In the view of many writers on the relationship between gender and organization, the dominant influence of the male is rooted in the hierarchical relations found in the patriarchal family, which, as Wilhelm Reich has observed, serves as a factory for authoritarian ideologies. In many formal organizations one person defers to the authority of another exactly as the child defers to parental rule. The prolonged dependency of the child upon the parents facilitates the kind of dependency institutionalized in the relationship between leaders and followers and in the practice where people look to others to initiate action in response to problematic issues. In organizations, as in the patriarchal family, fortitude, courage, and heroism, flavored by narcissistic self-admiration, are often valued qualities, as is the determination and sense of duty that a father expects from his son. Key organizational members also often cultivate fatherly roles by acting as mentors to those in need of help and protection.

Critics of patriarchy suggest that in contrast to matriarchal values, which emphasize unconditional love, optimism, trust, compassion, and a capacity for intuition, creativity, and happiness, the psychic structure of the male-dominated family tends to create a feeling of impotence accompanied by a fear of and dependence on authority. These critics argue that under the influence of matriarchal values organizational life would be far less hierarchical, be more compassionate and holistic, value means over ends, and be far more tolerant of diversity and open to creativity. Many of these traditionally female values are evident in nonbureaucratic forms of organization where nurturing and networking replace authority and hierarchy as the dominant modes of integration.

In viewing organizations as unconscious extensions of family relations, we thus have a powerful means of understanding key features of the corporate world. We are also given a clue as to how organizations are likely to change along with contemporary changes in family structure and parenting relations. We see the major role that women and gender-related values can play in transforming the corporate world. So long as organizations are dominated by patriarchal values, the roles of women in organizations will always be played out on "male" terms. Hence, the view of many feminist critics of the modern corporation: The real challenge facing women who want to succeed in the organizational world is to change organizational values in the most fundamental sense.

ORGANIZATION, DEATH, AND IMMORTALITY

In his book *The Denial of Death*, Ernest Becker suggests that human beings are "Gods with anuses." Among all the animals we alone are conscious of the fact that we will die, and we are obliged to spend our lives with knowledge of the paradox that while we may be capable of spiritual transcendence beyond our bodies, our existence is dependent on a finite structure of flesh and bone that will ultimately wither away. In Becker's view, humans spend much of their life attempting to deny the oncoming reality of death by pushing their morbid fears deep into the recesses of their unconscious. He in effect reinterprets the Freudian theory of repressed sexuality, linking childhood fears associated with birth and the development of sexuality with fears relating to our own inadequacies, vulnerability, and mortality.

These views lead us to understand culture and organization in a novel way. For example, they encourage us to understand many of our symbolic acts and constructions as flights from our own mortality. In joining with others in the creation of culture as a set of shared norms, beliefs, ideas, and social practices, we attempt to locate ourselves in something larger and more enduring than ourselves. In creating a world that can be perceived as objective and real, we reaffirm the concrete and real nature of our own existence. In creating symbol systems that allow us to engage in meaningful exchanges with others, we also help to find meaning in our own lives. Although we may in quiet times confront the fact that we are going to die, much of our daily life is lived in the artificial realness created through culture. This illusion of realness helps disguise our unconscious fear that everything is highly vulnerable and transitory.

Thus, as Becker shows, when viewed from the perspective of our own impending death, the artifacts of culture can be understood as defense systems that help to create the illusion that we are greater and more powerful than we actually are. The continuity and development that we find in systems of religion, ideology, national history, and shared values help us believe we are part of a pattern that continues well beyond the bounds of our own life. No wonder, therefore, that people are so quick to defend their basic beliefs, even if it means going to war and confronting the reality of death. In doing so, they can help preserve the myth of immortality when they are alive.

This perspective suggests that we can understand organizations and much of the behavior within organizations in terms of a quest for immortality. In creating organizations we create structures of activity that are larger than life and that often survive for generations. In becoming identified with such organizations we ourselves find meaning and permanence. As we invest ourselves in our work, our roles become our realities, and as we objectify ourselves in the goods we produce or the money we make, we make ourselves visible and real to ourselves. No wonder that questions of survival are such a high priority in organizations, for there is much more than the survival of the organization at stake.

In decoding the unconscious significance of the relationship between immortality and organization, we realize that in attempting to manage and organize our world we are really attempting to manage and organize ourselves. Of particular importance here is the fact that many of our most basic conceptions of organization hinge on the idea of making the complex simple. Thus, the bureaucratic approach to organization emphasizes the virtue of breaking activities and functions into clearly defined component parts. In much of science and in everyday life, we manage our world by simplifying it; in making it simple we make it amenable to control. In doing so, we create the myth that we are actually in control and that we are more powerful than we really are. Much of the knowledge through which we organize our world can thus be seen as protecting us from the idea that, ultimately, we probably understand and control very little. Arrogance often hides weakness, and the idea that human beings, so small, puny, and transient, can organize and boast mastery of nature is, in many respects, a sign of their own vulnerability.

People use detailed myths, rituals, and modes of involvement in everyday life to defend themselves against consciousness of their vulnerability. A splendid illustration of this has been presented by Richard Boland and Raymond Hoffman in a study of the operation of a machine shop producing custom-tooled parts, where jokes and humor are used to cope with difficult working conditions. The jobs on which the men are involved are often hazardous, yet are made even more dangerous by practical jokes. The study illustrates how jokes help the men deal with a difficult work situation and questions of self-identity and allow them to exert a measure of control. In other organizational contexts, processes of goal setting, planning, and other kinds of ritual activity perform similar functions. In setting personal or organizational goals, we reassert confidence in our future. In investing our time and energy in a favored project, we convert the flight of time into something concrete and enduring. Whereas Freudian analysis would view excessive concerns with productivity, planning, and control as expressions of sublimated anal concerns, the work of Becker leads us to understand them as an attempt to preserve and tie down life in the face of death.

ORGANIZATION AND ANXIETY

In his later work, particularly in his book *Beyond the Pleasure Principle*, Freud came to place increasing emphasis on the struggle between life and death instincts within the individual. This relationship became a special focus for study by Melanie Klein and the so-called English school of psychoanalysis based at the Tavistock Institute in London, who have spent a great deal of time tracing the impact of childhood defenses against anxiety on the adult personality. The Kleinian school has placed great emphasis on the role of the mother and on relationships between the child and its mother's breast in identifying the links between the conscious and unconscious. Klein's work thus helps rectify a great bias in Freud's research, which in being overly concerned with the role of the father as the key figure in early childhood experience had tended to ignore or underplay the importance of the nurturing role of the mother.

Klein's work builds on the premise that from the beginning of life the human child experiences unease associated with the death instinct and fear of annihilation and that this fear becomes internalized in the form of "persecutory anxiety." To cope with this anxiety, the child develops defense mechanisms, including splitting, introjection, and projection (see Exhibit 7.1). In Klein's view, this first occurs in relation to the mother's breast or surrogate, which becomes identified with good and bad experiences, resulting in severance between feelings of love and hate. While experiences of the "good breast" provide a focus for affirmation and integration of the child's existence, experiences of the "bad breast" (where feeding is frustrating, slow, or difficult) become the focus of persecutory anxieties within the child. These anxieties are projected onto the "bad breast," which is often attacked with anger. Although the split between the good and bad breast occurs in the unconscious fantasy life of the child, it is real in its effects: It gets translated into specific patterns of feelings, object relations, and thought processes that have a significant impact on later life.

In Klein's view, the formation of the ego begins in these very early experiences, the "good breast" providing an integrative focus that helps to fight the destructive forces projected onto the "bad breast." The child splits the good feelings from the bad, internalizing, idealizing, and enjoying the good, often as a means of denying the existence of threatening states, while attacking the bad, often by projecting them onto the outside world. The life of the infant thus tends to be a world of extremes, in which ego characteristics associated with idealization, projection, and denial are all visible. In Klein's view, these characteristics are associated with normal as well as maladapted development. The infant passes through a persecutory (paranoid-schizoid) phase during the first few months of life and then into a "depressive position," where the child begins to appreciate that the good and bad breast are one and the same and that he or she has hated and attacked what is also loved. Klein believed that the necessary synthesis between loved and hated aspects of the breast gives rise to mourning and guilt, which represent vital advances in the child's emotional and intellectual life. She believed that if the persecutory fears within the child remain strong the infant has great difficulty leaving the paranoid-schizoid position and working through the necessary depressive phase. Then these early experiences may become the focus for fear, hate, envy, greed, anger, sadism, frustration, guilt, paranoia, obsession, depression, fantasy, and other feelings that are carried in the unconscious and transferred to other objects and relations. Klein's theory of human development thus suggests that many of the disorders that Freud attributed to human sexuality have their origins in earlier patterns of "object relations."

Klein's approach to the analysis of object relations suggests that adult experience reproduces defenses against anxiety originally formed in early childhood, with the techniques of splitting, projection, introjection, idealization, and denial shaping the way we forge relations with our outside world. From this perspective, it is possible to understand the structure, process, culture, and even the environment of an organization in terms of the unconscious defense mechanisms developed by its members to cope with individual and collective anxiety.

This approach to organizational analysis has been systematically developed by many members of the Tavistock Institute. For example, in his analysis of group behavior, Wilfred Bion has shown that groups often regress to childhood patterns of behavior to protect themselves from uncomfortable aspects of the real world. When a group is fully engaged with a task, its energies tend to be occupied and directed in ways that keep the group in touch with an external reality of some kind. However, when problems that challenge the group's functioning arise, the group tends to withdraw its energies from task performance and use them to defend itself against the anxieties associated with the new situation. We have all experienced this in one way or another in our personal lives and in countless organizational situations where we become so anxious about the dynamics of a situation that we lose sight of the tasks that are supposed to be performed. Concerns about group functioning obliterate concerns relating to the role of the group in the wider world. Bion has shown that in such anxiety-provoking situations groups tend to revert to one of three styles of operation that employ different kinds of defense against anxiety.

In some groups, a *dependency* mode is adopted. It is assumed that the group needs some form of leadership to resolve its predicament. The group's attention is split from the problems at hand and projected onto a particular individual. Group members often proclaim helplessness in coping with the situation and idealize the characteristics of the chosen leader. Sometimes, the group projects its energies onto an attractive symbol of its past, celebrating the way things used to be instead of coping with the current reality. Such a climate makes it easy for a potential leader to step in and take charge of the group's affairs. However, he or she often inherits an extremely difficult situation, as the very existence of a leader will provide an excuse for personal inaction on the part of others. The leader will also have to embody traits fantasized by people in the group who project desired aspects of their own egos onto the leader figure. As a result, the leader often fails to live up to expectations and is soon replaced by another person, often one of the least able members of the group. He or she in turn usually fails, and so the problems continue, perhaps leading to fragmentation and infighting within the group. Group functioning thus tends to become immobilized as all kinds of petty wrangling and divisionary issues serve as substitutes for real action.

In another pattern of response, a group may attempt to deal with its problems through what Bion calls *pairing*. This involves a fantasy where members of the group come to believe that a messiah figure will emerge to deliver the group from its fear and anxiety. The group's dependence on the emergence of such a figure again paralyzes its ability to take effective action.

A third pattern of response is what Bion describes as *fight-flight*, in which the group tends to project its fears on an enemy of some kind. This enemy embodies the unconscious persecutory anxiety experienced by the group. The enemy may take the form of a competitor in the environment, a government regulation, a public attitude, or a particular person or organization that appears to be "out to get us." While uniting the group and making a strong form of leadership possible, the fight-flight process tends to distort the group's appreciation of reality and hence its ability to cope. Time and energy tend to be devoted to fighting or protecting the group from the perceived danger rather than taking a more balanced look at the problems that are evident in the situation.

A good example of this process is the way automobile manufacturers and many other branches of the manufacturing industry in North America first reacted to the challenge posed by the import of goods from Japan and other parts of Asia. While this new source of competition was very real in its effects, preoccupation with "the enemy" and the need to fight or protect oneself through legislation and import quotas diverted attention from an equally important aspect of the situation: the need to reexamine the nature of one's own products to find how they might be modified or improved to compete in the new market conditions. The fight-flight response illustrated in this example tapped an unconscious paranoia that is common to many group situations.

The relevance of these ideas for understanding the dynamics of leadership, group processes, the enactment of organizational culture, relations between organization and environment, and other day-to-day aspects of organizational functioning is clear. The defense mechanisms elucidated by Klein and Bion pervade almost every aspect of organizational activity. People construct realities wherein threats and concerns within the unconscious mind become embodied in structures for coping with anxiety in the outside world. People may project these unconscious concerns as individuals or through patterns of unconscious collusion that tap shared fears, concerns, and general anxiety.

These ideas can also help explain many of the more formal aspects of organization. For example, Elliott Jaques and Isobel Menzies, former members of the Tavistock Institute, have shown how aspects of organizational structure can be understood as social defenses against anxiety. Jaques has shown that many organizational roles are the focus of various kinds of paranoid or persecutory anxiety in that people project bad objects and bad impulses onto the occupant of the role, who, more often than not, will introject these projections or deflect them elsewhere. Thus, the first officer on a ship is typically held responsible for many things that go wrong, even if he is not responsible for them. By common unconscious consent, he is usually the source of all trouble, allowing the crew to find relief from their own internal persecutors. The process also allows the captain to be more easily idealized as a good protective figure. All kinds of organizational scapegoats serve similar functions—people in roles everyone "loves to hate," convenient "troublemakers" and "misfits," and people who are "just not playing the game." They provide a focus for unconscious anger and sadistic tendencies, relieving tension in the wider organization and binding it together.

Jaques has shown that this kind of defense against paranoid anxiety is often a feature of labor-management relations, bad impulses being projected onto different groups who are then perceived as villains or sources of trouble and who become the objects of vengeful attitudes and actions. The process also occurs in many patterns of interorganizational relations. For example, Robert Chatov characterizes many of the relations between government and business as "regulatory sadism," where regulators inflict burdensome and superfluous requirements on regulatees. The process can also be observed in the way organizations in competitive environments may attempt to dominate, punish, and control their rivals or other organizations with whom they work and in the way some organizations punish themselves. For example, one part of an organization may set out to create punishing problems for another, or build various kinds of punishment into its general policies and procedures. This becomes very evident in times of economic recession when key people often take great pleasure in "tightening up" organizational practices and privileges established in the preceding "fat" years. Similar attitudes can be found in the field of labor-management relations, where a weakened position of trade unions can open the door to "union bashing," and in major restructurings that are motivated as much by desires to take revenge and punish individuals and groups as by the genuine rationalization of work practices.

Isobel Menzies has developed related insights in a pioneering study on nursing staff in hospitals, showing how defenses against anxiety underpin many aspects of the way nursing work is organized. As is well known, nurses often have to deal with distressing tasks that can arouse mixed feelings of pity, compassion, love, guilt, fear, hatred, envy, and resentment.

Hence, in the nursing profession the splitting up of the nurse-patient relation into discrete tasks distributed among different nurses, the depersonalization, categorization, and denial of the significance of the patient as an individual in favor of the patient as a "case," and the detachment and denial of personal feelings often have unconscious as well as bureaucratic significance. They are coping mechanisms. Sometimes, they contribute to efficient health care. At other times, they get in the way. In both cases, they may be extremely difficult to remove or change.

In yet another area of research, Abraham Zaleznik of the Harvard Business School has shown that patterns of unconscious anxiety often exert a decisive influence on coalition building and the politics of organizational life. In some situations leaders are unable to develop close relations with their colleagues and subordinates because of unconscious fears, or because some form of unconscious anger or envy leads them to resent any trace of rivalry. Such concerns may motivate the leader to maintain control by dividing and ruling subordinates in ways that ensure that they are "kept in place." Often, the unconscious fears prevent the leader from being able to accept genuine help and advice. For example, policy suggestions put forward by subordinates may be interpreted as rivalry and hence dismissed or suppressed regardless of their substantive merit. When relations are dominated by this kind of unconscious competition, the leader frequently becomes isolated, providing an ideal situation for subordinates to club together in a way that may actually lead to his or her demise. In this manner, unconscious projections often have self-realizing effects.

It is easy to see that the patterns of meaning that shape corporate culture and subculture may also have unconscious significance. The common values that bind an organization often have their origin in shared concerns that lurk below the surface of conscious awareness. For example, in organizations that project a team image, various kinds of splitting mechanisms are often in operation, idealizing the qualities of team members while projecting fears, anger, envy, and other bad impulses onto persons and objects that are not part of the team. As in war, the ability to create unity and a feeling of purpose often depends upon the ability to deflect destructive impulses onto the enemy. These impulses then confront the team as "real" threats.

In organizations characterized by internal strife or an ethos of cutthroat competition, these destructive impulses are often unleashed within, creating cultures that thrive on various kinds of sadism rather than by projecting their sadism elsewhere. For example, deep-seated envy may lead people to block the success of their colleagues because they fear that they will be unable to match that success. This hidden process may undermine the ability to develop teamlike cooperation, which requires organizational members to enjoy success through affiliation with successful others as well as through their own achievements. Again, unresolved persecutory anxieties, which invariably inhibit learning because they prevent people from accepting criticism and correcting their mistakes, may lead to a culture characterized by all kinds of tension and defensiveness.

Considerations such as these suggest that there may be much more to corporate culture than is evident in the popular idea that it is possible to "manage culture." Culture, like organization, may not be what it seems to be. Culture may be of as much significance in helping us avoid an inner reality as it is in helping us cope with the external reality of our day-to-day lives.

ORGANIZATION, DOLLS, AND TEDDY BEARS

As children, most of us had a favorite soft toy, blanket, piece of clothing, or other special object on which we lavished attention and from which we were virtually inseparable. Psychoanalyst Donald Winnicott has developed the Kleinian theory of object relations in a way that emphasizes the key role of such "transitional objects" in human development. He suggests that they are critical in developing distinctions between the "me" and the "not me," creating what he calls an "area of illusion" that helps the child develop relations with the outside world. In effect, these objects provide a bridge between the child's internal and external worlds. If the favored object or phenomenon is modified (e.g., Teddy is washed or cleaned), then the child may feel that his or her own existence is being threatened in some way.

In Winnicott's view, the relationship with such objects continues throughout life, the doll, teddy bear, or blanket gradually being replaced by other objects and experiences that mediate relations with one's world to help maintain a sense of identity. In later life, a valued possession, a collection of letters, a cherished dream, or perhaps a valued attribute, skill, or ability may come to act as a substitute for our lost doll or teddy, symbolizing and reassuring us about who we actually are and where we stand in the wider world. While they play a crucial role in linking us with our reality, on occasion these objects and experiences may also acquire the status of a fetish or fixation that we are unable to relinquish. In such cases, adult development becomes stuck and distorted, a rigid commitment to a particular aspect of our world making it difficult for us to move on and deal with the changing nature of our surroundings. In other words, adults, like children, can become overly committed to the comfort and security provided by their new teddy bears in disguise!

If Winnicott is correct, the theories of transitional phenomena and associated areas of illusion add to our understanding of how we engage and construct organizational reality. They also provide a powerful perspective on the role of the unconscious in shaping and resisting change.

These issues have been studied in depth by Harold Bridger of the Tavistock Institute, who has run numerous seminars exploring the unconscious significance of transitional phenomena in organizational life. His perspective leads us to understand that many organizational arrangements can themselves serve as transitional phenomena: They play a critical role in defining the nature and identity of organizations and their members and in shaping attitudes that can block creativity, innovation, and change. For example, in many organizations a particular aspect of organizational structure or corporate culture may come to assume special significance and be preserved and retained even in the face of great pressure to change. A family firm may cling to a particular aspect of its history and mission, even though it is now operating in new conditions where this aspect is no longer relevant. Trade-union officials or a group of employees may want to fight to the death to defend a particular principle or a set of concessions won in previous battles, even though they are no longer of any real value to their members. A manager or work group may insist that they have the right and discretion to make particular decisions or that work be performed in a specific manner, even though when pressed they recognize that their requirements are ritualistic rather than substantive in nature.

In each of these cases the phenomenon to be preserved may be of transitional significance to those involved. Just as children may rely on the presence of the doll or teddy bear as a means of reaffirming who and where they are, managers and workers may rely on equivalent phenomena for defining their sense of identity. When these phenomena are challenged, basic identities are challenged. The fear of loss that this entails thus often generates a reaction that may be out of all proportion to the importance of the issue when reviewed from a more detached point of view. This unconscious dynamic may help explain why some organizations have been unable to cope with the changing demands of their environment and why there is often so much unconscious resistance to change in organizations.

The general principles are well illustrated in the case of an engineering company that, like many others in its industry, experienced difficulties in adapting to changes being created by new developments in computer technology. One of the interesting features of the culture of the company was its commitment to the use of slide rules. Even though the new computer technology offered a radically new and vastly more efficient way of making engineering calculations, many of the engineers insisted on continuing to use their "slides." The theory of transitional phenomena leads us to understand this in terms of an unconscious process where the use of slide rules was associated with a past that was fast disappearing and a reluctance to relinquish an old identity and move on with the changing times. As might be expected, the firm lost its position in the industry and eventually got taken over by another firm.

The theory of transitional phenomena contributes important insights to the practice of organizational change and development. It suggests that change will occur spontaneously only when people are prepared to relinquish what they hold dear for the purpose of acquiring something new or can find ways of carrying what they value in the old into the new. The engineering firm in the above example was committed to a symbolic object that could not perform transitional functions in the current situation. Some new object, insight, or experience was needed to aid in the transition to microprocessing. Interestingly, consultants and other change agents often become transitional objects for their client firms: The client refuses to "let go" and becomes crucially dependent on the change agent's advice in relation to every move.

In helping facilitate any kind of social change it may thus be necessary for the change agent to create transitional phenomena when they do not exist naturally. Just as a father or mother may have to help his or her child find a substitute for Teddy, a change agent—whether a social revolutionary or a paid consultant—must usually help his or her target group to relinquish what is held dear before they can move on. Significantly, this can rarely be done effectively by "selling" or imposing a "change package," an ideology, or a set of techniques. The theory of transitional phenomena suggests that in situations of voluntary change the person doing the changing must be in control of the process, for change ultimately hinges on questions of identity and the problematic relation between me and not-me. To create transitional situations, a change agent must help create that area of illusion identified by Winnicott, which, in his terms, is "good enough" for people to explore their situations and the options they face. People frequently need time to reflect, think over, feel out, and mull through action if a change is to be effective and long-lasting. If the change agent tries to bypass or suppress what is valued, it is almost sure to resurface at a later date.

The theory of transitional phenomena thus provides a way of understanding the dynamics of change and offers important ideas that can help individuals and groups make effective transitions from one state to another.

ORGANIZATION, SHADOW,
AND ARCHETYPE

In the above analysis we have focused on Freudian and neo-Freudian interpretations of the unconscious. It is now time to turn to the implications of the work of Carl Jung.

Whereas Freud was preoccupied with the demands that the body, as carrier of the psyche, placed on the unconscious, Jung cut loose from this constraint, viewing the psyche as part of a universal and transcendental reality. As his thinking developed, he came to place increasing emphasis on the idea that the human psyche is part of a "collective unconscious" that transcends the limits of space and time. Many criticize this aspect of Jung's work as bordering on the occult. However, a more informed interpretation encourages us to see how this concept links with developments in modern physics. Jung dematerialized our understanding of the psyche just as Einstein, whom Jung knew well, dematerialized our understanding of the physical world. In the light of evidence on premonitions and other psychic phenomena, Jung came to see matter and psyche as two different aspects of one and the same thing. The physical energy that Einstein saw as underlying all matter came to be paralleled in Jung's work by a conception of psychic energy, which, like physical energy, was open to many kinds of transformation through conscious and unconscious activity. Hence Jung's holistic view of the psyche as a universal phenomenon that is ultimately part of a transcendental reality linking mind to mind and mind to nature.

One of the most distinctive features of Jung's analysis is his emphasis on the role of archetypes. *Archetype*, which literally means "original pattern," is defined by Jung in a variety of ways and plays a critical role in linking the individual to the collective unconscious. At the most basic level, archetypes are defined as patterns that structure thought and hence give order to the world. Jung's use of archetypes was inspired by Plato's view of images or schemata, and he talks about them in various ways, for example, as "living ideas" that constantly produce new interpretations and as "ground plans" that give experience a specific configuration. He also speaks of them as "organs of the prerational psyche" and as "inherited forms and ideas" that acquire content in the course of an individual's life as personal experience is taken up in these forms. In other words, archetypes are structures of thought and experience, perhaps embodied in the structure of the psyche or inherited experience, that lead us to mold our understanding of our world in a patterned way. Jung devoted great time and energy to demonstrating the universal and timeless character of these archetypal structures, showing how they are found in the dreams, myths, and ideas of primitive, ancient, and modern man. Although the empirical contents may vary in detail, the principles that lend them shape and order seem to be one and the same. For Jung, these archetypes shape the way we "meet ourselves" in encounters with the external world and are crucial for understanding links between conscious and unconscious aspects of the psyche.

Jung's work thus has major implications for understanding how people enact organization reality. We will focus here on two of the more important ones: the way Jung encourages us to understand the general relations between internal and external life and the role that archetypes play in shaping our understanding of the external world.

The first theme has been explored in some detail by Robert Denhardt. In his book *In the Shadow of Organization*, he invites us to examine the repressed human side of organization lying beneath the surface of formal rationality. Jung used the term *shadow* to refer to unrecognized or unwanted drives and desires, the other side of the conscious ego, standing in relation to the ego as a kind of submerged opposite that at the same time strives for completeness with the ego. For Jung, the development of the ego always tended to be two-sided. He thus placed particular emphasis on understanding conscious and unconscious life in terms of an interplay between opposing tendencies. He believed that full development of self-knowledge and human personality, a process that he described as individuation, rests on a person's ability to recognize the rival elements within his or her personality and to deal with their contradictions in a unified manner. In his view, neurosis and human maladaptation stem from an inability to recognize and deal with the repressed shadow, which typically contains both constructive and destructive forces. Like the other theorists we have considered in this chapter, he also believed that many of these unresolved tensions in ourselves are projected onto other people and external situations and that to understand our external reality we must first understand what he called "the other within."

Thus, in the shadow of organization we find all the repressed opposites of rationality struggling to surface and change the nature of rationality in practice. Sociologist Max Weber noted that the more the bureaucratic form of organization advances, the more perfectly it succeeds in eliminating all human qualities that escape technical calculation. However, Jung's work suggests that these can never be eliminated, only banished or submerged. His work also leads us to understand that these irrational qualities never accept their banishment idly and are always looking for a way to modify their rational other side. We see this in much of the unofficial politicking that shapes organizational life and also in stress, lying, cheating, depression, and acts of sabotage. From a Jungian standpoint, such factors reflect inevitable yet neglected or suppressed tensions in a two-sided process. Just as the unconscious of the individual strives to achieve completeness with the ego, the shadowy unconscious in an organization can also be seen as crying for recognition, warning us that the development of one side of our humanness (e.g., the capacity to exercise technical reason) often does violence to other sides. The pathologies and alienations we find in organizational contexts can, from a Jungian standpoint, be interpreted as a manifestation of this essential wholeness of the psyche.

The theme of the unity in opposites is a powerful one running throughout Jung's work. It has been constructively used by many organization theorists interested in understanding how people relate to their realities and in improving organizational decision making. Jung distinguished two ways of perceiving reality (through sensation and intuition) and two ways of judging reality (thinking and feeling). These two dimensions are often combined to identify personality types (Exhibit 7.2) and to demonstrate styles of decision making. This scheme provides a nice illustration of how repressed elements of the psyche may signify unused skill and potential within the human that, if tapped, could contribute much to an individual's ability to cope with the problems he or she faces. Jung's work shows that the repressed shadow of organization acts as a reservoir not only of forces that are unwanted and hence repressed but of forces that have been lost or undervalued. For example, as the male archetype has asserted itself, values associated with the female have been submerged. By recognizing and coming to grips with the resources of this reservoir, Jungian organization theorists are at one in suggesting that we can tap new sources of energy and creativity and make our institutions much more human, vibrant, and morally responsive and responsible than they are now.

Jung's analysis of personality in terms of the way people relate to their world conveniently brings us to consider the role of archetypes in shaping the details of our reality. As noted earlier, archetypes are recurring themes of thought and experience that seen to have universal significance. For example, as Northrop Frye has shown, mythology and literature are dominated by a small number of basic themes—apocalyptic, demonic, romantic, tragic, comic, and ironic. The characters, situations, and actions may change, but the stories remain pretty much the same. In other aspects of life, too, powerful themes that help people make sense of their experience are used time and again to create patterns of meaning. These archetypal structures give people a sense of place in their own lives and in history and thus help them to make sense of who and where they are in the grand order of things.

If Jung's theory of archetypes is correct, then we would expect the pattern of organizational life to be created and re-created in accordance with

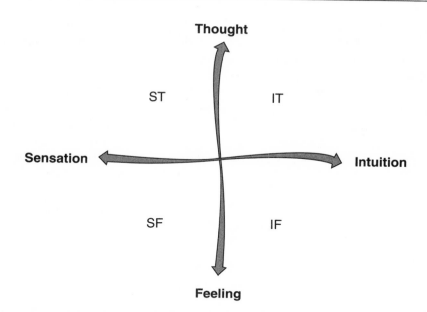

Jung suggests that people tend to process data about the world in terms of sense or intuition, and to make judgments, in terms of thought or feeling. According to which functions are dominant (or in the shadow), we can identify four ways of dealing with the world and of shaping one's reality: *ST* individuals tend to be empiricists who sense and think their way through life, making judgments and interpretations on the basis of "hard facts" and logical analysis; *SF* individuals also tend to pay a great deal of attention to data derived from the senses, but arrive at judgments in terms of "what feels right" rather than in terms of analysis; *IT* individuals tend to work their way through life by thinking about the possibilities inherent in a situation. Their actions tend to be guided by a combination of insight and feeling that pays much more attention to values than to facts. When one style of action is dominant, the other styles occupy background roles. Clearly, since each style presents an alternative way of understanding the same situation, opportunities are lost in this imbalance.

This scheme has been used by Ian Mitroff and various colleagues (Mitroff and Kilmann 1978, Mason and Mitroff 1981, and Mitroff 1984) to analyze managerial and decision-making styles, and to develop dialectical approaches to planning and decision making that attempt to take rival points of view into account. The scheme has been used by Ingalls (1979) as the foundation for a Jungian analysis of the use and direction of human energy in organizations, and by Myers-Briggs (1962) to develop a personality test that has many managerial applications. A variation of the scheme has also been developed by McWhinney (1982) as a means of tackling complex problems.

Exhibit 7.2   The Jungian Interplay of Opposites

the structures found in the history of myth and literature. Unfortunately, very little research has as yet been conducted on this topic. Ian Mitroff of the University of Southern California has made an important theoretical contribution to our understanding of the links between archetype and organizations and has suggested that organizational life can be understood in terms of the relations between fools, magicians, warriors, high priests, lovers, and other symbolic characters. His analysis suggests that we may be able to understand the unconscious significance of much organizational behavior in terms of the great themes that have shaped history. It appears that even though we may use the latest electronic technology and management technique to plan and execute our affairs we do so in ancient ways, for we are all primitives at heart, reproducing archetypal relations to make sense of the basic dilemmas of life.

THE UNCONSCIOUS: A CREATIVE
AND DESTRUCTIVE FORCE

Our exploration of organization and the unconscious has drawn on many images of the psychic prison, tracing relations between our conscious and unconscious life in terms of repressed sexuality, patriarchy, fear of death, mother's breast, teddy bears, and shadows and archetypes—the list is by no means exhaustive. These metaphors encourage us to become more sensitive about the hidden meaning of our everyday actions and preoccupations and to learn how we can process and transform our unconscious energy in constructive ways. They lead us to see how aggression, envy, anger, resentment, and numerous other dimensions of our hidden life may be built into work and organization. These hidden concerns influence whether we attempt to design work to avoid or to deal with problematic aspects of our reality and how we enact our organizational world. They lie at the center of many issues associated with group dynamics, effective leadership, and innovation and change.

The overall significance of these ways of understanding organizations has been vividly grasped by Frances Delahanty and Gary Gemmill of Syracuse University, who suggest that we should understand the role of the unconscious in organizational life as a kind of "black hole." As is well known, this metaphor has been used in physics to characterize invisible yet intense gravitational fields that capture all passing matter. In a similar way, the invisible dimension of organization that we have described as the unconscious can swallow and trap the rich energies of people involved in the organizing process.

However, the challenge of understanding the significance of the unconscious in organization also carries a promise: that it is possible to release trapped energy in ways that may promote creative transformation and change and create more integrated relations among individuals, groups, organizations, and their environments. This promise is in perfect harmony with the metaphor of the psychic prison, for a vision of confinement is invariably accompanied by a vision of freedom. For Plato, this freedom rests in the pursuit of knowledge about the world. For the psychoanalysts, it has rested in knowledge of the unconscious and in the capacity of humans to create a better world through an improved understanding of how we construct and interpret our realities.

Why do we get trapped by favored ways of thinking? Why do we protect our illusions? Why do we find it so difficult to change established and even uncomfortable modes of behavior? Why do we create so many problems for each other? The ideas that we have explored point toward some answers and offer some interesting ways of gaining new perspective on critical problems.

The image of a psychic prison is itself a powerful image for approaching this task because it encourages us to recognize how we may be caught in a self-sealing environment. We see each other, and we see the world around us. But what are we really seeing? Are we seeing an independent world? Or are we just seeing and experiencing projections of ourselves? Are we imprisoned by the language, concepts, beliefs, and a general culture through which we enact our world?

Paradoxically, by posing these kinds of questions we take the first steps in finding an escape. We are encouraged to look for messages coming from outside our particular "cave" and to use them for gaining new leverage on our world. This can bring enormous benefits to individuals and organizations, offering a way out of the "groupthink" and "cognitive traps" that may lock us into ineffective and undesirable patterns of behavior.

Strengths and Limitations of the Psychic Prison Metaphor

The psychic prison metaphor offers a powerful set of perspectives for exploring the hidden meaning of our taken-for-granted worlds. It encourages us to dig below the surface to uncover the processes and patterns of control that trap people in unsatisfactory modes of existence and to find ways through which they can be transformed.

One of the major strengths of the metaphor, as far as organization studies is concerned, rests in its many contributions to our understanding of the dynamics and challenges of organizational change. All the perspectives considered in this chapter have a lot to offer here, because they show that in seeking to change organizational practice we are usually trying to change much, much more.

Structures, rules, behaviors, beliefs, and the patterns of culture that define an organization are not just corporate phenomena. They are personal in the most profound sense. Any attempt to change these aspects of the organizational world can thus mobilize all kinds of opposition as individuals and groups defend the status quo in an attempt to defend their very selves. As has been show, structures and rules may be crucial in *creating* boundaries and rigidities that help to symbolize a manager's sense of who he or she really is; an outdated practice may reflect an effort to cling to a cherished experience or mode of life; high regard for a particular person or leader may be carrying all kinds of unconscious anxieties, aggressions, and energies of those being led; bloody mergers, acquisitions, downsizings, or combative relations with competitors or the world at large may veil all kinds of individual and group fears and inadequacies; a corporate group's understanding of its external environment may be dominated by the unconscious projections of a few key managers; a strong corporate subculture may be mobilizing neglected aspects of a corporate "shadow" that are truly worthy of attention and of being brought to light.

In understanding these hidden dimensions of everyday reality, managers and change agents can open the way to modes of practice that respect and cope with organizational challenges in a new way. They can learn to see when and how unconscious concerns are being projected or buried in a dysfunctional manner and find ways of releasing the energy in a more positive form. They can learn the art of carrying valuable dimensions of "old ways" into the new. They can begin to untangle sources of scapegoating, victimization, and blame and find ways of addressing the deeper anxieties to which they are giving form. They can approach the "resistance" and "defensive routines" that tend to sabotage and block change with a new sensitivity, and find constructive ways of dealing with them.

In showing that change initiatives often attack unconscious psychological defences, the ideas explored in this chapter thus add a valuable new dimension to our understanding of the challenges of innovation and change. They also put the whole issue of organizational rationality in new perspective. As has been shown in earlier chapters, the drive to create tightly controlled rational organizations has been a major feature of the twentieth century. For the most part, organization theory has sought to provide managers with perspectives and techniques that try to eliminate or control uncertainty and put management on a rational, objective basis.

The ideas presented in this chapter show the imbalance involved here, and suggest that instead of trying to enhance the rationality of organizations as an end in itself, more attention should be devoted to understanding and developing the links between the rational and irrational, because they are part of the very same phenomenon.

The psychic prison metaphor shows us that we have overrationalized our understanding of organization. Both in our behavior in organizations and in our explanations of organizations, factors such as aggression, greed, fear, hate, and libidinal drives have no official status. When they do break into the open, they are usually quickly banished through apologies, rationalizations, and punishments designed to restore a more neutered state of affairs. An outburst of anger may be interpreted as a sign that someone is under pressure, an emotional breakdown treated with a few days' leave, and an act of sabotage punished with further controls. Yet apologize, rationalize, punish, and control as we may, we do not rid organizations of these repressed forces lurking in the shadow of rationality. This human underside will always exist, and as has been suggested above, has to be taken into account if an organization is to develop in a holistic and convivial way. It is pointless to talk about creating "learning organizations" or of trying to develop corporate cultures that thrive on change if the unconscious human dimension is ignored. If underlying preoccupations and concerns are not addressed, the rhetoric of creating a new organization is almost sure to fall on deaf ears—even in situations where change may seem beneficial and logical for all concerned.

An excellent illustration of this is found in a study of coal mines conducted by Eric Trist. He discovered that the habit of working in "bad systems" had the compensation of allowing many of the workers to leave some of their own sense of "badness" in the system. Hence, although they hated their work, they could not change it. The system had a strange way of tying them in. In a similar way, people may build a dependency on some aspect of culture or social life that leads them to resist innovations that would undermine this dependency, even though in terms of "logical" criteria change seems the right thing for all concerned.

The psychic prison metaphor thus heightens our awareness of the relationship between "the rational" and what *seems* "irrational," and warns of the dangers of dismissing or downplaying the significance of the latter, because the "irrational" can be an incredibly powerful force for the people involved. Developing this point, the metaphor also encourages us to recognize that rationality is often irrationality in disguise. We have seen this in how the rationality of a Frederick Taylor can disguise an extreme form of compulsiveness, just as a manager's workaholism, excessive concern for clear-cut targets and goals, or aggressive manner in dealing with colleagues or external competitors can disguise all kinds of personal insecurities. Rationality and irrationality (a term for human forces that we cannot order and control) are flip sides of each other, and when one is overemphasized, distortions and dysfunctions inevitably arise.

The ideas presented in this chapter encourage us to understand the polarity involved here and to find ways of achieving better integration and balance. This has enormous implications for dealing with the challenges of a turbulent world, because it is clear that current conceptions and beliefs about organization and management overassert the importance of "being rational" and "in control." As will be clear from discussion of the brain metaphor in Chapter 4 and the ideas on flux and transformation in Chapter 8, if management is to rise to the challenge of encouraging emergent, self-organizing forms, these traditional concerns for rational control need to be tempered by a comfort in dealing with uncertainty, flux, and change as a norm. Similarly, the qualities of the male archetype that have dominated so much contemporary management need to be supplemented with those of the female. Rational decision processes need to make more room for intuitive creative leaps. The ethos of cutthroat competition needs to make more room for a gentler counterpart.

Interestingly, the forces that can help create the required integration are often present in most organizations: in the repressed "shadow side." For example, if one examines the relationship between the dominant corporate culture and patterns of subculture within an organization, one can often see the polarities discussed above struggling for attention. Many subcultural groups provide rallying points for positive ideas and developments that cannot find formal expression elsewhere, or for counterbalancing negative aspects of the dominant culture. As such they offer a hidden reservoir of energy and ideas for mobilizing constructive change. As Larry Hirschhorn of the University of Pennsylvania has shown in his book *The Workplace Within*, it is vitally important for managers to recognize the constructive and reparative side of forces that may at first sight seem to be opposing their policies, especially in circumstances of high interdependence. In recognizing that the shadow sides of our organizations send us messages about "the good" and "the bad," we can find ways of organizing and managing in a much more integrated way.

Finally, the psychic prison metaphor plays a powerful role in drawing attention to the ethical dimension of organization. As has been shown, there is nothing neutral about the way we organize. It is always human in the fullest sense and, as has been suggested, an increased awareness of the human dimension needs to be built into everything we do. While the metaphor offers obvious guidance on the management of change, it also warns us that we may be walking on dangerous ethical ground, especially when we systematically use our knowledge of archetypal feelings or social defence mechanisms to achieve instrumental ends.

Against these strengths and insights of the psychic prison metaphor, particularly as it has been developed in this chapter, it is necessary to register a number of limitations. First, our discussion has placed considerable emphasis on understanding and dealing with unconscious patterns of behavior and control. But what about the more explicit ideological factors that control and shape organizational life? People are often locked into cognitive traps because it is in the interests of certain individuals and groups to sustain one pattern of belief rather than another. This was discussed briefly in Chapter 6 but, as highlighted in the bibliographic notes to this chapter, is worthy of much more detailed attention. Our understanding of the psychic prison metaphor can and should be extended to embrace all the ideological processes through which we create and sustain meaning, not just the unconscious.

Second, the metaphor can be criticized for placing too much emphasis on the role of cognitive processes in creating, sustaining, and changing organizations and society. For many, it may seem more appropriate to talk about organizations as prisons than as psychic prisons, since the exploitation and domination of people is often grounded as much in control over the material basis of life as in control over ideas, thoughts, and feelings. This view builds on a long-standing debate between humanists and materialists and will be placed in better perspective in the following two chapters, where we give more attention to the idea that organizations and society may be shaped by forces that have a logic and momentum of their own. In the meantime, we must note that a change in consciousness or an appreciation of the role of the unconscious may not itself be enough to effect major change in the basic structure of organization and society.

Another limitation of the metaphor is that its promise of liberation from undesirable psychological and cognitive constraints often encourages utopian speculation and critique. While the metaphor does contribute certain insights into how to improve the conduct of day-to-day affairs, particularly in showing how we can challenge taken-for-granted mind-sets or achieve a better understanding of the psychodynamics of change, many of its implications ignore the realities of power and the force of vested interests in sustaining the status quo. Of course, the fact that reform may be dismissed as utopian adds power to the argument that our imprisoned state prevents us from imagining and realizing alternative modes of existence. If proposals for change must always be judged feasible and realistic, we are restricted to modifications of the status quo. However, the criticism of utopianism still remains.

A final limitation, and indeed danger, of the metaphor is that it raises the specter of an Orwellian world where we attempt to manage each other's minds. We noted in Chapter 5 how an awareness of the importance of corporate culture has sent many managers and management theorists hurrying to find ways of managing culture. In highlighting the role of the unconscious in organization, there is a danger that many will now want to find ways of managing the unconscious as well.

This, of course, is impossible, because the unconscious is by nature uncontrollable. While it is possible to act in a way that is sensitive to the existence and role of the unconscious in everyday life, knowledge of the unconscious does not produce blueprints for reform. As has been shown, the psychic prison metaphor promotes a style of critical thinking and awareness that can help us penetrate many of the complexities of organizational life. But it does not provide the easy answers and solutions to problems that many managers may wish to find.

8

Unfolding Logics of Change

Organization as Flux and Transformation

Around 500 B.C. the Greek philosopher Heraclitus noted that "you cannot step twice into the same river, for other waters are continually flowing on." He was one of the first Western philosophers to address the idea that the universe is in a constant state of flux, embodying characteristics of both permanence and change. As he noted, "Everything flows and nothing abides; everything gives way and nothing stays fixed. . . . Cool things become warm, the warm grows cool; the moist dries, the parched becomes moist. . . . It is in changing that things find repose." For Heraclitus, the secrets of the universe were to be found in hidden tensions and connections that simultaneously create patterns of unity and change.

In our own time, the late David Bohm, a theoretical physicist, has developed a theory that invites us to understand the universe as a flowing and unbroken wholeness. Like Heraclitus, he views process, flux, and change as fundamental, arguing that the state of the universe at any point in time reflects a more basic reality. He calls this reality the *implicate* (or *enfolded*) order and distinguishes it from the *explicate* (or *unfolded*) order manifested in the world around us. Bohm argues that the latter realizes and expresses potentialities existing within the former.

Imagine a whirlpool in a river. While possessing relatively constant form, it has no existence other than in the movement of the river. The analogy illustrates how an explicate order flows out of the implicate order in accordance with a coherent process of transformation.

This theory, which has provided a means of resolving many problems in modern physics, has important consequences, for it suggests that in order to understand the secrets of the universe we have to understand the generative processes that link implicate and explicate orders.

In this chapter we are going to explore four such processes that we will call "logics of change." The first draws on the theory of autopoiesis, an interesting new perspective that puts the relationship between systems and their environments in a new light. The second draws on some of the latest insights of chaos and complexity theory, with a view to explaining how ordered patterns of activity can emerge from spontaneous self-organization. The third draws on related cybernetic ideas suggesting that change is enfolded in the strains and tensions found in circular relations. The fourth suggests that change is the product of tensions between opposites. Each perspective offers a metaphorical frame for explaining how the explicit reality of organizational life is formed and transformed by underlying processes that have an order or logic of their own.

As you read, remember the whirlpool. Think about what it might take to change its configuration. Because that's what the following ideas are ultimately about. They seek to explain the nature of organizational whirlpools. Why do they exist? How do they sustain themselves? What can be done to influence their course?

In embarking on this task we will be exploring some ideas about the nature of change itself, and our journey will take us into some abstract scientific thinking. But stay with the process. There are raw images and ideas here—of imprisoning loops and vicious circles, of computer simulations that find spontaneous patterns, of birds, bees, butterflies, and termites, and of paradoxes and contradictions—that, although imperfectly formed, can challenge the foundations on which many existing theories of organization build.

In conducting this investigation, we are in effect looking for new metaphors that can create new ways of thinking about change.

Autopoiesis: Rethinking Relations With the Environment

Traditional approaches to organization theory have been dominated by the idea that change originates in the environment. As we saw in Chapter 3, the organization is typically viewed as an open system in constant interaction with its context, transforming inputs into outputs as a means of creating the conditions necessary for survival. Changes in the environment are viewed as presenting challenges to which the organization must respond. Although there is great debate as to whether adaptation or selection is the primary factor influencing survival, there is agreement that the major problems facing modern organizations stem from changes in the external environment.

This basic idea is challenged by the implications of a new approach to systems theory developed by two Chilean scientists, Humberto Maturana and Francisco Varela. They argue that all living systems are organizationally closed, autonomous systems of interaction that make reference only to themselves. The idea that living systems are open to an environment is, in their view, the product of an attempt to make sense of such systems from the standpoint of an external observer. Their theory challenges the validity of distinctions drawn between a system and its environment and offers a new perspective for understanding the processes through which living systems change.

Maturana and Varela base their argument on the idea that living systems are characterized by three principal features: autonomy, circularity, and self-reference. These lend them the ability to self-create or self-renew. Maturana and Varela have coined the term *autopoiesis* to refer to this capacity for self-production through a closed system of relations. They contend that the aim of such systems is ultimately to produce themselves; their own organization and identity is their most important product.

How is it possible to say that living systems such as organisms are autonomous, closed systems?

Maturana and Varela argue that this is because living systems strive to maintain an identity by subordinating all changes to the maintenance of their own organization as a given set of relations. They do so by engaging in circular patterns of interaction whereby change in one element of the system is coupled with changes elsewhere, setting up continuous patterns of interaction that are always self-referential. They are self-referential because a system cannot enter into interactions that are not specified in the pattern of relations that define its organization. Thus, a system's interaction with its "environment" is really a reflection and part of its own organization. It interacts with its environment in a way that facilitates its own self-production; its environment is really a part of itself.

In saying that living systems are closed and autonomous, Maturana and Varela are not saying these systems are isolated. The closure and autonomy to which they refer are organizational. They are saying that living systems close in on themselves to maintain stable patterns of relations and that it is this process of closure or self-reference that ultimately distinguishes a system as a system.

To discover the nature of a total system, it is necessary to interact with it and trace the circular pattern of interaction through which it is defined. In doing so, we encounter the problematic question of where the system begins and ends. Maturana and Varela recognize that in any systems analysis one will usually have to stop unwinding the pattern of circular relations at some point because systems, like Chinese boxes, can be seen as being made up of wholes within wholes. However, they believe that this kind of self-referential paradox is fundamental. There is no beginning and no end to the system because it is a closed loop of interaction.

Thus, to take an example, in the organization of a biological organism such as the honeybee we find self-referring systems within self-referring systems. The bee as an organism constitutes a chain of self-referring physiological processes with their own circular organization and lives within a society of bees where relations are also circular. In turn, the relationship between the society of bees and the wider ecology is also circular. Eliminate the bees and the whole ecology will change, for the bee system is linked with the botanical system, which is linked with insect, animal, agricultural, human, and social systems. All these systems are self-referential and turn back on each other. A change in any one element can transform all the others.

We could attempt to understand such systems by drawing an artificial boundary between system and environment—for example, around the individual bee, or the society of bees, or the bee-flora-fauna system—but in doing so we break the circular chain of interaction. An understanding of the autopoietic nature of systems requires *that we understand how each element simultaneously combines the maintenance of itself with the maintenance of the others.* It is simply not good enough to dismiss a large part of the circular chain of interaction as "the environment." The environment is part of the bee system, and the different levels are in effect coproduced. Changes do not arise as a result of external influences. They are produced by variations *within* the overall system that modify the basic mode of organization. Processes of reproduction, mutation, chance interconnection, and innovation can lead to all kinds of self-organizing activity.

To further illustrate these ideas, it is useful to consider how Maturana and Varela reinterpret the way the human brain and nervous system operate. As was discussed in Chapter 4, one of the most familiar images of the brain is that of an information processing system, importing information from the environment and initiating appropriate responses. The brain is viewed as making representations of the environment, recording these in memory, and modifying the information thus stored through experience and learning. In contrast, Maturana and Varela argue that the brain is closed, autonomous, circular, and self-referential. They argue that the brain does not process information from an environment as an independent domain and does not represent the environment in memory. Rather, it establishes and assigns patterns of variation and points of reference as expressions of its own mode of organization. The brain organizes its environment as an extension of itself.

If one thinks about it, the idea that the brain can make true representations of its environment presumes some external point of reference from which it is possible to judge the degree of correspondence between the representation and the reality. This implicitly presumes that the brain must have a capacity to see and understand its world from a point outside itself. Clearly, this cannot be so. Hence, the idea that the brain represents reality is open to serious question. Maturana and Varela's work identifies this paradox and suggests that the brain creates images of reality as expressions or descriptions of its own organization and interacts with these images, modifying them in the light of actual experience.

To those of us who have become used to thinking about organisms and organizations as open systems this kind of circular reasoning may seem very strange indeed. We have learned to see living systems as distinct entities because we insist on understanding them from *our* point of view as observers rather than attempting to understand their inner logic. As my colleague Peter Harris-Jones has put it, in doing this we tend to confuse and mix the domain of organization with that of explanation. If we put ourselves "inside" such systems we come to realize that we are within a closed system of interaction and that the environment is *part* of the system's organization because it is part of its domain of essential interaction.

The theory of autopoiesis accepts that systems can be recognized as having "environments" but insists that relations with any environment are *internally* determined. There may be countless chains of interaction within and between systems, A being linked to B, to C, D, E, and so forth, but there is no independent pattern of causation. Changes in A do not cause changes in B, C, D, or E because the whole chain of relations is part of the same self-determining pattern.

Gregory Bateson and other theorists who have interested themselves in the ecological aspects of systems have made a similar point in emphasizing that "wholes" evolve as complete fields of relations that are mutually determining and determined. The system's pattern has to be understood as a whole and as possessing a logic of its own. It cannot be understood as a network of separate parts.

ENACTMENT AS A
FORM OF NARCISSISM:
ORGANIZATIONS INTERACT
WITH PROJECTIONS OF THEMSELVES

Maturana and Varela have developed their theory as part of a new interpretation of biological phenomena and have strong reservations about applying it to the social world. However, used as metaphor, the theory of autopoiesis has intriguing implications for our understanding of organization.

First, a creative interpretation of the theory helps us see that organizations are always attempting to achieve a form of self-referential closure in relation to their environments, enacting their environments as extensions of their own identity. Second, the perspective helps us understand that many of the problems that organizations encounter in dealing with their environments are intimately connected with the kind of identity that they try to maintain. Third, it helps us see that explanations of the evolution, change, and development of organizations must give primary attention to the factors that shape the patterns embracing both organization *and* environment in the broadest sense.

In Chapter 5 we gave attention to Karl Weick's idea that organizations enact their environments as people assign patterns of meaning and significance to the world in which they operate. The ideas on autopoiesis are very consistent with this perspective, encouraging us to view organizational enactments as part of the self-referential process through which an organization attempts to tie down and reproduce itself.

Consider, for example, the cartoon in Exhibit 8.1. We find here a typical process of organizational self-reference. A meeting has been convened to discuss certain policy issues:

- Where do we stand?
- What's happening in the environment?
- What business are we in?
- Is it the right business?
- How can we penetrate new markets?

Autopoietic systems are closed loops—self-referential systems that strive to shape themselves in their own image.

Hand with reflecting globe. Self-portrait by M. C. Escher (lithograph, 1935).

Exhibit 8.1   Systems That Look at Themselves

SOURCE: Escher self-portrait reprinted by permission of Haags Gemeentemuseum, The Hague, and courtesy of Vorpal Gallery, San Francisco and New York City, by permission of the heirs of M. C. Escher, © M. C. Escher heirs c/o Cordon Arts-Baarn-Holland. Boardroom cartoon reproduced by permission of the artist.

Questions such as these, which parallel those required to generate the kind of double-loop learning discussed in Chapter 4, allow those asking them to make representations of themselves, their organization, and the environment in a way that helps orient action to create or maintain a desirable identity. The charts that decorate the walls of the meeting room are really mirrors. Like the reflecting globe in Escher's lithograph, they allow members of the organization to see themselves within the context of their ongoing activity. The figures and pictures that an organization produces on market trends, competitive position, sales forecasts, raw material availability, and so forth are really projections of the organization's own sense of identity, interests, and concerns. They reflect its understanding of itself. It is through this process of self-reference that organizational members can intervene in their own functioning and thus participate in creating and maintaining their identity.

When we view the enactment process as an attempt to achieve a form of closure in relation to the environment, the whole idea of enactment assumes new significance. We come to realize that enactment is not just an arbitrary mode of perception whereby we see or emphasize certain things while ignoring or downplaying others. It is a core process that projects, defines, and produces a particular way of existing.

IDENTITY AND CLOSURE:
EGOCENTRISM VERSUS
SYSTEMIC WISDOM

Nowadays, many organizations are preoccupied with understanding their environment as a "world out there" that has an existence of its own. The ideas discussed above show the dangers in this kind of thinking and suggest that if one really wants to understand one's environment one must begin by understanding oneself.

Many organizations encounter great problems in dealing with the wider world because they do not recognize how they are a part of their environment. They see themselves as discrete entities faced with the problem of surviving *against* the vagaries of the outside world, which is often constructed as a domain of threat and opportunity.

This is most evident in the practices of what I call *egocentric organizations*, which have a rather fixed notion of who they are or what they can be and are determined to impose or sustain that identity at all costs. This leads them to overemphasize the importance of themselves while underplaying the significance of the wider system of relations in which they exist.

When we look at ourselves in a mirror we create a relation between "figure," the face that we see, and "ground," the context in which our face is located. When we focus on our face, our context is pretty well eliminated from view. The egocentric enactments through which organizations attempt to structure and understand their environments often manifest a similar imbalance. In their quest to see and promote their own sense of identity and perceived self-interest against that of the wider context, they create an overassertive relation between figure and ground. Just as a face in a mirror is dependent on a host of conditions for its existence, such as the biological processes that create and sustain the face and the physical and cultural conditions required for the existence of the mirror, the defining features of organizations are dependent on a host of less obvious contextual relations that must be maintained if the organization is to continue to exist. The figure and its ground are part of the same system of relations and exist only in relation with each other. In enacting and dealing with their environment in an egocentric way, organizations often do not understand their own complexity and the numerous recursive loops on which they depend.

As a result of this kind of egocentrism, many organizations end up trying to sustain unrealistic identities or to produce identities that ultimately destroy important elements of the contexts of which they are part.

A good example of the former is found in those firms making watches and typewriters that failed to take account of developments in digital and microprocessing technology. Seeing themselves as "watchmakers" or "typewriter firms," they continued in the production of traditional products with traditional technologies, failing to understand that these identities were no longer relevant or realistic. As a result, many were obliterated by new forms of competition. We can correctly say in retrospect that all firms serving the traditional markets *should have* seen and included the new developments as part of their environment. But this misses the important point: that their understanding of the environment was a product of their identity as watchmakers or typewriter manufacturers. The closure that this entailed blocked their ability to gain or create new information that would allow them to challenge and question the status quo. To be successful, they needed very different conceptions of themselves and of what their future might entail.

Good examples of how egocentrism can destroy the context on which an organization depends are found in many modern industries. For example, producers of toxic chemicals create all kinds of environmental and social hazards as a side effect of their interest in making profits. They implicitly treat the physical and social environment as a kind of external dumping ground, setting the basis for long-run problems that challenge their future viability. The pollution and health problems created by toxins are likely to eliminate or severely constrain the operations of this industry in the long term. Similarly, in agriculture the use of fertilizers, pesticides, fungicides, and other chemicals together with mechanized methods of farming can bring short-term profits while destroying the soil and other aspects of the ecology on which farming ultimately depends.

We see the same process in the commercial fishing business, which is also in the process of destroying itself because, historically, the key actors involved have seen themselves as being separate from the fish. The firms involved have enacted identities in pursuit of short-term goals, with the result that their actions have, in many parts of the world, already depleted the resource on which their business relies.

Egocentric organizations draw boundaries around narrow definitions of themselves and attempt to advance the self-interest of this narrow domain. Part of the problem rests in the very idea of what it means to be "an organization." The concept implies an entity, "a thing," something with a discrete existence. The principles of autopoiesis highlight the self-referential loops that this creates. An organization "sees itself" as separate, views its "environment" with separateness in mind, acts to sustain its separateness, interprets reactions to those actions from a separatist viewpoint, and so on. Many of the social ills of our time are associated with this kind of egocentric enactment and the kind of free-standing individualism it implies.

Egocentric organizations tend to see survival as hinging on the preservation of their own fixed and narrowly defined identity rather than on the evolution of the more fluid and open identity of the system to which they belong. As discussed in Chapter 7, part of the problem rests in the fact that it is often difficult for them to relinquish identities and strategies that have brought them into being or provided the basis for past success. Yet this is what survival and evolution often require. As in nature, many lines of organizational development, although viable and successful for a while, can prove to be dead ends. In the long run, survival can only be survival *with*, never survival against, the environment or context in which one is operating. In seeing how one's suppliers, one's market, one's labor force, one's local, national, and worldwide community, and even one's competition are really parts of the same system of organization, it becomes possible to move toward an appreciation of systemic interdependence. Many organizations have succeeded in making major breakthroughs by breaking and reshaping the boundaries traditionally drawn between themselves and their customers and competition, creating a new sense of identity for themselves and the system as a whole.

The challenge presented by the theory of autopoiesis is to understand how organizations change and transform themselves along with their environments, and to develop approaches to organization that can foster the kind of open-ended evolution discussed above. At times, this may seem a daunting task. But human systems, like organizations, have a special character in that they are able to reflect on their identities and on the processes and practices that sustain them. In doing so, they can often initiate meaningful patterns of change. By learning to "see themselves" and the way they enact their relations with the broader "environment," they create new potentials for transformation.

The three logics of change discussed in the remainder of this chapter have important contributions to make to this process. They offer different yet complementary ways of understanding how patterns of change unfold and how we can use this understanding to influence future development.

Shifting "Attractors": The Logic of Chaos and Complexity

Our metaphorical development of the theory of autopoiesis has emphasized the close links between organization and environment. Although it is common to draw a clear distinction between the two, it seems systematically wiser to view organization and environment as elements of the same interconnected *pattern*. In evolution, it is pattern that evolves.

In recent years major insights into how this occurs have emerged from two related lines of development: the theory of chaos and self-organization on the one hand and complexity theory on the other. Using physical experiments and computer simulations as metaphors for understanding what happens in nature, they contribute important elements to a holistic theory of change.

The essence of their view is as follows:

Complex nonlinear systems like ecologies or organizations are characterized by multiple systems of interaction that are both ordered and chaotic. Because of this internal complexity, random disturbances can produce unpredictable events and relationships that reverberate throughout a system, creating novel patterns of change. The amazing thing, however, is that despite all the unpredictability, coherent order *always* emerges out of the randomness and surface chaos.

Consider, for example, the illustrations presented in Exhibit 8.2.

Whether we are examining the flocking of birds, the changing relationships between predators and prey, the development of weather patterns, complex chemical reactions, termite colonies, the hive behavior of bees, or the way in which organizations and social systems get transformed over

Order emerges from chaos!

When the behavior of complex systems is simulated through computer models that speed up the course of evolution, patterns form and re-form over and over again:

- Create a multitude of computerized "birds," "bats," or "fish that can move in any way they wish." Establish three simple rules: don't bump into one another; keep up with your neighbors; don't stray too far away. The result: dynamic flock patterns where the detailed movements are completely unpredictable, yet reflect the synchronized behavior of real birds, bats, and fish.

- Create computer "viruses" in a closed environment that are able to self-replicate, mutate at random, and compete for limited space. The result: simulation of evolutionary patterns, whereby one species secures dominance, is almost pushed to extinction by new forces, is modified and makes a comeback, is accompanied by dozens of new species . . . , and so on! A diverse ecology of artificial life emerges with all the familiar characteristics of predator and prey and the parasitic and symbiotic relations found in nature.

- Observe a colony of termites building their nest. Earth is moved randomly. Variations in the terrain emerge. These then become the focus of attention. The termites add to the emerging mounds. "Columns" begin to develop. These are connected to form arches and tunnels producing a wonderful piece of termite "architecture." Random movements eventually produce coherent structures.

- We see a similar pattern in the emergent intelligence of the human brain and in the behavior of the "mobots" discussed in Chapter 4. Unpredictable events and behaviors acquire coherent form.

Exhibit 8.2   Chaos, Complexity, and Emergent Organization

SOURCE: Based on K. Kelly (1994), Kauffman (1993), Langton (1992), and Lewin (1992).

time, it seems that we can detect common processes of spontaneous self-organization. If a system has a sufficient degree of internal complexity, randomness and diversity and instability become *resources* for change. New order is a natural outcome.

In their investigations, chaos theorists have paid particular attention to the way system behaviors tend to fall under the influence of different "attractors." For example, the attractor pattern mapped in Exhibit 8.3

illustrates how a system can be caught in a trajectory where events are unique yet patterned, and how the behavior of the system can "flip" from one pattern to another.

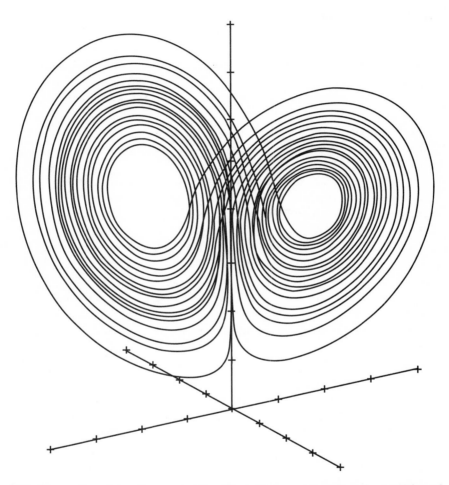

This image, based on the work of mathematician and meteorologist Edward Lorenz, has established itself as a powerful example of how complex systems combine order and disorder. The data plotted in this three-dimensional space show that although there is a clear pattern in the data the behavior of the system is never repeated in exactly the same way. The "flip" or crossover from one "wing" of the pattern to the other results from random, nonlinear events that bring the system under the influence of a new set of attractions.

Exhibit 8.3   The Lorenz Attractor

SOURCE: Diagram reproduced from Gleick (1987: 28). Used by permission.

To understand the significance of an "attractor," engage in the following experiment. Imagine that you are sitting in the early morning sun on an open veranda. Before you there is a scene of complete tranquility: a perfectly smooth lake reflecting the bright blue sky and the greens of the forest surrounding the lake. Loons are calling. Occasionally they dive and resurface. The scene draws you into a mood of complete peace and harmony.

Now, let your attention drift to the room behind you. You focus on the click, click, click of the electric clock; on the gurgling of a noisy refrigerator. A kitchen tap is also dripping. The sounds pull you out of the tranquil scene. Though your eyes may still be focused on the water, your mind is elsewhere.

In a very elementary sense you are caught between two "attractors" that define the context of two completely different situations. As you get pulled toward the one, the other becomes insignificant. When you are completely drawn into the lakeside scene, there are no discernible household noises. You only hear the loons. But if you are drawn to the clock, tap, and refrigerator, as many brainwashing techniques have discovered, the annoying noises *become* the dominant, indeed, the all-embracing reality.

Complex systems seem to have a natural tendency to get caught in tensions of this kind, falling under the influence of different attractors that ultimately *define the contexts in which detailed system behaviors unfold*. We see this in the examples described in Exhibit 8.2. Create a context defined by a few simple points of reference that are equivalent to the "minimum specs" discussed in Chapter 4, and random fluctuations will self-organize into a coherent form.

Chaos theorists have noted that complex systems can fall under the influence of different types of attractors. Some pull a system into states of equilibrium or near equilibrium, for example, as a result of negative feedback loops that counteract destabilizing fluctuations. Other attractors have a tendency to flip a system into completely new configurations, as in the case of the "Lorenz attractor" illustrated in Exhibit 8.3. This illustrates how a system can be drawn under the influence of different sets of reference points that in effect define competing contexts. The detailed behavior of the system depends on which context dominates.

In explaining how systems can transform themselves in this way, chaos theorists have become particularly interested in understanding what happens when a system is "pushed" far from its equilibrium toward an "edge of chaos" situation. Here, it encounters "bifurcation points" that are rather like "forks in a road" leading to different futures. At such points the energy within the system can self-organize through unpredictable leaps into different system states. If the old dominant attractor can dissipate the energy and instability, potential changes get dissolved and the system reverts to a variation of its former state. If, on the other hand, a new set of influences gains the upper hand, it can "attract" the energies to a new configuration.

Bifurcation points and associated "attractors" always exist as latent *potentials* within any complex nonlinear system. They signal potentials for self-organization and the evolution of new form. However, the path of system evolution is completely unpredictable, because, given the complexity and nonlinearity, seemingly insignificant changes can unfold to create large effects.

The famous image is of the "butterfly effect," whereby a small change as insignificant as a butterfly flapping its wings in Peking can influence weather patterns in the Gulf of Mexico. Or, as science writer Kevin Kelly has put it, in complex nonlinear systems, "2 + 2 = apples."

Under conditions of nonlinearity and randomness, incremental changes that may themselves seem insignificant can precipitate major discontinuous or qualitative changes because of the emergent properties triggered by marginal adjustments. The butterfly in China doesn't "cause" a new weather pattern. That's the old linear logic at work. The significance of the butterfly is that it triggers a small change, that perhaps triggers another small change, and another, and another that by chance proves to be a significant random element catalyzing changes that ultimately shift a system from the influence of one attractor pattern to another. Quantum and qualitative change, *incrementally!* 2 + 2 does not necessarily lead to 4 or even 5 or 6. It leads to the emergence of qualitatively new system states.

MANAGING IN THE MIDST OF COMPLEXITY

These insights have enormous implications for modern management, giving rise to at least five key ideas for guiding the management of change. In a nutshell, they suggest that it is important to

- Rethink what we mean by organization, especially the nature of hierarchy and control
- Learn the art of managing and changing contexts
- Learn how to use small changes to create large effects
- Live with continuous transformation and emergent order as a natural state of affairs
- Be open to new metaphors that can facilitate processes of self-organization

Rethinking organization: As will be recalled from our discussion of the emergent character of learning and intelligence in Chapter 4, complexity theory invites managers to rethink the nature of order and organization. Instead of seeing these qualities as states that can be externally imposed on a situation through hierarchical means, or through the predetermined logic that we bring to the design of bridges or buildings, managers are invited to view them as *emergent* properties. New order emerges in *any* complex system that, because of internal and external fluctuations, is pushed into "edge of chaos" situations. Order is natural! It is emergent and free! But most interesting of all, its precise nature can *never* be planned or predetermined.

Note that in all of our discussions of complexity, whether in the preceding pages, or in our discussion of the brain in Chapter 4, no mention has been made of any grand design. There has been no mention of a master manager or grand architect. There *has* been discussion of how order can evolve under the influence of a number of simple rules, like the "minimum specs" discussed in Chapter 4, and illustrated in Exhibit 8.2 in this chapter. But no mention has been made of any absolute ordering or predesign.

This can have frightening consequences for managers who have become used to the props of planning, structure, hierarchy, and other traditional modes of control. But the message of chaos and complexity theory is that while some kind of ordering is *always* likely to be a feature of complex systems, structure and hierarchy can have no fixed form, hence cannot function as predetermined modes of control. Patterns have to emerge. They cannot be imposed.

To take a simple example, consider the activities of a self-organizing work team involved with the development of a new product, or an autonomous work group operating in a "just in time" flexible factory. Hierarchial and other structural patterns are likely to develop as different team members, functions, or activities take a leading role, or as different priorities create a focus of attention. But the pattern evolves and finds its own form.

Under such conditions, hierarchy and associated patterns of organization and control are temporary conditions or *outcomes*. They are no more than "snapshot points" on a self-organizing journey. Moreover, the hierarchies that emerge are likely to be created and driven from any point within the system. Authoritarian "top-down" hierarchies found in mechanistic organizations give way to emergent hierarchies generated by the need to cluster and direct activities to address the contingencies at hand. Managers functioning in the midst of this kind of complexity are part of the flux. They need mind-sets that allow them to facilitate the process and flow with the change, rather than try to predesign and control in a more traditional way.

The art of managing and changing "context": A second extremely important implication of a chaos-complexity perspective rests in the idea that *the fundamental role of managers is to shape and create "contexts" in which appropriate forms of self-organization can occur.*

As has been noted, the implicit rules, reference points, or "minimum specs" that define an "attractor" create a context in which a system can acquire detailed empirical form. Managers have to become skilled in helping to shape the parameters that can define an appropriate context, while allowing the details to unfold within this frame. In this way, they can help to shape emergent processes of self-organization, while avoiding the trap of imposing too much control.

The focus on attractor patterns thus creates a powerful perspective for the management of stability and the management of change, suggesting that *transformational change ultimately involves the creation of "new contexts" that can break the hold of dominant attractor patterns in favor of new ones.* The key principles underlying this approach are summarized in Exhibit 8.4.

To illustrate the challenge of maintaining stability, consider the case of a hospital emergency operating room. The challenge here is to create a relatively stable space within which the surgical team can self-organize around the contingencies and challenges being faced. The context will be bombarded by all kinds of random influences: unanticipated or uncontrollable risks of infection; patients with unknown medical histories; an unpredictable caseload; unexpected changes in personnel. The challenge is to hold such a situation under the influence of a strong attractor pattern that minimizes disrupting influences, so that the surgical team can do an effective job.

In other situations where the dominant attractor pattern is sustaining an undesirable state, the challenge will be to open the door to instability, or even to *create* the instability that will help a new pattern of behavior emerge. Continuing with our hospital-based example, consider the challenge of shifting major medical services out of the hospital into the community by using new modes of service delivery. This change may be hindered by the forces of the dominant attractor system within the hospital, such as those sustained by established mind-sets, power bases, vested interests, and existing codes of practice. Typically, these will undermine the change by pulling the new initiative back under the control of the established system, creating a long-term pattern of business as usual.

To break the power of the established attractor, our manager will have to find ways of creating a new context. One strategy may be to transform the mind-sets of key physicians and administrators by dramatizing the

Let's use the image of a Lorenz attractor as a creative metaphor for thinking about organizational change. Here are some of the questions that are raised:

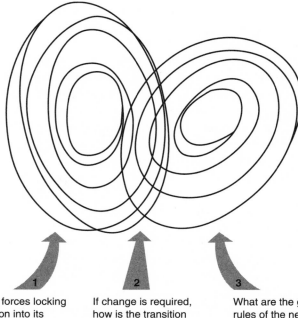

What are the forces locking an organization into its existing "attractor" pattern?

Structures?
Hierarchies?
Rules?
Controls?
Culture?
Defensive routines?
Power relations?
Psychic traps?

Is the "attractor" appropriate? Should it be changed?

If change is required, how is the transition from one attractor to another to be achieved?

How can small changes be used to create large effects?

What are the ground rules of the new attractor going to be?

How can we manage through the "edge of chaos" of stage 2 while remaining open to emergent self-organization?

Exhibit 8.4   Attractor Patterns and Organizational Change

fiscal realities, by demonstrating the viability of new innovations, or by highlighting the new forms of emerging competition that are underpinning the need for change. Another way may be to change the context by mobilizing a powerful coalition of key individuals that can launch and protect a prototype of a new system. Or steps may be taken to transfer the responsibility for delivery of these services to a completely new organization, for example, through some kind of subcontracting arrangement.

Such proposals or actions would create great instability within the established system. This would have to be nudged and pushed toward the critical point at which key players are inclined to reconsider the viability of the hospital's established sense of identity, so that the system can evolve into a new form, for example, where principles of community-based health care define key elements of the new context.

It is important to note that the manager acting on the insights of chaos and complexity theory cannot be in control of the change. He or she cannot define the precise form that the new attractor pattern will take. While it is possible to shape or nurture key elements of the emerging context by opening the old system to new information, new experiences, new modes of service delivery, new criteria for assessing quality, and so on, the resulting "attractor" will find its own form. The important point is that the manager helps to create the conditions under which the new context can emerge. To the extent that the system remains locked into the old context, no significant change is possible. This is the key problem that blocks so many organizations that are trying to transform themselves. Because of the power of the established context, they end up trying to do the new in old ways.

As chaos writer Jeffrey Goldstein has noted, much of the literature on organizational change has focused on the problem of "resistance," instead of focusing on how new "attractors" can "pull" the latent energies of a system to a point where they can organize into a new form. Resistance arises when the forces of an established attractor are more powerful than those of a new or emergent one. The challenge is to shift the balance.

This is what the art of creating new contexts helps us to do.

New contexts can be created by generating *new understandings* of a situation, or by engaging in *new actions*.

New understandings can transform the autopoietic processes of self-reference through which a system produces and reproduces its basic sense of identity. This can be achieved by exposing the system to new information about itself or its environment and by encouraging the kind of double-loop learning discussed in Chapter 4. Through such means the system can begin to challenge and change its operating norms, paradigms, and assumptions, and free itself from the cognitive and other psychic traps that sustain its established attractor pattern. As noted in our earlier discussion of autopoiesis, the very idea that an organization thinks about itself as a discrete organization may be a key feature of its dominant attractor, leading it to try to survive as a discrete entity instead of allowing itself to evolve into a new form. For example, as a result of a new understanding of its situation, the hospital in our earlier example may be able to develop a new identity where it becomes part of an evolving network of services rather than hanging onto an unsustainable one.

New contexts can also be created by engaging in *new actions* that help to push the system into a new state more directly. Experiments, prototypes, changes in rewards, changes in key personnel, a fiscal crisis, staff layoffs, and numerous other events, actions, and experiences can themselves embody powerful messages that catalyze other changes in the context as the system adjusts itself to the new reality.

While new understanding can create a heightened sense of the need for change, and a direction in which an organization may feel it needs to go, new actions help to get it there. The conventional way of thinking about organizational change puts these in sequential order. But from a chaos perspective they often need to be reversed. New action can catalyze new understandings. For example, a hospital that creates a powerful prototype of new service delivery in action, or subcontracts an important set of services to an organization that could develop into a potential competitor, can create a dramatic new understanding of the status quo. The generation of new understandings and new actions, in whatever order they evolve, are the keys to contextual change.

Using small changes to create large effects: A third major implication of the chaos-complexity perspective, and one that brings a great deal of pragmatism to the task of managing and changing contexts, rests in the idea that in "edge of chaos" situations, small but critical changes at critical times can trigger major transforming effects. The image from the natural world is of the "butterfly effect." But in complex human systems the principle assumes a new and even more powerful dimension, because human beings have the ability to reflect on their contexts and to choose the points at which they intervene. Developing this idea, it follows that any person wishing to change the context in which he or she is operating *should search for "doable" high-leverage initiatives that can trigger a transition from one attractor to another.*

Chaos theory also gives clear indications of where one should look for these initiatives. As will be recalled, the tensions between competing attractors generate "bifurcation points" leading to different paths of future development. Most often these manifest themselves as paradoxes or tensions between the status quo and alternative future states. For example, in the hospital situation discussed above, the drive toward a new system of community-based health care may generate all kinds of oppositions from the status quo, expressed as potential crises. For example, physicians or senior administrators may feel that community-based services will lead to "poorer quality," "less control," "falling standards," and "loss of power." Normally these fears and concerns will generate actions seeking to reinforce the current situation.

The chaos manager must recognize these "forks in the road" and create a context supporting the new line of development by finding interventions that transcend the paradoxes or make them irrelevant. For example, by creating a successful prototype, or by getting key opinion leaders behind the initiative, he or she may be able to create the crucial time and space in which success can be demonstrated, publicized, and made irreversible. The task of creating new context often hinges on the management of this kind of paradox.

The basic ideas involved here allow us to talk about the skills of creating new contexts in precise terms. In particular, they suggest that if managers can learn to identify emerging paradoxes, or, if necessary, create paradoxes that embody the tensions between the status quo and a desired future, they can identify important points of leverage that can be used to undermine the force of the status quo in favor of a new future. The task hinges on finding new understandings or new actions that can reframe the paradox in a way that unleashes system energies in favor of the new line of development.

Chaos theorists who have begun to look at the implications of this perspective for the management of change talk a great deal about the need to push systems into far from equilibrium states by generating instabilities and crises that will "flip" a system from one trajectory to another. The above ideas refine what is involved here, and help to show how the chaos manager can begin to tread the fine line that often arises between nudging or "flipping" the trajectory of a complex system, on the one hand, and the creation of sheer anarchy on the other.

The challenge of managing complex systems often seems completely overwhelming. The complexity defies comprehensive analysis, and it is often difficult to know where to intervene. The above principles encourage us to cut through this complexity and focus on a few key principles that offer the promise of achieving quantum change *incrementally!* In much of the management literature quantum and incremental change are seen as opposites. Quantum change is seen as being produced through large initiatives. Incremental change is viewed as the route to marginal improvements. While this is true under conditions of linearity, in complex nonlinear systems small incremental changes can produce large quantum effects. If people focus on finding high-leverage initiatives within their sphere of influence that have the capacity to shift the context, potentials for major change can be unleashed.

There are at least two ways in which this potential can unfold. First, small changes may in themselves *catalyze* a major change, because the change itself proves pivotal. For example, a successful experiment prototyping a new health care delivery system in our earlier example may prove to be the crucial change that transforms the context of opinion among key power holders in the hospital. Second, small changes can also create a *critical mass effect*. Though small and insignificant in themselves, together they build an overwhelming force.

In the management of complex systems, both processes can be mobilized in a way that overcomes the conventional dichotomy drawn between incremental and quantum change.

Living with emergence as a natural state of affairs: The significance of this point has been underscored in many ways. In complex systems no one is ever in a position to control or design system operations in a comprehensive way. Form emerges. It cannot be imposed, and there are no end states. At best, would-be managers have to be content with an ability to nudge and push a system in a desired direction by shaping critical parameters that can influence the course of system evolution.

In developing mind-sets and skills appropriate for this task, they can benefit from understanding the principles of holographic self-organization, discussed in Chapter 4, especially in terms of the role that a focus on the role of "limits" and "minimum specs" can play in creating a space in which coherent self-organization can emerge. These concepts can be crucial in helping managers encourage the emergence of desired forms without dictating their detailed nature.

Managers can also benefit from a perspective that views every initiative as a systemic "probe" and learning opportunity. In discussing the art of creating new contexts, much has been made of the use of experiments and prototypes as a means of shifting attractor patterns. Successful experiments can go a long way in creating a foothold on a new reality. In particular, they offer important insights into the feedback loops and defensive routines that sustain a dominant attractor pattern and what can be done to help a new one emerge.

The chaos manager must also develop a heightened awareness of the importance of "boundary management." As noted earlier, new experiments often get neutralized by the status quo. It is thus vital that the chaos manager become skilled in the art of managing boundaries: building them when it is necessary to shield an initiative from the forces of an old attractor, and breaking them when the initiative is strong enough to survive on its own. For example, a manager seeking to promote the transformation to community-based health care in the hospital discussed above may need to hide and protect radical experiments in their early stages or they will never get off the ground. But once successful, he or she may wish to drive their extensions in a very visible way. New images and metaphors of the manager's role are often needed to help in this task, and to cope with the ambiguity, paradox, pressures, and uncertainties that the absence of fixed states and clear end points entails.

Being open to new metaphors that can facilitate self-organization: Given what has been said above, this point probably needs no further emphasis. The challenge of nurturing processes of continuous self-organization demands that we find new metaphors for conceptualizing the task. The research on chaos and complexity is full of resonant images based on the behavior of termite colonies, beehives, and other processes that illustrate the nature of self-organizing systems. They provide a valuable resource for carrying organization and management theory into a new domain.

The images and ideas associated with the other two logics of change to be discussed in this chapter also make important contributions here. The discussion of mutual causality offered in the next section offers important images and insights into the nature of transformational change in nonlinear systems. The discussion on contradiction and the logic of dialectical change offers a powerful perspective on the tensions and paradoxes that shape processes of self-organization. It is to these that we now turn.

Loops, Not Lines: The Logic of Mutual Causality

The theories of autopoiesis, chaos, and complexity encourage us to understand how change unfolds through circular patterns of interaction, and how organizations evolve or disappear along with changes occurring in the broader context. They invite managers to think more systematically about this context and the evolving patterns to which they belong. As we have seen, this requires that we think about change in terms of loops rather than lines and to replace the idea of mechanical causality, for example, that A causes B, with the idea of mutual causality, which suggests that A and B may be co-defined as a consequence of belonging to the same system of circular relations.

Numerous cyberneticians have attempted to develop methodologies for studying this kind of mutual causality and how systems engage in their own transformation. One of the most notable contributions is found in the work of Magorah Maruyama, who focuses on positive and negative feedback in shaping system dynamics. Processes of negative feedback, where a change in a variable initiates counteracting forces leading to changes in the opposite direction, are important in accounting for the stability of systems. Processes characterized by positive feedback, where more leads to more and less to less, are important in accounting for escalating patterns of system change. Together, these feedback mechanisms, can explain why systems gain or preserve a given form and how this form can be elaborated and transformed over time.

The power of this kind of thinking was dramatically illustrated in the Club of Rome's project on the predicament of mankind, which pioneered the idea that we should understand world economics as a system of loops. Its report, *Limits to Growth*, focused on trends in world population, pollution, food production, and resource depletion, suggesting that these are driven by loops of positive feedback. Its analysis demonstrated how systems of positive feedback that do not have stabilizing loops can result in exponential change that cannot be sustained in the long run.

The characteristics of this kind of change are beautifully illustrated in the story of an ancient Persian enchanter who presented a chessboard to his king. In return he asked to receive 1 grain of rice for the first square on the board, 2 for the second, 4 for the third, and so on. The king readily agreed, ordering rice to be brought from his store. The fourth square required 8 grains, the tenth 512, the fifteenth 16,384, and the twenty-first topped the million mark. By the fortieth square a million million grains had to be brought forth. The entire rice supply was exhausted long before the sixty-fourth square was reached!

Exponential change is change that *increases* at a constant rate, in this case doubling at each stage. And the moral is easy to see. The change seems fine for a while but soon runs completely out of control, just as a constantly increasing rate of pollution or overfishing that begins by killing a few fish will soon kill them all. Many aspects of our socioeconomic system seem to be changing in this way, as attempts to maximize the rate of growth of specific economic and social variables generate changes that transform the whole system of relations in which the activity takes place.

Magorah Maruyama has developed this kind of loop analysis, showing how positive feedback accounts for the differentiation of complex systems. For example, a small crack in a rock may collect water, which freezes and makes the crack larger, permitting more water to collect and the crack to get bigger and bigger, allowing small organisms and earth to collect, a seed to grow, and the rock to be transformed by the growth of vegetation and perhaps even a tree. The runaway process creates differentiation, which may then be sustained in a given form by processes of negative feedback. Or, to take another of Maruyama's examples, a large homogeneous plain attracts a farmer, who settles on a given spot. Other farmers follow, and one of them opens a tool shop. The shop becomes a meeting place, and a food stand is established next to the shop. Gradually, a village grows as merchants, suppliers, farmhands, and others are attracted to it. The village facilitates the marketing of agricultural products, and more farms develop around the village. Increased agricultural activity encourages the development of industry, and the village gradually becomes a city. In the process, the homogeneous plain has been transformed by a series of positive feedback loops that amplify the effects of the initial differentiation.

The secret of the growth of the city, like the growth of the crack that collects water and vegetation, does not rest in any simple cause but in the deviation-amplifying *process*. Maruyama argues that this kind of process explains the evolution of both nature and society, processes of positive feedback producing changes that are quite out of proportion with the initial "kick" or incident that activates them. As in the case of the "butterfly effect," small changes can produce large effects. Initial kicks of high probability (e.g., that water will collect in a crack or that a farmer will settle on a plain) can escalate to produce deviations that have a very low probability (e.g., that a particular tree will grow in a particular crack or that a city will develop at a particular point on a homogeneous plain). Random mutations in nature and accidental events and connections in social life, given favorable circumstances, initiate open-ended processes of self-organization in which positive and negative feedback interact to produce changing patterns that may at some point assume relatively stable forms.

The relevance of this kind of analysis for understanding the events and processes that shape organizations and their contexts is obvious. As illustrated in Exhibits 8.5, 8.6, and 8.7, the approach can be used to understand the dynamics of many different kinds of organizational problems.

For example, Exhibit 8.5 presents a contextual analysis of some of the relations contributing to price inflation. Most analyses of this problem tend to fall into the trap of "thinking in lines," searching for simple causes that lie at the root of the problem. The level of employment, money supply, trade union power, wage rates, interest rates, and government spending have all at one time or another been identified as the root cause. This linear thinking then sets the basis for linear solutions: for example, increase unemployment, reduce the money supply, reduce trade union power, introduce wage restrictions, increase interest rates, or reduce government spending. The kind of contextual analysis diagrammed in Exhibit 8.5 offers an alternative way of thinking about the problem by revealing the *pattern of relations* that create and sustain inflation. Our attention now is directed toward an understanding of how the network of

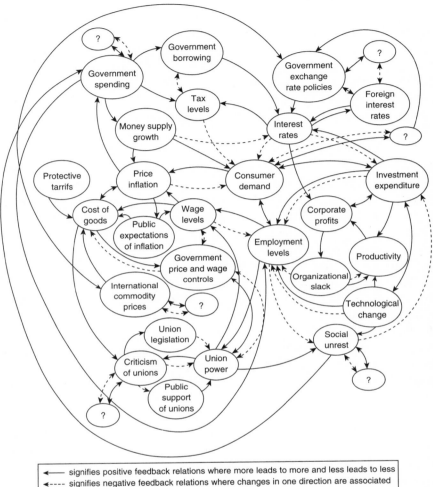

signifies positive feedback relations where more leads to more and less leads to less
signifies negative feedback relations where changes in one direction are associated
with changes in the opposite direction

When we understand the problem of price inflation as a system of mutual causal-ity defined by many interacting forces, we are encouraged to think in loops rather than in lines. No single factor is the cause of the problem. Price inflation is enfolded in the nature of the relations that define the total system. Many of the links represented in this diagram are deviation amplifying (heavy lines); negative feedback relations (dotted lines) are more sparse. Positive feedback thus gains the upper hand. The system can be stabilized by strengthening existing negative feed-back loops and creating others. Many government policies implicitly attempt to have this effect. For example, wage and price controls and unemployment policies introduce negative feedback loops that attempt to moderate the wage-price spiral.

(Continued)

Government or media criticism of trade unions as unreasonable "villains" attempts to weaken the positive feedback loop between public support and union power.

In understanding this kind of mutual causality, we recognize that it is not possible to exert unilateral control over any set of variables. Interventions are likely to reverberate throughout the whole. It is thus necessary to adjust interventions to achieve the kind of *system* transformation that one desires, often by modifying key subsystems.

Exhibit 8.5   Price Inflation as a System of Mutual Causality

---

positive feedback loops that amplify price rises can be stabilized through negative feedback. We are encouraged to find ways of redefining the total system to strengthen the pattern of relations that we wish to maintain.

Exhibit 8.6 illustrates how this kind of analysis can be used to understand some of the relations shaping a specific industrial sector—the power industry. As the diagram shows, a network of positive and negative feedback loops links the fortunes of many seemingly discrete elements of the industry. Quite often, energy plans, even at a national level, are based on the capacities and responses of individual industries—coal, hydro, oil, nuclear power, gas, solar. The demand for energy tends to be treated as an autonomous factor, the function of the various industries being to respond in an economic way. The kind of contextual analysis presented in Exhibit 8.6 allows one to arrive at a different way of formulating the dynamics through which the total system is evolving and to formulate different corporate responses. It is possible to influence the pattern of relations generating demand as well as supply and to design interventions that take advantage of the scope for collaborative action in the solution of shared problems.

Exhibit 8.7 applies the same method of analysis to how Great Britain's "mad cow" problem escalated completely out of control into a major European crisis threatening collapse of the beef industry. The problem was "kick-started" in the early 1980s when diseased sheep brains were used in the production of cattle food. In the 1980s, several cows were observed "dancing" and stumbling in British fields and farmyards. The problem was identified as bovine spongiform encephalopathy (BSE) and labeled by the British press as "mad cow disease." Public fears about eating beef began to develop but were quickly countered by the British government and medical opinion: Beef, it was declared, was perfectly safe to eat. No real action or concern was necessary.

But still the problem festered. Media publicity continued.

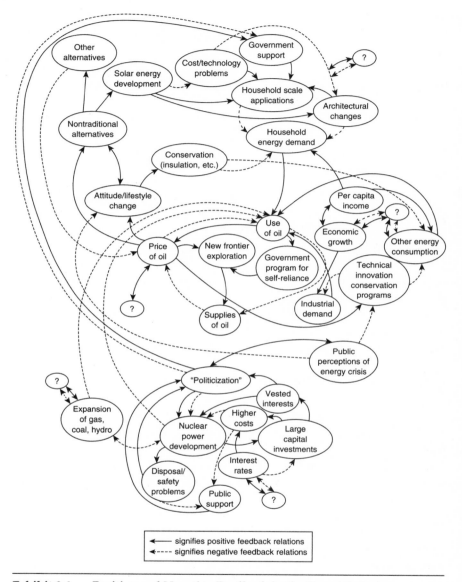

Exhibit 8.6   Positive and Negative Feedback in the Power Industry

In 1989, the British government began to take action by banning sale of diseased cattle. They hoped that this would make the problem go away. But the festering concerns continued until 1996, when the medical committee that had originally pronounced beef as being safe to eat reversed

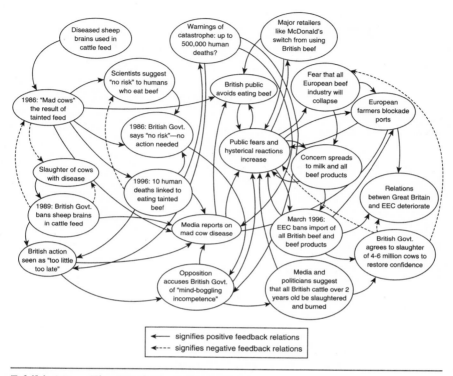

Exhibit 8.7   The "Mad Cow" Phenomenon

its position, announcing a connection between ten deaths of young British people from Creutzfeldt-Jakob disease, which seemed to be linked to BSE.

Panic hit the British media and Main Streets, with angry scenes in Parliament denouncing the "mind-boggling incompetence" of the British government in not taking swift action ten years before. The media carried forecasts of up to 500,000 human deaths and calls for the slaughter of all 11 million British cattle at a cost of up to $40 billion. It was estimated that the eventual cost to Great Britain could be one percent of the GDP.

The British government, backed by most scientific opinion, clung to its belief that beef was perfectly safe and that the ten deaths had resulted from contact with diseased animals, not from eating beef. The British public, fed by the media frenzy and dramatic scenes in Parliament, was unconvinced. Beef sales plummeted. McDonald's and other major food and retail chains joined the parade, declaring that they were no longer using British beef. The European Community, fearing the collapse of the whole European beef market, tried to contain the problem to British shores. It declared a state of emergency, banning the import and sale of British cattle. Countries throughout the world quickly followed.

The British government still declared that British beef was safe. But there were no buyers in sight. The whole British beef market had collapsed: no confidence at home, let alone worldwide. Within days the government was obliged to completely reverse its position, agreeing to the slaughter of 4.7 million cattle, even though existing scientific evidence showed that virtually all British cattle were now completely healthy and disease free.

We see here the power of positive feedback loops and how they can run completely out of control. The case is undoubtedly an extreme one, but the same process can be observed in countless situations: in how the Watergate burglary led to the fall of the Nixon administration in the United States; in the accumulating errors and oversights underlying the *Challenger* space shuttle disaster; and in the rapid collapse of the USSR, the Berlin Wall, and the political and economic structure of most of Eastern Europe. At a more modest scale, the phenomenon is experienced in millions of personal, family, and organizational situations where years of stalemate get flipped into patterns of anarchy and breakdown. Often, our explanations and analysis of such situations tend to focus on a search for villains or for a specific "cause." But more realistically, the phenomenon resides within the overall pattern of positive and negative feedback. Revisit the dynamics in Exhibit 8.7. Negative feedback loops are very weak.

When we analyze situations as loops rather than lines, we invariably arrive at a rich picture of the system under consideration. This can have its advantages in that the analysis highlights key connections and provides a way of identifying the configuration of positive and negative feedback loops defining a particular context or "attractor pattern." It also shows the points at which it may be desirable to intervene either to reinforce the existing attractor or to help the shift to a new one. But the richness and sheer complexity of the analysis can be overwhelming.

Thus, a balance often has to be struck to make the methodology pragmatic. One of the tactics that can be used here involves the search for key system patterns, by trying to identify the particular configuration of positive and negative feedback loops that are shaping a situation. For example, as Peter Senge of MIT has shown, it is often possible to detect distinct system *archetypes* that, once recognized, help to create general strategies of systems management.

For example, applying this approach to the analysis of detailed organizational problems, Senge shows that many systems tend to be inherently unstable because of *delayed feedback and response* between elements, which leads people to underplay or exaggerate their behaviors. The "mad cow" case offers a good example. No action, or "too little too late," can precipitate major swings in a system. The slaughter of a few thousand cattle in the 1980s could have saved the slaughter of 4 million later on. In other situations, of course, delayed action may be the best response because problems may prove to be nonproblems and disappear on their own.

Other systems may constantly *hit constraints* that prevent full development. For example, high production levels may hit manufacturing or resource constraints; the development of team skills or team spirit may plateau and then decline. In such situations the systemically wise response will focus on removing the constraints that are holding key processes back.

In yet other systems, positive feedback loops may be *escalating* and driving a system into a destructive state. For example, team members may be so competitive that in trying to outperform each other they end up eroding each other's success. In such situations the effective strategy may be to introduce system modifications through new loops that can create win-win outcomes.

In situations where individuals feed off a common resource without regard for the well-being of the whole system we find a *Tragedy of the Commons* problem, where the resource ends up being completely destroyed. This system archetype was originally identified by ecologist Garrett Hardin, who took the image of animals being allowed to graze common land and "grazing it to destruction" as a pattern that we find in the depletion of resources worldwide. There's short-term logic in farmers allowing their animals to eat as much of the common grass as possible. But the process pushes the system beyond the point of regeneration. The same process is destroying the world fishing industry and many aspects of the forestry and agricultural business. It is found in the dynamics of many social and corporate welfare systems and in the way individuals and organizations plunder long-term benefits for short-term gains. Solutions depend on the development of shared understandings of the problem, and an ability to reframe system dynamics so that short-term individual interest and long-term sustainability and development become more balanced and integrated.

The complexity of most social systems is such that the analysis can rarely be complete because the problem or focus with which one starts often ends up being part of a larger problem requiring a broader focus.

For example, in examining the details of Exhibits 8.5, 8.6, and 8.7, it is easy to see how new loops could be included to make the analysis even more comprehensive.

In using this kind of method, all kinds of shortcuts and compromises thus have to be struck. Otherwise, analysis leads to paralysis. However, despite this limitation, and the fact that since complex nonlinear systems are constantly unfolding, their form only becomes truly clear with hindsight. As in the case of our "mad cow" example, the methodology has great power. It invites us to understand the key patterns that are shaping system dynamics, especially those that are locking the system into vicious circles because of clusters of positive feedback loops. It encourages us to approach organizational and social problems with a mind-set that respects patterns of mutual causality and cultivates what Gregory Bateson has described as "systemic wisdom." Instead of thinking about problems mechanistically and trying to manipulate linear "causes" and "effects," it encourages us to develop mind-sets and skills that focus on recognizing and changing patterns. It provides a methodology for acting on insights about the nature of autopoiesis and for modifying the self-referential processes that create system identity. It provides a methodology for analyzing a system's "attractor patterns" and for changing their trajectory. It provides further insights into how small changes can create large effects.

- What are the significant loops defining a system?

- Are there principal subsystems or nests of loops that hang together? What are the key connections? What are the key patterns?

- Can we use this understanding to go beyond surface appearance and superficial problems to identify the generative forces that are *producing those problems*?

- Given our understanding of system dynamics, where is the best place to intervene?

- Can we find manageable initiatives that will change the generative pattern, for example, by adding or removing positive or negative feedback loops?

- How can we learn to "nudge" key aspects of such systems to create "new contexts," through our equivalent of the butterfly effect?

These become some of the important questions that need to be asked in the management of complexity.

Contradiction and Crisis:
The Logic of Dialectical Change

Let's now move from the study of circular loops to the study of opposites.

Any phenomenon implies and generates its opposite. Day and night, hot and cold, good and evil, life and death, positive and negative are pairs of self-defining opposites. In each case, the existence of one side depends on the existence of the other. We cannot know what is cold without knowing what is hot. We cannot conceive of day without knowing night. Good defines evil, and life defines death. Opposites are intertwined in a state of tension that also defines a state of harmony and wholeness. Could this tension lie at the basis of all change? Could flux and transformation be a manifestation of contradictory tendencies through which phenomena change themselves?

This idea has a long history. For example, Taoist philosophy, which originated in ancient China, has long emphasized how the way of nature (the word *Tao* means "way") is characterized by a continuous flux and wholeness shaped by the dynamic interplay of *yin* and *yang* (Exhibit 8.8). These words, which originally denoted the dark and sunny sides of a hill, symbolize how the *Tao* is underpinned by a flow of complementary yet opposite energies through which all trends eventually reverse themselves. As the ancient sage Lao-tzu put it, "Reversion is the movement of the *Tao*." Whenever a situation develops extreme qualities it invariably turns around and assumes opposite qualities, just as the brightest light of day begins to pass into the pitchest dark of night. Taoist philosophy emphasizes that all of natural and human life is shaped by this cycle of coming and going, growth and decay, everything being in the process of becoming something else.

The Taoists believed that the disposition or tendency of any situation could be understood in terms of *yin* and *yang*. And they believed that many human situations could be balanced and improved by influencing the relationship between these opposing elements. For example, a healthy and tasty diet attempts to reconcile *yin* and *yang*, and principles of acupuncture address disrupted flows between the *yin* and *yang* of the human body. The Taoist *I Ching* (meaning Book of Changes) formulates a way of thinking in terms of opposites, codifying archetypal patterns of the *Tao* found in the natural and social worlds. Although *I Ching* is now often viewed as the equivalent of a crystal ball, to be used for predicting the future, its true function was to provide a means of understanding the tendencies inherent in the present. As such, it is a document that has much

The dynamic character of *yin* and *yang* is illustrated by the ancient Chinese symbol called *T'ai-chi T'u*, or "Diagram of the Supreme Ultimate."

This diagram is a symmetrical arrangement of the dark *yin* and the bright *yang*, but the symmetry is not static. It is a rotational symmetry suggesting, very forcefully, a continuous cyclic movement: The *yang* returns cyclically to its beginning, the *yin* attains its maximum and gives place to the *yang*. The two dots in the diagram symbolize the idea that each time one of the two forces reaches its extreme, it contains in itself already the seed of its opposite. From very early times, the two archetypal poles of nature were represented not only by bright and dark but also by male and female, firm and yielding, above and below. *Yang*, the strong, male, creative power, was associated with Heaven, whereas *yin*, the dark, receptive, female and maternal element, was represented by the Earth. Heaven is above and full of movement, the Earth—in the old geocentric view—is below and resting, and thus *yang* came to symbolize movement and *yin* rest. In the realm of thought, *yin* is the complex, female, intuitive mind, *yang* the clear and rational male intellect. *Yin* is the quiet, contemplative stillness of the sage, *yang* the strong, creative action of the king.

Exhibit 8.8   Yin and Yang: The Primordial Opposites Guiding All Change

---

in common with modern attempts to understand the dynamics of transformation and change.

Many of these Taoist notions were brought into Western thought through the work of Heraclitus and have been developed and expressed in different ways by generations of social theorists and scientists subscribing to what is now known as a dialectical view of reality. For example, they have had a strong influence on the work of Hegel, the nineteenth-century German philosopher who did much to advance the dialectical method, and on the work of social theorists like Karl Marx, who developed the dialectical view that the world evolves as a result of internal tensions between opposites. In the following sections we will explore some of these views, starting at a societal level using a neo-Marxian perspective to analyze social change and then shifting to an organizational level to grasp some managerial applications of dialectical thinking.

DIALECTICAL ANALYSIS: HOW
OPPOSING FORCES DRIVE CHANGE

With the political collapse of the USSR and Eastern Europe, Marxist ideology and philosophy seem distinctly passé. Yet, ironically, the basic method that propelled Marxian analysis has never been more relevant for understanding the core problems facing Western society. Marxian method is a dialectical method that focuses on how the interplay of opposites fuels social change and how all societies have a tendency to transform and, in many respects, "destroy" themselves because of inner contradictions that cannot be contained. In the view of many social commentators, Western society, despite the political and ideological victories over Eastern communism, is now in such a position. It is being transformed by social and economic contradictions that will ultimately lay the groundwork for a completely new kind of society to emerge. While it is clear that this society will have precious little in common with the communist utopia that Marx envisaged, it is very likely to be shaped by responses to the core contradictions that he identified as lying at the base of the capitalist system. Remembering that the substance of what follows is about *method*, not about the radical ideologies with which Marx is now most often associated, let us engage in some Marxian thinking about social change.

At the risk of some oversimplification, the thrust of Marx's social analysis can be understood as the expression of three dialectical principles. As Exhibit 8.9 suggests, these combine to provide a complex explanation of the processes that set the basis for both gradual and revolutionary kinds of change. Marx's method was to search for the primary tensions or contradictions shaping a given society and to trace their repercussions on the detailed pattern of social life. In so doing, he tried to identify the "laws of movement" of a society, documenting how one stage of social organization inevitably passes into another.

Marx worked under the premise that one must begin by understanding the material conditions of life through which humans produce and reproduce their existence. Under the capitalist mode of production these conditions are found in the system of work organization where certain individuals employ others for the purpose of making a profit and accumulating capital. Marx thus analyzed the nature and implications of the process of capital accumulation as a means of revealing the basic contradictions and laws of movement that it generated.

Marx never wrote about the dialectical method employed in his work, preferring to demonstrate it in the concrete analysis of specific situations. Not surprisingly, his view of dialectical analysis has thus been subject to a wide range of interpretation. One of the clearest and most influential statements is found in Frederick Engels's *Dialectics of Nature*, which, despite its rather deterministic flavor, provides a useful perspective on how Marx's theory of social change reflects three principles:

1. The mutual struggle, or unity of opposites

2. The negation of the negation

3. The transformation of quantity into quality

The first principle accounts for processes of self-generated change whereby phenomena change themselves as a result of tension with their opposite. This principle underpins the idea of contradiction and is used by Marx to explain how one social arrangement inevitably gives way to another. For example, an act whereby one person attempts to rule or control another tends to set up a process of resistance or countercontrol that undermines the initial attempt at control. The act of control *itself* sets up consequences that work against its effectiveness.

The second principle explains how change may become developmental in the sense that each negation rejects a previous form, yet also retains something from that form. Thus, an act of control may be negated by an act of countercontrol, which is in turn negated by a further act of control (the negation of the negation), and so on. Each successive pattern of control will retain an element of the previous negation.

The third principle accounts for processes of revolutionary change whereby one form of social organization gives way to another. Marxists call them "totality shifts." In nature there are many processes where changes in quantity eventually lead to a change in quality. Water will absorb increases in temperature until the boiling point, when it then changes into steam. A camel can be loaded with more and more weight until the final straw breaks its back. Similar processes can be observed in patterns of social organization. A process of control and countercontrol may continue until control is no longer possible, leading to a new phase of collaborative or destructive activity. Cumulative changes in society may thus provide the platform for a revolution that changes the underlying basis of that society.

When we combine these three dialectical principles we arrive at a rich and complex picture of the nature of change. Marx's analysis of society stresses that social arrangements generate inner contradictions that defeat the purposes for which they were set up, leading to a continuing pattern of

(Continued)

negation and counternegation. The negation of the negation allows for the progressive development of the system until a limit is reached where its inner contradictions can no longer be contained.

These three principles help explain the transformation of *all* social systems.

Exhibit 8.9   Three Principles of Dialectical Change

For Marx, "capital," by which he meant the surplus value that arises as a result of trading goods and services at a profit, embraces a fundamental contradiction because it puts people in a state of opposition. For example, buyers are pitted against sellers, just as employers (Marx's capitalists) depend for their profit on paying their employees less than what the product of their labor is worth in the marketplace. This view ignores the idea that employer and employee can come together in a value-creating relationship where both gain, but it grasps the dialectical tension that exists in situations where the relative gain accruing to one party (even in a value-adding relationship) defines an associated "loss" for the other. In the view of Marxian economist Ernest Mandel, this dialectical tension in the nature of "capital" is captured in the ancient belief that Mercury, the god of trade (and etymological source of the word *merchant*), is also the king of thieves. It is also captured in the old anarchist slogan that "property is theft." Dialectically, capital, wealth, and profit are based on antagonisms that have a momentum of their own.

Marx's *Das Kapital* illustrates the antagonisms in practice. For example, he shows how the quest for profit or "surplus value" places the capitalist producer in constant antagonism with labor and competitors in the marketplace. These basic contradictions then unfold to create many problems. For example, the drive for surplus value leads the capitalist to reduce labor costs wherever possible. Labor, of course, resists, creating a continuing struggle in the workplace.

Similarly, profits are also reduced through increased competition. This leads the capitalist producer to find ways of constantly beating the competition. Because price reductions of one's product, even though sometimes bringing short-term gain, ultimately reduce the level of profit, the capitalist system is launched into a constant search for new products and new markets. Hence, historically, the push has been toward constant innovation and toward the search for new customers throughout the world. It is a never-ending process and is always intensified by the fact that when new ways of making a profit are found there is a natural tendency for them to be negated by the appearance of new forms of competition. Marx's economic analysis of the process makes much of the fact that, because of the inability of capitalists to isolate themselves from the long-term tendency toward declining rates of profit in all niches where a strong monopoly or exclusivity cannot be sustained, the system as a whole is constantly thrust toward a state of crisis.

Capitalism, in this view, is a social system riddled with, and driven by, contradictions. It is an endless treadmill because the driving logic is based on constant struggle. Competition, which was at first seen as the "protector" against abuse of monopoly power and an important dimension of the "invisible hand" that Adam Smith saw guiding economic relations toward the good of all, becomes part of a runaway system that drives to ever-increasing levels of accomplishment in terms of productivity but with enormous contradictions and potentially negative consequences for the system at large.

This kind of dialectical analysis provides a novel perspective on the broad sweep of history. For example, we can see the Marxian dialectic playing itself out in the early struggles between capital and labor. To increase the efficiency of production, capitalists centralized the productive process under the factory system. Labor forces were *created* through this centralization. Gradually they unionized and began to oppose the system that had created them. The industrial system in the first part of the twentieth century was continuously shaped and reshaped by changing patterns of this dialectical opposition. For example, the mechanization of production *created* human relations problems, exacerbating the "them" and "us" division between capitalists and managers, on the one hand, and labor, on the other. This strengthened unionization, which strengthened management's resolve to break the power of unions.

The success of unionization, which succeeded in sustaining relatively high wages and undermined management control, led to all kinds of management innovation to eliminate labor or improve its efficiency, on the one hand, and to find ways of breaking labor control, on the other. The major solutions have been found in automation and the shift of production to Third World countries where wage rates are much lower than in the West and unions far less powerful. This, in turn, has created a high degree of structural unemployment in the West and a new crisis of long-term consumption. The irony of the spectacular achievements of Western corporations is that they have more or less mastered the problems of providing high-quality and relatively low-priced products, but in doing so, have eliminated, or are in the process of eliminating, their markets. The problem has been exacerbated by the fact that the structural crisis in employment has thrown an increasing burden on Western welfare states, which, faced with the declining tax revenue resulting from reduced employment levels, have moved into states of increasing crisis. This, in turn, has added to the basic problem because when you remove welfare payments you remove markets!

This somewhat oversimplified sketch of some of the broad dynamics within Western development illustrates Marx's dialectical analysis in action. Referring back to Exhibit 8.9 we see how the fundamental opposition that is built into the nature of "capital" and the idea that a system can be driven through a logic of capital accumulation *creates* all kinds of unfolding contradictions. The concept of "capital" and the idea of making a profit define a contested terrain, which embraces a "struggle of opposites" that unfolds through various patterns of negation.

Every solution leads to a new problem. Modern managers experience this every day as they cope with the flux confronting them. But they rarely grasp the underlying social dynamic producing their problems. They are so embroiled in what might be called the micromanagement of capitalism that they miss the macroforces that are shaping the microflux. In a nutshell, they fail to see how the drive to increase efficiency through factory production (a solution) in effect *created* the power of unions (a new problem), which eventually led to increased automation and Third World production (a new solution) that undermines Western markets (a new problem). And so on.

This analysis is schematic, but it makes the basic point: Problem solutions are constantly negated, and the process continues. Capitalism has demonstrated an enormous resiliency in its ability to self-organize into elaborate new forms to the extent that, in terms of his detailed vision and prediction of how the future of society would unfold, Marx got it almost all wrong. But his method of analysis is as powerful as ever.

If we look ahead to future negations of capitalism, what are we going to see? Is the decline in Western markets going to be reversed by some new value-added service economy that finds a new way of creating and distributing wealth? Is the expansion into massive new markets—China, Eastern Europe, India, and South America—going to provide a breath of new life? Will Third World countries become the new economic superpowers, riding the way already charted by the Pacific Rim "Asian Tigers"? Is their economic power going to be undermined by a new Third World unionism that creates similar constraints to development as those experienced in the West? What is going to happen to the social fabric of Western and Eastern societies given that the "invisible hand" conceived by Adam Smith is no longer doing its job in guiding the system for the good of all? These are the questions pertaining to the change of quantity into quality, underpinned by Marx's third dialectical rule.

We are in the midst of a dialectical unfolding, the future of which cannot be seen. Who knows whether the crisis currently being experienced by Western capitalism will prove to be a point of complete transformation of the system, or just another stage in its evolution? What is clear, however, is that the mode of dialectical analysis explored here provides another powerful lens for understanding the unfolding logic of change of which we are all part. From a "chaos theory" perspective, Marxian analysis identifies key elements of the "attractor system" that has shaped much of the nineteenth and twentieth centuries. But Marx's vision of the "new attractor"—his ideal of a communist society—was completely wrong. As noted above, it remains to be seen whether a new "attractor" will emerge to redefine the logic of the basic system or whether capitalism will continue to self-organize and refine itself into new variations on its existing pattern.

THE DIALECTICS OF MANAGEMENT

These ideas have important implications for management. First, they encourage us to put our heads above the flux and see the dialectical contradictions that are shaping detailed organizational life. Unfortunately, Marxian analysis has become so identified with an anticapitalist position that advocates of capitalism have been unable to see or grasp the contributions that this kind of thinking can make to an understanding of contemporary management problems. As should be clear from the foregoing discussion, the escalating levels of competition and the social problems and market potentials that are being lost as a result of corporate cutbacks and downsizings are systemic. They need to be understood in these terms and approached in a way that, using the language of chaos theory, addresses the basic "attractor pattern" producing the problems. They can be resolved only by modifying the basic "rules" of the game. Now that the ideological battle between Western capitalism and Eastern communism has been resolved, political and corporate leaders have an opportunity to go beyond ideological debate and address problems at a more substantial and systemic level.

One way of approaching these issues rests in thinking about developments in modern capitalism as manifestations of "primary" and "secondary" contradictions. For example, as has been suggested, widespread structural unemployment is an offshoot of the primary contradiction captured in the conflict between profit and costs. In turn, this generates secondary contradictions expressed in social oppositions, such as in the conflicts between employed and unemployed, between indigenous populations and new immigrants in their search for jobs, in the tensions between management and unions, and in all kinds of racial and social problems that arise along with difficult economic circumstances. These secondary, or "off-shoot" contradictions cannot be completely resolved in themselves. They need to be tackled at a higher level, through an appreciation of the primary contradictions that are creating the context in which they are able to flourish.

In a similar way, managers are encouraged to recognize that corporate "downsizings" and associated global restructurings are *not* solutions to problems. As suggested above, they too are manifestations of deeper problems. Ultimately, they are best tackled through social and political initiatives that can address the "rules of the game" embedded in the primary contradictions shaping capitalism itself. The dialectical thinking described above provides a framework for approaching the policy issues involved.

The second major contribution of dialectical analysis rests in insights and methods for the micromanagement of capitalism at an organizational level. Managers cannot wait for the macro-problems described above to be resolved. They have to deal with the micro-flux even if it is the reflection of secondary contradictions. Dialectical analysis contributes to this in showing how many detailed organizational problems hinge on the effective management of paradox, and in recognizing that innovation and development always rest in a process of "creative destruction."

Managing paradox: In our discussion of chaos theory, mention was made of how systems that are moving away from the influence of a dominant attractor pattern toward a potential new configuration encounter "bifurcation points" or "forks in the road," at which energies for change either dissipate and dissolve in a way that allows the old attractor to reassert itself or shift the system into a new form. An understanding of the dialectical nature of change offers important insights into the process, suggesting that the "forks in the road" usually arise around key paradoxes or contradictions that block the way to a new future. The successful management of change requires skill in dealing with these contradictory tensions.

Consider the following examples.

An organization is seeking to empower its staff by giving employees more control over the decisions influencing their work. This new development, which represents a shift toward a potential new "attractor pattern," encounters opposition from the status quo. Existing decision-making systems and controls, and associated politics of hierarchy and careerism, block or undermine the new developments. Staff struggle to implement the new system. If they are successful in creating a context where they can exercise more autonomy and influence, there is a chance that new forms of empowered decision making will emerge and be accompanied by a transformation of the existing organization. If not, tradition will rule and the "empowerment exercise" will just be added to the organizations's list of failed experiments and initiatives.

Potential new futures *always* create oppositions with the status quo. This dialectical principle gets played out in many forms:

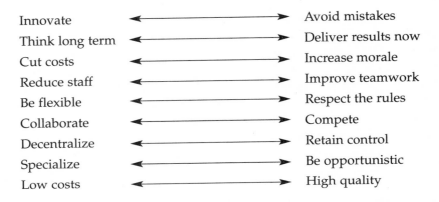

Innovate	Avoid mistakes
Think long term	Deliver results now
Cut costs	Increase morale
Reduce staff	Improve teamwork
Be flexible	Respect the rules
Collaborate	Compete
Decentralize	Retain control
Specialize	Be opportunistic
Low costs	High quality

These are just a few examples of how new initiatives or new directions get mired in paradoxical tensions that undermine the desired change. Although there may be ways of resolving the paradoxes, the fact that the tensions are *experienced as contradictory* may in itself be sufficient to negate transformational change. For example, if people *feel* that the new demands for "more innovation," "improved morale," "more collaboration," "increased decentralization," and so on, are inconsistent with what seems reasonable or possible, inertia is the most likely outcome.

A dialectical view of change asserts that this kind of paradox is inevitable. It reflects the "struggle of opposites" and the fact that any system development always contains elements of a counterdevelopment, because each position tends to *generate* its opposite. Thus, to return to the empowerment example, the very act of seeking to empower staff is likely to *mobilize* awareness of existing modes of control, which, in turn, undermines the drive toward empowerment.

Managers interested in transformational change have to be skilled in managing these tensions. They need to be able to target those that are most important. As in the case of broad societal contradictions, there are often "primary" and "secondary" contradictions at a management level, and managers need to find ways of reframing them so that new patterns of development can unfold. Left to themselves, new initiatives often generate their negation, resulting in the stalemate described above, or in circumstances particularly favorable to the emergent dimension of the paradox, to a complete pendulum swing to the polarity that it represents. Thus, in our empowerment example, if the drive to empowerment was introduced in a context where the traditional control systems were particularly vulnerable to attack, the organization could end up with a situation of empowerment without any semblance of control. Such an extreme development may result in a situation as undesirable as the one the organization is trying to leave behind.

The first step in the successful management of paradox rests in *recognizing that both dimensions of the contradictions that accompany change usually have merit*. Casting your eye over the list of contradictions presented earlier, it is unlikely that as a manager you would want to build your organization around any one side of the dimensions presented. It is likely that you would want your organization to incorporate *both*. Just as staff may need to be empowered *and* controlled, you may want innovation with minimum mistakes; long-term development with an early return; high morale in a low-cost environment; improved teamwork with fewer staff; collaboration that is underpinned by a healthy competitive spirit along the right dimensions; faster, better quality production; and so on.

It is this requirement that distinguishes the management of paradox from the management of resistance to change. The idea of managing and removing "resistance" was pioneered in the 1940s by social psychologist Kurt Lewin, who suggested that any potential change is resisted by forces working in the opposite direction. The idea is similar to the dialectical principle that everything generates its opposite. But within Lewin's framework, the forces tend to be external to the change, holding situations in states of dynamic equilibrium. His solution was to advocate that successful change rests in "unfreezing" an established equilibrium by enhancing the forces driving change, or by reducing or removing the resisting forces, and then "refreezing" in a new equilibrium state.

The dialectical view differs in that it sees paradox as a product of *internal* tensions produced by the fact that elements of both sides of the paradox may embrace equally desirable states. As in the examples cited above, the management task is to find ways of integrating the competing elements. Paradox cannot be successfully resolved by eliminating one side.

The second vital step in the successful management of paradox thus rests in finding ways of creating contexts that can mobilize and retain desirable qualities on both sides while minimizing the negative dimensions. All the skills of managing in the midst of complexity, discussed earlier in this chapter, are relevant here. To the extent that the paradoxes created by change remain unaddressed, they become the stalemating context. The challenge is to find a way of transcending this by *creating new contexts* that can reframe key contradictions in a positive way.

Thus, applying the principles for managing complexity, discussed earlier, managers can help to develop *new understandings* that will reshape the mind-sets through which a particular paradox is approached. For example, by encouraging a view of empowerment that respects a few critical principles or rules (i.e., the "minimum specs" needed to deliver required control), it may be possible to integrate needs for both empowerment *and* control.

Alternatively, the manager may seek to create a new context in which empowerment and control can flourish through *new actions* that prototype required behaviors. For example, he or she may create a new empowered environment in relation to special projects, or prototypes of new team-based forms of production that break old patterns of control while re-creating their essential contributions in a new form. Following the principles discussed earlier, the challenge is to find small changes that can unfold in a way that creates large effects, which deliver on both sides of the paradox at the same time.

Paradox is one of the major forces stalling change at all levels of an organization. It tends to immobilize at both a psychological and action level. Yet approached in the manner described above, it can be transformed into a major lever of change. For in dissolving or transforming paradox, we change the basic rules of the game. As an example, note how modern industry has transformed the traditional paradox between "low cost" and "high quality." For decades they were seen as opposites. But as a result of the Japanese idea that it is possible to reduce costs by improving quality, a whole new line of development has been unleashed. The reframing created a context where people recognized how they could reduce costs by eliminating waste and defects, by simplifying production through better product design, by taking the cost and time out of production, by eliminating excess resources in the production process, and so on. The new frame created a context in which the methods of just-in-time (JIT) management and new relations between networks of firms involved in the production process could unfold, and are still unfolding. Reframed paradoxes create new contexts in which radically new modes of operation can emerge.

Innovation as "creative destruction": Dialectical thinking can also make a major contribution to how we understand and approach the process of innovation. The point is implicit in our discussion of paradox, but has been most fully developed by management writers, who, following economist Joseph Schumpeter, invite us to see evolution and development as a process of creative destruction where new innovations in effect lead to the destruction of established practice. New innovations tend to displace old innovations. In turn, they define the frontier for the next phase of innovation, creating a pattern where problems tend to generate new solutions, which set the basis for new problems, which lead to new solutions, to new problems, and so on. The process applies to the evolution of social life and the development of products, services, and business processes of all kinds.

This has important implications.

For example, it means that innovations create the basis for their own downfall! Whenever an organization succeeds in creating a breakthrough in relation to one of its products or services, for example, as Apple Computer did with the invention of the personal computer, this begins to define the frontier for new competition. Thinking dialectically, we can see that the breakthrough in effect *creates* the frontier for new competition. As Apple has found, numerous companies have moved into the PC market with products and services that ultimately try to overcome the weaknesses of the original product, thus eroding the competitive edge that the innovation established.

At a practical level, this means that any organization wishing to sustain a competitive advantage must recognize how their successes are going to become weaknesses. They must be prepared to innovate in ways that will undermine current success, so that new innovations can emerge.

The power of this strategy for promoting successful innovation has been widely recognized and practiced in many Japanese corporations that, as a consequence of Eastern comfort with dialectical thinking, have long used it as a method for continuous improvement of products and business processes. More recently, it has been advocated as a strategy for dealing with the turbulence and change of the modern corporate environment. For example, as Richard d'Aveni of Dartmouth College has suggested, many companies who succeed in sustaining competitive advantage in turbulent environments do so by systematically destroying the breakthroughs created by their own products and initiatives, by coming up with better ones. Take, for example, the experience of Intel. As d'Aveni suggests, the company's success in becoming a dominant force in the microchip business was propelled by its determination to produce innovations that could beat its own best innovations. Thus in 1992 alone, the company produced nearly thirty new variations on its 486 chip, as well as introducing the Pentium as a foundation for the next generation of chips. The company operates on a philosophy of launching multiple projects that in effect aim to make their developing products obsolete *before* they hit the market. It also tries to find ways of changing the rules of its industry by shifting business frontiers into domains that other competitors find it difficult to reach.

In the language of dialectical analysis this kind of strategy celebrates the "negation of the negation": the second dialectical rule illustrated in Exhibit 8.9. It provides a powerful way of driving constant innovation, and for directing creative energy and attention to the ideas and insights around areas of weakness that, if addressed, may help to avert downfall by propelling one's organization to higher and higher levels of innovation. It provides a way of challenging the "psychic prisons" explored in Chapter 7, and other dimensions of the "attractor patterns" through which organizations get trapped by their own success.

But, if taken to an extreme, the strategy leads to dangerous ground, because it can unleash a spiral of destructive forces. To illustrate, return to the position adopted by Richard d'Aveni, who suggests that the best competitive strategy under conditions of great turbulence, or what he calls "hypercompetition," is to develop strategies that systematically destroy or disrupt the advantages of others. The result: a world where survival seems to hinge on an ethic of kill or be killed. Life is war!

In the anarchist movements of the 19th century the slogan that "the most creative desire is the desire to destroy" became a rallying point for those wishing to overthrow capitalism. In the 1960s it provided the driving principle behind Mao Tse-tung's Cultural Revolution, where an ethic of continuous conflict and destruction was used to dominate the Chinese people and destroy existing patterns of civilization, with disastrous results. d'Aveni's position in effect uses the same principle to support innovation under conditions of advanced capitalism. In essence it defines a "new anarchism," or as it is sometimes described in Europe, a "new brutalism." Destruction feeds on itself. Just as the "Tragedy of the Commons" created a cycle of destruction because the identity and needs of individuals took precedence over those of the collective, strategies of constant destruction can generate similar pathological patterns.

The process of negation and the creative destruction that it implies seems to be a natural quality of all systems. It is found in nature, as well as in social life. But, for the most part, it needs no help! It is spontaneous. It is a part of the self-organizing process.

The danger of promoting "creative destruction" as a management policy is that the destructive potentials within a system get *overemphasized*. It is a major paradox of social life. Evolution involves destruction. But destruction is a side effect or consequence, not a conscious aim. If we use an ethic of destruction to enhance evolutionary processes, the risk is that all manner of new instabilities and pathologies can arise.

Strengths and Limitations of the
Flux and Transformation Metaphor

We now often take change for granted, viewing it as an independent force transforming the world around us and presenting us with all kinds of novel problems with which we have to deal. One of the major strengths of the ideas explored in this chapter is that they seek to fathom the nature and source of change so that we can understand its logic. As has been shown, this has immense significance for how we understand and manage organizations, for if there is an inner logic to the changes that shape our world, it may be possible to understand and manage change at a new and higher level. Instead of just responding to discrete events as novel happenings, we may be able to influence the processes that produce them.

The four sets of ideas explored in this chapter provide alternative yet complementary means of approaching this task.

The theory of autopoiesis suggests that the way we see and manage change is ultimately a product of how we see and think about ourselves, hence how we enact relationships with the environment. Much of the turbulence of the social world is a product of this enactment process.

As shown, relationships between organizations and environment tend to be very truncated and egocentric. There is a poor appreciation of how organization and environment are part of the same broad pattern and how, in evolution, it is *pattern* that evolves. Our interpretation of the theory of autopoiesis suggests that, because of their capacities for self-reflection, organizations, like individuals, have an opportunity to enact new, more systemic identities that break the rigid boundaries between organization and environment, opening the way to more systemic patterns of evolution. In the long run, survival can only be survival *with*, never survival *against*, the environment or context in which one is operating. Organizations, like individuals, have to appreciate that they are always more than themselves. New mind-sets redefining boundaries to embrace customers, "competitors," and other significant elements of "the environment" are part of the required trend.

In the most fundamental sense, the distinction typically drawn between organization and environment is very problematic. Organizations do not exist in any way that is separate from their environments. As discussed in Chapter 3, we may feel that this is now well recognized through the idea that organizations are "open" rather than "closed" systems, but, paradoxically, this distinction just perpetuates the illusion of separateness. As has been shown, the concept of "openness" is flawed conceptually and also practically, for it works against organizations acquiring a deeper appreciation of the evolving or self-destructing pattern of relations to which they belong. The fundamental challenge is to think in terms of gestalt patterns, not just in terms of immediate organization-environment relations.

This point seems a very conceptual one, but it is elaborated in detail through the insights offered by the other three perspectives explored in this chapter. The theories of chaos and complexity, mutual causality, and dialectical opposition each provide complementary ways of understanding how pattern evolves.

Through the lens of chaos and complexity theory we begin to learn that "organizations" and their relationships with "the environment" are part of an "attractor pattern." Key organizing rules—embedded in various aspects of structure, culture, information, mind-sets, beliefs, and perceived identity—tend to hold organization-environment relations in a particular configuration. When pushed into "edge of chaos" situations the basic pattern can flip into new forms. The managerial challenge rests in nudging systems into desired trajectories by initiating small changes that can produce large effects.

The theory of mutual causality encourages us to understand these "attractor patterns" and the processes of change in terms of the positive and negative feedback loops that define complete fields of relations. As we inspect the "mapping" that this kind of perspective creates (Exhibits 8.5, 8.6, and 8.7), we quickly see the arbitrariness of any distinction between organization and environment. We see that the logic of the whole is embedded in the nature of the deviation-amplifying or -stabilizing loops. We see that the key to management results in shaping and reframing the nature of these loops.

Through the lens of dialectical analysis we gain another appreciation of pattern and how it evolves. This time, the emphasis is placed on understanding the paradoxes and tensions that are created whenever elements of a system try to push in a particular direction. Each phase of development sets up conditions leading to its own transformation. The "attractor patterns" of chaos theory are now seen in terms of the core dialectical principles shaping a form of life, such as the dialectics of capital in capitalism and the emergent paradoxes and conflicts they generate. The perspective encourages us to recognize how the management of organization, society, and personal life ultimately involves the management of contradiction. It invites us to find ways through which key tensions can be reframed to create new paths of development.

To use David Bohm's phrase, all these ways of viewing change provide explanations of the relationship between the "implicate" and the "explicate" order of reality. Each in effect provides a metaphorical frame for thinking about the way change emerges in practice. Although they focus attention on different concepts and ideas, all share the view that change self-organizes and is an emergent phenomenon that cannot be predetermined or controlled.

This insight, of course, is two-edged. It can be seen as both a strength and a limitation. The whole idea that change is an emergent phenomenon offers a powerful mind-set for managing change. It encourages us to gain a reflective understanding of the logic driving the flux around us and to nudge and shape that logic whenever we can. Yet it also requires us to recognize that we can never be "in control." The message is that, even though our actions shape and are shaped by change, we are just part of an evolving pattern.

The challenge, of course, is to cope with this paradox: By recognizing that even though we cannot exert unilateral power or control over any complex system, we can act through the power and control that we actually do have. Using the image popularized by chaos theorists, the invitation is to recognize that although we may be no more than "butterflies" in terms of our power on the overall system, we can have enormous effects, especially when we use our insights about systems dynamics and the nature of change to determine how and where to intervene. And, of course, the more butterflies the better!

The strength in this idea, of course, may also be seen as a major weakness, for while it brings a message of hope that emphasizes the potential of "powerless power," it is not a message that many managers want to hear. The whole history of organization and management theory is based on the idea that it is possible to organize, predict, and control. The insights of this chapter suggest that given the reality of complex systems this is not possible.

Ironically, all the perspectives on change explored in this chapter suggest that change is rule-bound. There is order in the chaos, whether we analyze that order by understanding attractor patterns, feedback loops, or unfolding contradictions. However, the order becomes apparent only with hindsight. As we look at the evolution of nature, of organizations, or of the artificial intelligence reflected in the computer simulations conducted by complexity theorists, we can discern distinct rules or patterns of behavior. But the key question is: Are they generative or residual? Do they reflect the rules that have created the pattern that we see? Or are they just "rules" that we invent to capture and *describe* that pattern?

Hindsight is always 20/20. Rules and patterns can always be found in nature and in history. The problem is: Can we find rules that will predict the emergence of a pattern before it becomes reality?

This is a quest that drives much of science and indeed much of the ideology of Western civilization. There is an aspiration to predict and see the future and thus to be "in control."

But is this realistic?

Is it just part of our psychic prison? If so, the ultimate challenge of this chapter may be to recognize the emergent nature of change and let this aspiration go!

9

The Ugly Face

Organizations as Instruments of Domination

Our organizations are killing us!

Ramparts magazine noted many years ago that the Western world is slowly eating itself to death. Our food is often adulterated with thousands of different synthetic flavors, colors, thickeners, acidifiers, bleaches, preservatives, package contaminants, antibiotics, and poison pesticides. Food and tobacco companies spend billions of dollars each year promoting health-damaging products, thereby contributing to the high incidence of cancer and various forms of liver, kidney, heart, and lung disease. Although many argue that the scientific evidence is not conclusive enough to ban other than the most obvious hazards, many scientists believe that we are dealing with a human time bomb because the most damaging effects are likely to be long-term. Ingested toxins may well have an influence on mutations of the human gene pool, producing irreversible damage in generations to come.

Similar threats stem from environmental pollution. Every day, industrial organizations spew millions of tons of toxic waste into our waterways and the atmosphere or bury them in leaky containers underground. The economics of waste disposal is such that many organizations feel that they have no choice but to continue in these damaging practices so long as they remain legal. As a result, it is now estimated that as many as 2,000 toxins pollute the Great Lakes, and there are thousands of dangerous toxic-waste sites adding pollution to the groundwater. For example, over 160 such sites have been identified within three miles of the Niagara River, which feeds into Lake Ontario. The fish have cancer, and in areas of concentrated pollution such as the infamous Love Canal near the Niagara River, concern about pollution-related diseases has reached crisis proportions. As in the case of food and tobacco production, human health is adversely affected by corporate practices that place profits before human welfare.

Working in many organizations can be dangerous, too. Each year hundreds of thousands of workers throughout the world die of work-related accidents and illnesses. Over 100,000 deaths occur in North America alone. Hundreds of thousands of workers suffer from occupational diseases of varying severity, such as heart disease, eye strain, back pain, stress, or lung ailments. Only the worst hazards are closely monitored or controlled. Others occur within the law and are frequently treated as inevitable aspects of the lines of business in which they occur. Accidents and occupational disease, like pollution, are often viewed in a way that places more emphasis on costs and the "bottom line" than on the health of employees.

Throughout the Third World, large multinational corporations often ride roughshod over the interests of local people. As in the early years of the Industrial Revolution in Europe, people are legally and illegally dispossessed of their land and traditional ways of life. They are transformed into an urban poor who work for subsistence wages in sweatshops and factories. In the view of many analysts, the multinationals virtually rob their host countries of resources and labor power. At the same time, they engage in modes of strategic management that increase the dependence of these countries on their continued presence. Industrial accidents, occupational disease, pollution, and general degradation of the people and the land continue to occur at a level that vividly reproduces the conditions of raw exploitation and human despair experienced in the worst industrial centers of England in the late eighteenth and nineteenth centuries. Again, the logic of economics and the imperative of making large profits tend to be the dominant concerns.

In all these illustrations we are talking about what former British Prime Minister Edward Heath once described as the "ugly face" of organizational life. Whether by design or by default, organizations often have a large negative impact on our world. Our purpose in this chapter is to gain insight into this aspect of organization by exploring how organizations can be understood as instruments of domination. Although we are usually encouraged to think about organizations as rational enterprises pursuing goals that aspire to satisfy the interests of all, there is much evidence to suggest that this view is more an ideology than a reality. Organizations are often used as instruments of domination that further the selfish interests of elites at the expense of others, and there is an element of domination in *all* organizations.

Organization as Domination

Throughout history, organization has been associated with processes of social domination where individuals or groups find ways of imposing their will on others. This becomes clearly evident when we trace the lineage of the modern organization from its roots in ancient society, through the growth and development of military enterprise and empire, to its role in the modern world.

Consider, for example, the incredible feat of organization, planning, and control required to build the Great Pyramid at Giza. It is estimated that its construction involved work by perhaps 10,000 persons over a period of twenty years. The pyramid is built from over 2.3 million blocks of stone, each weighing two and one-half tons. These had to be quarried, cut to size, and transported over many miles, usually by the Nile river, when it was in flood. When we admire this and other pyramids today it is the incredible ingenuity and skill of the early Egyptians that strikes us from both an aesthetic and an organizational standpoint. From another standpoint, however, the pyramid is a metaphor of exploitation, symbolizing how the lives and hard labor of thousands of people were used to serve and glorify a privileged elite.

In the view of some organization theorists this combination of achievement and exploitation is a feature of organization throughout the ages. Whether we are talking about the building of the pyramids or the running of an army, a multinational corporation, or even a family business, we find asymmetrical power relations that result in the majority working in the interests of the few. Of course, important differences in practice can be observed, and over the ages much has changed. The conscription and slavery that provided much of the labor power required to build pyramids and empires have given way to use of paid employment where employees have the right to leave. Slave drivers have given way to managers, and employees now typically work in the interests of shareholders rather than of pharaohs, emperors, or absolute monarchs. However, in all cases, pursuit of the goals of the few through the work and labor of the many continues. Organization, in this view, is best understood as a process of domination. The varied organizations observed in history and the modern world are best understood as instruments that reflect variations in the *mode* of domination employed.

This aspect of organization has been made a special focus of study by radical organization theorists inspired by the insights of Karl Marx and two other very famous sociologists: Max Weber and Robert Michels. As was discussed in Chapter 2, Weber is famous among organization theorists for his work on the nature of bureaucracy. However, his main concern was to understand how different societies and epochs are characterized by different forms of social domination. He viewed bureaucracy as a special mode of social domination and was interested in the role of bureaucratic organizations in creating and sustaining structures of domination.

For Weber, domination can occur in several ways. First and most obviously, domination arises when one or more persons coerce others through the direct use of threat or force. However, domination also occurs in more subtle ways, as when a ruler imposes his or her will on others while being *perceived as having a right to do so*. This is the kind of domination that most interested Weber, and much of his effort was devoted to understanding the process through which forms of domination become legitimized as normal, socially acceptable power relations: patterns of formal authority in which rulers see themselves as having the *right* to rule, and those subject to this rule see it as their *duty* to obey.

As a result of his historical studies, Weber identified three types of social domination that could become legitimate forms of authority or power. He called these the charismatic, the traditional, and the rational-legal (Exhibit 9.1). He believed that a ruler's ability to use one or another of these kinds of authority depended on his or her ability to find support or legitimation in the ideologies or beliefs of those being ruled and to place this authority on a firm base by developing an appropriate administrative apparatus linking the ruler and the ruled. Thus, Weber believed that each mode of domination was accompanied by a particular kind of legitimacy and by a specific form of administrative organization.

However, he recognized that the three types of domination are rarely found in their pure form and that when they impinge on one another, the

Charismatic domination occurs when a leader rules by virtue of his or her personal qualities. Legitimacy of rule is grounded in the faith that the ruled vest in the leader (e.g., a prophet, hero, heroine, or demagogue). The administrative apparatus under this mode of domination is very loose, unstructured, and unstable, usually working through the activities of a few disciples or intermediaries.

Traditional domination occurs when the power to rule is underwritten by a respect for tradition and the past. Legitimacy is vested in custom and in a feeling of the "rightness" of traditional ways of doing things. People thus often command power as a result of inherited status, as in systems of monarchy or family succession. The administrative apparatus under this mode of domination typically takes two forms—patriarchal or feudal. In the former, the officials or administrators are usually personal retainers— servants, relatives, or favorites—dependent on and remunerated by the ruler. In the latter, the officials retain a measure of independence. In return for giving their allegiance to the ruler they are usually allowed autonomy within a specified sphere of influence and are not directly dependent on the ruler for remuneration or subsistence.

Under the mode of *rational-legal domination*, power is legitimized by laws, rules, regulations, and procedures. The ruler can thus attain legitimate power only by following the legal procedures that specify how the ruler is to be appointed. The power is also formally bounded by rules. The typical administrative apparatus is the bureaucracy, a rational-legal framework in which formal authority is concentrated at the top of the organizational hierarchy. In contrast with the feudal case, the means of administration do not belong to the bureaucrat; his or her position can be neither inherited nor sold. There is a strict separation between private and official income, fortune, and life generally.

Exhibit 9.1   Weber's Typology of Domination

SOURCE: Mouzelis (1979: 16–18).

result is often an uneasy tension. Weber was also much concerned by the trend toward increasing bureaucratization and rationalization. For him, the process of bureaucratization presented a very great threat to the freedom of the human spirit and the values of liberal democracy, because those in control have a means of subordinating the interests and welfare of the masses. Hence his view that bureaucracy could all too easily turn into an iron cage. He saw bureaucracy as a power instrument of the first order and believed that the bureaucratization of administration when completely carried through establishes a form of power relation that is "practically unshatterable." The strength of bureaucratic organization is, of course, now being undermined by developments in information technology that erode hierarchy and introduce new organizational power bases. But the process of rationalization and control to which Weber speaks is as strong as ever.

Similar concerns to Weber's have been voiced by the French sociologist Robert Michels, who saw in the politics of bureaucratic organization distinct oligarchic tendencies. In his famous "iron law of oligarchy" he developed the view that modern organizations typically end up under the control of narrow groups, even when this runs against the desires of the leaders as well as the led. In his study of supposedly democratic organizations, such as trade unions and political parties, he found that the democracy was often no more than window dressing. Despite the best intentions, these organizations seemed to develop tendencies that gave their leaders a near monopoly of power. As leaders rise to power they tend to become preoccupied with their own way of looking at things, and it seems that the most that can be hoped for is that they will attempt to keep the interests of their members in mind. But in Michels's view, even democratically elected leaders with the best intentions have a tendency to become part of an elite furthering their own interests and to hang onto their power at all costs. Hence, he was very pessimistic with regard to the domineering character of modern organization, in a way that parallels the pessimism of Weber.

The real value of these perspectives is that they show how even the most rational and democratic forms of organization can result in modes of domination where certain people acquire and sustain a commanding influence over others, often through subtle processes of socialization and belief. To take Weber's ideas as an illustration, we can become dominated by such basic and hidden forces as those underpinning the quest for rationality. Indeed, for Weber the process of rationalization is itself a mode of domination. As we become increasingly subject to administration through rules and engage in strict calculations relating means and ends and costs and benefits, we become increasingly dominated by the process itself. Impersonal principles and the quest for efficiency tend to become our new slave drivers.

These ideas resonate with those of Karl Marx, especially those discussed in Chapter 8. For Weber, the logic-driving modern society is found in the process of domination through rationalization. For Marx, it is found in the domination generated by the quest for surplus value and the accumulation of capital. In recent years, many "radical" theorists and researchers have become very interested in the links between these different insights and in the way the process of rationalization is often used to serve the interests of capital accumulation. Collectively, their work brings the ideas of Marx and Weber right up to date, showing how organization in the modern world is based on processes of domination and exploitation of many kinds. In the remainder of this chapter we will explore the ideas of these radical organization theorists, focusing on how the forces of domination embedded in the ways we organize often lead organizations to exploit their employees and the social and economic contexts in which they operate.

How Organizations Use and Exploit Their Employees

Arthur Miller's well-known play *Death of a Salesman* explores the tragic life and death of Willy Loman. Willy had been a salesman with the Wagner company for thirty-four years, traveling through New England year after year as Wagner's "New England man." However, at the age of sixty Willy feels that he can no longer cope with the demands of life on the road. After a number of nervous breakdowns he reluctantly decides to ask for a posting in New York City so that he can work at his home base. His family has grown up, and his financial needs are modest. He thus feels confident that Wagner will be able to find a niche for him, even though his sales performance is nowhere near what it once was.

However, on raising the subject with Howard Wagner, Willy is rudely disappointed. Howard has little time for Willy's plight. Willy talks about his time with the firm, his close association with Howard's father, and the promises that had been made. But it has no effect on Howard. Within a matter of minutes Willy finds himself suggesting that his wages could be reduced from sixty-five dollars per week to fifty and finally to forty since he needs only to earn enough to get by.

Howard is uncomfortable with Willy's pleading but insists that there's no room for favors. After various attempts at escaping the situation by claiming that he has no more time and must move on to his next appointment, Howard finally ends the conversation by telling Willy that the company no longer needs him. Willy is shattered. He feels like "an empty orange peel." The company has eaten thirty-four years of his life as if it were a piece of fruit and is now throwing the rest of him away.

He ends up committing suicide.

Miller's play stands as a metaphor for the way organizations often consume and exploit their employees, taking and using what they need while throwing the rest away. Of course, there are exceptions. But many workers and managers at all levels of organization find their health and personal lives being sacrificed on the altars created by modern organizations. Willy's story, though extreme in its end result, is not extreme in substance. In the world today, individuals and even whole communities find themselves being thrown away like empty orange peels when the organizations they serve have no further use for them. Individuals find themselves permanently unemployed even though they feel that they have many good years of useful work ahead of them. Communities find that they are unable to survive once the organizations on which they have depended for their economic livelihood decide to move their capital elsewhere. Increasingly, many managers find themselves ending lives of workaholic involvement with their employer as the victims of cutbacks or "early retirement plans." Even if cushioned by a "golden handshake" and comfortable pension, the blow to one's ego and self-confidence can be shattering. Somewhat ironically, those with the most privileged access to important information or with pivotal positions in their companies are often those who receive the hardest blow to their self-esteem. Many important executives, on being told that they are no longer needed, are also told that their termination is immediate. They will not be required to turn up at work ever again because, despite their glowing reputation, the organization fears that resentment may lead them to carry away documents that could be used to help competitors or to damage the organization in some way. In these cases, insult is added to injury.

In the opinion of many radical organization theorists, even though we have advanced a long way from the naked exploitation found in slavery and in the developing years of the industrial revolution, the same pattern continues today. They find particularly striking evidence of this in the way organizations structure job opportunities to produce and reproduce the class structure of modern societies; in the way organizations approach the problems of hazardous work situations, industrial accidents, and occupational disease; and in the way organizations perpetuate structures and practices that promote workaholism and associated forms of social and mental stress.

ORGANIZATION, CLASS, AND CONTROL

A strong case can be made for the idea that organization has always been class-based. The first types of formal organization probably arose in hierarchical societies where one social group imposed itself on another, often through conquest. Such societies became further stratified as certain individuals placed themselves in the service of the ruling class as priests, scribes, bookkeepers, traders, and merchants.

Because these people were not involved in producing the goods necessary to provide their livelihood, they formed an intermediate class of people between the ruling class and the peasants or slaves involved in the actual production of goods. We find the same system reproduced in modern organization in terms of the distinctions between owners, managers, and workers.

Thousands of years intervene between the emergence of the first formal organizations and the corporations that we see around us today. These embrace many major social epochs in different parts of the world. We can pick up the story in the period of the Industrial Revolution in Great Britain around the 1760s and in the industrialization of the United States from the early 1800s. Although the two countries began the process of industrialization in very different circumstances, there are many common links in the way growing industrialization develops and extends the tripartite class system handed down from earlier times.

As is well known, the Industrial Revolution in Great Britain was set against the background of an agrarian society with a "domestic" or "cottage" system of production, supplemented by a small amount of mining and construction and a system of industrial workshops run by merchant-craftsmen organized in craft guilds. These workshops were typically stratified according to skill and status, in terms of masters, journeymen, and apprentices. The guilds controlled entry and working conditions and managed to secure a reasonable livelihood for their members, especially when compared with the poor farmers or landless poor who had lost their source of livelihood as a result of the enclosure of land during the sixteenth century.

The Industrial Revolution changed this picture as capitalist producers sought to overcome the uncertainties of output and quality associated with domestic production; to serve the new markets created by expanding world trade and a growing population; and, most important of all, to take advantage of mechanical systems of production. The development of factory production transformed the structure of the work force and intensified the growth of urban areas. Increasing numbers of people who had formerly been self-employed in workshops and cottage industry assumed new roles as part of an emerging wage-earning class. Labor increasingly became viewed as a commodity to be bought and sold. Because these changes eliminated earlier systems of production, for the new wage earners the process was irreversible, making them dependent on the wage system.

Similar developments occurred in the United States, even though the emergence of a class of wage earners was delayed by the availability of land. At the beginning of the nineteenth century, capitalist production for profit using wage labor was insignificant outside the major cities. Most of the population lived in rural areas, and over 80 percent of the labor force was employed in agriculture, over 20 percent being slaves and indentured laborers. About 80 percent of the nonslave workforce were property holders and professionals—farmers, merchants, craftsmen, small manufacturers, doctors, lawyers, and others.

Slavery remained important in agriculture for much of the century. There were almost 4.5 million slaves in 1860, and even after emancipation many continued in feudal servitude under sharecropping and other systems of farming. In manufacturing, systems of capitalist production had an increasing impact, replacing cottage industry and small business with a system of wage labor. Immigrants, Native Americans, women and children, and displaced artisans and agricultural workers swelled a labor force that, as in Great Britain, found it increasingly difficult to find alternative sources of livelihood. Thus, as the figures in Exhibit 9.2 demonstrate, historically the growth of capitalist organization has been accompanied by a decline in the number of self-employed persons and an increase in the number of wage and salary earners. This trend has now started to move in a new direction as a result of the flattening and decentralization of large bureaucracies and the rise of small business.

The growth of a capitalist system of production depends on the existence of a supply of wage labor, unless it is to rely on slaves or on some system of subcontracting. Slavery runs against important social norms and can be inefficient, and subcontracting, until the revolutions created in information technology, just-in-time management, and new forms of electronic control, was highly unpredictable from the capitalist's standpoint. Early capitalism in North America combined elements of these different systems, but as the century progressed, a consistent trend toward the use of wage labor occurred—and with it the rise of the profession and activities of management as we know it today.

In many respects, it is possible to say that the system of wage labor created modern management, since for the first time outside slavery, profits depended on efficiency in the use of labor time. Under systems of domestic manufacture and subcontracting, the profit of the merchant-capitalist who bought and sold the goods produced did not necessarily depend on how the goods were produced. The merchant paid an appropriate price and lived off the profit margin. Great inconvenience arose when private producers failed to deliver the appropriate quantity or quality on time, but the problems involved were outside the merchant's direct sphere of interest.

With the appearance of the factory system, however, every second of wasted time or inefficient use of time represented a loss of profit. The

Year	% Wage and Salaried Employees (1)	% Self-Employed (2)	% Salaried Managers and Administrators	Total Labor Force
1780	20.0	80.0	—	100.0
1800	17.4	82.6	—	100.0
1860	48.0	52.0	—	100.0
1880	59.8	39.1	1.1	100.0
1890	60.7	38.1	1.2	100.0
1900	63.3	35.4	1.3	100.0
1910	69.2	29.0	1.8	100.0
1920	72.6	24.8	2.6	100.0
1930	74.8	22.3	2.9	100.0
1940	75.6	21.4	3.0	100.0
1950	79.1	16.5	4.4	100.0
1960	81.1	13.6	5.3	100.0
1970	83.5	10.4	6.1	100.0
1980	81.4	10.8	8.6	100.0

Figures relate to percentage distribution of the employed, excluding family workers.

(1) Excluding salaried managers and administrators.

(2) Business proprietors, professional practitioners, independent artisans, and farm owners.

Figures for 1780–1860 are rough estimates, excluding slaves, who composed between 20 and 30 percent of the total labor force; white indentured servants are included among wage and salary employees.

Self-employment figures for 1880 exclude southern tenant farmers; their businesses were directly managed by moneylenders and landowners.

Figures for self-employed in 1970 and 1980 have been adjusted to include owners receiving salaries from their own corporations.

Exhibit 9.2   The Changing Structure of the U.S. Labor Force

SOURCE: Adapted from Edwards, Reich, and Weisskopf (1986: 124).

employment of wage labor thus led the capitalist to place primary emphasis on the efficiency of labor time and to seek increasing control over the process of production. The establishment of a wage system thus carried with it implications for the organization of the labor process and, as a corollary, institutionalized class divisions in the workplace, particularly between managers involved in the design and control of work and the workforce engaged in productive activity.

There are thus close links between organization, class, and control. If we examine the history of work organization since the beginning of the Industrial Revolution, we find a common pattern in both Europe and North America. The development of a system of wage labor tends to be followed by increasingly strict and precise organization, close supervision, and increasingly standardized jobs. Skilled and semiskilled workers are increasingly replaced by cheaper unskilled workers, leading to what is sometimes described as "degradation" or "deskilling" of work and "homogenization" of the labor market. The extent of the deskilling has been graphically illustrated in a British study that showed how, in some organizations, over 80 percent of manual workers exercised less skill in their jobs than they used in driving to work.

The labor market has also become increasingly segmented into two categories, sometimes described as primary and secondary sectors. The primary labor market is a market for career-type jobs that are especially crucial or that call for a high degree of skill and detailed knowledge, often of a corporation-specific nature. This market has grown along with the proliferation of bureaucratic and technocratic enterprises whose members are enticed to work not only for money but for nonmonetary rewards such as job satisfaction, the promise of career advancement, and security of employment. Members of the primary labor market are usually deemed worthy of significant investment. They are regarded and treated as "corporate assets" or "human capital." Such employees are expected to become committed and loyal. Corporations typically go to great lengths to foster and reward these traits and use extensive and rigorous selection mechanisms to eliminate high-risk candidates. However, as developments in information technology have created increasingly sophisticated subcontracting or "outsourcing" processes, increasing numbers of professionals once regarded as a core part of the "primary" labor market are finding themselves working on limited contracts where long-term commitments are neither desired nor possible.

The secondary labor market is a market for lower-skilled and lower-paid workers in offices, factories, and open-air jobs who are more dispensable and more easily replaced. It calls for little capital investment in the form of training and education, and workers can be hired and fired along with the vagaries of the business cycle. This type of labor provides a "buffer" that allows the organization to expand output in good times and to contract in bad, leaving the organization's operating core and elite primary labor force relatively unaffected. Increasingly, "secondary labor" is employed on a subcontracting basis.

The existence of the two categories of labor gives an organization a great deal more control over its internal and external environment than it would otherwise have. The fact that primary workers are committed to the firm increases the predictability of its internal operations, whereas the existence of the secondary buffer facilitates its general ability to adapt. However, this means of control creates a differential system of status and privilege within the organization that parallels and sustains broader class divisions outside. It means that the vagaries of the business cycle have the harshest effects on the poorer sections of society who belong to the secondary sector and on special groups such as women, ethnic minorities, the handicapped, and poorly educated youths, who form a large part of this labor market.

For example, if we examine the occupational structures of many Western societies we find that, on average, minorities and socially disadvantaged groups have a greater chance of having to perform dirty work for relatively low wages, with little security of employment and few fringe benefits. Secondary-sector jobs are usually left for those who can't get any other. Employment patterns in this sector of the economy thus end up reflecting social attitudes and patterns of prejudice and discrimination in society as a whole.

Some European countries have institutionalized this pattern by allowing migrant or "guest" workers from other countries to enter the workforce on temporary visas to perform the jobs that no one else wants. It is estimated that as many as ten million migrant workers are employed in Europe, making up as much as 11 percent of the workforce in Germany and 27 percent in Switzerland. Historically, the ranks of the British working class have always been swelled by immigrants, most recently by immigrants from the West Indies, India, Pakistan, and other Asian, European, and Commonwealth countries. In the United States, it is estimated that anywhere between 2 and 12 percent of the labor force consists of undocumented workers from Mexico, the Caribbean, and elsewhere, and African American workers have formed a substantial part of the working class ever since the days of slavery. Since the 1920s they have become increasingly involved in manufacturing and service sector jobs and, despite affirmative action programs, still remain overrepresented in the secondary labor market.

Institutionalized discrimination? Or an unintended consequence of industrial development? The debate continues. It is clear that even though the domination and exploitation of disadvantaged groups may not be a stated aim of the modern corporation, it is definitely a side effect. Despite many major advances in employment equity legislation, the implicit or explicit exploitation of employees persists. Modern organizations continue to play an important part in creating and sustaining a relatively underprivileged working class that is now more appropriately described as an "underclass" because many of the working class are no longer working and have poor prospects of ever doing so. In creating and reinforcing the market system for labor, modern organizations continue to favor and reinforce a power structure that encourages people with certain attributes while disadvantaging others. The process reproduces patterns of favor and privilege that symbolize and reinforce underlying socioeconomic divisions. From this perspective, modern corporations play a crucial role in producing and sustaining the ills and inequities of modern society.

Although the focus has been placed on studying the evolution of organization under capitalism, it is important to recognize that a similar pattern is also evident in noncapitalist societies. As the Berlin Wall has tumbled in a political as well as a physical sense, it has become increasingly clear that state-run communist societies reveal similar features. China and the former USSR have always had a clear class structure, with Weber's vision of the iron cage of bureaucracy and Michels's "iron law of oligarchy" much in evidence. Organization, whatever ideological cloak it wears, seems to give form to systemic patterns of exploitation and social domination.

WORK HAZARDS, OCCUPATIONAL
DISEASE, AND INDUSTRIAL ACCIDENTS

In one of the most vivid and moving chapters of *Das Kapital*, Karl Marx gives detailed attention to how many employers of his day were working their employees to death in horrific conditions. Quoting from the reports of factory inspectors and magistrates, his account bristles with incredible detail. In the lace industry in Nottingham, "children of nine or ten years were dragged from their squalid beds at two, three, or four o'clock in the morning, and forced to work for subsistence wages until ten, eleven, or twelve at night, their frames dwindling, their faces whitening, and their humanity sinking into a stone-like torpor, utterly horrible to contemplate." Mr. Broughton Charlton, the county magistrate whose words are quoted above, castigated the system as one of "unmitigated slavery, socially, physically, morally, and spiritually." "We declaim against the Virginian and Carolinian cotton planters. Is their lash, and the barter of human flesh, more detestable than this slow sacrifice of humanity which takes place in order that veils and collars may be fabricated for the benefit of capitalists?"

In quoting reports on the pottery industry in Staffordshire, Marx produces similar facts, relating, for example, the story of William Wood, nine years old, who had been working for over a year from 6 a.m. until 9 p.m., six days a week. Quoting from health reports on how potters were dying at an alarming rate from pulmonary diseases caused by dust, fumes, vapors, and so on, he notes the observations of three physicians who had reported how each successive generation of potters was more dwarfed and less robust than the previous one. For example, Dr. J. T. Arledge reported in 1863 how the potters as a class, both men and women, represent a "degenerated population . . . stunted in growth, ill-shaped, and frequently ill-formed in the chest . . . prematurely old, and . . . short lived . . . [dogged by] disorders of the liver and kidneys, and by rheumatism . . . [and] especially prone to pneumonia, phthisis, bronchitis, and asthma."

Reports on match factories in the large cities documented how half the workers were children and young persons under eighteen and how tetanus, a disease long associated with match making, was rife. Reports on the wallpaper industry tell how young girls and children were obliged to work from 6 a.m. until at least 10 p.m., with no stoppage for meals. Working seventy or eighty hours a week, they were often fed at their machines.

Reports on the baking industry document how bakers often worked from 11 p.m. until 7 p.m. the following evening, with just one or two short intervals of rest. They were among the most short-lived workers, rarely reaching the age of forty-two.

Reports on the clothing industry document how girls and young women were being worked to death on sixteen-hour shifts and on shifts of up to thirty hours in peak seasons. They often worked without a break, being kept awake by occasional supplies of sherry, port, or coffee. On the railways, men often worked fourteen to twenty hours a day, forty or fifty hours of continuous work being common in peak travel periods. In the steel mills, boys nine to fifteen years old were reported working continuous twelve-hour shifts in high temperatures, often at night, and not seeing daylight for months on end. It was Marx's opinion that capital lived "vampire-like . . . sucking living labor" and that, in general, capital took no account of the health or length of life of the worker unless society forced it to do so.

Many people conducting research on health and safety at work today believe that, although the working conditions in the majority of organizations are much better than those described above, many basic problems remain. Many employers take account of work hazards only when legislation requires them to do so. Workers in the Third World still often suffer under conditions exactly like those described above, working in subcontracted sweatshops for global corporations, and child labor is rife. Even in developed Western countries, accidents and occupational disease continue to take an alarming toll on human life.

For example, in the United States the Occupational Safety and Health Administration (OSHA) reports that every year work-related accidents and illnesses cost an estimated 56,000 American lives. On an average day, 17 people are killed in safety accidents, 16,000 are injured, and 137 die from occupational disease. Each year, 700,000 days are lost to injuries and illnesses related to musculoskeletal disorders because of overuse of particular parts of the body. It is estimated that safety alone costs the American economy over $100 billion a year.

Data on occupational illness and diseases are more difficult to tie down than those on accidents because the links are often harder to document in an authoritative way. However, U.S. government estimates suggest that as many as 100,000 people a year die as a result of work-related illnesses. It is estimated that anywhere between 23 and 38 percent of cancer deaths may be work related. To put the figures in perspective, the number of people killed by occupational diseases and accidents each year exceeds the number of American lives lost in the duration of the Vietnam War.

We're a long way from the Industrial Revolution in terms of general working conditions, but these figures speak for themselves. Despite the major advances in occupational health and safety legislation, the issue of costs versus safety looms large on the unofficial agenda in many corporate decisions. Often, it is the issue of cost that wins. As one safety officer in an automobile factory described it, although the explicit policy is "safety first," the reality is "safety when convenient." Many industrial accidents occur because of problems unintentionally built into the structure of the plant and buildings because of poor maintenance or because it is easier or more efficient to work without using safety equipment. Because it is either expensive or incovenient to remedy such problems, nothing tends to get done until someone gets hurt or until the organization is forced to introduce changes by government regulation.

Similar problems arise in relation to the hazards underlying occupational disease. Here, the problems are so pervasive that it is often difficult to know where to begin dealing with them. It is estimated that industry at present creates and uses over 63,000 chemicals, perhaps 25,000 of which would be classified as toxic. Many of these are new, and their long-term effects are unknown. The effects of their interaction are impossible to predict in a comprehensive manner because of the number of possible permutations. In the view of some safety experts, the approach commonly adopted is a kind of trial and error using people in the workplace as human guinea pigs until concrete risks are identified.

It is often the most gruesome problems that are brought to our attention, such as the dangers presented to coal miners by black lung, the hazards of brown lung for those exposed to cotton dust, the dangers of working with asbestos, or the risks of radiation from nuclear power plants and uranium mining. However, toxic substances of one type or another affect the majority of occupational groups. In a survey of production workers conducted by the Survey Research Center at the University of Michigan, 78 percent reported some exposure to work hazards. Occupational groups such as carpenters, construction workers, laboratory technicians, agricultural workers, dry cleaners, firefighters, hospital staff, and even hairstylists increasingly work with chemical substances whose long-term effects are unknown. Even in the modern office building, poor ventilation or exposure to radiation from video display terminals can add to the risk of occupationally induced illness of one kind or another.

While such risks can be seen as an inevitable side effect of industrial development, those directly involved with the promotion of health and safety at work suggest that employers are often reluctant to admit to hazards even when there is plenty of evidence or early warning signs.

The classic case is found in the history of the asbestos industry, which, even now, accounts for approximately 50,000 deaths annually in the United States alone. The risks have been long known. As early as 1918, insurance companies in both the United States and Canada stopped selling life policies to asbestos workers. Yet the industry continued to allow employees to operate without respirators, sometimes in dust so thick that it was impossible to see beyond a few yards. The industry also systematically overlooked the tragic consequences.

For example, in his book *Death on the Job*, Daniel Berman tells the story of asbestos worker Marco Vela. Vela began working in the Johns-Manville asbestos factory in Pittsburg, California, around 1935. In 1959, the company started a policy of conducting medical examinations to detect lung disease. That year a physician paid by the company obtained a chest X ray on Vela and noted the existence of an occupation-related disease. The report contained no recommendation about changing the work environment, and Vela was not informed he was developing asbestosis.

In 1962, Vela was examined by another company-paid physician. A chest X ray again showed the presence of lung disease. The patient was told nothing. The same physician saw Vela again in 1965 and ordered another chest X ray. A diagnosis of work-related pneumoconiosis was made. Vela was told nothing.

In 1968, Vela was given another routine physical. Although he had a cough and was short of breath and although his X ray showed a "ground glass appearance," Vela was told by the company nurse that everything was fine and received no information to the contrary from the physician. Later that year he was hospitalized, and he never returned to work again.

Documents in product liability suits against the asbestos industry in the United States suggest an organized cover-up of the ill effects. For example, a 1980 report on corporate crime by a subcommittee of the U.S. House of Representatives noted that a number of firms in the asbestos industry made out-of-court settlements to asbestos workers who had registered claims, many in the 1930s, well before they admitted to having recognized the hazard presented by asbestos.

The problems continue in the Third World, where international corporations engage in the same dangerous practices, free from the health regulations now imposed in the West. For example, the evidence on hazardous factories operated for Western corporations suggests that health and safety practice is often fifty years behind standard practice in their home countries. Besides the hazards in the factories, dangerous chemicals are often dumped in places where other humans, especially children at play, are subject to direct exposure.

The history of the modern asbestos industry is every bit as bad as that of the lace and pottery industries in the mid-nineteenth century. Asbestos-related deaths among shipyard and insulation workers continue at high rates; it is estimated that 20 to 25 percent die from lung cancer, 10 to 18 percent from asbestosis, and 10 percent from gastrointestinal cancer. Additional asbestos-related deaths in industries as diverse as steel, automotive-parts manufacture, construction, and building maintenance continue at high levels.

Although this case history is one of the more extreme and serious ones, it is by no means untypical. Just as the tobacco industry long denied links between smoking and lung cancer in the interests of profitability, toxic industries seem to resist acknowledging key problems and are reluctant to take action until forced to do so.

Economics rules! Just as the early manufacturers of the nineteenth century often worked their employees to death because of losses associated with idle machines, modern industrialists often seem compelled to keep their plants in operation despite statistics suggesting that all is not well. Although workers may prove careless and bad management and negligence often occur, many of the problems are systemic. If accidents are built into the structure of a plant or if the use of toxic chemicals is essential for continued productivity or for gaining a competitive edge, the welfare of the worker frequently takes second place.

Despite an early start in Great Britain with the Factory Acts of 1833, legislation has often appeared too late to deal with critical problems and is often difficult to enforce, especially in relation to the threat presented by exposure to toxics. The effect of these is often difficult to prove in a conclusive way. Many employees bringing compensation claims have found it hard to show employer liability. Of the half million people in the United

States severely disabled as a result of occupational disease, fewer than 5 percent have received formal compensation.

Since the passage of the 1970 Occupational Safety and Health Act in the United States and similar legislation elsewhere, the situation has improved. For example, OSHA intervention in the United States has been accompanied by a 50 percent reduction in the workplace fatality rate. Action in relation to specific problems such as brown lung disease in the cotton industry, lead poisoning in battery and smelting operations, accidents on building sites, and grain dust explosions, to name a few, has led to major improvements.

But problems still abound. The fact that it is often cheaper to pay accident compensation than to eliminate accidents or diseases by making work safe, and that penalties on firms that continue to operate high-risk plants are not stiff enough to close them down, perpetuate the underlying problem.

Also, issues of liability and the threat of "class action" suits from employees with a common grievance lead organizations to adopt a defensive posture. Many corporations, like the tobacco industry, marshall their resources to demonstrate that no risk exists. When accidents do occur, organizational prudence suggests that it is much better to let the injured worker sue for compensation than for the organization to acknowledge any responsibility.

Legislation often requires the appointment of safety officers in high-risk organizations. But because they are paid by the corporation concerned, they often get caught in role conflicts around the economics versus safety issue. Many end up performing a role designed to make their employer look good in the eyes of government inspectors. As a result, the relations between safety officers and inspectors often become an elaborate organizational game, reminiscent of those played between time-and-motion staff and production workers in the setting of work standards, discussed in Chapter 6.

As a safety officer in a manufacturing plant tells it,

> The tactics employed depend on the government inspector. There's one who usually likes to issue a few minor directives. He's nearing retirement, does not want a fuss, and wants to avoid the paperwork that stems from issuing serious directives. . . . In this case the tactic is to create obvious minor infractions so that the inspector does not have to search for problems. . . . [Thus] items such as exit signs with burnt-out bulbs, or guard rails that are not high enough, are left unrepaired near inspection time. . . . In the case of another younger inspector, renowned to be thorough, and wishing to make a name for himself as having promotion potential, everything must be up to scratch. Thus, in this case, a particular machine or process which is known to be in marginal condition is examined before the inspection so that modifications can be planned and

budgeted. Then, when the inspection occurs, the inspector, indirectly, is encouraged to shut down the machine and thus satisfy his own requirements. The approach is successful in minimizing inconvenience and projecting a good image in that we get few instructions for improvement.

Organizations work hard to look good in official records by reducing the number or severity of potential hazards *identified* through various kinds of window dressing. They may do this by influencing the way accidents or hazards are classified or by reducing the number of days lost to injury by encouraging injured employees to turn up for work in return for assignments to easy jobs. The attempt to control accidents through legislation often encourages this type of response, leaving underlying attitudes and hazards unchanged.

Of course, while there are many employers who do not take health and safety seriously, there are also many who do. Similarly, there are many workers who take advantage of the rules, regulations, and compensation schemes. The Marxian idea that the majority of employers are unscrupulous "vampires" who willfully suck the blood of labor is no doubt an exaggeration, as is the widespread idea that the majority of workers are fakers and scroungers. While there are many cases at the extremes, the truth stands somewhere in between: In a place consistent with the general idea that in many situations "the bottom line" tends to come first and safety second. The radical critics of modern organization make a strong case in asserting that many organizations continue to advance their interests by exploiting and dominating the health and welfare of employees.

WORKAHOLISM AND
SOCIAL AND MENTAL STRESS

Our discussion up to now has placed principal emphasis on work-related hazards of a physical kind. As such, many of the victims belong to the "secondary" labor market, a fact that again emphasizes the different impact of organizations on different sections of the working population. However, those in the "primary" labor market also become victims of certain hazards, especially those producing various kinds of stress. Although white-collar workers are, on average, less likely than blue-collar workers to be killed or seriously injured by accidents while working on the job or to be directly exposed to toxic hazards, they are often far more likely to suffer from work-related coronary disease, ulcers, and mental breakdown.

Coronary disease, often labeled the "management killer," is being increasingly recognized as a problem affecting many people in stressful work situations. Not only white-collar workers but also blue-collar workers and women faced with the problem of managing a family as well as holding down a part- or full-time job often suffer here. The problem is endemic to stressful situations of all kinds and seems to be the product of a complex network of factors. One's working conditions, role, career aspirations, and quality of relations at work interact with one's personality to influence personal stress levels and physical and mental well-being. The "Type A" personality, driven by the compulsion to control his or her work environment, ambitious, achievement oriented, competitive, impatient, and perfectionistic, is always a good candidate for coronary problems. Those who work with such a person run risks as well, for the Type A personality often creates considerable tension for others in the workplace. The tension, frustration, and anger that often accompany a sense of powerlessness, such as that experienced by people in dead-end blue-collar and clerical jobs, also increases the risk of physical and mental breakdown.

It is estimated that somewhere between 75 and 90 percent of visits to physicians in the United States are stress related, with an estimated cost to industry of between $200 billion and $300 billion per annum. Insurance industry surveys of American workers have found that over 40 percent of employees find their jobs very or extremely stressful. For women, stress is identified as the number-one problem, highlighted as a major concern by an average of 60 percent over all occupational groups. The figures are as high as 74 percent for women in their forties in professional and managerial roles and 67 percent for single mothers. Overwork, impossible schedules, high uncertainty, fear of job loss, economic problems, work-family conflicts, and other contextual factors are important factors across many occupational groups.

High stress also correlates with increasing physical violence in the workplace. Data collected by the U.S. Department of Justice reveal that the number of work-related assaults is now in the region of one million per annum. Homicide ranks as the second leading cause of workplace death overall and ranks number one for women. Each month, five or six employers are killed in employer-directed homicides.

Although much can be done to modify the levels of stress and tension experienced at work—for example, through appropriate design of jobs and the attempt to develop balanced relations between work and outside life—it seems that a certain amount of stress is endemic. Indeed, organizations thrive on and at times actively create stress as a means of promoting organizational effectiveness. Although in the view of many experts a certain amount of stress may be beneficial, undue stress has a costly long-term impact on organizations because of illness and lost working time and its negative impact on overall quality of life. The feeling in many quarters is that the problem is almost out of control. The hypercompetition in the global economic environment with the constant drive toward continuous improvement and creative destruction is reflected in hyperstress in the workplace.

Few people feel completely secure in their roles. They have seen Arthur Miller's "orange peel phenomenon" all too often in relation to friends, family, or community. The flattening of organizations and associated resource reductions have removed a lot of the slack that used to provide a cushion through which people could moderate organizational pressures. Also, information technology has created an expectation of instantaneous action, even on difficult problems. It has also led to increased surveillance. For example, through the use of sophisticated software and "on-line" information systems, salespeople, telephone operators, production teams, and service staff can be subject to constant control. Their productivity can be measured and updated every minute of the day. In some offices and manufacturing situations the latest online productivity statistics of individuals or groups may be displayed continuously as a constant reminder of how well or badly one is doing against expectations. Needless to say, work stress in such situations is at an all-time high.

Even when people enjoy their jobs, work pressures in the modern corporation can carry the "enjoyment" too far. To get ahead or just keep their current position, many executives and aspiring newcomers feel that they must demonstrate complete identification with what their organization stands for and comply with organizational norms that demand rushed or missed meals and long hours of work six or seven days a week.

The product, of course, is the workaholic. Work becomes an addiction and a crutch, leading to unbalanced personal development and creating many problems for family life. The workaholic tends to be always under pressure, to have little spare time for his or her spouse and children, and to be frequently absent from home. Very often, progress on the career ladder requires frequent change in jobs, often involving moves from one anonymous city to another. The negative impact on home life and the incidence of marital and family breakdown is of course enormous. In the case of dual-career families, the strains and tensions are often amplified many times. While the individuals involved ultimately make the choices that shape these events, they are in many cases driven by their desire to comply with the norms and values that have become standard practice in the corporate world.

ORGANIZATIONAL POLITICS AND
THE RADICALIZED ORGANIZATION

The idea that organizations use and exploit their employees thus commands a great deal of support and accounts for important attitudes, beliefs, and practices in many organizations. In Chapter 6 we referred to the "radical frame of reference" built on the principle that organizations are class-based phenomena characterized by deep-rooted divisions between the interests of capital and labor (see Exhibit 6.6 and related discussion). The ideas discussed in this chapter help make the rationale of this perspective clearer. They help us understand why labor and management have often found themselves in such bitter conflict and why, with the downsizings in executive ranks, many managers now find themselves sharing the same uncertainty and skepticism with regard to their role in the modern corporation. From the point of view of a member of the "secondary" labor market who suffers periodic unemployment with the ups and downs of the business cycle, or who is engaged in a low-status job that values and uses few of his or her abilities, or who has suffered from a work-related accident or toxic hazard without compensation, it may make much more sense to understand organizations as battlegrounds than as united "teams" or friendly pluralist coalitions.

How can one feel one belongs to a team if one is uncertain whether one will still be employed next week?

How can one believe that one is part of a community of shared interests when differences in status and privilege are obvious and rife?

It seems quite reasonable in these circumstances to see oneself as part of an exploited and disadvantaged group of people, and to band together with one's fellows to see what gains and benefits can be extracted from one's employers. This is what has made unions thrive, making organizations become divided worlds reflecting and entrenching class divisions found in the wider society.

In extreme cases, these divisions have often become as sharp as those between warring factions, creating "radicalized organizations" such as those often found in mining and heavy manufacturing industries. Here, the difference between white- and blue-collar workers has always been very clear, being symbolized and reinforced every day in terms of the rights and privileges of the different groups.

On average, white-collar workers have enjoyed cleaner and safer work conditions, more regular work hours, more fringe benefits, longer vacations, and higher wages than their blue-collar colleagues. They have enjoyed corporate cultures that reflect their privilege and which, by implication, affirm the inferior status of their colleagues.

Consider, for example, the British vehicle assembly firm where separate dining rooms were provided for shop-floor workers and white-collar staff. The rooms were next to each other but were worlds apart. In the "staff" dining room one could enjoy lunch and a glass of wine served by uniformed waitresses at an attractive table. In the "plant dining room" one had to line up for self-service food to be eaten at long bare tables with plastic knives and forks. Metal cutlery could be used—provided one paid a deposit!

Needless to say, there was no feeling on the part of the workforce that they belonged to the same team as management, let alone that of the shareholders. They knew they were on opposite sides and behaved accordingly. A battleground atmosphere was the norm.

Interestingly, with the fiscal cutbacks and job reductions of the 1990s, many white-collar workers have begun to adopt the same position. Even white-collar bureaucracies that used to be regarded as secure and privileged middle-class institutions have become radicalized through strikes, lockouts, and battles over job security. In the aftermath, relations often remain strained and hostile, with people acting with minimum trust on the premise that they are always in danger of being exploited in some way.

In the 1970s and 1980s when open conflicts between management and labor were at their height, representatives of senior management tended to adopt a unitary or pluralist ideology, emphasizing the need for "team efforts" or a "stakeholder approach" to problem resolution, as a means of reframing the "us and them" attitudes. But since the 1980s, the battleground has shifted, and new tactics and strategies have emerged.

The shift to automated manufacturing and the decision on the part of many major companies to relocate operations in lower-wage, nonunionized Third World countries have undermined the power of Western trade unions. Faced with a lower demand for labor and the increasing structural unemployment created by plant relocations, support for militant action among union membership has declined. Fear and uncertainty have replaced the sense of power, confidence, and strength that characterized earlier times. This has opened the way for management to more or less dictate the terms of labor-management negotiations and to obtain a reversal in basic conditions of employment that in the heyday of unionism would have been completely unthinkable.

The trend has been so dramatic and extreme that in continental Europe it has become known as the "new brutalism." The ruthless drive for efficiency and "bottom line" profits at the expense of human concerns and considerations is seen as more or less shifting capitalism back into the nineteenth and early twentieth centuries. Management ideology is seen as serving the needs of capital accumulation above all else. News of the "latest layoffs" are frequently accompanied by news of "record profits," highlighting the conflict of interest between labor and capital expressed by Marx and the radical frame of reference.

Interestingly, the critique is no longer confined to left-wing radicals. It has become mainstream. For example, amid the corporate downsizings of the mid-1990s, *Newsweek* magazine ran a cover-page article on "Corporate Killers." It featured the photographs of leading chief executives accompanied by details of their salaries, often many millions of dollars per annum, and the number of employees that had been "downsized" during the previous few years: 74,000 at GM, 60,000 at IBM, 50,000 at Sears, and 40,000 at AT&T, to name just a few. The fact that such a conservative magazine would use such an extreme image to capture the reality of corporate life symbolizes the increasing concern and cynicism that people hold about the role and interests of the modern corporation.

In Germany, where the system of codetermination has established joint labor-management committees at the most senior corporate levels, the above trend has been resisted. There has been a deliberate attempt to integrate the interests of labor and capital. Work sharing has often replaced layoffs, and there has been a deliberate attempt to maintain wage levels and social benefits. But with the development of globalized low-wage production systems, it is very difficult to preserve national policies. The global economy doesn't respect national boundaries insofar as the economics of production are concerned. While rules about "local content" may require global corporations to produce locally if they are to sell in these markets, the tendency in many globalized industries is to shift to low-cost manufacturing centers, wherever they may be. The battle between labor and management is thus now being fought on a global stage and is intimately connected with the role of multinationals in the world economy. It is to this dimension of the radical critique of organizations that we now turn.

Multinationals and the World Economy

The operation of the world economy is dominated by the activities of giant corporations, usually referred to as multinationals (MNCs) or transnationals (TNCs). They account for over 70% of world trade. In 2003, Fortune Magazine reported that the 53 largest corporations had annual sales ranging from $55 billion to $263 billion. The largest corporations, including names such as Exxon Mobile General

Motors, Wal-Mart, BP, Royal Dutch/Shell, General Electric, Toyota, Total, ING Group, and Hitachi, have annual sales figures that exceed the gross national income (GNI) of many nations (see Exhibit 9.3). No wonder, therefore, that they have been described as sovereign states that have a major impact on international politics and the world economy.

Multinational corporations with headquarters in the United States, Europe, and Japan, called the Triad, dominate the list of the largest companies. Up until the early 1970s, hegemony of United States' multinational corporations was undisputed. From the 1970s to the mid-1990s Japanese companies became a dominant force. More recently, companies from China and other Asian countries have begun to appear among the multinational giants.

The largest multinationals include oil, automobile, electronics, telecom, insurance, retail, and a variety of other business activities. Typically they operate in countries throughout the world. Most have diversified interests and are controlled by shareholders; some are fully or partly government owned.

Of course, transnational corporations have been with us for a long time. The Venetian city-state in the fifteenth century was heavily involved in international finance, and large international trading companies such as the Dutch East India Company and the Hudson Bay Company developed commercial operations on many continents as early as the seventeenth century. However, it is in the late nineteenth and early twentieth centuries that we witness the growth and proliferation of multinationals along with developments in the capitalist world economy. Large, specialized corporations were among the first to appear, amassing a great concentration of economic resources and near monopoly power with operations in many countries. Around the middle of the twentieth century a new development emerged along with antitrust legislation designed to curb the influence of such organizations, namely, the emergence of diversified conglomerates. Diversified conglomerate multinationals developed as firms attempted to control supplies of crucial raw materials, to develop a portfolio of different types of investment, to hedge the risks associated with location by operating in many places at once, to engage in defensive foreign investment that protected them from the vagaries of the business cycle or the policies of any single host government, and to open up new markets for products that were reaching a stage of maturity in older markets.

Some of the conglomerates developed as large firms acquired interests in new areas of activity; others developed very rapidly through series of financial transactions that built giant conglomerates from humble beginnings. The latter development occurred with amazing speed during the

Rank		GNP or Revenues (billions $US)	Rank		GNP or Revenues (billions $US)
1	United States	11,012.5	52*	Nippon Telephone & Telegraph	98.2
2	Japan	4,360.8			
3	Germany	2,085.4	53	Malaysia	96.
4	United Kingdom	1,680.	54*	ING Group	95.8
5	France	1,521.6	55*	CitiGroup	94.7
6	China	1,416.7	56	Egypt	93.8
7	Italy	1,243.1	57	Singapore	90.2
8	Canada	773.9	58	Venezuela	89.6
9	Spain	700.4	59*	International Business Machines	89.1
10	Mexico	637.1			
11	Korea (Republic)	576.4	60	Philippines	87.7
12	India	570.7	61*	American International Group	81.3
13	Brazil	479.5			
14	Australia	436.4	62	Colombia	80.5
15	Netherlands	425.5	63*	Siemans	80.5
16	Russian Federation	374.8	64*	Carrefour	79.7
			65	Pakistan	77.5
17	Switzerland	298.9	66*	Hitachi	76.4
18	Belgium	267.2	67*	Hewlett Packard	73.0
19*	Wal-Mart Stores	263.	68	Czech Republic	72.8
20	Sweden	258.8	69*	Honda Motor*	72.2
21*	BP	232.5	70*	McKesson	69.5
22*	Exxon Mobil	222.8	71	Chile	68.7
23	Austria	216.9	72*	US Postal Service	68.5
24	Saudi Arabia	208.	73*	Verizon	67.7
25*	Royal Dutch/ Shell Group	201.7	74*	Assicurazioni Generali	66.7
26	Poland	201.6	75*	Sony	66.3
27	Norway	197.9	76*	Matsushita Electric Industrial	66.2
28	Turkey	197.7			
29*	General Motors	195.3	77*	Nissan Motor	65.7
30	Denmark	180.8	78*	Nestle	65.4
31	Hong Kong (China)	176.2	79*	Home Depot	64.8
			80	Hungary	64.3
32	Indonesia	173.5	81*	Berkshire Hathaway	63.8
33*	Ford Motor	164.5	82*	Nippon Life Insurance	63.8
34*	Daimler Chrysler	156.6	83*	Royal Ahold	63.4
			84*	Deutsche Telecom	63.1
35*	Toyota Motor	153.1	85	New Zealand	62.2
36	Greece	145.9	86	Algeria	61.5
37	Finland	141.	87*	Peugeot	61.3
38	Argentina	140.1	88*	Altria Group	60.7
39	Thailand	135.8	89*	Metro	60.6
40*	General Electric	134.1	90*	Aviva	59.7
41	Iran	133.1	91*	Eni	59.3
42	South Africa	125.9	92*	Munich Re Group	59.0
43	Portugal	123.2	93*	Credit Suisse	58.9
44*	Total	118.4	94*	State Grid (China)	58.3
45*	Allianz	114.9	95	Peru	58.1
46*	Chevron Texaco	112.9	96*	HSBC Holdings	57.6
47*	Axa	111.9	97*	BNP Parabas	57.2
48	Israel	108.5	98*	Vodaphone	56.8
49	Ireland	107.8	99*	Cardinal Health	56.8
50*	Conoco Phillips	99.4	100*	Fortis	56.6
51*	Volkswagon	98.6			

Exhibit 9.3   1994 Comparison of Country GNPs and Annual Sales of the Largest Multinationals

*Multinational corporations

SOURCE: World Bank Development Indicators Database and *Global 500: World's Largest Corporations. Fortune,* July 2004.

1960s as financiers took advantage of the stock exchange boom accompanying the Vietnam War, acquiring or merging with company after company. To take one very spectacular example, in just ten years Harold Geneen transformed ITT from a loosely knit group of international telephone companies into a centralized conglomerate with 331 subsidiaries and another 771 subsidiaries of subsidiaries, with operations in seventy countries. For eleven years, from 1959 to 1970, ITT climbed from fifty-second to ninth place on the *Fortune* list of top companies. As journalist Anthony Sampson reports in his analysis of the affairs of ITT, Geneen's spectacular success was paralleled in many other corporations. Gulf and Western was quickly built up from a small firm making car fenders into a conglomerate of 92 companies in a range of industries as diverse as mining, sugar production, publishing, and show business. Litton Industries developed from a million-dollar electronics firm into a conglomerate of over 100 companies in less than ten years.

The overall trend toward larger and more diversified organizations that dominated the 1960s is reflected in the figures on industrial concentration. In 1948, the two hundred biggest industrial corporations in the United States controlled 48 percent of the manufacturing assets, but by 1969 they controlled 58 percent. By the early 1980s the top one hundred manufacturing companies controlled 48 percent of total manufacturing assets.

This strong pattern of centralized *control* has been sustained throughout the century, but as Peter Drucker has noted, it has been accompanied by an increasingly broad-based pattern of ownership through the influences of pension funds and other channels of institutionalized investment. The trend has produced a form of "postcapitalist society" where the logic of accumulating capital still drives the system, but with rewards accruing to a new detached group of "owners."

THE MULTINATIONALS
AS WORLD POWERS

These developments have had major repercussions on power structures throughout the world. Many modern organizations are larger and more powerful than nation-states, but, unlike nation-states, they are often not accountable to anyone but themselves. For example, research has suggested that the activities of many multinationals are highly centralized, their foreign subsidiaries being tightly controlled through policies, rules, and regulations set by headquarters. The subsidiaries have to report on a regular basis, and their staff are often allowed very little influence on key decisions affecting the subsidiary. Chief executives in foreign countries often become branch managers, developing local initiatives but within the policies set at the center. Because it is headquarters that actually controls the executive's future in the corporation, central concerns will almost always override local ones. The resources of the multinationals are also usually managed in a way that creates dependency rather than local autonomy.

Whenever we examine the multinationals, therefore, we are quickly brought face-to-face with their monolithic power and the fact that the twentieth century has witnessed a worldwide transformation where, as business historian Alfred Chandler has put it, the "visible hand" of management has replaced the "invisible hand" that Adam Smith saw as guiding competitive market economies. The power is not just economic. It is cultural and political as well. Note, for example, the global marketing alliance struck between McDonald's and Disney. In coming together in this way, the two companies have created a global force that will have a massive socializing impact on youths throughout the world.

Of all organizations, the multinationals come closest to realizing Max Weber's worst fears with regard to how bureaucratic organizations can become totalitarian regimes serving the interests of elites, where those in control are able to exercise power that is "practically unshatterable." Even though ownership is now widely diversified, and in an idealistic sense reflects what Peter Drucker calls "pension fund socialism," governance is still highly centralized. The "owners" are not really in a position to know what is happening, especially on a detailed level, because multinationals usually control a network of subsidiary companies. Power is firmly concentrated in the hands of senior management.

Historically, the name of the multinational game has been to achieve global dominance through worldwide sourcing of raw materials at the lowest possible price, with a view to producing and selling goods and services in the most profitable markets. The old model was one where the multinational would operate from its home base, for example, the United States, and penetrate foreign markets at a distance. Now the tendency is to create a strong simultaneous presence in a number of key areas of the world.

For example, renowned strategy expert Kenichi Ohmae has suggested that the late twentieth century has seen a shift toward what he calls "triad power"—a simultaneous penetration and presence in Japan, the European Community, and North America. Instead of selling "clone" products and services throughout the world, international companies now find ways of getting inside these three power bases with differentiated goods that tap regional markets to an optimum degree. This calls for new strategies and the use of joint ventures and international consortia through which different companies leverage each other's strength. This creates strange bedfellows. Consider, for example, the alliance between companies like GM and

Toyota. Competitors such as these can leverage each other's distribution, production, and other strengths in mutually beneficial ways. If a U.S.-based manufacturer can link with European and Japanese companies with strengths in distribution, considerable gains can accrue to all.

As Kurt Mirow and Harry Maurer have shown in their book *Webs of Power*, multinationals have long engaged in this kind of collaboration through the medium of international cartels, even though these are illegal in many countries. They have also reduced competition by entering into home-market protection agreements that establish exclusive territories that competitors will avoid, or where competitors will content themselves with existing market shares, leaving the dominant firm with no competition except from small domestic firms outside the cartel. "Hunting ground" agreements have often defined the degree of competition that is to be allowed in foreign markets, with preference usually being given to patterns of traditional market dominance. Agreements in relation to the exchange and transfer of technology and patent rights have reduced competition in this sphere as well. With the new patterns of international alliances, all this has developed to a new level of sophistication. The practices add to the already immense power of the multinationals in an important way, not least because they help to prevent mutually destructive battles between the giants, by controlling the ground and terms on which they will fight.

The efforts of multinationals to control their environments also extend into the realm of politics itself. As is well known, big corporations often use their immense lobbying power to shape the political agenda and to create political outcomes favorable to themselves. In this, perhaps more than any other single activity, the political significance of multinationals as world powers comes to the fore, as they are often in a position to exert major influence on host governments, especially when a nation is critically dependent on their presence or on some aspect of their operations. While the issues on which a multinational wishes to exert its influence are usually economic, the corporation often becomes directly and sometimes illegally involved in the political process. For example, when the economic aims and objectives of a multinational are in conflict with the line of development favored by a host government, it is very easy for the multinational to become embroiled in activities designed to shape the economic and social policies of the government. As a result, it may be drawn into the political arena and become explicitly political and ideological in its activities, although usually acting behind the scenes. The classic and infamous case is ITT's involvement in the affairs of Chile, where it plotted in 1970 to stop the election of Marxist president Salvador Allende. Conspiring with the CIA, ITT sought to create economic chaos within Chile and thus to encourage a military coup, with the company offering to contribute "up to seven figures" to the White House to stop Allende coming to power.

The multinationals are a major political force in the world economy and, for the most part, a political force without political accountability. The Chilean episode, although extreme in its characteristics, highlights a much more general set of problems relating to the contradictions that arise when strong authoritarian powers like the multinationals are allowed to exist in democratic states, for they are in a position to make complete nonsense of the democratic process, obliging governments to be more responsive to corporate interests than to those of the people who elected them.

We can see now why advocates of the radical frame of reference point to the existence of the multinationals as yet further evidence of the general antagonism of interests between people and corporations. The sheer power of the multinationals, and the associated cartels, alliances, and interlocking patterns of ownership and control that bind them together, combine to create a world economy dominated by organizations where the power of the corporate official often dwarfs that of the elected politician and that of the public at large.

MULTINATIONALS: A RECORD OF EXPLOITATION?

Advocates of the multinationals often see them as positive forces in economic development, creating jobs and bringing capital, technology, and expertise to communities or countries that might have difficulty developing these resources on their own account. Their critics, though, tend to see them as authoritarian juggernauts that are ultimately out to exploit their hosts for all they can get. The argument identifies the horns of a major dilemma in that the policies that serve the interests of a multinational firm may not be in the best interests of the community or nation in which the firm is located. Hence, given the immense power of the multinational firm, its hosts often find themselves having to rely on a benevolent social responsibility on the part of the multinational.

The record of the multinationals in this regard, however, leaves a great deal to be desired. The highly centralized systems of decision making frequently mean that centralized corporate interests relating to the profitability, growth, or strategic development of the multinational as a whole take first place in decision making, with localized community or national interests taking second. Thus, when strategic considerations lead the executive staff of a multinational to divest its holdings in a particular industry, to close down a particular plant, or to restructure its operations internationally, the consequences can be devastating for the communities and countries involved. Consider, for example, how the shift in search of cheaper, non-unionized labor has led many firms to leave relatively high-priced cities in Canada and the northern United States for locations in the southern states,

Mexico, Brazil, or Asia. The effect has been to create large areas of regional and urban decline. The effects are particularly marked in small communities where the decision of the multinational to close down operations of a major plant can remove the economic lifeblood of the community. Regional exodus also creates massive structural unemployment, increasing welfare rolls and intensifying the fiscal problems faced by governments. The bitter irony is often that many of these decisions are made not because a particular plant or set of operations is unprofitable, but because the corporation believes that it is possible to earn greater profit elsewhere.

Similar developments are found in the decaying industrial and mining centers of Europe, where the closure of coal mines and steel mills leads to the economic and social decline of whole regions. As in the case of Willy Loman in Arthur Miller's play, these communities often feel that they have been used and sucked dry and are now being thrown away because they are no longer needed. The feelings of resentment and exploitation are particularly severe when the plants or mines being closed are profitable but not profitable enough from a corporate standpoint.

That corporate and community interests are not always synonymous is a truism common to all organizations, not just the multinationals. But the scale of operations among the latter is so enormous that it makes the consequences of their decisions especially great. We have illustrated the point by focusing on how changes in corporate strategy, even if only to *increase* rates of profit, can set the basis for widespread socioeconomic change. In a similar way, the decisions of multinationals to move their liquid capital from one country to another to take advantage of interest rate differentials can have a major effect on the international balance of payments of the countries concerned. Or a decision to pursue a particular line of corporate development can have a major effect on national and regional economic planning, distorting the pattern of relations that the host region or nation wishes to encourage.

For these and many other reasons, communities and nations often find themselves wishing to attract multinationals while also fearing the consequences because they know that the underlying sets of interests may be in fundamental conflict. Some nations, such as Canada, where foreign ownership in many sectors of industry runs at levels well over 50 percent, have formally recognized that such conflicts exist and have tried, without success, to codify the conditions under which the multinationals will be allowed to operate within their domains (Exhibit 9.4). However, there is a dilemma in that the more a host government attempts to control the practices of the multinationals, the less attractive their investment in that country becomes. Hence, multinational and nation-state often end up in a relation of dominance and dependency, or as rival power blocs, each attempting to shape the conditions under which the other is to operate.

Up to now, it seems that the multinationals have been winning the battle. Increasingly, nations are having to recognize that they cannot really manage or control what goes on within their own boundaries.

The impact of multinationals on Western countries may be damaging, but their impact on the Third World has undoubtedly been much worse. Critics see them as modern plunderers, exploiting natural and other resources for their own ends. Of course, the multinationals do not see themselves in this way. They see their activities as helping develop the underdeveloped world amid the difficulties created by unfavorable publicity about the wrongdoings of a socially irresponsible minority, by propaganda against big business leveled by critics on the "left," and sometimes by hostile and ungrateful foreign governments who fail to honor contracts. Although multinationals, recognize that their activities

---

In 1974, the Canadian government established the Foreign Investment Review Agency (FIRA) and adopted guidelines for good corporate behavior. They serve to highlight areas in which conflicts of interest between government and multinationals may arise.

Canada's Twelve Good Corporate Behavior Principles (as They Related to Alleged Objectionable U.S. Subsidiary Policies)	
Guiding Principle	*Alleged Objectionable Practice*
1. Full realization of the company's growth and operating potential in Canada.	1. U.S.-based corporate planners institute expansion and cutback plans without regard for Canada's plans and aspirations.
2. Make Canadian subsidiary a self-contained, vertically integrated entity with total responsibility for at least one productive function.	2. The Canadian subsidiary is primarily an assembler of imported parts or distributor of goods produced elsewhere so operations can be easily shut down or transferred.
3. Maximum development of export markets from Canada.	3. Filling export orders to third-country markets from the U.S. stock earns credits for U.S. balance of payments rather than Canada's.
4. Extend processing of Canada's raw materials through maximum number of stages.	4. Have as few as possible materials-processing stages in Canada to minimize political leverage.

Exhibit 9.4   Potential Conflicts of Interests Between Multinationals and Nation-States   *(Continued)*

Exhibit 9.4 (Continued)

Guiding Principle	Alleged Objectionable Practice
5. Equitable pricing policies for international and intracompany sales.	5. Negotiated or spurious prices by Canadian U.S. subsidiaries are designed to get around Canadian income taxes.
6. Develop sources of supply in Canada.	6. Preferences for U.S. or third-country sources for purposes of corporate convenience or political leverage.
7. Inclusion of R&D and product development.	7. The concentration of R&D and product design in the United States means Canada can never develop these capabilities.
8. Retain substantial earnings for growth.	8. Profits earned in Canada do not remain to finance Canadian expansion.
9. Appointment of Canadian officers and directors.	9. Use of U.S. officers and directors to prevent development of local outlook in planning and execution.
10. Equity participation by Canadian investing public.	10. Creation of wholly owned subsidiaries denies policy determination and earnings to Canadians.
11. Publication of financial reports.	11. Consolidation of Canadian operating results into parent company statement or failure to publish any relevant information.
12. Support of Canadian cultural and charitable institutions.	12. Failure locally to support such causes as the United Appeal while parent corporations give generously to comparable U.S. campaigns.

The establishment of such a code makes enormous sense from a national standpoint but is extremely difficult to apply in a globalized economy. Canada more or less gave up the attempt, disbanding FIRA in 1984 and moving into the North American Free Trade Agreement (NAFTA). The dilemma posed by the presence of multinationals is thus by no means easy to solve. Many governments want multinationals within their boundaries but are concerned about the consequences.

SOURCE: Based on Ashton (1968: 57).

must be subjected to appropriate rules of conduct, they argue that their influence is for better rather than for worse and that multinationals and host nations can operate in a way that benefits both. The debate is a hot one, and arguments can be made for either side.

Here are the detailed points of concern.

The first criticism of multinational operations in the Third World is that their effect on the economies of host nations, like that of the colonial empires on whose legacy they build, is basically an exploitative one. If we examine the role of multinationals in Third World countries we find that traditionally they have been heavily involved in the extraction of raw materials and foodstuffs. More recently they have become involved in manufacturing. In both cases, control of operations, technology, and revenues rests with the multinationals and their parent nations, the end result being that the Third World countries are *more* dependent on them than when the process first started.

Consider how multinationals have dealt with Third World commodities and natural resources. In both cases, they have used the resources of their host countries to enhance profits and standards of living in the West. The commodity trade is dominated by a handful of global companies. For example, about six companies in each group control between 85 and 90 percent of the global wheat trade, 75 percent of crude oil, and 95 percent of iron ore. The market structure has had a powerful impact on world prices, and Third World producers have seen real commodity export values drop below 1930 levels. Between 1980 and 1990, it is estimated that this involved the equivalent of a $300 billion transfer of funds from poor Third World countries to the developed nations. Until pressured by host governments to do so, multinational corporations used to conduct little refining or processing of raw products in the country of extraction. The materials were exported in a raw state, often at considerable profit but with little benefit to the host country either financially or in terms of economic development.

The story in relation to agriculture is even worse, as producing for export to the West has often made local populations completely dependent on foreign employers and foreign markets for even the most basic subsistence. Consider, for example, how agriculture in many Latin American and Caribbean countries has been restructured toward the production of cash crops such as sugar, coffee, tropical fruits, nuts, and carnations. Under the influence of the small number of multinationals that dominate these and other areas of agriculture, the Third World, despite widespread hunger, has become a net exporter of foodstuffs. Even Africa is currently a net exporter of barley, beans, peanuts, fresh vegetables, and cattle. The production of cash crops has meant that the best land is used to produce crops for export rather than for local consumption. Hence, poverty in the Third World has often been *produced* by the process of "development," as small farmers dispossessed of land requisitioned by colonialists or bought by the multinationals become laborers working for subsistence wages on large plantations rather than earning a living in their old way. Cash crops are useless for local purposes. One cannot survive by eating sugar, coffee, rubber, strawberries, or carnations—the crops that have replaced the more traditional produce. One can survive only by selling one's labor, earning wages, and buying food. But because local food production has largely been replaced by the cash crops, it is extremely expensive. Thus people even in agriculturally fertile countries are often forced into poverty. Many critics of the multinationals see them as actually creating and sustaining many of the problems now being experienced in the Third World. Even liberal economists recognize the way multinationals widen rather than close the gap between rich and poor. As Teresa Hayter has put it, they are involved in "the creation of world poverty." It is estimated that the richest 20 percent of the world's population now have an average per capita income 60 times greater than the poorest 20 percent.

The way the populations of Third World countries have become dependent on wage labor as a source of livelihood parallels what occurred in the Industrial Revolution in Europe when the creation of a dependent working class arose along with the disappearance of traditional means of livelihood. Exactly the same process is occurring in the Third World today. The introduction of multinational enterprise tends to eliminate local agriculture and traditional craft and industry, creating a dispossessed labor force and a market for unskilled labor. Skilled artisans and farmers go to work on plantations and in factories for subsistence wages exactly as they did in Europe and North America centuries before. And just like the factory owners in the Industrial Revolution who exploited this workforce, corporations continue to do so in the Third World today.

Hence, a second criticism of the multinationals: They exploit local populations, using them as wage slaves, often as a substitute for unionized Western labor. In multinational-owned Third World factories, men, women, and children sometimes work ten, twelve, or more hours for less than one dollar a day. No wonder that industry drifts from Western cities to Third World factories at an incredible rate. For example, the AFL-CIO has estimated that the United States alone loses around one million jobs every five years to these sources of cheap and exploited labor.

Other criticisms of multinationals in the Third World hinge on the fact that while they claim to be taking capital and technology to underdeveloped countries, they do in fact extract a net outflow of capital and ensure that they always retain control of the technology they introduce. It has been estimated that multinationals sometimes raise as much as 80 percent of their capital from local sources. Their own direct investment is thus often relatively small, boosting the return generated by overall profits on their own capital to quite staggering heights. In certain industries, the estimated rate of return on capital invested by the multinationals sometimes runs as high as 400 percent per annum. Given that it is usual to repatriate a major proportion of profits to headquarters, and hence the parent nation, it is thus easy to see how a net outflow of capital from the host nation can arise. It becomes extremely difficult for Third World countries to derive any long-term benefit from the presence of the multinationals, as host governments usually do not build any real equity in their industry.

The severity of this problem has been exacerbated by the kinds of foreign aid extended by agencies such as the World Bank, the IMF, and the United States Agency for International Development. Frequently, this aid is tied in ways that promote links with multinational enterprises, and in the long run it contributes to the net outflow of capital. This problem is vividly illustrated by the fact that the outstanding interest on the international debt of Third World countries is now greater than the capital originally borrowed, and that their annual interest payments often exceed the amount of incoming aid. It is estimated that Third World debtor countries make net transfers of over \$20 billion per annum. In other words, international aid has resulted in their paying to the West much more than they have received.

Similar criticisms apply to the export of technology. Although much is often made of how multinationals bring valuable expertise to the Third World, they bring only what they want and ensure that they retain control. Much of the technology exported to the Third World is Western technology that is often not appropriate to local conditions, and much is well-established technology that is no longer at the cutting edge. Technology reaching maturity in the West often finds a ready market in the Third World, especially when supported by foreign aid. Western technology also makes the Third World user dependent on the Western supplier for spare parts, modernization, and often the expertise necessary to maintain and develop the technology. Thus, critics argue that multinationals are doing no more than a form of intelligent marketing that ultimately serves their own interests. For example, most research and development continues to be done in the parent country, so no real opportunity is created for a Third World country to build technological expertise of its own. The export of technology thus really exports a new form of dependency.

Another criticism of multinational operations relates to the way they often disguise excess profits and avoid paying appropriate taxes in their host nations through creative "transfer pricing." It has been estimated that a staggering one-third of world trade is intracompany trade. In terms of value, each multinational corporation is often its own most important customer, with one subsidiary buying from another. Such trading gives the corporation great scope for manipulating profit figures for a subsidiary in a given country. By buying materials from one fellow subsidiary at high prices and selling its products to another at low prices, a subsidiary can make an operating loss or a high profit according to the impression it wishes to give to the outside world. Thus, the profits of subsidiaries in high-tax countries may be kept artificially low and those in low-tax countries inflated. Or profits can be switched from one industry to another to take advantage of special incentives offered by host governments. Such transactions often play a big part in the politics of organization, especially in relation to negotiations with trade unions, and in producing rationales for plant closure. The simple statement that a plant is "unprofitable" is often backed by creative accounting that deceives all but the most discerning members of trade unions, investors, and members of the general public. Multinationals, like other organizations, use accounting to shape perceptions of reality to further their own ends.

Finally, the multinationals are heavily criticized for driving unduly hard bargains with their host nations and communities, often playing one group or country against another to achieve exceptional concessions. These bargains may take many forms: rights to retain a controlling interest for a set period of time; excessive rates of return; local tax concessions or access to subsidies and other forms of host government support; freedom from government regulation; or regulations of reduced stringency. The multinational often achieves a position where it can do pretty well as it wishes. Some of the most obvious examples of abuses are found in the field of occupational health and safety and in the general conduct of multinationals in relation to the safety of the communities and markets they serve. Free of government regulations, they often end up operating hazardous factories or dumping hazardous products onto an unsuspecting public. It has been suggested that safety standards in some multinational plants in the Third World are decades behind those in the West. The ever-present danger posed by such plants was vividly illustrated by the 1984 tragedy at the Union Carbide plant in Bhopal, India, which took over 2,500 lives and maimed thousands more.

For all these reasons, critics of multinational operations tend to stress that these organizations can create economic, political, and social havoc, distorting rather than benefiting the development of their host country. Of course, the blame is not seen as lying entirely with the multinationals, as they are usually invited into the countries where they operate and often do so with the active cooperation and encouragement of ruling governments, dictatorships, or powerful elites. The critics thus also place a heavy measure of blame on the ruling classes within those countries for participating in the domination and exploitation of their nations' human and material resources. Sometimes, the multinationals engage in explicit or implicit agreements with ruling authorities regarding the conditions under which they will operate. Elsewhere the arrangements tend to be more subtle and the result of careful and continuous political lobbying.

The radical critique thus emphasizes that the modern state and multinational corporations act as partners in systematic domination. The defenders of modern practice, however, tend to see such activities in a more favorable light. States and multinationals are viewed as partners in progress, modernization, and development, and, in the view of advocates of this partnership, the majority of multinationals usually behave in an exemplary way. These advocates would argue that it is necessary to focus on the exemplary behavior as a model of what overall practice could look like and to develop codes of conduct and accountability to create a constructive framework for world development, such as those developed by the United Nations in relation to the dumping of hazardous products and by the ILO in relation to good corporate citizenship.

Strengths and Limitations of the Domination Metaphor

Most of what has been discussed in this chapter under the label of domination can, from another standpoint, be seen as but an unintended consequence of an otherwise rational system of activity. The negative impact that organizations often have on their employees or their environments, or that multinationals have on patterns of inequality and world economic development, is not necessarily an intended one. It is usually a consequence of rational actions through which a group of individuals seeks to advance a particular set of aims, such as increased profitability or corporate growth.

What, then, do we mean by rationality? If rationality has unintended negative impacts that lead even the most celebrated and excellent organizations to create problems for others, why is such action rational?

The overwhelming strength of the domination metaphor is that it draws our attention to this double-edged nature of rationality, illustrating that it always reflects a partial point of view. Actions that are rational for increasing profitability may have a damaging effect on employees' health.

Actions designed to spread an organization's portfolio of risks (e.g., by divesting interests in a particular industry) may spell economic and urban decay for whole communities of people who have built their lives around that industry. What is rational from one organizational standpoint may be catastrophic from another.

Viewing organization as a mode of domination that advances certain interests at the expense of others forces this important aspect of organizational reality into the center of our attention. It leads us to appreciate the wisdom of Max Weber's insight that the pursuit of rationality can itself be a mode of domination and to remember that, as discussed in the conclusions to Chapter 6, in talking about rationality we should always be asking the question *"Rational for whom?"*

The metaphor thus provides a useful counterweight to much of traditional organization theory, which has for the most part ignored values or ideological premises. Most discussions of organization attempt to be ideologically neutral, often by presenting theories of organization as theories that can be used to serve many different ends, and by identifying questions of business ethics as topics for special and isolated study. Through such means, it is possible to talk or write about how one can design a bureaucratic or matrix organization, or create or manage an organizational culture, or play organizational politics, without paying too much attention to the way the ideas will be used. The fact that they may be used to improve the production of food or of bombs, and that in improving the rationality and efficiency of an organization one may be providing the basis for action that is profoundly irrational for many other groups of people, is not addressed. One of the major strengths of the domination metaphor is that it forces us to recognize that domination may be intrinsic to the way we organize and not just an unintended side effect. It shows us that there is often a "seamy" side to otherwise excellent organizations and suggests that this should be a mainstream concern of managers and organization theorists.

Used in an even more proactive mode, the domination metaphor also shows a way of creating an organization theory *for* the exploited. In exposing the seamy side of organizational life, whether in terms of structured inequality, institutionalized racism, occupational accidents and disease, or exploitation in the Third World, and in attempting to develop theories to account for these phenomena, the organization theorist has a means of using organization theory as an instrument for social change. Those interested in pursuing this agenda thus make much of the possibility of developing a radical organization theory to counter the influence of more conventional theory, which they see as serving and reinforcing vested interests embodied in the status quo.

Another strength of the domination metaphor is that it helps us appreciate the issues that fuel this radical frame of reference in practice. As we have discussed, many organizations become radicalized in ways that stress "them and us" attitudes. In understanding how organizations foster dual labor markets, symbolized and extended in differential systems of privilege, or how these operate as opportunity structures that open the doors to success for some employees while closing them to others, we catch a glimpse of the kinds of segregation and division that millions of people experience on a daily basis. As we begin to appreciate the reality of factory workers who see no future in their organization other than an extension of their dingy present, or the sense of exploitation experienced by those who are forced to work under oppressive conditions because they have no other means of survival, we can begin to understand that industrial unrest is not necessarily the work of troublemakers or of unions that have outlived their usefulness.

Many organizations are literally divided societies that perpetuate class warfare in the workplace. They are societies that naturally generate radical leaders hell-bent on changing the circumstances of their followers, even if this means a long and arduous battle that may ultimately be lost. Hence, employees may frequently engage in what their employers see as a senseless or futile struggle for wage increases they feel they deserve, or they may even put a company out of business rather than return to work on unfair terms. The popular notion that organizations serve the interests of all often blinds us to the fact that the radical ideology is not just ideology but an accurate description of the reality of masses of people.

The domination metaphor encourages us to recognize and deal with perceived and actual exploitation in the workplace rather than dismiss it as a "radical" distortion of the way things are. Clearly, if those managing organizations were to attempt to deal with the radical frame of reference by accepting rather than denying its legitimacy, as tends to be the situation at present, this would help initiate a new era of employee relations and conceptions of corporate responsibility. A new and aggressive form of social consciousness would oblige corporate decision makers to take personal responsibility for the inhuman consequences of so many conventional practices.

The strengths of the domination metaphor thus provide the basis for a truly radical critique of organization and organization theory. However, in the view of many it goes too far and has a number of serious limitations. The first and most important of these arises when the perspective is linked to a crude conspiracy theory of organization and society. Although there is much evidence to suggest that patterns of domination are class based, that there is a tendency for the interests of ruling elites to converge in centralized ownership and control, and that government policies often work in ways that sustain and serve the interests of dominant social groups, this does not necessarily support the idea that there is a conspiracy in the way one group or social class is pitted against another.

Let us return to a question raised implicitly throughout this chapter: Does organizational domination occur by default or by design? A conspiracy theory tends to imply the latter, suggesting that the process of domination in society is rooted in some callous structure of motivation or in a conscious policy of exploitation. However, this is not necessarily the case. For example, if we return and consider the ideas discussed in Chapter 8, it is easy to see that domination may be encoded in the logics of change through which social life is unfolding: Organizational actions that promote structured inequalities, industrial accidents, occupational disease, environmental pollution, or exploitation in the Third World may all result from the way systemic forces dictate that business be done. In this regard it is important to note that many of the pathologies explored in this chapter are found on both sides of the political spectrum. The fall of the Berlin Wall has shown that Eastern communism, like Western capitalism, has excelled at producing systems of corporate domination!

For many, any explanation of social domination that emphasizes its systemic character is far too deterministic, serving to remove all responsibility from the powerful decision makers who are actively engaged in producing the organizational world, and who, in principle, have the power to change things. However, it does serve to raise a very real dilemma, for many top-level decision makers often feel caught "between a rock and a hard place," recognizing the social consequences of their actions and yet knowing that a sensitive social conscience or undue concern for people may prove economically paralyzing and prevent their organizations from operating in a decisive and efficient way.

To the extent that domination is seen as part of a social conspiracy or the responsibility of a few individuals, the latent consequence is to assign blame, arouse defenses, and entrench the fundamental problems. At best, it mobilizes social and political opposition to the problem, aiming for revolutionary change, but usually achieving no more than marginal change. Although such mobilization may be appropriate, a more systemic understanding would help to create a greater sense of collective responsibility and to find ways of reframing the basic problems to create new kinds of remedial actions. For example, such reframing may show that domination is embedded in processes of mutual causality or in dialectical logics of change that can be reshaped by giving attention to special system pathologies, new codes of social responsibility, new concepts of social accounting, and the like. As discussed in Chapter 8, we may be able to remove key problems by changing the "rules of the game" that produce them. Approached in this manner, the insights of the metaphor transcend the limitations imposed by interpretations grounded in any conspiracy theory.

A second potential limitation of the metaphor stems from the danger that in asserting an equivalence between domination and organization we may blind ourselves to the idea that nondominating forms of organization may be possible. With this in mind, it is sometimes argued that the real thrust of the domination metaphor should be to critique the values that underly different modes of organization, and highlight the differences between exploitive and nonexploitive forms, rather than to engage in critique in a broader sense.

Finally, it is often said that the metaphor merely articulates an extreme form of left-wing ideology, serving to fan the flames of the radical frame of reference and thus adding to the difficulties of managers in an already turbulent world. The criticism has merit in that the perspective is ideological, but it is certainly no more ideological than any other. The chapters in this book show that all theories of organization are inherently ideological in that they tend to give us rather one-sided views. Thus, although the domination metaphor may lead us to focus on the negative side of organization in an extreme way, it is really no more extreme than any other viewpoint, including the highly orthodox.

PART III

IMPLICATIONS FOR PRACTICE

Using Metaphor to Negotiate the
Demands of a Paradoxical World

10

The Challenge
of Metaphor

$\mathbf{O}$rganizations are many things at once!
They are complex and multifaceted.
They are paradoxical.
That's why the challenges facing management are often so difficult.

In any given situation there may be many different tendencies and dimensions, all of which have an impact on effective management.

The metaphors considered in previous chapters reveal this complexity. Each provides a comprehensive view of organization and management from the perspective created through the metaphor. Each generates important insights. But taken to an extreme, these insights encounter severe limitations. Any given metaphor can be incredibly persuasive, but it can also be blinding and block our ability to gain an overall view.

Hence, like many prominent management theorists, we can get seduced by the idea that management must engineer, reengineer, and operate an efficient organization machine, only to find our designs undermined by a changing environment or by the human beings that ultimately have to bring the machine to life. Or, in becoming converts to the idea of developing "learning organizations" that can evolve in a brain-like way, we can easily overlook the political realities that block effective learning. Or, as enthused organizational politicians or social critics, we can find that while we are preoccupied with our political maneuvering or debates, key transformations in the external environment are "calling the tune."

As discussed in Chapter 1, this partiality of insight is inherent in the nature of metaphor and the theories and ideas it generates. It helps to explain the swings in management from fad to fad, and why the latest theory is *always* in the process of giving way to another. Management theories tend to sell the positive insights of a metaphor, while ignoring the limitations and distortions that it creates. These insights attract. That's why they develop a following and become the trend of the day. But when managers get down to the business of applying the insights in practice, reality presents itself as being much more complicated. Most management theories are developed in a way that inevitably creates disillusionment and disappointment. They usually have an element of "truth," but it is a truth that, in effect, denies the complexity of the realities to which the theories are to be applied.

Hence the main invitation and challenge of this book: To recognize and cope with the idea that all theories of organization and management are based on implicit images or metaphors that persuade us to see, understand, and imagine situations in partial ways.

As has been shown, metaphors create insight.

But they also distort.

They have strengths.

But they also have limitations.

In creating ways of seeing they tend to create ways of *not* seeing.

Hence there can be no single theory or metaphor that gives an all-purpose point of view. There can be no "correct theory" for structuring everything we do.

The challenge facing modern managers is to become accomplished in the art of using metaphor: To find appropriate ways of seeing, understanding, and shaping the situations with which they have to deal.

Metaphors Create Ways of Seeing and Shaping Organizational Life

Different metaphors have a capacity to tap different dimensions of a situation, showing how different qualities can coexist. For example, using some of the images explored in previous chapters we can see that a specific aspect of organizational structure may reflect an attempt to "mechanize" a particular set of activities; it may be a particular manager's defence against anxiety; it may symbolize a key aspect of corporate culture; it may express a mode of "single-loop learning"; it may be a crucial part of a department's power base; it may be an anachronism that prevents the organization from dealing with the demands of the wider environment. All these features can have a simultaneous presence.

At one level, this may seem to be complicating the nature of organizational reality to a terrible degree. But this is the nature of the reality with which managers have to deal.

Continuing the above example, that element of organizational structure that seems such a hopeless and obvious anachronism may be the symbol and "carrier" of important elements of culture or corporate politics; or it may be playing a vital psychological role in how managers are coping with the uncertainties of the time. As such, its removal will generate all kinds of cultural, political, and psychological consequences. It is vital that managers understand this. Otherwise they will find themselves falling into the unanticipated problems that have plagued so many corporate change programs seeking to restructure, reinvent, reengineer, or reform organizational life.

This view of organizational reality, of course, is completely consistent with what natural scientists have demonstrated in relation to the physical and biological worlds. These, too, possess paradoxical qualities. Consider, for example, the famous experiments on the nature of light. When scientists study light as a wave it reveals itself as a wave. When it is studied as a particle, it reveals itself as a particle. Both tendencies or qualities coexist. The metaphor that the scientist uses to study these latent tendencies *shapes* what he or she sees.

The same is true of organizations.

Think "structure" and you'll see structure. Think "culture," and you'll see all kinds of cultural dimensions. Think "politics" and you'll find politics. Think in terms of system patterns and loops, and you'll find a whole range of them.

This is the manager's dilemma. We tend to find and realize what we are looking for. This does not mean that there is no real basis to what we find. Rather, it is just that reality has a tendency to reveal itself in accordance with the perspectives through which it is engaged. As Albert Einstein once noted, it is the theory through which we observe a situation that decides what we can observe. Or as philosopher George Berkeley expressed this idea way back in the eighteenth century, objectivity is as much a part of the observer as of the object observed. In any given situation there are many potential objectivities. In using different perspectives to create different modes of engagement we are able to tap into these and understand the same situation in many ways. Some of these ways may be extremely powerful, because they connect and resonate with the reality being observed. Other perspectives may prove weak or irrelevant, having little evocative or substantial power.

Scientists have generated powerful insights by studying light as a wave or a particle. But not as a grapefruit!

In a similar way, managers face the challenge of finding or creating powerful metaphors that can help them understand and shape their organizations. The metaphors offered in previous chapters provide examples, but by no means exhaust the possibilities.

Against the background of this discussion, the idea introduced in Chapter 1 that managers need to be skilled in the art of reading and understanding organizational life assumes new significance. For if managers are not engaged in an active reading that embraces different points of view, much of the richness and complexity of organizational life is passing them by. They are simply not seeing what is really going on.

Also, they are surrendering their ability to *shape* what is going on. As will be evident from the above, our observations are by no means neutral. The metaphors and ideas through which we "see" and "read" situations influence how we act. Managers who see organizations in a mechanistic way have a tendency to "mechanize." Those dominated by a cultural lens tend to act in a way that shapes and reshapes culture. Favored metaphors tend to trap us in specific modes of action. We see this in how all the metaphors explored in previous chapters end up having their own prescriptive tone.

Mechanistic imagery encourages us to structure and rationalize everything we do. Organic imagery encourages a focus on adaptation and the satisfaction of needs. Images of the brain focus on issues of organizational learning. The psychic prison metaphor points to ways out of cognitive and unconscious traps. Theories of autopoiesis encourage us to challenge and rethink our identities. Images of mutual causality encourage us to transform problematic loops.

This review is by no means exhaustive. It just serves to illustrate how ways of thinking tend to generate ways of acting.

Hence the all-important message: Limit your thinking and you will limit your range of action.

Seeing, Thinking, and Acting in New Ways

Metaphor encourages us to think and act in new ways. It extends horizons of insight and creates new possibilities.

You may have experienced this in reading some of the previous chapters, especially those that have sought to stretch the horizons of contemporary thinking to embrace images of "corporate DNA," holographic self-organization, emergent intelligence, psychic traps, shifting "attractor patterns," or destructive contradictions. The images of organization explored in this book offer a range of competing insights that, as illustrated in Exhibit 10.1, encourage us to see the world of organization and management from a variety of perspectives.

Organizations and organizational problems can be seen and understood in many different ways.

Each way of seeing will produce distinctive insights with their own pattern of strengths and limitations. The challenge is to integrate the insights to obtain an understanding and action strategy that can suit our purposes.

Exhibit 10.1   Metaphor Can Generate Multiple Ways of Seeing and Acting

There are a lot of differences in the points of view explored. Different chapters pull us in very different directions, creating a great range of insights. But there is enormous complementarity as well.

Hence, in reading the foregoing chapters you may have been struck by how the insights of different metaphors often support and reinforce each other. Note, for example, how the challenge of creating organic organizations that can flow with environmental change is informed by an understanding of how we can use principles of holographic organization to enhance flexibility, or how corporate culture can help to create integration in the absence of formal structures and written rules. Note how blocks to organizational change can be understood through an analysis of "single" and "double-loop learning," in terms of entrenched patterns of corporate culture, or as manifestations of unconscious defences. Note how we can integrate structure, culture, and politics as key dimensions of organizational design. Or, note how the four logics of change explored in Chapter 8 each add new angles on problems of corporate transformation. The theory of autopoiesis focuses on the key role of system identity in sustaining entrenched patterns. Chaos theory recasts understanding through an analysis of "attractor patterns." An understanding of mutual causality and patterns of paradox and contradiction add yet further insights. Together they generate a range of complementary ideas that are very distinct, yet also capable of contributing to an integrated theory of change.

In all these instances we see how the insights of different metaphors can contribute to a rich understanding of the situations with which we are trying to deal, suggesting their own favored methods of tackling the issues at hand. In approaching the same situation in different ways they extend insight and suggest actions that may not have been possible before. For example, an understanding of the holographic nature of the brain, or of the "DNA" encoded in corporate culture, really can help an enterprise break free of traditional structures and controls. An understanding of the unconscious psychic traps that are holding an organization in an undesirable "attractor pattern" can provide the all-important breakthrough for generating new opportunities around organizational learning. The insights generated by different metaphors are not just theoretical. They are incredibly practical.

As we gain comfort in using the implications of different metaphors in this way, we quickly learn that the insights of one metaphor can often help us overcome the limitations of another. This, in turn, encourages us to recognize and, indeed, search for the limitations of existing insights: So that we can use them as springboards for new insight.

This is exactly what I have sought to illustrate in moving from one metaphorical frame to another, both within and between the chapters of this book. Metaphors lead to new metaphors, creating a mosaic of competing and complementary insights. This is one of the most powerful qualities of the approach. When you recognize that your theories and insights are metaphorical, you have to approach the process in an open-ended way. You have to recognize your limitations and find ways of going beyond them. This results in a style of thinking that is always open and evolving, and extremely well-suited for dealing with the complexity of organizational life.

As suggested in Chapter 1, this book delivers its message on the key role of metaphor at two levels. It stands as a treatise on metaphorical thinking that demonstrates, through its content, that organization and management theory is no more than a domain of extended metaphor. It also shows how metaphor can be mobilized at a practical level to create more effective ways of understanding and tackling organizational problems.

The next chapter pursues the latter agenda in more depth, illustrating how managers can blend the insights of different metaphorical frames to create powerful perspectives on what is happening in their organizations.

11

Reading and Shaping Organizational Life

The ability to "read" and understand what is happening in one's organization is a key managerial competence. As has been suggested, if one can broaden understanding, it is possible to broaden the range of actions through which one approaches key issues.

How can this be achieved?

The advice drawn from earlier chapters and summarized in Exhibit 10.1 is this: Learn how to generate, integrate, and use the insights of competing metaphors. Use them to understand and shape the situations that you are seeking to organize and manage.

We have discussed the process in general terms, so the purpose of this chapter is to go one step further by offering a concrete illustration at a practical level. In the next sections you will find a short case study followed by two readings of the case from different points of view. One adopts the perspective of a manager-consultant seeking to deal with the problems presented in the case. The other presents a reading from the perspectives of a social critic and policy analyst. Together they illustrate how we can mobilize the insights of different metaphors to identify and understand key dimensions of a situation to serve the purposes at hand.

It must be emphasized that the aim of the case study is to provide just one simple illustration of the methodology in action. Readers interested in further applications, and more advice on use of the method, will find these in this book's companion volume *Imaginization: The Art of Creative Management*.

The Multicom Case

Multicom is a small firm employing 150 people in the public relations field. It was started by Jim Walsh, a marketing specialist, and Wendy Bridges, a public relations expert. They had worked together for several years at a medium-size communications firm and decided to branch out on their own to realize their own ideas as to what a good PR firm could and should be. They felt that their combined expertise and extensive contacts provided an excellent base on which to do this.

Before submitting their resignations at their old firm they persuaded two colleagues, Marie Beaumont and Frank Rossi, to join them as minority shareholders. Walsh and Bridges each held 40 percent of the equity in the new venture; Beaumont and Rossi were each given 10 percent. Rossi was an editor and writer with an excellent reputation, and Beaumont was a well-regarded film and video person.

At first, business was difficult, and they were glad of the corporate clients that they had taken with them from their old firm. Competition was keen, and their old firm seemed subtly to be doing everything it could to block their progress. However, they worked hard, and their reputation steadily grew along with the size of their staff and their earnings. By the end of their second year, the four partners were each earning almost double their previous salaries and building a significant capital investment as well. They felt that they were well on the way to achieving the kind of top-notch outfit on which they had set their sights.

These early years were exciting ones.

When they established Multicom the four partners adopted a client-centered mode of organization. They each had certain clients for whom they felt a special responsibility, and in effect became project managers for these clients. Each developed a reasonable competence in all aspects of the agency's work so that they could substitute for each other when necessary. New staff were encouraged to develop the same all-around skills and capacities in addition to their specializations. While this was often time-consuming and expensive, it created great flexibility. The search for new business and continuing contacts with clients took a significant proportion of staff away from the office most of the time, so the existence of a number of good "all arounders" was a real asset. Besides that, it often made work more interesting and enjoyable and added to the general team spirit of the office.

The staff at Multicom worked hard, often starting early in the morning and working late at night. They also played hard, throwing regular parties to celebrate the completion of major projects or the acquisition of new clients. These helped keep morale high and project Multicom's image as an excellent and exciting place to work. The firm's clients often attended these parties and were usually impressed by the vitality and quality of interpersonal relations.

During the company's third year, however, things began to change. The long hours and pace of life at Multicom were getting to Walsh and Bridges. Each had heavy family commitments and wanted more leisure time. They increasingly talked about the need to "get more organized" so that they could exercise a closer control over staff and office activities, which, in their view, at times verged on the chaotic. Beaumont and Rossi, however, both of whom were single and at thirty and thirty-one, respectively, almost ten years younger than the senior partners, relished the lifestyle and were keen to maintain the firm's present character. They would have been happy to shoulder a greater share of the work and responsibility in return for a greater equity in the company, but Walsh and Bridges were reluctant to hand them this sort of control.

As time went on, it became clear that there were important philosophical differences with regard to the way the office should be run. Whereas Walsh and Bridges regarded the ad hoc style of organization that had developed during the first two years as temporary—"necessary until we've sorted out our ideas as to how we want to put this organization together"—Beaumont and Rossi saw it as a desirable way of doing business in the longer term. Whereas Walsh and Bridges complained about the frequent absence of staff from the office and the lack of clear systems of responsibility and office protocol, Beaumont and Rossi relished what they often described as their "creative chaos." To them, the firm was producing excellent results, clients were happy and knocking at the door, and this was all that mattered.

By the fourth year, tensions were close to the breaking point. The four principals frequently found themselves in long meetings about office organization, and the differences were as deep as ever. Walsh and Bridges argued for "more system," and Beaumont and Rossi argued for the status quo. The differences were straining personal relations and were having an unfavorable impact on life in the office generally. Many staff felt that Multicom was in danger of losing its special character and was no longer quite the same "fun place" at which to work.

All four principals sensed this change, and they talked about it frequently. However, there was simply no consensus as to what should be done. As a result of general frustration, they began to break an unwritten but golden rule set in the early days of Multicom: that all four would always be involved in major policy decisions. Walsh and Bridges began to meet together and resolved that the only way forward was for them to exercise their authority and to insist that a reorganization of the office be initiated. They agreed to propose this at a meeting with Beaumont and Rossi the following day.

Walsh and Bridges were surprised. The idea produced little resistance from their two colleagues. It was almost as if it was expected. Beaumont and Rossi insisted that the decision should not be taken without a lot of thought because it represented a major departure. They reiterated their view that no change in office organization was necessary other than a streamlining of a few financial procedures. They were by no means happy with the proposal, but it was clear that they weren't going to fight it.

The following week Walsh and Bridges called a meeting of all staff to outline their plans. In operational terms these involved a clearer definition of job responsibilities, a more formalized procedure governing the exchange of staff between projects, and a closer control over the conditions under which staff were to be away from the office during business hours. A number of other office procedures were also introduced.

The meeting was unique in Multicom's history in tone and nature. For weeks there was talk about a rift among the four principals and about how winds of change were blowing through the firm. Some members of the staff welcomed the greater degree of structure; others resented the new developments. Staff continued to work hard at their jobs with the professionalism they knew Multicom demanded, but everyone knew that things were not quite the same. Multicom was no longer working—or playing—the Multicom way.

Walsh and Bridges, however, were well pleased. They felt a lot more secure with the way things stood, and could see the time ahead when they would be able to take a lot of pressure off themselves and let the office run itself within the framework they had begun to develop.

Beaumont and Rossi continued to work hard as usual, and their project teams were least affected by the new developments. Within a year, however, they had left Multicom and set up a new company of their own, taking a number of key staff and clients with them.

Thanks to a large number of faithful clients, Multicom continued to produce sound financial results, but it gradually lost its reputation as a leading-edge agency. It could be relied on to produce good solid work but was, in the eyes of a number of disaffected clients, "uninspiring."

Beaumont and Rossi's new firm, Media 2000, picked up many of these clients and, adopting the organizational style pioneered at Multicom, re-created a "fun business" employing eighty people. The firm quickly established itself as a talented and innovative agency. Beaumont and Rossi take satisfaction in the firm's reputation and financial success and look back on their days with Multicom as "a great learning experience." In retrospect, they view their differences with Walsh and Bridges as part of a "lucky break" that spurred them to find an even more lucrative and satisfying work situation.

Interpreting Multicom

How should we interpret this case?

Clearly, in view of what has been said earlier, many different metaphors or theoretical frameworks can be used to understand the pattern of events at Multicom. The tendency for many people is to seize on a particular point of view—for example, that "Multicom offers a clear case of organizational politics"—and elevate this to THE VIEW of the situation, instead of recognizing that, as illustrated in Exhibit 11.1, many different interpretations and meanings may all have a measure of validity in understanding what is happening. A reflective reading of Multicom requires that we remain open to as many possibilities as we can and then find ways of integrating the insights to suit our purposes.

I find it helpful to think about these two stages as involving a *diagnostic reading*, whereby we strive to gain as comprehensive an understanding as possible, accompanied by a *critical evaluation* that integrates key insights. The diagnostic reading allows us to remain in an open-minded mode. The evaluation brings us into a more focused perspective. The trouble, for many people, is that they jump into the latter too quickly, instead of rec-ognizing how an openness to multiple interpretations can create a much broader range of insight and action opportunities.

Consider, for example, the *diagnostic reading* offered in Exhibit 11.1. This reading is schematic, highlighting how different metaphors can draw us into different features of the case. Thus, as we learn to see Multicom through different frames, we may be struck, for example, by holographic qualities that were originally out of view. We may be intrigued by the DNA-like cultural codes that are being transferred from the old Multicom

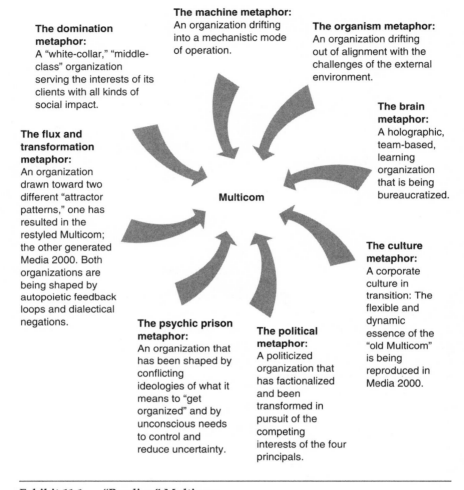

The domination metaphor:
A "white-collar," "middle-class" organization serving the interests of its clients with all kinds of social impact.

The machine metaphor:
An organization drifting into a mechanistic mode of operation.

The organism metaphor:
An organization drifting out of alignment with the challenges of the external environment.

The brain metaphor:
A holographic, team-based, learning organization that is being bureaucratized.

The flux and transformation metaphor:
An organization drawn toward two different "attractor patterns," one has resulted in the restyled Multicom; the other generated Media 2000. Both organizations are being shaped by autopoietic feedback loops and dialectical negations.

Multicom

The culture metaphor:
A corporate culture in transition: The flexible and dynamic essence of the "old Multicom" is being reproduced in Media 2000.

The psychic prison metaphor:
An organization that has been shaped by conflicting ideologies of what it means to "get organized" and by unconscious needs to control and reduce uncertainty.

The political metaphor:
A politicized organization that has factionalized and been transformed in pursuit of the competing interests of the four principals.

Exhibit 11.1   "Reading" Multicom

to Media 2000. We may note interesting connections between the tendency toward bureaucratization and the conscious and unconscious motives driving Walsh and Bridges to tighter control. We may want to dwell on the political dynamic or on the way Multicom is moving out of strategic alignment with the needs of a changing external environment. Or the focus may lead to Multicom's client list and the seamy side of its operations.

A good diagnostic reading seeks to generate a comprehensive range of insights that allows us to discern the unfolding tendencies and character of a situation:

What is happening at Multicom, and in the emergence of Media 2000? What understandings or lessons can we take away from the experience?

How can we use the knowledge thus gained?

The answers to such questions, of course, ultimately depend on the point of view and set of interests that we bring to the task of understanding in the first place. If we are examining Multicom from a detached academic standpoint, we may enjoy exploring the paradox of competing viewpoints as an end in itself. But, if we are in a position that requires that we *act* in relation to Multicom in some way, we will want to drive beyond this kind of relativism. For example, if we are a new manager or management consultant charged with advising on recent history and what Multicom or Media 2000 should do next, we will want to find a way of integrating our insights to serve this end. If, however, we are a social critic or policy analyst, we will want our reading to serve quite different purposes in terms of our policy agenda or critique.

This is where the *critical evaluation* stage of the reading process comes into play. It involves creating what may be described as a kind of *storyline* that can advance our ends. Whereas the diagnostic phase generates a range of insights that can open avenues for creative interpretation, the "storyline" seeks to bring them together in a meaningful way.

DEVELOPING A DETAILED
READING AND "STORYLINE"

To illustrate, let us adopt the perspective and role of the new manager or management consultant charged with making recommendations on the case. As we "read" through various metaphors, we find ourselves being "pulled into" their ways of seeing. We begin to identify key insights, such as those illustrated in Exhibit 11.1. Some of the insights strike us as particularly resonant or meaningful and worthy of further investigation. We choose to investigate in more depth.

Thus, following the insights of the organismic metaphor, we find ourselves asking more questions about the relationship between Multicom and Media 2000 and the broader environment:

What is the nature of the environment?

What are the critical tasks influencing the ability to survive?

Have Multicom and Media 2000 found an appropriate niche?

Are they adopting appropriate strategic organizational and managerial styles?

Pursuing this line of inquiry, we may choose to perform a contingency analysis using the framework offered in Chapter 3 (Exhibit 3.6) and map the relationships between internal and external characteristics. As a result, we conclude that the trend toward increased bureaucratization in Multicom is a dangerous one, creating an incongruent relationship with the challenges of the environment. Using the same framework (Exhibit 11.2), we note that Media 2000, with its flexible holographic style, is much better adapted. Viewing both organizations as part of a wider ecology of competitive and collaborative relations, involving similar and dissimilar organizations and rapid developments in multimedia technology, we find ourselves reflecting on various paths for future strategic development. Can the firms survive as distinct entities? Are new alliances necessary to cope with new technologies and the patterns of organization shaping the multimedia sector as a whole?

In this way, the detailed insights of the organismic metaphor help us build a comprehensive reading of where the two organizations stand.

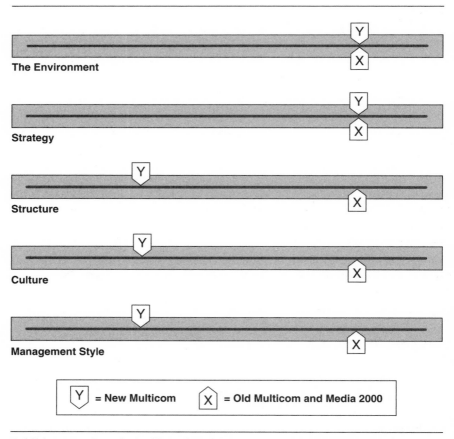

Exhibit 11.2   Rough Profiles of Multicom and Media 2000 (Based on the contingency model prsented in Exhibit 3.6, p. 57)

The other metaphors also lead to rich insights.

For example, pursuing the perspective of the brain metaphor and the requirements for creating learning organizations, we note how the holographic characteristics of the early Multicom implicitly built on the principles of requisite variety and redundant functions. The client teams were microcosms of the whole. They built requisite ability at every level in a way that encouraged flexibility, learning, and development. We note how the same principles underpin the organizational style of Media 2000.

Or, viewing the situation through the lens of the culture metaphor, we note how the holographic style of operation in Multicom's early years was underpinned by a highly cohesive corporate culture built around the shared values of the four principals. The corporate philosophy stressed the importance of working and playing hard in a way that affirmed the corporate identity. We note how the culture is still alive in Media 2000 and how it has been undermined by the bureaucratization at Multicom.

Switching to the political metaphor we note that the troubles of Multicom and the new success of Media 2000 were spawned by the divergent styles and interests of the four principals. History has repeated itself. Just as Multicom was born politically as Walsh, Bridges, Beaumont, and Rossi broke away from their old firm, taking key clients with them, Multicom has split into two separate elements. We note how this potential was seeded by the unequal ownership structure and power base that ultimately allowed an autocratic decision to be made.

As we probe the psychic prison metaphor we find ourselves asking new questions. Were unconscious factors driving Walsh and Bridges's desire for control? Could the problem of overwork and conflicting family obligations have been resolved in another way? Were Walsh and Bridges trapped by the idea that good organization ultimately means more bureaucracy?

The challenge, of course, is to convert this diagnostic reading into a storyline that can help us deal with the complexity. Thus, as the new manager or management consultant faced with advising Multicom or Media 2000, we may find ourselves developing an integrated perspective along the lines illustrated in Exhibit 11.3. Using the organismic metaphor as a dominant frame, we see the main challenge facing both organizations as that of evolving with a changing environment. We see Media 2000 as well adapted. We see Multicom as facing major problems.

Our advice to Media 2000 is to build on the organization's holographic style, using the strong corporate culture as a way of creating systems of shared meaning and understandings that continue to bind the organization

Multicom is an organization that has become bureaucratized and incongruent with its wider environment. It must recapture the flexibility and vitality of its old culture and style to achieve future effectiveness.

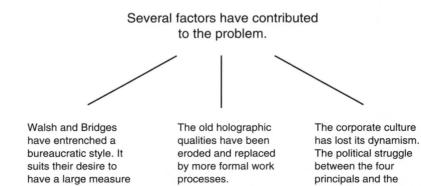

Several factors have contributed
to the problem.

| Walsh and Bridges have entrenched a bureaucratic style. It suits their desire to have a large measure of certainty and control. | The old holographic qualities have been eroded and replaced by more formal work processes. | The corporate culture has lost its dynamism. The political struggle between the four principals and the departure of Beaumont and Rossi have left their mark. |

Given the politicized history, any transformation of Multicom must first win the confidence of Walsh and Bridges. Hence: Use the above analysis to present the history of Multicom in a new light and to argue for a new mode of alignment with the environment.

Media 2000 seems adapted to its environment in every respect. Look to the future here: How can Media 2000 evolve with the broader environment?

Exhibit 11.3   An "Adapt to the Environment" Storyline

together while maintaining a flexible, free-flowing style. We urge Beaumont and Rossi to look at the broader ecology of relations of which they are part, and to strike the alliances and connections that they will need to flow with change.

Our advice to Multicom is to understand what has happened and how the organization has become incongruent with the environment. We have to tread carefully here because there may be deep forces behind the bureaucratization. Our task will be to explore these with Walsh and Bridges, learn more about the psychological and political factors that have driven the change, and advise accordingly. If the increased bureaucratization is indeed a psychological force, as opposed to a pragmatic time-management ("Let's get Multicom under control") strategy, we will probably have a difficult task launching any kind of restructuring. Entrepreneurial figures that create successful new enterprises are notoriously

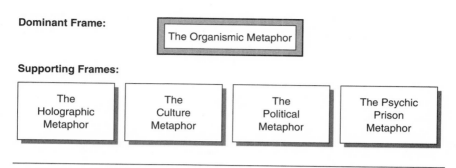

Exhibit 11.4   "Storylines" Prioritize the Insights of Different Metaphors

reluctant to let the reins of control go, even when it is in the best interests of the future enterprise. As we interact with Walsh and Bridges it is likely that a deeper reading will unfold, suggesting an appropriate course of action.

As should be clear from the above account, a storyline implies a course of action. If Multicom is indeed out of alignment with its environment, the task of the new manager or consultant will be to help it strike a more effective configuration. The detailed insights about the psychological, political, cultural, and other factors that have created the malalignment provide clues as to how the bureaucratization should be approached and how the situation can be rectified. They are incorporated into the storyline within the overall framework presented by the organismic metaphor, offering detailed insights as to how the manager or consultant can shape his or her change strategy.

We will have more to say on the relationship between a storyline and the mode of action that it recommends later in this chapter. So, for the moment, let's stay with the process of developing an appropriate storyline.

As summarized in Exhibit 11.4, a storyline ultimately involves a prior-itization of insights generated through one's diagnostic reading. In the above analysis, our emerging storyline has given priority to insights generated by the organismic metaphor. The insights of other metaphors are brought in as subsidiary themes. They are mobilized to inform and shape action around the primary task of helping Multicom and Media 2000 thrive in a rapidly developing media business.

The development of a storyline is always a highly relativistic affair, depending on the precise circumstances being faced. To illustrate, let's turn the clock back on the situation and assume a point of intervention in the middle of the chain of events leading to the schism within Multicom. Our manager-consultant would have found him- or herself dealing with a very different set of circumstances and evolving a very different storyline.

As illustrated in Exhibit 11.5, it is likely that he or she would be seeing "politics" all over the place. The issue of whether Multicom was adapted to the environment would at first probably be nowhere in view. The primary aim of our new manager-consultant would be to understand the political dynamic:

- What are the key forces driving the four principals apart?
- Are they rooted in truly different sets of interests and styles?
- Do they hold different assumptions and beliefs about what it means to "get organized"?
- Is there a deep psychological dimension behind the actions of Walsh and Bridges?
- Can the organization be held together?
- Is there a different way of helping Walsh and Bridges manage the conflicts between work and family?
- Is there a gender dimension here?
- Can we use the insights of the holographic and culture metaphors to demonstrate how Multicom is already well organized?
- Can we use the contingency model generated by the organismic metaphor (Exhibits 3.6 and 11.2) to make the case against bureaucratization?
- Will the insight that the firm has discovered a highly effective way of organizing for flexibility with a strong client orientation help the principals preserve their success?

And so on.

As summarized in Exhibit 11.5, the political metaphor provides the principal frame for analyzing the situation. The other frames tend to be used in a subsidiary role. For example, the organismic metaphor, which provided the dominant frame for understanding the situation once Multicom and Media 2000 had split (see Exhibits 11.3 and 11.4), now has less status. Although from a professional standpoint our manager-consultant may *want* to see this metaphor as offering a dominant frame for understanding, since the ability to survive along with a changing environment is the long-term challenge facing Multicom, the political realities may require that it be used only as a supporting frame to bring a measure of detachment into a hot political situation. For example, the contingency analysis presented in Exhibit 11.2 could be used to help reframe the politics by allowing the four principals to see the proposed bureaucratization and its consequences from another viewpoint.

Multicom is being politicized in an extreme way. The challenge is to understand and defuse the political dimensions.

The insights of other metaphors can help this process.

| The **holographic** metaphor can help Walsh and Bridges understand that there are real alternatives to bureaucratization. Minimize the impact of bureaucratic thinking! | The **culture** metaphor can be used to show how the organization is being held together through core values and shared meanings. It can continue to flourish in this way. | The **psychic prison** metaphor can be used to explore the unconscious dimensions. | The **organismic** metaphor and contingency analysis can be used to frame a debate on the kind of organization that is required to meet external challenges. |

Dominant Frame:

> The Political Metaphor

Supporting Frames:

| The Holographic Metaphor | The Culture Metaphor | The Psychic Prison Metaphor | The Organismic Metaphor |

Exhibit 11.5   A "Political" Storyline

The main point being made here, however, is that a storyline dominated by political considerations usually requires that change strategies be approached with the political factors firmly in mind. As suggested earlier, different storylines tend to favor different actions.

An effective diagnostic reading and storyline hinges on an ability to play with multiple insights with a view to integrating them into a coherent pattern. In a way, the metaphors, theories, and frames through which we implicitly scan the situations that we are trying to understand act as a kind of "radar" or "homing device" that draws our attention toward key features of a situation. These factors become elevated in importance, with others remaining invisible or in a background role. As I suggested in Chapter 1, the way of seeing becomes a way of not seeing. The skilled reader of organizational life has a well-equipped radar system embracing many potential points of view and learns to marshal relevant insights in a way that provides a basis for effective action.

In describing the process, a clear distinction has been drawn between the "reading" and "evaluation" phases and the suggestion made that there is a temporal sequence here, with the evaluation implied in the storyline following the diagnostic reading. This is an oversimplification because in reality the elements are intertwined. As we read a situation through different metaphors we inevitably begin to form an evaluation as we become attracted to one line of interpretation over another. But the distinction drawn between the two stages is a very useful one, because it warns us of the dangers of jumping prematurely into an evaluative mode. The challenge is to remain open to a range of possibilities, so that an effective reading and storyline providing real insights and real leverage on situations and problems can emerge.

The process has been illustrated from the perspective of a manager-consultant, showing how readings and storylines have an unfolding character. They're not fixed. They're not absolute. They change over time. They vary with the objectives and perspectives of the reader. Although the process and skills are consistent, the content and product vary.

MULTICOM FROM ANOTHER VIEW

To illustrate and reinforce these important points, let's change perspective once again. Instead of adopting the role of a manager-consultant, let's view the developments at Multicom through the eyes of a social critic or policy analyst interested in the field of media relations.

The Multicom story now has a very different significance. There is probably little interest in the internal politics or the new Multicom's malalignment with its task environment. The horizon is set much wider. Both firms are likely to be viewed from a broader institutional perspective that focuses on understanding the role that Multicom and Media 2000 play in serving the interests and public relations needs of their clients. The domination and flux metaphors are likely to provide key frames (Exhibit 11.6):

- What clients do the two firms serve?
- What services do they offer?
- What are the explicit and *unstated* functions of these services?
- How do they serve to legitimize their clients' activities?
- Is there a seamy side?
- Are there cover-ups?

Multicom and Media 2000 belong to the ideological superstructure of modern capitalism. They are handmaidens of power. Their main role is to perform services that legitimize and enhance the interests of their clients. Their true nature can be revealed by studying their ultimate impacts on people, society, and the environment.

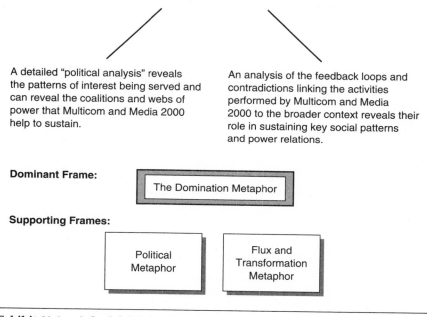

A detailed "political analysis" reveals the patterns of interest being served and can reveal the coalitions and webs of power that Multicom and Media 2000 help to sustain.

An analysis of the feedback loops and contradictions linking the activities performed by Multicom and Media 2000 to the broader context reveals their role in sustaining key social patterns and power relations.

Dominant Frame:

The Domination Metaphor

Supporting Frames:

Political Metaphor

Flux and Transformation Metaphor

Exhibit 11.6   A Social Critic's Storyline

- Is there government lobbying?
- What role do the activities of Multicom and Media 2000 play in creating a pattern of positive and negative feedback loops that create "space" in which their clients' activities can thrive?
- Are they, in effect, paid to dampen, mask, or gloss the negative social impacts of their clients?

The social critic is likely to "zero in" on signs of domination wherever they can be found. The insights and methodologies of the political and flux and transformation metaphors may be used to analyze key relationships and marshal the evidence relating to Multicom and Media 2000's social role and impacts.

If our social critic was more of a policy analyst, however, it is likely that he or she would choose to use the flux and transformation metaphor as a primary frame (Exhibit 11.7). The modes of analysis illustrated in

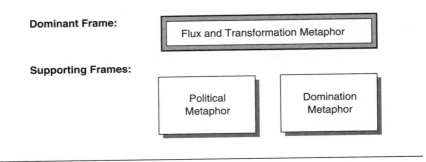

Exhibit 11.7   A Policy Analyst's Storyline

Chapter 8, for example, in relation to the study of dialectical oppositions or loops of mutual causality (Exhibits 8.5, 8.6, and 8.7), may provide ideal frames for analyzing the institutional patterns and processes to which Multicom and Media 2000 contribute, and for understanding where, from a policy point of view, it is most effective to intervene.

The point being made here is that the way of "seeing" and "reading" that our social critic or policy analyst brings to the situation will be very different from that of our manager-consultant. Their different perspectives and interests favor different theoretical frames. They see completely different dimensions of the same situation. Indeed, the perspectives of the critic and policy analyst will lead them to break the boundaries of the case study presented earlier in the chapter and seek a completely different pattern of information. From these perspectives, most of what has been provided in the Multicom case description would probably be deemed irrelevant to the needs at hand.

In juxtaposing these different perspectives, we thus underscore the inherent partiality of any reading process. Whoever we are, it is impossible to obtain a complete point of view. Our perspectives always have horizons and limits dictated by the factors that we implicitly or explicitly value and deem important. We are back to Albert Einstein's point that our observations are always shaped by the "theory" through which we see.

One of our challenges as managers, consultants, critics, or policy analysts, and as individuals in everyday life, is to cope with this problem. If we dwell on the impossibility of achieving an all-embracing understanding or comprehensive insight, we will surely be depressed and overwhelmed. But if we turn the problem around and focus on what *can* be achieved by refining our interpretive skills, a much more positive message emerges.

"Reading" and Emergent Intelligence

In Chapter 4 we discussed how the human brain is characterized by a form of "emergent intelligence" whereby coherent order and pattern result from a multitude of possibilities.

It is useful to think about the process of reading organizational life in similar terms, for, as has been shown, an effective reading requires that we remain open to different possibilities that can form and re-form in a way that allows us to act appropriately.

The process is organic, not mechanistic. There is a dynamic quality that unites "the reader" and the situation being "read" in an unfolding process through which the reader can begin to grasp, shape, and understand the pattern of events or circumstances being encountered.

By being open to the frames and concepts generated by different metaphors we can be sensitive to the different dimensions of a situation. We can be aware of when "politics," "culture," "domination," or the insights of other frames "call our attention" and, in effect, say "take account of this point of view." We can open ourselves to a variety of insights on which creative interpretation and synthesis thrive. We can learn, as illustrated in relation to the Multicom case, to use different frames and subframes to explore, elevate, or diminish the significance of what we are seeing. We can be sensitive to the all-important relationship between figure and ground and realize that when we elevate the importance of a particular metaphor or group of metaphors we tend to push others into a background role. We can recognize that in making something highly visible and a focus of attention, we do so in a way that inevitably makes other features much less visible.

In this way, we can use our "reading" skills to open new horizons as well as deepen understanding of the territory we already know. We can learn to keep open, reflective, and evolving as we search for meaningful insights.

As discussed earlier, the purpose of an effective reading is to develop creative insights that open new action opportunities or give new leverage on difficult problems. The reading is not an end in itself. It does not rest in the mechanical application of a few favored metaphors or analytical schemes. Its purpose is to connect with the truly significant dimensions of a situation.

Effective readings are *generative*. They produce insights and actions that were not there before. They open new action opportunities. They make a difference.

The criteria for judging an effective reading are thus not objective. They are pragmatic. Returning to the specifics of the Multicom case, for a manager this pragmatism may rest in understanding how the political dynamic of the "old Multicom" can be reframed through a contingency analysis that defuses the politics. For a social critic or policy analyst, the pragmatism may rest in discovering positive and negative feedback loops that can change the social impacts of key Multicom clients.

Another important point that must be emphasized is that the process of reading a situation is always "two-way." In trying to discern the meaning of a situation, we create an interplay between the situation itself and the frames through which we are trying to tie it down.

To illustrate, consider the process of reading a book. The book presents us with words and sentences. But the reader also brings his or her personal perspective to the reading, and this plays a vital role in determining the meaning that the text conveys.

The same is true in organization and everyday life. Situations may "call" for our attention. But the interpretive frame of the reader also *shapes* what is read into that situation. As has been suggested, if we are dominated by an interest in structure, culture, or politics, this is what we will probably see. The dominant frame will push other potential insights from view.

In this sense the reader is also an author. He or she is not in a passive role. This is what makes the challenge of reading organizational life so powerful. The manager truly does have an opportunity to shape how situations unfold. All these issues are discussed in more detail in the Bibliographic Notes to Chapter 11.

12

Postscript

$\mathbf{A}$s we move into the twenty-first century we find ourselves living through a period of unprecedented change with major implications for the whole field of organization and management. Theories that were once viewed as providing sound foundations are becoming obsolete. New theories are emerging at a rapid pace. Each month, it seems, brings a crop of new perspectives through which managers are urged to understand and act on their problems.

Needless to say, the situation is often overwhelming. Managers at all levels are invited to embrace new paradigms, develop new competencies, integrate left- and right-brain thinking, become skilled political actors, and learn to be team players. In any single year, leading business journals invite managers to consider dozens of ways of structuring and managing their enterprise: to create "learning organizations," "inverted pyramids," "shamrocks," "spider plants," "third-wave organizations," "virtual enterprises," "cluster organizations," and "lean organizations," to name just a few.

Modern chaos theorists would describe this as an "edge of chaos" situation. We are shifting from a world dominated by bureaucratic-mechanistic principles into an electronic universe where new organizational logics are required. The intense theoretical and practical innovation is part of the transition and, given the fluid, self-organizing nature of a world dominated by electronic media, is likely to remain so.

This poses enormous challenges for any person wishing to stay abreast of new developments and cope with the flux in a positive way. Managers have to get beneath the surface and understand what is happening at a deeper level. Instead of being buffeted by the latest theories and trends, they need to be able to develop and take their own position.

This book shows how this can be done.

In a famous discussion on the nature of scientific understanding, quantum physicist Werner Heisenberg once observed that understanding ultimately rests in the ability to recognize how many different phenomena are really part of a coherent whole. Genuine understanding cuts through surface complexity to reveal an underlying pattern.

This is exactly what an understanding of the role of metaphor helps us to do. When we recognize that competing theories are competing metaphors, we can approach them in a new way. We can learn to see and tap their strengths and be aware of their inevitable weaknesses. We can set the grounds for a much more reflective approach to management practice, where people rather than theories are in the driver's seat.

The various chapters in this book have covered a great deal of ground and, in a conclusion such as this, it is not possible to cover all the ideas that have been presented. Nor is it desirable to do so. As suggested in Chapter 1, part of the message of this book rests directly in the *experience* of reading different chapters and of coping with competing points of view. So the focus in the remainder of this *Postscript* is on four key ideas of general relevance, which capture some of the major implications for management. They can be summarized as follows.

First, in times of change it is vital to be in touch with the assumptions and theories that are guiding our practice and to be able to shape and reshape them for different ends. *Images of Organization* shows us how to do this, and it encourages us to bring a fluid perspective to the problems and challenges being faced. Traditional management perspectives often lock us into fixed frameworks. They offer a way of seeing that in effect says, "This is THE WAY to see." As a result, we often get trapped by the metaphors on which they are based.

A part of the problem rests in the fact that in a world dominated by practical considerations, there is often a reluctance to get involved with issues of a theoretical nature. People tend to think that theory gets in the way of practice. Yet, as Kurt Lewin has pointed out, "there is nothing so practical as a good theory." Also, as previous chapters illustrate, practice is *never* theory free. In any sustained endeavor we are guided by implicit root images that generate theories of what we are doing. It is vital that we know what they are and the strengths and limitations they express. This has implications at all levels of management and policy making.

The second major point is implicit in the above, but deserves special emphasis. Managers at all levels must gain comfort in dealing with the insights and implications of diverse perspectives. In Chapters 3 and 4 mention was made of the "law of requisite variety," which states that the adaptive capacity of any system depends on its ability to embrace the complexity of the environment being faced. This assumes new significance here. In being open to the insights of different metaphors, and in learning to use metaphor to *create* new insights, we enrich our capacities for generating innovative ways of dealing with new challenges and of forging new evolutionary patterns.

Third, this book has emphasized the importance of being able to "read" and understand the complexity of organizational life. But as suggested in Chapter 11, it is also important to remember that the "reading" of a situation always implies a degree of authorship as well.

In reading our organizations it is important to place ourselves in an active mode. We are not passive observers interpreting and responding to the events and situations that we see. We play an important role in shaping those interpretations, and thus the way events unfold.

Finally, we need to recognize that despite its roots in mechanistic thinking, organization is really a creative process of *imaginization*. We organize as we imaginize, and it is always possible to imaginize in new ways. In appreciating this, we open the way to numerous possibilities and to a key competence for managing in turbulent times.

The process has been illustrated throughout this book, especially in those chapters that have sought to extend the boundaries of current practice by using creative metaphors to capture and develop new ways of organizing. Consider, for example, our discussion of the brain in Chapter 4, where images of holograms, mobots, "corporate DNA," and fractal-like reproduction were used to create design principles for developing intelligent organizations.

The approach developed here begins to illustrate the possibilities. But, like the book as a whole, it only offers a sliver of the full potential. As I have shown in a companion volume, *Imaginization: The Art of Creative Management*, we can use the style modeled here for rethinking almost every aspect of management. Organizational structure, strategy, management style, teamwork, organizational change, and even products and services can be vitalized and re-formed through creative images that allow us to act in new ways.

The concept of organization is a product of the mechanical age. Now that we are living in an electronic age, new organizing principles are necessary. The ideas presented here help us to make the transition and meet the challenges of this new reality.

Bibliographic Notes

1: Introduction

This is a book about metaphor set within a metaphor: that of "reading organization." Intellectually, it develops the tradition pioneered by writers such as Pepper (1942) and Kuhn (1970) on the impact of root metaphors and cognitive paradigms on how we understand the world around us.

Specifically, the impetus for the book stemmed from my work on earlier projects, Burrell and Morgan (1979) and Morgan (1980, 1983a, 1983b, 1983c, 1984), each of which develops different perspectives on organization. Whereas they were pitched at a theoretical level and directed at an academic audience, the present book develops the practical implications of the basic ideas. My concern is to show how we can *use* the creative insights generated by metaphor to create new ways of understanding organization. In these notes, I sketch the foundations on which I build, elaborate points of special interest, and provide a trail of references for further reading.

On metaphor: There is a growing literature demonstrating the impact of metaphor on the way we think, on our language, and on systems of scientific and everyday knowledge. Aristotle was the first to identify the role of metaphor in the production of knowledge. In his *Rhetoric* he suggests that "midway between the unintelligible and the commonplace, it is metaphor which most produces knowledge." In *The Poetics* he identifies the four tropes we now recognize as metaphor, metonymy, synecdoche, and irony. Each of these tropes can be understood as a variety of metaphor, but they play somewhat different roles (see, for example, White 1978; Morgan 1983b). In this work I use the term *metaphor* to embrace the general process of image crossing whereby A is seen as B.

Vico (1968) in the early eighteenth century was the first to recognize the importance of metaphor and related tropes as modes of experience and hence as having more than figurative significance. A number of philosophers in the nineteenth century, such as Nietzsche (1974), mention the importance of metaphor. But it is not until the work of twentieth-century philosophers like Cassirer (1946), Wittgenstein (1958), and others emphasizing language and other modes of symbolism in reality construction that these ideas acquire any prominence.

Over the past fifty years, a number of important works have suggested that we must pay more attention to the role of metaphor and related tropes, including Black (1962), Boulding (1956a), Brown (1977), Burke (1962), Grant and Oswick (1996), Manning (1979), Pepper (1942), Schön (1963, 1979), and White (1978). Some of the most important contemporary debates are occurring in linguistics, hermeneutics, and psychoanalysis. Works such as Charteris-Black (2005), Eco (1976), Jakobson and Halle (1962), Lacan (1966), Lemaire (1977), Maasen and Weingart (2000), Ricoeur (2003), and Tilley (1999) are central to the overall debate. Collections of papers on metaphor, such as those by Ortony (1979) and Sacks (1979), present useful overviews of some of the issues.

The impact of metaphor on language and communication generally has been subjected to detailed analysis by Lakoff and Johnson (1980). This is an important work that shows how metaphor pervades ordinary language. Our speaking and writing are inherently metaphorical. We live through our metaphors. They define what Wittgenstein has called a "form of life."

The role of metaphor in creative imagination and science has been treated in a number of popular and academic works. Koestler (1969) and Jonathan Miller (1978a) are both outstanding in combining these dimensions. More recent works include Sproull (1997), Kreitman (1999), and Brown (2003).

Brown (1977), Lopez (2003), and Rigney (2001) have shown the links between metaphor and social theory. My own work has explored the metaphorical basis of organization theory (Morgan 1980, 1983b, 1986, 1996). Over the past few years, organization and management theorists have become increasingly aware of the importance of metaphor in the development of the discipline. For an excellent overview see the collections of papers presented by Grant and Oswick (1996) and Oswick and Grant (1996), and the work of Alvesson (1993b), Beyer (1992), Boroditsky (2000), Cornelissen (2005), Gherardi (2000), Holyoak and Thagard (1995), Krippendorf (1993), McClintock et al. (2004), Oswick et al. (2002), Sackmann (1989), and Tsoukas (1991, 1993). Cornellison (2005) provides an excellent discussion of a constructivist view of metaphor and how the similarities in metaphor typically stimulate an emergent stream of thinking that often goes well beyond the concepts that the metaphor initially suggests. For a practical illustration of this kind of emergence, see my discussion of "Organizations as Spider Plants" (Morgan 1993a: 63–89). As I discuss in Chapter 1, metaphor can open up new ways of thinking and seeing. It is an expansive rather than a reductive process.

The way I develop and use metaphor for the present book has much in common with the hermeneutic approach to social analysis. For an outstanding discussion of the 1986 edition of this book from this perspective, see Boland (1989). The issues are explored in greater detail in the bibliographic notes relating to Chapters 10 and 11 and in Morgan (1993a, 1996).

2: The Machine Metaphor

Mechanism in science: Many social theorists have noted that we live in a technological society dominated by the needs of machines and mechanical modes of thought (e.g., Ellul 1964; Giedeon 1948; Mumford 1934). The elements of mechanistic theory first appear in the ideas of the Greek "atomists" of the fifth through third centuries B.C., such as Democritus and Leucippus. They believed that the world was composed of indivisible particles in motion in an infinite void and that all form, movement, and change could be explained in terms of the size, shape, form, and movement of atoms. This mechanistic vision has influenced scientific thought right into the twentieth century and receives its fullest and most comprehensive expression in the contributions to physics of Sir Isaac Newton, who developed a theory of the universe as a celestial machine. On the way, numerous scientists invented and studied machines as a means of understanding the laws of nature. Aristotle used mechanistic principles to understand the movement of animals. Archimedes (in Heath 1897), Galileo (1968), and others used machines to make important contributions to mathematics and physics and did much to advance the idea that it is possible to build an objective science based on mechanistic principles. Galileo, for example, sought a science that could reduce all explanations of reality to a physical base, pursuing the atomist's ideal of a universe that could be explained in terms of matter in motion.

Mechanism in social theory: Within the field of philosophy, mechanistic ideas have exerted a powerful influence on theories of the human mind and the nature of knowledge and reality. The French philosopher René Descartes set important foundations for these developments in his famous *Discourse on Method* published in 1637, arguing for the separation of mind and body and subject and object, in an attempt to place the process of human reasoning on as firm a basis as possible. Descartes, like Galileo and Newton, built his views on the principles of atomism, believing that the material world was to be understood in terms of the mechanical interaction and movement of corpuscles originally created and set in motion by God. He was fascinated with the study of automata and mechanical toys and contemplated the possibility of building mechanical men. Plants and animals were viewed by Descartes as superior forms of machines. Humans were viewed as being like machines but were distinguished by their great capacity to use words and signs as a basis for discourse and by their capacity to reason (Descartes 1968: 73–74).

The logic of Descartes's view of human nature was eventually developed to an extreme a century later by the French materialist Julien de LaMettrie. In 1748, he published a book, *L'Homme Machine*, arguing that man *is* a machine, that both body and soul are a product of mechanical processes, and that all human behavior is reducible to laws of matter in motion. Instincts, actions, and the operation of the human brain were thus seen as operating in accordance with completely deterministic laws, which allowed no room for voluntary behavior or subjective influence of any kind. His views were unpopular in many quarters, and he was forced at different times to leave his native Paris and Holland, where *L'Homme Machine* was published. Interestingly, LaMettrie found a welcome in the court of Frederick the Great, where he was given a prominent position. There is thus an interesting and direct link between the mechanistic theories of the human being developed by Descartes and LaMettrie and the military practice of Frederick's Prussian army, which, as discussed in Chapter 2, actually attempted to reduce soldiers to automata who would obey instructions on command.

In social science, the idea that man is a machine has exerted a powerful influence over behavioral psychology, especially through the idea that human beings are the product of environmental forces. These ideas were carried to modern psychology through the ideas of philosophers such as Hume, Locke, and Bentham and receive their fullest expression in the stimulus-response psychology of B. F. Skinner (1953) and reinforcement theory. Arthur Koestler (1967) presents a comprehensive critique of this kind of approach to understanding human behavior. Schön (1963) presents an excellent analysis of how the principles of Newtonian physics have been used in psychological theories. The work of the influential social theorist Vilfredo Pareto (e.g., Pareto 1935) provides a powerful illustration of how principles derived from mechanical sciences have been used to understand economics, politics, and society. And in the ideas of one of Frederick Taylor's followers, Henry Gantt (see Alford 1934: 264–277), we find the mechanistic vision of social life carried to an extreme in his proposal for an organization called "The New Machine": "a conspiracy of men of science, engineers, chemists, land and sea-tamers and general masters of arts and materials" (p. 264). In this scheme, all industry would be put under the control of engineers, who would design and run it with mechanical efficiency.

Mechanism in everyday life: With regard to the links between mechanism and everyday life, it is interesting to note how we have come to treat our bodies as machines. This is most evident in many approaches to physical fitness in which the primary aim is to "shape" the body through jogging, calisthenics, body building, and gymnastics. Calisthenics were first developed by Swedish landowners wishing to make their peasants like soldiers, and gymnastics were developed in Germany in an attempt to prepare farmworkers for war. Modern sports are being increasingly "mechanized," the epitome being American football. This provides an almost perfect exposition of Taylor's principles of scientific management. For a discussion, see Keidel (1985, 1988).

Mechanism in organization theory—Max Weber and bureaucratic organization: Sociologist Max Weber (1947, 1949) discusses the parallels between mechanization and organization. In understanding his work it is important to realize that he was not interested in studying formal organizations as ends in themselves. Rather, he was concerned with understanding the process of organization, which takes different forms in different contexts and in different epochs, as part of a wider social process. Thus, the bureaucratic form of organization was seen as but a manifestation of a more general process of rationalization within society as a whole, emphasizing the importance of means-ends relations.

There has been much misinterpretation of Weber's work in organization theory, especially with regard to his idea that the bureaucratic form of organization constitutes an ideal type. In Weber's work, the concept of "ideal type" is used as a methodological tool for understanding many aspects of society. He believed that in order to understand the social world it was necessary to develop clear-cut concepts against which one could compare empirical reality. All of the ideal types that he developed were intended to serve this end. Thus, he advocated using the concept of bureaucracy as an ideal type to capture a particular *form* of organization— that based on the *idea* of a machine—with a view to understanding the extent to which a society is bureaucratized. He recognized that the ideal type would not be found in practice in a pure form, since organizations would probably correspond with the ideal in varying degrees—hence its purpose as a comparative tool. By using different ideal types to discern different forms of organization, he believed that one possessed a powerful methodology for understanding the social world.

Many of the misinterpretations relate to the fact that Weber's use of the concept "ideal" has been equated with the concept of best. Thus, Weber is often presented as endorsing bureaucracy as a best type of organization. This is completely inaccurate. Weber was skeptical about the merits of bureaucracy and in no way intended the concept to be used in this way. One important reason why this misinterpretation has occurred is found in the fact that the publication of Weber's work in English followed the publication and popularization of the work of the classical management theorists, who had advocated that the bureaucratic approach to organization was the one best way of organizing. Even though Weber did not share this view, many organization theorists have interpreted him as belonging to the same school of classical management theory. They have understood his theory of bureaucracy and his use of the notion of ideal type through the lens provided by their understanding of the classical management theorists. As a result, the thrust and significance of his work has been placed in a completely inappropriate perspective. Most important, the fact that he understood organization as a process of domination has been completely overlooked (see Chapter 9). More often than not, he has been used as a "straw man"—an advocate of the bureaucratic mode of organization—to be knocked down in the course of building theories that overcome the well-known limitations of bureaucracy. Unfortunately for Weberian sociology, even some of Weber's most constructive and accurate interpreters, such as Robert Merton (1968a), focus on the dysfunctions of the bureaucratic model in a way that has unintentionally fed the misinterpretations of Weber's stand on bureaucracy. This work and its implications for organization theory are discussed extensively by Burrell and Morgan (1979).

Stinchcombe (1965) presents important insights on how the bureaucratic mode of organization emerges along with the mechanization of industry and the Industrial Revolution. George (1972) presents an extensive analysis of the history of management thought from prehistoric times, including good discussion of the writers who set the basis for classical management theory and scientific management. Adam Smith (1776) and Charles Babbage (1832) are worth reading as classic texts of the Industrial Revolution.

Classical management theory: Of the works of the classical management theorists, those of Fayol (1949), Mooney and Reiley (1931), and Gulick and Urwick (1937) have been among the most influential. Each illustrates how classical management theory is essentially a theory of machine design. These ideas have been carried forward to the present day and reinterpreted within the context of MBO, MIS, and PPBS.

Scientific management: The principles of scientific management are set out by Taylor (1911). Important insights on the nature of the man and his ideas can be obtained by reading the biographies by Copley (1923) and Kakar (1970). Taylor emerges as a man with an obsessive vision backed by a determination to implement it at all costs. These aspects of his personality and background are discussed in Chapter 7. A folklore has developed around Taylor and Taylorism that often confuses fact and fiction, a point that needs to be borne firmly in mind when reading Taylor's own writings. As Wrege and Perroni (1974) show, Taylor himself appears to have had what might be kindly described as a vivid imagination, creating elaborate tales that often bear little resemblance to other accounts of the same situations. Despite the fiction, the reality of the consequences of Taylor's ideas are beyond dispute. Braverman (1974) and Worthy (1959) provide excellent critical accounts of the nature and significance of Taylorism in industrial management in both the United States and the former USSR.

Frank and Lillian Gilbreth's pioneering work on the study of human motion in the workplace, found in Frank Gilbreth's *Motion Study* (1911), proved important in developing the detailed practice of Taylorism. The impact on industrial engineering, industrial psychology, modern ergonomics, and work study can be seen in almost any modern text on industrial management. On a point of detail, it should be noted that, although the work of all these theorists elaborates a mechanistic view of organization that is highly consistent in terms of detailed principles, minor disagreements did arise, such as between the principle of the unity of command and Taylor's principle of functional foremanship, which violated the principle that each subordinate should have only one boss.

Mechanistic organization in practice: The data relating to Henry Ford's introduction of assembly-line production are drawn from Sward (1948). He provides an excellent account of the background to assembly line production. The data on GM's Lordstown plant are drawn from Aronowitz (1973). Hailey (1971) and Frost, Mitchell, and Nord (1992) also present interesting ethnographic accounts of work experience in similar situations.

Extensive critiques of the consequences of Taylor's work and developments in relation to the "de-skilling" of jobs and the modern work process can be found in Knights and Willmott (1989), Scarbrough and Corbett (1992), Shostak (1996), and Wall, Clegg, and Kemp (1987). Interestingly, the trend is often described as being a part of "Fordism"—a concept that links the mechanistic influence of Taylor with that of Henry Ford. For a discussion of this and the "McDonaldization of society," see Ritzer (1996).

The problems encountered by mechanistic organizations in changing circumstances are explored in the classic study by Burns and Stalker (1961) and in Kanter's (1983) analysis of the problems of modern U.S. corporations.

March and Simon (1958) and Merton (1968a, 1968b) explore some of the dysfunctional aspects of bureaucracy.

The human problems resulting from mechanistic organization have been explored by Argyris (1957) and numerous other writers on the psychology of organization.

For a discussion of the "reengineering movement," which provides a critique of mechanistic organization but also, paradoxically, reflects a late-twentieth-century reincarnation of the mechanistic approach in management, see Hammer and Champy (1993). The failures of reengineering are discussed in Champy (1995).

For a discussion of the distinction between "functional" (instrumental-bureaucratic) rationality, where people are expected to "fit into" a predetermined mechanical design, and "substantial rationality," where people are encouraged to challenge and question the system of relations of which they are part, see the work of Karl Mannheim (1940). The philosophy of total quality management and the brainlike learning systems discussed in Chapter 4 seek to encourage the latter.

The quotation from the Chinese sage Chuang-tzu is taken from Heisenberg (1958a).

3: The Organismic Metaphor

Biology has developed as a systematic science concerned with the study and explanation of organic functioning. It studies the anatomy and physiology of living things and investigates the modes and conditions of their survival, reproduction, development, and decay. Biology classifies vital organisms into species and inquiries into their geographic description, their lines of descent, and their evolutionary changes. What better description could there be of organization theory since the 1950s?

Biology and social theory: Biological thought has influenced social and organizational theory since at least the nineteenth century through the work of Spencer (1873, 1876, 1884), Durkheim (1934, 1938, 1951), and Radcliffe-Brown (1952). These are the formative works that have influenced the powerful school of thought in sociology known as structural functionalism, brought into prominence in the 1950s and 1960s by Talcott Parsons (1951). A comprehensive discussion of this development and its relevance for the study of organization is presented by Burrell and

Morgan (1979). Nisbet (1969) and Pepper (1942) discuss the impact of organic thought in more general terms. Edward Wilson (1975) has developed formal links between biology and social life through his concept of "sociobiology," and in recent years a number of writers have begun to explore novel linkages between biological and social systems under the umbrella of what's being called the study of "complexity" (Kauffman 1993; Lewin 1992). For further discussion, see Chapter 8.

Individual and organizational "needs": The influence of the organic metaphor on the analysis of individual and organizational "needs" can be seen in the classic accounts of the Hawthorne studies (Roethlisberger and Dickson 1939; Mayo 1933) and in the work of Maslow (1943), Argyris (1957, 1964), Alderfer (1969, 1972), McGregor (1960), and Herzberg et al. (1959). The main Tavistock publications and related work have been published by Trist and Murray (1990, 1993) and Trist and Emery (forthcoming) in three major volumes under the title *The Social Engagement of Social Science*. Volume 1 focuses on the sociopsychological perspective, Volume 2 on the sociotechnical perspective, and Volume 3 on the socioecological perspective.

Open systems theory: The concept of the "open system" has been elaborated through the use of biological principles by von Bertalanffy (1950, 1968) and many others. J. G. Miller's (1978b) mammoth work on "living systems" provides an excellent and thorough overview. Boulding (1956a) presents an excellent illustration of how systems theory can be applied to different levels of system that go beyond those of the biological organism. Virtually anything can be defined as a system by drawing a boundary— hence the application of systems theory to psychology, social psychology, organization studies, and societal studies. The approach is a flexible one and open to a wide variety of interpretations. For an example of how basic systems theory can be applied to the study of organizations, see the works by Katz and Kahn (1978), Kast and Rosenzweig (1973), and Beer (1980). Ackoff (1999), Emery (1969), and Scott (2002) provide excellent reviews of open systems concepts. Poole and Van de Ven (2004) provide an excellent overview of different perspectives on organizational innovation and change.

The early development of systems theory was very much influenced by perspectives emphasizing equilibrium and homeostasis. In recent years, however, much more attention has been devoted to the analysis of instability. See, for example, Maruyama (1963), Kauffman (1993), Lewin (1992), Prigogine (1978, 1984), Senge (1990), and the references on autopoiesis and mutual causality in my notes to Chapter 8. These new developments have carried systems thinking into a completely new realm, with very exciting possibilities.

Contingency theory: The history of the contingency approach to organizational analysis is outlined in Burrell and Morgan (1979). The important works are by Burns and Stalker (1961), Woodward (1965), Lawrence and Lorsch (1967a, 1967b), and Miles and Snow (1978). The important ideas on differentiation and integration are found in Lawrence and Lorsch (1967a, 1967b).

Good discussions on matrix organization are presented by Galbraith (1971), Kingdon (1973), Davis and Lawrence (1977), and Kolodny (1981). On "virtual organizations" and "network" forms, see Hastings (1993), Miles and Snow (1986, 1992), Nadler et al. (1992), Savage (1990), and Tapscott (1996). On the concept of the "cluster organization," see Mills (1991). On the "federal" and "shamrock" forms, see Handy (1990). On the variation between mechanistic and organic forms, see Morgan (1989: 64–67).

The use of contingency theory for organizational development has been very popular and takes various forms. Donaldson (2001), Kast and Rosenzweig (1973), Leavitt (1964), Nadler and Tushman (1977), and Nadler and Tushman (1997) provide illustrations. The approach offered in the present chapter elaborates the model developed by Burrell and Morgan (1979).

Bennis (1966) and Levinson (1972) present good illustrations of how the general concept of organizational health underlies the theory and practice of organizational development.

Rosabeth Moss Kanter (1983) identifies the characteristics of successful corporations dealing with changing environments and makes important contributions to our understanding of "adhocracies" and the organic approach to management. The distinction that she draws between "segmentalist" and "integrative" organizations parallels the distinction between Burns and Stalker's concept of mechanistic and organic organizations. Her insights on the pathologies that segmentalist organizations encounter in dealing with change, and on the processes through which integrative organizations manage learning and novelty, add much to our understanding of the problems that have preoccupied contingency theorists over the past few decades.

The variety of the species: There is a growing literature identifying different species of organizations and distinguishing between different "patterns," "clusters," "archetypes," or "configurations" of organizational characteristics. See, for example, Mintzberg (1979), Miles and Snow (1978, 1986), McKelvey (1982a, 1982b), Miller and Mintzberg (1983), Miller and Friesen (1984), Miller (1990), Hinings and Greenwood (1988), and Tushman and Romanelli (1985).

The following is an overview of discussions of different organizational attributes:

Environment: A number of key characteristics have been identified, including the degree of stability or change, homogeneity-heterogeneity, interconnectedness between elements, abundance or scarcity of key resources, patterns of resource ownership, competition, symmetrical or assymetrical interdependence, and political, legal, technological, economic, social, and market conditions. Turbulence, uncertainty, resource dependence, and specific contextual features have attracted much attention. See, for example, Dill (1958), Emery and Trist (1965), Hall (1982), Lawrence and Lorsch (1967a, 1967b), Pfeffer and Salancik (1978), Scott (1981), and Thompson (1967). For further discussions of the turbulence of modern environments, see D'Aveni (1994), Drucker (1980), Fombrun (1992), Land and Jarman (1992), Morgan (1988a), Toffler (1980, 1990), and Toffler and Toffler (1994).

Strategy: Organizations may be classified according to the strategic stance they adopt. Thus, Miles and Snow (1978) distinguish between reactor, defender, analyzer, and prospector organizations, Porter (1980) distinguishes between competitive strategies based on "cost leadership," "differentiation," and "focus," while Miller and Friesen (1984), Miller (1990), and Emery and Trist (1965) identify other strategic patterns. On the links between organizations and strategic choice, see Child (1972).

Structure: Organizations may be classified according to whether their structures are bureaucratic-mechanistic, organic, matrix, virtual, clusters, network, federal, functionalized, divisionalized according to their authority base, size, and their scores on various measuring scales. In addition to the references cited under "contingency theory," see Burns and Stalker (1961), Chandler (1962), Davis and Lawrence (1977), Galbraith and Lawler (1993), Mintzberg (1979), Pugh, Hickson, and Hinings (1969), and Weber (1947).

Technology: The core technology employed by an organization may be used to explain many different organizational characteristics. Among the classifications of technology are those that distinguish between mass, process, and unit or small-batch production (Woodward 1965), the complexity and analyzability of work processes (Perrow 1967), operations, knowledge, and materials technology (Hickson, Pugh, and Pheysey 1969), task interdependence (Thompson 1967), and stage of technological evolution (McKelvey and Aldrich 1983), relationship between subjective and objective dimensions (Scarbrough and Corbett 1992), and degree of automation and informatics (Zuboff 1988).

Employee Commitment: Organizations can be classified according to the relationships developed between organization and employees. Blau and Scott's (1962) typology of organizations focuses on the prime beneficiary, arguing that different organizational characteristics are associated with the way organizations are controlled and rewards distributed. They distinguish between mutual benefit associations, business concerns, service organizations, and commonwealth organizations in which the prime beneficiaries are, respectively, rank-and-file members, owners and managers, clients, and the public at large. Etzioni (1961) focuses on the kind of motivation or use of power employed, distinguishing between coercive, utilitarian, and normative organizations (e.g., prisons, business firms, and churches), based on alienative, calculative, and moral involvement. Also, see DiMaggio and Powell (1983, 1991) and Scott and Christensen (1995) for an "institutional perspective" on the problem.

Population ecology: The main works developing the population-ecology view of organizations are Aldrich (1979), McKelvey and Aldrich (1983), Hannan and Freeman (1977), and Freeman and Hannan (1983). They in turn draw upon the ideas of Hawley (1968), on human ecology, and Campbell (1969), who introduced the variety-selection-retention model to social science. Pfeffer and Salancik (1978) develop related ideas in terms of a resource dependence view of organization that has close links to the population ecology approach. For a comprehensive review of the population-ecology field, see Baum (1996), Singh and Lumsden (1990), and Singh (1990). Kimberley and Miles (1980) and Freeman (1982) have produced interesting ideas on organizational life cycles, tracing the birth, growth, development, and decline of organizations. Pennings (1982) has studied birth frequencies. De Geus (1997) presents an interesting view of organizations as living systems.

The debate between the population ecologists and the contingency theorists is very well represented by Astley and Van de Ven (1983) and by Lawrence and Dyer (1982).

The approach known as "institutional theory" is often closely identified with the literature on population ecology because it seeks to ground our understanding of organization in its broad historical and social context. DiMaggio and Powell (1983) have offered an important typology rooted in ideas about social domination. Scott and Christensen (1995) and Tolbert and Zucker (1996) provide important discussions and overviews of the field with a variety of European and North American perspectives on the problem. Their view of institutional formation goes beyond the population ecology approach to embrace important political and cultural dimensions, rooting the character of organizations in broader institutional control mechanisms.

Organizational ecology—the creation of shared futures: Eric Trist's work on organizational ecology can be found in Trist (1976, 1979, 1983), Trist and Emery (forthcoming), and Emery and Trist (1973). Epistemologically, there are strong links between his perspective and the theory of coevolution developed by Bateson (1972, 1979). My notes to Chapter 8 on autopoiesis and "systemic wisdom" provide further references. Kenneth Boulding's view that evolution involves the "survival of the fitting" can be found in Boulding (1981). Kropotkin's (1903) early work on the relationship between evolution and mutual aid is also important, providing an impressive counterweight to the interpretations of Darwin that place emphasis on the role of competition in social evolution.

The implications of the idea that organizations can evolve through collaboration as well as competition are developed by Astley (1984), Astley and Fombrun (1983), Fombrun and Astley (1983), Gray (1989), and Van de Ven and Astley (1981). Also, see Vickers (1983). Gray (1989) and Weisbord's (1992) collection of papers provide many examples of the development of domain-based initiatives and the significance of "reference organizations." These ideas become increasingly important in view of the fact that the competitive ethic has received new impetus from writers concerned with the phenomena of "hyperturbulence" and "hypercompetition" (e.g., D'Aveni 1994), an issue addressed in Chapter 8.

Hurst (1995) provides an excellent analysis of organizational ecocycles and processes of creative destruction and renewal.

4: The Brain Metaphor

Brains looking at brains! The study of the brain poses a unique problem in reflexivity and of knowledge construction: We use brains to understand brains. Not surprisingly, the process has drawn on many different kinds of metaphor as scientists have searched for appropriate images to make sense of this complex part of anatomy. My analysis in this chapter draws on the work of Begley (1983), Burns (1968), Dennett (1991), Pribram (1971, 1976), and Taylor (1979). Useful accounts of holographic and other characteristics of the brain are found in Andersen (1992), Broekstra (1996), Calvin (1996, 2004), Carruthers (2000), Edelman (2004), Ferguson (1980), Goldberg (2001), Hampden-Turner (1981), Sternberg (1990), and Wilber (1982), who provide outstanding accounts of the different metaphors that have shaped theories of the mind in science and social thought.

Under the influence of the findings of split brain research arising from the work of Roger Sperry (1968, 1969), Ornstein (1972), and others, there has been much interest in understanding the implications of the functioning of the creative right and analytic left hemispheres. The specialization of functions between these two hemispheres is important, but it is important not to underestimate the degree of interconnection as well. To reemphasize this here, it is worth noting that some scientists believe that there may be more interconnections in a single human brain than atoms in the universe. Research continues to reveal the adaptability and flexibility of the human brain. Quartz and Sejnowski (2002) describe how biology and culture work together with experience to help build the brain. Restak (2004) discusses how repetitive mental exercise can activate previously unused brain circuits to extend human learning and performance. Cognitive scientist Clark (2004) uses a cyborg metaphor to explain how humans develop and use new technologies to continuously enhance mental capacities, referring to the internet and cell phone as examples of "entry level cyborg technology." Despite all our theories, the simple fact is that the brain is as complicated as anything we know.

Brains and organizations as communication and decision-making systems: Compared with the complexity and mystery of modern brain research, use of the brain metaphor in organization theory is still in an early stage of development.

Reference has been made in Chapter 4 to the valuable work of Herbert Simon (1947) and his colleagues at Carnegie-Mellon University (March and Simon 1958; Cyert and March 1963) in developing a view of organizations as decision-making systems. Their work has been developed in formal theories of decision making (e.g., Braybrooke and Lindblom 1963; Lindblom 1959, 1968) and in principles of organizational design (e.g., Thompson 1967; Galbraith 1974, 1977).

Much of this work has focused on the rational, analytic aspects of decision making and underplayed the creative and intuitive side. Simon (1987) has recently recognized the imbalance and extended his ideas to embrace the intuitive and nonlogical aspects of decision making in terms of capacities for pattern recognition. As noted in Chapter 4, Simon's original formulation of the decision-making process used logic (with its emphasis on drawing conclusions from premises) *as a metaphor* for capturing the process (Simon 1987: 57–64). This, of course, accounts for its mechanical, reductive nature and its synergy with the bureaucratic view of organization. The image of a logical mind in effect dominates how cognitive capacities are conceptualized and understood at both individual and organizational levels.

A broader-based theory of decision making, which incorporates the intuitive, nonlogical side, will help to shift organization theory beyond the view of bounded rationality that has tended to dominate the field. Gigerenzer and Selten's (2001) collection of papers extends Simon's bounded rationality to include emotional, social, and cultural factors. Other important steps in this direction have been taken by researchers who deliberately emphasize the importance of developing organizational capacities rooted in the creative "right brain" as well as the rational "left brain" (e.g., de Bono 1970,1985; Mintzberg 1976; Taggart and Robey 1981; Agor 1989; Evans and Russell, 1989; Henry 1991; Ford and Gioia 1995). Increasing attention is also being given to the role of emotional intelligence (Goleman 1995; Goleman et al. 2002; and Stein and Book 2000).

The process of recognizing the nonrational and, at times, irrational aspects of organizational decision making has also been built into new theories of decision making by Cohen, March and Olsen (1972), Hedberg et al. (1976), March (1981), March and Olsen (1976), and Shapira (2002), who use images of organizations as "garbage cans," "organized anarchies," "seesaws," and "camping grounds" to capture the nonrational aspects. Brunsson (1985), Starbuck (1983, 1985), Weick (1979, 1995, 2000), and other "enactment theorists" have also pursued the nonrational dimension by revealing how thought is imposed on action retrospectively. Decisions, it seems, often become rational only as we use hindsight to rationalize and explain them.

Pattern recognition, creativity, and frame-breaking insights are vital characteristics for developing capacities for organizational learning. The interest in knowing more about exactly how individuals and organizations process information and make decisions is rapidly expanding, and interesting perspectives are being developed around the idea that organizations can be understood as cognitive structures or "thinking systems" (Nystrom and Starbuck 1981, 1984; Sims and Gioia 1986). Hampden-Turner (1990a, 1990b) has offered a view of "corporate mind" that seeks to broaden the definition of intelligent corporate thinking and action beyond "the rational" to incorporate the management of dilemma and conflicting values within a cybernetic framework. Gladwell (2005) has also drawn attention to how individuals unconsciously select "thin slices" of information to make snap decisions.

For discussions of ideas about "organizational memory" and "organizational mind," see Sandelands and Stablein (1987) and Walsh and Ungson (1991); on organizational intelligence see March (1999).

Research has also given attention to the role of organizational knowledge creation and sharing (Nonaka and Takuchi 1995)—a product of individual and collective intelligence, and crucial for organizations seeking to improve performance in the postindustrial marketplace. The focus of much learning organization research has moved from information technology networks to managing the brainpower of the networked knowledge workers who work within and across geographically dispersed organizations. Choo's (1998) model for the "knowledge organization" interlinks sensemaking, knowledge creation, and decision making to result in productive action. Cross and Israelit's (1999) collection of papers discusses learning-focused approaches to building knowledge-based organizations. Davenport and Prusak (2000) provide advice and case studies on applying knowledge to achieve results.

Much of the research on knowledge-based organizations combines learning and social theory to examine collaborative group learning and knowledge creation. Cross and Parker (2004) discuss the informal self-organizing collaboration networks that exist in organizations and suggest ways of making them visible. Wenger's (1998) important work on communities of practice describes the social aspect of individual learning within informal communities, and how group learning can build organizational capacity. Insight into the importance of collaborative thinking and learning for knowledge creation can be found in Bray et al. (2000). Issacs (1999), Perkins (2006), and Senge et al. (2004) focus on the contribution of communication and dialogue to learning and knowledge creation. Adams and Morgan (in press) focus on how internet technology can support self-organizing learning processes. Boiset (1998) uses an "I (information) space" metaphor to explore the complex dynamics and linkages of organizational knowledge assets. Allee (2003) combines social network analysis, communities of practice, self-organization, and value network analysis to present the organization as a living knowledge network.

New Yorker journalist Surowiecki (2004) points to the development of the Google search engine to illustrate his view that a crowd's collective intelligence can deliver better outcomes than the individual intelligences of those perceived as the experts. Rheingold (2003) speculates upon the potential impact of mobile and wireless devices on the formation of new types of knowledge exchange networks.

A number of works address creative thinking as an important element for knowledge creation and innovation. Dacey and Lennon (1998) offer a multidisciplinary theory of creativity. Simonton (2004) describes the serendipitous aspect of important scientific discoveries. Perkins's (2000) work on breakthrough thinking uses a Klondike gold rush metaphor to explain the "self-organizing criticality" and active knowledge required to navigate unknown terrain. Mauzy and Harriman (2003) discuss developing systematic creativity in organizations as a means of promoting and sustaining innovation.

Cybernetics: For an introduction to cybernetics it is best to start with Wiener (1967), McCorduck (1979), McCullouch (1974), and Warrick (1980) and then proceed to some of the classic works such as Wiener (1961), Ashby (1952, 1960), and Beer (1959, 1972). Useful overviews of concepts and ideas are provided by Buckley (1967, 1968), Steinbrunner (1974), and Morgan (1982).

From a cybernetic perspective, everything can be understood in informational terms. It is no accident that the word *information* contains the word *form*, for the cyberneticians believe that form rests in information, or difference. The mathematical basis of this proposition has been demonstrated by Spencer-Brown (1969) and its logic has been clearly described by Gregory Bateson (1972: 317–318) in the notion that a unit of information is a difference that makes a difference. Responsiveness to difference seems to be basic to all systems. We see this in the operation of a simple thermostat and in the operation of more complex systems such as the human brain. Information systems map differences exactly as a geographical map traces the difference between water and land, degrees of elevation, and other physical features of the terrain thus represented. Information rests in the communication of difference.

Developments in cybernetics and cybernetic technology have contributed greatly to our understanding of how systems learn. The work of Pask (1961) and Ashby (1952, 1960) on the nature of learning is important, as is the work of writers on the principles of self-organization and artificial intelligence (e.g., von Foerester and Zopf 1962; McCorduck 1979; Kelly 1994). Bateson (1972) has developed the concept of learning to learn.

Cybernetic thinking has become an important part of the information revolution and underpins a great deal of work exploring the impact of information technology on human organizations. For excellent overviews, see Brown and Duguid (2000), Courtney et al. (2005), Kelly (1994), Menzies (1996), Negroponte (1995), Tapscott (1996), Taylor and van Every (1993), and Zuboff (1988).

Cybernetic epistemology: Although cybernetics is primarily seen as a technique for designing self-regulating systems, its basic insight that systems in the natural and social world can be understood as changing patterns of information has major epistemological implications. We have not had a chance to explore these in this chapter, but they lead to exciting new theories relating to the nature of control, causality, and the process of evolution. Bateson (1972, 1979), Gadalla and Cooper (1978), Harries-Jones (1995), Maruyama (1963), Morgan (1982, 1983c), and Wilden (1972) discuss these, including the cybernetic theory of coevolution that critiques Darwin's overmaterialistic interpretation of nature. Some of the implications of this cybernetic epistemology are discussed in Chapter 8.

Learning and learning to learn: Studies of organizational learning tend to build around the work of Bateson (1972). The concept has been brought to prominence through the work of Argyris and Schön (1974, 1978), Argyris (1982, 1990, 1993, 1994, 1999, 2004), and Schön (1983). They develop the distinction between single- and double-loop learning and give considerable attention to "defensive routines" and other barriers to learning created in many conventional approaches to organization. De Geus (1988), Michael (1973), Ogilvy (2002), Schwartz (1996), and Williams (1982) have presented comprehensive analyses of the need for learning in the planning process and indicated ways in which this might be achieved. Vickers (1965, 1972) has also given considerable attention to the kind of inquiry that provides the basis for effective learning.

Belden, Hyatt, and Ackley (1993), de Geus (1988), Easterby-Smith et al. (1999), Hedberg (1981), Hedberg et al. (1976), Kim (2001), Nystrom and Starbuck (1981, 1984), Pedler and Aspinwall (1996), Pedler, Burgoyne, and Boydell (1991), Revans (1982), and Senge (1990) have also made important theoretical and practical contributions to the development of "learning organizations." Senge's approach has strong links with the ideas about complex systems and mutual causality discussed in Chapter 8.

For an introduction to Revans's approach to action learning, see Revans (1982, 1983), Pedler (1983, 2005), and Pedler et.al (2005). Schwandt and Marquardt (2000) and Marquardt (1999, 2004) have also developed an action-centered model of organizational learning.

For an introduction to the Tavistock approach to action learning see Trist and Murray (1993), Morgan and Ramirez (1984), and Weisbord (1992). For discussions of the concept of "intelligent enterprise," see Quinn (1992), Pinchot and Pinchot (1993), and Thannhuber (2005).

Cybernetic strategy: The argument in favor of developing a cybernetic strategy based on an avoidance of noxiants is developed in different ways by Bateson (1972), Michael (1973), and Morgan (1983c). The more we examine this principle, the more we come to see its key role in the evolution of forms of all kinds. When we talk about adaptation or "good fit," we are referring to an absence of disjunction; that is, any misfit between form and context has been removed. In any design process it is the misfit that draws attention and calls for correction. Design typically evolves through the elimination of noxiants, and, as architect Christopher Alexander (1964) has suggested, good design can be specified in terms of potential misfit variables. The process is guided by a vision of the end product, but the specific form emerges as a consequence of corrective actions that eliminate undesirable qualities.

Many human decisions evolve in a similar way as noxiants are eliminated. When we make decisions we cut off undesirable courses of action (the word *decide* comes from the Latin *decidere* meaning "cut off"). The decision "yes" always implies a series of "no's." In these and other ways, the avoidance of noxiants underpins much of everyday life. We typically avoid what is unpleasant or threatening, carving a course to the future in the space that remains. Our most basic sensibility thus has a cybernetic quality of which we are often unaware. The logic of goal setting often tends to erode this quality, favoring a more linear process that tries to straighten the path between present and future. As noted in Chapter 4, in the development of the Internet, which offers a perfect example of the problems of design in complex, open-ended systems, users are given advice on what they should *not* do. The key parameters, thus defined, create a space for the possible and the evolution of forms of practice that cannot be forecast or predesigned.

Holographic organization: For a discussion of holography, see Bentov (1977), Bohm (1978, 1980a, 1980b), Bohm and Peat (1987), Briggs and Peat (1984), and Wilber (1982). As in the case of cybernetics the technical principles have all kinds of epistemological implications. For example, as Karl Pribram (in Wilber 1982) has suggested, if we see holography as a basic organizing principle and recognize the holographic character of the brain, it takes but a small step to realize that perhaps the world *is* a hologram. This makes good sense, for if we accept that the brain is holographic it is likely that it is a holographic element of a holographic whole. The work of Bohm and Pribram explores this possibility and promises to open the way to radically new modes of understanding.

With the explosion of information technology, holographic organization has become a reality, because it is now possible to organize in a decentralized fashion as never before. The technology is leading us into a new world that demands new metaphors for conceptualizing and dealing with the problems and challenges being faced. Theories consistent with holographic principles invite us to think about organizations as "hives," "termite colonies," "spider plants," and "mobots," and through other images that capture the self-organizing processes discussed in Chapter 4 (see, for example, Kelly 1994; Mills 1991; Morgan 1993a, 1993b). This kind of thinking will become increasingly important as we continue to wrestle with the implications of the new information economy. For example, Adams and Morgan (2006) have used these ideas to develop internet-based learning systems for promoting distributed organizational learning, knowledge creation, and knowledge sharing.

Important new evidence on the effectiveness of holographic organization is found in the work of Nonaka (1988) and Nonaka and Takuchi (1995). Their studies of "knowledge creating" companies in Japan illustrate how the holographic principles of requisite variety, redundancy, and learning processes driven by shared visions and "minimum specs" can help to create powerful systems of information exchange that allow groups of people to reinvent their relationships with the environment and develop new services and products. Their view of individual and organizational learning embraces both "tacit" and "explicit" dimensions, drawing attention to the fact that we learn through "feel" and lived experience as well as through abstract conceptual processes. They encourage us to understand knowledge creation more holistically than through the cognitive approach dominant in the West.

On the detailed principles of holographic organization discussed in Chapter 4, see Morgan (1993b) and Morgan and Ramirez (1984). The important distinction between organizational designs based on a redundancy of parts and a redundancy of functions has been developed by Emery (1969, 1976). The principle of requisite variety is developed in the work of Ashby (1952, 1960), and the principle of learning to learn derives from the work of Bateson (1972) and Argyris and Schön (1978). The principle of minimum critical specification derives from Herbst (1974).

Comprehensive discussions on the principles and practice of autonomous work groups are found in Herbst (1962), Susman (1976), and Mohrman and Cummings (1989).

Discussions on mobots are found in Brooks (1991) and Kelly (1994). For links with organization studies see Gee (1996) and Zohar and Morgan (1996). Brooks's description of Genghis is found in Kelly (1994: 39).

The Norwegian shipping firm suffering the plane crash is discussed by Andersen (1992). Peter Drucker's discussion of the challenges of the new "knowledge economy" is found in Drucker (1993, 2001).

5: The Culture Metaphor

"Culture" as a modern concept used in an anthropological and social sense to refer broadly to "civilization" and "social heritage" is attested no earlier than 1871. This meaning of the word did not appear in an English dictionary until the 1920s. Its use within the German language is somewhat older, having made an appearance by 1800. Its increasing use within the social sciences has led to definitions of varying generality, which develop in a host of ways Tylor's (1871) view that "culture, or civilization . . . is that complex whole which includes knowledge, belief, art, law, morals, custom, and any other capabilities and habits acquired by man as a member of society." Kroeber and Kluckhohn (1952), in their classic work on the meaning and use of this concept within the social sciences, claim to have identified almost 300 definitions, and they provide a detailed analysis of 164.

Culture and organization: There is a growing literature of relevance to understanding how organization can be understood as a cultural phenomenon. Durkheim (1934), Weber (1947), Parsons (1973), and Harris (1979) provide valuable sociological analyses. Durkheim (1934) is particularly valuable for understanding the relationship between culture and industrialization. Kerr et al. (1964) explore the similarities in the structure of all kinds of industrial societies. The approach known as "institutional theory" (see Scott and Christensen 1995 and the references cited in the bibliographic notes to Chapter 3) has developed the broad tradition by examining the links between organization and social context, revealing how both are intertwined in the most fundamental sense. Sahlins (1972) helps us to see the distinctive nature of modern society through comparisons with Stone Age society.

There is an enormous literature on the relationship between organization and culture from a cross-national perspective. See, for example, Adler (1997), Aktouf (1996), Ashkenas et al. (2002), Child (1981), Clegg and Redding (1990), Cole (1979), Daniels et al. (2000), Goldsmith (2003), Hall (1959, 1960), Hofstede (1980), Lammers and Hickson (1979), Mead (2005), Sanyal (2001), Triandis and Albert (1987), Trompenaars (1993), and Webber (1969). Campbell (2004) offers a theory of institutional change in a globalization context. In Gannon and Newman's (2002) collection, managers, psychologists, and economists offer their perspectives on operating in a global environment. Hampden-Turner and Trompenaars (2000) and Mankin and Cohen (2004) discuss complex collaborations across geographic, cultural, and organizational boundaries. Sahay (2003) describes the cultural challenges presented by global outsourcing of software development. On the relation between culture and Japanese organization and management, see Abeglen (1974), Austin (1976), Dore (1973), McMillan (1984), Morita, Reingold, and Shimomura (1986), Vogel (1979), and Yoshino (1968, 1976). The discussion presented in my chapter has drawn on Dore (1973), Kamata (1982), Ouchi (1981), Pascale and Athos (1981), Maruyama (1982), and Sayle (1982). The story of the Honda worker is taken from Peters and Waterman (1982).

The text discussion on American culture draws upon the analysis by Bateson (1972: 88–106). Numerous examples of his thesis regarding the prominence of exhibitionistic behavior in American culture are found in Peters and Waterman (1982).

Corporate culture and subculture: The possibility of studying organizations as cultures has been brought into prominence by a number of recent works, notably Alvesson (1993a, 2002), Alvesson and Berg (1992), Ashkanasy, Wilderom, and Peterson (2000), Bate (1994), Calas and Smircich (1987, 1988), Collins (2001), Czarniawska-Joerges (1992), Deal and Kennedy (1982, 1999), Denison (1990), Frost et al. (1985, 1991), Hall (1967), Handy (1978), Henry and Walker (1991), Jelinek et al. (1983), Keyton (2005), Kilmann et al. (1985), Linstead and Grafton-Small (1992), Marshall and McLean (1985), Martin (1992, 2001), Martin and Frost (1996),

Neuhauser et al. (2000), Ott (1989), Ouchi and Wilkins (1985), Pascale and Athos (1981), Peters and Waterman (1982), Pondy et al. (1983), Schein (1985, 1999), Senge et al. (1999), Smircich (1983a, 1983b, 1983c), Smircich and Calas (1987), Trice and Beyer (1993), and Willmott (1993). These works provide a comprehensive indication of some of the latest developments in this field.

The case study of the insurance company discussed in Chapter 5 is based on Smircich (1983a, 1983b) and Smircich and Morgan (1982). The discussion of corporate culture at Hewlett-Packard draws on Ouchi (1981), Peters and Waterman (1982), and Wilkins (1983). The discussion of the corporate culture of ITT under Geneen draws on Sampson (1978) and Deal and Kennedy (1982). Michael Maccoby's characterization of the gamesman is found in Maccoby (1976).

On female values and leadership styles, see Calas and Smircich (2004), Harragan (1977), Helgesen (1990), Rhode (2003), and the references on gender presented in the bibliographic notes to Chapters 6 and 7. The quote on Anita Roddick is from Helgesen (1990: 5). On organizational countercultures or subcultures, see Collinson (1988), Cox (1993), Frost et al. (1991), Frost et al. (1995), Gregory (1983), Kidder (1981), Martin and Frost (1996), Martin and Siehl (1983), and Turner (1971). On occupational subcultures, see Barley (1983) and van Maanen and Barley (1984). W. F. Whyte's study of status relations in the restaurant industry is in Whyte (1948). On the cultural diversity of the modern workforce, see Adler (1997), Cox (1993), Cross et al. (1994), and Stockdale and Crosby (2004).

Creating organizational reality: Garfinkel (1967) discusses how we "accomplish" realities and Weick (1979, 1995) discusses the concepts of enactment and retrospective "sense making." Gergen (1985, 1991) and Gergen and Davis (1985) address the social construction of reality from a psychological standpoint. These ideas draw on a long tradition of social thought, most often associated with the work of James (1950), Wittgenstein (1958), Schutz (1967), and Berger and Luckmann (1967). Useful discussions on the enactment of organizational culture can be found in Louis (1983) and Smircich (1983a). Huff (1982), Hamel and Prahalad (1994), and Smircich and Stubbart (1985) show how organizations enact their environments, a theme that is explored again in Chapter 8. Sudnow's analysis of the enactment of realities in the judicial system is found in Sudnow (1965).

For a discussion of how language shapes organizational reality, see Bittner (1965), Eccles and Nohria (1992), Evered (1983), Fox (2004), Hummel (1977), and Silverman and Jones (1976). Hall (1959, 1960) has also drawn attention to the "silent language" of nonverbal forms and gestures.

The volumes by Alvesson and Berg (1992), Frost et al. (1985, 1991), Frost et al. (1995), Gagliardi (1990), Gherardi (1995), Kilmann et al. (1985), Morgan

(1993a), Parker (1990), Pondy et al. (1983), Schein (1985), Turner (1989), and van Maanen (1991) contain many illustrations of the influence of stories, sagas, legends, rituals, ceremonies, symbols, images and metaphors, and other attributes of culture in the enactment of reality. Also see Barley (1983), Cooperrider and Srivastva (1987), Dandridge (1986), Gabriel (1995), Hatch (2004), Magruder Watkins and Mohr (2001), Mitchell (1989), Srivastva and Cooperrider (1990), and Turner (1990).

The impact of leadership on corporate culture is discussed by Barnard (1938), Bennis and Nanus (1985), Peters (1978), Peters and Waterman (1982), Selznick (1957), Schein (1985), Smircich and Morgan (1982), and Westley and Mintzberg (1989). The notion of transformational leadership is discussed by Burns (1978).

There are many major studies of corporate transformation that illustrate the pivotal role of leadership in reframing culture. See, for example, the study of Jack Welch at General Electric by Tichy and Sherman (1993), of Anita Roddick and The Body Shop by Lessem (1987) and Roddick (1991), the studies of entrepreneurial leaders offered by Davis (1987) and Lessem (1987), and Pettigrew's (1985) study of corporate transformation at ICI. Griffin (2002), Kleiner (1996), and Torbert (2004) discuss the nature of transformational leadership. Goleman et al. (2002) explain the importance of emotional intelligence in leaders, while Lennick and Kiel (2005) discuss moral intelligence. For the role of ethics and governance issues in leadership see Ciulla (2004) and Gandossy and Sonnenfeld (2004). The impact of leadership can be both positive and negative. For the negative side, see Miller (1990).

For an outstanding discussion of the links between gender, symbolism, and organizational culture, including a detailed bibliography of most of the major research see Gherardi (1995). For a detailed discussion of female values and how "webs of inclusion" and other interactive patterns can replace hierarchies see Aaltio and Mills (2002), Cleveland et al. (2000), Gregory (2003), Helgesen (1990), Iannello (1992), Marshall (1984, 1993, 1994), Powell (2002), Roddick (1991), Rosener (1990), and Sheppard (1992). For expositions of a feminist perspective and critiques of male-dominated styles of organization, see Alvesson and Billing (1992), Bowles (1993), Calas and Smircich (1993, 1996), Ferguson (1984), Gilligan (1993), Hearn et al. (1989), and Mills and Tancred (1992).

For a discussion of how women have been encouraged to adopt "male" strategies for survival in a male-dominated world, or what Betty Harragan has described as "no woman's land," see Harragan (1977) and Hennig and Jardim (1976).

For a discussion of how accounting systems shape social constructions of reality, see Hopwood (1989) and Morgan (1988b).

On the philosophy of employee empowerment, see Block (1987).

Discussions of the parallels between the use of managerial techniques and primitive magic draw on Devons (1961), Gluckman (1972), and an unpublished paper by Gimpl and Dakin (1983). Also, see Clark and Salaman (1996).

Meyer and Rowan (1977) provide an insightful analysis of the role of organizational structure as myth and ceremony.

The story about Picasso is drawn from Hampden-Turner (1981).

The story about the Kwakiutl's visit to New York is related by Lévi-Strauss (1967) and Turner (1983).

The interpretation of the culture metaphor adopted in this chapter has been a broad one. Many of the ideas that we have discussed elaborate a cluster of insights that in principle could have been developed in their own right. For example, at various points in discussion we have referred to the idea that organizational activity can be understood as a language, as the playing of a game, as drama, as theater, or even as text. A preliminary indication of how these metaphors can be used to develop approaches to organizational analysis is provided by Morgan, Frost, and Pondy (1983). Goffman (1959), Mangham (1978), Mangham and Overington (1983, 1987), and Rosen (1985) illustrate the use of dramaturgical metaphor.

Since the 1980s, a "postmodernist" critique of organization and culture has gained considerable prominence, drawing attention to the value base and associated biases or "silences" accompanying any view of organization. For an overview, see Alvesson and Deetz (1996), Burrell (1997), Calas and Smircich (1999), Flax (1990), Hassard and Parker (1993), Hatch (1997), and Smircich and Calas (1999).

6: The Political Metaphor

Any discussion of politics and political systems must pay early reference to the work of Aristotle. His idea that politics is a way of creating order is central to political thought, showing how society can avoid degenerating into what Thomas Hobbes (1951) described as "a war of all against all." Most political philosophies, whether we are talking about the manipulative diplomacy of a Machiavelli, the anarchism of a Proudhon (1969), the elitism of a Mosca (1939), or the rationalism of a Popper (1945), are centrally concerned with solutions to this problem of order. Almost any good text on political science can be consulted to obtain more background on the evolution of the Aristotelian view (e.g., Crick 1964). Bottomore (1966) provides an excellent discussion of the relationship between elites, democracy, and society and their general role in politics.

Organizations as systems of government: The idea of drawing the links between modes of organization and systems of political rule has been long appreciated by political scientists interested in understanding the political significance of organization and the relationship between organizations and the state. As a result, most of the systems of organizational rule explored in Chapter 6 have been investigated in one way or another.

For example, on autocracy, see Michels (1949); on bureaucracy, see Weber (1947); on technocracy, see Galbraith (1967); and on approaches to industrial democracy and self-organization, see Vanek (1975) and Woodworth, Meek, and Whyte (1985); on the political role of corporations in a global economy, see Carroll (2004), Chandler and Mazlish (2005), Deetz (1992a), Haley (2001), Kelly (2003), Ohmae (1993), Perrow (2002), and Young and Scott (2004). Discussions of the German approach to code-termination are found in Agthe (1977), Aktouf (1996), Bergmann (1975), Donahue (1976), Garson (1977), Mintzberg (1983), and Tivey (1978). This is now evolving into a new form with the unification of Germany and the challenge of surviving in a global economy. On varieties of representative and direct democracy, see Emery and Thorsrud (1969), Coates and Topham (1970), and Coates (1976, 1981a, 1981b). Much of the literature in the field of industrial democracy is also vitally concerned with these issues, as many of the debates between labor and management hinge on issues relating to who has the right to rule and under what circumstances (see, e.g., Cloke 2002; Fox 1974; Potterfield 1999).

The story on Henry Ford is taken from *Business Week*, April 1979. Lee Iacocca's (1984) autobiography confirms the details of this story and provides many interesting illustrations of how Henry Ford II exercised a monarchial prerogative over company affairs.

Organizational politics: The idea of viewing organizations with a focus on the political actions of organizational members has become increasingly popular since the early 1960s. Important discussions can be found in Bacharach and Lawler (2000), Bower (1983), Burns (1961), Burns and Stalker (1961), Butcher (2001), Crozier (1964), Frost (1987), Frost and Egri (1991), Kleiner (2003), Jay (1967), March (1962), Murray and Gandz (1980), Pettigrew (1973), Pfeffer (1978, 1981), and Vigoda-Gadot (2003). The idea that organizational politics hinges on the relationship between interests, conflict, and power runs throughout this literature, at least in an implicit way. Useful discussions on how political action follows individual or group interests can be found in almost all these works.

Interests: Culbert and McDonough (1980) discuss how self-interest shapes organizational behavior. Downs (1967) provides a discussion of the types of political actors found in bureaucratic organizations: for example, climbers, conservers, zealots, advocates, and statesmen. Useful discussions on the role of interest groups, cliques, and coalitions in organizations can be found in Bacharach and Lawler (1980), Cyert and March (1963), Dalton (1959), Frost (1987), Pfeffer (1981), Tichy (1973), and Wildavsky (1964). For a discussion of the importance of thinking about organization through the eyes of stakeholders see Freeman (1984), Wheeler and Sillanpaa (1997), and Wheeler, et. al. (2003).

Conflict: Useful discussions on organizational conflict can be found in Brown (1983), Filley (1975), Litterer (1966), and Pondy (1964, 1967). Much of the current literature on organizational conflict tends to draw upon the ideas first developed by Coser (1956) on the latent functions of social conflict. His work builds on important sociological insights developed by Simmel (1950) and Merton (1968a). The work of Mary Parker Follett (1973) is also very important. She was one of the first to develop what is now known as a pluralist approach to conflict management. For a collection of her papers, see Graham (1995). A history of the background and evolution of sociological approaches to the analysis of conflict and their impact on organization theory is provided by Burrell and Morgan (1979).

Discussions of the nature of interdepartmental and role conflict are found in Dalton (1959), Frost (1987), Putnam and Poole (1987), Morgan (1979), Crozier (1964), Pettigrew (1973), and Lawrence and Lorsch (1967a, 1967b). Related discussions of role conflicts between bureaucrats and professionals can be found in Benson (1973), Corwin (1970), and Kornhauser (1963). On conflicts relating to the process of budgeting and resource allocation, see Hofstede (1967), Pondy (1964), and Wildavsky (1964). The case illustrations on conflicts relating to the setting of work standards are taken from Whyte (1955).

Power: The study of power has received long-standing treatment in the field of political science, and its nature has been the subject of great debate. The pluralist view of power draws on the work of Dahl (1957), Emerson (1962), and Lasswell (1936) and has been extended to the analysis of organizations in many different ways by Bacharach and Lawler (1980), Blau (1964), Crozier (1964), Cumming (1981), French and Raven (1968), Korda (1975), Kotter (1977), Mintzberg (1983), and Pfeffer (1978) and in numerous collections of readings, such as Allen and Porter (1983). The adequacy of the pluralist view has been challenged through a number of radical critiques such as those of Bachrach and Baratz (1962, 1970), Burrell and Morgan (1979), Clegg (1975, 1979), Giddens (1979), Kelly (2003), Lukes (1974), and Perrow (2002). For an overview of the whole field, see Clegg (1989).

The following references are useful in following up chapter discussion on specific sources of power. On formal authority, see Weber (1947), Follett (1949), and Mouzelis (1979). On influence as power, see Cohen (2005) and Provis (2004). On the control of scarce resources, see Emerson (1962), Pfeffer and Salancik (1978), and Pfeffer (1981). On the use of organization structure, rules, and regulations, see Crozier (1964), Hickson et al. (1971), Perrow (1979, 1984), Pettigrew (1973), and Pfeffer (1978, 1981). On the control of decision processes, see Bachrach and Baratz (1962, 1970), Lukes (1974), March and Simon (1958), Perrow (1979), and Pettigrew (1973). On the control of knowledge and information and the use of expert power and gatekeeping activities, see Crozier (1964), Easton (1965), Forester (1983), French and Raven (1968), Habermas (1970a, 1970b), Pettigrew (1973), and Wilensky (1967). Lorsch et al. (2005) examine gatekeeper responsibility in the context of corporate scandals. On the control of boundaries, see Miller and Rice (1967), Thompson (1967), and Pfeffer (1981). Goffman (1967) contains a discussion of avoidance rituals. My discussion on the schismatic tendencies of organizations and how boundaries may be managed to protect the autonomy of individuals and departments draws on Morgan (1981), and the idea of loosely coupled systems draws on Weick (1976). On the ability to cope with uncertainty, see Hickson et al. (1971), Thompson (1967), and Pfeffer (1981). On the control and political nature of technology, see Child (1985), Crozier (1964), Scarbrough and Corbett (1992), and Woodward (1965). Bard and Soderqvist (2002) suggest that those organizations that harness interactive network technologies will become the new power elites. On interpersonal alliances, networks, and coalitions, see Pfeffer and Salancik (1978) and Pfeffer (1981). Kanter (1977) contains a useful discussion of the role of sponsors, mentors, and godfather figures. Literally hundreds of pieces of research since the Hawthorne studies (Roethlisberger and Dickson 1939) have demonstrated the role and power of informal organization. On the control of "counterorganizations," see Galbraith (1962) on countervailing power and Fox (1974), Coates (1976, 1981a, 1981b), and Hyman (1975) on labor unionism. On symbolism and the management of meaning, see Edelman (1971, 1977), Habermas (1970a, 1970b), Pondy et al. (1983), and Smircich and Morgan (1982). Alvesson (1987), Brunsson (1989), and Knights and Willmott (1987) discuss the use and management of "culture" as a form of ideology and control. The discussion in the text on dramatism and impression management develops the work of Goffman (1959). Carr (1968), Frost (1987), and Maccoby (1976) contain useful discussions of gamesmanship in organizations. On gender, see Burk (2005), Ferguson (1984), Harragan (1977), Hartsock (1990), Hearn and Parkin

(1987), Helgesen (1990), Iannello (1992), Kanter (1977), Millett (1969), Savage and Witz (1992), Sheppard (1984), Thomas, et al. (2004), Wilson (2001), and the references on gender in the bibliographic notes to Chapter 5. On class, race, and other structural factors that define the stage of action, see Bachrach and Baratz (1962, 1970), Clegg (1979, 1989), Deetz (1992a, 1992b), Foucault (1979a, 1979b), Giddens (1979), Gramsci (1971), Lukes (1974), Nkomo (1992), Kelly (1994), Ohmae (1985), and Townley (1994). This topic is also explored in depth in Chapters 8 and 9 of the present work. On the empowering aspects of power, see Block (1987), Cloke (2002), Freire (1970), Potterfield (1999), and Robbins (1987).

Pluralism: On the origins of pluralism in political thought, see Bentley (1908), Figgis (1913), Follett (1918), Laski (1917, 1919), and Maitland (1911). The concept of pluralism has been brought to organization theory in many different ways and is discussed in detail by Burrell and Morgan (1979). The distinction between unitary and pluralist frames of reference has been developed by Ross (1958, 1969) and in the important works by Fox (1966, 1974). Fox (1974) and Burrell and Morgan (1979) develop the implications of the radical frame of reference.

The pluralist approach to conflict has its roots in Coser (1956) and has had an important impact on the history of both sociology and organization theory. Within organization theory, the focus has been on studying the functions of social conflict and the skills of conflict management—see, for example, Brown (1983), Filley (1975), Follett (1973), Graham (1995), Robbins (1978), and Thomas (1976).

My analysis of rationality as a political concept benefited from the work of Lucas (1987) and Perrow (1979) and the warnings issued by Silverman (1971) regarding the dangers of reifying the organization and its goals. My critique of organizations as functionally integrated systems builds on the work of Gouldner (1973) and Morgan (1981) and on general sociological analyses of the dysfunctions of bureaucracy. Burrell and Morgan (1979: 184–189) provide a review of this work. Discussion of the relationship between power, personality, and human motivation is developed by Nietzsche (1976), Adler (1927), Horney (1942), Lips (1981), Nord (1978), and McClelland (1975). The manipulative and gamelike aspects of power are explored in books such as Korda (1975) and Kennedy (1980). Literature relating to the radical critique of pluralism is further explored in Chapter 9 of the present work. The problems of elite dominance have also been exposed by modern corporate scandals such as those leading to the collapse of Enron and WorldCom, creating major interest in new governance models. See, for example, Batten and Fetherston (2003), Grandori (2004), Leblanc and Gillies (2005), Monks and Minow (2003), Rowland (2005), Schirm (2004), and Young and Scott (2004).

7: The Psychic Prison Metaphor

The idea that people create worlds that then imprison them has proved a popular theme in social thought and literature. It is explored in Shakespeare's *Othello*, in Herman Melville's *Moby Dick*, and in the cries of alienation that pervade the novels of Beckett (1958, 1965), Camus (1946), Kafka (1953, 1973), and Sartre (1938, 1966). The ideas expressed in these and other works draw upon a long history of social thought stretching back to Plato. This now receives its most forceful treatment in the intellectual schemes developed by Freud, Marx, and other contributors to what Burrell and Morgan (1979) have described as the radical humanist paradigm.

Plato was among the first to intellectualize the predicament of human beings as prisoners of their thoughts and actions. His allegory of the cave, found in Book VII of *The Republic*, provides an evocative image that has inspired many to explore the relationship between illusion and reality. The works of Freud, Jung, and various "critical theorists" have developed new attacks on the basic problem, linking the idea that humans become trapped by their preoccupations, images, and ideas with the need for radical critique of this situation. This is the essential foundation of the radical humanist tradition, which builds from the idea that while individuals create their reality, they often do so in confining and perhaps alienating ways. In this sense, the image of the psychic prison radicalizes many of the ideas discussed in Chapter 5 on the notion of culture, suggesting that the enactments, accomplishments, and language games that shape everyday life often serve hidden purposes and can be much more confining and oppressive than typically presumed.

On ideology: My original aim in writing this chapter was to explore two aspects of the psychic prison: one associated with the unconscious and the other with the role of ideology. However, the problem of making the chapter a manageable one has led me to focus on the former. The issue of ideology is thus not given the attention it truly deserves. Indeed, a strong case can be made for the idea that the metaphor of "organization as ideology" should be developed in its own right. This would require that we attempt to understand how organizational life reflects a process of *power-based reality construction* and to trace how people become trapped by ideas that serve specific sets of interests. In addition, it would be necessary to understand the ideological links between organizational life and social life more generally and to focus on the general problem of human alienation. Much of the work of Karl Marx on the theory of alienation (Marx 1975; Marx and Engels 1846, 1848; Fromm 1961), of Michel Foucault (1979a, 1979b; Miller 1993) on the deep structure of power, of Jürgen

Habermas (1970a, 1970b, 1972) on knowledge and human interests, and of the Frankfurt school on "critical theory" would be relevant to this endeavor. (See, for example, Horkheimer 1972; Horkheimer and Adorno 1973; Jay 1973; Held 1980.)

Interest in the links between critical theory and the study of organization has mushroomed since the 1980s, with a focus on how ideology, accounting and information systems, and other organizational practices shape forms of personal and interpersonal control that allow people to be manipulated in alienating modes of existence. Alvesson and Willmott (1992) present an excellent overview. For a focus on the ideological dimension of culture, see Alvesson (1987). For a critical perspective on planning and decision making, see Forester (1989). For a discussion of the ideological dimensions of accounting and information systems, see Arrington and Puxty (1991), Power and Laughlin (1992), and Hopwood (1989). Townley (1994) examines human resource management practice through the lens of Foucault's view of discipline and power. Deetz (1992a) also examines the nature of disciplinary practice. The writings on institutional theory (e.g., DiMaggio and Powell 1983; Scott and Christensen 1995) address the idea that organizations are knowledge systems that help people internalize patterns of obligation.

The postmodern critique of organization and organization studies (see references provided in the bibliographic notes to Chapter 5) is also relevant in understanding how organizational meaning systems are inherently biased and ideological.

Cognitive traps: In organization theory, the idea of challenging taken-for-granted ways of thinking is becoming well established, especially in the work of theorists recognizing the role of paradigms and metaphors in shaping how we think (e.g., Burrell and Morgan 1979; Morgan 1980, 1986, 1993a; Nystrom and Starbuck 1984; Weick 1979; Schön 1963, 1979). At a practical level it has become vitally important to challenge traditional paradigms and mind-sets as a means of coping with the demands of our postcapitalist society (Drucker 1993). Thomas Kuhn's concept of "paradigm change" (Kuhn 1970) has become an important managerial concept and ideology for reshaping management practice. Almost any book on creative management develops the implication of this approach, showing how all problems and problem solutions are products of how they are framed and that we can challenge and escape from cognitive traps by learning the art of framing and reframing and by fine-tuning skills of dialectical and other modes of critical thinking (e.g., Argyris 2004; Beer and Nohria 2000; Evans and Russell 1989; Mason and Mitroff 1981; Mitroff and Linstone 1993; and Morgan 1988a, 1989). The process of framing and reframing underpins the processes of learning to learn discussed in Chapter 4 and can help avoid the problem of "groupthink" identified by Janis (1972).

Another approach to understanding cognitive traps is offered by writers focusing on the management of paradox (e.g., Harvey 1995; Hampden-Turner 1990a, 1990b; Quinn 1988; Smith and Berg 1987; Zohar 1995). By recognizing the paradoxes tying one into the status quo, we take a first step toward escaping them. This is the invitation offered by Miller (1990) through his concept of the "Icarus paradox."

The parable on the relationship between a fish and water can be found in McLuhan and Zingrone (1995: 35).

Freud and the unconscious: The literature on the Freudian approach to the unconscious is enormous. To understand Freud's view on the theory of repression, it is important to consult his essays (in *The Complete Psychological Works of Sigmund Freud*, 1953) on "The Unconscious" (Vol. 14) and "Repression" (Vol. 14) and the "Introductory Lectures on Psychoanalysis" (Vols. 15 and 16). On the links between the unconscious and culture see "Totem and Taboo" (Vol. 13), "Civilization and Its Discontents" (Vol. 21), and "The Future of an Illusion" (Vol. 21). Fromm (1971), Brown (1959), Hampden-Turner (1981), Frey-Rohn (1974), and Mitchell (1974) provide excellent overviews of Freud's work.

In interpreting Freudian work it is important to note the division in Freudian circles between conservative and radical wings. The former tend to be preoccupied with the role of psychoanalysis as an instrument of control, whereas the latter see psychoanalysis as a potentially liberating force. The difference is splendidly discussed in Fromm (1971). In considering the more important radical Freudians one should note the work of Eric Fromm (1961, 1962, 1971), Karen Horney (1967), Melanie Klein (1965, 1980, 1981), R. D. Laing (1965), and Wilhelm Reich (1933, 1961, 1972a, 1972b). Numerous social theorists have built on and developed these insights, particularly Norman O. Brown (1959) and members of the so-called Frankfurt School of social thought, notably Horkheimer (1972), Horkheimer and Adorno (1973), Habermas (1972), and Marcuse (1955, 1964, 1970).

Organization and repressed sexuality: Freud's ideas on the development of sexuality are presented in *Three Essays on the Theory of Sexuality* (Vol. 7) and in *Character and Anal Eroticism* (Vol. 9). The latter article presents initial ideas leading to the theory of characterology, as developed by Abraham (1927), Reich (1972a), and Fromm (1971). In understanding the role of sexuality in Freudian theory it is important to recognize that sexuality was linked to the concept of primitive and aggressive forces of life and death as well as with forms of eroticism. It is also important to remember that in many discussions Freud's interpretation of anal eroticism is much oversimplified, being reduced to a concern for the relationship between anal desires and toilet training. In point of fact, Freud believed that anal sexuality was the focus of many aspects of bodily eroticism, displaced into anal concerns. Norman O. Brown (1959) presents an excellent discussion of this, together with a detailed exposition of the Freudian theory on the relations between wealth, money, and feces and the links that Freud drew between anal sexuality and the death instinct.

My analysis of the anal-compulsive character of Frederick Taylor draws on information in the biographies by Copley (1923) and Kakar (1970). In case we think Taylor an exception, it is important to note that other key figures in developing the work ethic on which industrial society has been built share many of Taylor's personality characteristics. For example, the biographies of Henry Ford, Benjamin Franklin, Martin Luther, and many of the Quakers in England and North America reveal excellent examples of people dominated by concerns that have roots in unconscious anal preoccupations. See, for example, Zaleznik and Kets de Vries (1975) and Jardim (1970).

Brown's *Life Against Death* (1959) provides an intriguing analysis of how the rise of capitalism seems linked with characteristics of the anal personality. In particular, his essay on the role of anality in the life and ideas of Martin Luther and the rise of Protestantism deserves special attention. As is well known, Max Weber (1958b) has linked Protestantism and the rise of capitalism. Brown's contribution is to show how Luther's support for capitalism through the Protestant movement is quite unintended. In a remarkable analysis, Brown reveals that Luther received the great illumination that led him to the doctrine of justification by faith while on the privy. He shows that Luther perceived a link between money, feces, and the devil and saw the devil as being the lord of capitalism. Luther was thus critical of capitalism, viewing usury as the devil and usurers as serving the devil's cause. He also saw a certain inevitability in the ways of the world, believing that the world was in bondage to the devil—hence the principle of being true in one's calling and of receiving salvation through faith rather than by attempting to find salvation in the present world. Brown's psychoanalytic interpretation of Luther's underlying motives thus provides an interesting twist to Weber's thesis, suggesting that Protestantism sanctioned capitalism by default, in a way that was probably opposite to Luther's intentions.

On the role of sexual repression and the rise of formal organization, see Burrell (1984, 1992), Cleugh (1963), Hearn and Parkin (1987), Hearn et al. (1989), Miller (1993), Taylor (1954), and Foucault (1979a, 1979b). See

Chatov (1981) on the links between repressed sexuality and governmental and other forms of regulation and Schwartz (1982) on the links between anal eroticism and compulsive job involvement.

Good discussions on the relationship between narcissism and contemporary society can be found in Lasch (1979), Walter (1983), and Schwartz (1990). For an analysis of the relationship between personality types and power, see McClelland (1975). For an analysis of the relation between character types and managerial styles, see Maccoby (1976).

One of the interesting questions embedded in discussions about organization and sexuality is whether it is possible to achieve a repression-free mode of organization. Such an ideal has been advocated by Marcuse (1955) and also underlies the vision of certain anarchistic theories, such as those of Stirner (1963). In Fromm's (1971) view, such theorists are searching for an infantilistic utopia where there are no limits on gratification. For example, he suggests that Marcuse ignores conflict and tragedy as human realities and that his dream of a nonrepressive society confuses the Freudian notion of repression with the idea of political suppression or oppression. In the Freudian view, there seems an inherent conflict between the satisfaction of libidinal drives and the requirements of civilized organization. As Fromm notes, humans seem to face a choice between instinctual satisfaction and barbarism. Sometimes, the balance achieved between these competing principles leads to neurosis, and at other times, to modes of happy adjustment.

The patriarchal family: For discussion of the significance of patriarchy and the patriarchal family, see Bachofen (1968), Engels (1972), Coward (1983), Fromm (1971), Gherardi (1995), and Reich (1968). Mitchell (1974) provides an excellent discussion of the Oedipus complex from a woman's point of view, and Dodson-Gray (1982) has presented an analysis of the links between patriarchy and modern society.

Death and immortality: On the links between death and immortality, see Becker (1973), Freud's *Beyond the Pleasure Principle* (Complete Works, Vol. 18), Lifton and Olson (1975), and Rank (1950). Denhardt (1981) and Schwartz (1985) begin to develop the organizational implications of these views.

Defenses against anxiety: For Melanie Klein's approach to psychoanalysis and object relations, see Klein (1965, 1980, 1981). Her essays "Notes on Some Schizoid Mechanisms" (1980: 1–24) and "Our Adult World and Its Roots in Infancy" (1980: 247–263) are particularly important for the discussion presented in my chapter. Guntrip (1961) presents an excellent introduction to her work. Trist and Murray (1990, 1993) present several applications. Discussions of Bion's theory of leadership and group behavior can be found in Bion (1959) and Pines (1985). Hirschhorn (1991) links Bion's ideas to the management of teams.

Jaques (1955) discusses how social systems act as defenses against anxiety, and Menzies (1960) applies this idea in the analysis of nursing. Chatov (1981) discusses the idea of regulatory sadism. Argyris (1993, 1994), Baum (1987), and Hirschhorn (1988) provide excellent in-depth analyses of the links between organization and unconscious defenses.

Zaleznik's work on power relations, leadership, and the unconscious can be found in Zaleznik (1970), Zaleznik and Kets de Vries (1975). Other interesting perspectives on the psychodynamics of leadership and research studies on how fear, envy, anger, and other impulses are often projected elsewhere can be found in Lowenberg (1972), Eagle and Newton (1981), and Gemmill and Oakley (1992). Kets de Vries and Miller (1984) investigate these issues in detail. The book contains excellent case material and goes a long way toward showing how the influence of the unconscious gives rise to different varieties of organization, lending great support to the idea that it may be possible to develop a "new contingency theory of organization" based on an understanding of unconscious processes.

The theory of transitional objects: The work of Winnicott on transitional objects can be found in Winnicott (1958, 1964, 1971). Harold Bridger of the Tavistock Institute has developed the implications of this for organizational analysis and organizational change. For a discussion, see Bridger (1980, 1981, 1990) and Ambrose and Amado (1995). William Bridges (1991) provides a detailed methodology for managing organizational transitions. He draws his inspiration from a different source, but his method has a great deal in common with Bridges's. What a coincidence! Two of the preeminent contributors to the theory of transition both have *bridge* in their name!

Jung, shadow, and archetypes: The work of Jung on psychoanalysis and the unconscious is, like Freud's, voluminous and wide-ranging. Among the numerous volumes of his *Collected Works,* those on *Psychological Types, Analytical Psychology*, and the *Structure and Dynamics of the Psyche* are most relevant for the ideas discussed in my chapter. Extracts from these works are presented in Jung (1971), which also contains a useful editorial by Joseph Campbell. Good overviews of Jung's most important ideas can be found in Jung (1964, 1967, 1968), Whitmont (1969), and Frey-Rohn (1974). These are especially useful for understanding the Jungian position on archetypes. In particular, Frey-Rohn discusses many definitions of Jung's use of the notion of archetype in a clear way. Neumann (1954), Maccoby (1976), Frye (1957), and Thompson (1971) illustrate the role of archetypes in social life. Bettleheim (1977) analyzes fairy tales. Mitroff and Kilmann (1976) use Jung's psychological types to analyze patterns of reasoning and thought.

Gherardi (1995) discusses the relationship between archetypes, gender, and organization and creates a powerful new perspective on many familiar aspects of organizational life. The relevance of Jung's work for organizational analysis has been explored by Bowles (1990, 1991, 1993), Bradshaw and Newell (1993), Denhardt (1981), Ingalls (1979), Mitroff (1984), and McSwain and White (1982). Zweig and Abrams (1991) provide an excellent discussion of the "shadow" side of human nature and its impact on many aspects of human life.

Hirsch and Andrews (1983) have illustrated how the language of corporate takeovers is often dominated by archetypal visions of rape, conquest, pillage, and romantic union. Smith and Simmons (1983) have shown how the dynamics of a case of organizational change followed the pattern of a fairy tale about Rumplestiltskin.

The idea of viewing the unconscious as a black hole is explored by Delahanty and Gemmill (1982).

Eric Trist's discussion of how workers may leave "badness" in the systems in which they work can be found in Trist (1990).

For collections of readings on the role played by emotions in organizations see Ashkanasy, Hartel, and Zerbe (2000), Hartel et al (2005), and Lord et al. (2002). Lubit (2004) discusses the role of emotional intelligence in dealing with toxic work situations, and Frost (2003) and Whicker (1996) examine toxic leadership and work relationships.

Works by Alford (2001), Ciulla (2000), Miethe (1999), Rayman (2001), and Sennett (1998) address the ethical, moral, and other conflicts that people can experience in maintaining authenticity and integrity in the modern workplace, including the suffering experienced by whistleblowers and the corrosion of character experienced by those forced to conform.

8: The Flux and Transformation Metaphor

This chapter develops a view that, until the past few years, has received little attention in organization theory. It takes its point of departure from the ideas of Heraclitus, which have much in common with the ancient Chinese philosophy of Taoism. Despite Heraclitus's important influence on the evolution of Western science and social thought, his ideas can be understood and read only through secondary sources. Wheelwright (1959) provides an excellent overview.

Implicate and explicate orders and modern realist philosophy: Bohm's analysis of the relations between the implicate and explicate order is presented in Bohm (1980a), Bohm and Peat (1987), and Briggs and Peat

(1984) and in a number of important articles, especially Bohm (1978, 1980b). His idea that the implicate order is an enfolded domain of potentiality has close links with the holographic metaphor discussed in Chapter 4. Bohm uses holonomic and other metaphors to express his point of view.

In appreciating Bohm's theory it is important to realize that he places considerable emphasis on the creativity inherent in the implicate order. Indeed, he has suggested that this realm may be sheer creativity, a set of potentialities that become explicate in a probabilistic way. His theory, like that of Heraclitus, reverses the usual relationship between reality and change. Whereas in science and everyday life we tend to view change as an attribute of reality and see the world changing, Bohm encourages us to understand that the world is itself but a moment in a more fundamental process of change. The word *moment* actually derives from the idea of movement! This perspective has implications for science generally, which, up to now, has confined much of its attention to understanding relations *within* the explicate order. Bohm encourages us to discover the "laws of the whole," which embrace the processes that *produce* the explicate world. The forms realized in the explicate order are permitted a degree of autonomy and self-rule, but are always regarded as dependent on deeper forces within the implicate order for their existence. Under appropriate conditions, certain explicate orders become likely or possible, realizing the logic of the system. This aspect of the theory has much in common with the work of Prigogine (1978, 1984) and Sheldrake (1981).

Bohm's analysis of relations between implicate and explicate orders parallels the distinction drawn in modern realist philosophy by Bhaskar (1978) and Outhwaite (1983) between three domains of reality: the empirical, the actual, and the real. The thrust of their "realist" analysis is to suggest that our reality is shaped by generative mechanisms in the domain of the real and that the domains of the actual and the empirical are in effect realized tendencies that lend specific form to processes in this other domain. This kind of analysis searches for an explanation of the deep structure of social life and provides a means of reinterpreting the role and significance of the unconscious, culture, and other generative social forces. It has a great deal in common with more materialistic theories that stress how society "unfolds" in accordance with some kind of structural logic.

In the present chapter, ideas about chaos, complexity, mutual causality, and dialectical opposition are used as different frameworks for thinking about relations between the implicate and explicate order.

Autopoiesis: The theory of autopoiesis was first developed in Chile in the 1960s and early 1970s by Maturana and Varela. The core works are Maturana and Varela (1980), which provides an excellent though very difficult and technical overview of concepts, and Varela (1979), which applies the theory to biology. Other useful expositions can be found in Varela (1976, 1979, 1984), Varela and Johnson (1976), Geyer and van der Zouwen (1986), Luhmann (1995), Ulrich and Probst (1984), and Zeleny (1980, 1981). Kickert (1993) provides an excellent and highly readable discussion of key concepts with a range of applications.

The theory of autopoiesis has many implications for the analysis of living systems of all kinds, whether biological, cognitive, or social. In the manner of general systems theory, it seeks to unite and transcend discipline boundaries using the simple but remarkably powerful notion that all systems in effect look at themselves and regulate their functioning through a process analogous to thought. It is in this sense that Maturana and Varela can describe living as a process of cognition and view cognition as a biological process. They view the basic cognitive operation as that of making distinctions, as does Spencer-Brown (1969). Maturana and Varela argue that by specifying distinctions we make entities distinct from their background. Because this process can proceed in many possible directions, the notion of a complete system is thus rather arbitrary. Any unity, such as a biological system, can be differentiated into cells, organs, and so forth by drawing further distinctions. Moving in the opposite direction, we can draw distinctions between an individual organism and its background and create differentiations within its background. The whole process of specifying differences (i.e., the process of differentiation) is based upon this simple cognitive process, which is the basis of all form and specifies the organization of a system.

The theory of autopoiesis has been applied to social systems by Geyer and van der Zouwen (2001), Jessop (1990), Luhmann (1995), and Russell and Ison (2004). The ideas developed by Maturana and Varela have much in common with Bateson's (1972, 1979) views on coevolution and the idea that nature thinks and the mind evolves, with Touraine's (1977) work on the self-production of society, and with Weick's (1979, 1995) theory of sense-making and enactment. Similar ideas on the nature of self-referential systems have also been offered in very different contexts by Godel (1962) and Hofstadter (1979, 1983). My own work on the nature of epistemology (Morgan 1983a) also explores a similar theme. The point in my chapter about confusing and mixing the domain of organization with that of explanation is made by Harries-Jones (1984).

Bateson's (1972) analysis of the pathology of conscious purpose points to the lack of recursive awareness in much decision making, and has much in common with the pathologies of egocentric self-imagery discussed in my chapter. Rapoport's (1960) work on fights, games, and debates is important in developing collaborative strategies (also see Hofstadter 1983).

It should be noted that in much of my discussion about organizations as autopoietic systems I have talked about *organizations* maintaining their identity. This is an oversimplification, as, strictly speaking, organizations do not think and act: Organizational members do this, and what we recognize as the organization is a product of their thoughts and actions. When we talk about an organization acting, or sustaining its identity, it would thus be more correct to do so in terms of the key people involved.

Chaos, complexity, and emergent organization: For an excellent overview of ideas about chaos and complexity, see Cowan et al. (1994), Gleick (1987), Kauffman (1991, 1993), Kelly (1994), Langton (1992), Lewin (1992), Richardson et al. (2005), Strogatz (2003), and Waldrop (1992). They provide wonderful illustrations of how metaphors drawn from the natural world, computer simulations, and artificial intelligence are generating new organizing principles. Barabasi (2002) and Watts (1999, 2003) explore the new science of networks and complexity.

For important discussions on the nature of self-organizing systems see Artigliani (1987), Camazine et al. (2001), Jantsch (1980), Jantsch and Waddington (1976), Johnson (2001), Leifer (1989), Prigogine (1978, 1984), and Smith and Gemmill (1991).

In organization and management theory, the work of Ambrose and Amado (1995), Bennet (2004), Bonabeau and Meyer (2001), Eisenhardt and Brown (1998, 1999), Gharajedaghi (1999), Goldstein (1994), Hurst (1995), Kiel (1994), Lewin and Regine (2001), Olson and Eoyang (2001), Shaw (2002), Stacey (1992, 2001), Stacey et al. (2000), Thietart and Forgues (1995), Weick and Sutcliffe (2001), Wheatley (1992), Zimmerman and Hurst (1993), Zimmerman et al. (1998), and Zohar (1997) provides a wide-ranging discussion on how insights from chaos and complexity can be used to enrich our understanding of leadership, strategy, and the management of change. They signal an important new approach to organizing that treats organization as an emergent, self-organizing phenomenon that can never be predicted or controlled. The approach has much in common with our discussion of the emergent nature of intelligence in Chapter 4.

For further discussion on self-organization and the creation of "new contexts" and on how small changes can be used to create large effects see Fullan (1993), Gladwell (2002), Johansson (2004), Morgan (1994), Morgan and Zohar (1995), and work in progress on what I call the "15% approach to change." This can be accessed through the World Wide Web on www.imaginiz.com. For extensive discussion of how individuals and organizations can create new patterns of development by challenging self-identity, and how new metaphors can be used to promote free-flowing forms of self-organization and management through the principle of "minimum specs" see my development of the concept of *imaginization* in Morgan (1993a).

My discussion of organization through the lens of competing "attractors" draws on Goldstein (1994), Kiel (1994), and exchanges through the Chaos Network (Michaels 1996).

Discussion in Chapter 8, and also in Chapter 4, has made much of the emergent nature of hierarchy. Hierarchy is always a feature of complex systems, and as Herbert Simon (1962) has suggested, it is the adaptive form for finite intelligence to assume in the face of complexity. He illustrates this principle with a tale of two watchmakers. Both make good watches, but one is far more successful because instead of assembling the watches piece by piece as if he were building a mosaic, he constructs his watches by forming subassemblies of about ten parts each, which can then be joined with other subassemblies to create subsystems of a higher order. These can then be assembled to form the complete watch.

Simon uses the parable to illustrate the importance of hierarchy, and to argue that systems will evolve much more rapidly if there are stable intermediate forms. Cybernetician W. Ross Ashby has made the similar point that no complex adaptive system can succeed in achieving a steady state in a reasonable period of time unless the process can occur subsystem by subsystem, each subsystem being relatively independent of the others.

If we limit our discussion to the level of complexity implied in Simon's tale of the watchmakers, which in essence addresses the operation of a mechanical system subject to frequent interruption from the broader environment, hierarchy is something that *can* be engineered and predesigned. Indeed, if one knows enough about the nature of the interruptions, optimal management strategies can be produced to ensure peak performance.

But if we address the problem of managing systems of greater complexity, where goals and required activities are far less clear, or people and situations are linked by numerous nonlinear feedback loops creating ambiguity and turbulence, such design strategies cannot work. Managers and systems designers find it impossible to predict, design, and control all relevant activities. Under such conditions, principles of emergent self-organization have to become the norm. These are likely to result in hierarchical arrangements, because if activities are completely random, as Ashby's point suggests, complex tasks will take an almost infinite amount of time to complete. But the hierarchical pattern has to *emerge*. It cannot be imposed. This is a key idea of the new management thought.

Mutual causality: The second cybernetics: A discussion of the theory of mutual causality is presented by Maruyama (1963) and Buckley (1967). Maruyama's discussion of "the second cybernetics" is of crucial importance in allowing cybernetic theory to break free of the steady-state models that dominated early development of the discipline. Useful applications of his theory are found in Maruyama (1982) and Weick (1979) and in the journal *Cybernetics and Human Knowing*, which is devoted to research on the second cybernetics and autopoiesis. Also see Forester's (1961) work on the dynamics of global systems. The Club of Rome's report *The Limits to Growth* is authored by Meadows et al. (1972) and contains the tale of the Persian courtier. Maruyama's analysis of runaway systems in nature, such as the crack that collects water and the development of a homogeneous plain, is taken from Maruyama (1963).

Peter Senge's development of this type of thinking and his discussion of system archetypes is presented in Senge (1990). For a full discussion of the "Tragedy of the Commons" syndrome, see Hardin (1968).

An analysis of the schismatic properties of social systems in which positive feedback relations transform and often destroy existing relations can be found in Bateson (1936, 1972) and in Morgan (1981).

Systemic wisdom: Bateson's discussion of the epistemology of systemic wisdom can be found in Bateson (1972). Also, see Harries-Jones (1995). Vickers (1965, 1972) develops a related notion through his concept of "appreciation." Gadalla and Cooper (1978) and Morgan (1982, 1983c) apply these notions in developing new epistemologies for management and corporate strategy. Wilden (1972) presents a difficult theoretical discussion of issues related to the epistemology of systemic wisdom. He has a neat way of summarizing one of the important implications of mutual causality through the idea that causes cause causes to cause causes. Weick (1979) provides good illustrations of how social systems can be managed through the modification of feedback loops. Interest in systemic wisdom has now become a major focus of the business sustainability movement since the publication of the Brundtland report (1987). See, for example, Doppelt (2003), Hart and Milstein (2003), and McDonough and Braungart (2002).

Dialectics and Marxian analysis: Most books on Eastern philosophy provide good discussions of Taoism. The *I Ching* and the *Chuang-Tzu* make interesting reading. Capra (1975, 1982) also provides an excellent discussion of Eastern philosophy and its links with modern science.

The concept of dialectics has made a contribution to a wide variety of social thought. Recall, for example, Jung's use of the "unity of opposites" discussed in Chapter 7. Extensive discussions of the Hegelian approach to dialectics can be found in Hegel (1892, 1929), Findlay (1958), Kaufman (1965), McLellan (1973), and Wetter (1958).

Marx's description of his own use of the dialectic can be found in the postface to the second edition of *Das Kapital*, although he does not devote any extensive description to the nature of the method, preferring to illustrate its use in practice. Ernest Mandel's introduction to Volume 1 of Marx's *Das Kapital* (Marx 1976) also provides an informative discussion. Marx's dialectical method has been subjected to a wide range of interpretation (see, e.g., Althusser 1969; Colletti 1975a, 1975b; Engels 1873, 1876, 1886; Godelier 1972; Lefebvre 1968a, 1968b; Lenin 1936; Plekhanov 1961; Markovic 1974; Meszaros 1972; Novack 1966; Wetter 1958). Marx's friend Frederick Engels for a long time stood as the authoritative source of interpretation of the Marxist dialectic. Apart from rival interpretations provided by Lenin (1936) and Lukacs (1971), which sought to recognize and revive the importance of the Hegelian influence on Marx, it is only recently that the overly deterministic trend set in motion by Engels has begun to be reversed. With Engels, Marx's dialectical method was characterized as dialectical materialism and eventually presented as being equivalent to a historical materialism in which the laws of society are equivalent to the laws of nature. In the view of many, Engels's work has done a disservice to the development of Marxist theory, lending it a much more deterministic flavor than Marx probably intended.

An interesting perspective can be gained on the varieties of Marxism and other radical social theories by focusing on the various elements of the dialectic presented in Exhibit 8.9. Very often, these different aspects of the dialectic are developed in a somewhat isolated and extreme form. As discussed in my chapter, Marx's own work emphasizes their interconnection, explaining how the struggle of opposites (principle 1) sets the basis for change, which, through the negation of the negation (principle 2), becomes evolutionary, until the intensity or quantity of change precipitates a qualitative change in the system as a whole (principle 3). Developed separately, these three dialectical principles give rise to (a) theories focusing on change through contradiction (principle 1; e.g., Allen 1975; Godelier 1972); (b) anarchistic theories that *celebrate* the act of negation (principle 2) and its creative potential (e.g., Bakunin 1950, 1964; Stirner 1963 and the philosophy of Mao Tse Tung's "Cultural Revolution" in China); and (c) revolutionary or catastrophic theories that focus on the inevitability of revolutionary change (principle 3), often to understand how revolution can best be brought about, as in varieties of revolutionary Marxism (Bukharin 1962, 1972). Yet another branch of radical thought focuses on documenting the opposition inherent in the dialectic, building on a theme of domination to be examined in Chapter 9.

In addition to consulting *Capital* itself, especially Volume 1, the reader interested in obtaining a grip on Marxian economics should consult Mandel (1962) and analyses of the contradictions of capitalism offered by Godelier (1972), Baran and Sweezy (1966), Benson and Jenkins (1978), Glyn and Sutcliffe (1972), Habermas (1973), Holloway and Picciotto

(1978), O'Connor (1973), and Offe (1974a, 1975, 1976). Mandel (1962) provides an excellent analysis of the concept of surplus value and of the contradictions that arise from the quest for surplus value.

Mandel's discussion of the links between wealth and theft is in Mandel (1962: 83–88). Marx's explanation of how capitalism helps to create its demise by organizing the working class as a by-product of its organization of production is in *Das Kapital* (Vol. 1, chap. 32).

Good illustrations of the dialectical mode of organizational analysis can be found in the work of Allen (1975), Benson (1983), Braverman (1974), and Heydebrand (1977, 1983). Such works show how we can begin to understand how dialectical contradictions lie at the source of recurrent crises in the modern world and how we can begin to deal with them. As suggested in Chapter 8, the reach and implications of this kind of dialectical analysis are very broad. As we examine the sweep of industrial development in terms of tensions between unfolding opposites, we see how the growing industrialization and urbanization of the nineteenth century in effect produced the unionized and militant labor force that then began to shape future industrial development. We can see how the dehumanization of work that accompanied industrialization produced the human-relations movement. We can see how the success and power of unions produced the internationalization of the labor force and the substitution of robots for labor. We can see how the success of these strategies in reducing costs of production produces unemployment in Western countries that removes the primary markets for which the products are manufactured. We can see how unemployment and the need to sustain consumption produces the welfare state, which, because it consumes surplus value, has to live off surplus value produced elsewhere, creating fiscal and other crises, which reverberate in their effects throughout society. We can see how the wealth of the advanced countries produces the poverty and industrialized ghettos of the Third World. We can see how the pressure of industry in the Third World produces the demise of local agriculture as people leave the land to move to urban areas. We can see how the prosperity of the West may produce its own downfall with the rise of a Third World working class capable of taking ownership of the local means of production used in creating that prosperity. We can see how humans' attempts to master nature can turn back on human beings as problems of pollution, resource depletion, and general degradations of the environment that threaten to dominate humans themselves.

In all these illustrations we are not talking about linear processes where As cause Bs. Rather, we are looking at self-generating oppositions where one side of the phenomenon tends to produce the existence of the other.

Thus industrialization tends to produce unionization as a force opposing the process of industrialization. Wealth tends to produce poverty, which produces forces that undermine wealth. All phenomena generate latent tendencies and contradictions that tend to change themselves. Our habit of "thinking in lines" tends to hamper our ability to think dialectically. We thus fail to appreciate how the seeds of the future are always enfolded in the oppositions shaping the present.

A dialectical imagination invites us to embrace contradiction and flux as defining features of reality. As with the theory of mutual causality, this leads us to think in terms of loops, but loops of a special kind in which we recognize that every action has a tendency to produce a movement in the opposite direction. As suggested in Chapter 8, this has important consequences for the way we organize in all spheres of life, encouraging us to recognize that the parameters of organization define the rallying points for disorganization, that control always generates forces of counter-control, and that every success is the basis for a potential downfall.

As noted in Chapter 8, in this kind of dialectical analysis it is important to consider which tensions and oppositions are primary and which are subsidiary, since oppositions tend to arise within oppositions, creating patterns of change where the importance of the primary opposition may be masked by a variety of more superficial differences. The successful analysis of change, and of the dispositions and tendencies inherent in the present, thus requires that we come to grips with the basic forces shaping organization and society. If Marx's analysis is correct, we may well find that these lie in the structures through which we produce and sustain our material conditions of existence (i.e., in our economics and the basic logic of capitalism).

The dialectics of management: Managing paradox: Returning to a management level, the importance of studying the role of paradox has been pioneered by writers such as Hampden-Turner (1990a, 1990b), Hennestad (1990), Kets de Vries (1980), Pascale (1990), McWhinney (1992), Quinn (1988), Quinn and Cameron (1988), and Smith and Berg (1987). They provide ways of thinking about the management of competing tensions and of how paradoxes can often be reframed through creative insights. Clegg (2002), Fletcher and Olwyler (1997), Johnson (1992), McKenzie (1996), and Streatfield (2001) offer valuable guidelines on how managers can deal with the polarities involved. My own work Morgan (1994) links the management of paradox to the principle of using small changes to create large effects.

Lewin's analysis of "force fields" shaped by "driving" and "restraining" forces can be found in Lewin (1951). Goldstein (1994) provides a valuable critique of Lewin's work within the context of chaos theory.

McWhinney (1992) presents an outstanding analysis of the dialectical nature of change and the many levels on which contradictions can unfold.

Innovations as "creative destruction": Joseph Schumpeter (1934, 1942) has pioneered the idea of dialectical change as a process of "creative destruction." For example, his work on the role of entrepreneurs shows how their innovations in effect destroy the old order into which they are introduced. As noted in Chapter 8, management writers like d'Aveni (1994) who advocate creative destruction as a strategic weapon run the risk of overemphasizing the destructive side. Dialectical analysis shows that destruction is a natural consequence of change. But it is more of a *side effect* than an intention. When destruction becomes the aim, we move into a completely new reality that has much more in common with forms of destructive anarchism that can generate many negative consequences from a societal standpoint. Hurst (1995) warns against some of the dangers here, encouraging a form of "ethical anarchy." Also, see Eric Trist's view of organizational ecology, discussed in Chapter 3, and Hart's (2005) and Hart and Milstein's (1999) analysis of the positive benefits of creative destruction as a source of major innovation and value creation in the new world economy. This stands as a counterpoint to destructive anarchy.

Adam Smith's view of the "invisible hand" is found in Smith (1776). For new global business competition models see Hagel and Brown (2005), Kim and Mauborgne (2005), and Luo (2004).

9: The Domination Metaphor

Reports on domination in the corporate world, especially with regard to how organizations often have a negative impact on human beings and the environment, appear regularly in most newspapers and current affairs magazines. The "ugly face" has become headline news since the gross scandals and corporate exploitation revealed at Enron, WorldCom, and other major corporations (see, for example, Rowland, 2005). The illustrations presented at the beginning of this chapter are drawn from the following sources: Zwerdling (1971) discusses the topic of food pollution; the data on pollution in the Great Lakes Basin are drawn from local data sources and figures presented at professional conferences; the data on health hazards at work are drawn from annual reports of the International Labor Organization; and data on the relationship between multinationals and the Third World are provided by Hayter (1981) and the journal *New Solutions*. The latter provides an extensive critique of the activities of modern organizations across a range of important topics. Numerous other references on these issues are presented in later sections of the notes on this chapter.

Domination in history: It is instructive to analyze the origins of organizations in ancient society and, in particular, to understand how the rise of organization is associated with the generation of economic surplus and accompanied by a more general process of social stratification. From the earliest times there seems to be a relationship between organization and domination in the form of class rule. See, for example, the analyses of ancient and prehistoric societies offered by Childe (1946), Kautsky (1982), Wittfogel (1957), and Sahlins (1972). Diamond (2005) presents the thesis that the long-term viability of civilizations depends on the environmental effects of the choices made in pursuit of economic activities. My data on the building of the Great Pyramid at Giza are taken from the *Encyclopedia Britannica*. George (1972) also offers useful discussions of the forms of organization used in ancient society and an overview of the evolution of management practice to the present day.

It is fascinating to observe how the development of organization occurs alongside the development of slavery or the control of one group or class by another and with the development of military power. The mode of organization employed often varied. For example, slaves were not extensively used in purely agricultural societies in ancient days because of the communal nature of agriculture and the difficulty of enforcing people to take the great care required in the cultivation process. Their main use was in the context of domestic work, workshops, mines, and building, where effective systems of supervision could be most easily developed. From the earliest of times, therefore, the contingency idea that different types of organization and management are required in different circumstances has been well understood. As is argued in my chapter, the evolution of modern society has been accompanied by changes in the mode of domination employed, there being a shift away from the use of raw exploitation to what Max Weber would describe as more subtle forms of domination. An appreciation of the historical process through which this has occurred is thus very instructive for understanding organizations in the present day.

Weber, Michels, and Marx—founders of radical organization theory: Max Weber's analysis of the links between organization and social domination is found throughout his extensive writings, notably in Weber (1946, 1947, 1949, 1961, 1968). McNeil (1978), Mouzelis (1979), and Salaman (1978) present excellent discussions of this aspect of his work with a focus on the problem of understanding modern organizations. Weber was very much aware of the intimate connection between the development of bureaucratization and the role of the state in society, and he has provided an excellent basis for understanding the growth of "corporatism" in capitalist and noncapitalist societies. Important discussions of these ideas and other post-Weberian developments are found in Miliband (1973) and Benson (1975). In viewing the role of the state as an aspect of a wider process of domination in society, the work of Weber has much affinity with that of Marx, and many organization theorists have contributed useful insights by exploring this interface. Burrell and Morgan (1979) provide an extensive discussion of this in their analysis of their "radical structuralist paradigm."

Weber's views on bureaucracy as an iron cage are in Weber (1946:228). Robert Michels's views on the iron law of oligarchy are in Michels (1949). Perrow (1979) provides an excellent discussion of the way organizations engage in strategies of domination both internally and in relation to their environment.

For a discussion of Marx's analysis of how domination is embedded in the quest for surplus value, see my discussion in Chapter 8 and the references provided in the bibliographical notes to that chapter. On the links between the work of Marx and Weber, see Burrell and Morgan (1979) and Salaman (1978).

For a discussion of how society can be understood as having moved beyond capitalism into a knowledge economy and all the transformations this entails in terms of organizational and global relations, see the wonderful analysis offered by Peter Drucker (1993, 2001) in terms of his vision of postcapitalist society. Mokyr (2002) and Thurow (1999) are among many who have written about the knowledge economy.

For a discussion of how "institutional theorists" see the process of social control and domination, see Scott and Christensen (1995), DiMaggio and Powell (1991), and Tolbert and Zucker (1996).

Organization, class, and control: Most modern discussions of the relationship between organization, class, and control draw on Weberian or Marxist theories in one way or another (see, e.g., Clegg and Dunkerley 1980; Clegg 1981; Salaman 1979, 1981). My discussion of the evolution of the working class in Great Britain draws on Thompson (1968) and of the evolution of wage labor in the United States on Gordon, Edwards, and Reich (1982) and Edwards, Reich, and Weisskopf (1986). For a discussion of the process of de-skilling and the degradation of work, see Braverman (1974) and Wood (1982). Gordon et al. (1982) present an excellent discussion of the proletarianization of the workforce in the United States, and Blackburn and Mann (1979) provide an excellent analysis of the role of the working class in the labor market in Great Britain. The figures quoted in my chapter on the number of manual workers that exercise less skill in their jobs than in driving to work and the extent to which there is an interchangeability of skills in the workplace are derived from this source.

For a discussion of ideas on the dual nature of primary and secondary labor markets, see Berger and Piore (1980), Piore (1979), and Gordon et al. (1982). For a discussion of the segmentation of labor markets, see Gordon et al. (1982), Edwards et al. (1975), Edwards (1979), Williamson (1981), and Friedman (1977). Friedman (1977) and Edwards (1979) are particularly useful in illustrating the different strategies of managerial control relating to different labor markets. Ackers and Wilkinson (2003), Bridges (1994), Firebaugh (2003), Freeman (2005), Hartman, et al. (2003), Heckscher et al. (2003), Howell (2005), Howells and Wood (1993), Levy and Murnane (2004), Rifkin (1995), and Shostak (1996) provide excellent overviews of issues relating to how developments in advanced capitalism are leading to a restructuring of work, jobs, and labor markets.

For historical and contemporary perspectives on the role of migrant workers and the globalization of the labor force in the modern economy, see Berger and Mohr (1975), Bharati (2004), Castles and Kosack (1973), Castles and Miller (2003), Hepple (2002), Piore (1979), Power and Hardman (1978), and Zimmerman (2002). Barley and Kunda (2004) provide an interesting perspective on the new itinerant knowledge worker. Friedman (2005) and Prestowitz (2005) speculate on the challenge to the west presented by the economic rise of developing countries such as India and China. Sharpe (2001) and Ehrenreich and Hochschild (2003) discuss the migration of women from developing countries to take up domestic and sex trade positions in wealthy nations. Schmitz, et al. (2004) describe child labor from a global perspective.

Other discussions of the links between capitalism and domination in the labor process are found in Goldman and Van Houten (1977), Gorz (1985), Marglin (1976), Buroway (1979), Knights, Willmott, and Collinson (1985), and Knights and Willmott (1989). The analysis of Marglin (1976) and O'Connor (1973) also provide useful political-economic explanations of contemporary organizational structure and the division of labor. Salaman (1979) provides a useful analysis of how the labor process can be seen as a process of domination and focuses on the resistance presented by the workforce. Foucault (1979a, 1979b) presents a useful analysis of the history of control, tracing links between the school, the army, the prison, and the factory. Perrow (1979) provides a discussion of the role of unobtrusive controls in organization, and Friedman (1977) provides a good discussion of how organizations often attempt to control their employees in the primary labor market through systems of "responsible autonomy." Lash and Urry (1987) and Sullivan (2002) provide an excellent analysis of the changing nature of capitalism and the shift to flexible as opposed to "organized" forms of control.

Hazardous work: Marx's vivid account of the horrors of early capitalism is found in *Das Kapital* (chap. 10). All my quotes are taken from this source. There is a growing literature on the hazards of modern work situations. See, for example, Ashford (1976), Berman (1978), Dear (1995), Epstein (1978), Follman (1978), Frost et al. (1992), Navarro and Berman (1983), Nelkin and Brown (1984), Pauchant and Mitroff (1992), Reasons et al. (1981), Sayles and Strauss (1981), Scott (1974), Tataryn (1979), Viscusi (1983), and Wright (1973). My data are drawn from these sources and the original reports cited therein. Details on the asbestos "cover-up" are found in Reasons et al. (1981). The problems of asbestos production in the Third World are discussed in Navarro and Berman (1983).

My data on occupational accidents and diseases are confined to the United States and Canada, as international comparisons are extremely misleading. The scope and coverage of these kinds of statistics vary considerably from one country to another and between industries within any given country. Even the basic concept of the recordable occupational injury varies. Comparisons with Third World countries are particularly difficult because the available statistics are unreliable. They are generally produced as a by-product of administrative work processes and regulations, and are often uncoordinated with regard to the requirements of occupational health and safety. Anyone wishing to examine these statistics further is referred to the *International Labour Organization Statistical Year Book*. This produces the best statistics that are available and also gives a good guide to some of the qualifications that need to be made in interpretation.

For an overview of the literature relating to occupational sources of stress and related illness, see Burke and Weir (1980), Cooper (2000), Cooper and Marshall (1976), Cooper and Payne (1980), Dear (1995), Peterson (2003), and Wainwright (2002). For a discussion of the problems relating to workaholism, see Oates (1971), Machlowitz (1978), and Feinberg and Dempewolf (1980). Frost et al. (1992) present a useful collection of readings relating to this area of work. Frost (2003) addresses workplace toxicity and its effects on workers. Gleick (1999) discusses "hurry sickness," a condition caused by the proliferation of technology and media. Cascio (2002) discusses the consequences of uncertain workplace environments due to downsizing, restructuring, and outsourcing. Menzies (1996) presents an excellent analysis of the impact of information technology from a radical perspective.

The radical frame of reference: As discussed in Chapter 6, the concept of the radical frame of reference as a description of organizational reality and as an ideology for guiding organizational practice derives from the work of Fox (1974). Much of the best literature on this topic is British, for it is in Great Britain that the battle lines between management and workers have often been most clearly drawn. For an illustration of workers' perspectives on the logic of the profit motive and alternatives and its relevance for understanding the loss of jobs, industrial decline, and the need for industrial revitalization, see Bryer, Brignall, and Maunders (1982), Levie and Lorentzen (1984), Massey and Meegan (1982), and the results of the workers' inquiry conducted by the Trades Councils of Coventry, Liverpool, Newcastle, and North Tyneside (1980). As part of the radical response to managerial control, many unions have attempted to develop alternative plans and alternative work systems. See, for example, Coates (1978, 1981a, 1981b) and Wainwright and Elliott (1982). For a discussion of related economic strategies, see Holland (1975) and Hughes (1981). Many radical interpretations of the nature of the labor process are available on both sides of the Atlantic. For example, see Braverman (1974), Gorz (1985), Hyman (1975), and Levidon and Young (1981). On "brutal" American management methods, see Eberle (1996).

Multinationals: The literature on the activities of multinational corporations is now voluminous. The United Nations and Stopford et al. publish many valuable statistics on a regular basis. My data relating to the current size of multinational corporations are drawn from *Fortune* magazine and United Nations reports on transnational corporations in world development.

As is evident from the debate presented in my chapter, different writers on the multinationals tend to present different perspectives on their operation, according to whether they are advocates or critics. A good historical and all-round view can be achieved by consulting some of the following works: Bartlett and Ghoshal (1989), Beneria (2004), Bhagwati (2004), Birkinshaw et al. (2003), Brandt (1980), Brooke and Remmers (1970), Campbell (1995), Casson (1983), Ferguson (2004), Friedman (1999), Gilpin and Gilpin (2000), Goldberg and Negandhi (1983), Grunberg (1981), Gunnermann (1975), Hirst and Thompson (1994), Kujawa (1975), Lall (1983), Mansell (1994), Medwar and Freese (1982), Mirow and Maurer (1982), Ohmae (1993), Stiglitz (2003), Tavis (1982), Thomas (1979), Servan-Schreiber (1968), Wilczynski (1976), and Wolf (2004). Sampson (1978) provides an excellent analysis of the international operations of ITT and has interesting information on other organizations as well. My data on industrial concentration are taken from the U.S. Conglomerate Hearings and from the 1985 Statistical Abstract of the U.S. Department of Commerce (also see Mizruchi 1982).

To sample the power of contemporary criticisms, especially in the wake of the corporate scandals that opened the 21st century, see Cavanaugh and Mander (2003), Klein (1999), Rowland (2005) and Young and Scott (2004). The dominant theme is that large corporations under the control of small elites who wield major power have a propensity for bullying and greed in pursuit of raw self interest. Bakan (2004) examines the dysfunctional and what he describes as the "psychopathic" character of the modern corporation. Many believe that the problems are systemic—intrinsic to the economic logic of self-interest and externalization of social costs that drives so much corporate development and growth. The film "The Corporation," based on Bakan's book, provides a graphic exposition of its exploitative character across many dimensions.

Sampson (1978) provides a classic early analysis of the abuse of power in the international operations of the former ITT and is the source of material presented in my ITT discussion.

Beneria (2004), Birkinshaw, et al. (2003), Campbell (1995), Emmott (2003), Ferguson (2004), Gilpin and Gilpin (2000), Goldberg and Negandhi (1983), Grunberg (1981), and Gunnermann (1975) present interesting statistics and case studies on the role of multinationals as world powers. Mirow and Maurer (1982) present excellent case studies of the role of cartels in the world economy. Brooke and Remmers (1970) provide a useful discussion of the strategies adopted by multinationals in dealing with their environment. Boggs (2001), Korton (2001), and Nace (2003) discuss the growing influence of corporations on politics. Balanyá et al. (2003) discuss how multinational corporations have shaped EU policies.

Good critical accounts of how the multinationals have exploited the world economy can be found in Hayter (1981), George (1976), and Bello et al. (1982). Hayter (1981) is particularly useful in presenting numerous pieces of data and case studies and is the source of many of the statistics that I have presented on the international operations of multinational corporations. The influential Brandt report (1980) has also provided a valuable source of data. Works by Davis (2002) and Schneider and McCumber (2004) describe cases of industrial pollution in America. Gonzalez (2001), Gunningham et al. (2003), and Markowitz and Rosner (2003) discuss the influence of corporations on American environmental policy. Newton (2005) discusses ethical environmental issues for business. Lang and Heasman (2004) discuss the multinational aspects of control over the world's food supply and examine the role of corporations. As an example of corporate excess, Brownell and Horgen (2004) and Nestle (2003) present their view of how the food industry is contributing to health problems in America. Giroux (2000) explains corporate influence on youth culture. Lafeber (2002) shows how multinationals influence the world's consumer preferences by using the example of Nike.

For an excellent critical discussion of how decision making in large corporations can have major negative impacts on whole communities, see the analysis of the cutbacks in the British steel industry presented by Bryer et al. (1982) and the case studies on profit-oriented divestment decisions presented by Grunberg (1981).

Alfred Chandler's discussion of how the visible hand of management has replaced the invisible hand that Adam Smith saw guiding competitive market economies is found in Chandler (1977).

For Kenichi Ohmae's discussion of "Triads," see Ohmae (1985).

On a positive but also cautious and at times pessimistic note, many analysts of the modern corporation argue that major transformation is inevitable because current practice is inherently unsustainable due to the destructive global, social, economic, and environmental effects that have been created. Present paths cannot continue because they are paths to extinction of so many aspects of life as we know it—environmentally and socially. Stimulated by the Brundtland report (Brundtland, 1987), a strong sustainability movement has emerged seeking to reinvent corporate practice through a balanced focus on economic, social, and environmental development in a way that embraces the developing world. See, for example, Hart (2005), Hawken (1994), Hawken et al. (1999), Hoffman and Bazerman (2005), Wheeler and Sillanpaa (1997), and the bibliographical notes on Chapter 8 for further details.

10: The Challenge of Metaphor

Intellectually, this chapter owes much to the work of social scientists such as Gregory Bateson (1972, 1979), Thomas Kuhn (1970), Donald Schön (1963, 1979), Geoffrey Vickers (1965, 1972), Watzlawick et al. (1974), and other contributors to our understanding of the art of framing and reframing.

As Richard Boland (1989) has observed, in an excellent review of the first edition of *Images of Organization*, the approach developed here has a good deal in common with the hermeneutic approach to social analysis that views social life as a "text" that has to be interpreted and "read." Taking the domain of organization theory as a reference point, it shows how we can open the way to different modes of understanding by using different metaphors to bring organizations into focus in different ways. Each metaphor opens a horizon of understanding and enacts a particular view of organizational reality. Just as Wittgenstein (1958) has shown that language is a social *activity*, I view metaphor as an active, constitutive force that leads us to enact the world in a particular manner. My view of metaphor as a way of being and acting in the world gives it an *active* quality. Metaphor *makes* meaning. It is in this sense that I regard the process of "reading" organizational life as embracing the idea of "authoring," an issue pursued in Chapter 11. Observation is never neutral. It is always an active, constitutive force.

The general view of knowledge underpinning this book has a great deal in common with ideas underlying scientist Neils Bohr's (1958) "principle of complementary" and Werner Heinensberg's (1958b) "uncertainty principle." They emphasize how we need different modes of explanation that, while excluding each other, add to the richness and depth of understanding. The implications of this position for studying organization is explored in depth in Morgan (1983a, 1996).

Einstein's views of the relationship between theory and observation and information on the study of light as wave and particle are presented in Heisenberg (1971). Berkeley's view of objectivity can be found in Berkeley (1910).

11: Reading and Shaping Organizational Life

The method offered in this chapter is one that has been developed through my action research and action learning projects and is explained and illustrated in detail in my book *Imaginization: The Art of Creative Management* (1993a).

For a discussion of other schemes using the ideas of framing and reframing as a basis for organization analysis, see the "soft systems methodology" developed by Peter Checkland (Checkland and Scholes 1990) and the reframing methodology of Bolman and Deal (1991). All these approaches have a great deal in common with Schön's (1983) aim of developing the skills of reflective practice.

As noted above, my view of "reading" situations implies the idea of "authoring," and I am in full agreement with Shotter (1990), who suggests that we must avoid any suggestion that managers are just *passive* readers of their organizations. The concept of "reading organization" is a metaphor and has both strengths and limitations. It should be interpreted and used in a way that enhances the strengths and overcomes the limitations. Hence, as in every chapter of this book, discussion in Chapter 11 has stretched the metaphor, for example, by suggesting that effective "readers" need to develop well-tuned "radar" systems that can draw attention toward significant aspects of the situation that they are "reading." I like the radar metaphor because it emphasizes how it is necessary for managers to be able to pick up a wide range of signals. This is what the use of metaphor allows us to do. The eight broad frames explored in Chapters 2 through 9 create an excellent range of sensitivity, and they can be supplemented by other frames that you find useful.

Although I have not developed the idea in this book, I also find it helpful to view the reading process as a kind of "two-way conversation," whereby the reader brings his or her views to a situation, and also recognizes that the situation may have a "view or opinion of its own" (see Morgan 1983a, 1986, 1993a). The challenge is to learn from the creative tension that this kind of "conversation" can produce. The process is paralleled in the case presented in Chapter 11 where I encourage "readers" to explore and integrate the insights of competing metaphors.

Given the discussion in Chapter 11 and what has been said above, it is clear that the methodology for understanding organization developed in this book is *not* a regimented approach where we have to apply all metaphorical frameworks to all situations. The aim is *not* to advocate viewing organizations as machines, organisms, brains, or cultures in any mechanistic fashion. Rather, the aim is to use understanding of metaphor to create a sensitivity for the competing dimensions of a situation, so that we can proceed with our interpretations in a flexible manner, as illustrated in Chapter 11. The methodology is discussed and illustrated in detail in Morgan (1993a). Any person trying to apply every metaphor to every situation in a formal or mechanized way will get overwhelmed by the complexity.

The approach needs to be used much more flexibly, in a way that combines analytical and intuitive insights. Interestingly, an openness to metaphor and familiarity with frames such as those presented in Chapters 2 through 9 can help us develop and have much more confidence in intuitive insights, and it can help us to tap the latent potentials of a situation.

As discussed in Chapter 11, my position as to what constitutes an effective "reading" of a situation builds on a pragmatic, as opposed to an objective, view of truth that is rooted in the aims and objectives of the "reader" (Morgan 1983a). This is a natural consequence of any position that places humans—whether scientists or individuals in everyday life— as *interpreters* and *creators* of an "objective reality," rather than neutral objective observer. In line with the excellent work of Kenneth Gergen, the position in Chapter 11 also views knowledge as a generative force that is capable of creating new potentials. As Gergen suggests, insights and knowledge that challenge taken-for-granted assumptions extend human potential and create important new action possibilities. This is exactly the position through which the process of "reading" and "authoring" organizational life needs to be approached. A "reading" that grasps key dimensions of a situation in a way that challenges existing assumptions can open new avenues for effective action. Metaphor offers a particularly powerful way of doing this because it encourages us to stretch and challenge existing frames of reference. In this way, my use of metaphor and the process of "reading" and "authoring" situations helps to create a *praxis* linking theory and action in a new way.

Those familiar with what is now being called "postmodernism" will note how the overall style and message of *Images of Organization* has a distinctly postmodern flavor. Postmodernism thrives on paradox and the relativism of competing points of view. It emphasizes how in opening horizons and perspectives we also close others, and how the attempt to gain particular kinds of insights or "truths" inevitably leads to distortions.

Images of Organization puts these ideas into practice. It develops a mode of interpretation sensitive to biases and distortions, while pushing ultimate responsibility for all acts of interpretation back on *you*, the reader, which is the only place that it can really rest.

We see this postmodern flavor in both the style and content of the book. Its premise is that reality is simultaneously subjective and objective. We *engage* objective realities subjectively. We put ourselves into what we "see" in a way that actually *influences* what we see! The book also recognizes how metaphor creates insight through distortion. Also, every chapter in effect deconstructs itself in that successive chapters offer compelling yet competing points of view, each of which is recognized as having both strengths and limitations. Even in Chapter 11 where the aim is to integrate the ideas within a management methodology, emphasis is placed on the inevitable biases that arise in use. The standpoints of the manager-consultant and critic-policy analyst used to illustrate the approach in practice symbolize the relativism involved there, and how effective readings inevitably have a political dimension because, in serving a point of view, they privilege certain insights, interpretations, and actions over others. The concept of "reading organization" is also recognized as inherently limited, and critiqued, in these notes, through other metaphors emphasizing the importance of authorship, "radar," and the open-ended "conversation" with situations we are seeking to understand.

The aim of *Images of Organization* is to create a postmodern approach to understanding the paradoxes, ambiguities, and competing dimensions of our postmodern world.

12: Postscript

One of the major paradoxes facing modern managers is that they need to combine a high tolerance of ambiguity and openness to competing views with the need to create a "closure" that allows them to go forward in a positive way. While the professional post-modernist can relish the relativism of competing perspectives, the manager has to go one step further and *act* in the midst of all this uncertainly.

The perspective offered in this book, especially the methodology offered in Chapter 11, shows how this can be done. The key is to find ways of generating and prioritizing different metaphorical frames so that a range of insights can be integrated, albeit in a dominant or supporting role.

This, of course, is a key problem that I have had to deal with in writing this book. In principle, there are few limits to the metaphors that could have been considered, and I have also had to prioritize certain metaphors over others.

For example, I regard gender as a major force in all aspects of organization and have discussed its role in Chapters, 5, 6, and 7. But I have not written a chapter on "Organization as Gender." I have featured ecological thinking in Chapters 3, 4, and 8. But I have not written a chapter on "Organizations as Ecologies."

You the reader will face similar challenges as you seek to deal with the perspectives presented. For example, if your interests favor the development of "learning organizations" you may feel that the brain metaphor should be prioritized and argue that the insights of the culture, political, organismic, psychic prison, and other metaphors be mobilized within this frame. Or, if you are a political theorist, you may wish to prioritize "politics" or "domination" and see other metaphors as filling in the details.

This is as it should be, and underscores how there are many different ways to achieve closure and many different frames that may be worthy of attention. Valuable insights can be achieved by viewing organizations through the lens of gender, race, ecology, theater, games, market forces, and many other images that may come to mind.

This is why I believe it is important to see the task of understanding and shaping organization as a process of *imaginization* (Morgan 1993a). As suggested in the Postscript, the concept allows us to approach a range of issues in an open and creative manner.

While recognizing that this approach is ideally suited for the demands of an electronic age, as Boland (1989) and others have suggested, it is also important to recognize that this flies straight in the face of both power and convention. Historically, mechanistic and organismic metaphors have dominated the study and practice of organization and management. It remains to be seen whether the new context and demands of the twenty-first century will transform this.

For Heisenberg's views on scientific understanding, see Heisenberg (1971). For Lewin's view on theory and practice, see Lewin (1951).

Bibliography

Aaltio, I. and A. J. Mills (eds.) *Gender, Identity and the Culture of Organizations.* London: Routledge, 2002.

Abeglen, J. G. *The Japanese Factory.* Glencoe, IL: Free Press, 1974.

Abraham, K. *Selected Papers.* London: Hogarth Press, 1927.

Ackers, P. and A. Wilkinson. *Understanding Work and Employment: Industrial Relations in Transition.* Oxford, UK: Oxford University Press, 2003.

Ackoff, R. L. *Re-creating the Corporation: A Design of Organizations for the 21st Century.* New York: Oxford University Press, 1999.

Ackoff, R. L. and F. E. Emery. *On Purposeful Systems.* Chicago: Aldine, 1972.

Adams, J. and G. Morgan "Second Generation" e-Learning: Characteristics and Design Principles for Supporting Soft-Skills Development, *International Journal of eLearning (2006).*

Adler, A. *Understanding Human Nature.* New York: Greenburg, 1927.

Adler, N. (ed.) *International Dimensions of Organizational Behavior* (3rd ed.). Belmont, CA: Wadsworth, 1997.

Agor, W. (ed.) *Intuition in Organizations.* Newbury Park, CA: Sage, 1989.

Agthe, K. E. "Mitbestimmung: Report on a Social Experiment." *Business Horizons,* 5–14, 1977.

Ahituv, N. and S. Neumann. *Principles of Information Systems for Management.* Dubuque, IA: W. C. Brown, 1982.

Aktouf, O. *Traditional Management and Beyond.* Montreal: Morin, 1996.

Alderfer, C. P. "A New Theory of Human Needs." *Organizational Behavior and Human Performance,* 4: 142–175, 1969.

Alderfer, C. P. *Existence, Relatedness and Growth.* New York: Free Press, 1972.

Aldrich, H. *Organizations and Environments.* Englewood Cliffs, NJ: Prentice Hall, 1979.

Alexander, C. *Notes on the Synthesis of Form.* Cambridge, MA: Harvard University Press, 1964.

Alford, C. F. *Whistleblowers: Broken Lives and Organizational Power.* Ithaca, NY: Cornell University Press, 2001.

Alford, L. P. *Henry Lawrence Gantt, Leader in Industry.* New York: Harper & Row, 1934.

Allee, V. *The Future of Knowledge: Increasing Prosperity Through Value Networks.* Boston: Butterworth-Heinemann, 2003.

Allen, R. F. and C. Kraft. *The Organizational Unconscious.* Englewood Cliffs, NJ: Addison-Wesley, 1982.

Allen, R. W. and L. W. Porter (eds.) *Organizational Influence Processes.* Glenview, IL: Scott Foresman, 1983.

Allen, V. L. *Social Analysis: A Marxist Critique and Alternative.* London: Longman, 1975.

Althusser, L. *For Marx.* London: New Left Books, 1969.

Althusser, L. and E. Balibar. *Reading Capital.* London: New Left Books, 1970.

Alvesson, M. "Organizations, Culture and Ideology." *International Studies of Management and Organizations,* 3: 4–18, 1987.

Alvesson, M. *Cultural Perspectives on Organizations.* Cambridge, UK: Cambridge University Press, 1993a.

Alvesson, M. "The Play of Metaphors," in J. Hassard and M. Parker (eds.) *Postmodernism and Organizations.* London: Sage, 1993b.

Alvesson, M. *Understanding Organizational Culture.* London: Sage, 2002.

Alvesson, M. and P. O. Berg. *Corporate Culture and Organizational Symbolism.* Berlin: Walter de Gruyter, 1992.

Alvesson, M. and Y. D. Billing. "Gender and Organization: Towards a Differentiated Understanding." *Organization Studies,* 13: 73–104, 1992.

Alvesson, M. and S. Deetz. "Critical Theory and Postmodernism Approaches to the Study of Organization," pp. 191–217 in S. Clegg, C. Hardy, and W. Nord (eds.) *Handbook of Organization Studies.* Thousand Oaks: Sage, 1996.

Alvesson, M. and H. Willmott. "On the Idea of Emancipation in Management and Organization Studies." *Academy of Management Review,* 17: 432–464, 1992.

Ambrose, A. and G. Amado. *The Transitional Approach to the Management of Change* (HEC School of Management, Jouy-en-Josas, France), 1995.

Andersen, E. *On Organizations as Brains.* 1992. Available at http://www1.usa1.com/self/orgbrain.htm.

Argyris, C. *Personality and Organization.* New York: Harper & Row, 1957.

Argyris, C. *Integrating the Individual and the Organization.* New York: John Wiley, 1964.

Argyris, C. *Reasoning, Learning and Action.* San Francisco: Jossey-Bass, 1982.

Argyris, C. *Overcoming Organizational Defenses.* Boston: Allyn & Bacon, 1990.

Argyris, C. *Knowledge for Action.* San Francisco: Jossey-Bass, 1993.

Argyris, C. "Good Communication That Blocks Learning." *Harvard Business Review,* 77–85, 1994.

Argyris, C. *On Organizational Learning.* Oxford, UK: Blackwell Business, 1999.

Argyris, C. *Reasons and Rationalizations: The Limits to Organizational Knowledge.* Oxford, UK: Oxford University Press, 2004.

Argyris, C. and D. A. Schön. *Theory in Practice.* San Francisco: Jossey-Bass, 1974.

Argyris, C. and D. A. Schön. *Organizational Learning: A Theory of Action Perspective.* Reading, MA: Addison-Wesley, 1978.

Argyris, C. and D. A. Schon. *Organizational Learning II: Theory, Method and Practice.* Reading, MA: Addison Wesley, 1996.

Aristotle. *On the Movement of Animals.* Cambridge, MA: Harvard University Press, 1937.

Aristotle. *The Politics*. Oxford: Clarendon, 1946a.

Aristotle. *Rhetoric*. Oxford, UK: Oxford University Press, 1946b.

Aristotle. *The Poetics*. Cambridge, UK: Cambridge University Press, 1968.

Aronowitz, S. *False Promises*. New York: McGraw-Hill, 1973.

Arrington, C. E. and A. E. Puxty. "Accounting, Interests and Rationality: A Communicative Relation." *Critical Perspectives on Accounting*, 2: 31–58, 1991.

Artigliani, R. "Revolution and Evolution: Applying Prigogine's Dissipative Structures Model." *Journal of Social and Biological Structure*, 10: 249–264, 1987.

Ashby, W. R. *Design for a Brain*. New York: John Wiley, 1952.

Ashby, W. R. *An Introduction to Cybernetics*. London: Chapman & Hall, 1960.

Ashford, N. *Crisis in the Workplace: Occupational Disease and Injury*. Cambridge: MIT Press, 1976.

Ashkanasy, N. M., C. E. J. Hartel, and W. J. Zerbe. *Emotions in the Workplace: Research, Theory and Practice*. Westport, CT: Quorum, 2000.

Ashkanasy, N. M., C. P. M. Wilderom, and M. F. Peterson (eds.) *Handbook of Organizational Culture and Climate*. Thousand Oaks, CA: Sage, 2000.

Ashkenas, R. N., et al. *The Boundaryless Organization: Breaking the Chains of Organization Structure*. San Francisco: Jossey-Bass, 2002.

Ashton, D. S. "U.S. Investments in Canada." *Worldwide P&I Planning*, September 1968.

Astley, W. G. "Toward an Appreciation of Collective Strategy." *Academy of Management Review*, 9: 526–535, 1984.

Astley, W. G. and C. J. Fombrun. "Technological Innovation and Industrial Structure: The Case of Telecommunications," pp. 205–229 in *Advances in Strategic Management*. Greenwich, CT: JAI Press, 1983.

Astley, W. G. and A. H. Van de Ven. "Central Perspectives and Debates in Organization Theory." *Administrative Science Quarterly*, 28: 245–273, 1983.

Atkinson, A. B. *The Economics of Inequality*. New York: Oxford University Press, 1983.

Austin, L. (ed.) *Japan: The Paradox of Progress*. New Haven, CT: Yale University Press, 1976.

Austin, R. and L. Devin. *Artful Making: What Managers Need to Know About How Artists Work*. Upper Saddle River, NJ: FT Prentice Hall, 2003.

Babbage, C. *On the Economy of Machinery and Manufactures*. London: Charles Knight, 1832.

Bacharach, S. B. and E. J. Lawler. *Power and Politics in Organizations*. San Francisco: Jossey-Bass, 1980.

Bacharach, S. B. and E. J. Lawler (eds.) *Organizational Politics*. Stamford, CT: JAI Press, 2000.

Bachofen, J. J. *Myth, Religion, and Mother-Right*. London: Routledge & Kegan Paul, 1968.

Bachrach, P. and M. S. Baratz. "Two Faces of Power." *American Political Science Review*, 56: 947–952, 1962.

Bachrach, P. and M. S. Baratz (eds.) *Power and Poverty*. New York: Oxford University Press, 1970.

Bailey, A. "Coronary Disease: The Management Killer." *Journal of General Management*, 3: 72–80, 1973.

Bakan, J. *The Corporation: The Pathological Pursuit of Profit and Power.* New York: Free Press, 2004.

Baker, K. "Textile Industry vs. Brown Lung." *The Washington Post*, November 28: 19, 1980.

Bakunin, M. *Marxism, Freedom and the State.* London: Freedom Press, 1950.

Bakunin, M. *The Political Philosophy of Bakunin.* New York: Free Press, 1964.

Balanyá, B., et al. *Europe, Inc.: Regional and Global Restructuring and the Rise of Corporate Power* (2nd ed.). Sterling, VA: Pluto Press, 2003.

Bales, R. F. *Interaction Process Analysis.* Cambridge, MA: Addison-Wesley, 1950.

Barabasi, A. L. *Linked: The New Science of Networks.* Cambridge, MA: Perseus, 2002.

Baran, P. and P. M. Sweezy. *Monopoly Capital.* New York: Monthly Review Press, 1966.

Bard, A. and J. Soderqvist. *Netocracy: The New Power Elite and Life After Capitalism.* London: Pearson Education, 2002.

Barley, S. "Semiotics and the Study of Occupational and Organizational Cultures." *Administrative Science Quarterly*, 28: 393–414, 1983.

Barley, S. R. and G. Kunda. *Gurus, Hired Guns, and Warm Bodies: Itinerant Experts in a Knowledge Economy.* Princeton, NJ: Princeton University Press, 2004.

Barnard, C. *The Functions of the Executive.* Cambridge, MA: Harvard University Press, 1938.

Baron, H. "The Demand for Black Labor," pp. 368–381 in R. C. Edwards, M. Reich, and D. Gordon (eds.) *Labor Market Segmentation.* Lexington, MA: D. C. Heath, 1975.

Bartlett, C. A. and A. Ghoshal. *Managing Across Borders: The Transnational Solution.* Cambridge, MA: Harvard Business School Press, 1989.

Barton, S. "Chaos, Self-Organization and Psychology." *American Psychologist*, 49: 5–14, 1994.

Bate, P. *Strategies for Cultural Change.* Oxford, UK: Butterworth-Heinemann, 1994.

Bateson, G. *Naven.* Cambridge, UK: Cambridge University Press, 1936.

Bateson, G. *Steps to an Ecology of Mind.* New York: Ballantine, 1972.

Bateson, G. *Mind and Nature.* New York: Bantam, 1979.

Batten, J. A. and T. A. Fetherston. *Social Responsibility: Corporate Governance Issues.* Amsterdam: JAI Press, 2003.

Baum, H. *The Invisible Bureaucracy.* New York: Oxford University Press, 1987.

Baum, J. "Toil and Trouble? Taiwan Adopts Liberal Stance on Migrant Workers." *Far Eastern Economic Review*, May 15: 56–58, 1995.

Baum, J. "Organizational Ecology," pp. 77–114 in S. Clegg, C. Hardy, and W. Nord (eds.) *Handbook of Organization Studies.* Thousand Oaks, CA: Sage, 1996.

Baxter, B. *Alienation and Authenticity.* London: Tavistock, 1982.

Becker, E. *The Denial of Death.* New York: Free Press, 1973.

Beckett, S. *Endgame.* New York: Faber, 1958.

Beckett, S. *Waiting for Godot.* New York: Faber, 1965.

Beer, M. *Organization Change and Development.* Santa Monica, CA: Goodyear, 1980.

Beer, M. and N. Nohria (eds.) *Breaking the Code of Change.* Boston, MA: Harvard Business School Press, 2000.

Beer, S. *Cybernetics and Management*. New York: John Wiley, 1959.

Beer, S. *Brain of the Firm*. New York: Herder & Herder, 1972.

Begley, S. J. and R. Sawhill. "How the Brain Works." *Newsweek*, February 7: 40–47, 1983.

Belden, G., M. Hyatt, and D. Ackley. *Towards the Learning Organization*. Toronto: Institute of Cultural Affairs, 1993.

Bello, W., D. Kinley, and E. Elinson. *Development Debacle: The World Bank in the Philippines*. San Francisco: Institute for Food and Development Policy, 1982.

Bendix, R. *Work and Authority in Industry*. New York: John Wiley, 1956.

Beneria, L. *Global Tensions: Challenges and Opportunities in the World Economy*. New York: Routledge, 2004.

Bennet, A. *Organizational Survival in the New World: The Intelligent Complex Adaptive System*. Boston, MA : Butterworth-Heinemann, 2004.

Bennis, W. G. *Changing Organizations*. New York: McGraw-Hill, 1966.

Bennis, W. G. and B. Nanus. *Leaders: The Strategies for Taking Charge*. New York: Harper & Row. 1985.

Benson, J. K. "The Analysis of Bureaucratic-Professional Conflict." *Sociological Quarterly*, 14: 376–394, 1973.

Benson, J. K. "The Interorganizational Network as a Political Economy." *Administrative Science Quarterly*, 20: 229–249, 1975.

Benson, J. K. "A Dialectical Method for the Study of Organizations," pp. 331–346 in G. Morgan (ed.) *Beyond Method*. Beverly Hills, CA: Sage, 1983.

Benson, J. K. and C. J. Jenkins. "Interorganizational Networks and the Theory of the State." Presented at the American Sociological Association meeting, San Francisco, 1978.

Bentley, A. F. *The Process of Government*. Cambridge, MA: Harvard University Press, 1908.

Bentov, I. *Stalking the Wild Pendulum*. New York: Dutton, 1977.

Berger, J. and J. Mohr. *A Seventh Man*. Harmondsworth: Penguin, 1975.

Berger, P. and T. Luckmann. *The Social Construction of Reality*. Garden City, NY: Anchor, 1967.

Berger, S. and M. Piore. *Dualism and Discontinuity in Industrial Societies*. New York: Cambridge University Press, 1980.

Bergmann, A. E. "Industrial Democracy in Germany—The Battle for Power." *Journal of General Management*, 20–29, 1975.

Berkeley, G. *A New Theory of Vision*. New York: Everyman, 1910.

Berman, D. M. *Death on the Job*. New York: Monthly Review Press, 1978.

Bettleheim, B. *The Uses of Enchantment: The Meaning and Importance of Fairy Tales*. New York: Vintage, 1977.

Beyer, J. M. "Metaphors, Misunderstanding and Mischief: A Commentary." *Organization Science*, 3: 467–475, 1992.

Beynon, H. *Working for Ford*. London: Allen Lane, 1973.

Bhagwati, J. *In Defence of Globilization*. New York: Oxford University Press, 2004.

Bharati, B. *International Labor Mobility: Unemployment and Increasing Returns to Scale*. London: Routledge, 2004.

Bhaskar, R. *A Realist Theory of Science*. Hassocks, Sussex: Harvester Press, 1978.

Bigger, C. P. *Between Chora and the Good: Metaphor's Metaphysical Neighborhood*. New York: Fordham University Press, 2005.

Bion, W. R. *Experiences in Groups*. New York: Basic Books, 1959.

Birchall, D. W. and V. J. Hammond. *Tomorrow's Office Today*. New York: John Wiley, 1981.

Birkinshaw, J., et al. (eds.) *The Future of the Multinational Company*. Chichester, UK: Wiley, 2003.

Bittner, E. "On the Concept of Organization." *Social Research*, 32: 239–255, 1965.

Black, M. *Models and Metaphors*. Ithaca, NY: Cornell University Press, 1962.

Blackburn, R. M. and M. Mann. *The Working Class in the Labor Market*. London: Macmillan, 1979.

Blake, R. and J. S. Mouton. *The Managerial Grid*. Houston: Gulf Publishing, 1964.

Blau, P. M. *Exchange and Power and Social Life*. New York: John Wiley, 1964.

Blau, P. M. and W. R. Scott. *Formal Organizations*. San Francisco: Chandler, 1962.

Blauner, R. *Alienation and Freedom*. Chicago: University of Chicago Press, 1964.

Block, P. *The Empowered Manager*. San Francisco: Jossey-Bass, 1987.

Boggs, C. *The End of Politics: Corporate Power and the Decline of the Public Sphere*. New York: Guilford Press, 2001.

Bohm, D. "The Implicate Order: A New Order for Physics." *Process Studies*, 8: 73–102, 1978.

Bohm, D. *Wholeness and the Implicate Order*. London: Routledge & Kegan Paul, 1980a.

Bohm, D. "The Enfolded Order and Consciousness," in G. Epstein (ed.) *Studies in Non-deterministic Psychology*. New York: Human Sciences Press, 1980b.

Bohm, D. and F. D. Peat. *Science, Order and Creativity*. New York: Bantam, 1987.

Bohr, N. *Atomic Theory and Human Knowledge*. New York: Wiley, 1958.

Boiset, M. H. *Knowledge Assets: Securing Competitive Advantage in the Information Economy*. Oxford, UK: Oxford University Press, 1998.

Boland, R. J. "Beyond the Objectivist and the Subjectivist: Learning to Read Accounting as Text." *Accounting, Organizations and Society*, 14: 591–604, 1989.

Boland, R. J. and R. Hoffman. "Humor in a Machine Shop," pp. 187–198 in L. Pondy, P. Frost, G. Morgan, and T. Dandridge (eds.) *Organizational Symbolism*. Greenwich, CT: JAI Press, 1983.

Bolman, L. G. and T. E. Deal. *Reframing Organizations*. San Francisco: Jossey-Bass, 1991.

Bonabeau, E. and C. Meyer. "Swarm Intelligence: A Whole New Way to Think About Business." *Harvard Business Review*, May: 107–114, 2001.

Bordwin, M. "Overwork: The Cause of Your Next Workers' Comp Claim?" *Management Review*, 85: 50, 1996.

Boroditsky, L. "Metaphoric Structuring: Understanding Time Through Spatial Metaphors." *Cognition*, 75: 1–27, 2000.

Bottomore, T. B. *Elites and Society*. Harmondsworth: Penguin, 1966.

Boulding, K. E. *The Image*. Ann Arbor: University of Michigan Press, 1956a.

Boulding, K. E. "General Systems Theory—The Skeleton of Science." *Management Science*, 2: 197–208, 1956b.

Boulding, K. E. *Evolutionary Economics*. Beverly Hills, CA: Sage, 1981.

Bower, J. "Managing for Efficiency, Managing for Equity." *Harvard Business Review*, August: 83–90, 1983.

Bowles, M. "Recognizing Deep Structures in Organizations." *Organization Studies*, 11: 395–412, 1990.

Bowles, M. "The Organizational Shadow." *Organization Studies*, 12: 387–404, 1991.

Bowles, M. "The Gods and Goddesses: Personifying Social Life in the Age of Organization." *Organization Studies*, 14: 395–418, 1993.

Bradshaw, P. and S. Newell. *Exploring Deep Structures of Power Using Jungian Dream Analysis*. Working Paper, Schulich School of Business, Toronto, 1993.

Brandt, W. *North-South: A Program for Survival*. Cambridge: MIT Press, 1980.

Braverman, H. *Labor and Monopoly Capital*. New York: Monthly Review Press, 1974.

Bray, J. N., et al. *Collaborative Inquiry in Practice: Action, Reflection, and Making Meaning*. Thousand Oaks, CA: Sage, 2000.

Braybrooke, D. and C. E. Lindblom. *A Strategy of Decision*. New York: Free Press, 1963.

Brickley, J. A., et al. *Designing Organizations to Create Value: From Strategy to Structure*. New York: McGraw-Hill, 2003.

Bridger, H. "The Kinds of Organizational Development Required for Working at the Level of the Whole Organization Considered as an Open System," in K. Trebesch (ed.) *Organizational Development in Europe*, Vol. 1. Berne: Paul Haupt Verlag, 1980.

Bridger, H. "Consultative Work With Communities and Organizations." *The Malcolm Millar Lecture*. Aberdeen: Aberdeen University Press, 1981.

Bridger, H. "The Implications of Ecological Change on Groups, Institutions and Communities," in M. Pines and L. Rafaelson (eds.) *The Individual and the Group*. New York: Plenum, 1982.

Bridger, H. "Courses and Working Conferences as Transitional Learning Institutions," in E. Trist and H. Murray (eds.) *The Social Engagement of Social Science*, Vol. 1. Philadelphia: University of Pennsylvania Press, 1990.

Bridges, W. *Managing Transitions*. Reading, MA: Addison Wesley, 1991.

Bridges, W. *Job Shift*. Reading, MA: Addison-Wesley, 1994.

Briggs, J. P. and F. D. Peat. *Looking Glass Universe*. New York: Simon & Schuster, 1984.

Broekstra, G. "The Triune-Brain Evolution of the Living Organization," in D. Grant and C. Oswick (eds.) *Metaphor and Organizations*. London: Sage, 1996.

Brooke, M. Z. and H. L. Remmers. *The Strategy of Multi-national Enterprise*. New York: American Elsevier, 1970.

Brooks, R. A. "New Approaches to Robotics." *Science*, 1991.

Brown, B. *Marx, Freud, and the Critique of Everyday Life*. New York: Monthly Review Press, 1973.

Brown, J. S. and P. Duguid. *The Social Life of Information*. Boston: Harvard Business School Press, 2000.

Brown, L. D. "Managing Conflict Among Groups," pp. 225–237 in D. A. Kolb, I. M. Rubin, and J. McIntyre (eds.) *Organizational Psychology*. Englewood Cliffs, NJ: Prentice Hall, 1983.

Brown, N. O. *Life Against Death*. Middletown, CT: Wesleyan University Press, 1959.

Brown, R. H. *A Poetic for Sociology*. New York: Cambridge University Press, 1977.

Brown, T. L. *Making Truth: Metaphors in Science*. Urbana, IL: University of Illinois Press, 2003.

Brownell, K. D. and K. B. Horgen. *Food Fight: The Inside Story of the Food Industry, America's Obesity Crisis, and What We Can Do About It*. New York: Contemporary, 2004.

Brundtland, G. (ed.) *Our Common Future: The World Commission on Environment and Development*. Oxford, UK: Oxford University Press, 1987.

Brunsson, N. *The Irrational Organization*. New York: John Wiley, 1985.

Brunsson, N. *The Organization of Hypocrisy*. New York: John Wiley, 1989.

Bryer, R., T. J. Brignall, and A. R. Maunders. *Accounting for British Steel*. London: Gower Press, 1982.

Buckley, W. *Sociology and Modern Systems Theory*. Englewood Cliffs, NJ: Prentice Hall, 1967.

Buckley, W. (ed.) *Modern Systems Research for the Behavioral Scientist*. Chicago: Aldine, 1968.

Bukharin, N. *Historical Materialism: A System of Sociology*. New York: Russell & Russell, 1962.

Bukharin, N. *Imperialism and World Economy*. London: Merlin, 1972.

Burk, M. *Cult of Power: Sex Discrimination in Corporate America and What Can Be Done About It*. New York: Scribner, 2005.

Burke, K. *A Grammar of Motives and a Rhetoric of Motives*. Cleveland, OH: Meridian, 1962.

Burke, K. "Dramatism," in D. Sills (ed.) *International Encyclopaedia of the Social Sciences*. New York: Macmillan, 1968.

Burke, R. J. and T. Weir. "Coping With the Stress of Managerial Occupations," pp. 299–335 in C. L. Cooper and R. Payne (eds.) *Current Concerns in Occupational Stress*. London: Wiley, 1980.

Burns, J. M. *Leadership*. New York: Harper & Row, 1978.

Burns, R. D. *The Uncertain Nervous System*. London: Arnold, 1968.

Burns, T. "Micropolitics: Mechanisms of Organizational Change." *Administrative Science Quarterly*, 6: 257–281, 1961.

Burns, T. and G. M. Stalker. *The Management of Innovation*. London: Tavistock, 1961.

Buroway, M. *Manufacturing Consent*. Chicago: University of Chicago Press, 1979.

Burrell, G. "Sex and Organizational Analysis." *Organization Studies*, 5: 97–118, 1984.

Burrell, G. "The Organization of Pleasure," pp. 66–89 in M. Alvesson and H. Willmott (eds.) *Critical Management Studies*. London: Sage, 1992.

Burrell, G. *Pandemonium: Towards a Retro-organization Theory*. London: Sage, 1997.

Burrell, G. and G. Morgan. *Sociological Paradigms and Organizational Analysis.* London: Heinemann Educational Books, 1979.

Business Week Reporters. "Ford After Henry II: Will He Really Leave?" *Business-Week,* April 30: 62–72, 1979.

Butcher, D. *Smart Management: Using Politics in Organizations.* Basingstoke, UK: Palgrave, 2001.

Calas, M. and L. Smircich. "Post-culture: Is the Organizational Culture Literature Dominant but Dead?" Paper presented at the International Conference on Organizational Symbolism and Corporate Culture, Milan, 1987.

Calas, M. and L. Smircich. "Reading Leadership as a Form of Cultural Analysis," in J. Hunt, B. Baliga, P. Dachler, and A. Schriesheim (eds.) *Emergent Leadership Vistas.* Lexington, MA: Lexington Books, 1988.

Calas, M. and L. Smircich. "Dangerous Liaisons: The Feminine-in-Management Meets Globalization." *Business Horizons,* March: 73–83, 1993.

Calas, M. B., and L. Smircich. "From the Woman's Point of View: Feminist Approaches to Organization Studies," pp. 218–257 in S. Clegg, C. Hardy, and W. Nord (eds.) *Handbook of Organization Studies.* Thousand Oaks, CA: Sage, 1996.

Calas, M. B. and L. Smircich "Past Postmodernism? Reflections and Tentative Directions." *Academy of Management Review,* 24: 649–671, 1999.

Calas, M. B. and L. Smircich. "Revisiting 'Dangerous Liasions' or Does the 'Feminine-in-Management' still meet 'Globalization'?" In P. J. Frost, W. R. Nord, & L. A. Krefting (eds.) *Managerial and Organizational Reality: Stories of Life and Work,* Upper Saddle River, NJ: Prentice Hall, 467–481, 2004.

Calvin, W. H. *The Cerebral Code: Thinking a Thought in the Mosaics of the Mind.* Cambridge: MIT Press, 1996.

Calvin, W. H. *A Brief History of the Mind: From Apes to Intellect and Beyond.* New York: Oxford University Press, 2004.

Camazine, Scott, et al. *Self-Organization in Biological Systems.* Princeton, NJ: Princeton University Press, 2001.

Campbell, B. "The Global Economy at the Close of the 20th Century." *New Solutions,* Summer: 16–33, 1995.

Campbell, D. T. "Variation and Selective Retention in Socio-cultural Evolution." *General Systems,* 16: 69–85, 1969.

Campbell, J. L. *Institutional Change and Globalization.* Princeton, NJ: Princeton University Press, 2004.

Camus, A. *The Outsider.* London: Hamilton, 1946.

Capra, F. *The Tao of Physics.* New York: Wildwood House, 1975.

Capra, F. *The Turning Point.* New York: Bantam, 1982.

Carr, A. Z. *Business as a Game.* New York: Mentor, 1968.

Carroll, W. K. *Corporate Power in a Globalizing World: A Study in Elite Social Organization.* Don Mills, ON: Oxford University Press, 2004.

Carruthers, P. (ed.) *Evolution and the Human Mind: Modularity, Language and Meta-Cognition.* Cambridge, UK: Cambridge University Press, 2000.

Cascio, W. F. *Responsible Restructuring: Creative and Profitable Alternatives to Layoffs.* San Francisco: Berrett Koehler, 2002.

Cassirer, E. *Language and Myth.* New York: Dover, 1946.

Casson, M. *The Growth of International Business.* London: Allen & Unwin, 1983.

Castles, S. *Migrant Workers and the Transformation of Western Societies.* Ithaca, NY: Cornell Studies in International Affairs: Western Societies Papers, 1989.

Castles, S. and G. Kosack. *Immigrant Workers and Class Structures in Western Europe.* New York: Oxford University Press, 1973.

Castles, S. and M. J. Miller. *The Age of Migration: International Population Movements in the Modern World.* New York: Guilford Press, 2003.

Cavanaugh, J. and J. Mander. *Alternatives to Economic Globalization: A Better World Is Possible* (2nd ed.). San Francisco: Berrett-Kohler, 2003.

Champy, J. *Reengineering Management.* New York: Harper, 1995.

Chandler, A. *Strategy and Structure.* Cambridge: MIT Press, 1962.

Chandler, A. *The Visible Hand.* Cambridge, MA: Harvard University Press, 1977.

Chandler, A. D., Jr., and B. Mazlish (eds.) *Leviathans: Multinational Corporations and the New Global History.* Cambridge, UK: Cambridge, 2005.

Charteris-Black, J. *The Persuasive Power of Metaphor.* Houndsmills, UK: Palgrave MacMillan, 2005.

Chatov, R. "Cooperation Between Government and Business," pp. 487–502 in P. C. Nystrom and W. H. Starbuck (eds.) *Handbook of Organizational Design.* New York: Oxford University Press, 1981.

Checkland, P. and J. Scholes. *Soft Systems Methodology in Action.* Chichester, UK: Wiley, 1990.

Child, J. "Organization Structure, Environment and Performance: The Role of Strategic Choice." *Sociology,* 6: 1–22, 1972.

Child, J. "Culture, Contingency and Capitalism in the Cross-National Study of Organizations," pp. 303–356 in B. Staw and L. L. Cummings (eds.) *Research in Organizational Behavior.* Greenwich, CT: JAI Press, 1981.

Child, J. "Management Strategies, New Technology and the Labour Process," in D. Knights, H. Willmott, and D. Collinson (eds.) *Job Redesign.* Aldershot, UK: Gower, 1985.

Childe, V. G. *Man Makes Himself.* London: Fontana, 1946.

Choo, C. W. *The Knowing Organization: How Organizations Use Information to Construct Meaning, Create Knowledge, and Make Decisions.* New York: Oxford University Press, 1998.

Ciulla, J. B. *The Working Life: The Promise and Betrayal of Modern Work.* New York: Times Books, 2000.

Ciulla, J. B. *Ethics, the Heart of Leadership.* Westport, CT: Praeger, 2004.

Clark, A. *Natural-Born Cyborgs: Minds, Technologies, and the Future of Human Intelligence.* Oxford, UK: Oxford University Press, 2004.

Clark, P. A. *Organizations in Action: Competition Between Contexts.* London: Routledge, 2000.

Clark, T. and G. Salaman. "The Management Guru as Organizational Witchdoctor." *Organization,* 3: 85–107, 1996.

Clegg, S. *Power, Rule and Domination.* London: Routledge & Kegan Paul, 1975.

Clegg, S. *The Theory of Power and Organization.* London: Routledge & Kegan Paul, 1979.

Clegg, S. "Organization and Control." *Administrative Science Quarterly*, 26: 545–562, 1981.

Clegg, S. *Frameworks of Power*. London and Newbury Park, CA: Sage, 1989.

Clegg, S. R. (ed.) *Management and Organization Paradoxes*. Amsterdam: John Benjamins, 2002.

Clegg, S. and D. Dunkerley. *Organization, Class and Control*. London: Routledge & Kegan Paul, 1980.

Clegg, S. and S. G. Redding. *Capitalism in Contrasting Cultures*. Berlin: Walter de Gruyter, 1990.

Cleugh, J. *Love Locked Out: An Examination of the Irrepressible Sexuality of the Middle Ages*. New York: Crown, 1963.

Cleveland, J., et al. *Men and Women in Organizations: Sex and Gender Issues at Work*. Mahwah, NJ: Erlbaum, 2000.

Cloke, K. *The End of Management and the Rise of Organizational Democracy*. San Francisco: Jossey-Bass, 2002.

Coates, K. *The New Worker Cooperatives*. Nottingham: Spokesman Books, 1976.

Coates, K. (ed.) *The Right to Useful Work*. Nottingham: Spokesman Books, 1978.

Coates, K. *Work-ins, Sit-ins and Industrial Democracy*. Nottingham: Spokesman Books, 1981a.

Coates, K. *How to Win*. Nottingham: Spokesman Books, 1981b.

Coates, K. and T. Topham. *Worker Control*. London: Panther, 1970.

Cohen, A. R. *Influence Without Authority* (2nd ed.). Hoboken, NJ: Wiley, 2005.

Cohen, M. D., J. G. March, and J. P. Olsen. "A Garbage Can Model of Organizational Choice." *Administrative Science Quarterly*, 17: 1–25, 1972.

Cole, R. E. *Work, Mobility and Participation: A Comparative Study of American and Japanese Industry*. Berkeley: University of California Press, 1979.

Colletti, L. *From Rousseau to Lenin*. London: New Left Books, 1972.

Colletti, L. "A Political and Philosophical Interview." *New Left Review*, 86: 3–28, 1974.

Colletti, L. "Introduction," pp. 7–56 in K. Marx, *Early Writings*. London: Allen Lane, 1975a.

Colletti, L. "Marxism and the Dialectic." *New Left Review*, 93: 3–29, 1975b.

Collins, J. C. *Good to Great: Why Some Companies Make the Leap and Others Don't*. New York: HarperBusiness, 2001.

Collinson, D. "Engineering Humour: Masculinity, Joking and Conflict in Shopfloor Relations." *Organization Studies*, 9: 181–199, 1988.

Collison, C. and G. Parcell. *Learning to Fly: Practical Knowledge Management From Leading and Learning Organizations* (2nd ed.). Milford, CT: Capstone, 2004.

Cooper, C. L. (ed.) *Theories of Organizational Stress*. New York: Oxford University Press, 2000.

Cooper, C. L. and J. Marshall. "Occupational Sources of Stress: A Review of the Literature Relating to Coronary Heart Disease and Mental Ill-Health." *Journal of Occupational Psychology*, 49: 11–28, 1976.

Cooper, C. L. and R. Payne (eds.) *Current Concerns in Occupational Stress*. New York: John Wiley, 1980.

Cooperrider, D. L. and S. Srivastva. "Appreciative Inquiry in Organizational Life." *Research in Organizational Change and Development*, 1: 129–169, 1987.

Copley, F. B. *Frederick Taylor: Father of Scientific Management*, 2 vols. New York: Harper & Row, 1923.

Cornelissen, J. P. "Beyond Compare: Metaphor in Organization Theory." *Academy of Management Review*, 3(4): 751–764, 2005.

Corwin, R. G. *Militant Professionalism*. New York: Appleton-Century-Crofts, 1970.

Coser, L. A. *The Functions of Social Conflict*. New York: Routledge & Kegan Paul, 1956.

Courtney, J. F., J. D. Haynes, and D. B. Paradice (eds.) *Inquiring Organizations: Moving From Knowledge Management to Wisdom*. Hershey, PA: Idea Group, 2005.

Cowan, G. A., D. Pines, and D. Meltzer (eds.) *Complexity: Metaphors, Models, and Reality*. Reading, MA: Addison Wesley, 1994.

Coward, R. *Patriarchal Precedents: Sexuality and Social Relations*. London: Routledge & Kegan Paul, 1983.

Cox, T. *Cultural Diversity in Organizations*. San Francisco: Berrett-Koehler, 1993.

Crick, B. *In Defense of Politics*. Harmondsworth: Penguin, 1964.

Cross, E. Y., J. H. Katz, F. Miller, and F. W. Seashore. *The Promise of Diversity*. Burr Ridge, IL: Irwin, 1994.

Cross, R. L. and S. Israelit (eds.) *Strategic Learning in a Knowledge Economy: Individual, Collective and Organizational Learning Processes*. Boston: Butterworth-Heinemann, 1999.

Cross, R. L. and A. Parker. *The Hidden Power of Social Networks*. Boston: Harvard Business School Press, 2004.

Crozier, M. *The Bureaucratic Phenomenon*. London: Tavistock, 1964.

Culbert, S. and J. McDonough. *The Invisible War: Pursuing Self-Interest at Work*. Toronto: John Wiley, 1980.

Cumming, P. *The Power Handbook*. Boston: CBI Publishing, 1981.

Cyert, R. M. and J. G. March. *A Behavioral Theory of the Firm*. Englewood Cliffs, NJ: Prentice Hall, 1963.

Czarniawska-Joerges, B. *Exploring Complex Organizations: A Cultural Perspective*. Newbury Park, CA: Sage, 1992.

Dacey, J. S. and K. H. Lennon. *Understanding Creativity: The Interplay of Biological, Psychological, and Social Factors*. San Francisco: Jossey-Bass, 1998.

Dahl, R. A. "The Concept of Power." *Behavioral Science*, 2: 201–215, 1957.

Dalton, M. *Men Who Manage*. New York: John Wiley, 1959.

Dandridge, T. "Ceremony as an Integration of Work and Play." *Organization Studies*, 7: 159–170, 1986.

Daniels, J. D., et al. *Global Business: Environments and Strategies*. Oxford, UK: Oxford University Press, 2000.

D'Aveni, R. A. *Hyper-Competition: Managing the Dynamics of Strategic Maneuvering*. New York: Free Press, 1994.

Davenport, T. and L. Prusak. *Working Knowledge*. Boston: Harvard Business School Press, 2000.

Davis, D. L. *When Smoke Ran Like Water: Tales of Environmental Deception and the Battle Against Pollution*. New York: Basic Books, 2002.

Davis, S. M. and P. R. Lawrence. *Matrix*. Reading, MA: Addison-Wesley, 1977.

Davis, W. *The Innovators*. London: Ebury Press, 1987.

Deal, T. E. and A. A. Kennedy. *Corporate Cultures*. Reading, MA: Addison-Wesley, 1982.

Deal, T. and A. Kennedy. *The New Corporate Cultures: Revitalizing the Workplace After Downsizing, Mergers and Re-engineering*. Reading, MA: Perseus Books, 1999.

Dear, J. A. "Work Stress and Health '95." *Vital Speeches of the Day*, 62: 39–42, 1995.

de Bono, E. *Lateral Thinking*. Harmondsworth: Penguin, 1970.

de Bono, E. *Six Thinking Hats: An Essential Approach to Business Management*. Boston: Little, Brown, 1985.

Deetz, S. *Democracy in an Age of Corporate Colonialization*. Albany: State University of New York Press, 1992a.

Deetz, S. "Disciplinary Power in the Modern Corporation," pp. 21–25 in M. Alvesson and H. Willmott (eds.) *Critical Management Studies*. London: Sage, 1992b.

DeGeus, A. "Planning as Learning." *Harvard Business Review*, March-April: 70–74, 198.

DeGeus, A. *The Living Company: Habits for Survival in a Turbulent Business Environment*. Boston: Harvard Business School Press, 1997.

Delahanty, F. and G. Gemmill. "The Black Hole in Group Development." Presented at the Academy of Management Meetings, New York, 1982.

Denhardt, R. B. *In the Shadow of Organization*. Lawrence, KA: Regents Press, 1981.

Denison, D. *Corporate Culture and Organizational Effectiveness*. New York: John Wiley, 1990.

Dennett, D. C. *Consciousness Explained*. Boston: Little, Brown, 1991.

Descartes, R. *Discourse on Method*. London: Penguin, 1968.

Devons, E. "Statistics as a Basis for Policy," pp. 122–137 in *Essays in Economics*. London: Allen & Unwin, 1961.

Diamond, J. *Collapse: How Societies Choose to Fail or Survive*. New York: Viking, 2005.

Dill, W. R. "Environment as an Influence on Managerial Autonomy." *Administrative Science Quarterly*, 2: 409–443, 1958.

DiMaggio, P. J. and W. W. Powell. "The Iron Cage Revisited." *American Sociological Review*, 48: 147–160, 1983.

DiMaggio, P. J. and W. W. Powell (eds.) *The New Institutionalism in Organizational Analysis*. Chicago: University of Chicago Press, 1991.

DiVanna, J. A. *Synconomy: Adding Value in a World of Continuously Connected Business*. New York: Palgrave Macmillan, 2003.

Dodson-Gray, E. *Patriarchy as a Conceptual Trap*. Wellesley, MA: Roundtable Press, 1982.

Donahue, T. R. "Collective Bargaining, Codetermination, and the Quality of Work." *World of Work Report*, 1, 1976.

Donaldson, L. *The Contingency Theory of Organizations*. Thousand Oaks, CA: Sage, 2001.

Doppelt, B. *Leading Change Toward Sustainability*. Sheffield, UK: Greenleaf Publishing Ltd., 2003.

Dore, R. *British Factory, Japanese Factory.* London: Allen & Unwin, 1973.

Dore, R. "Introduction," pp. ix–xi in S. Kamata (ed.) *Japan in the Passing Lane.* New York: Pantheon, 1982.

Downs, A. *Inside Bureaucracy.* Boston: Little, Brown, 1967.

Drucker, P. F. *The Practice of Management.* New York: Harper & Row, 1954.

Drucker, P. F. *Managing in Turbulent Times.* New York: Harper & Row, 1980.

Drucker, P. F. *Post-capitalist Society.* New York: Harper Business, 1993.

Drucker, P. F. *Management Challenges for the 21st Century.* New York: HarperBusiness, 2001.

Dunn, B. *Global Restructuring and the Power of Labour.* Houndsmills, UK: Palgrave Macmillan, 2004.

Dunnette, M. D. (ed.) *Handbook of Industrial and Organizational Psychology.* Chicago: Rand McNally, 1976.

Dunning, J. *Multinational Enterprises and the Global Economy.* Reading, MA: Addison Wesley, 1993.

Durkheim, E. *The Division of Labour in Society.* London: Macmillan, 1934.

Durkheim, E. *The Rules of Sociological Method.* New York: Free Press, 1938.

Durkheim, E. *Suicide.* New York: Free Press, 1951.

Eagle, J. and P. M. Newton. "Scapegoating in Small Groups." *Human Relations,* 34: 283–301, 1981.

Easterby-Smith, M., J. Burgoyne, and L. Araujo. *Organizational Learning and the Learning Organization: Development in Theory and Practice.* London: Sage, 1999.

Easton, D. A. *A Systems Analysis of Political Life.* New York: John Wiley, 1965.

Eberle, T. S. "Dislocation Policies in Western Europe: Past, Present and Future." *Annals of the American Academy of Political and Social Science,* 544: 127–139, 1996.

Eccles, R. G. and N. Nohria. *Beyond the Hype.* Boston: Harvard Business School Press, 1992.

Eccles, T. *Under New Management.* London: Pan Books, 1981.

Eco, U. *A Theory of Semiotics.* Bloomington: Indiana University Press, 1976.

Edelman, G. *Wider Than the Sky: The Phenomenal Gift of Consciousness.* New Haven, CT: Yale University Press, 2004.

Edelman, M. *Politics as Symbolic Action.* Chicago: Markham, 1971.

Edelman, M. *Political Language: Words That Succeed and Policies That Fail.* New York: Academic Press, 1977.

Edwards, R. C. *Contested Terrain.* New York: Basic Books, 1979.

Edwards, R. C., M. Reich, and D. Gordon (eds.) *Labor Market Segmentation.* Lexington, MA: D. C. Heath, 1975.

Edwards, R. C., M. Reich, and T. Weisskopf. *The Capitalist System.* Englewood Cliffs, NJ: Prentice Hall, 1986.

Ehrenreich, B. and A. R. Hochschild (eds.). *Global Woman: Nannies, Maids, and Sex Workers in the New Economy* (2nd ed.) New York: Metropolitan Books, 2003.

Eisenhardt, K. and S. Brown. *Competing on the Edge.* Cambridge, MA: Harvard Business School Press, 1998.

Eisenhardt, K. and S. Brown. "Patching: Restitching Business Portfolios in Dynamic Markets." *Harvard Business Review*, May-June: 72–82, 1999.

Ellul, J. *The Technological Society*. New York: Alfred A. Knopf, 1964.

Emerson, R. M. "Power-Dependence Relations." *American Sociological Review*, 27: 31–40, 1962.

Emery, F. E. (ed.) *Systems Thinking*. Harmondsworth: Penguin, 1969.

Emery, F. E. *Futures We Are In*. Leiden: Martinus Nijhoff, 1976.

Emery, F. E. and E. Thorsrud. *Form and Content in Industrial Democracy*. London: Tavistock, 1969.

Emery, F. E. and E. L. Trist. "The Causal Texture of Organizational Environments." *Human Relations*, 18: 21–32, 1965.

Emery, F. E. and E. L. Trist. *Toward a Social Ecology*. London: Tavistock, 1973.

Emmott, B. *20/21 Vision: Twentieth-Century Lessons for the Twenty-first Century*. New York: Farrar, Straus and Giroux, 2003.

Engels, F. *Dialectics of Nature*. London: Lawrence & Wishart, 1873.

Engels, F. *Anti-Duhring*. London: Martin Lawrence, 1876.

Engels, F. *Ludwig Feuerbach and the Outcome of Classical German Philosophy*. London: Martin Lawrence, 1886.

Engels, F. *The Origins of the Family, Private Property and the State*. London: Lawrence & Wishart, 1972.

Epstein, S. S. *The Politics of Cancer*. San Francisco: Sierra Club Books, 1978.

Epstein, S. "The Unconscious, the Preconscious, and the Self-Concept," in J. Suls and A. Greenwald (eds.) *Psychological Perspectives on the Self*. Hillsdale, NJ: Lawrence Erlbaum, 1983.

Etzioni, A. *A Comparative Analysis of Complex Organizations*. New York: Free Press, 1961.

Evans, R. and P. Russell. *The Creative Manager*. London: Unwin, 1989.

Evered, R. "The Language of Organization: The Case of the Navy," pp. 125–143 in L. Pondy et al. (eds.) *Organizational Symbolism*. Greenwich, CT: JAI, 1983.

Fayol, H. *General and Industrial Management*. London: Pitman, 1949.

Feinberg, M. R. and R. F. Dempewolf. *Corporate Bigamy*. New York: William Morrow, 1980.

Ferguson, K. *The Feminist Case Against Bureaucracy*. Philadelphia: Temple University Press, 1984.

Ferguson, M. *The Aquarian Conspiracy*. New York: J. P. Tarcher, 1980.

Ferguson, N. *Colossus: The Price of America's Empire*. New York: Penguin, 2004.

Figgis, J. N. *Churches in the Modern State*. London: Longmans, 1913.

Filley, A. C. *Interpersonal Conflict Resolution*. Glenview, IL: Scott Foresman, 1975.

Findlay, J. N. *Hegel: A Re-examination*. London: Allen & Unwin, 1958.

Firebaugh, G. *The New Geography of Global Income Inequality*. Cambridge, MA: Harvard University Press, 2003.

Flax, J. *Thinking Fragments*. Berkeley: University of California Press, 1990.

Fletcher, J. and K. Olwyler. *Paradoxical Thinking: How to Profit From Your Contradictions*. San Francisco: Berrett-Koehler, 1997.

Follett, M. P. *The New State*. London: Longmans, 1918.

Follett, M. P. "The Basis of Authority," in L. Urwick (ed.) *Freedom and Coordination: Lectures in Business Organization by Mary Parkes Follett*. London: Management Publications Trust, 1949.

Follett, M. P. *Dynamic Administration: The Collected Papers of Mary Parker Follett*, edited by E. M. Fox and L. Urwick. London: Pitman, 1973.

Follman, J. F. *The Economics of Industrial Health: History, Theory, Practice*. New York: Amacom, 1978.

Fombrun, C. J. *Turning Points*. New York: McGraw-Hill, 1992.

Fombrun, C. J. and W. G. Astley. "Strategies of Collective Action: The Case of the Financial Services Industry," pp. 125–129 in *Advances in Strategic Management*. Greenwich, CT: JAI Press, 1983.

Ford, C. M. and D. A. Gioia (eds.) *Creative Action in Organizations*. Thousand Oaks, CA: Sage, 1995.

Forester, J. W. *Industrial Dynamics*. Cambridge: MIT Press, 1961.

Forester, J. "Critical Theory and Organizational Analysis," pp. 234–246 in G. Morgan (ed.) *Beyond Method: Strategies for Social Research*. Beverly Hills, CA: Sage, 1983.

Forester, J. W. *Planning in the Face of Power*. Berkeley: University of California Press, 1989.

Foucault, M. *Discipline and Punish*. New York: Vintage, 1979a.

Foucault, M. *The History of Sexuality*. London: Allen Lane, 1979b.

Fox, A. "Industrial Sociology and Industrial Relations." *Royal Commission on Trade Unions and Employers' Associations*. London: HMSO, 1966.

Fox, A. *Beyond Contract: Work, Power and Trust Relations*. London: Faber & Faber, 1974.

Fox, R. *Organizational Discourse: A Language-Ideology-Power Perspective*. Westport, CT: Praeger, 2004.

Freeman, E. *Strategic Management: A Stakeholder Approach*. Marshfield, MA: Pitman, 1984.

Freeman, J. "Organizational Life Cycles and Natural Selection Processes," in B. M. Staw and L. L. Cummings (eds.) *Research in Organizational Behavior*. Greenwich, CT: JAI Press, 1982.

Freeman, J. and M. T. Hannan. "Niche Width and the Dynamics of Organizational Populations." *American Journal of Sociology*, 6: 1116–1145, 1983.

Freeman, R. B., J. Hersch, and L. Mishel. *Emerging Labor Market Institutions for the Twenty-first Century*. Chicago: University of Chicago Press, 2005.

Freire, P. *The Pedagogy of the Oppressed*. New York: Herder & Herder, 1970.

French, J. R. P. and B. Raven. "The Bases of Social Power," in D. Cartwright and A. Zander (eds.) *Group Dynamics*. New York: Harper & Row, 1968.

Freud, S. *The Complete Psychological Works of Sigmund Freud*. London: Hogarth, 1953.

Frey-Rohn, L. *From Freud to Jung*. New York: Putnam, 1974.

Friedman, A. L. *Industry and Labour: Class Struggle at Work and Monopoly Capitalism*. London: Macmillan, 1977.

Friedman, T. L. *The Lexus and the Olive Tree.* New York: Farrar, Strauss and Giroux, 1999.

Friedman, T. L. *The World Is Flat: A Brief History of the 21st Century.* New York: Farrar, 2005.

Fromm, E. *Marx's Concept of Man.* New York: Ungar, 1961.

Fromm, E. *Beyond the Chains of Illusion: My Encounter With Marx and Freud.* New York: Trident Press. 1962.

Fromm, E. *The Crisis of Psychoanalysis.* New York: Cape, 1971.

Frost, P. J. "Power, Politics and Influence," pp. 503–548 in F. Jablin, L. Putnam, K. Roberts, and L. Porter (eds.) *Handbook of Organizational Communication.* Newbury Park, CA: Sage, 1987.

Frost, P. J. *Toxic Emotions at Work: How Compassionate Managers Handle Pain and Conflict.* Boston: Harvard Business School Press, 2003.

Frost, P. J. and C. Egri. "The Political Process of Innovation," pp. 229–295 in L. Cummings and B. Staw (eds.) *Research in Organizational Behavior.* Greenwich, CT: JAI Press, 1991.

Frost, P. J., V. F. Mitchell, and W. R. Nord (eds.) *Organizational Reality* (4th ed.). New York: HarperCollins, 1992.

Frost, P. J., V. F. Mitchell, and W. R. Nord (eds.) *Managerial Reality.* New York: HarperCollins, 1995.

Frost, P. J., L. F. Moore, M. R. Louis, C. C. Lundberg, and J. Martin. *Organizational Culture.* Beverly Hills, CA: Sage, 1985.

Frost, P. J., L. F. Moore, M. R. Louis, C. C. Lundberg, and J. Martin (eds.) *Reframing Organizational Culture.* Newbury Park, CA: Sage, 1991.

Fry, E. H. *The Politics of International Investment.* New York: McGraw-Hill, 1983.

Frye, N. *Anatomy of Criticism.* Princeton, NJ: Princeton University Press, 1957.

Frye, N. *The Great Code: The Bible and Literature.* Toronto: Academic Press, 1982.

Fullan, M. *Change Forces.* New York: Falmer Press, 1993.

Gabriel, Y. "The Unmanaged Organization: Stories, Fantasies and Subjectivity." *Organization Studies,* 16: 477–502, 1995.

Gadalla, I. E. and R. C. Cooper. "Toward an Epistemology of Management." *Social Science Information,* 17: 349–383, 1978.

Gagliardi, P. (ed.) *Symbols and Artifacts.* Berlin: Walter de Gruyter, 1990.

Galbraith, J. K. *American Capitalism.* Boston: Houghton Mifflin, 1962.

Galbraith, J. K. *The New Industrial State.* London: Hamish Hamilton, 1967.

Galbraith, J. R. "Matrix Organization Designs: How to Combine Functional and Project Forms." *Business Horizons,* 14: 29–40, 1971.

Galbraith, J. R. "Organization Design: An Information Processing View." *Interfaces,* 4: 28–36, 1974.

Galbraith, J. R. *Organization Design.* Reading, MA: Addison-Wesley, 1977.

Galbraith, J. R. and E. E. Lawler. *Organizing for the Future.* San Francisco: Jossey-Bass, 1993.

Galileo, G. *Discourses on Two New Sciences.* Evanston, IL: Northwestern University Press, 1968.

Gandossy, R. and J. Sonnenfeld (eds.) *Leadership and Governance From the Inside Out*. Hoboken, NJ: Wiley, 2004.

Gannon, M. J. and K. L. Newman (eds.) *The Blackwell Handbook of Cross-cultural Management*. Oxford, UK: Blackwell Business, 2002.

Garfinkel, H. *Studies in Ethnomethodology*. Englewood Cliffs, NJ: Prentice Hall, 1967.

Garson, G. D. "The Codetermination Model of Workers' Participation: Where Is It Leading?" *Sloan Management Review*, 63–78, 1977.

Gee, J. P. "On Mobots and Classrooms: The Converging Languages of the New Capitalism and Schooling." *Organization*, 3: 385–407, 1996.

Geertz, C. *The Interpretation of Cultures*. New York: Basic Books, 1973.

Gemmill, G. and J. Oakley. "Leadership: An Alienating Social Myth?" *Human Relations*, 45: 113–129, 1992.

George, C. S. *The History of Management Thought*. Englewood Cliffs, NJ: Prentice Hall, 1972.

George, S. *How the Other Half Dies: The Real Reasons for World Hunger*. Harmondsworth: Penguin, 1976.

Gergen, K. J. "The Social Constructionist Movement in Modern Psychology." *American Psychologist*, 40: 266–275, 1985.

Gergen, K. J. *The Saturated Self*. New York: Basic Books, 1991.

Gergen, K. J. and K. Davis (eds.) *The Social Construction of the Person*. New York: Springer-Verlag, 1985.

Geyer, F. and J. van der Zouwen (eds.) *Sociocybernetic Paradoxes*. London: Sage, 1986.

Geyer, F. and J. van der Zouwen (eds.) *Sociocybernetics: Complexity, Autopoiesis, and Observation of Social Systems*. Westport, CT: Greenwood Press, 2001.

Gharajedaghi, J. *Systems Thinkings Managing Chaos and Complexity: A Platform for Designing Business Architecture*. Boston: Butterworth Heinemann, 1999.

Gherardi, S. *Gender, Symbolism and Organizational Cultures*. Thousand Oaks, CA: Sage, 1995.

Gherardi, S. "Where Learning Is: Metaphor and Situated Learning in a Planning Group." *Human Relations*, 53: 1057–1080, 2000.

Giddens, A. *Central Problems in Social Theory*. London: Macmillan, 1979.

Giedeon, S. *Mechanization Takes Command*. New York: Oxford University Press, 1948.

Gigerenzer, G. and R. Selten (eds.) *Bounded Rationality: The Adaptive Toolbox*. Cambridge: MIT Press, 2001.

Gilbreth, F. B. *Motion Study*. New York: Van Nostrand, 1911.

Gilligan, C. *In a Different Voice*. Cambridge, MA: Harvard University Press, 1993.

Gilpin, R. and J. M. Gilpin. *The Challenge of Global Capitalism: The World Economy in the 21st Century*. Princeton, NJ: Princeton University Press, 2000.

Gimpl, M. L. and S. Dakin. *"Management and Magic."* New Zealand: University of Canterbury, 1983 (unpublished).

Giroux, H. A. *Stealing Innocence: Youth, Corporate Power and the Politics of Culture*. New York: St. Martin's, 2000.

Gladwell, M. *The Tipping Point: How Little Things Can Make a Big Difference*. Boston: Little, Brown, 2002.

Gladwell, M. *Blink: The Power of Thinking Without Thinking*. Boston: Little, Brown, 2005.

Gladwin, T. N. and I. Walter. *Multinationals Under Fire*. New York: John Wiley, 1980.

Gleick, J. *Chaos: Making a New Science*. New York: Penguin, 1987.

Gleick, J. *Faster: The Acceleration of Just About Everything*. New York: Pantheon, 1999.

Glencross, P. M. and D. C. Christiani. "Health Hazards of Abatement Work: Asbestos and Lead." *New Solutions*, 6(3): 23–24, 1996.

Gluckman, M. (ed.) *The Allocation of Responsibility*. Manchester: Manchester University Press, 1972.

Glyn, A. and B. Sutcliffe. *British Capitalism, Workers and the Profits Squeeze*. Harmondsworth: Penguin, 1972.

Godel, K. *On Formally Undecidable Propositions*. New York: Basic Books, 1962.

Godelier, M. "Structure and Contradiction in Capital," pp. 334–368 in R. Blackburn (ed.) *Ideology in Social Science*. London: Fontana/Collins, 1972.

Goffman, E. *The Presentation of Self in Everyday Life*. Garden City, NY: Doubleday, 1959.

Goffman, E. *Interaction Ritual*. Garden City, NY: Doubleday, 1967.

Goldberg, E. *The Executive Brain: Frontal Lobes and the Civilized Mind*. Oxford, UK: Oxford University Press, 2001.

Goldberg, W. H. and A. R. Negandhi (eds.) *Governments and Multinationals: The Policy of Control Versus Autonomy*. Cambridge, MA: Oelgeschlager, Gunn, & Hain, 1983.

Goldman, P. and D. Van Houten. "Managerial Strategies and the Worker." *Sociological Quarterly*, 18: 108–125, 1977.

Goldsmith, M., et al. *Global Leadership: The Next Generation*. Upper Saddle River, NJ: FT Prentice Hall, 2003.

Goldstein, J. *The Unshackled Organization*. Portland, OR: Productivity Press, 1994.

Goleman, D. *Emotional Intelligence: Why It Can Matter More Than IQ*. New York: Bantam, 1995.

Goleman, D., A. McKee, and R. E. Boyatzis. *Primal Leadership: Realizing the Power of Emotional Intelligence*. Boston: Harvard Business School Press, 2002.

Gomez, P. and G. Probst. "Organizational Closure in Management: A Complementary View to Contingency Approaches." Presented to the American Society for Cybernetics, Philadelphia, 1984.

Gonzalez, G. A. *Corporate Power and the Environment: The Political Economy of U.S. Environmental Policy*. Lanham, MD: Rowman and Littlefield, 2001.

Gordon, D. M., R. C. Edwards, and M. Reich. *Segmented Work, Divided Workers*. New York: Cambridge University Press, 1982.

Gorz, A. *Paths to Paradise*. London: Pluto Press, 1985.

Gottlieb, R. (ed.) *Reducing Toxics: A New Approach to Policy and Industrial Decisionmaking*. Washington, DC: Island Press, 1995.

Gouldner, A. "Reciprocity and Autonomy in Functional Theory," pp. 190–225 in A. W. Gouldner (ed.) *For Sociology*. Harmondsworth: Penguin, 1973.

Graham, P. (ed.) *Mary Parker Follett: Prophet of Management*. Boston: Harvard Business School Press, 1995.

Gramsci, A. *Selections From the Prison Notebooks*. London: Lawrence & Wishart, 1971.

Grandori, A. (ed.) *Corporate Governance and Firm Organization: Microfoundations and Structural Forms*. Oxford, UK: Oxford University Press, 2004.

Grant, D. and C. Oswick (eds.) *Metaphor and Organizations*. London: Sage, 1996.

Gray, B. *Collaborating: Finding Common Ground for Multiple Problems*. San Francisco: Jossey-Bass, 1989.

Gregory, K. "Native-View Paradigms: Multiple Cultures and Culture Conflicts in Organizations." *Administrative Science Quarterly*, 28: 259–276, 1983.

Gregory, R. F. *Women and Workplace Discrimination: Overcoming Barriers to Gender Equality*. New Brunswick, NJ: Rutgers University Press, 2003.

Griffin, D. *The Emergence of Leadership: Linking Self-organization and Ethics*. London: Routledge, 2002.

Grunberg, L. *Failed Multinational Ventures: The Political Economy of International Divestments*. Lexington, MA: D. C. Heath, 1981.

Guillet de Monthoux, P. *Action and Existence: Anarchism for Business Administration*. New York: John Wiley, 1983.

Gulick, L. and L. Urwick (eds.) *Papers in the Science of Administration*. New York: Institute of Public Administration, Columbia University, 1937.

Gunnermann, J. P. (ed.) *The Nation-State and Transnational Corporation in Conflict*. New York: Praeger, 1975.

Gunningham, N., R. A. Kagan, and D. Thornton. *Shades of Green: Business, Regulation and Environment*. Stanford, CA: Stanford University Press, 2003.

Guntrip, H. *Personality Structure and Human Interaction*. New York: International University Press, 1961.

Habermas, J. "On Systematically Distorted Communications." *Inquiry*, 13: 205–218, 1970a.

Habermas, J. "Towards a Theory of Communicative Competence." *Inquiry*, 13: 360–375, 1970b.

Habermas, J. *Knowledge and Human Interests*. London: Heinemann Educational Books, 1972.

Habermas, J. *Legitimation Crisis*. London: Heinemann Educational Books, 1973.

Hackman, J. R. and J. L. Suttle. *Improving Life at Work*. Santa Monica, CA: Goodyear, 1976.

Hagel, J., III, and J. S. Brown. *The Only Sustainable Edge: Why Business Strategy Depends on Productive Friction and Dynamic Specialization*. Boston: Harvard Business School Press, 2005.

Hailey, A. *Wheels*. Garden City, NY: Doubleday, 1971.

Haley, U. C. V. *Multinational Corporations in Political Environments: Ethics, Values and Strategies*. River Edge, NJ: World Scientific, 2001.

Hall, E. T. *The Silent Language*. Garden City, NY: Doubleday, 1959.

Hall, E. T. "The Silent Language in Overseas Business." *Harvard Business Review*, 38: 87–96, 1960.

Hall, E. T. *Beyond Culture*. Garden City, NY: Doubleday, 1967.

Hall, R. H. *Organizations: Structure and Process*. Englewood Cliffs, NJ: Prentice Hall, 1982.

Hamel, A. and C. K. Prahalad. *Competing for the Future*. Boston: Harvard Business School Press, 1994.

Hammer, M. and J. Champy. *Reengineering the Corporation*. New York: Harper, 1993.

Hampden-Turner, C. *Maps of the Mind*. New York: Macmillan, 1981.

Hampden-Turner, C. *Charting the Corporate Mind*. New York: Free Press, 1990a.

Hampden-Turner, C. *Creating Corporate Culture*. Reading, MA: Addison-Wesley, 1990b.

Hampden-Turner, C. and F. Trompenaars. *Building Cross-cultural Competence: How to Create Wealth From Conflicting Values*. New Haven, CT: Yale University Press, 2000.

Handy, C. *Gods of Management*. London: Pan Books, 1978.

Handy, C. *The Age of Unreason*. Boston: Harvard Business School Press, 1990.

Hannan, M. T. and J. H. Freeman. "The Population Ecology of Organizations." *American Journal of Sociology*, 82: 929–964, 1977.

Hardin, G. "The Tragedy of the Commons." *Science*, 13: 1968.

Harding, M. E. *The I and the Not I: A Study in the Development of Consciousness*. Princeton, NJ: Princeton University Press, 1965.

Harragan, B. *Games That Mother Never Taught You*. New York: Warner, 1977.

Harries-Jones, P. "Human Judgement and Conversation Theory: The Significance of Gregory Bateson's Concept of Co-evolution." Toronto: York University, 1983 (unpublished).

Harries-Jones, P. "The Other Side of the Mirror: Communication as Presentation." Toronto: York University, 1984. (unpublished)

Harries-Jones, P. *Ecological Understanding and Gregory Bateson*. Toronto: University of Toronto Press, 1995.

Harris, M. L. *Cultural Materialism*. New York: Random House, 1979.

Hart, S. L. *Capitalism at the Crossroads: The Unlimited Business Opportunities in Solving the World's Most Difficult Problems*. Upper Saddle River, NJ: Wharton School Publishing, 2005.

Hart, S. L. and M. B. Milstein. "Global Sustainability and the Creative Destruction of Industries." *Sloan Management Review*, 41(1): 23–33, 1999.

Hart, S. L. and M. B. Milstein. "Creating Sustainable Value." *Academy of Management Executive*, 17(2): 56–69, 2003.

Hartel, C., E. J. Wilfred, J. Zerbe, and N. M. Ashkanasy (eds.) *Emotions in Organizational Behavior*. Mahwah, NJ: Erlbaum, 2005.

Hartman, L. P., G. Denis, and R. E. Wokutch. *Rising Above Sweatshops: Innovative Approaches to Global Labor Challenges*. Westport, CT: Praeger, 2003.

Hartsock, N. "Foucault on Power: A Theory for Women," in L. Nicholson (ed.) *Feminism/Postmodernism*. New York: Routledge, 1990.

Harvey, J. *The Abilene Paradox*. New York: Free Press, 1995.

Hassard, J. and M. Parker. *Postmodernism and Organizations*. London: Sage, 1993.

Hastie, R. *Rational Choice in an Uncertain World: The Psychology of Judgment and Decision Making*. Thousand Oaks, CA: Sage, 2001.

Hastings, C. *The New Organization*. London: McGraw-Hill, 1993.

Hatch, M. J. *Organization Theory: Modern, Symbolic and Postmodern Perspectives*. Oxford, UK: Oxford University Press, 1997.

Hatch, M. J. and M. Schultz (eds.) *Organizational Identity: A Reader*. Oxford, UK: Oxford University Press, 2004.

Hawken, P. *The Ecology of Commerce: A Declaration of Sustainability*. New York: HarperBusiness, 1994.

Hawken, P., A., Lovins, and L. H. Lovins. *Natural Capitalism: Creating the Next Industrial Revolution*. Boston: Little, Brown, 1999.

Hawley, A. H. "Human Ecology," pp. 328–337 in D. Sills (ed.) *International Encyclopedia of the Social Sciences*. New York: Macmillan, 1968.

Hayter, T. *The Creation of World Poverty: An Alternative View to the Brandt Report*. London: Pluto Press, 1981.

Hearn, J. and W. Parkin. *"Sex" at "Work": The Power and Paradox of Organization Sexuality*. New York: St. Martin's, 1987.

Hearn, J., D. Sheppard, P. Tancred-Sheriff, and G. Burrell (eds.) *The Sexuality of Organization*. London: Sage, 1989.

Heath, T. L. *The Works of Archimedes*. Cambridge: Cambridge University Press, 1897.

Heckscher, C. C., et al. *Agents of Change: Crossing the Post-industrial Divide*. Oxford, UK: Oxford University Press, 2003.

Hedberg, B. "How Organizations Learn and Unlearn," pp. 3–27 in P. C. Nystrom and W. H. Starbuck (eds.) *Handbook of Organization Design*, Vol. 1. New York: Oxford University Press, 1981.

Hedberg, B., P. C. Nystrom, and W. H. Starbuck. "Camping on Seesaws: Prescriptions for a Self-Designing Organization." *Administrative Science Quarterly*, 21: 41–65, 1976.

Hegel, G. W. F. *The Logic of Hegel*. Oxford, UK: Clarendon, 1892.

Hegel, G. W. F. *Science of Logic*. London: Allen & Unwin, 1929.

Heisenberg, W. *A Physicist's Conception of Nature*. London: Hutchinson, 1958a.

Heisenberg, W. *Physics and Philosophy*. New York: Harper, 1958b.

Heisenberg, W. *Physics and Beyond*. New York: Harper and Row, 1971.

Held, D. *Introduction to Critical Theory*. Berkeley: University of California Press, 1980.

Helgesen, S. *Female Advantage: Women's Ways of Leadership*. New York: Doubleday, 1990.

Hennestad, B. W. "The Symbolic Impact of Double Bind Leadership." *Journal of Management Studies*, 27: 265–279, 1990.

Hennig, M. and A. Jardim. *The Managerial Woman*. New York: Pocket Books, 1976.

Henry, J. (ed.) *Creative Management*. London: Sage, 1991.

Henry, J. and D. Walker (eds.) *Managing Innovation*. London: Sage, 1991.

Hepple, B. A. *Social and Labour Rights in a Global Context: International and Comparative Perspectives.* Cambridge, UK: Cambridge University Press, 2002.

Herbst, P. G. *Autonomous Group Functioning.* London: Tavistock, 1962.

Herbst, P. G. *Socio-technical Design.* London: Tavistock, 1974.

Herriot, P. *The Employment Relationship: A Psychological Perspective.* Hove, UK: Routlege, 2001.

Herzberg, F., B. Mausner, and B. Snyderman. *The Motivation to Work.* New York: John Wiley, 1959.

Heydebrand, W. V. "Organizational Contradictions in Public Bureaucracies: Toward a Marxian Theory of Organizations." *Sociological Quarterly,* 18: 83–107, 1977.

Heydebrand, W. V. "Organization and Praxis," pp. 306–320 in G. Morgan (ed.) *Beyond Method.* Beverly Hills, CA: Sage, 1983.

Heydebrand, W. V. and C. Seron. "The Double-Bind of the Capitalist Judicial System." *International Journal of the Sociology of Law,* 9: 407–436, 1981.

Hickson, D. J., C. R. Hinings, C. A. Lee, R. E. Schneck, and J. M. Pennings. "A Strategic Contingencies Theory of Intra-organizational Power." *Administrative Science Quarterly,* 16: 216–229, 1971.

Hickson, D. J., D. S. Pugh, and D. C. Pheysey. "Operations Technology and Organization Structure: An Empirical Reappraisal." *Administrative Science Quarterly,* 14: 378–397, 1969.

Hiebert, M. "Give and Take—Foreign Workers Are Providing Much of the Muscle for Asia's Building Boom." *Far Eastern Economic Review,* May 25: 56, 1995.

Hinings, C. R. and R. Greenwood. *The Dynamics of Strategic Change.* Oxford, UK: Basil Blackwell, 1988.

Hirsch, P. M. and J. Andrews. "Ambushes, Shootouts, and Knights of the Roundtable: The Language of Corporate Takeovers," pp. 145–155 in L. Pondy et al. (eds.) *Organizational Symbolism.* Greenwich, CT: JAI Press, 1983.

Hirschhorn, L. *The Workplace Within.* Cambridge: MIT Press, 1988.

Hirschhorn, L. *Managing in the New Team Environment.* Reading, MA: Addison-Wesley, 1991.

Hirst, P. and G. Thompson. "Globalization, Foreign Direct Investment and International Governance." *Organization,* 1: 277–303, 1994.

Hobbes, T. *Leviathan.* London: Basil Blackwell, 1951.

Hodge, B., R. Fleck, and C. B. Honess. *Management Information Systems.* Reston, VA: Reston Publishing, 1984.

Hoffman, A. J. and M. H. Bazerman. *Changing Environmental Practice: Understanding and Overcoming the Organizational and Psychological Barriers.* Working Paper. Boston: Harvard Business School, 2005.

Hofstadter, D. R. *Gödel, Escher, Bach.* New York: Basic Books, 1979.

Hofstadter, D. R. "Metamagical Themas." *Scientific American,* 248: 16–26, 1983.

Hofstede, G. *Culture's Consequences.* London: Sage, 1980.

Hofstede, G. H. *The Game of Budget Control.* Assen, The Netherlands: Van Gorcum, 1967.

Holland, S. *The Socialist Challenge.* London: Quartet, 1975.

Holloway, J. and S. Picciotto (eds.) *State and Capital: A Marxist Debate*. London: Arnold, 1978.

Holyoak, K. and P. Thagard. *Mental Leaps: Analogy in Creative Thought*. Cambridge: MIT Press, 1995.

Hopkins, T. K. and I. Wallerstein. *World-System Analysis*. Beverly Hills, CA: Sage, 1982.

Hopwood, A. G. "Accounting and the Pursuit of Social Interests," in W. Chia, T. Lowe, and T. Puxty (eds.) *Critical Perspectives in Management Control*. Basingstoke: Macmillan, 1989.

Horkheimer, M. *Critical Theory: Selected Essays*. New York: Herder, 1972.

Horkheimer, M. and T. Adorno. *Dialectic of Enlightenment*. London: Allen Lane, 1973.

Horney, K. *Self-Analysis*. New York: Norton, 1942.

Horney, K. *Feminine Psychology*. New York: Norton, 1967.

Howell, D. R. (ed.) *Fighting Unemployment: The Limits of Free Market Orthodoxy*. Oxford, UK: Oxford University Press, 2005.

Howells, J. and M. Wood. *The Globalization of Production and Technology*. London: Belhaven Press, 1993.

Huff, A. S. "Industry Influences on Strategy Reformulation." *Strategic Management Journal*, 3: 119–131, 1982.

Hughes, J. *Britain in Crisis*. Nottingham: Spokesman Books, 1981.

Hummel, R. *The Bureaucratic Experience*. New York: St. Martin's, 1977.

Hurst, D. *Crisis and Renewal: Meeting the Challenge of Organizational Change*. Boston: Harvard Business School Press, 1995.

Hyman, R. *Industrial Relations: A Marxist Introduction*. London: Macmillan, 1975.

Iacocca, L. *An Autobiography*. New York: Bantam, 1984.

Iannello, K. P. *Decisions Without Hierarchy*. New York: Routledge, 1992.

Ingalls, J. D. *Human Energy*. Austin, TX: Learning Concepts, 1979.

Issacs, W. *Dialogue: The Art of Thinking Together*. New York: Currency, 1999.

Jakobson, R. *Selected Writings*. The Hague: Mouton, 1956.

Jakobson, R. and M. Halle. *Fundamentals of Language*. The Hague: Mouton, 1962.

James, W. *The Principles of Psychology*. New York: Dover, 1950.

Janis, I. L. *Victims of Groupthink*. Boston: Houghton Mifflin, 1972.

Jantsch, E. *Design for Evolution*. New York: Braziller, 1975.

Jantsch, E. *The Self-Organizing Universe*. Oxford: Pergamon, 1980.

Jantsch, E. and C. Waddington. *Evolution and Consciousness*. Reading, MA: Addison-Wesley, 1976.

Jaques, E. "Social Systems as a Defense Against Persecutory and Depressive Anxiety," pp. 478–498 in M. Klein (ed.) *New Directions in Psycho-analysis*. London: Tavistock, 1955.

Jardim, A. *The First Henry Ford: A Study in Personality and Business Leadership*. Cambridge: MIT Press, 1970.

Jay, M. *The Dialectical Imagination*. London: Heinemann, 1973.

Jay, P. *Management and Machiavelli*. London: Hodder & Stoughton, 1967.

Jelinek, M., L. Smircich, and P. Hirsch (eds.) "Organizational Culture." *Administrative Science Quarterly*, 28, 1983.

Jessop, B. *State Theory*. Cambridge: Polity, 1990.

Johansson, F. *The Medici Effect: Breakthrough Insights at the Intersection of Ideas, Concepts and Cultures*. Boston: Harvard Business School Press, 2004.

Johnson, B. *Polarity Management*. Amherst, MA: HRD Press, 1992.

Johnson, S. *Emergence: The Connected Lives of Ants, Brains, Cities, and Software*. New York: Scribner, 2001.

Jung, C. G. *Collected Works*. London: Routledge & Kegan Paul, 1953.

Jung, C. G. *Man and His Symbols*. London: Aldus Books, 1964.

Jung, C. G. *Memories, Dreams, Reflections*. London: Routledge & Kegan Paul, 1967.

Jung, C. G. *The Archetypes and the Collective Unconscious*. Princeton, NJ: Bollingen, 1968.

Jung, C. G. *The Portable Jung*. New York: Viking, 1971.

Kafka, F. *The Trial*. Harmondsworth: Penguin, 1953.

Kafka, F. *The Castle*. New York: Secker, 1973.

Kakar, S. *Frederick Taylor: A Study in Personality and Innovation*. Cambridge: MIT Press, 1970.

Kamata, S. *Japan in the Passing Lane*. New York: Pantheon, 1982.

Kanter, R. M. *Men and Women of the Corporation*. New York: Basic Books, 1977.

Kanter, R. M. *The Change Masters*. New York: Simon & Schuster, 1983.

Kanter, R. M. *Evolve! Succeeding in the Digital Culture of Tomorrow*. Boston: Harvard Business School Press, 2000.

Kast, F. E. and J. E. Rosenzweig. *Contingency Views of Organization and Management*. Chicago: Science Research Associates, 1973.

Katz, D. and R. L. Kahn. *The Social Psychology of Organizations*. New York: John Wiley, 1978.

Kauffman, S. A. "Antichaos and Adaptation." *Scientific American*, August: 78–84, 1991.

Kauffman, S. A. *The Origins of Order: Self Organization and Selection in Evolution*. New York: Oxford University Press, 1993.

Kaufman, W. *Hegel*. London: Weidenfeld & Nicholson, 1965.

Kautsky, J. H. *The Politics of Aristocratic Empires*. Chapel Hill: University of North Carolina Press, 1982.

Keidel, R. W. *Game Plans*. New York: John Wiley, 1985.

Keidel, R. W. *Corporate Players*. New York: John Wiley, 1988.

Kelly, K. *Out of Control: The New Biology of Machines, Social Systems, and the Economic World*. Reading, MA: Addison-Wesley, 1994.

Kelly, M. *The Divine Right of Capital: Dethroning the Corporate Aristocracy*. San Francisco: Berrett Koehler, 2003.

Kelly, M. P. F. "Making Sense of Gender in the World Economy." *Organization*, 1: 249–275, 1994.

Kennedy, M. M. *Office Politics: Seizing Power and Wielding Clout*. New York: Warner Books, 1980.

Kerr, C., J. T. Dunlop, F. H. Harbison, and C. A. Myers. *Industrialism and Industrial Man*. London: Oxford University Press, 1964.

Kets de Vries, M. *Organizational Paradoxes*. London: Tavistock, 1980.

Kets de Vries, M. and D. Miller. *The Neurotic Organization*. San Francisco: Jossey-Bass, 1984.

Keyton, J. *Communication and Organizational Culture: A Key to Understanding Work Experiences*. Thousand Oaks, CA: Sage, 2005.

Kickert, W. J. M. "Autopoiesis and the Science of (Public) Administration: Essence, Sense and Nonsense." *Organization Studies*, 14: 261–278, 1993.

Kidder, T. *The Soul of a New Machine*. Harmondsworth: Penguin, 1981.

Kiel, L. D. *Managing Chaos and Complexity in Government*. San Francisco: Jossey-Bass, 1994.

Kiernans, E. *Globalism and the Nation State*. Toronto: CBC Enterprises, 1984.

Kilmann, R. H., M. J. Saxton, and R. Serpa (eds.) *Gaining Control of the Corporate Culture*. San Francisco: Jossey-Bass, 1985.

Kim, D. *Organizing for Learning: Strategies for Knowledge Creation and Enduring Change*. Waltham, MA: Pegasus Communications, 2001.

Kim, W. C. and R. Mauborgne. *Blue Ocean Strategy: How to Create Uncontested Market Space and Make Competition Irrelevant*. Boston: Harvard Business School Press, 2005.

Kimberley, J. R. and R. H. Miles. *The Organizational Life Cycle*. San Francisco: Jossey-Bass, 1980.

Kingdon, D. R. *Matrix Organization*. London: Tavistock, 1973.

Klein, M. *Contributions to Psycho-analysis: 1921–1945*. London: Hogarth, 1965.

Klein, M. *Envy, Gratitude and Other Works*. London: Hogarth, 1980.

Klein, M. *Love, Guilt and Reparation and Other Works*. London: Hogarth, 1981.

Klein, N. *No Space, No Choice, No Jobs, No Logo: Taking Aim at the Brand Bullies*. New York: Picador, 1999.

Kleiner, A. *The Age of Heretics: Heroes, Outlaws, and the Forerunners of Corporate Change*. New York: Currency, 1996.

Kleiner, A. *Who Really Matters: The Core Group Theory of Power, Privilege, and Success*. New York: Currency, 2003.

Knights, D. and H. Willmott. "Organizational Culture as Management Strategy." *International Studies of Management and Organization*, 3: 40–63, 1987.

Knights, D. and H. Willmott (eds.) *Labour Process Theory*. London: Macmillan, 1989.

Knights, D., H. Willmott, and D. Collinson (eds.) *Job Redesign: Critical Perspectives on the Labour Process*. Aldershot, UK: Gower, 1985.

Koestler, A. *The Ghost in the Machine*. London: Hutchinson, 1967.

Koestler, A. *The Act of Creation*. London: Hutchinson, 1969.

Kolodny, H. "Managing in a Matrix." *Business Horizons*, March: 17–24, 1981.

Koontz, H. and C. O'Donnell. *Principles of Management*. New York: McGraw-Hill, 1955.

Korda, M. *Power: How to Get It, How to Use It*. New York: Random House, 1975.

Kornhauser, W. *Scientists in Industry*. Berkeley: University of California Press, 1963.

Korton, D. C. *When Corporations Rule the World* (2nd ed.). San Francisco: Berrett-Kohler, 2001.

Kotter, J. P. "Power, Dependence and Effective Management." *Harvard Business Review*, July–August, 1977.

Kreckel, R. "Unequal Opportunity Structure and Labor Market Segmentation." *Sociology*, 14: 525–550, 1980.

Kreitman, N. *The Roots of Metaphor: A Multidisciplinary Study in Aesthetics.* Aldershot, UK: Ashgate, 1999.

Krippendorf, K. "Major Metaphors of Communication and Some Constructivist Reflections on their Use." *Cybernetics and Human Knowing*, 2: 3–25, 1993.

Kroeber, A. L. and C. Kluckhohn. *Culture: A Critical Review of Concepts and Definitions.* New York: Vintage, 1952.

Kropotkin, P. A. *Mutual Aid.* New York: McLure, Phillips, 1903.

Kuhn, T. S. *The Structure of Scientific Revolutions.* Chicago: University of Chicago Press, 1970.

Kujawa, D. (ed.) *International Labor and the Multinational Enterprise.* New York: Praeger, 1975.

Lacan, J. *Ecrits.* Paris: Seuil, 1966.

Lafeber, W. *Michael Jordan and the New Global Capitalism.* New York: Norton, 2002.

Laing, R. D. *The Divided Self.* Harmondsworth: Penguin, 1965.

Lakoff, G. and M. Johnson. *Metaphors We Live By.* Chicago: University of Chicago Press, 1980.

Lakoff, G. and M. Johnson. *Philosophy in the Flesh: The Embodied Mind and Its Challenge to Western Thought.* New York: Basic Books, 1999.

Lall, S. (ed.) *The New Multinationals: The Spread of Third World Enterprises.* New York: John Wiley, 1983.

LaMettrie, J. *L'Homme Machine.* London: Owen, 1748.

Lammers, C. J. and D. Hickson (eds.) *Organizations Alike and Unalike.* London: Routledge & Kegan Paul, 1979.

Land, G. and B. Jarman. *Breakpoint and Beyond.* New York: Harper Business, 1992.

Lang, T. and M. Heasman. *Food Wars: The Global Battle for Mouths, Minds and Markets.* London: Earthscan Publications, 2004.

Langton, C. (ed.) *Artificial Life II.* Reading, MA: Addison-Wesley, 1992.

Lasch, C. *The Culture of Narcissism.* New York: Warner Books, 1979.

Lash, S. and J. Urry. *The End of Organized Capitalism.* Cambridge, UK: Polity, 1987.

Laski, H. J. *Studies in the Problem of Sovereignty.* New Haven, CT: Yale University Press, 1917.

Laski, H. J. *Authority in the Modern State.* New Haven, CT: Yale University Press, 1919.

Lasswell, H. D. *Politics: Who Gets What, When, How.* New York: McGraw-Hill, 1936.

Lawler, E. E. *Motivation in Work Organizations.* Monterey, CA: Brooks/Cole, 1973.

Lawrence, P. R. and D. Dyer. *Renewing American Industry.* New York: Free Press, 1982.

Lawrence, P. R. and J. W. Lorsch. *Organization and Environment.* Cambridge, MA: Harvard Graduate School of Business Administration, 1967a.

Lawrence, P. R. and J. W. Lorsch. "Differentiation and Integration in Complex Organizations." *Administrative Science Quarterly*, 12: 1–47, 1967b.

Leavitt, H. J. "Applied Organizational Change in Industry: Structural, Technical and Human Approaches," in W. W. Cooper, H. J. Leavitt, and M. W. Shelly (eds.) *New Perspectives in Organization Research*. New York: John Wiley, 1964.

Leblanc, R. and J. Gillies. *The Coming Revolution in Corporate Governance*. New York: Wiley, 2005.

Lefebvre, H. *Dialectical Materialism*. London: Jonathan Cape, 1968a.

Lefebvre, H. *The Sociology of Karl Marx*. London: Allen Lane, 1968b.

Leifer, R. "Understanding Organizational Transformation Using a Dissipative Structure Model." *Human Relations*, 42: 899–916, 1989.

Lemaire, A. *Jacques Lacan*. London: Routledge & Kegan Paul, 1977.

Lenin, V. I. "On Dialectics," in *Selected Works*. London, 1936.

Lennick, D. and F. Kiel. *Moral Intelligence: Enhancing Business Performance and Leadership Success*. Upper Saddle River, NJ: Wharton School Publications, 2005.

Lessem, R. *Intrapreneurship*. Aldershot, UK: Gower, 1987.

Levidon, L. and B. Young (eds.) *Science, Technology and the Labour Process*. London: Blackrose Press, 1981.

Levie, H. D. and N. Lorentzen (eds.) *Fighting Closures*. Nottingham: Spokesman Books, 1984.

Levinson, H. *Organizational Diagnosis*. Cambridge, MA: Harvard University Press, 1972.

Lévi-Strauss, C. *The Scope of Anthropology*. New York: Jonathan Cape, 1967.

Levy, F. and R. J. Murnane. *The New Division of Labor: How Computers Are Creating the Next Job Market*. Princeton, NJ: Princeton University Press, 2004.

Lewin, K. *Field Theory in Social Sciences*. New York: Harper and Row, 1951.

Lewin, R. *Complexity: Life at the Edge of Chaos*. New York: Macmillan, 1992.

Lewin, R. and B. Regine. *Weaving Complexity and Business: Engaging the Soul at Work*. New York: Texere, 2001.

Lifton, J. and E. Olson. *Living and Dying*. New York: Bantam, 1975.

Lindblom, C. E. "The Science of 'Muddling Through.'" *Public Administration Review*, 19: 78–88, 1959.

Lindblom, C. E. *The Policy-Making Process*. Englewood Cliffs, NJ: Prentice Hall, 1968.

Linstead, S. and R. Grafton-Small. "On Reading Organizational Culture." *Organization Studies*, 13: 331–355, 1992.

Lips, H. M. *Women, Men, and the Psychology of Power*. Englewood Cliffs, NJ: Prentice Hall, 1981.

Litterer, J. A. "Conflict in Organization: A Re-examination." *Academy of Management*, 9: 178–186, 1966.

Lopez, J. *Society and Its Metaphors: Language, Social Theory and Social Structure*. New York: Continuum, 2003.

Lord, R. G., R. J. Klimoski, and R. Kanfer (eds.) *Emotions in the Workplace: Understanding the Structure and Role of Emotions in Organizational Behavior*. San Francisco: Jossey-Bass, 2002.

Lorsch, J. W., L. Berlowitz, and A. Zelleke (eds.) *Restoring Trust in American Business*. Cambridge: MIT Press, 2005.

Louis, M. R. "Organizations as Culture-Bearing Milieux," pp. 39–54 in L. Pondy et al. (eds.) *Organizational Symbolism*. Greenwich, CT: JAI Press, 1983.

Lowenberg, P. "Love and Hate in the Academy." *Centre Magazine*, September 4–11, 1972.

Lubit, R. H. *Coping With Toxic Managers, Subordinates and Other Difficult People*. Upper Saddle River, NJ: FT Prentice Hall, 2004.

Lucas, R. "Political and Cultural Analysis of Organizations." *Academy of Management Review*, 12: 144–146, 1987.

Luhmann, N. *Social Systems*. Stanford, CA: Stanford University Press, 1995.

Lukacs, G. *History and Class Consciousness*. London: Merlin, 1971.

Lukes, S. *Power: A Radical View*. London: Macmillan, 1974.

Luo, Y. *Coopetition in International Business*. Denmark: Copenhagen Business School Press, 2004.

Maasen, S. and P. Weingart. *Metaphors and the Dynamics of Knowledge*. London: Routledge, 2000.

Maccoby, M. *The Gamesman*. New York: Simon & Schuster, 1976.

Machiavelli, N. *The Prince*. New York: St. Martins Press, 1964.

Machlowitz, M. *Workaholics*. Reading, MA: Addison-Wesley, 1978.

Magruder Watkins, J. and B. Mohr. *Appreciative Inquiry: Change at the Speed of Imagination*. San Francisco: Jossey-Bass, 2001.

Maitland, F. W. *Collected Papers*. Cambridge: Cambridge University Press, 1911.

Mandel, E. *Marxist Economic Theory*. London: Merlin, 1962.

Mangham, I. *Interactions and Interventions in Organizations*. New York: John Wiley, 1978.

Mangham, I. and M. Overington. "Dramatism and the Theatrical Metaphor," pp. 219–233 in G. Morgan (ed.) *Beyond Method*. Beverly Hills, CA: Sage, 1983.

Mangham, I. and M. Overington. *Organizations as Theatre*. Chichester, UK: Wiley, 1987.

Mankin, D. A. and S. G. Cohen. *Business Without Boundaries: An Action Framework for Collaborating Across Time, Distance, Organization, and Culture*. San Francisco: Jossey-Bass, 2004.

Mannheim, K. *Man and Society in an Age of Reconstruction*. London: Routledge & Kegan Paul, 1940.

Manning, P. K. "Talking and Becoming: A View of Organizational Socialization," pp. 239–256 in J. Douglas (ed.) *Understanding Everyday Life*. Chicago: Aldine, 1970.

Manning, P. K. "Metaphors of the Field: Varieties of Organizational Discourse." *Administrative Science Quarterly*, 24: 660–671, 1979.

Mansell, R. *The New Telecommunications: A Political Economy of Network Organizations*. London: Sage, 1994.

Mao Tse Tung. *On Contradiction*. Peking: Foreign Language Press, 1937.

March, J. G. "The Business Firm as a Political Coalition." *Journal of Politics*, 24: 662–678, 1962.

March, J. G. "Decision Making Perspective: Decisions in Organizations and Theories of Choice," pp. 205–244 in A. Van de Ven and W. Joyce (eds.) *Perspectives on Organization Design and Behavior*. New York: John Wiley, 1981.

March, J. G. *The Pursuit of Organizational Intelligence*. Malden, MA: Blackwell, 1999.

March, J. G. and J. P. Oslen. *Ambiguity and Choice in Organizations*. Bergen: Universitetsforlaget, 1976.

March, J. G. and H. A. Simon. *Organizations*. New York: John Wiley, 1958.

Marcuse, H. *Eros and Civilization*. Boston: Beacon, 1955.

Marcuse, H. *One-Dimensional Man*. Boston: Beacon, 1964.

Marcuse, H. "Freedom and Freud's Theory of Instincts," in *Five Lectures: Psychoanalysis, Politics and Utopia*. Boston: Beacon, 1970.

Marglin, S. A. "What Do Bosses Do?" pp. 13–54 in A. Gorz (ed.) *The Division of Labor*. Hassocks: Harvester, 1976.

Markovic, M. *From Affluence to Praxis*. Ann Arbor: University of Michigan Press, 1974.

Markowitz, G. E. and D. Rosner. *Deceit and Denial: The Deadly Politics of Industrial Pollution*. Berkeley: University of California Press, 2003.

Marks, J. "Time Out." *U.S. News & World Report*, December 11: 85–96, 1995.

Marquardt, M. *Action Learning in Action: Transforming People and Problems for World Class Organizational Learning*. Palo Alto, CA: Davies-Black Publishing, 1999.

Marquardt, M. *Optimizing the Power of Action Learning: Solving Problems and Building Leaders in Real Time*. Palo Alto, CA: Davies-Black Publishing, 2004.

Marshall, J. *Women Managers: Travellers in a Male World*. Chichester, UK: Wiley, 1984.

Marshall, J. "Patterns of Cultural Awareness as Coping Strategies for Women Managers," pp. 90–110 in S. Kahn and B. Long (eds.) *Women, Work and Coping*. Montreal: McGill-Queen's University Press, 1993.

Marshall, J. "Re-visioning Organizations by Developing Female Values," in R. Boot, J. Lawrence, and J. Morris (eds.) *Managing the Unknown*. London: McGraw-Hill, 1994.

Marshall, J. and A. McLean. "Exploring Organization Culture as a Route to Organizational Change," pp. 2–20 in V. Hammond (ed.) *Current Research in Management*. London: Francis Pinter, 1985.

Martin, J. *Cultures in Organizations: Three Perspectives*. New York: Oxford University Press, 1992.

Martin, J. *Organizational Culture: Mapping the Terrain*. Thousand Oaks, CA: Sage, 2001.

Martin, J. and P. Frost. "The Organizational Culture War Games: A Struggle for Intellectual Dominance," pp. 599–621 in S. Clegg and C. Hardy (eds.) *Handbook of Organization Studies*. London: Sage, 1996.

Martin, J. and C. Siehl. "Organizational Culture and Sub-culture: An Uneasy Symbiosis." *Organizational Dynamics*, 12: 52–64, 1983.

Maruyama, M. "The Second Cybernetics: Deviation Amplifying Mutual Causal Processes." *American Scientist*, 51: 164–179, 1963.

Maruyama, M. "Mindscapes, Management, Business Policy, and Public Policy." *Academy of Management Review*, 7: 612–619, 1982.

Marx, K. *Early Writings*. Harmondsworth: Penguin, 1975.

Marx, K. *Das Kapital*. Harmondsworth: Penguin, 1976.

Marx, K. and F. Engels. *The German Ideology*. London: Lawrence & Wishart, 1846.

Marx, K. and F. Engels. "The Manifesto of the Communist Party," pp. 35–63 in K. Marx and F. Engels, *Selected Works*. London: Lawrence & Wishart, 1848.

Maslow, A. H. "A Theory of Human Motivation." *Psychological Review*, 50: 370–396, 1943.

Maslow, A. H. *Toward a Psychology of Being*. New York: Van Nostrand, 1968.

Mason, R. O. and I. Mitroff. *Challenging Strategic Planning Assumptions*. New York: John Wiley, 1981.

Massey, D. and R. Meegan. *The Anatomy of Job Loss*. London: Methuen, 1982.

Maturana, H. and F. Varela. *Autopoiesis and Cognition: The Realization of the Living*. London: Reidl, 1980.

Mauzy, J. and R. A. Harriman. *Creativity Inc.: Building an Inventive Organization*. Boston: Harvard Business School Press, 2003.

Mayo, E. *The Human Problems of an Industrial Civilization*. New York: Macmillan, 1933.

McClelland, D. *Power: The Inner-Experience*. New York: John Wiley, 1975.

McClintock, D., R. Ison, and R. Armson. "Conceptual Metaphors: A Review With Implications for Human Understandings and Systems Practice." *Cybernetics and Human Knowing*, 11(1): 25–47, 2004.

McCorduck, P. *Machines Who Think*. San Francisco: Freeman, 1979.

McCulloch, W. S. "Recollections of the Many Sources of Cybernetics." *Forum*, 6, 1974.

McDonough, W. and M. Braungart. *Cradle to Cradle: Re-making the Way We Make Things*. New York: North Point Press, 2002.

McGregor, D. *The Human Side of Enterprise*. New York: McGraw-Hill, 1960.

McKelvey, B. "Guidelines for the Empirical Classification of Organizations." *Administrative Science Quarterly*, 20: 509–525, 1982a.

McKelvey, B. *Organizational Systematics: Taxonomy, Evolution, Classification*. Berkeley: University of California Press, 1982b.

McKelvey, B. and H. Aldrich. "Populations, Natural Selection and Applied Organizational Science." *Administrative Science Quarterly*, 28: 101–128, 1983.

McKenzie, J. *Paradox: The Next Strategic Dimension*. London: McGraw-Hill, 1996.

McLellan, D. *Karl Marx: His Life and Thought*. London: Macmillan, 1973.

McLuhan, E. and F. Zingrone (eds.) *Essential McLuhan*. Toronto: Anansi Press, 1995.

McMillan, C. J. *The Japanese Industrial System*. Berlin: Walter de Gruyter, 1984.

McNeil, K. "Understanding Organizational Power: Building on the Weberian Legacy." *Administrative Science Quarterly*, 23: 65–90, 1978.

McSwain, C. J. and O. F. White, Jr. "The Case for Lying, Cheating, and Stealing: Organization Development as an Ethos Model for Management Practice." Presented at the Academy of Management meeting, New York City, 1982.

McWhinney, W. "Resolving Complex Issues." Los Angeles: Fielding Institute, 1982. (unpublished).

McWhinney, W. *Paths of Change*. Thousand Oaks, CA: Sage, 1992.

Mead, R. *International Management: Cross-cultural Dimensions* (3rd ed.). Oxford, UK: Blackwell, 2005.

Meadows, D. H., D. L. Meadows, R. Randers, and W. Behrens. *The Limits to Growth*. New York: Universe Books, 1972.

Medwar, C. and B. Freese. *Drug Diplomacy*. London: Social Audit, 1982.

Menzies, H. *The Information Highway and the New Economy*. Toronto: Between the Lines, 1996.

Menzies, I. "A Case Study in the Functioning of Social Systems as a Defense Against Anxiety." *Human Relations*, 13: 95–121, 1960.

Merton, R. K. *Social Theory and Social Structure*. New York: Free Press, 1968a.

Merton, R. K. "Manifest and Latent Functions," pp. 73–138 in *Social Theory and Social Structure*. New York: Free Press, 1968b.

Meszaros, I. *Marx's Theory of Alienation*. London: Merlin, 1970.

Meszaros, I. *Lukacs' Concept of Dialectic*. London: Merlin, 1972.

Meyer, J. W. and B. Rowan. "Institutionalized Organizations: Formal Structure as Myth and Ceremony." *American Journal of Sociology*, 83: 340–363, 1977.

Michael, D. N. *On Learning to Plan—and Planning to Learn*. San Francisco: Jossey-Bass, 1973.

Michaels, M. *The Chaos Network Newsletter*. Savoy, IL: The Chaos Network, 1996.

Michels, R. *Political Parties*. New York: Free Press, 1949.

Miethe, T. D. *Whistleblowing at Work: Tough Choices in Exposing Fraud, Waste, and Abuse on the Job*. Boulder, CO: Westview Press, 1999.

Miles, R. E. and C. C. Snow. *Organizational Strategy, Structure and Process*. New York: McGraw-Hill, 1978.

Miles, R. E. and C. C. Snow. "Organizations: New Concepts for New Forms." *California Management Review*, 28: 62–73, 1986.

Miles, R. E. and C. C. Snow. "Causes of Failure in Network Organizations." *California Management Review*, 34: 53–72, 1992.

Miles, R. H. *Macro Organizational Behavior*. Santa Monica, CA: Goodyear, 1980.

Milgate, M. *Alliances, Outsourcing, and the Lean Organization*. Westport, CT: Quorum, 2001.

Miliband, R. *The State in Capitalist Society*. London: Quartet, 1973.

Miller, A. *Death of a Salesman*. New York: Viking, 1949.

Miller, D. *The Icarus Paradox*. New York: Harper Business, 1990.

Miller, D. and P. H. Friesen. "Archetypes of Strategy Formulation." *Management Science*, 24: 921–933, 1978.

Miller, D. and P. H. Friesen. *Organizations: A Quantum View*. Englewood Cliffs, NJ: Prentice Hall, 1984.

Miller, D. and H. Mintzberg. "The Case for Configuration," pp. 57–73 in G. Morgan (ed.) *Beyond Method: Strategies for Social Research*. Beverly Hills, CA: Sage, 1983.

Miller, E. J. and A. K. Rice. *Systems of Organization*. London: Tavistock, 1967.

Miller, J. G. *The Body in Question*. New York: Jonathan Cape, 1978a.

Miller, J. G. *Living Systems*. New York: McGraw-Hill, 1978b.

Miller, J. *The Passion of Michel Foucault*. New York: Doubleday, 1993.

Millett, K. *Sexual Politics*. New York: Avon, 1969.

Mills, A. J. and P. Tancred (eds.) *Gendering Organizational Analysis*. Newbury Park, CA: Sage, 1992.

Mills, D. Q. *Rebirth of the Corporation*. New York: John Wiley, 1991.

Mills, T. "Europe's Industrial Democracy: An American Response." *Harvard Business Review*, 56, 1978.

Mintzberg, H. *The Nature of Managerial Work*. New York: Harper & Row, 1973.

Mintzberg, H. "Planning on the Left Side and Managing on the Right." *Harvard Business Review*, 54: 49–58, 1976.

Mintzberg, H. *The Structuring of Organizations*. Englewood Cliffs, NJ: Prentice Hall, 1979.

Mintzberg, H. *Power in and Around Organizations*. Englewood Cliffs, NJ: Prentice Hall, 1983.

Mintzberg, H. "Crafting Strategy." *Harvard Business Review*, 4: 66–75, 1986.

Mirow, K. R. and H. Maurer. *Webs of Power: International Cartels and the World Economy*. Boston: Houghton Mifflin, 1982.

Mitchell, J. *Psychoanalysis and Feminism*. New York: Pantheon, 1974.

Mitchell, R. "Masters of Innovation: How 3M Keeps Its New Products Coming." *Business Week*, April 10: 58–63, 1989.

Mitroff, I. I. *Stakeholders of the Mind*. San Francisco: Jossey-Bass, 1984.

Mitroff, I. I. and R. H. Kilmann. "On Organizational Stories," in R. H. Kilmann, L. R. Pondy, and D. P. Slevin (eds.) *The Management of Organization Design*. New York: American Elsevier, 1976.

Mitroff, I. I. and R. H. Kilmann. *Methodological Approaches to Social Science*. San Francisco: Jossey-Bass, 1978.

Mitroff, I. I. and H. A. Linstone. *The Unbounded Mind*. New York: Oxford University Press, 1993.

Mizruchi, M. *The American Corporate Network, 1904–1974*. Beverly Hills, CA: Sage, 1982.

Mohrman, S. A. and T. G. Cummings. *Self-Designing Organizations*. Reading, MA: Addison-Wesley, 1989.

Mokyr, J. *The Gifts of Athena: Historical Origins of the Knowledge Economy*. Princeton, NJ: Princeton University Press, 2002.

Monks, R. A. G. and N. Minow. *Corporate Governance* (3rd ed.). Malden, MA: Blackwell, 2003.

Mooney, J. C. and A. P. Reiley. *Onward Industry*. New York: Harper & Row, 1931.

Morgan, G. "Internal Audit Role Conflict: A Pluralist View." *Managerial Finance*, 5: 160–170, 1979.

Morgan, G. "Paradigms, Metaphors and Puzzle Solving in Organization Theory." *Administrative Science Quarterly*, 25: 605–622, 1980.

Morgan, G. "The Schismatic Metaphor and Its Implications for Organizational Analysis." *Organization Studies*, 2: 23–44, 1981.

Morgan, G. "Cybernetics and Organization Theory: Epistemology or Technique?" *Human Relations*, 35: 521–538, 1982.

Morgan, G. (ed.) *Beyond Method: Strategies for Social Research*. Beverly Hills, CA: Sage, 1983a.

Morgan, G. "More on Metaphor: Why We Cannot Control Tropes in Administrative Science." *Administrative Science Quarterly*, 28: 601–607, 1983b.

Morgan, G. "Rethinking Corporate Strategy: A Cybernetic Perspective." *Human Relations*, 36: 345–360, 1983c.

Morgan, G. "Opportunities Arising From Paradigm Diversity." *Administration & Society*, 16: 306–327, 1984.

Morgan, G. *Images of Organization* (1st ed.). Beverly Hills, CA: Sage, 1986.

Morgan, G. "Accounting as Reality Construction." *Accounting, Organizations and Society*, 13: 477–485, 1988a.

Morgan, G. *Riding the Waves of Change*. San Francisco: Jossey-Bass, 1988b.

Morgan, G. (ed.) *Creative Organization Theory*. Newbury Park, CA: Sage, 1989.

Morgan, G. *Imaginization: The Art of Creative Management*. Newbury Park, CA: Sage, 1993a.

Morgan, G. "Organizational Choice and the New Technology," pp. 354–368 in E. Trist and H. Murray (eds.) *The Social Engagement of Social Science*, Vol. 2. Philadelphia: University of Pennsylvania Press, 1993b.

Morgan, G. "The 15% Solution"; "How to Live With Contradiction"; "Quantum Leaps: Step by Step"; "It's All in the Water." Toronto: *The Globe and Mail*, 1994 (www.Imaginiz.com).

Morgan, G. "Is There Anything More to Be Said About Metaphor?" in D. Grant and C. Oswick (eds.) *Metaphor and Organizations*. London: Sage, 1996.

Morgan, G., P. Frost, and L. Pondy. "Organizational Symbolism," pp. 3–35 in L. Pondy et al. (eds.) *Organizational Symbolism*. Greenwich, CT: JAI Press, 1983.

Morgan, G. and R. Ramirez. "Action Learning: A Holographic Metaphor for Guiding Social Change." *Human Relations*, 37: 1–28, 1984.

Morgan, G. and A. Zohar. *Achieving Quantum Change: Incrementally!!!* Working paper. Toronto: Schulich School of Business, 1995.

Morita, A., E. M. Reingold, and M. Shimomura. *Made in Japan*. New York: E. P. Dutton, 1986.

Mouzelis, N. *Organization and Bureaucracy* (2nd ed.). London: Routledge & Kegan Paul, 1979.

Mumford, L. *Technics and Civilization*. New York: Harcourt Brace Jovanovich, 1934.

Murray, V. and J. Gandz. "Games Executives Play: Politics at Work." *Business Horizons*, 11–23, 1980.

Myers-Briggs, I. *Manual for the Myers-Briggs Type Indicator*. Princeton, NJ: Educational Testing Service, 1962.

Nace, T. *Gangs of America: The Rise of Corporate Power and the Disabling of Democracy*. San Francisco: Berrett Koehler, 2003.

Nadler, D. A., M. S. Gerstein, and R. B. Shaw. *Organizational Architecture*. San Francisco: Jossey-Bass, 1992.

Nadler, D. A. and M. L. Tushman. "A General Diagnostic Model for Organizational Behavior: Applying a Congruence Perspective," in J. R. Hackman, E. E. Lawler, and L. W. Porter (eds.) *Perspectives on Behavior in Organizations*. New York: McGraw-Hill, 1977.

Nadler, D. L. and M. L. Tushman. *Competing by Design: The Power of Organizational Architecture*. New York: Oxford University Press, 1997.

Navarro, V. and D. M. Berman (eds.) *Health and Work Under Capitalism*. New York: Baywood, 1983.

Negandhi, A. R. "External and Internal Functioning of American, German, and Japanese Multinational Corporations: Decision-Making and Policy Issues," in W. H. Goldberg and A. R. Negandhi (eds.) *Governments and Multinationals*. Cambridge, MA: Oelgeschlager, Gunn, & Hain, 1983.

Negroponte, N. *Being Digital*. New York: Alfred A. Knopf, 1995.

Nelkin, D. and M. S. Brown. *Workers at Risk*. Chicago: University of Chicago Press, 1984.

Nestle, M. *Food Politics: How the Food Industry Influences Nutrition and Health*. Berkeley: University of California Press, 2003.

Neuhauser, P. C., R. Bender, and K. L. Stromberg. *Culture.com: Building Corporate Culture in the Connected Workplace*. Toronto: Wiley, 2000.

Neumann, E. *The Origins and History of Consciousness*. Princeton, NJ: Princeton University Press, 1954.

Newsweek, "The Hitmen." February 26: 44–48, 1996.

Newton, L. H. *Business Ethics and the Natural Environment*. Malden, MA: Blackwell, 2005.

Nichols, T. *Ownership, Control and Ideology*. London: Unwin, 1980.

Nietzsche, F. *The Gay Science*. New York: Vintage, 1974.

Nietzsche, F. *The Will to Power*. New York: Vintage, 1976.

Nisbet, R. A. *Social Change and History*. London: Oxford University Press, 1969.

Nkomo, S. M. "The Emperor Has No Clothes: Rewriting 'Race' in the Study of Organizations." *Academy of Management Review*, 17: 487–513, 1992.

Nonaka, I. "Creating Organizational Order out of Chaos: Self Renewal of Japanese Firms." *California Management Review*, 30: 57–73, 1988.

Nonaka, I. and H. Takuchi. *The Knowledge-Creating Company*. New York: Oxford University Press, 1995.

Nord, W. "Dreams of Humanization and the Realities of Power." *Academy of Management Review*, 3: 674–679, 1978.

Normann, R. *Reframing Business: When the Map Changes the Landscape*. New Chichester, UK: Wiley, 2001.

Northrup, H. R. and R. L. Rowan. *Multinational Collective Bargaining Attempts*. Philadelphia: University of Pennsylvania Press, 1979.

Novack, G. *An Introduction to the Logic of Marxism*. New York: Merit, 1966.

Nystrom, P. C. and W. H. Starbuck (eds.) *Handbook of Organizational Design*, Vol. 1. New York: Oxford University Press, 1981.

Nystrom, P. C. and W. H. Starbuck. "To Avoid Crises, Unlearn." *Organizational Dynamics*, Spring: 53–65, 1984.

Oates, W. *Confessions of a Workaholic*. New York: Harper & Row, 1971.

O'Connor, J. *The Fiscal Crisis of the State*. New York: St. Martin's, 1973.

Offe, C. "Advanced Capitalism and the Welfare State." *Politics and Society*, 2: 479–488, 1974a.

Offe, C. "Class Rule and the Political System." *German Political Studies*, 1: 31–57, 1974b.

Offe, C. "The Theory of the Capitalist State and the Problem of Policy Formation," in L. N. Lindberg et al. (eds.) *Stress and Contradiction in Modern Capitalism.* Lexington, MA: D. C. Heath, 1975.

Offe, C. *Industry and Inequality.* London: Arnold, 1976.

Office of Management and Budget. *Standard Industrial Classification Manual.* Washington, DC: Government Printing Office, 1972.

Ogilvy, J. A. *Creating Better Futures: Scenario Planning as a Tool for a Better Tomorrow.* Oxford, UK: Oxford University Press, 2002.

Ohmae, K. *Triad Power.* New York: Free Press, 1985.

Ohmae, K. *The Borderless World.* London: Collins, 1993.

Ollman, B. *Alienation: Marx's Conception of Man in Capitalist Society.* Cambridge, UK: Cambridge University Press, 1976.

Olson, E. E. and G. Eoyang. *Facilitating Organizational Change: Lessons From Complexity Science.* San Francisco: Jossey-Bass/Pfeiffer, 2001.

Ornstein, R. *The Psychology of Consciousness.* New York: Freeman, 1972.

Ortony, A. "Why Metaphors Are Necessary and Not Just Nice." *Educational Theory*, 25: 45–53, 1975.

Ortony, A. (ed.) *Metaphor and Thought.* Cambridge, UK: Cambridge University Press, 1979.

Oswick, C. and D. Grant. *Organization Development: Metaphorical Explorations.* London: Pitman, 1996.

Oswick, C., T. Keenoy, and D. Grant. "Metaphor and Analogical Reasoning in Organization Theory: Beyond Orthodoxy." *Academy of Management Review*, 27, 294–303, 2002.

Ott, J. *The Organizational Culture Perspective.* Pacific Grove, CA: Brooks/Cole, 1989.

Ouchi, W. and A. Wilkins. "Organizational Culture." *Annual Review of Sociology*, 11: 457–483, 1985.

Ouchi, W. A. *Theory Z: How American Business Can Meet the Japanese Challenge.* Reading, MA: Addison-Wesley, 1981.

Outhwaite, W. "Toward a Realist Perspective," pp. 321–330 in G. Morgan (ed.) *Beyond Method.* Beverly Hills, CA: Sage, 1983.

Pareto, V. *The Mind and Society.* New York: Harcourt Brace Jovanovich, 1935.

Parker, M. *Creating Shared Vision.* Clarendon Hills, IL: Dialog International, 1990.

Parsons, T. *The Social System.* New York: Free Press, 1951.

Parsons, T. "Culture and Social System Revisited," in L. Schneider and C. M. Bonjean (eds.) *The Idea of Culture in the Social Sciences.* Cambridge, UK: Cambridge University Press, 1973.

Pascale, R. *Managing on the Edge.* London: Viking, 1990.

Pascale, R. and A. Athos. *The Art of Japanese Management.* New York: Warner Books, 1981.

Pask, G. *An Approach to Cybernetics.* New York: Harper & Row, 1961.

Pauchant, T. C. and I. A. Mitroff. *Transforming the Crisis Prone Organization.* San Francisco: Jossey-Bass, 1992.

Pava, C. *Managing New Office Technology*. New York: Free Press, 1983.

Pedler, M. "Critical Action Learning." *Action Learning: Research and Practice*, 2005: 1–6.

Pedler, M. J. (ed.) *Action Learning in Practice*. Aldershot, UK: Gower, 1983.

Pedler, M. J. and K. Aspinwall. *"PERFECT plc"?* London: McGraw-Hill, 1996.

Pedler, M. J., J. A. Burgoyne, and T. H. Boydell. *The Learning Company*. London: McGraw-Hill, 1991.

Pedler, M. J., J. A. Burgoyne, and C. Brook. "What Has Action Learning Learned to Become?" *Action Learning: Research and Practice*, 2(1): 49–68, 2005.

Penney, J. "Work and Health in the Global Economy: A Report." *New Solutions*, 5(4): 4–15, 1995.

Pennings, J. M. "Organizational Birth Frequencies: An Empirical Investigation." *Administrative Science Quarterly*, 27: 120–144, 1982.

Pepper, S. C. *World Hypotheses*. Berkeley: University of California Press, 1942.

Perkins, D. *Archimedes' Bathtub: The Art and Logic of Breakthrough Thinking*. New York: Norton, 2000.

Perkins, D. N. *King Arthur's Round Table: How Collaborative Conversations Create Smart Organizations*. New York: Wiley, 2003.

Perrow, C. "A Framework for the Comparative Analysis of Organizations." *American Sociological Review*, 32: 194–208, 1967.

Perrow, C. *Complex Organizations: A Critical Essay*. New York: Random House, 1979.

Perrow, C. *Normal Accidents*. New York: Basic Books, 1984.

Perrow, C. *Organizing America: Wealth, Power, and the Origins of Corporate Capitalism*. Princeton, NJ: Princeton University Press, 2002.

Peters, T. J. "Symbols, Patterns and Settings." *Organizational Dynamics*, 7: 3–22, 1978.

Peters, T. J. and R. H. Waterman. *In Search of Excellence*. New York: Harper & Row, 1982.

Peterson, C. L. *Work Stress: Studies of the Context, Content, and Outcomes of Stress*. Amityville, NY: Baywood Publishers, 2003.

Pettigrew, A. M. *The Politics of Organizational Decision Making*. London: Tavistock, 1973.

Pettigrew, A. M. *The Awakening Giant: Continuity and Change in ICI*. Oxford, UK: Basil Blackwell, 1985.

Pfeffer, J. *Organization Design*. Arlington Heights, IL: AHM, 1978.

Pfeffer, J. *Power in Organizations*. Marshfield, MA: Pitman, 1981.

Pfeffer, J. *Organizations and Organization Theory*. Marshfield, MA: Pitman, 1982.

Pfeffer, J. and G. R. Salancik. *The External Control of Organizations: A Resource Dependence Perspective*. New York: Harper & Row, 1978.

Pinchot, G. and E. Pinchot. *The End of Bureaucracy and the Rise of the Intelligent Organization*. San Francisco: Berrett-Koehler, 1993.

Pinder, C. and L. Moore. "The Resurrection of Taxonomy to Aid the Development of Middle-Range Theories of Organizational Behavior." *Administrative Science Quarterly*, 24: 99–118, 1978.

Pines, M. *Bion and Group Psychotherapy*. London: Routledge & Kegan Paul, 1985.

Piore, M. *Birds of Passage: Migrant Labor in Industrial Society*. Cambridge, UK: Cambridge University Press, 1979.

Plato. *The Laws*. London: Heinemann, 1926.

Plato. *The Republic*. Oxford: Clarendon, 1941.

Plekhanov, G. V. *Selected Philosophical Works*. London: Lawrence & Wishart, 1961.

Poff, D. C. "Reconciling the Irreconcilable: The Global Economy and the Environment." *Journal of Business Ethics*, 13: 439–445, 1995.

Pondy, L. R. "Budgeting and Intergroup Conflict in Organizations." *Pittsburgh Business Review*, 1964.

Pondy, L. R. "Organizational Conflict: Concepts and Models." *Administrative Science Quarterly*, 12: 296–320, 1967.

Pondy, L. R., P. Frost, G. Morgan, and T. Dandridge (eds.) *Organizational Symbolism*. Greenwich, CT: JAI, 1983.

Poole, M. S. and A. H. Van de Ven (eds.) *Handbook of Organizational Change and Innovation*. Oxford, UK: Oxford University Press, 2004.

Popper, K. R. *The Open Society and Its Enemies*. London: Routledge & Kegan Paul, 1945.

Porter, M. *Competitive Strategy*. New York: Free Press, 1980.

Potterfield, T. A. *The Business of Employee Empowerment: Democracy and Ideology in the Workplace*. Westport, CT: Quorum, 1999.

Powell, G. N. *Women and Men in Management* (3rd ed.). Thousand Oaks, CA: Sage, 2002.

Power, J. and A. Hardman. *Western Europe's Migrant Workers*. London: Minority Rights Group, 1978.

Power, M. and R. Laughlin. "Critical Theory and Accounting," pp. 113–135 in M. Alvesson and H. Willmott (eds.) *Critical Management Studies*. London: Sage, 1992.

Presthus, R. *The Organizational Society*. New York: St. Martin's, 1978.

Prestowitz, C. *Rogue Nation: American Unilateralism and the Failure of Good Intentions*. New York: Basic Books, 2003.

Prestowitz, C. *Three Billion New Capitalists: The Great Shift of Wealth and Power to the East*. New York: Basic Books, 2005.

Pribram, K. *Languages of the Brain*. Englewood Cliffs, NJ: Prentice Hall, 1971.

Pribram, K. "Problems Concerning the Structure of Consciousness," in G. Globus et al. (eds.) *Consciousness and the Brain*. New York: Plenum, 1976.

Prigogine, I. "Time, Structure and Fluctuations." *Science*, 201: 777–795, 1978.

Prigogine, I. *Order out of Chaos*. New York: Random House, 1984.

Prince, C. J. "Migrant Workers Find Work but No Welcome." *The Christian Science Monitor*, April 3: 7, 1996.

Proudhon, P. J. *Selected Writings*. London: Macmillan, 1969.

Provis, C. *Ethics and Organisational Politics*. Cheltenham, UK: Edward Elgar Publishing, 2004.

Pugh, D. S., D. J. Hickson, and C. R. Hinings. "An Empirical Taxonomy of Work Organizations." *Administrative Science Quarterly*, 14: 115–126, 1969.

Putnam, L. L. and M. S. Poole. "Conflict and Negotiation," pp. 549–599 in F. Jablin, L. Putnam, K. Roberts, and L. Porter (eds.) *Handbook of Organizational Communication*. Newbury Park, CA: Sage, 1987.

Quartz, S. R., and T. J. Sejnowski. *Liars, Lovers, and Heroes: What the New Brain Science Reveals About How We Become Who We Are*. New York: Morrow, 2002.

Quinn, J. B. *Intelligent Enterprise*. New York: Free Press, 1992.

Quinn, R. E. *Beyond Rational Management*. San Francisco: Jossey-Bass, 1988.

Quinn, R. E. and K. S. Cameron. *Paradox and Transformation*. New York: Harper and Row, 1988.

Radcliffe-Brown, A. R. *Structure and Function in Primitive Society*. London: Cohen & West, 1952.

Rank, O. *Psychology and the Soul*. Philadelphia: University of Pennsylvania Press, 1950.

Rapoport, A. *Fights, Games and Debates*. Ann Arbor: University of Michigan Press, 1960.

Ravn, I. "Notes on the Emergence of Order." Philadelphia: Wharton School, University of Pennsylvania, 1983 (unpublished).

Rayman, P. M. *Beyond the Bottom Line: The Search for Dignity at Work*. New York: Palgrave, 2001.

Reasons, C. E., L. L. Ross, and C. Paterson. *Assault on the Worker*. Toronto: Butterworth, 1981.

Reich, W. *The Mass Psychology of Fascism*. New York: Farrar, Straus, Giroux, 1933.

Reich, W. *The Function of the Orgasm*. New York: Panther, 1961.

Reich, W. *The Sexual Revolution*. New York: Farrar, Straus, Giroux, 1968.

Reich, W. *Character Analysis*. New York: Farrar, Straus, Giroux, 1972a.

Reich, W. *Dialectical Materialism and Psychoanalysis*. London: Socialist Reproduction, 1972b.

Restak, R. M. *The New Brain: How the Modern Age Is Rewiring Your Mind*. Emmaus, PA: Rodale, 2004.

Revans, R. W. *The Origins and Growth of Action Learning*. Bromley: Chartwell-Bratt, 1982.

Revans, R. W. *The ABC of Action Learning*. Bromley: Chartwell-Bratt, 1983.

Revans, R. W. *Developing Effective Managers*. New York: Praeger, 1987.

Rheingold, H. *Smart Mobs: The Next Social Revolution*. Cambridge, MA: Perseus, 2003.

Rhode, D. L. (ed.) *The Difference Difference Makes: Women and Leadership*. Stanford, CA: Stanford Law and Politics, 2003.

Rice, A. K. *Productivity and Social Organization*. London: Tavistock, 1958.

Richardson, K., J. A. Goldstein, P. M. Allen, and D. Snowden (eds.) *Emergence, Complexity & Organization*. Mansfield, MA: ISCE Publishing, 2005.

Ricoeur, P. *The Rule of Metaphor: The Creation of Meaning in Language*. New York: Routledge, 2003.

Rifkin, J. *The End of Work*. New York: Putnam, 1995.

Rigney, D. *The Metaphorical Society: An Invitation to Social Theory*. Lanham, MD: Rowman and Littlefield, 2001.

Ritzer, G. *The McDonaldization of Society.* Thousand Oaks, CA: Sage, 1996.

Robbins, A. *Unlimited Power.* New York: Ballantine, 1987.

Robbins, S. P. "Conflict Management and Conflict Resolution Are Not Synonymous Terms." *California Management Review,* 21: 67–75, 1978.

Roberts, J. *The Modern Firm: Organizational Design for Performance and Growth.* Oxford, UK: Oxford University Press, 2004.

Roddick, A. *Body and Soul.* New York: Crown, 1991.

Roethlisberger, F. J. and W. J. Dickson. *Management and the Worker.* Cambridge, MA: Harvard University Press, 1939.

Rosen, M. "Breakfast at Spiro's: Dramaturgy and Dominance." *Journal of Management,* 11: 31–48, 1985.

Rosener, J. B. "Ways Women Lead." *Harvard Business Review,* 69: 119–125, 1990.

Ross, N. S. "Organized Labour and Management: The U.K.," in E. M. Hugh-Jones (ed.) *Human Relations and Modern Management.* North Holland: Elsevier, 1958.

Ross, N. S. *Constructive Conflict.* Edinburgh: Oliver & Boyd, 1969.

Rowland, W. *Greed Inc.: Why Corporations Rule Our World and How We Let It Happen.* Markham, ON: Thomas Allen Publishers, 2005.

Royal Commission on Matters of Health and Safety Arising From the Use of Asbestos in Ontario. *Report.* Toronto: Ontario Government Bookstore, 1984.

Russell, B. and A. N. Whitehead. *Principia Mathematica.* Cambridge, UK: Cambridge University Press, 1913.

Russell, D. B. and R. L. Ison. "Maturana's Intellectual Contribution as a Choreography of Conversation and Action." *Cybernetics & Human Knowing,* 11(2): 36–48, 2004.

Sackmann, S. "The Role of Metaphors in Organization Transformation." *Human Relations,* 42: 463–485, 1989.

Sacks, S. (ed.) *On Metaphor.* Chicago: University of Chicago Press, 1979.

Sahay, S., B. Nicholson, and S. Khrishna. *Global IT Outsourcing: Software Development Across Borders.* Cambridge, UK: Cambridge University Press, 2003.

Sahlins, M. *Stone Age Economics.* London: Tavistock, 1972.

Salaman, G. "Towards a Sociology of Organizational Structure." *Sociological Quarterly,* 26: 519–554, 1978.

Salaman, G. *Work Organizations: Resistance and Control.* New York: Longman, 1979.

Salaman, G. *Class and the Corporation.* London: Fontana, 1981.

Sampson, A. *The Sovereign State of ITT.* New York: Stein & Day, 1978.

Sandelands, L. E. and R. E. Stablein. "The Concept of Organization Mind," Vol. 5 of *Research in the Sociology of Organizations.* Greenwich, CT: JAI Press, 1987.

Sanyal, R. N. *International Management: A Strategic Perspective.* Upper Saddle River, NJ: Prentice Hall, 2001.

Sapir, E. *Culture, Language and Personality.* Berkeley: University of California Press, 1949.

Sartre, J. *Nausea.* Harmondsworth: Penguin, 1938.

Sartre, J. P. *Being and Nothingness.* New York: Washington Square Press, 1966.

Savage, C. M. *5th Generation Management.* Bedford, MA: Digital Press, 1990.

Savage, M. and A. Witz. *Gender and Bureaucracy.* Cambridge, MA: Blackwell, 1992.

Sayle, M. "The Yellow Peril and the Red Haired Devils." *Harper's,* November: 23–35, 1982.

Sayles, L. R. and G. Strauss. *Managing Human Resources.* Englewood Cliffs, NJ: Prentice Hall, 1981.

Scarbrough, H. and J. M. Corbett. *Technology and Organization.* London and New York: Routledge, 1992.

Schattschneider, E. E. *The Semi-sovereign People.* New York: Holt, Rinehart & Winston, 1960.

Schein, E. *Organizational Culture and Leadership.* San Francisco: Jossey-Bass, 1985.

Schein, E. H. *The Corporate Culture Survival Guide.* San Francisco: Jossey-Bass, 1999.

Schirm, S. A. (ed.) *New Rules for Global Markets: Public and Private Markets in the World Economy.* Houndsmills, UK: Palgrave Macmillan, 2004.

Schmitz, C. L., E. K. Traver, and D. Larson (eds.) *Child Labor: A Global View.* Westport, CT: Greenwood, 2004.

Schneider, A. and D. McCumber. *An Air That Kills: How the Asbestos Poisoning of Libby, Montana Uncovered a National Scandal.* New York: Putnam, 2004.

Schön, D. A. *Invention and the Evolution of Ideas.* London: Tavistock, 1963.

Schön, D. A. *Beyond the Stable State.* New York: Random House, 1971.

Schön, D. A. "Generative Metaphor: A Perspective on Problem Setting in Social Policy," pp. 254–283 in A. Ortony (ed.) *Metaphor and Thought.* Cambridge, UK: Cambridge University Press, 1979.

Schön, D. A. *The Reflective Practitioner.* New York: Basic Books, 1983.

Schumpeter, J. *The Theory of Economic Development.* Cambridge, MA: Harvard University Press, 1934.

Schumpeter, J. *Capitalism, Socialism and Democracy.* New York: Harper, 1942.

Schutz, A. *Collected Papers I: The Problem of Social Reality.* The Hague: Martinus Nijhoff, 1967.

Schwandt, D. R. and M. J. Marquardt. *Organizational Learning: From World-Class Theories to Global Best Practices.* Boca Raton, FL: St. Lucie Press, 2000.

Schwartz, H. S. "Job Involvement as Obsession Compulsion." *Academy of Management Review,* 7: 429–432, 1982.

Schwartz, H. S. "The Usefulness of Myth and the Myth of Usefulness." *Journal of Management,* 11: 31–42, 1985.

Schwartz, H. S. *Narcissistic Processes and Corporate Decay.* New York: New York University Press, 1990.

Schwartz, P. *The Art of the Long View: Planning for the Future in an Uncertain World.* New York: Currency Doubleday, 1996.

Scientific American. *The Brain: A Scientific American Book.* San Francisco: Freeman, 1979.

Scott, R. *Muscle and Blood.* New York: Dutton, 1974.

Scott, W. R. *Organizations: Rational, Natural and Open Systems.* Englewood Cliffs, NJ: Prentice Hall, 1981.

Scott, W. R. *Organizations: Rational, Natural, and Open Systems* (5th ed.). Englewood Cliffs, NJ: Prentice Hall, 2002.

Scott, W. R. and S. Christensen (eds.) *The Institutional Construction of Organizations.* Thousand Oaks, CA: Sage, 1995.

Selznick, P. *Leadership in Administration.* New York: Harper & Row, 1957.

Senge, P. *The Fifth Discipline.* New York: Doubleday, 1990.

Senge, P. M., et al. *The Dance of Change: The Challenges to Sustaining Momentum in Learning Organizations. New York:* Currency-Doubleday, 1999.

Senge, P. M., et al. *Presence: Human Purpose and the Field of the Future.* Cambridge, MA: SoL, Society for Organizational Learning, 2004.

Sennett, R. *The Corrosion of Character: The Personal Consequences of Work in the New Capitalism.* New York: Norton, 1998.

Servan-Schreiber, J.-J. *The American Challenge.* New York: Atheneum, 1968.

Shapira, Z. (ed.) *Organizational Decision Making.* Cambridge, UK: Cambridge University Press, 2002.

Sharpe, P. *Women, Gender, and Labour Migration: Historical and Global Perspectives.* London: Routledge, 2001.

Shaw, P. *Changing Conversations in Organizations: A Complexity Approach to Change.* New York: Routledge, 2002.

Sheldrake, R. *A New Science of Life.* London: Bland & Briggs, 1981.

Sheldrake, R., R. Weber, and D. Bohm. "Conversations." *Re-Vision,* 5: 23–48, 1982.

Sheppard, D. "Image and Self-Image of Women in Organizations." Presented to the Annual Conference of the Canadian Research Institute for the Advancement of Women, Montreal, 1984.

Sheppard, D. "Women Managers' Perceptions of Gender and Organizational Life," pp. 151–166 in A. J. Mills and P. Tancred (eds.) *Gendering Organizational Analysis.* Newbury Park, CA: Sage, 1992.

Shostak, A. B. (ed.) "Impacts of Changing Employment." *Annals of the American Academy of Political and Social Science,* 544: Special Issue, 1996.

Shotter, J. "The Manager as Author," pp. 217–226 in *Knowing of the Third Kind.* Utrecht: Rijksuniversiteit to Utrecht, 1990.

Silverman, D. *The Theory of Organizations.* London: Heinemann Educational Books, 1971.

Silverman, D. and J. Jones. *Organizational Work.* London: Macmillan, 1976.

Simmel, G. *The Sociology of Georg Simmel.* New York: Free Press, 1950.

Simon, H. A. *Administrative Behavior.* New York: Macmillan, 1947.

Simon, H. A. "The Architecture of Complexity." *Proceedings of the American Philosophical Society,* 106: 467–482, 1962.

Simon, H. A. "Making Management Decisions: The Role of Intuition and Emotion." *Academy of Management Executive,* 1: 57–64, 1987.

Simonton, D. K. *Creativity in Science: Chance, Logic, Genius, and Zeitgeist.* Cambridge, UK: Cambridge University Press, 2004.

Sims, H. P. and D. A. Gioia (eds.) *The Thinking Organization.* San Francisco: Jossey-Bass, 1986.

Sinclair, U. *The Jungle.* New York: Grosset & Dunlap, 1906.

Singh, J. V. (ed.) *Organizational Evolution.* Newbury Park, CA: Sage, 1990.

Singh, J. V. and C. J. Lumsden. "Theory and Research in Organizational Ecology." *Annual Review of Sociology,* 16: 161–195, 1990.

Skinner, B. F. *Science and Human Behavior*. New York: Macmillan, 1953.

Smircich, L. "Organizations as Shared Meanings," pp. 55–65 in L. Pondy et al. (eds.) *Organizational Symbolism*. Greenwich, CT: JAI Press, 1983a.

Smircich, L. "Studying Organizations as Cultures," pp. 160–172 in G. Morgan (ed.) *Beyond Method: Strategies for Social Research*. Beverly Hills, CA: Sage, 1983b.

Smircich, L. "Concepts of Culture and Organizational Analysis." *Administrative Science Quarterly*, 28: 339–358, 1983c.

Smircich, L. and M. Calas. "Organizational Culture: A Critical Assessment," pp. 228–263 in F. M. Jablin, L. Putnam, K. Roberts, and L. Porter (eds.) *Handbook of Organizational Communication*. Newbury Park, CA: Sage, 1987.

Smircich, L. and M. Calas, "Past postmodernism? Reflections and tentative directions." *The Academy of Management Review*, 24: 649–673, 1999.

Smircich, L. and G. Morgan. "Leadership: The Management of Meaning." *Journal of Applied Behavioral Studies*, 18: 257–273, 1982.

Smircich, L. and C. Stubbart. "Strategic Management in an Enacted World." *Academy of Management Review*, 10: 724–736, 1985.

Smith, A. *The Wealth of Nations*. London: Stratton & Cadell, 1776.

Smith, C. and G. Gemmill. "Change in the Small Group: A Dissipative Structure Perspective." *Human Relations*, 44: 697–716, 1991.

Smith, K. K. and D. N. Berg. *Paradoxes of Group Life*. San Francisco: Jossey-Bass, 1987.

Smith, K. K. and V. M. Simmons. "A Rumplestiltskin Organization: Metaphors on Metaphors in Field Research." *Administrative Science Quarterly*, 28: 377–392, 1983.

Spencer, H. *The Study of Sociology*. London: Kegan Paul & Tench, 1873.

Spencer, H. *Principles of Sociology*. London: Williams & Norgate, 1876.

Spencer, H. *The Principles of Biology*. London: Williams & Norgate, 1884.

Spencer-Brown, G. *Laws of Form*. New York: Dutton, 1969.

Sperry, R. W. "Hemisphere Deconnection and Unity in Conscious Awareness." *American Psychologist*, 23: 723–733, 1968.

Sperry, R. W. "A Modified Concept of Consciousness." *Psychological Review*, 76: 532–536, 1969.

Sproull, R. L. *A Scientist's Tools for Business: Metaphors and Modes of Thought*. Rochester, NY: University of Rochester Press, 1997.

Srivastva, S. and D. L. Cooperrider. *Appreciative Management and Leadership*. San Francisco: Jossey-Bass, 1990.

Stacey, R. D. *Managing the Unknowable: Strategic Boundaries Between Order and Chaos in Organizations*. San Francisco: Jossey-Bass, 1992.

Stacey, R. D. *Complex Responsive Processes in Organizations: Learning and Knowledge Creation*. London: Routledge, 2001.

Stacey, R. D., D. Griffin, and P. Shaw. *Complexity and Management: Fad or Radical Challenge?* London: Routledge, 2000.

Starbuck, W. H. "Organizations as Action Generators." *American Sociological Review*, 48: 91–102, 1983.

Starbuck, W. H. "Acting First and Thinking Later," in J. M. Pennings (ed.) *Organizational Strategy and Change*. San Francisco: Jossey-Bass, 1985.

Stein, S. and H. E. Book. *The EQ Edge: Emotional Intelligence and Your Success*. Toronto: Stoddart, 2000.

Steinbrunner, J. *The Cybernetic Theory of Decision*. Princeton, NJ: Princeton University Press, 1974.

Sternberg, R. J. *Metaphors of Mind: Conceptions of the Nature of Intelligence*. Cambridge, UK: Cambridge University Press, 1990.

Stiglitz, J. E. *Globalization and Its Discontents*. New York: Norton, 2003.

Stinchcombe, A. L. "Social Structure and Organizations," pp. 142–193 in J. G. March (ed.) *Handbook of Organizations*. Chicago: Rand McNally, 1965.

Stirner, M. *The Ego and His Own*. New York: Libertarian Book Club, 1963.

Stockdale, M. and F. J. Crosby (eds.) *The Psychology and Management of Workplace Diversity*. Malden, MA: Blackwell, 2004.

Stopford, J. M., J. H. Dunning, and K. O. Itaberich. *The World Directory of Multinational Enterprises*. New York: Facts on File, 1980.

Streatfield, P. J. *The Paradox of Control in Organizations*. London: Routledge, 2001.

Strogatz, S. H. *Sync: The Emerging Science of Spontaneous Order*. New York: Theia, 2003.

Sudnow, D. "Normal Crimes: Sociological Features of the Penal Code in a Public Defender Office." *Social Problems*, 12: 255–276, 1965.

Sullivan, J. J. *The Future of Corporate Globalization: From the Extended Order to the Global Village*. Westport, CT: Quorum Books, 2002.

Surowiecki, J. *The Wisdom of Crowds: Why the Many Are Smarter Than the Few and How Collective Wisdom Shapes Business, Economies, Societies, and Nations*. New York: Doubleday, 2004.

Susman, G. *Autonomy at Work*. New York: Praeger, 1976.

Sward, K. *The Legend of Henry Ford*. New York: Rinehart, 1948.

Taggart, W. and D. Robey. "Minds and Managers: On the Dual Nature of Human Information Processing and Management." *Academy of Management Review*, 6: 187–196, 1981.

Tapscott, D. *The Digital Economy*. New York: McGraw-Hill, 1996.

Tataryn, L. *Dying for a Living: The Politics of Industrial Death*. Ottawa: Deneau & Breenberg, 1979.

Tavis, L. A. *Multinational Managers and Poverty in the Third World*. Notre Dame, IN: University of Notre Dame Press, 1982.

Taylor, F. W. *Principles of Scientific Management*. New York: Harper & Row, 1911.

Taylor, G. R. *Sex in History*. New York: Vanguard, 1954.

Taylor, G. R. *The Natural History of the Mind*. New York: Dutton, 1979.

Taylor, J. R. and E. J. van Every. *The Vulnerable Fortress*. Toronto: University of Toronto Press, 1993.

Thannhuber, M. J. *The Intelligent Enterprise: Theoretical Concepts and Practical Implications*. Heidelberg: Physica Verlag, 2005.

Thietart, R. A. and B. Forgues. "Chaos Theory and Organizations." *Organization Science*, 6: 19–42, 1995.

Thomas, K. W. "Conflict and Conflict Management," pp. 889–935 in M. D. Dunnette (ed.) *Handbook of Industrial and Organizational Psychology*. Chicago: Rand McNally, 1976.

Thomas, K. W. "Toward Multidimensional Values in Teaching: The Example of Conflict Behaviors." *Academy of Management Review*, 12: 484–490, 1977.

Thomas, R., A. J. Mills, and J. H. Mills (eds.) *Identity Politics at Work: Resisting Gender, Gendering Resistance*. London: Routledge, 2004.

Thomas, S. *The Multi-national Companies*. Hove, UK: Wayland, 1979.

Thomas, W. I. *Social Behavior and Personality*. New York: Social Science Research Council, 1951.

Thompson, E. P. *The Making of the English Working Class*. London: Pelican, 1968.

Thompson, J. D. *Organizations in Action*. New York: McGraw-Hill, 1967.

Thompson, W. I. *At the Edge of History*. New York: Harper & Row, 1971.

Thorsrud, E. "Policy-Making as a Learning Process," in A. B. Cherns et al. (eds.) *Social Science and Government Policies and Problems*. London: Tavistock, 1972a.

Thorsrud, E. *Workers' Participation in Management in Norway*. Geneva: Institute for Labour Studies, 1972b.

Thurow, L. C. *The Future of Capitalism*. New York: Morrow, 1986.

Thurow, L. C. *Building Wealth: The New Rules for Individuals, Companies, and Nations in a Knowledge-Based Economy*. New York: HarperBusiness, 1999.

Tichy, N. M. "An Analysis of Clique Formation and Structure in Organizations." *Administrative Science Quarterly*, 18: 194–208, 1973.

Tichy, N. M. and S. Sherman. *Control Your Destiny or Someone Else Will*. New York: Doubleday, 1993.

Tickner, J. and H. Gray. "Nowhere to Hide: Chemical Accident Risks in the US—Avoiding the Worst-Case." *New Solutions*, 6(3): 90–96, 1996.

Tilley, C. Y. *Metaphor and Material Culture*. Oxford, UK: Blackwell, 1999.

Tivey, L. *The Politics of the Firm*. New York: St. Martin's, 1978.

Toffler, A. *Future Shock*. New York: Bantam, 1970.

Toffler, A. *The Third Wave*. New York: Morrow, 1980.

Toffler, A. *Powershift*. New York: Bantam, 1990.

Toffler, A. and H. Toffler. *Creating a New Civilization*. Atlanta: Turner Publishing, 1994.

Tolbert, P. S. and L. G. Zucker. "The Institutionalization of Institutional Theory," pp. 175–190 in S. Clegg, C. Hardy, and W. Nord (eds.) *Handbook of Organization Studies*. Thousand Oaks, CA: Sage, 1996.

Torbert, W. R., et al. *Action Inquiry: The Secret of Timely and Transforming Leadership*. San Francisco: Berrett Koehler, 2004.

Touraine, A. *The Self-Production of Society*. Chicago: University of Chicago Press, 1977.

Townley, B. *Reframing Human Resource Management*. London: Sage, 1994.

Trades Councils of Coventry, Liverpool, Newcastle, and North Tyneside. *State Intervention in Industry: A Workers' Inquiry*. Coventry: Trades Council, 1980.

Triandis, H. C. and R. D. Albert. "Cross-Cultural Perspectives," pp. 264–295 in F. M. Jablin, L. L. Putnam, K. H. Roberts, and L. W. Porter (eds.) *Handbook of Organizational Communications*. Newbury Park, CA: Sage, 1987.

Trice, H. and J. Beyer. *The Cultures of Work Organizations*. Englewood Cliffs, NJ: Prentice Hall, 1993.

Trist, E. L. "A Concept of Organizational Ecology." *Australian Journal of Management*, 2, 1976.

Trist, E. L. "New Directions of Hope: Recent Innovations Interconnecting Organizational, Industrial, Community and Personal Development." *Regional Studies*, 13: 439–451, 1979.

Trist, E. L. "The Evolution of Sociotechnical Systems as a Conceptual Framework and as an Action Research Program," pp. 19–75 in A. H. Van de Ven and W. F. Joyce (eds.) *Perspectives on Organization Design and Behavior*. New York: John Wiley, 1982.

Trist, E. L. "Referent Organizations and the Development of Inter-organizational Domains." *Human Relations*, 36: 269–284, 1983.

Trist, E. L. "Culture as a Psycho-social Process." in E. Trist and H. Murray (eds.) *The Social Engagement of Social Science*, Vol. 1. Philadelphia: University of Pennsylvania Press, 1990.

Trist, E. L. and K. W. Bamforth. "Some Social and Psychological Consequences of the Longwall Method of Coal Getting." *Human Relations*, 4: 3–38, 1951.

Trist, E. L. and F. Emery. *The Social Engagement of Social Science*, Vol. 3. Philadelphia: University of Pennsylvania Press, forthcoming.

Trist, E. L., G. W. Higgin, H. Murray, and A. B. Pollock. *Organizational Choice*. London: Tavistock, 1963.

Trist, E. L. and H. Murray. *The Social Engagement of Social Science*, Vol. 1. Philadelphia: University of Pennsylvania Press, 1990.

Trist, E. L. and H. Murray. *The Social Engagement of Social Science*, Vol. 2. Philadelphia: University of Pennsylvania Press, 1993.

Trompenaars, F. *Riding the Waves of Culture*. London: Economist Books, 1993.

Trompenaars, F. and C. Hampden-Turner. *Riding the Waves of Culture: Understanding Diversity in Global Business* (2nd ed.). New York: McGraw-Hill, 1998.

Tsoukas, H. "The Missing Link: A Transformational View of Metaphors in Organizational Science." *Academy of Management Review*, 16: 566–585, 1991.

Tsoukas, H. "Analogical Reasoning and Knowledge Generation in Organization Theory." *Organization Studies*, 14: 323–346, 1993.

Turner, B. A. *Exploring the Industrial Sub-culture*. London: Macmillan, 1971.

Turner, B. A. (ed.) *Organizational Symbolism*. Berlin: Walter de Gruyter, 1989.

Turner, B. A. "The Rise of Organizational Symbolism," pp. 83–96 in J. Hasard and D. Pym (eds.) *The Theory and Philosophy of Organizations*. London: Routledge, 1990.

Turner, S. "Studying Organization Through Levi Strauss's Structuralism," pp. 189–201 in G. Morgan (ed.) *Beyond Method*. Beverly Hills, CA: Sage, 1983.

Tushman, M. L. and D. A. Nadler. "Implications of Political Models of Organization," pp. 177–190 in R. Miles (ed.) *Resource Book in Macro Organizational Behavior*. Glenview, IL: Scott Foresman, 1980.

Tushman, M. L. and E. Romanelli. "Organizational Evolution: A Metamorphosis Model of Convergence and Reorientation," in L. Cummings and B. Staw (eds.) *Research in Organizational Behavior*. Greenwich, CT: JAI Press, 1985.

Tylor, E. B. *Primitive Culture*. London: John Murray, 1871.

Ulrich, H. and G. J. B. Probst (eds.) *Self-Organization and Management of Social Systems*. New York: Springer-Verlag, 1984.

United Nations. *Transnational Corporations in World Development: Third Survey*. New York: United Nations, Center on Transnational Corporations, 1983.

Vaill, P. B. "Process Wisdom for a New Age." *ReVision*, 7: 39–49, 1984.

Van de Ven, A. H. and W. G. Astley. "Mapping the Field to Create a Dynamic Perspective on Organization Design and Behavior," pp. 427–468 in A. H. Van de Ven and W. F. Joyce (eds.) *Perspectives on Organization Design and Behavior*. New York: John Wiley, 1981.

Vanek, J. *Self Management*. Harmondsworth: Penguin, 1975.

Van Maanen, J. "The Smile Factory: Work at Disneyland," pp. 58–76 in Frost et al. (eds.) *Reframing Organizational Culture*. Newbury Park, CA: Sage, 1991.

Van Maanen, J. and S. R. Barley. "Occupational Communities: Culture and Control in Organizations," in B. Staw and L. L. Cummings (eds.) *Research in Organizational Behavior*. Greenwich, CT: JAI Press, 1984.

Varela, F. "Not One, Not Two." *Co-Evolution Quarterly*, 1976.

Varela, F. *Principles of Biological Autonomy*. Amsterdam: Elsevier, 1979.

Varela, F. "Two Principles of Self-Organization," in H. Ulrich and G. Probst (eds.) *Self-Organization and Management of Social Systems*. New York: Springer-Verlag, 1984.

Varela, F. and D. Johnson. "On Observing Natural Systems." *Co-Evolution Quarterly*, Summer: 26–31, 1976.

Vickers, G. *The Art of Judgment*. London: Chapman & Hall, 1965.

Vickers, G. *Value Systems and Social Process*. London: Tavistock, 1972.

Vickers, G. *Human Systems Are Different*. New York: Harper & Row, 1983.

Vico, G. *The New Science*. Ithaca, NY: Cornell University Press, 1968.

Vigoda-Gadot, E. *Developments in Organizational Politics: How Political Dynamics Affect Employee Performance in Modern Worksites*. Cheltenham, UK: Edward Elgar Publishers, 2003.

Viscusi, W. K. *Risk by Choice: Regulating Health and Safety in the Workplace*. Cambridge, MA: Harvard University Press, 1983.

Vogel, E. *Japan as Number One*. Cambridge, MA: Harvard University Press, 1979.

von Bertalanffy, L. "The Theory of Open Systems in Physics and Biology." *Science*, 3: 23–29, 1950.

von Bertalanffy, L. *General Systems Theory: Foundations, Development, Applications*. New York: Braziller, 1968.

von Foerester, H. and G. W. Zopf (eds.) *Principles of Self-Organization*. New York: Pergamon, 1962.

Wainwright, D. *Work Stress: The Making of a Modern Epidemic*. Buckingham, UK: Open University Press, 2002.

Wainwright, H. and D. Elliott. *The Lucas Plan: A New Trade-Unionism in the Making?* London: Allison & Busby, 1982.

Waldrop, M. M. *Complexity: The Emerging Science at the Edge of Order and Chaos*. London: Penguin, 1992.

Wall, T. D., C. W. Clegg, and N. J. Kemp (eds.) *The Human Side of Advanced Manufacturing Technology*. Chichester, UK: Wiley, 1987.

Wallerstein, I. *The Modern World-System*. New York: Academic Press, 1974.

Wallerstein, I. *The Capitalist World Economy*. London: Cambridge University Press, 1979.

Wall Street Journal. "Palace Revolt Forced Henry Ford to Remove Knudsen as President." *Wall Street Journal*, September 17, 1969.

Walsh, J. P. and G. R. Ungson. "Organizational Memory." *Academy of Management Review*, 16: 57–91, 1991.

Walter, G. A. "Psyche and Symbol," pp. 257–271 in L. Pondy et al. (eds.) *Organizational Symbolism*. Greenwich, CT: JAI, 1983.

Walton, R. E. and J. M. Dutton. "Managing Inter-departmental Conflict: A Model and Review." *Administrative Science Quarterly*, 14: 73–82, 1969.

Wamsley, G. L. and M. N. Zald. *The Political Economy of Public Organizations*. Lexington, MA: D. C. Heath, 1973.

Ward, C. *Anarchy in Action*. London: Allen & Unwin, 1973.

Warrick, P. S. *The Cybernetic Imagination in Science Fiction*. Cambridge: MIT Press, 1980.

Watkins, J. M. and B. J. Mohr. *Appreciative Inquiry: Change at the Speed of Imagination*. San Francisco: Jossey-Bass, 2001.

Watson, L. *Lifetide*. New York: Simon & Schuster, 1979.

Watts, D. J. *Small Worlds: The Dynamics of Networks Between Order and Randomness*. Princeton, NJ: Princeton University Press, 1999.

Watts, D. J. *Six Degrees: The Science of a Connected Age*. New York: Norton, 2003.

Watzlawick, P., J. Weakland, and R. Fisch. *Change: Principles of Problem Formulation and Problem Resolution*. New York: Norton, 1974.

Webber, R. A. (ed.) *Culture and Management*. Homewood, IL: Irwin, 1969.

Weber, M. *From Max Weber*, (eds.) H. Gerth & C. W. Mills. New York: Oxford University Press, 1946.

Weber, M. *The Theory of Social and Economic Organization*. London: Oxford University Press, 1947.

Weber, M. *The Methodology of the Social Sciences*. New York: Free Press, 1949.

Weber, M. *From Max Weber: Essays in Sociology*. New York: Oxford University Press, 1958a.

Weber, M. *The Protestant Ethic and the Spirit of Capitalism*. New York: Scribner's, 1958b.

Weber, M. *General Economic History*. New York: Collier, 1961.

Weber, M. *Economy and Society: An Outline of Interpretive Sociology*. New York: Bedminster, 1968.

Weick, K. E. "Educational Organizations as Loosely Coupled Systems." *Administrative Science Quarterly*, 21: 1–19, 1976.

Weick, K. E. *The Social Psychology of Organizing*. Reading, MA: Addison-Wesley, 1979.

Weick, K. E. *Sensemaking in Organizations*. Thousand Oaks, CA: Sage, 1995.

Weick, K. E. *Making Sense of the Organization*. Oxford, UK: Blackwell, 2000.

Weick, K. E. and K. M. Sutcliffe. *Managing the Unexpected: Assuring High Performance in an Age of Complexity*. San Francisco: Jossey-Bass, 2001.

Weisbord, M. (ed.) *Discovering Common Ground*. San Francisco: Berrett-Koehler, 1992.

Wenger, E. *Communities of Practice: Learning, Meaning, and Identity*. Cambridge, UK: Cambridge University Press, 1998.

Westley, F. and H. Mintzberg. "Visionary Leadership and Strategic Management." *Strategic Management Journal*, 10: 17–32, 1989.

Wetter, G. E. *Dialectical Materialism*. London: Routledge & Kegan Paul, 1958.

Wheatley, M. J. *Leadership and the New Science: Discovering Order in a Chaotic World*. San Francisco: Berrett Koehler, 1992, 1999.

Wheeler, D., B. Colbert, and E. Freeman. "Focusing on Value: Reconciling Corporate Social Responsibility, Sustainability and a Stakeholder Approach in a Network World." *Journal of General Management*, 28(3): 1–28, 2003.

Wheeler, D. and M. Sillanpaa. *The Stakeholder Corporation: A Blueprint for Maximizing Stakeholder Value*. London: Pitman, 1997.

Wheelwright, P. *Heraclitus*. Princeton, NJ: Princeton University Press, 1959.

Whicker, M. L. *Toxic Leaders: When Organizations Go Bad*. Westport, CT: Quorum Books, 1996.

White, H. *The Tropics of Dicourse*. Baltimore: Johns Hopkins University Press, 1978.

White, L. *Human Debris: The Injured Worker in America*. New York: Seaview/ Putnam, 1983.

White, O. F. and C. J. McSwain. "Transformational Theory and Organizational Analysis," pp. 292–305 in G. Morgan (ed.) *Beyond Method*. Beverly Hills, CA: Sage, 1983.

Whitmont, E. C. *The Symbolic Quest*. New York: Putnam, 1969.

Whyte, W. F. *Human Relations in the Restaurant Industry*. New York: McGraw-Hill, 1948.

Whyte, W. F. *Money and Motivation*. New York: Harper & Row, 1955.

Wiener, N. *Cybernetics*. Cambridge: MIT Press, 1961.

Wiener, N. *The Human Use of Human Beings*. Boston: Houghton Mifflin, 1967.

Wilber, K. (ed.) *The Holographic Paradigm and Other Paradoxes*. Boulder, CO: Shambhala, 1982.

Wilczynski, J. *The Multinationals and East-West Relations*. London: Macmillan, 1976.

Wildavsky, A. *The Politics of the Budgetary Process*. Boston: Little, Brown, 1964.

Wilden, A. *System and Structure*. London: Tavistock, 1972.

Wilensky, H. L. *Organizational Intelligence*. New York: Basic Books, 1967.

Wilkins, A. L. "Organizational Stories as Symbols Which Control the Organization," pp. 81–92 in L. Pondy et al. (eds.) *Organizational Symbolism*. Greenwich, CT: JAI Press, 1983.

Williams, T. A. *Learning to Manage Our Futures*. New York: John Wiley, 1982.

Williamson, I. (ed.) *The Dynamics of Labor Market Segmentation*. New York: Academic Press, 1981.

Willmott, H. "Strength Is Ignorance; Slavery Is Freedom: Managing Culture in Modern Organizations." *Journal of Management Studies*, 30: 515–552, 1993.

Wilson, E. M. (ed.) *Organizational Behavior Reassessed: The Impact of Gender*. London: Sage, 2001.

Wilson, E. O. *Sociobiology: The New Synthesis*. New York: Belknap, 1975.

Winnicott, D. W. "Transitional Objects and Transitional Phenomena," in *Collected Papers*. London: Tavistock, 1958.

Winnicott, D. W. *The Child, the Family and the Outside World*. Harmondsworth: Penguin, 1964.

Winnicott, D. W. *Playing and Reality*. London: Tavistock, 1971.

Wittfogel, K. A. *Oriental Despotism*. New Haven, CT: Yale University Press, 1957.

Wittgenstein, L. *Philosophical Investigations*. Oxford, UK: Basil Blackwell, 1958.

Wittgenstein, L. *Tractatus Logico-Philosophicus*. London: Routledge & Kegan Paul, 1961.

Wokutch, R. E. *Worker Protection, Japanese Style: Occupational Safety and Health in the Auto Industry*. Ithaca, NY: ILR Press, 1992.

Wolf, M. *Why Globalization Works*. New Haven, CT: Yale University Press, 2004.

Wood, S. (ed.) *The Degradation of Work?* London: Hutchinson, 1982.

Woodward, J. *Industrial Organization: Theory and Practice*. London: Oxford University Press, 1965.

Woodworth, W., C. Meek, and W. F. Whyte. *Industrial Democracy*. Beverly Hills, CA: Sage, 1985.

Worthy, J. C. *Big Business and Free Men*. New York: Harper & Row, 1959.

Wrege, C. D. and A. G. Perroni. "Taylor's Pig-Tale." *Academy of Management Journal*, 17: 6–27, 1974.

Wright, H. B. "Health Hazards of Managers." *Journal of General Management*, 2: 9–13, 1973.

Wright, J. P. *On a Clear Day You Can See General Motors*. New York: Avon, 1979.

Wright, S. and D. Morley. *Learning Works*. Toronto: ABL Publication, Faculty of Environmental Studies, York University, 1989.

Yoshino, M. Y. *Japan's Managerial System: Tradition and Innovation*. Cambridge: MIT Press, 1968.

Yoshino, M. Y. *Japan's Multinational Enterprises*. Cambridge, MA: Harvard University Press, 1976.

Young, D. and P. Scott. *Having Their Cake . . . How the City and Big Bosses Are Consuming U.K. Businesses*. London: Kogan Page, 2004.

Zaleznik, A. "Power and Politics in Organizational Life." *Harvard Business Review*, 48: 47–60, 1970.

Zaleznik, A. and M. Kets de Vries. *Power and the Corporate Mind*. Boston: Houghton Mifflin, 1975.

Zeleny, M. *Autopoiesis, Dissipative Structures and Spontaneous Social Order*. Boulder, CO: Westview, 1980.

Zeleny, M. (ed.) *Autopoiesis: A Theory of Living Organization*. North Holland: Elsevier, 1981.

Zimmerman, B., C. Lindberg, and P. Plsek. *Complexity and Organizations*. Dallas, TX: VHA Inc., 1998.

Zimmerman, B. J. and D. K. Hurst. "Breaking the Boundaries: The Fractal Organization." *Journal of Management Inquiry*, 2: 334–355, 1993.

Zimmerman, K. F. and T. Bauer (eds.) *The Economics of Migration*. Northampton, MA: Edward Elgar Publishers, 2002.

Zmud, R. W. *Information Systems in Organizations*. Glenview, IL: Scott, Foresman, 1983.

Zohar, A. *Paradoxical Dimensions of Organization.* Working Paper, Toronto: Schulich School of Business, 1995.

Zohar, A. and G. Morgan. "How Seriously Should We Take Mobots?" *Organization*, 3: 408–410, 1996.

Zohar, D. *Rewiring the Corporate Brain: Using the New Science to Rethink How We Structure and Lead Organizations.* San Francisco: Berrett Koehler, 1997.

Zuboff, R. *In the Age of the Smart Machine.* New York: Basic Books, 1988.

Zweig, C. and J. Abrams (eds.) *Meeting the Shadow.* New York: Tarcher, 1991.

Zwerdling, D. "Food Pollution." *Ramparts*, June: 35–37, 1971.

Index

Action:
    action stage, structural factors and,
        190–192
    authority, patterns of, 21
    bureaucratization and, 86
    creative action, barriers to, 28–29
    data management theories/systems
        and, 77
    intelligent action, linked
        independent processes and,
        74–75, 107
    learning organizations and, 89
    managerial flexibility and, 28
    metaphors and, 341–343, 341
        (exhibit)
    minimum critical specification and,
        110–111
    reading of situations, management
        actions and, 3–4
    spontaneous human actions, 17
    See also Dialectical change;
        Exploitation; Mutual causality
Action learning, 84, 89
Adaptation:
    fallacy of, 67–68
    inertial pressures, change
        prevention and, 60–61
    mechanistic approaches to, 28
    organizational change and, 72
    requisite variety principle and,
        109–110
    team-based organizations
        and, 53
    See also Contingency theory
Adhocracy, 50–51
Advisory functions, 17
Allende, S., 320

American insurance company case,
    126–128
Anarchist movements, 286
Anxiety, 16, 221
    bibliographic notes on, 399–400
    childhood defenses against, 221–222
    coalition building and, 226–227
    death fears, 7, 219–221, 399
    dependency mode and, 223–224
    fight-flight response and, 224
    labor-management relations and,
        225–226
    object relations and, 222–223,
        227–229
    social defense against, 224–226
Apathy, 29–30, 128
Apple Computer, 131, 285
Appropriate structure principle, 47–48
Archetypes, 230–231, 232, 270–271,
    400–401
Argyris, C., 36, 84, 86
Artificial intelligence, 74–75
Ashby, W. R., 108
Ashton, D. S., 324
Assembly-line production. See Factory
    systems; Fast-food industry;
    Mass-production factories
AT&T, 315
Athos, A., 119
Attractor patterns, 7
    changing contexts, management of,
        257–259, 258 (exhibit)
    chaos/complexity theories and,
        251–255, 252–253 (exhibits), 288
    dialectical change and,
        280, 281, 286
    mutual causality and, 270, 272, 288

mechanistic organization, origins
of, 15–18
political consequences, democracy
and, 17–18
professional bureaucracy, 50
reengineering movement and, 22
social consequences of, 17–18
top-down management and, 21
See also Classical management
theory; Machine metaphor;
Open-systems approach;
Political systems metaphor;
Scientific management
Burns, T., 42, 43, 45, 46, 47, 49, 50,
54, 163
Burrell, G., 57, 196, 216, 367
Butterfly effect, 255, 260, 265

Canon Inc, 88
Capacity development, 84, 87–88, 90
Capitalism, 275, 277–280, 286, 288,
299–300
See also Domination metaphor
Career interests, 157–158, 158 (exhibit)
Careerism, 30
Cartels, 320
Causality. *See* Mutual causality
Central Intelligence Agency
(CIA), 320
Centralization of control,
19, 21, 28, 50, 318
Chandler, A., 319
Change:
adaptation, mechanistic
approaches and, 28
adhocracy, flexibility of, 50–51
anticipation of, 88–89
cultural change, shared meaning
and, 137–139, 142–143
exponential change, 264
inertial pressures and, 60–61
natural selection, population
ecology perspective and, 59–62
open/flexible organization and,
43–47, 44–45 (exhibit)
organizational style, organizational
subunits/subenvironments
and, 48–49
project/matrix form of organization
and, 46

quantum change, high-leverage
initiatives and, 261–262
small change, large effects and, 255,
260–262
transition phenomenon and,
227–229
See also Cybernetics; Dialectical
change; Information
processing; Learning
organizations; Logics of
change; Mutual causality;
Psychic prisons metaphor
Chaos theory, 7, 242
attractor patterns and, 251–255,
252–253 (exhibits)
bibliographic notes on,
404–405
boundary management and,
262–263
contexts of self-organization,
managing for, 257–260, 258
(exhibit)
flipping trajectories and, 261
small changes, large effects and,
260–262
See also Dialectical change; Logics
of change; Mutual causality
Charismatic authority, 167–168
Charismatic domination, 295
Chatov, R., 225
Circular flows of feedback, 7, 242,
243–245
See also Feedback; Mutual
causality
Class-based organizations, 298–304,
412–414
Classical management theory:
bibliographic notes on, 372–373
centralized vs. divisionalized
organization and, 21
environmental factors and,
38–39
Hawthorne Studies and, 35
hierarchical network organization
and, 18, 20 (exhibit), 21
human vs. technical aspects of
organization and, 22, 35
organizational learning/inquiry
and, 22
principles of, 18, 19 (exhibit)

Goal setting, 95–97, 113
Goffman, E., 177
Goldstein, J., 259
Good enough decisions, 76, 229
Government systems, 7, 151–156, 391
federal organizations, 51
legislative protections, 216, 308–309
See also Political systems metaphor
Grogan, B., 132
Group management, 151
Groupthink, 87, 107, 198, 211
Guest workers, 303
Gulf and Western Industries, 318

Haldeman, R., 177
Hamel, G., 88
Hampden-Turner, C., 136, 215
Handy, C., 51, 123
Hardin, G., 271
Harragan, B., 131, 188
Harris-Jones, P., 245
Hawthorne Studies, 35
Hayter, T., 326
Health of organizations, 54–58, 57 (exhibit)
Hegel, G. W. F., 274
Heisenberg, W., 364
Helgesen, S., 131, 132
Herzberg, F., 36
Hesselbeim, F., 132
Hewlett-Packard Development Company, 128–129, 137
Hierarchical network organization, 18, 20 (exhibit), 21, 77, 163
Hierarchy of needs, 35–36, 37 (exhibit), 66
High-leverage initiatives, 261–262
Hirschhorn, L., 238
Hitachi Corporation, 316
Holistic teams, 103–105, 106 (exhibit)
Holographic brains, 97–98
bibliographic notes on, 385–386
corporate DNA and, 99–100
double-loop learning and, 111
holistic teams, diversified roles and, 103–105, 106 (exhibit)
holographic design principles, 99–112, 100 (exhibit), 111–112
holographic structure and, 101–103, 102 (exhibit)
hypertext organization and, 107
learning-to-learn principle and, 111
minimum critical specification and, 110–111
networked intelligence, information systems and, 100–101
organization design and, 98
redundancy principle and, 105–108
regenerative capacity and, 98–99
requisite variety principle and, 108–110
self-organizing work groups and, 105, 108, 109, 111, 114
specialization-generalization balance and, 104–105
whole-in-all-parts principle, 99–105
See also Brain metaphor; Learning organizations
Holographic system, 73
Homeostasis, 40, 68
Honda Motor Company, 121
Hudson Bay Company, 316
Human capital, 302
Human potential movement, 193
Human resource management, 36
human capital and, 302
team-based organization and, 53
Humans:
bureaucratic organization, social effects of, 17–18, 28
decision-making process and, 76
formal rationality, repressed human and, 231–232
hierarchy of needs and, 36, 37 (exhibit)
informal organization and, 35, 37
job enrichment, employee-centered leadership and, 36
mechanistic organization and, 5, 12–13, 17, 22, 30–31
management observation checklist and, 13, 14–15 (exhibit)
motivation, factors in, 22, 34–36
reengineering movement and, 22
scientific management and, 24–25
sociotechnical systems and, 36–38, 39, 65–66
unity of opposites, personality and, 232, 233 (exhibit)

simplification, interchangeable
    workers and, 25
time-and-motion study and, 23
See also Classical management
    theory; Employees;
    Exploitation; Labor;
    Metaphors; Political systems
    metaphor; Scientific
    management
Workaholism, 310–312
World Bank, 327

World Bank Development Indicators
    Database, 317
World economy. *See* Global economy;
    Multinational corporations
    (MNCs)
World Wide Web. *See* Internet

Yin/Yang interplay, 273–274, 274
    (exhibit)

Zaleznik, A., 226

About the Author

Gareth Morgan, Distinguished Research Professor, Schulich School of Business, York University, Toronto, is author of several books, including *Imaginization: New Mindsets for Seeing, Organizing and Managing, Riding the Waves of Change, Beyond Method, Creative Organization Theory,* and *Sociological Paradigms and Organizational Analysis* (with Gibson Burrell). He has been elected Life Fellow of the International Academy of Management for his international contributions to the science and art of management. He is a prominent keynote speaker on issues relating to learning, change, and new approaches to organization and management. His consulting and research have been at the forefront of many contemporary management trends—developing learning organizations; designing and managing decentralized networks; creating flexible team-based enterprise; using theories of chaos, paradox, and self-organization to find new methods of managing change; and action learning and use of the internet for leadership and management development.

Since 1999, he has been involved with the NewMindsets action learning project—a "second-generation" approach to e-learning aimed at developing new methods of leadership education and management development. The aim is to find new ways of using the internet to promote continuous learning as a key competence for dealing with turbulent times. The work and its practical applications have received several best-practice awards from Brandon-hall.com / *Online Learning Magazine,* the American Society for Training and Development, and Information Highways / The Canadian e-Content Institute.

Gareth holds degrees from the London School of Economics and Political Science, the University of Texas at Austin, and the University of Lancaster. Born in Wales, he now lives in Toronto with his wife, Karen, and their son and daughter, Evan and Heather.

For further information please visit:

http://www.imaginiz.com

http://www.newmindsets.com